TESTI E DOCUMENTI PER LO STUDIO DELL'ANTICHITA'
LV - 2

Francis Thomas Gignac

A GRAMMAR OF THE GREEK PAPYRI
OF THE ROMAN
AND BYZANTINE PERIODS

Volume II

Morphology

ISTITUTO EDITORIALE CISALPINO - LA GOLIARDICA
Milano

Francis Thomas Gignac

A GRAMMAR OF THE GREEK PAPYRI
OF THE ROMAN
AND BYZANTINE PERIODS

Volume II

Morphology

ISTITUTO EDITORIALE CISALPINO - LA GOLIARDICA

Milano

ISBN 88-205-0247-X
Copyright © by

Istituto Editoriale Cisalpino-La Goliardica
Via Bassini 17/2

Finito di stampare
nel mese di giugno 1981
presso il Centro Grafico Linate
S. Donato (Milano - Italy)

PREFACE

This second volume was able to be prepared for publication so soon after the first volume because of a generous grant from the Condon Fund administered by the Chicago Province of the Society of Jesus. I am most grateful to the Rev. Dr. Raymond V. Schoder, who recommended my application for assistance in typing and indexing, and to the Rev. Ronald J. Ferguson, who approved it. I also gratefully acknowledge a grant from the Faculty Research Fund of The Catholic University of America. The manuscript of this volume was typed by Maurya P. Horgan, Frank Fletcher, and Elizabeth Petit. J. Rebecca Lyman assisted in proofreading and checking references.

FRANCIS THOMAS GIGNAC

The Catholic University of America
Washington, September, 1977

TABLE OF CONTENTS

SECTION TWO: CONJUGATION

V. AUGMENT AND REDUPLICATION

VI. FORMATION OF THE TENSE STEM

VII. VOICE

X. -MI VERBS

SUPPLEMENT TO VOLUME I:
BIBLIOGRAPHY AND ABBREVIATIONS

B. REFERENCE WORKS, PERIODICALS,
AND GRAMMATICAL LITERATURE

sub *BL*: vi, ed. E. Boswinkel, P. W. Pestman, H.-A. Rupprecht. Leiden, 1976.

Boyaval, Bernard. *Corpus des étiquettes de momies grecques*. Institut de papyrologie et d'égyptologie de l'Université de Lille 3. Lille, 1977.

sub Brandenstein: ii, *Wortbildung und Formenlehre*. Sammlung Göschen 118/118a. Berlin, 1959.

Gagnepain, J. *Les Noms grec en -ος et en -ᾱ: Contribution à l'étude du genre en indo-européen*. Etudes et Commentaires 31. Paris, 1959.

Mandilaras, B. G. *The Verb in the Non-Literary Papyri*. Hellenic Ministry of Culture and Sciences. Athens, 1973.

Maspero = Maspero, Francesco. *Grammatica della lingua greca moderna*. Milano, 1976.

Perpillou, Jean-Louis. *Les Substantifs grecs en -εύς*. Etudes et Commentaires 80. Paris, 1973.

Ruozzi Sala, S. M. *Lexicon Nominum Semiticorum quae in papyris Graecis in Aegypto repertis ab anno 323 a.Chr.n. usque ad annum 70 p.Chr.n. laudata reperiuntur*. Teste e documenti per lo studio dell'antichità 46. Milano, 1974.

Tabachovitz, David. *Etudes sur le grec de la basse époque*. Skrifter utgivna av K. Humanistiska Vetenskaps-Samfundet i Uppsala 36 : 3. Uppsala-Leipzig, 1943.

Wuthnow, Heinz. *Die semitischen Menschennamen in griechischen Inschriften und Papyri des vorderen Orients*. Studien zur Epigraphik und Papyruskunde, hg. Fr. Bilabel. Leipzig, 1930.

C. OTHER ABBREVIATIONS AND SYMBOLS

1. AUTHORS AND WORKS

Ael.Dion., Aelius Dionysius, gram. ii A.D.

Aesop., Aesopus, fab.

Anaxipp., Anaxippus, com. iv B.C.

Ascl., Asclepiodotus, tact. i B.C.

Diocl., Diocles, epigr. i A.D.

Emp., Empedocles, poet. & phil. v B.C.

Epicur., Epicurus, phil. iv/iii B.C.

Gorg., Gorgias, rhet. & soph. v B.C.

Lib., Libanius, soph. iv A.D.

M.Ant., Marcus Antoninus, emp. ii A.D.

Paul.Al., Paulus Alexandrinus, astrol. iv A.D.

Placit., *Placita Philosophorum*

Ruf., Rufus, med. ii A.D.

Stad., *Stadiasmus/Periplus Maris Magni*, i B.C./i A.D.

Tryph., Tryphiodorus, epic.

Xenoph., Xenophanes, poet. & phil. v B.C.

PART TWO

MORPHOLOGY

INTRODUCTION

This analysis of the morphology of the papyri of the Roman and Byzantine periods is based essentially on phonology. The spoken form of a word is determined on the evidence presented in Volume One, and most purely orthographic variations are eliminated. For instance, ει and ι were found to represent the same sound /i/. It is therefore not significant for the morphology of the language that the dative singular of third declension s-, i-, and diphthongal stems is sometimes written -ι instead of -ει. Both spellings represent the same spoken form and consequently one morpheme {-i}. The variation in spelling is significant only for phonology and for the evidence it provides for the prevalent orthography of the time and the degree of conformity to the historical norm on the part of the writer concerned.

Similarly, the dative singular of the first and second declensions is generally written without the -ι adscript. This reflects the reduction of the long diphthongs in -ι to their corresponding simple vowels. During the period when the orthography was fluctuating in the representation of the ι adscript, mainly during the first two centuries A.D., the presence or absence of the -ι is not significant for morphology. The -ι had ceased to be pronounced, and there was thus only the one morpheme {-a, -i, -o} according to the declensional type of the word.

The genitive singular of third declension i-stems is variously written -εως, -εος, -ιος, -ηος, -ειος, -ειως, etc. Again, these various spellings do not represent different morphemes. Since o and ω were alternate representations of /o/, without distinction in quantity, and ε, η, ει, and ι all represented /i/ before a back vowel, there was in all these instances only one spoken form /-ios/, regardless of spelling, and so only one morpheme. Analogy may have been an operative factor on the orthographic level, but not in actual speech.

Some occasional variants in verb forms are also purely orthographic. Since o and ω both represented /o/, the occasional failure to indicate the augment in verbs beginning with o is not significant for morphology. A further consequence of the identification of o and ω is that there was no longer a distinction in pronunciation between the present and the imperfect in forms of verbs which were marked by the augment alone, as ὀφείλομεν (present) and ὠφείλομεν (imperfect). In the Roman and Byzantine periods, there was only the one spoken form /ophilomεn/.

To describe the living language accurately, a careful distinction is made between speech and writing. This volume therefore does not catalogue all the spelling variations observed in the papyri but only those which represent actual changes in form.

Just as every change in spelling does not necessarily reflect a change in form, adherence to a traditional orthography tends to conceal morphological developments. In most instances, however, this is not a major difficulty in dealing with the papyri. Because there are documents of various types from all times and places with numerous misspellings, changes in speech are generally reflected in writing.

But even when an orthographic variation represents an actual change in pronunciation and therefore a new morpheme, the question remains whether or not this new morpheme has become a part of the living language or is simply a blunder or an idiosyncrasy of the particular writer. The criteria used for deciding which forms are part of the language are similar to those used in Volume One to determine which spelling mistakes constituted phonologically significant orthographic variations.

The most useful criterion is frequency and regularity of occurrence. If a new form occurs only sporadically, it probably does not reflect a linguistic change. If the form does represent a new morpheme accepted into the language as a whole, it should occur frequently.

Another criterion is historical Greek grammar. If a new form first found in the papyri has survived in Modern Greek, either in the same form or in a secondary form, or if it is attested elsewhere in the Koine, it is probably part of the contemporary Greek language. If, however, a form attested in the papyri is not paralleled elsewhere in Greek, it often has other explanations.

Anomalous forms can often be explained by the context in which they occur. For instance, there is little reason to expect in Koine Greek a variation in nouns of the first declension between -η and -α after *stops*. When, therefore, the anomalous dative ἀδελφᾶι occurs in *BGU* 644.9 (A.D. 69) following the adjective ὁμοπατρίαι, likewise ending in -αι, it may well be a simple mistake in writing which has no correspondence in pronunciation. The writer may have simply duplicated the -αι ending of the adjective. Forms such as these, for which a plausible psychological or mechanical explanation can be found in the associative force of the context, are not classified as grammatical innovations.

But when the *r*-stem θυγάτηρ has an accusative in -αν between other accusatives in -ν in the phrase τὴν θυγατέραν ἄχ[ου]σαν in *POxy.* 237 vii.5 (A.D. 186), this is not to be attributed solely to the influence of the context, even though the historically correct θυγατέρα occurs some lines later (vii.32) in a quotation from a different source. Accusative singular endings in -αν are common in consonant stems of the third declension and have led to the assimilation of these nouns into the Modern Greek first declension, with the back-formation of a nominative in -α on the basis of the accusative in -αν.

There are other instances in which an abnormal form does not occur frequently, does not have descendants in later Greek, is not paralleled elsewhere in the Koine, and has no obvious explanation from context. In some of these instances, bilingual interference could be a factor, especially where there is evidence of interference in phonology in the same document. This might occur in the occasional formation of infinitives in -εν instead of -ειν, because non-contract thematic Greek verbs incorporated as loanwords in three dialects of Coptic end in -ε (SA₂A: BF -ɪⲛ). But in this case, besides the uncertainty whether the Coptic form was derived from the Greek infinitive or imperative, or was just a short form, there could have been little if any distinction in pronunciation between -ειν and -εν in accented or unaccented syllables because of the interchange of ει and ε before nasals. Bilingual interference seems more likely in occasional changes in the gender of nouns not connected with a general shift (as second declension feminine nouns), especially when these changes are in the direction of the gender of the corresponding Coptic word, as in ὅρα ἕκτη τοῦ ἡμέρας *POxy.* 893 = *MChr.* 99.7 (late 6th/7th cent.). In Coptic, the word for 'day,' ⲉⲟⲟⲩ, is masculine.

This volume follows the traditional method of presentation, beginning with the declension of nouns, adjectives, pronouns, and numerals, and concluding with the conjugation of verbs. There is a summary at the end of the section on declension and another at the end of the section on conjugation. Parallels in inscriptions and documents from other places, and from Greek literature in general, are cited for each form. When a form is noted which differs from the classical form, a list of authors who use this same form or similar forms is given in every instance to show how the grammar of the papyri fits into the perspective of the Greek language as a whole. The position of the language of the papyri in the general history of Greek is illustrated in the summaries by comparative tables of paradigms for classical Attic, the papyri, and Modern Greek.

Since word formation by suffixes constitutes the completed part of Palmer's *A Grammar of the Post-Ptolemaic Papyri* (1946: see Vol. i, 42), word formation by composition and the formation of adverbs will be published in a separate monograph.

SECTION ONE

DECLENSION

I. THE DECLENSION OF NOUNS

A. THE FIRST DECLENSION[1]

1. General features.

a. The dat. sg. is regularly written without the -ι adscript, especially after the first century A.D., reflecting the identification of the long diphthongs in -ι with their corresponding simple vowels.[2]

b. The dual has become extinct. The only relic is the gen. ταῖν στήλαιν *PGiss.* 99.19, with the dat. στή[λαι]ν δυοῖν ... ἱδρυμέ[ν]αιν 15-16, Atticistic speech of advocate (2nd/3rd cent.).

2. Nouns in -ᾱ/-η.

a. Nouns in -ᾱ (normally only after ε, ι, or ρ as in Attic) sometimes have forms in -ης, -η.

1) Names:

    Ὠριγενίης *POxy.* 1475.10 (A.D. 267)
    Ἀμαζονίης *POxy.* 43 V = *WChr.* 474 i.22 (A.D. 295)
    Ἀρμενίης *PCairPreis.* 12.6 (3rd/4th cent.)
    Ἀντιοχίη *POxy.* 102.3 (A.D. 306)
    Εὐτροπίης *PMerton* 40.7 (late 4th/5th cent.)

These names could be inherited from Ionic, but forms in -η are also found after ι in Egyptian names, e.g., Σ[ε]ναμουνίης *POxy.* 1959.6 (A.D. 499), and fluctuation in the declension of the same name is observed in some documents, as Εὐτροπίης *POxy.* 1953.1 (lst hand), with Εὐτροπίας 3 (2nd hand) (A.D. 419).

---

[1] Schwyzer i, 554, 558-62, cf. also 459-62; Chantraine[2], § 27-47; Buck, *GD*, § 104-5; *MS*, 118-24; Schweizer, 138-41; Nachmanson, 119-22; Hauser, 77-79; Mayser i[2], 2, 2-11; Crönert, 159-64; *BDF*, § 43, 45.

[2] See Vol. i, 183-6, and Introd. to Morphology above, p. XVII.

2) Common nouns:

ἀρταβίης (for ἀρταβείας) *PMich.* 252.6, so duplic. *PSI* 905.10 (A.D. 26/27)
[ε]ὐδαιμο[νο]ίης (better restored -μο[νε]ίης for εὐδαιμονίας) *PHermRees*
     2.28-29 (4th cent.)
ἀλλωνίης (for ἀλωνίας) *SB* 9593.21 (6th/7th cent.)
θυείη (for θυείᾳ) *POxy.* 1890.8,9 (A.D. 508)

b. Conversely, nouns in -η sometimes have forms in α:[1]
μετὰι τελευτάν (for μετὰ τελευτήν) *PHamb.* 70.12 (A.D. 144/5+)
εἶλαν (for εἴλην) *POxy.* 1666.6,11 (3rd cent.)
τὴν ὄχθαν (for ὄχθην[2]) *OMich.* 781.3-4 (A.D. 305/6?)
τῆς β̄ μονᾶς (for μονῆς) *PRyl.* 630-7.463 (A.D. 317-23)
ἑκάστης ἀρτάβας (for ἀρτάβης) *PCairMasp.* 303.18 (A.D. 553)

c. The acc. sg. of nouns in -ία is sporadically written -ιν:[3]
προστασίν (for προστασίαν) *SB* 7619 = *PRein.* 103.17 (A.D. 26)
λυχναψίν (for λυχναψίαν) *PMerton* 27.15 (3rd cent.)
εὐκερίν (for εὐκαιρίαν?) *PSI* 1430.1 (7th cent.)
εὐγνωμονείν (for εὐγνωμονίαν) *PLond.* 1000 = *MChr.* 73.6 (A.D. 538)

d. Some feminine nouns in -ᾱ/-η appear sporadically as masculine or neuter,
e.g., τοῦ ἡμέρας *POxy.* 893 = *MChr.* 99.7 (late 6th/7th cent.), perhaps through
bilingual interference from Coptic masc. ϩⲟⲟⲩ,[4] or have *o*-stem by-forms, e.g.,
λί(τρα) χωρικά, τὸ λί(τρον) *POxy.* 2729.29,33 (4th cent.), and perhaps also λίτρον
PFay. 331 descr. V (2nd cent.).

3. Nouns in -ᾰ.

a. Feminine nouns in -ρᾰ, originating in the attachment of the suffix *-jə*
to form qualitative abstracts and other feminine substantives of stems ending
in -ρ-,[5] very frequently have -ρης, -ρη in the gen. and dat. sg. The word ἄρουρα
is almost always declined in this way; some other nouns have these forms as
well as forms in -ρας, -ρᾳ:

ἀρούρης *PLBat.* vi, 1.21 (A.D. 89/90?); *PStrassb.* 291.7 (A.D. 124); *POslo*
     133.6 (2nd cent.); *POxy.* 1270.28 (A.D. 159); *SB* 7677 = *PCairIsidor.*
     108.8 (A.D. 276); *PCairMasp.* 169 bis.46 (A.D. 569); etc., passim
ἀρούρη *PHamb.* 64.11,15 (A.D. 104); *POxy.* 488.17 (late 2nd/3rd cent.)[6]
but ἑκάστης ἀρούρας *POxy.* 102.12 (A.D. 306); *PRossGeorg.* iii, 32.8 (A.D.
     504); *PCairMasp.* 329 i.11,12 (A.D. 524/5: *BL* iv, 15); etc.

---

[1] See Introd. to Morphology above, p. XX, for such spellings found where there is a
predominance of -α endings in the context.
[2] τὴν ὄχθαν also Aet. (*LSJ*, s.v.).
[3] Cf. the very common -ιν for -ιον below, pp. 25-29.
[4] See Introd., p. XXI.
[5] Schwyzer i, 473; Buck, *CG*, 178-9.
[6] Cf. also from the mag. papp. ἀρούρης *PGM* 77.6 (2nd cent.); *PGM* 4.3023 (4th cent.).

σπείρης *PMich.* 569.6 (A.D. 90?); *PFuadCrawford* 26.4 (1st/2nd cent.?); *PSI* 1063.23, etc. (A.D. 117); *PLBat.* xvi, 14.3 (A.D. 131); *OStrassb.* 445.8 (A.D. 145); *PPhil.* 16.1 (A.D. 161); *BGU* 2024.7 (A.D. 204); *PPar.* 69 = *WChr.* 41 iii.9 (A.D. 232); *POxy.* 2978.3 (3rd cent.?); etc.; cf. *SB* 3919.6, inscr. (A.D. 111); *PDura* 26.6 (A.D. 227); 30.3 (A.D. 232); 129.2 (A.D. 225) σπείρῃ *MChr.* 372 iii.13, also σπείρης iii.7, iv.11, with σπείρᾳ v.5,9 (2nd cent.); *SB* 7362.9,13 (A.D. 188)

but σπίρας *PLond.* 256a = *WChr.* 443.3 (A.D. 15); sim. *PMilVogl.* 25 v.12 (A.D. 126/7); *BGU* 1574.12 (A.D. 176/7)

γεφύρης *SB* 7174 = *PMich.* 233.8 (A.D. 24: *BL* v, 69)

    cf. γεφύρῃ *PColt* 102.1 (6th cent.)

λείτρης *BGU* 781 ii.8,13,16; vi.12; with λείτρας iii.1,16,19; v.7,9,11,14; vi.1,2,16 (1st cent.)

but λείτρας *SB* 9159 — *PMilVogl.* 102.8 (2nd cent.)

ὀλύρης *PFlor.* 379.35,49 (2nd cent.); *PErl.* 50.6,10 (3rd cent.)

but ὀλύρας *BGU* 1206.15 (28 B.C.)

μοίρης *PMilVogl.* 99.10 (A.D. 119); cf. *PLond.* 98 R (i, 126-30).12; 130 (i, 132-9).58,80,100, etc., horoscopes (1st/2nd cent.)

    ἀπομοίρης *PBouriant* 30.7,8 (2nd cent.); *SB* 6951 V.40,50,56,65 (A.D. 138-61); *PRyl.* 213.165 part. rest., etc. (late 2nd cent.); *PRyl.* 427, frag. 47.11 (A.D. 198-209?); *POxy.* 1046.9,11 abbrev. (A.D. 218/19)

but μοίρας *PLond.* 1708.204,218, with μοίρᾳ 255,263a (A.D. 567?); *PCair-Masp.* 158.21 (A.D. 568); 151-2.88,97 (A.D. 570); *PMon.* 6.64 (A.D. 583)

αἴρης *PFouad* 43.47 (A.D. 190/1); *PHamb.* 19.16 (A.D. 225); *POxy.* 1031 = *WChr.* 343.17 (A.D. 228)

πείρης *PRossGeorg.* iii, 1.23 (A.D. 270: *BL* iii, 156)

but πείρας *PCairMasp.* 89 R b.7 (Byz.)

    [π]εῖρα *POxy.* 473 = *WChr.* 33.3 (A.D. 138-60)

        πίρα *PSI* 696.8 (3rd cent.); *PPrinc.* 169.3 (5th cent.)

πρῷρας *PMon.* 4-5 V.12 (A.D. 581)

These forms in -ρης, -ρη have been explained as Ionicisms in the Koine,[1] or as the result of levelling of the declensional system on the analogy of other nouns in -α whose stem ends in a consonant, as δόξα and nouns in -σσα, -λλα.[2] The latter explanation is more satisfactory in view of the fact that other nouns in -α rarely have forms in -ης, -η in the papyri. If Ionic influence were the cause, nouns in -ρᾱ as well as nouns in -ρᾰ should exhibit this same tendency. But these forms in -ρης, -ρη are generally limited to nouns in -ρᾰ.[3] This distribution indicates that the declensional pattern developed before the loss of quantitative distinction, when -ρᾰ could still be distinguished from -ρᾱ.[4]

---

[1] Schweizer, 40-42; Thumb, *Hell.*, 70-72.

[2] Mayser i, 12-13; *BDF*, § 43.1.

[3] Cf. ptcs. in -υῖα, -υίης below, pp. 132-3.

[4] For sim. spellings in the Ptol. papp., see Mayser i[2], 1, 11-12.

b. Some nouns and names in ‑ειᾰ only sporadically have forms in ‑είης,
‑είη:

ἱερείης *PAmh*. 97.2 (A.D. 180/92)
Ἀριστοκλείης *POxy*. 1537.4 (late 2nd/early 3rd cent.)
ἐμφ[αν]είης *PFlor*. 34.17, with ἐμφανείας 9 (A.D. 342)
Ἡρακλείη, Ἡρακλείης *PTebt*. 397 = *MChr*. 321.7,8, with Ἡρακλείας
   10,23 (A.D. 198)

c. Conversely, levelling in nouns in ‑σσα is reflected by the sporadic dat.
‑σσᾳ:

ἱερίσσᾳ *PMeyer* 20.45 (1st half 3rd cent.)
γναφίσᾳ (for γναφίσσῃ) *POxy*. 2425 ii.17 (3rd/4th cent.)
ὑπατίσσᾳ *POxy*. 2243a.86 (A.D. 590)

In Modern Greek, analogical levelling has extended the vowel of the nom.
to the oblique cases. Consequently, nouns in ‑σσα, as well as those in ‑ρα, etc.,
are declined ‑α, ‑ας, e.g., γλῶσσα, γλώσσας; μοῖρα, μοίρας; δόξα, δόξας.[1]

d. Levelling of the acc. sg. to the vowel quality of the gen. and dat. is also
found sporadically:

δεσποίνην *POxy*. 123.22 (3rd/4th cent.)
ἀρούρην *PSI* 774.5 (5th cent.)

e. τόλμα, which is attested with a nom. and acc. in ‑η, ‑ην elsewhere in
Hellenistic Greek,[2] is found with both ‑α and ‑η forms in the acc.:

τόλμην *CPJud*. 156c.32 (mid 1st cent.); *SB* 9527.6 (A.D. 385‑412)
τόλμαν *POxy*. 1119 = *WChr*. 397.8 (A.D. 253: *BL* i, 332)

f. Some feminine Latin loanwords of the first declension in ‑α are declined
‑α, ‑ης, ‑η, ‑αν, others are declined ‑α, ‑ας, ‑ᾳ, ‑αν, but most fluctuate between
the two declensional types; only a few appear as ‑η, ‑ης, ‑η, ‑ην.

1) Declined ‑α, ‑ης, ‑η, ‑αν:

ἅλης *ala* *PHamb*. 1.8 (A.D. 57); 2.7 (A.D. 59); *PGrenf*. ii, 51.5 (A.D. 143);
   PSI 300.2 (A.D. 324: *BL* i, 395); cf. *SB* 4575.3, inscr. (n.d.)
ἅλαν *BGU* 623.5 (2nd/3rd cent.)
ἅλα (acc.) *BGU* 4.10‑11 (2nd/3rd cent.)
ληίνης *laena* *PGiss*. 76.5 (ca. A.D. 117)
ταβέλλ[η]ς, ταβέλλαν *tabella* *BGU* 388 = *MChr*. 91 i.39; ii.38,40 (2nd
   half 2nd cent.)
   ταβέλλη *POxy*. 273 = *MChr*. 221.7 (A.D. 95)
   ταβέλλαν *SB* 5217.16 (A.D. 148)

---

[1] Thumb, *Handbook*, § 81.
[2] τόλμη Clitarch.; τόλμην pap. S. cod. LXX; Dor. τόλμᾱ (*LSJ*, s.v.).

cf. also τάβλα and βάτελλα below, pp. 8-9. For τ(ο)ὐρμης, see Vol. i, 222; for φοῦνδαν, see Vol. i, 99.

Note. Also declined -α, -ης, -η, -αν are the following loanwords from other Latin declensions:

> κλάσσης *classis* BGU 455.8 (before A.D. 133); BGU 741 = MChr. 244.7
>   (A.D. 143/4); BGU 326 = MChr. 316 ii.16 (A.D. 194); etc.
> κλάσση BGU 265 = WChr. 459.5 (A.D. 148)
> κλάσσαν SB 7354.6 (early 2nd cent.)
> σακέλλης *sacellum* PLond. 1336.9 (A.D. 709); PLond. 1380 = WChr.
>   285.6 (A.D. 710/11); PLond. 1405.2 (8th cent.)
> σακέλλη PLond. 1359.5,11; 1363.7 (A.D. 710); 1375.12 (A.D. 711), etc.

2) Declined -α, -ας, -ᾳ, -αν:

> κατήνας *catena* PSI 959.29 (4th cent.)
> κόπλας *copula* PAberd. 70.3 (2nd cent.)
> ματρώνας *matrona* PStrassb. 8.11 (A.D. 271-6); POxy. 907 = MChr.
>   317.4 (A.D. 276); POxy. 2712.3 (A.D. 292/3)
>   ματρώνᾳ BGU 860.1: BL i, 74 (A.D. 260-8); PRyl. 165.9 (A.D. 266);
>   POxy. 1705.3 (A.D. 298); PSI 1338.2 (A.D. 299)
> παρατούρας *paratura* PGrenf. ii, 100.7 (A.D. 683)
> πίλας *pila* POxy. 1890.12 (A.D. 508); PRein. 108.4 (6th cent.)
>   πίλαν PMerton 39.10 (late 4th/5th cent.)
> πόρτα *porta* SB 8704.1, inscr. (7th cent.)
>   πώρτας OTaitPetr. 417.5 (n.d.)
> ῥόγας (*erogatio*) PCairMasp. 76.4 (6th cent.); PLond. 1319 = WChr.
>   284.15 (A.D. 710); sim. PLond. 1660.9 (ca. A.D. 553); POxy. 2010.2
>   abbrev. (A.D. 618); BGU 304.11 (Arab.); etc.
>   ῥόγαν POxy. 1913.60 (ca. A.D. 555?); PBerlZill. 13.8 (6th cent.);
>   PLond. 1357.2 (A.D. 710)

3) The following loanwords fluctuate between the two declensional types:[1]

> κέλλα *cella* PErl. 40.9,11 (2nd cent.); PMich. 620.14, etc. (A.D. 239/40);
>   BGU 1726.1 (4th cent.)
>   cf. nom. κέλλαν PLond. 978 (iii, 232-4).8,10 (A.D. 331)
>   also κέλλη SB 5168.26 (A.D. 138-61)
> κέλλης POxy. 1144.16 (late 1st/early 2nd cent.); OStrassb. 793.3 (A.D.
>   195/6); POxy. 2240.40 (A.D. 211); PFlor. 77.14,16 (A.D. 241/2)
> but κέλλας BGU 1036 = MChr. 118.25, with dat. κ[έλλ]ηι 19, dat.
>   κέλλαι 28 (A.D. 108); PPetaus 36.5 (ca. A.D. 185); POxy. 1067.11

---

[1] Cf. also from the mag. papp. λάμνης *lamina* PGM 9.8 (4th/5th cent.); λάμνας PGM 7.459,462 (3rd cent.); λάμνη PGM 4.2153 (4th cent.).

(3rd cent.); *POxy.* 2146.9 (3rd cent.); *PLips.* 102 ii.1 (prob. late
4th cent.); *PMon.* 8.11,12 (late 6th cent.); sim. *SB* 4755.17 (Byz.)
cf. possibly also κέλλου *PLond.* 157a (ii, 255).1 (2nd cent.?)
κέλλη *BGU* 845.21: *BL* i, 72 (2nd cent.); *POxy.* 495.8 (A.D. 181-9);
BGU 98.14 (A.D. 211)
but κέλλᾳ *PHermRees* 52.7 (A.D. 399)
κέλλαν *BGU* 1036 = *MChr.* 118.10,27 part. rest. (A.D. 108); *POxy.*
1128.15 (A.D. 173); *PMilVogl.* 203.4 (2nd half 2nd cent.); *PFlor.*
10.7 (3rd cent.); *PGiss.* 52.6,13 (A.D. 397); etc.
ἀννώνης *annona PBerlLeihg.* 9.3 (A.D. 240/1); *POxy.* 1192.4 (A.D. 280);
POxy. 1115.9 (A.D. 284); *OMich.* 802.4; 1029.4 (A.D. 296); *POxy.*
2408.1,9 (A.D. 397); etc.
but ἀννώνας *PMich.* 390.4 (A.D. 215); *SB* 9429.4-5 (A.D. 247)

4) Only a few Latin loanwords are declined -η, -ης, -ῃ, -ην:

χώρτη *cohors SB* 4591.3-4, inscr. (Rom.); 4601.2, inscr. (A.D. 144); etc.
χώρτης *PBeattyPanop.* 1.46 part. rest. (A.D. 298); 2.292 (A.D. 300);
cf. *SB* 8523.4; 8524.10, inscrr. (Rom.); etc.
χώρτῃ, χώρτην *MChr.* 372 v.16; iv.5 (2nd cent.)
χώρτην *PMich.* 466.48 part. rest. (A.D. 107); *BGU* 423 = *WChr.*
480.28 (2nd cent.); *OTait* 1682.1 (2nd/early 3rd cent.); *PBaden*
87.4 (3rd cent.); etc.
κορτίνην *cortina PCairMasp.* 6 V.48 (ca. A.D. 567)
σκάλη *scala POxy.* 1925.42 (7th cent.)
cf. μανδήλην *mantele SB* 7033.42 (A.D. 481)
See also δαλματική, etc., immediately below.

5) Some first declension Latin loanwords also have second declension by-
forms or are declined exclusively according to the second declension:[1]

τάβλα *tabula BGU* 1079 = *WChr.* 60.29 (A.D. 41)
τάβλη[ς] *BGU* 847 = *WChr.* 460.15 (A.D. 182/3)
τάβλαν *PPar.* 18b = *WChr.* 499.5 (2nd/3rd cent.)
τάβλας *SB* 4514 (A.D. 269)
but τάβλου *SB* 4924.2 (Byz.)
and τάβλα (neut. pl.) *BGU* 338.8 (2nd/3rd cent.); poss. also *PLBat.* vi,
49 b ii.6 (prob. A.D. 205)
λωρίκαν *lorica POxy.* 812.7 (5 B.C.)
but λωρεῖκος (nom.) *PLond.* 191 (ii, 264-5).14 (A.D. 103-17)
λωρίκων (or -ῶν) *PBeattyPanop.* 1.343-4 (A.D. 298)
δαλματική *dalmatica CPR* 21 = *StudPal.* xx, 31.16 (A.D. 230)
δαλματικῆς *StudPal.* xx, 85 R i.21 (1st half 4th cent.: *BL* v, 144);
sim. *PLond.* 247 = *PAbinn.* 81.4 (ca. A.D. 346)

---

[1] Cf. also dimin. formations in -ιον, e.g., κελλίον, ταβλίον, etc. (Palmer, 86).

δερ[μα]τικήν *POxy.* 1583.9 (2nd cent.); in full *BGU* 93.7 (2nd/3rd cent.)

cf. δελματικήν *PDura* 33.8 (A.D. 240-50)

but δελματικόν *PSI* 900.7 (3rd/4th cent.); *POxy.* 1741.15, sim. 5 (early 4th cent.)

δελματικά *PRyl.* 627.4, sim. 344 (A.D. 317-23); *WO* 1611.6-9 abbrev. (Rom.)

βατέλλης *patella POxy.* 2423 R iv.15 (2nd/3rd cent.)

but πάτελλον *BGU* 781 vi.2 (1st cent.)

κούκκομα *cucuma PCairIsidor.* 137.4 (late 3rd/early 4th cent.)

κόκκουμαν *PGissBibl.* 25.8-9 (3rd cent.); sim. *POxy.* 1160.23 (late 3rd/early 4th cent.)

but κούκκουμος *StudPal.* xx, 67 R.16 (2nd/3rd cent.)

καμπάνω *campana PCairMasp.* 325 iv R.37 (after A.D. 585); *BGU* 550.2 (Arab.); sim. *PHermRees* 27.8 (5th cent.)

κάμπανον *PLond.* 1369.5 (A.D. 710)

σπορτούλου *sportula PFouad* 85.9 (6th/7th cent.); *PLond.* 1332.12, sim. 14; 1333.13, sim. 15 (A.D. 708)

6) Other loanwords of the Latin first declension are declined according to the Greek third declension:

μάνικες *manica BGU* 40.3 (2nd/3rd cent.: *BL* i, 11)

τῆς φαβρίκος *fabrica PBeattyPanop.* 1.214 (A.D. 298)

g. Some feminine personal names in -α are normally declined -α, -ης, -η, -αν, others (in addition to those in -ία, -έα, and -ρᾱ) -α, -ας, -ᾳ, -αν, while most fluctuate between the two declensional types.

1) Declined -α, -ης, -η, -αν:

Ἀμερύλλη *BGU* 301.3 (A.D. 157)

Δῶμνα *BGU* 9 = *WChr.* 293 i.10 (late 3rd cent.)

Δόμνη *POxy.* 1350 descr. (5th/6th cent.)

Κρονιαίνης *OTheb.* 98.2 abbrev. (A.D. 111); *SB* 9495 (1a) = *PMilVogl.* 193.2,11 (A.D. 147); *SB* 9378 = *PMilVogl.* 103.6 (2nd cent.); *BGU* 560 i.6 (2nd cent.); sim. *PSI* 1227.15 (A.D. 188); *PLBat.* vi, 48.23 (A.D. 202/3)

Λυκαίνης, Λυκαίνη, Λύκαιναν *BGU* 1051.2,15,28 (30 B.C. - A.D. 14)

Λυκαρίαινα *SB* 7561.6 (2nd cent.)

Λυκαριαίνης *BGU* 407.4 (3rd cent.?)

Μαρκέλλης *PBouriant* 41a.10 (A.D. 197); *POxy.* 1460.4 part. rest. (A.D. 219/20 or 223/4: *BL* iv, 62)

Μαρκέλλαν *BGU* 326 = *MChr.* 316 i.4 (A.D. 189); *BGU* 384.10 (2nd/3rd cent.)

Νεμεσίαινα *BGU* 1899.1 (A.D. 172+)
    Νεμεσιαίνης *CPR* 155.6 (2nd cent.?); 95.4 (early 3rd cent.); 159.3
    (1st half 3rd cent.); *SB* 4370.6 (A.D. 228/9); *PMichael.* 28.2 (A.D.
    311/12?); etc.
Νιλίαινα *SB* 7790.9, inscr. (A.D. 222); cf. nom. Νιλιαίνι *SB* 9554 (26).18-19
    (A.D. 147)
    Νιλιαίνης *StudPal.* xx, 42.1 (2nd cent.)
    Νειλλίαιναν *BGU* 115 = *WChr.* 203 i.10 (A.D. 189)
Παλλαντιαίνης *BGU* 499.12 (2nd cent.)
Πρισκίλλης *PGiss.* 84 ii.21 (early 2nd cent.)
Προκόνδη *POxy.* 1020.7 (A.D. 198-201)
Σαραπιαίνης *PLips.* 33 = *MChr.* 55 ii.19 (A.D. 368)
Σατυριαίνης *PLond.* 358 = *MChr.* 52.11 (ca. A.D. 150); *BGU* 505.10
    (2nd cent.)
Τανουβιαίνης *PLond.* 258 (ii, 28-36).223 (A.D. 94)
Τερτίλλης *PLond.* 188 (ii, 141-6).91 (3rd cent.?)

2) Declined -α, -ας, -ᾳ, -αν:

Μακρῖνα *SB* 6193.2-3, inscr. (Xtn.)
    Μακρίνας *BGU* 114 = *MChr.* 372 i.6 (2nd cent.)
Μαροέμμᾳ *BGU* 895.29 (2nd cent.)
Μενεχώσᾳ *PRein.* 54.17 (3rd/4th cent.)
Πρείσκας *PSAAthen.* 37.2 (A.D. 138-61); *PLond.* 470 = *MChr.* 328.11
    (A.D. 168); *POxy.* 907 = *MChr.* 317.4,21 (A.D. 276)
Σεκουντίλλας *PGiss.* 106.1 & V (6th cent.); *PBaden* 30.7 (A.D. 577?)
Σεουηρίνας *CPR* 9 i.5-6 (A.D. 271)
Σωτείρας *PLond.* 604 B (iii, 76-87).324 (ca. A.D. 47); sim. *PVars.* 23.5
    (2nd/3rd cent.)
Ταβούας *BGU* 277 ii.1 (2nd cent.)

3) Declined according to either declensional type:

'Αμμωνίλλης *PSI* 875.1 (1st/2nd cent.); *SB* 9298.11-12 (A.D. 249); *POxy.*
    1714.4 (prob. A.D. 285-304)
    ['Αμμων]ίλλη *PMilVogl.* 161 i.8; sim. ii.4 (A.D. 117-38)
but 'Αμμωνίλλας *PStrassb.* 122.6 (A.D. 161-9); *OTait* 1630.4 (A.D. 250)
"Αννης *POxy.* 2419.9 (6th cent.); *PApoll.* 79.10; 80.10 (A.D. 703-15)
but "Αννας *POxy.* 1982.7 (A.D. 497); *POxy.* 1990.13 (A.D. 591); *BGU*
    402.8 (A.D. 582-602); *POxy.* 2244.9 (6th/7th cent.)
    "Αννᾳ *PHermRees* 31.5 (6th cent.)
'Αρίλλης *PHarris* 65.4 (A.D. 342)
but 'Αρίλλας *PLond.* 1673.129 (6th cent.); *POxy.* 2058.64 (6th cent.)
Βικτωρίνη *PGrenf.* ii, 97 = *StudPal.* iii, 318.8, with gen. Βικτωρίνης 1
    (6th cent.); *PCairMasp.* 6 V.33,99 (ca. A.D. 567)
    Βικτωρίνης *PHermRees* 42.1 (6th cent.)
but Οὐικτωρείνᾳ, -ας *PRyl.* 181.6,9 (A.D. 203/4)

Γεμέλλης *PFay.* 113.15; 114.20 (A.D. 100); *BGU* 913.12 (A.D. 206); *BGU* 1722.3 (Rom.)

but Γεμέλλας *BGU* 282.12 (A.D. 161-80); *PCairGoodsp.* 30 xix.6 (A.D. 191-2); etc.

Θέκλης *PSI* 60.12 (A.D. 595); *POxy.* 2478.14 (A.D. 595: *BL* v, 82)

but Θέκλας *PHermRees* 22.6 (A.D. 394); *POxy.* 1900.8 (A.D. 528); *PAntin.* 42.4 (A.D. 542); *POxy.* 2238.10 (A.D. 551); *PMichael.* 42 B.4 (A.D. 566); etc.

Θέκλᾳ *POxy.* 1911.201 (A.D. 557); *POxy.* 2480.170 (prob. A.D. 565/6)

Θεωνίλλης *POxy.* 2346.43-44 (2nd half 3rd cent.); *POxy.* 1747.59 (late 3rd/early 4th cent.); *POxy.* 2421.26 (early 4th cent.); *PHamb.* 21.1 (A.D. 315); *PFlor.* 64.18 (early 4th cent.?); etc.

but Θεονίλλᾳ *PSI* 895.5, with nom. Θεωνίλλα marg. (3rd/4th cent.)

Κοπρίλλης *PGen.* 41.3 (A.D. 222/3); *PRossGeorg.* iii, 4.23 (3rd cent.); *PPrinc.* 30.3 (ca. A.D. 264)

but Κοπρίλλᾳ *StudPal.* xx, 71.4 (A.D. 268-70)

Κυρίλλης *PLond.* 1164 (iii, 154-67) g.1 (A.D. 212); *SB* 8087.2-3 (ca. A.D. 279); *PRyl.* 288.5 (late 3rd cent.)

Κυρίλλη *PMich.* 207.1 (2nd cent.); *POxy.* 931.11 (2nd cent.)

but Κυρίλλας *PErl.* 75.15 (A.D. 535-7); *PLond.* 1020 (iii, 272-3).4,7 (7th cent.)

Κυρίλλᾳ *BGU* 1662.5,9 (A.D. 182)

Λουκίλλη[ς] *PJand.* 95.5 (2nd/3rd cent.)

but Λουκίλλᾳ *PSI* 295.8 (A.D. 235/8?)

Μαξίμα *StudPal.* v, 127 = xx, 68 I R xvii.14; xviii.18 (3rd cent.); *POxy.* 1442.3 (A.D. 252)

Μαξίμας *SB* 6821.2 (A.D. 161); *PMarmarica* vii.17 (A.D. 190/1?); *POxy.* 2338.32 (late 3rd cent.); *PAmh.* 149.4 (6th cent.); etc.

Μαξίμᾳ *POxy.* 1895.4 (A.D. 554)

but Μαξίμης *PStrassb.* 23.9 (1st/2nd cent.)

Μαξίμη *PHermRees* 84.11 (6th cent.)

Νεμεσίλλης *BGU* 497.13 (2nd cent.); *BGU* 603.5 part. rest. (A.D. 168); *PSI* 93.19-20 (3rd cent.); *PLips.* 33 = *MChr.* 55 ii.10, etc. (A.D. 368); etc.

but Νεμεσίλλᾳ *PMeyer* 27.10 (2nd/3rd cent.)

Σαβείνης *BGU* 542.1 (A.D. 165); sim. *StudPal.* xx, 46 R.6 (2nd/3rd cent.)

Σαβίνη *BGU* 632.1-2 (2nd cent.)

but Σαβείνας *CPR* 195.6 (2nd cent.); *PSI* 1104.2 (A.D. 175); *PSI* 811.2 (3rd cent.?)

Σεκούνδης *MChr.* 372 iv.18 (2nd cent.)

but Σεκόνδας *POxy.* 294.9 (A.D. 22); sim. *SB* 4252 = *OMeyer* 56.4 (2nd cent.)

Σερηνίλλης *BGU* 1897.107 abbrev. (A.D. 166); *BGU* 1899.27 (A.D. 172+); *PSI* 465.4 (A.D. 265?); *SB* 7671 = *PCairIsidor.* 5.10,14 (A.D. 299); etc.

but Σερηνίλλας *PCairIsidor.* 122.1, sim.12 (A.D. 314/15); *OHeid.* 288.8 (Rom.); *POxy.* 2058.8 (6th cent.)

Σερηνίλᾳ *POxy.* 1751.1 (A.D. 347)

4. Nouns in -ας.

a. In Latin loanwords, the gen. sg. fluctuates between -ου and -α, and the acc. sg. between -αν and -α; the other cases are regular. By-forms of κολλήγας also occur.

> ὁ σκρείβας *scriba POxy.* 1417.10 (early 4th cent.); (σκρίβας) *PLond.*
>   1914.18 (A.D. 335?); *POxy.* 2110.41 (A.D. 370); *PLips.* 40 ii.22;
>   iii.14,15,25 (late 4th/early 5th cent.)
>   τοῦ σκρείβου *POxy.* 1191.7 (A.D. 280)
>   σκρίβου *PLips.* 40 iii.19 (late 4th/early 5th cent.)
>   ἀντισκρίβου *PSI* 768.15 (A.D. 465)
>   (gen.) σκρείβα *POxy.* 59.9 (A.D. 292); *POxy.* 2674.5 (A.D. 308)
>   σκρίβα *PErl.* 109.3 (early 4th cent.)
>   τὸν σκρίβαν *PLips.* 40 ii.20 twice, with τὸν σκρίβα ii.12; iii.8,14,17
>   (late 4th/early 5th cent.)
>   τὸν [σ]κρίβα *PCairMasp.* 353 V A.25 (A.D. 569)
>   τὸν ... ἀντισκρίβα *MChr.* 71.11 (A.D. 462)
>   ἰσκ[ρ]ίβαις *StudPal.* i, p. 8, iii.3 (A.D. 456)
> τοῦ κολήκου (for κολλήγου) *collega OTait* 1861.5,6 (3rd cent.)
>   τοῦ κολλήγα *PLips.* 40 iii.18 (late 4th/early 5th cent.)
>   (acc.) κολλήγα *POxy.* 1253.17 (4th cent.)
>   τῶν ... κολ[λη]γῶν *SB* 7252 = *PMich.* 220.25-26 (A.D. 296)
>   τοῖς κολλήγαις *POxy.* 123.14 (3rd/4th cent.)
>   τοὺς κολλήγας *PMich.* 466.45 (A.D. 107)
>   cf. κολληγίω(νι) *SB* 9207.7 (2nd cent.)
>   τοὺς κολληγιᾶτες *PSAAthen.* 67.9: *BL* iii, 220 (3rd/4th cent.)

b. The gen. sg. of names in -ας of whatever origin fluctuates between -ου and the Doric -α:[1]

1) Gen. -ου:

> Αἰνείου *PRyl.* 621.15 (early 4th cent.); *PCairMasp.* 327.45 (prob.
>   A.D. 539)
> Ἀκύλλου *PPrinc.* 64.6 (late 3rd cent.); *PLips.* 100 iii.2 (1st half 4th
>   cent.: *BL* v, 49)

---

[1] Foreign names in -ας have gen. -ου in Att. public inscrr. in the 5th and 4th cent. B.C. but a gen. in -α is found in one private inscr. in the name of an Athenian (*MS*, 120). At Perg., only -ου is found (Schweizer, 138). At Magn., the Doric gen. -α is found a few times in names in wh. a gen. in -ου is also found (Nachmanson, 119-20). Both endings are also found at Lycia, w. -ου more common (Hauser, 77). In the Ptol. papp., the gen. is reg. -ου, but -α is found occ. (Mayser i², 2, 3-4). In the NT, the gen. of foreign names in -ας is -α except after ι, when it is -ου (*BDF*, § 55.1). The gen. -α is sts. found even in the Atticists (Schmid iv, 586) and in Rom. names in Gr. inscrr. (Eckinger, 129). Cf. further Hatzidakis, *Einl.*, 77-78; Dieterich, 171-2; Jannaris, § 277.

Ἑρμαγόρου *PSI* 947.18 (A.D. 185/6?); *StudPal.* xx, 83 iv.17 part. rest. (3rd/4th cent.)

Ἑρμανίου *PRyl.* 75.24 (late 2nd cent.)

Κοπρέου *PAntin.* 106.1 (A.D. 304); *PCairGoodsp.* 13.4 (A.D. 341); *PHermRees* 57.13 (4th cent.); *PLips.* 65 = *WChr.* 404.13 (A.D. 390); etc.

2) Gen. -α:

Ἀβίκλα *PLond.* 1449.92 (A.D. 710-12)

Ἀγρίππα *PAmh.* 75.32,35,36 (A.D. 161-8); *PHamb.* 39 HH i.2 (A.D. 179)

Γάλβα *WO* 21.4; 423.3 (A.D. 68); sim. *PLond.* 260 = *StudPal.* iv, pp. 72-78.68; *PLond.* 261 = *StudPal.* iv, pp. 62-72.207 (A.D. 72/73); etc.

Γέτα *BGU* 45.25 part. rest. (A.D. 203); *BGU* 2 = *MChr.* 113.20 (A.D. 209); etc.

Μαικήνα *Archiv* v, 380, #41.4 (A.D. 15); *PFlor.* 6.2 (A.D. 210); *PFlor.* 71.338,421 (4th cent.)

Πάνσα *WO* 129.2; 130.1 (A.D. 124); *PRyl.* 172.4 (A.D. 208); sim. *PFlor.* 151.4 (A.D. 267)

3) Gen. -ου or -α:

Ἀκύλου *PSI* 1149.13 (1st cent.); *PHarris* 76.4 (A.D. 88); *PBeattyPanop.* 1.351 (A.D. 298)

but Ἀκύλα *BGU* 660 i.16 (2nd cent.); *BGU* 71.21 (A.D. 189); *PTebt.* 324.9 (A.D. 208); etc.

Ἀμύντου *SB* 2062 = *OTait* 1925.11 (1st/2nd cent.); *POxy.* 918 ii.6 part. rest. (2nd cent.), *WO* 1486.3 (2nd cent.); *PHarris* 108.2 (3rd cent.); etc.

but Ἀμύντα *SB* 7348.9 (A.D. 23); *PPrinc.* 13, xix.21 (ca. A.D. 35)

Ἀνδρέου *PGron.* 6.10 (5th cent.?); *BGU* 673.3 (A.D. 525); *PSI* 954.24 (6th cent.); *PFouad* 88.2 (6th cent.); etc.

but Ἀνδρέα *PAntin.* 109.22 (6th cent.); *SB* 9402.24 (6th/7th cent.); sim. *SB* 9436 ii.4 (4th cent.); etc.

Ἑρμίου *PCornell* 6.31 (A.D. 17); 21.131,220,418 (A.D. 25); *PRossGeorg.* ii, 12 iii.14,20 (A.D. 48); *PHarris* 72.16,20 (1st/2nd cent.); *BGU* 1621 iii.2 (2nd cent.); *POxy.* 513 = *WChr.* 183.1,47 (A.D. 184); *PJand.* 94.2 (late 2nd/early 3rd cent.); etc.

but Ἑρμία *PMich.* 311.44; 312.53 (A.D. 34); *PRossGeorg.* ii, 20.12 (ca. A.D. 146); *PFay.* 94.4 (A.D. 222-35); etc.

Ἡλίου *POxy.* 2195.2,12 (6th cent.); *POxy.* 2243 a.39 (A.D. 590); etc.

but Ἡλία *PSI* 1268.3 (A.D. 290); *PHermRees* 21.23 (A.D. 346); *POxy.* 2197.74,113 part. rest. (6th cent.); etc.

Ματρέου *POxy.* 1444.26 (A.D. 248/9); sim. *POxy.* 2035.16 (late 6th cent.)

but Ματρέα *POxy.* 611 descr.: *BL* i, 326 (2nd cent.); cf. *SB* 1456, inscr. (n.d.)

Φιλώτου *BGU* 1891.61,299 (A.D. 134); *PFay.* 26.12 (A.D. 150); *OTait* 1589.3 (A.D. 209) but Φιλώτα *SB* 7558.8 (A.D. 172/3?); *PFlor.* 100.20 (A.D. 231/2?); *OMich.* 183.4 (A.D. 301); etc.

5. Nouns in -ης.

a. A gen. sg. in -η, the Modern Greek gen. of nouns in -ης,[1] is sometimes attested in common nouns and foreign names from the first century A.D. on.

1) In common nouns:

ἀπηλιώτη (parallel to λιβός) *PMich.* 308.4, with ἀπηλιότου 2 (1st cent.)
φροτιστῆ (for φροντιστῆ) *PLond.* 851 (iii, 48-50).47 (A.D. 216-19)
Πολείονος στρατειότη *PTebt.* 538 descr. (3rd cent.)
π[ε]ρ[ὶ] Παύλω τοῦ στρατιότη *PLond.* 417 = *PAbinn.* 32.6 (ca. A.D. 346)
διὰ Πέκυσι ὀνηλάτη *POxy.* 2730.19-20 (4th cent.)
διὰ σοῦ ... βιάρχη *PMich.* 612.4-5 (A.D. 514)
τοῦ ἐμοῦ δεσπότη *PSI* 843.5 (5th/6th cent.)
    τοῦ δεσπότη *POxy.* 1867.12 twice (7th cent.)
Μηγᾶ ναύτη *POxy.* 1948.7 (early 6th cent.)
διὰ Μρίσωνος οἰκέτη *POxy.* 2779.15-16, with οἰκέτου 5 (A.D. 530)

2) In names:

Ἰωάννη *PFlor.* 78.65 (A.D. 330-40: *BL* iii, 56); *POxy.* 1986.24 (A.D. 549); *PLond.* 1765.9 (A.D. 554); *POxy.* 2057.3 (7th cent.); etc.
Μαλλίτη *PAbinn.* 82.8,12,19, with Μαλλίτου 4,6,10, etc. (ca. A.D. 346)

b. The voc. is regular in -α:[2]

δέσποτα *POxy.* 2131.7 (A.D. 207); *POxy.* 2133.4 (late 3rd cent.); *PStrassb.* 286.16 (mid 4th cent.); *PCairMasp.* 2 iii.16 (A.D. 567: *BL* i, 100); *PAntin.* 188.11 (6th/7th cent.); etc.
εὐεργέτα *PGM* 31b.2 (1st cent.)
πρόστατα *PGMXtn.* 8a.2 (6th cent.)

c. Heteroclitic *o*-stem forms are sometimes found in the pl. of masc. nouns:[3]

ὑ ὑπογεγραμμένυ ἄνδρες ἁλοπῶλυ (= οἱ -μένοι -πῶλοι for -πῶλαι)
SB 8030 = *PMich.* 245.2-3 (A.D. 47)

---

[1] Mirambel, *Langue grecque*, 106; *Gram.*, 49-50; Thumb, *Handbook*, § 68; Jannaris, § 278.

[2] The late Attic analogous formation δέσποτε (Schwyzer, "Vulg.," 256; *MS*, 124) does not occur.

[3] τοῖς ναύτοις and ἀμφότεροι λυχνάπτοι are found in the Ptol. papp. (Mayser i², 2, 10-11).

ἐπιτιμητοί (for ἐπιτιμηταί) *BGU* 747 = *WChr.* 35 ii.7 (A.D. 139)
τοῖς συνοδείτοις (for συνοδίταις) *PMich.* 575.2,4,10 (A.D. 184?)
[τ]οῖ[ς] γεννεροτάτοις στρατιώδροις (for στρατιώταις) *PSI* 683.19: *BL* ii,
    2, 141 (A.D. 199)
πλείονες στρατιῶτοι (for στρατιῶται) *POxy.* 122.7 (late 3rd/4th cent.)
τοῖς σιτομέτροις (for σιτομέτραις) *SB* 9015 = *PMed.* 69.9 (3rd cent.)
τοῖς ναύτοις (for ναύταις) *POxy.* 1071.4 (5th cent.)
οἱ προνοητοί (for προνοηταί) *POxy.* 1931.3 (5th cent.)
τοῖς ἐμοῖς χάρτοις (for χάρταις) *PCairMasp.* 306.8 (A.D. 515)
τοῖς ἐργάτοις (for ἐργάταις) *PSI* 165.2 (6th cent.)
τοῖς ποτ[α]μίτοις (for ποταμίταις) *PCairMasp.* 139, fol. v, R.8 (6th cent.)
οἱ ζυγοστάτοι (for ζυγοστάται) *SB* 9285.9, with τοὺς ζυγοστάτας 11
    (2nd half 6th cent.)

Many of these forms were probably produced under the influence of the
o-forms of the preceding masc. definite article. These nouns have remained
within the first declension in both sg. and pl. in Modern Greek.[1]

d. Other heteroclitic *o*-stem forms occur sporadically:

ἐπιμελιτὴν καὶ εἰσάκτον (for εἰσάκτην[2]) *SB* 8030 = *PMich.* 245.5
    (A.D. 47)
σιτομέτρο[ς] *BGU* 509.11 (2nd cent.)
χάρτον (for χάρτην) *POxy.* 1142.12 (late 3rd cent.)[3]
ναῦτος (for ναύτης) *PMich.* 596.2,14 (A.D. 328/43)
μέσατον (for μεσίτην) *StudPal.* iii, 402.4 (6th cent.)

e. Heteroclitic third declension forms are found only sporadically in names,
including the dat. sg. in -ει so common in papyri of the 3rd-2nd cent. B.C.:[4]

Εὐτυχίδης ... Εὐτυχίδους (for -ίδου) *PAmh.* 103 = *PSarap.* 29.1 (A.D. 90)
Ἀσκληπιάδει (for -άδη) *BGU* 21 i.1 (A.D. 340)
τὸν Ἡρακλείδη *PHamb.* 90.15-16, with Ἡρακλείδην 14 (mid 3rd cent.)

Note. The Latin loanwords *abolla* and *pincerna* are declined -ης, -ην:[5]

ἀβόλλης *StudPal.* xx, 46.20 (2nd/3rd cent.); *POxy.* 2424.40 (2nd/3rd
    cent.); *SB* 9834 b.5 (early 4th cent.)

---

[1] The MGr. pl. of these and other nouns of the 1st decl. is usu. -ες, but κλέφτοι, etc.,
is found dialectally (Thumb, *Handbook*, § 68-69; Mirambel, *Langue grecque*, 112; *Gram.*,
49-50).

[2] εἰσάκτης elsewh. only *Gloss.* Hsch. (*LSJ* and *Suppl.*, s.v.).

[3] ἡ χάρτη Plu. (Mayser i², 2, 10) is not found, but a heteroclitic 3rd decl. form ταῖς χάρτεσι is attested in *PGM* 5.423, w. τὸν χάρτην 304, etc. (4th cent.).

[4] Mayser i², 2, 2-3. The distinction betw. -ει and -η(ι) is purely orthographic in Rom.
and Byz. papyri (see Vol. i, 239-42).

[5] Cf. Palmer, 67-69.

ἀβόλλην *POxy.* 1153.18 (1st cent.); *POslo* 150.17 (1st cent.); *POxy.*
2593.24 (2nd cent.); *BGU* 814.8 (3rd cent.)
πινκέρνης *PLond.* 1656.3 (4th cent.)

6. Nouns in -ᾶς.[1]

a. Names in -ᾶς, originally hypocoristics and not necessarily foreign to
Attic-Ionic,[2] fluctuate between the *a*-stem declension and a mixed *a*- and dental
stem type. Many Egyptian names follow the same patterns.

1) The nom. is regularly -ᾶς, but spellings in -ᾶ appear rarely, probably
representing the loss of final /s/:[3]

Μηνᾶ *PLond.* 1850 descr. (Byz.); *StudPal.* iii, 323.1-2, with οἰνοπράτη
nom. 2 (6th cent.); *BGU* 29 = *StudPal.* iii, 117.1 (7th/8th cent.);
cf. *SB* 8723.3, inscr. (Xtn.)

2) The gen. and dat. fluctuate between -ᾶ, -ᾷ and -ᾶτος, -ᾶτι:[4]

Αἰλουρᾶ *PSI* 1124.3 (A.D. 150); *PSI* 1154d.9 (prob. 2nd cent.); *PHamb.*
34.27 (A.D. 159/60); *SB* 5124.186 (A.D. 193: *BL* v, 94); etc.
Αἰλουρᾷ *PBrem.* 51.22; 52.1; *PStrassb.* 187.2; sim. *PGiss.* 25.1 (all
ca. A.D. 117)
Ἀλεξᾶ *PMich.* 195.5,19 (A.D. 121); *PSAAthen.* 35.6 (A.D. 153/4); *PCol.*
1 V 3.101 (A.D. 155); 6.124 (ca. A.D. 160/1); etc.
but Ἀλεξᾶτος *PLond.* 258 (ii, 28-36).111,112 (A.D. 94); *PMich.* 196.20
(2nd hand), with Ἀλεξᾶ 5 (1st hand) (A.D. 122); *POxy.* 2134.45 (ca.
A.D. 170); etc.
Ἀμμωνᾶ *POxy.* 2346.48,51,55 (2nd half 3rd cent.); *POxy.* 2144.2 (late
3rd cent.); *PMich.* 376.43 (late 3rd/early 4th cent.)
but Ἀμμωνᾶτος *SB* 7590.5 (A.D. 99/100); *PAberd.* 37.1; 38.1 (A.D.
198); sim. *PRossGeorg.* v, 59.11 (4th cent.)
Ἀμμωνᾶτι *PMilVogl.* 52.22 (A.D. 138); 71.2,6 (A.D. 161-80); *PMerton*
28.1,24 (late 3rd cent.); etc.

---

[1] Cf. W. Petersen, "The Greek Masculines in Circumflexed -ᾶς," *CP* 32 (1937), 121-30;
O. Masson, "Quelques noms de métier grecs en -ᾶς et les noms propres correspondants,"
ZPE 11 (1973), pp. 1-19 and pl. i a) & ii.
[2] Schwyzer i, 128.
[3] See Vol. i, 124-6.
[4] Forms in -ᾶδος, -ᾶδι appear only rarely, prob. through the interchange of δ and τ
(see Vol. i, 80-83, 85-86). The Dor. gen. -ᾶ is found once at Perg., along w. -ᾶδος once (Schweizer, 139-40) and predominates at Magn. (Nachmanson, 120), but the dental stem decl. is
more freq. elsewh. in Asia Minor (Schweizer, *ibid.*, w. lit.). In the Ptol. papp., the dental
stem decl. -ᾶτος, -ᾶτι is more freq. than the Dor. -ᾶ (Mayser i², 2, 5-8, w. lit.). In the NT,
however, only the Dor. decl. is found (*BDF*, § 55.1b).

'Αμοιτᾶτος *POxy.* 47.13 (late 1st cent.); *POxy.* 98.4 (A.D. 141/2)

but 'Αμοιτᾷ *POxy.* 509.9 (late 2nd cent.); *SB* 7336.16 (late 3rd cent.)

'Ανουβᾶ *PGrenf.* ii, 49.5 (A.D. 141); *PVars.* 20.1 part. rest. (3rd cent.); *PBeattyPanop.* 1.326 (A.D. 298); etc.

but 'Ανουβᾶτος *PMich.* 123 R XIII (a).7 (A.D. 45-47); *PSI* 901.7,17 (A.D. 46); etc.

'Ανουβᾶτι *PGen.* 71.27: *BL* i, 166 (3rd cent.)

'Αντᾶ *PBouriant* 42.603 (A.D. 167); *POxy.* 1637.31 (A.D. 257-9); *PFlor.* 297.74 (6th cent.); etc.

but 'Αντᾶτος *POxy.* 105 = *MChr.* 303.6,12 part. rest. (A.D. 117-37); *SB* 7662.6 (late 2nd cent.); *PHermRees* 69.5,14 (A.D. 412)

'Απφουᾶ *POxy.* 1138.3 (5th/6th cent.); *StudPal.* viii, 948 = xx, 187.3 (5th/6th cent.); sim. *PLond.* 113 (1) (i, 199-204).94 (6th cent.); etc.

'Απφουᾷ *POxy.* 125.7 (A.D. 560); *POxy.* 2035.14 (late 6th cent.); *POxy.* 2244.61,78 (6th/7th cent.); etc.

Βησᾶ *PSI* 1035.15 (A.D. 179); *POxy.* 2415.25 (late 3rd cent.); *PFlor.* 71.30, etc. (4th cent.); etc.

Βησᾷ *PPrinc.* 174 iii.6 (ca. A.D. 260); *PAntin.* 33.29 (A.D. 346?)

but Βησᾶτος *PHarris* 107 V (3rd cent.?); *PRein.* 143.3 abbrev. (A.D. 228/9); *StudPal.* v, 127 = xx, 68 II R iv.22 (3rd cent.); etc.

Διδυμᾷ *POxy.* 1758.1 (2nd cent.)

but Διδυμᾶτος *POxy.* 115 = *WChr.* 479.4 (2nd cent.); cf. *SB* 8581.3, inscr. (A.D. 20)

Διδυμᾶτι *PPrinc.* 13 ii.17 (ca. A.D. 35); *PSI* 967.1,21 (1st/2nd cent.); *POxy.* 1064.1 (3rd cent.)

'Ερμᾶ *PAmh.* 126 = *PSarap.* 55.9 (A.D. 128); *PMich.* 605.4,19 (A.D. 117); *BGU* 1621 ii.1 (2nd cent.); *PBerlLeihg.* 4 V iii.10, v.17, ix.2 (A.D. 165); etc.

'Ερμᾷ *OMich.* 35.2 (1st cent.); 393.1 (3rd cent.)

but 'Ερμᾶτος *PMich.* 128 III.39 part. rest. (A.D. 46-47); *PHarris* 70.18 part. rest. (A.D. 62); *OROM* 14.1 (A.D. 100); *POxy.* 503.5 (A.D. 118); *PMerton* 70.4,43 (A.D. 159); *PFouad* 73.1 (4th cent.); etc.

Εὐδᾶ *PGen.* 35.1,14 (A.D. 161); *PMich.* 225.3113 (A.D. 173-4); *PLond.* 1170 (iii, 92-103).537 (3rd cent.); etc.

but Εὐδᾶτος (fem.) *BGU* 1898.177 (A.D. 172); (masc.) *PMich.* 422.22 (A.D. 197); *SB* 7013.63 (3rd cent.)

'Ηρᾶ (fem.) *PMerton* 68.3,4 (A.D. 137); (masc.) *BGU* 77.7, with 'Ηρᾶτι 5: *BL* i, 16 (A.D. 172-5); *BGU* 194 = *WChr.* 84.4 (A.D. 177); *PTebt.* 639 descr.12: *BASP* ix, 13-15 (ca. A.D. 198); *PWürzb.* 16.2 (A.D. 349); etc.

'Ηρᾶι *POxy.* 715 = *MChr.* 212.1 (A.D. 131); sim. *POslo* 111.273 (A.D. 235)

but 'Ηρᾶτος (fem.) *PTebt.* 321.6 (A.D. 147); *POxy.* 716 = *MChr.* 360.5 (A.D. 186); (masc.) *PMich.* 240.24,30,72 (A.D. 46/47); *PMerton* 88 xiv.2, with 'Ηρᾶ xiii.7; xv.5 (A.D. 298-301); etc.

Ἡρακλᾶ *PMerton* 16.4 (A.D. 149); *POxy.* 2135.11,13 (A.D. 188)
but Ἡρακλᾶτος *PMich.* 123 R VII.24,32; X.13; etc. (A.D. 45-47); *PFay.*
    31 = *MChr.* 201.5 (ca. A.D. 129)
Θεωνᾶ *OMich.* 566.2 (3rd cent.); 573.3 (late 3rd cent.); *PBeattyPanop.*
    1.329,352 (A.D. 298); etc.
    Θεονᾷ *PAmh.* 3(a) iii.14 = *SB* 9557.50 (A.D. 250-85); *StudPal.* xx,
        268 V.7 (7th cent.); sim. *PGrenf.* ii, 82.2,30 (ca. A.D. 400); *BGU*
        809.9 (Arab.); etc.
but Θεωνᾶτος *POxy.* 1481 V (early 2nd cent.); *BGU* 1891.36 (A.D. 134);
    PAberd. 20.4 (2nd cent.); sim. *POxy.* 1155.20 (A.D. 104)
    Θεονᾶτι *PFay.* 127.12-13 (2nd/3rd cent.)
Κερᾶ *PLond.* 438 (ii, 188-9).5 (A.D. 134: *BL* i, 262); *PChic.* 23.2; 41.4
    (A.D. 158/9); *PCairGoodsp.* 12 iv.10 (A.D. 340)
but Κερᾶτ(ος) *PLond.* 258 (ii, 28-36).236 (A.D. 94); in full *OTait* 1317.3
    (A.D. 134); etc.
Λεοντᾶ *PFay.* 91.8,36 (A.D. 99); *PLBat.* iii, 10.9,33 (A.D. 98-117); etc.
but Λεοντᾶτος *PMich.* 123 R XII.31 (A.D. 45-47); *PStrassb.* 55.11
    (2nd cent.); *PFlor.* 194.7-8 (A.D. 259); etc.
Μηνᾶ *PBerlLeihg.* 18.12 (A.D. 163); *PGron.* 6.13 (5th cent.?); etc.; cf.
    PColt 90 i.9; 91.3; etc. (6th/7th cent.)
    cf. Μηνοῦ *POxy.* 1837.4 (early 6th cent.)
    Μηνᾷ *POxy.* 2238.4 (A.D. 551); *PFouad* 86.12 (6th cent.); *PAntin.*
        45 V (6th cent.); etc.
Χαιρᾶ *PMerton* 15.2 (A.D. 114); *PChic.* 64.4 (A.D. 158/9); *SB* 7196 =
    PBerlLeihg. 4, V iv.14; ix.19 (A.D. 165); *PSI* 922.10 (A.D. 180/92);
    etc.
    Χαιρᾷ *PHamb.* 36.4 (2nd cent.)
but Χαιρᾶτος *PHarris* 70.5 (A.D. 62); *Archiv* vi, p. 428.39 (A.D. 116);
    SB 9025.33 twice (2nd cent.)
    Χαιρᾶτι *SB* 7365.31 abbrev. (A.D. 114: *BL* v, 100); 8002.1 (prob.
        3rd cent.)

3) The acc. is regularly -ᾶν, but some by-forms occur:

Καστωρᾶτα *PMich.* 123 V VI.22 (A.D. 45-47)
but Καστωρᾶν *PMich.* 127 II.20; III.12 abbrev. (A.D. 45-46)
Μηνᾶ *PAntin.* 92.4 (4th/5th cent.); *PFlor.* 303.11 (6th cent.)
Νεμεσᾶτα *PFay.* 96 = *WChr.* 313.9 (A.D. 122)

b. Occupational and other designations formed by the suffix -ᾶς[1] are normally declined -ᾶς, -ᾶ, -ᾷ, -ᾶν, but heteroclitic dental stem forms are sometimes
found in the gen. sg. and in the pl.

---

[1] Cf. Palmer, 49-50; Schwyzer i, 461.

1) Nom. sg.:

πατικουρᾶς *BGU* 594.3 (ca. A.D. 70-80)
ἀρτυματᾶς *SB* 5124.251 (A.D. 193: *BL* v, 94); *POxy.* 1517.14, with ταπιτᾶς
   3 (A.D. 272/8)
φακινᾶς, κασσιτερᾶς *BGU* 1087 ii.13 & v.15 part. rest.; iv.9: *BL* ii, 2, 23
   (3rd cent.)
ὀρνιθᾶς *SB* 7527.5 (prob. 3rd cent.); *PLond.* 870 (iii, 235).3 part. rest.
   (4th cent.)
παστιλλᾶς *POxy.* 1891.4,21 (A.D. 495)
cf. λιβανᾶς *SB* 410.1, inscr. (1st/2nd cent.)

2) Gen. sg.:

ἀργυρᾶ *BGU* 1034.15: *BL* ii, 2, 22 (3rd cent.)
μαχαιρᾶ *POxy.* 1676.6 (3rd cent.)
but μαχερᾶς (nom. for gen.?) *OTait* 2092.2 (late 3rd/early 4th cent.)
κιρκουλᾶ *circulator* *PSAAthen.* 34.7: *BL* iii, 219 (3rd/4th cent.)
πλακουντᾶ *PRossGeorg.* v, 63.7 (7th cent.)
μασγιδᾶ *PLond.* 1334.14 = *PRossGeorg.* iv, 3.3,16 part. rest. (A.D. 709);
   PLond. 1403.4 (A.D. 709-14); *PLond.* 1368.6 part. rest. (A.D. 710)
but κωδᾶτ(ος?), πορτᾶ(τος) *POxy.* 1519.4,7 (mid 3rd cent.)

3) Dat. sg.:

ὀρνειθᾷ *POxy.* 2139.1 (late 2nd/early 3rd cent.); sim. *POxy.* 1568.1:
   BL ii, 2, 101 (A.D. 265); *PCairMasp.* 166.9: *BL* ii, 2, 39 (A.D. 568)
πλακουντᾷ *POxy.* 1495.7 (4th cent.); *PRyl.* 640.12 part. rest. (4th cent.);
   PPrinc. 96.38 (2nd half 6th cent.)
ταλαρᾷ *OMich.* 978.4 (4th cent.)

4) Acc. sg.:

πλακουντᾶν *POxy.* 2672.6-7 (A.D. 218)
   πλακουτᾶ *sic* *SB* 9303.7 (3rd cent.)
σαγματᾶν *PFlor.* 376.8: *BL* i, 460 (3rd cent.)
ὀρνιθᾶν *StudPal.* xx, 107.4 (4th cent.)
ζυτᾶν *SB* 9140.15 (7th cent.)

5) Nom. pl.:

ἀρτυματᾶταις (= -ες) *BGU* 1087 ii.9 (3rd cent.)
κορσᾶτες *BGU* 9 iv.15 (prob. late 3rd cent.)

6) Dat. pl.:

πλακουντᾶσ(ι) *PRyl.* 641.5,27 (4th cent.)

c. ἀββᾶς has gen. -ᾶ, dat. -ᾷ, acc. -ᾶ (-ᾶν at Nessana):

ὁ ἀββᾶς *PColt* 53.2,9-10 (before A.D. 608?)
gen. ἀββᾶ *PAlex.* 32.3 (A.D. 448/63: *BL* v, 4); *PGrenf.* ii, 90.14,24 (6th
    cent.); *PApoll.* 65.2 (A.D. 710/11); etc.
    ἀβᾶ *StudPal.* x, 25.28 (7th cent.); viii, 854.1 (7th/8th cent.)
dat. ἀββᾷ *PCairMasp.* 342 V (6th cent.); *BGU* 103 = *WChr.* 134.11
    (6th/7th cent.); *PBerlZill.* 8.5 (A.D. 663); etc.
acc. ἀββᾶ *POxy.* 1900.5 (A.D. 528); *PSI* 89.1 (6th cent.)
    ἀβᾶν *PColt* 50.1,5; (ἀββᾶν for dat.) 52.13 (early 7th cent.)

d. The Arab title transliterated ἀμῖρ in *PApoll.* 1.1, etc. (ca. A.D. 704/6),
BGU 681 = *StudPal.* viii, 715.4 (Arab.), etc., is usually formed by the addition
of the suffix -ᾶς and declined -ᾶ, -ᾷ, with a heteroclitic gen. pl.:

nom. sg. ἀμιρᾶς *PLond.* 1081 (iii, 282-3).3 (7th cent.); *PApoll.* 10.h (A.D.
    704); 20.1 (A.D. 710); etc.
    ἀμιρᾶ *SB* 5591.7 (8th cent.)
gen. sg. ἀμιρᾶ *SB* 9577.4 (A.D. 643); *PApoll.* 7.1,5 (A.D. 709-12?); *Stud-*
    Pal. x, 204 ii.3 (8th cent.)
dat. sg. ἀμιρᾷ *StudPal.* x, 29.2 (7th cent.); *SB* 5578.3 (A.D. 725: *BL* v,
    96); *SB* 5609.5 (A.D. 735: *BL* v, 97); etc.
gen. pl. τῶν ἀμιράτων *PLips.* 103 = *WChr.* 257.12 (Arab.)

e. The Attic contracted βορρᾶς, with ρρ < ρϳ,[1] is the regular spelling in
documentary papyri.[2] The acc. is usually βορρᾶ; βορρᾶν is rare before the Byzantine period:[3]

ἐπὶ βορρᾶ *PAberd.* 53 i.3,4; ii.4 (A.D. 10/11); *PMich.* 251.27 (A.D. 19);
    PTebt. 383.21,23 (A.D. 46); *PLond.* 293 (ii, 187-8).13 (A.D. 114);
    PMilVogl. 99.7, etc. (A.D. 119); *PMed.* 54.14 (A.D. 138-61); *POxy.*
    1959.12 (A.D. 499); 1965.12 (A.D. 553); etc.
πρὸς βορρᾶ *PLond.* 262 = *MChr.* 181.4 (A.D. 11); *BGU* 251.12 (A.D.
    81); *CPR* 28.20 (A.D. 110); *PHamb.* 62 = *PLBat.* vi, 23.5 (A.D.
    123); *BGU* 907.7 (A.D. 180-93); *CPR* 160.5 (1st half 3rd cent.?); etc.

---

[1] Schwyzer i, 274, 562.

[2] βορέας is found in mag. papp. along w. βορρᾶς: βορέας, βορέαν *PGM* 13.862,863,
w. βορρᾶ (nom.) 840, -ᾶ 826, ᾷ 642 (A.D. 346); βορέα *PGM* 8.10 (4th/5th cent.); βορέαν *PGM*
5.163 (4th cent.); βορρᾶ (acc.) *PGM* 2.106; 4.3183 (4th cent.). βορέας is still found in 5th cent.
B.C. Att. inscrr. (*MS*, 124), but βορρᾶς appears on Att. vases (Kretschmer, *Vas.*, 177).
βορρᾶς is usu. in the Ptol. papp., w. βορέας read only in an Ionicizing pap. of the 1st half
of the 3rd cent. B.C. (Mayser i², 2, 5). βορρᾶς is also the NT spelling (*BDF*, § 45, regarding
it as an Atticism in the Koine; so also Thumb, *Hell.*, 65).

[3] The mag. papp. have acc. βορρᾶ never βορρᾶν, but βορέαν (see preceding note). In
the Ptol. papp., the acc. is usu. βορ(ρ)ᾶν (Mayser i², 1, 5), but εἰς βορρᾶ occurs in *PLille* 2.1
(3rd cent. B.C.) and *BGU* 1002.6 (55 B.C.) and πρὸς βορρᾶ *PTebt.* 86.32 (2nd cent. B.C.).

εἰς βορρᾶ *PSI* 1058.6 (5th/6th cent.); *SB* 4753.6; 4787.5 (Byz.);
    PCairMasp. 302.11 (A.D. 555); *PLond.* 1722.18,21 (A.D. 573);
    PMon. 9.32 (A.D. 585); 13.30 (A.D. 594); *SB* 9154.9 (6th/7th cent.);
    PLond. 133 (6b) = *MChr.* 147.24 (A.D. 633); etc.
ἐπὶ βορρᾶν *PMich.* 293.3 (A.D. 14-37); *PMich.* 326.20,30 (A.D. 48);
    PMich. 287.3 (1st cent.); *BGU* 282.18 (A.D. 161-80); *SB* 8987.13
    (A.D. 644/5)
πρὸς βορᾶν *PMerton* 122.1 (2nd cent.); cf. *PColt* 22.25 (A.D. 566)
εἰς βορρᾶν *PFlor.* 50.87 part. rest. and dotted, with ἐπὶ βορρᾶ 2, etc.
    (A.D. 268); *PBerlZill.* 6.24,25 (A.D. 527-65); *SB* 4697.6 (Byz.);
    PLond. 1768.3,11 (6th cent.); *PMon.* 11.25,28 (A.D. 586); 12.20,23
    (A.D. 590/1?); *SB* 4491.2 (6th/7th cent.); etc.

βορρᾶ appears to represent an alternate spelling for the acc. of nouns in
-ᾶς, although with the widespread loss of final /n/ it may not represent a new
morpheme.[1]

7. Nouns in -ῆς.

a. The name Ἑρμῆς, whether referring to the god or used as a personal
name, is usually declined -οῦ, -ῇ, -ῆν, but gen. -οῦς (also -ῇ), dat. -εῖ (also -ῆτι),
and acc. -ῇ are sometimes found.[2]

1) Gen.:

Ἑρμοῦ (god) *POxy.* 2555.13 (late 1st cent.); *PGiss.* 24 = *WChr.* 15.3
    (ca. A.D. 117); *POxy.* 494 = *MChr.* 305.34 (A.D. 156); *PJand.* 34.3
    (A.D. 190); *PLond.* 1164 (iii, 154-67) g.5,19,21 (A.D. 212); *PFlor.*
    50.97 (A.D. 268); *PHermRees* 2.11 (4th cent.); etc.
    (personal name) *POxy.* 105 = *MChr.* 303.8 (A.D. 117-37); *PGron.*
    7.1 (2nd cent.); *PPrinc.* 132.2 (2nd cent.); *PAmh.* 94 = *WChr.*
    347.1 (A.D. 208); *CPR* 20 = *StudPal.* xx, 54 i.4 part. rest. (A.D.
    250); *PSI* 293.30 (3rd cent.); *StudPal.* v, 119 R iv.20; 120 R ii.1
    (A.D. 266); *StudPal.* xx, 81 i.6 (4th cent.); 121.41 (A.D. 438); etc.
Ἑρμοῦς (god) *PLond.* 98 R (i, 126-30).12-15, etc., with Ἑρμοῦ 34,35,55,59
    (1st/2nd cent.); *SB* 9377 = *PMilVogl.* 84.24 (A.D. 138); *OMich.*
    656.3 (3rd cent.); etc.
    (personal name) *PRyl.* 173a.11, with Ἑρμοῦ 24 (2nd hand) (A.D. 99);
        SB 9609 = *PMilVogl.* 196.3,4 (A.D. 140); *BGU* 1893.136,233,

---

[1] See Vol. i, 111-14, and partic. my "Loss of Nasal Consonants in the Language of the
Papyri," *Akten des XIII. Internationalen Papyrologenkongresses* (*Münchener Beiträge zur
Papyrusforschung und Antiken Rechtsgeschichte.* 66. Heft [1974]), 144-5.
[2] In the Ptol. papp., the gen. is reg. -οῦ, but dat. -ῆι and -εῖ (Mayser i², 2, 5). In the
Herc. papp., the gen. Ἑρμοῦς is alone found; the acc. is Ἑρμῆν more freq. than Ἑρμῆ
(Crönert, 163).

315,336, with Ἑρμοῦ (diff. person) 108,157 (A.D. 149); *PMilVogl.*
142.18 part. rest. (A.D. 165?); etc.
Ἑρμῆ (personal name) *POxy.* 2480.46 (prob. A.D. 565/6)

2) Dat.:

Ἑρμῆ (personal name) *PAmh.* 94 = *WChr.* 347.1 (A.D. 208); *StudPal.*
xx, 30.9 (A.D. 230); *CPR* 229 = *StudPal.* xx, 23.2 (3rd cent.); *PRyl.*
117.1 (A.D. 269); *PRyl.* 627.281, etc. (A.D. 317-23); etc.
cf. Ἑρμεῖ (god) *SB* 8279.16, inscr. (A.D. 133/4)
Ἑρμῆτ(ι) (personal name) *PRyl.* 224a.2 (2nd cent.)

3) Acc.:

Ἑρμῆν (personal name) *PBon.* 39 c R.5 (5th cent.)
Ἑρμῆ (personal name) *PSI* 89.1 (6th cent.)

b. For other names in -ῆς inflected according to mixed *a-*, *s-*, and dental
stem declensional types, see below, pp. 72-74.

B. THE SECOND DECLENSION[1]

1. General features.

a. As in the first declension, the dat. sg. is regularly written without the
-ι adscript, especially after the first century A.D., reflecting the identification
of the long diphthongs in -ι with their corresponding simple vowels.[2]

b. Fluctuation between -ου and -ω(ι) in the gen. and dat. sg.[3] cannot be
considered significant for morphology. It is caused partly by the confusion of
ου and ω in the speech of some writers[4] and partly by a syntactic confusion of
the gen. and dat. cases.[5]

c. The voc. is regularly -ε, including θεέ *PGMXtn.* 8a.1 (6th cent.); θ(ε)έ
BGU 954 = *WChr.* 133.1 (prob. 6th cent.); etc.[6]

---

[1] Schwyzer i, 554-8, cf. also 457-61; Chantraine[2], § 11-26; Buck, *GD*, § 106; *MS*, 124-9;
Schweizer, 141-5; Nachmanson, 122-8; Hauser, 79-83; Mayser i[2], 2, 11-21; Crönert, 164-6,
176-7; *BDF*, § 44-45.
[2] See Vol. i, 183-6, and Introd. to Morphology above, p. XIX.
[3] For exx., see Vol. i, 208-10.
[4] See Vol. i, 213-14.
[5] See esp. J. Humbert, *Disparition du datif*, 168-78. The dat. is not used in MGr. speech
exc. in a very few stereotyped expressions (Thumb, *Handbook*, § 41; Jannaris, § 1247).
[6] The voc. (θεέ and θεός) is late, exc. in compd. names (*LSJ*, s.v.); θεέ LXX and NT,
but ὁ θεός is more freq. (*BDF*, § 44.2) because of Semitic interference: *hammelek* = 'the
king' or 'O king.'

d. An anomalous dat. pl. in -οισι is found in σὺγ χρηστηρίοισι καὶ δικαίοις πᾶσι *PBaden* 172.17-18 (A.D. 547).

e. Change in declensional type.[1]

1) Nouns of the second declension sometimes have forms of the third declension:

τοῦ βαλανήως (for βαλανείου) *OEdfou* 390.1-2; 391.2-3 (2/1 B.C.); with βαλανήου 392.2-3 (2/1 B.C.); etc.
τὸν ἀρχέφοδα (for ἀρχέφοδον) *PAberd.* 60.2 (1st/2nd cent.)
οἱ ἀρχέφοδες (for ἀρχέφοδοι) *BGU* 909 = *WChr.* 382.10 (A.D. 359)
τοῦ μεγάλου κλήρους (for κλήρου) *POxy.* 1482.18-19 (2nd cent.)
ἀργυρικοῦ φώρους (for φόρου) *POxy.* 1719.8 (A.D. 204)

2) Other variants are sporadic and may have phonological explanations, e.g., τυρὰ (for τυρία?) τρία *POxy.* 1870.15 (5th cent.); sim. *PAntin.* 92.17 (4th/5th cent.).[2]

Note. Latin loanwords also fluctuate in declensional type.[3]

1) *Magister* fluctuates between the second and third declensions, and third declension endings are also found in the name *Niger*. Some other nouns of the Latin second declension are declined predominantly according to the Greek third declension.

a) *magister*:

ὁ μαγίστερ *PSI* 481.10 (5th/6th cent.)
μαγίστρου *BGU* 927 = *WChr.* 178.5 (prob. 3rd cent.); *PBeattyPanop.* 1.193, etc. (A.D. 298); *POxy.* 2673.13 (A.D. 304); *BGU* 917.1; 405.3; 456.3 (A.D. 348); *BGU* 1092.3 (A.D. 372); etc.
but μαγίσστορος (for μαγίστωρος) *PLond.* 1790.10 (5th/6th cent.)
μαγίστερος *PCairMasp.* 3.4 part. rest. (A.D. 567: *BL* i, 100); *PCairMasp.* 76.11 (6th cent.)
μαγίστρω *SB* 8994.16 (6th cent.)
but μαγίστωρι *SB* 8262.2 (not later than 5th cent.)
μαγίστερι *PLond.* 1677.3 (A.D. 566/7)

---

[1] For ὁ ἄρακος/ἄραξ, ὁ & τὸ γάρος (τὸ γάρον), διάκονος/διάκων, etc., see below, pp. 98-101.
[2] For loss of accented ι before a back vowel, esp. after ρ, see Vol. i, 302-3. τυρόν, however, is read in Chionid. (*LSJ*, s.v. τυρίον).
[3] For Lat. nouns of other decl. types declined according to the 2nd decl. through the addition of the suffix -ιον, e.g., βεστίον *vestis* (also βέστη), σιλίγνιον *siligo* (also σίλιγνον), σόλιον *solea*, ταβέρνιον *taberna*, see Palmer, 84-90, and the indiv. words in Daris, *Lessico*. For πατρών *patronus* (3rd decl.), see Palmer, 120.

μαγίστερα *PCairMasp.* 76.7 (6th cent.)
μάγιστρε (voc.) *PBeattyPanop.* 1.140 (A.D. 298)
μαγίστρων *POxy.* 2423 V iii.15 (2nd/3rd cent.)
μαγίστερσι *PLond.* 1678.1 (A.D. 566-73)

b) *Niger:*

Νίγερ *OEdfou* 19.3; 20.4 (A.D. 75); *WO* 261.1,5; 266.1 (A.D. 174); *OMich.* 279.1 (3rd cent.); etc.
but Νίγερο(ς) *OTait* 1200.1 (A.D. 114); in full *PMich.* 225.2997 (A.D. 173-4); *PMich.* 395 i.10 (A.D. 183)
Νίγερος (gen.) *WO* 296.3 (A.D. 154/5); *PSI* 161.15 (A.D. 169); sim. *BGU* 454.26 (A.D. 193); *PPrinc.* 52.20 (3rd cent.); etc.
but Νίγρου *OTaitPetr.* 245.2 (ca. A.D. 15-36); *BGU* 1614 C i.6 (A.D. 69/70); *WO* 657.11 (A.D. 165); *POxy.* 1056.1 (A.D. 360); etc.
Μίγερι (for Νίγερι) *PFouad* 37.1 (A.D. 48); (Νίγερι) *SB* 9017 (38).1 (1st/2nd cent.); *PBerlLeihg.* 10.4 part. rest. (A.D. 120)
Νίγερα *SB* 9164.15 (1st half 2nd cent.); *SB* 7558.6 (A.D. 172/3?)

c) Other words:

κόλων *colonus POxy.* 2476.32,48 (A.D. 288: *BL* v, 82)
μαγνιφέρι (for ἰμαγινιφέρι) *imaginifer PBeattyPanop.* 2.297 (A.D. 300)
σιγνιφέρι *signifer PBeattyPanop.* 2.190 part. rest., 195, with σιγνιφέρου 248 (A.D. 300)

2) *Castra,* used also in the singular,[1] seems to have a first declension plural in ἐν ταῖς κάστραι[ς] *PLips.* 97 xxii.9 (A.D. 338).[2]

3) The following nouns of the Latin second declension have Greek first declension by-forms or are declined exclusively according to the Greek first declension:

βασκαύλης *vasculum POxy.* 109.22 (late 3rd/4th cent.)
but βάσκυλα (pl.) *PRyl.* 627.82 (A.D. 317-23)
    cf. πασκαύλιν *PCairIsidor.* 137.3 (late 3rd/early 4th cent.)
βουκελλατῶν *buccellarius PErl.* 81.49 (6th cent.)
but βουκελλάριος passim
καστελλίτης *castellanus PLond.* 1652.6 (1st half 4th cent.)
ξέστης *sextarius* passim

---

[1] See Daris, *Lessico,* s.v.
[2] For nouns of the Lat. 2nd decl. declined according to the Gr. 1st decl. through the addition of the suffix -ίτης, see Palmer 6-7, 110-15, and Daris, *Lessico,* s.vv.

4) Nouns of the Latin fourth declension are declined according to the Greek second declension masculine or neuter, except for *magistratus* declined according to the third declension:[1]

κάσου *casus PCairMasp.* 312.100 (A.D. 567)

    κάσοι *CPR* 30 = *MChr.* 290 ii.23 (6th cent.)

κήνσῳ *census PAmh.* 83 = *WChr.* 230.2 (A.D. 303-6); sim. *SB* 5356.6 (A.D. 311?)

    κήνσου *BGU* 917.6 (A.D. 348)

κομιτάτου *comitatus SB* 7181 A.8 (A.D. 220)

    κομιτάτῳ *PLond.* 233 = *PAbinn.* 58.6 (ca. A.D. 346); *PLips.* 34.6; 35.6 (ca. A.D. 375)

κομμεᾶτον *commeatus PMich.* 466.39 (A.D. 107)

    κομεάτου *PGiss.* 41 = *WChr.* 18.4 (ca. A.D. 117); *POxy.* 1666.14 part. rest. (3rd cent.)

    κομιάτοις *POxy.* 2425 iii.9 (3rd/4th cent.)

    cf. κομιᾶτον *PGM* 26.7 (late 3rd/early 4th cent.)

τοὺς διαφόρους κούρσου(ς) *cursus PCairMasp.* 359 ii R.1 (Arab.)

but τὸ κοῦρ[σον] *PLond.* 1350.4 (A.D. 710)

    τὰ κ[ο]ῦρσα' *PLond.* 1394.9 (A.D. 709/10?)

μίσσος *missus POxy.* 2707.3, etc. (6th cent.)

Πόρτου, Πόρτον *Portus (Ostia) SB* 7352 = *PMich.* 490.10,21 (2nd cent.)

2. Nouns in -ιος/-ιον.

A late Greek declension in -ις/-ιν, -ίου, -ίῳ, -ιν is found considerably more frequently in papyri of all periods than elsewhere in the Koine.[2] In the Roman and Byzantine papyri, forms in ις, ιν are found in names, forms of address, titles, occupational designations, and diminutives.[3]

a. Names:

'Αμμῶνις *PHibeh* 218.25 (1st/2nd cent.); sim. *PMich.* 551.24-25 (A.D. 103); *PMich.* 188.25 (A.D. 120); *POxy.* 64 = *WChr.* 475.4 (3rd/early 4th cent.); etc.

'Αντῶνις *PMich.* 201.1 (A.D. 99); *SB* 9017 (14).1 (1st/2nd cent.); *WO* 304.1 (A.D. 115); *BGU* 846.1 (2nd cent.); *BGU* 876.8 (A.D. 151/2); *SB* 5124.367 (A.D. 193: *BL* v, 94); *POxy.* 1519.13 (mid 3rd cent.);

---

[1] See below, p. 50.

[2] Forms in -ις, -ιν are found in Perg. only in a few later and mainly vulgar inscr. (Schweizer, 143-4, w. lit.); there are isolated late exx. at Magn. (Nachmanson, 125, w. lit.). In the Ptol. papp., these forms occur from ca. 258 B.C. on in names, common nouns, and ad's.; most of the exx. are from the 2nd and 1st cent. B.C. (Mayser i², 2, 15-16). See further Schwyzer i, 472; Thumb, *Hell.*, 36, 154-5, and esp. D. J. Georgacas, "On the Nominal Endings -ις, -ιν in Later Greek," *CP* 43 (1948), 243-60. Names in -ις are also found at Nessana, cf. 'Αβραάμις, Σέργις, Γεῶργις *PColt* 76 i.2,12,24 (A.D. 689?). Forms in -ιν are reflected in Gr. loanwords in Copt., cf. Β ϫⲁⲗⲕⲓⲛ, ⲫⲣⲁⲧⲉⲗⲗⲓⲛ (Böhlig, 121).

[3] For analogous forms in ad's., see below, p. 115.

PRossGeorg. v, 58.88 (4th cent.); *StudPal.* iii, 495.2 (6th cent.); etc.

'Αντῶνιν *SB* 9017 (23).6 (1st/2nd cent.); *PAberd.* 71.12 (2nd cent.)

'Απολινᾶρις *SB* 7661.9 (ca. A.D. 100); *OTait* 1024.1 (A.D. 183?); *PAlex.* 329 (p. 33).7 (Rom.); *OMich.* 4.3 (3rd/4th cent.); etc.

   cf. 'Απολινᾶρι *OTait* 2057.2 (Rom.)

'Απολλιναρίῳ *BGU* 289.1 (A.D. 147-50); *BGU* 38.1 (2nd/3rd cent.: *BL* i, 10); etc.

'Απολλινᾶριν *PMich.* 477.12 part. rest. (early 2nd cent.); *PMich.* 489.4 (2nd cent.); sim. *SB* 7352 = *PMich.* 490.17 (2nd cent.); etc.

Αὐρῆλις *OTait* 1665.1 (A.D. 138-61); *OTait* 2023.4 (2nd half 2nd cent.); *BGU* 578 = *MChr.* 227.8 (A.D. 189); *BGU* 146.1 (2nd/3rd cent.); *PCairIsidor.* 38.10 (A.D. 296); *PMich.* 596.1,13 (A.D. 328/43); etc.

Διονῦσις *PFouad* 59.4,6 (after A.D. 75/76); *WO* 1052.1 (A.D. 100/1); *PMerton* 79.7 (2nd cent.); *BGU* 568.6 (prob. 2nd cent.); *PFouad* 68.5 (late 2nd cent.); *OTait* 1843.3 (2nd/3rd cent.); sim. *PLBat.* xiii, 19.2 (3rd cent.); etc.

Διονῦσιν *BGU* 164.28 (2nd/3rd cent.)

Διονῦσι (acc.) *PLBat.* vi, 15.99 (ca. A.D. 114)

'Ιοῦλις *PAberd.* 22.1 (2nd cent.); *WO* 1130.1 (A.D. 211); *WO* 1144.1 (early 3rd cent.); *PLond.* 246 = *PAbinn.* 61.3,5,9 (A.D. 346); etc.

Κρόνις *PLBat.* vi, 6.9 (A.D. 99); *SB* 5124.227, etc. (A.D. 193: *BL* v, 94); *PFouad* 68.7 (late 2nd cent.); etc.

Μακάρις *BGU* 9 = *WChr.* 293 i.15 (late 3rd cent.); *SB* 5354.17 (5th cent.); *StudPal.* iii, 516.2 (6th cent.); *BGU* 320.9 (Byz./Arab.); *PMerton* 99 R.2 (7th cent.); *PLond.* 1162 V (iii, 252).6 (7th/8th cent.: *BL* i, 294) cf. Μακάρι (nom.) *OStrassb.* 572.3 (prob. 5th/6th cent.); *POxy.* 1866.7 (V) (6th/7th cent.); *PLond.* 1460.126 (ca. A.D. 709)

Μακάρι (gen.) *PGron.* 6.16 (5th cent.?); *SB* 9593.27 (6th/7th cent.)

Οὐαλέρις *CPR* 1 = *MChr.* 220.35 (A.D. 83/84); *BGU* 69 = *MChr.* 142.22 part. rest. (A.D. 120); *PMich.* 224.2761,3405 (A.D. 173-4); etc.

Πετρῶνις *PLond.* 178 (ii, 207-8).25 (A.D. 145); *WO* 257.1 (A.D. 165); *PAberd.* 22.6 (2nd cent.); *BGU* 827.26 (n.d.)

Cf. also Πτολεμαῖς (for Πτολεμαῖος) *PMich.* 395.5 (A.D. 158); *PAmh.* 116.2 (A.D. 178); *SB* 5124.132 (A.D. 193: *BL* v, 94); *BGU* 93.1; 344 i.11, etc. (2nd/3rd cent.); etc.

Πτολεμαῖν (for Πτολεμαῖον) *POxy.* 257 = *WChr.* 147.32 (A.D. 94/95); *SB* 7353 = *PMich.* 491.17 (2nd cent.); *BGU* 227.18 (A.D. 151); etc.

b. The title κύριος:

κῦρις *PMich.* 283-4.17 (1st cent.); *POxy.* 2858.39 (A.D. 171); *StudPal.* viii, 781 = xx, 157.1 (5th/6th cent.); *BGU* 723.3 (Byz.); *PGen.* 14.22 (Byz.); etc.

κῦριν *SB* 9017 (18).9 (1st/2nd cent.); *BGU* 632.15-16 (2nd cent.); *BGU* 827.11-12,17 (n.d.); *POxy.* 1936.11 (6th/7th cent.); *PApoll.* 11.8 (A.D. 705); etc.; cf. *PColt* 52.10 (early 7th cent.)

κῦρι (voc.) *PBrem.* 56a.1 (ca. A.D. 117); *PStrassb.* 355.1 (2nd cent.?);
PSI 1101.6 (A.D. 271); *OMich.* 25.10 (A.D. 279); *PGissBibl.* 30.12-13
(3rd/4th cent.); *PHermRees* 15.2 (late 4th/early 5th cent.); *POxy.*
1871.7 (late 5th cent.); *PJand.* 101.5,8 part. rest. (5th/6th cent.);
PSI 973.8, with κυρῷ 13 (6th cent.); cf. *PGM* 8.14 (4th/5th cent.)

c. Occupational designations (freq. in γέρδις):

γέρδις *PTebt.* 401.4 (early 1st cent.); *PPrinc.* 10 ii.32 (A.D. 34); *BGU*
698.14 (2nd cent.); *StudPal.* xxii, 26.10; 165.27,36 (2nd cent.); *SB*
5124.69,105,225 (A.D. 193: *BL* v, 94); *OStrassb.* 569.3 (prob. 4th
cent.); etc.
γέρδιν *PMich.* 123 R II.34 (A.D. 45-47); *BGU* 1040.38 (2nd cent.);
BGU 2083.2 twice (2nd/3rd cent.); *PMich.* 620.95 (A.D. 239/40);
etc.
but γέρδιος *PPrinc.* 1 i.17 (A.D. 24/25); *OWilb-Brk.* 75.1 (late 2nd cent.);
OTait 1942.2,8,10 (3rd cent.?); *WO* 1155.2 (Rom.); etc.
γερδίωι *PTebt.* 385.8 (A.D. 117)
βενεφικιᾶρις *beneficiarius* *SB* 7662.15 (late 2nd cent.)
λειβλάρεις *librarius* *POxy.* 43 R v.19 (A.D. 295)

d. Diminutives and other nouns in -ιον:[1]

ἀργύριν *POxy.* 2353.5-6 (A.D. 32); *BGU* 827.17 (n.d.)
cf. ἀργύρι (gen.) *PSI* 882.10 (ca. A.D. 330)
ὀψάριν *PMich.* 123 R i, c.8 (A.D. 45-47); cf. *PColt* 53.8 (before A.D.
608?); 160.10 (7th cent.); etc.
κεράμιν *SB* 7356 = *PMich.* 203.27 (A.D. 98-117); *PSI* 206.19 (late 3rd
cent.); *POxy.* 1851.3 (6th/7th cent.)
μισθάριν *PMich.* 202.14 (A.D. 105); *POxy.* 1862.38 (7th cent.); *PApoll.*
28.6 (ca. A.D. 713); cf. *PColt* 73.8 (A.D. 683?); 72.8 (A.D. 684?)
σφυρίδιν *POxy.* 529.5 (2nd cent.); *SB* 7662.10 (late 2nd cent.); *POxy.*
1923.19 (5th/early 6th cent.); sim. *BGU* 247.3,4,6 (2nd/3rd cent.); etc.
ἐπιστόλιν *PPhil.* 35.5-6,8-9,14 (late 2nd cent.)
κνίδιν *POxy.* 2983.9 (2nd/3rd cent.); *PLBat.* xi, 26.18 (3rd cent.)
λωδῖκιν *POxy.* 114.9 (2nd/3rd cent.); *BGU* 93.24: *BL* i, 18 (2nd/3rd
cent.); *SB* 7249 = *PMich.* 217.18 (A.D. 296); sim. *PAntin.* 43.4 (late
3rd/4th cent.)
μαφόρτιν *POxy.* 114.6, sim. 5,5-6 (2nd/3rd cent.); *PGrenf.* i, 53 = *WChr.*
131.7 (4th cent.); *POxy.* 2156.17-18,19 (late 4th/5th cent.); *POslo*
64.11 (5th cent.)

---

[1] For the overlapping of dimin. and non-dimin. -ιον suffixes, see Palmer, 79-84.

δερματίκιν *PTebt.* 413.8 (2nd/3rd cent.); sim. *POxy.* 1051.1,2 (3rd cent.);
    SB 7250 = *PMich.* 218.14 part. rest. (A.D. 296); etc.
οἰκίδιν *PAlex.* 28.5-6 (3rd cent.)
λογάριν *PFay.* 134.5 (early 4th cent.); cf. *PColt* 53.9,11 (before A.D.
    608?)
χαρτάριν *PPrinc.* 100.6 (4th cent.)
πιττάκιν *PAlex.* 40.3 (4th/5th cent.); *POxy.* 1996.5 (5th/early 6th cent.)
cf. πεδίν (for παιδίον) *SB* 9158.2 (5th cent.)

e. The -ιον suffix is sometimes further reduced to -ι:

πάλλι (for πάλλιον) *PMich.* 201.20, with παλλιῶλιν 9 (A.D. 99)
cf. τὸ ψυχί (for ψυχίον) *POxy.* 1874.17-18 (6th cent.)
cf. *enari* (οἰνάρι), *eladi* (ἐλᾶδι), *axnari* (ἀξινάρι), *clindi* (κλινίδι), *opxari*
    (ὀψάρι), etc. *PPar.* 4 bis, Lat.-Gr. glossary (5th/6th cent.)

f. πλοῖον is sometimes written πλοῖν (πλῦν):

πλοῖν *OEdfou* 141.3,4,7,8 (1st/2nd cent.); *OTait* 1733.4,11,15, with πλοίῳ
    11; 1734.4 (2nd cent.); *PFlor.* 298.53 (6th cent.)
πλῦν *POxy.* 528.22, with οι > υ 7 other times (2nd cent.)

The frequency of these forms in -ις, -ιν excludes the possibility that they are
merely orthographic variants of -ιος, -ιον. The above examples of nom. -ις/-ιν,
acc. -ιν, when considered in connection with examples of gen. -οῦ, dat. -ῷ in
some of the same words, as κύρις, κυροῦ, κυρῷ, κῦριν, (voc. κῦρι), and ἀργύριν,
ἀργυροῦ,[1] indicate a new declensional type {-is, -ju, -jo, -in}, neut. {-in, -ju,
-jo, -in} or {-i, -ju, -jo, -i}.[2] The nouns so affected are either diminutives or
other nouns, including names, which lend themselves easily to shortened forms.
The great productivity of the -ιον suffix[3] reflects a predilection for diminutive formations in Koine Greek. This suggests that the forms in -ις, -ιν (later
-ι) are shortened forms of -ιος, -ιον[4] rather than strictly phonetic simpli-

---

[1] For exx. of gen. -οῦ, dat. -ῷ, w. loss of preceding accented -ι, see Vol. i, 302-3.
[2] The nom. and acc. in {-is, -in} may have been pronounced by many writers simply as
{-i}, according to the evidence for the partial loss of final /s/ and /n/ (see Vol. i, 124-6, 111-14).
This decl. has survived in MGr. diminutives, e.g., μάτι, ματιοῦ {mati, matju}, while κύριος
and other nouns in -ιος generally follow the normal 2nd decl. in -ος, -ον (Thumb, *Handbook*,
§ 63, 94-95; Mirambel, *Gram.*, 50-51, 60-61; Pring, 42-46).
[3] See Palmer, 79-90.
[4] So Hatzidakis, whose orig. assumption of the influence of Lat. names in *-is* for *-ius*,
e.g., *Claudis* (*Einl.*, 314-19) is refuted by the evidence of the Ptol. papp. wh. have exx. of
these forms already in the 3rd cent. B.C., considerably antedating poss. Lat. influence. His
later suggestion ('Ἀθηνᾶ 12, 296-7) of the influence of hypocoristics in -ις, as Ζεῦξις for
Ζεύξιππος, is plausible but does not explain the parallel neut. -ιον > -ιν. Jannaris suggests
(§ 1040) that diminutives in -ιον were shortened on the analogy of names in -ιον > -ιν.
Schwyzer's hypothesis (i, 472) of a later (Doric?) contraction is unnecessary.

fications.[1] Phonetic patterns, however, conditioned the change. The -ο- is lost in the nom. and acc. when the accent is proparoxytone; the -ι- is lost in the gen. and dat. when the accent is paroxytone, corresponding to a general shift of prevocalic stressed /i/ to /j/ with concomitant shift of accent to the final vowel.[2] Some few adjectives followed analogously.

3. The Attic second declension.[3]

This declensional type is found frequently (with by-forms) only in ἄλως; it occurs sporadically in a few other words.

a. ἄλως,[4] declined basically according to the Attic declension, fluctuates with a third declension by-form ἄλων; a diminutive form ἀλώνιον is also found.

1) ἄλως:

> gen. sg. ἄλω *PRyl.* 122.10 (A.D. 127); *BGU* 698.17, with τῆς ἄλωι 20 (2nd cent.); *PGen.* 78.21: *BL* i, 167 (2nd/3rd cent.); *POxy.* 1734. 5,10,15 (late 2nd/3rd cent.); *POxy.* 1748.5 (3rd cent.); etc.
> ἄλωι *PRyl.* 168.12 (A.D. 120); *PAmh.* 126 — *PSarap.* 55.22 (A.D. 128); *BGU* 698.20 (2nd cent.)
> dat. sg. ἄλῳ *PHarris* 96.32 (1st/2nd cent.); *PRyl.* 122.20 (A.D. 127); *PMerton* 123.1 (A.D. 151); etc.
> acc. sg. ἄλω *PLond.* 131 R = *SB* 9699.502,576 (A.D. 78/79); *PFay.* 112.19 (A.D. 99); *PWürzb* 22 = *PSarap.* 97.12 (A.D. 117-38); *PLBat.* vi, 45.6 (A.D. 190); *POxy.* 1049.2 (late 2nd cent.); etc.
> ἄλωι *BGU* 698.18 (2nd cent.)
> ἄλων *BGU* 920.19 (A.D. 180); *BGU* 1018.17 (3rd cent.); *PAmh.* 147 = *WChr.* 279.9-10 (4th/early 5th cent.); etc.

---

[1] Georgacas, *CP* 43 (1948), 257-9, sees influence of the stress accent, w. consequent vowel weakening along the line -ιον > [iən] > [iin] > [in], w. -ιος > -ις on false analogy w. acc. sg. -ιν. But this vowel weakening had to occur before the development of the ι in this position to a vowel glide [i], as he well recognizes (p. 259). This explanation places too much of a burden on analogy to explain the freq. exx. of -ιος > -ις, and involves a phonological development contrary to the normal tendency of prevocalic ι throughout the history of the Gr. language (see Schwyzer i, 144-5, 169-74; Thumb, *Hell.*, 297; Dieterich, 45-72; Jannaris, § 155, 271). Georgacas (pp. 248-9) also does not explain the retention of -ιο(ς), -ιο in some MGr. words.

[2] See Vol. i, 302-3.

[3] The so-called Attic 2nd decl., arising first among Ionic speakers through quantitative metathesis (νεώς < νηός < νᾱός), contraction (λαγώς < λαγωός), or analogy from the similarity of the nom. sg. (ἕως, orig. an *s*-stem like αἰδώς, cf. Lat. *aurora*) (Schwyzer i, 514, 557[-8], Zus. 3) was lost in the transition from ancient to MGr. See further Chantraine², § 25; *MS*, 127-8; Dieterich, 173; Crönert, 165; *BDF*, § 44.1.

[4] In origin, ἄλως is an *ou*-stem like ἥρως (Schwyzer i, 479).

gen. pl. ἄλω(ν) *SB* 10573.17 (10/9 B.C.); sim. *POxy.* 1124.11 part. rest. (A.D. 26)

acc. pl. ἄλως *SB* 9643.3 (1st cent.); *PFay.* 112.20 (A.D. 99); *BGU* 918.21 (A.D. 111/12); *POslo* 34, betw. 7-8 (A.D. 188/9); *PFlor.* 120.8 (A.D. 254); etc.

ἄλωι *POxy.* 277.14: *BL* i, 320 (19 B.C.)

The acc. sg. -ω (or -ωι with -ι added erroneously[1]), attested already in Attic,[2] represents a heteroclitic third declension form.[3] The acc. pl. -ω(ι)[4] may have followed the acc. sg.[5] or may simply reflect the loss of final /s/.[6]

2) *n*-stem by-form ἄλων:[7]

ἄλων *BGU* 651 = *MChr.* 111.5 (A.D. 192)

ἄλωνο(ς) *OStrassb.* 520.1 (2nd cent.)
   cf. ἄλωνος *PColt* 26.25 (A.D. 570)
   ἄλωνω *sic* *BGU* 1040.10 (2nd cent.)

ἀλώνων *PSI* 37.1 (A.D. 82); *BGU* 759 = *PSarap.* 1.11 (A.D. 125); *POxy.* 2272.21 (2nd cent.); *PFlor.* 388.104 abbrev. (3rd cent.?); *PStrassb.* 10.20 (A.D. 268); *PLond.* 1239 (iii, 52-53).13 (A.D. 278-81); *PCair-Preis.* 39.18 (A.D. 347); *PSI* 78.7 (5th cent.); etc.

3) Diminutive ἀλώνιον:

ἀλωνί(ου) *OStrassb.* 625 ii.2, 682.1 (2nd cent.)
ἀλωνίῳ *PHermRees* 57.8 (4th cent.)
ἀλ[ω]νί[ων] *BGU* 740.5 (Byz.)
   cf. ἀλόνιον *PColt* 82.4,5 (7th cent.); 83.3,4, with ἀλόνον 1,2 (A.D. 684/5?)
   ἀλωνοῦ (for ἀλωνίου) 84.3 (7th cent.)

b. νεώς is attested only in τοῦ [ν]εώ in *PGiss.* 99.16-17 (2nd/3rd cent.), a very Atticistic speech of an advocate in which other archaic forms, e.g., a dual, occur.[8] The Attic vocalism is also preserved in the combinative form in νεωκόρος, also spelled νεοκόρος, and in νεωκορία:

---

[1] See Vol. i, 183-6.

[2] ἄλω A. inscr.; ἄλων Nic.; cf. acc. νεών inscrr. Ar. X. Philem. Aristid. Ach.Tat. etc.; νεώ inscrr. from the 4th cent. B.C., LXX, D.S. etc. (*LSJ*, s.vv.). ἄλω occurs 4 times in the Ptol. papp., ἄλωι once, ἄλων once (Mayser i², 2, 14).

[3] Perh. on the analogy of αἰδῶ, ἕω (Chantraine², § 25).

[4] ἄλως, ἄλω, and ἄλωι occur once each as acc. pl. in the Ptol. papp. (Mayser i², 2, 14). τὰς ἄλω is also found in codd. of J. (Crönert, ix).

[5] So Crönert, ix.

[6] See Vol. i, 124-6.

[7] Nom. ἄλων Thphr. LXX; oblique cases Arist., etc. (*LSJ*, s.v.). There are six occurrences of forms of ἄλων in the Ptol. papp. (Mayser i², 2, 14), and only τὴν ἄλωνα is attested in the NT (*BDF*, § 44.1; 52).

[8] See above, p. 3.

νεωκόρος *POxy.* 100.2 (A.D. 133); *BGU* 73 = *MChr.* 207.1 (A.D. 135); *POxy.* 2134.5 (ca. A.D. 170); etc.

νεωκόρου *SB* 176.7, inscr. (A.D. 161-80)

νεωκόρῳ *SB* 8010.3 part. rest. (A.D. 54-68?); *POxy.* 477 = *WChr.* 144.1 (A.D. 132/3); *POxy.* 1472.8 (A.D. 136); *BGU* 729 = *MChr.* 167.2 (A.D. 144); *PMich.* 620.1, etc. (A.D. 239/40); etc.

γεωκόρων *PMilVogl.* 56.1 (A.D. 151)

νεοκόρος *BGU* 136 = *MChr.* 86.21 (A.D. 135)

νεοκόρῳ *PMeyer* 6.7 (A.D. 125); *BGU* 455.1 (before A.D. 133)

νεωκορία *SB* 9016 ii.12; sim. i.12,23 part. rest. (A.D. 160)

Νεω[κο]ριῶν *BGU* 14 ii.11 (A.D. 255)

Elsewhere the non-Attic ναός is normal, including in the compound ναοφύ-λ(ακι) *BGU* 362 = *WChr.* 96 iv.16, etc. (A.D. 215); cf. also ναολέκτης *PLond.* 982 (iii, 242-3).2 (A.D. 370-375: *BL* v, 54).[1]

c. Neither λεώς nor λαός occurs in Roman or Byzantine papyri except in composition.[2] As the first element, the combinative form is λαο-, with sporadic variant spellings, e.g., λαγραφίας *PSI* 1432.9 (1st half 1st cent.); *WO* 6.2 abbrev. (A.D. 26); *WO* 12.4 abbrev. (A.D. 46); *OTait* 530.3 (A.D. 124); *OOslo* 9.3 (A.D. 210/11); 10.5 (A.D. 211); etc.; λευγραφίαν *WO* 1239.2 (A.D. 14-37); λωγραφίας *WO* 10.2-3 (A.D. 39); Λαδικεύ<ς> *PLond.* 1178 = *WChr.* 156.84 (A.D. 194); Λαδικίᾳ *PRyl.* 627.276, etc. (A.D. 317-23); Λαυδικ[ίᾳ] *PRyl.* 630-8.246 (A.D. 317-23); Λαυδικίας *PSI* 311.9,20, sim. 23, etc. (4th cent.?). As the second element in names, it appears normally as -λαος, e.g., Νικολάου *PLond.* 258 (ii, 28-36).91 (A.D. 94); Ἀκουσιλάου *PMich.* 354.2 (A.D. 52); Ἀκουσιλάῳ *PLond.* 1221 (iii, 24-25).1 (A.D. 105), as well as with orthographic variants, e.g., Νικόλαως (nom.) *WO* 1198.4 (Rom.); but -λας is found sporadically, e.g., Νικόλας *SB* 1726.3 (1st cent.).

---

[1] νεώς is the only form found in Att. prose inscrr. to 250 B.C., after wh. ναός is normal through the influence of the Koine, but in Rom. times both forms are used (*MS*, 127). ναός was also sts. used in Att. lit., normally in Trag., even dialogue, but only rarely in Com. and prose, e.g., Pl. Arist., more freq. X. (*LSJ*, s.v.). At Perg., only forms of ναός are found, exc. νεωκόρος and τοῦ νεώ in a Rom. poet. inscr. (Schweizer, 142-3 w. lit.). At Magn. and Lycia, only ναός occurs exc. in compds. (Nachmanson, 124; Hauser, 80). In the Ptol. papp., τοῦ νεώ appears once, appar. as a deliberate archaism; elsewh. only forms of ναός occur (Mayser i², 2, 15). τὸν νεών is attested in the Herc. papp. (Crönert, 165). Both Att. and non-Att. forms are found in Plb. Str. Plu. (*ibid.*, n. 1).

[2] Only [λ]αοῦ is read in *PRossGeorg.* v, 24.10 (3rd cent.); λαῶν occurs in a hymn *SB* 4127.19 (Xtn.: *BL* iii, 169), and λαοῦ in *SB* 6087.9, diptych (7th cent.). λαός is found sts. in Trag. and once or twice even in Com. (*LSJ*, s.v.). In the Att. inscrr., λεώς fluctuates in compds. w. -λαος and -λας (*MS*, 128). At Perg., only λαός is attested (Schweizer, 143); at Magn. -λαος and -λας occur (Nachmanson, 124). At Lycia, Λεω[δα]μί[ας] is found, but only -λαος as the 2nd element (Hauser, 80). In the Ptol. papp., only λαός, -λαος and -λας occur (Mayser i², 2, 14-15). See also now C. Vandersleyen, *ChrEg.* 48 (1973), 339-49. In the NT, λαός is used excl. (*BDF*, § 44.1).

d. Αἰγόκερως (Capricorn) is found in horoscopes, etc., always inflected according to the Attic second declension:

Αἰγόκερως *PPrinc.* 75.4 (A.D. 138-61)

Αἰγόκερως, -κερωι (gen.), -κερω[ι] (dat.), -κερωι & -κερω (acc.)[1] *PMich.* 149 passim (2nd cent.)

Αἰγόκερωι (dat.) *POxy.* 2555.2 (late 1st cent.); *PLond.* 110 (i, 130-2). 16,35 (A.D. 138)

Αἰγόκερω *PPar.* 19b.16,36 (A.D. 138); *PLBat.* i, 21.65 (3rd cent.); *PSI* 2790 ii.2 (A.D. 257); *PSI* 764.6 (A.D. 277); 765.12 (A.D. 314?); *PMich.* 153.6 (A.D. 431); *POxy.* 2060.8 (A.D. 498); etc.

Αἰγόγαιρω *WO* 1602.3 (2nd cent.)

cf. also in the magical papyri, e.g., Αἰγόκερως (for gen.) *PGM* 7.819, with Αἰγόκερω (dat.) *PGM* 7.291, etc. (3rd cent.)

e. ἕως, originally an *s*-stem,[2] is attested in Roman and Byzantine documentary papyri only in the adjective ἑωθινοῦ *SB* 7995 = *PSI* 1334.21-22 (3rd cent.) and in the adverb ἕωθεν, e.g., *PAmh.* 136.3 (3rd cent.), but the Attic gen. ἕω occurs in *PGM* 62.33 (late 3rd cent.), as well as ἕωθεν *PGM* 7.156,159 (3rd cent.).

f. λαγώς is attested only in an uncontracted gen. pl. λαγόων (for λαγώων) *PTebt.* 333 = *MChr.* 115.9 (A.D. 216)[3] and in the diminutive form λαγωδίων *PFlor.* 177.13-14 (A.D. 257). The name Λαγώς *PPrinc.* 8 viii.23 (ca. A.D. 27-32), *PAmh.* 129 = *PSarap.* 63.21,27 (A.D. 127/8), is inflected according to the consonantal stem declension, with gen. Λαγῶτος *PRyl.* 595.55 abbrev. (A.D. 57), *PBouriant* 41 a.3 (A.D. 197), dat. Λαγῶτι *PSarap.* 79a (pp. 290-2) ii.13 (early 2nd cent.).

g. μήτρως, in origin an *ou*-stem like ἥρως,[4] has an apparent gen. τοῦ μή-τρ[ω]ς (= -ωος or nom. for gen.?) *CPR* 8 = *StudPal.* xx, 25.10 (A.D. 218).

For adjectives of this type, see below, pp. 125-7.

---

[1] The -ι in the gen. & acc. is an erroneous addition of the -ι adscript (see Vol. 1, 185-6). An acc. Αἰγόκερων is found in Luc. (*LSJ* s.v.).

[2] Cf. Ion. ἠώς, ἠοῦς, ἠοῖ and Schwyzer i, 514. In Att., a gen. ἕω and dat. ἕωι were formed on the analogy of λεώς, νεώς, etc., and also sts. an acc. ἕων (Schwyzer i, 557).

[3] Cf. also λαγοῦ *PGM* 7.176 (3rd cent.). λαγωός is found in Ep. codd.X. Arist. etc.; Ion. λαγός is also found in Dor. Trag. Com. along w. λαγώς (*LSJ*, s.v. λαγώς). The Ion. form has alone survived in MGr. (Thumb, *Handbook*, § 63).

[4] As πάτρως, cf. Lat. *patruus* (Schwyzer i, 479-80). Gen. -ωος & -ω, acc. -ωα & -ων; the pl. is always 3rd decl. (but οἱ πάτρω on a Lydian inscr.) (*LSJ*, s.vv.).

4. Contract nouns of the second declension.

Some contract nouns of the second declension have open forms and/or heteroclitic forms of the consonantal third declension.[1]

a. νοῦς is normally contracted; there is no evidence of the heteroclitic forms νοός, νοί, etc., found elsewhere in the Koine:[2]

νοῦς *POxy.* 2193.12 (LXX) (5th/6th cent.); *PRossGeorg.* iii, 13 V.4,6,7 (6th cent.)

νῷ *PErl.* 18.16 (A.D. 248); τὸ νο (for τῷ νῷ) *SB* 7572.11-12 (prob. 1st half 2nd cent.); *PMich.* 514.8 (3rd cent.)

νοῦν *SB* 8027.8 (2nd/3rd cent.); *PTebt.* 334.9 (A.D. 200/1); *PRyl.* 605.8 (3rd cent.); *PCairMasp.* 154 R. 22 (A.D. 527-65); *PFouad* 86.17 (6th cent.); *PLond.* 1712.15 (A.D. 569); etc.; cf. *PColt* 57.22 (A.D. 689)

νοῦ (prob. for νοῦν) *POxy.* 1665.27 (3rd cent.)

cf. νουνεχίας *PCairMasp.* 2 i.7 (A.D. 567: *BL* i, 100)

νόῳ *BGU* 385 = *WChr.* 100.5 (2nd/3rd cent.)

b. πλοῦς and its compounds are usually contracted in the nom., gen., and acc. sg., but open forms are used in the dat. sg. and in the pl. of ἐπίπλους.[3]

1) Contract forms:

κατάπλους *BGU* 1114.9,11 part. rest. (5 B.C.)

παράπλους *POxy.* 525.1 (early 2nd cent.)

ἐπίπλους *PCairGoodsp.* 28.2 (2nd cent.)

πλοῦ *PBeattyPanop.* 1.253 (A.D. 298)

ἐπίπλου *SB* 7737.3 (1st cent.); *PLond.* 256a = *WChr.* 443.2 part. rest. (A.D. 15)

ἀνάπλου *PFouad* 87.9 (6th cent.)

---

[1] Nouns w. secondary -εο- and -οο- are reg. contr. in Att. and sts. in Ion. In the Koine, this contract decl. becomes less freq. In the Att. inscrr., νοῦς is always so contr., as are ἀδελφιδοῦς, ἔκπλους, etc. (*MS*, 126). At Magn., [ν]οῦν is found, as well as ἀδελφιδοῦ[ς] (Nachmanson, 122-3). In the Ptol. papp., ῥοῦς, φλοῦς, χοῦς (dike), and the neuters κανοῦν and ὀστοῦν are always contr., while both contr. and open forms are found in νοῦς and in πλοῦς and its compds. (usu. contr.); neither λα(ο)ξοῦς nor λα(ο)ξόος occurs, only λαξός (Mayser i², 2, 12-13). In the NT (only Paul), νοῦς is declined like a diphthongal stem of the 3rd decl.; χοῦν is used twice (*BDF*, § 52); but ὀστέον remains usu. uncontr. (*ibid.*, § 45). See further Crönert, 166. In MGr., the only traces of this old contract decl. are in νοῦς, etc., acc. sg. νοῦ(ν), along w. gen. νοός, pl. νοῦδες (also rarely νόες); it is also found dialectally in παπποῦς and in 'Ιησοῦς (Jannaris, § 322; Thumb, *Handbook*, § 63). It has mainly been replaced by the adoption of other words, e.g., ταξίδι for πλοῦς.

[2] E.g., LXX, NT, Ph. Plu. Plot. Dam. etc. (*LSJ*, s.v. νόος). These forms follow the decl. of βοῦς (Schwyzer i, 192, n. 1; 562; Chantraine², § 26).

[3] Cf. *LSJ Suppl.*, s.v. Heteroclitic 3rd decl. forms πλοός, πλοί, attested in D.S., etc. (*LSJ*, s.v.), do not occur.

κατάπλου *PCairMasp.* 293.3 (Byz.)

ἀνάπλου καὶ κατάπλου *PAmh.* 131 = *PSarap.* 80.20 (early 2nd cent.)

πλοῦν *POxy.* 727.11 (A.D. 154); *PTebt.* 317 = *MChr.* 348.10 part. rest.
  (A.D. 174/5); *PTebt.* 437 descr. (2nd/early 3rd cent.); *PHarris* 134.5
  (3rd cent.)

ἀνάπλουν *POxy.* 709 = *WChr.* 32.3 (ca. A.D. 50); *POxy.* 2349.28
  (A.D. 70); *POslo* 154.20 (2nd cent.); *PBeattyPanop.* 2.17 part.
  rest., 111 (A.D. 300)

ἀπόπλουν *PRossGeorg.* ii, 18.183 (A.D. 140)

ἔκπλουν *BGU* 1210 (45).171 (mid 2nd cent.); *PFlor.* 154 R.10 part.
  rest. (3rd cent.)

ἐπίπλουν *PPhil.* 10.9 (A.D. 139)

κατάπλουν *PFlor.* 6.14 (A.D. 210)

cf. Εὔπλουν *BGU* 665 ii.7 (1st cent.)

2) Open forms:

ἐπιπλόου *POxy.* 276.8 (A.D. 77)

ἐπιπλόωι *PSAAthen.* 63.6 (2nd cent.)

  ἀναπλόῳ *POxy.* 1666.12 (3rd cent.)

  κατ[α]πλόῳ *POslo* 62.8 (1st half 4th cent.: *BL* iii, 123)

  cf. Εὐπλόῳ *POxy.* 1585.1 (late 2nd/early 3rd cent.)

ἐπίπλοοι *PAmh.* 123.1 (2nd/3rd cent.)

ἐπιπλόους *PLond.* 342 (ii, 173-4).7-8 (A.D. 185); *PLond.* 301 = *MChr.*
  340.10 (A.D. 138-61)

Note. The classical τὰ ἔπιπλα fluctuates with an expanded spelling ἐπίπλοα:[1]

  ἔπιπλα *PLond.* 177 = *MChr.* 57.21 (A.D. 40/41); *POxy.* 105 = *MChr.*
    303.4 (A.D. 117-37); *POxy.* 2583.5 (2nd cent.); *PLBat.* iii, 7.10 (A.D.
    256/7); *SB* 7243 = *SB* 9746.25-26 (early 4th cent.); etc.

  ἐπίπλων *PMich.* 350.25 part. rest. (2nd hand), with ἐπιπλόων 9 (1st
    hand) (A.D. 37); *POxy.* 489.8 (A.D. 117)

  ἐπίπλοις *PLBat.* ii, 5.17 (A.D. 305)

ἐπίπλοα *BGU* 1654.11 (A.D. 98-117); *PTebt.* 381.13 (A.D. 123); *SB*
  9377 = *PMilVogl.* 84.5 (A.D. 138); *BGU* 483.6 (2nd cent.); etc.

  ἐπιπλόων *PMich.* 321.13,51 (A.D. 42); 352.5 (A.D. 46); 326.64 (A.D.
    48); *SB* 8265.12 (ca. A.D. 335/45); etc.

c. χοῦς "excavated earth" has acc. χοῦν, but the usual gen. is χοός (from
confusion with χοῦς, χοός, a measure of capacity):[2]

---

[1] ἐπίπλοα also codd. Hdt. (*LSJ*, s.v.).

[2] Cf. *LSJ*, s.vv.; Schwyzer i, 577, 582. For the decl. of χοῦς, measure, see below, pp.
83-84.

χοῦν *PLond.* 131 R = *SB* 9699.51 (A.D. 78/79); *POxy.* 985 descr. (2nd
half 1st cent.); *POxy.* 729.6 (A.D. 137); *PRossGeorg.* ii, 19.25 part.
rest. (A.D. 141); *POxy.* 1758.10 (2nd cent.); etc.
τοῦ χοῦ *POxy.* 1631.28, with χοῦν 15 (A.D. 280)
but χοός *PMich.* 322a.7,24 (A.D. 46); *PMich.* 274-5.6 (A.D. 46/47);
PBrem. 14.13 (ca. A.D. 117); *PTebt.* 342.27 (late 2nd cent.)

d. The determinative element -χόος sometimes appears in contracted forms,
but open forms are usual; anomalous and heteroclitic forms also occur:[1]

1) Contracted forms:

χρυσοχοῦς *PFuadCrawford* 8.11 (2nd cent.?); *PPrinc.* 166.1,12-13 (2nd/3rd
cent.); *PLond.* 188 (ii, 141-6).80, etc. (3rd cent.?); cf. *SB* 5144.2,
mummy label (n.d.)
perh. gen. χρυσοχ[ο]ῦ *PMich.* 181.9 (early 2nd cent.)
χρυσοχοῦν *POxy.* 1582.1 (2nd cent.); *BGU* 115 = *WChr.* 203 i.8 abbrev.,
16 (A.D. 189)

2) Open forms:

χρυσοχόος *BGU* 659 ii.27 (A.D. 229); *SB* 9157.6 (3rd cent.); *PCairMasp.*
143 R.10 part. rest., 14 (6th cent.); 288 iv.2; v.4 (6th cent?); *PPar.*
21c.4 (A.D. 599); etc.; cf. *PColt* 30.3 (A.D. 596)
χρυσοχόου *PLond.* 604 B (iii, 76-87).233 (ca. A.D. 47); *SB* 9408 (1).29
(A.D. 250); (2).83 (A.D. 253/6); *POxy.* 43 V = *WChr.* 474 ii.15 (A.D.
284-95); *PCornell* 53.7 (late 3rd cent.); *PSI* 1081.28 (3rd/4th cent.);
StudPal. iii, 98.2 (6th cent.); etc.
χρυσοχόῳ *POxy.* 806 descr. (21/20 B.C.); *PCairGoodsp.* 30 xxxviii.14,
xxxix.14 (A.D. 191-2); *POxy.* 1146.13 (early 4th cent.); *PErl.* 106.18
(early 4th cent.); *PGen.* 15.1 (Byz.); etc.
χρυσοχόον *POxy.* 2727.24 (3rd/4th cent.); *PErl.* 54.25 (4th cent.); *PCair-
Masp.* 297.7 abbrev. (A.D. 535); *SB* 10525.9 (6th/7th cent.)
χρυσοχόων *BGU* 434.4 abbrev. (A.D. 169); *POxy.* 1117.12,12-13 (ca.
A.D. 178)
χρυσοχόοις *PFouad* 46.2 (23/22 B.C.)

3) Heteroclitic forms:

χρυσοχώς (nom. sg.) *BGU* 1065.18-19 (2nd hand), with dat. χρυσοχεῖ
5 (1st hand) (A.D. 97); *StudPal.* xx, 269.19: *BL* ii, 2, 166 (6th/7th cent.)
χρυσοχέων *PMich.* 123 R IX.35 (A.D. 45-47)

Note. In horoscopes and astrological treatises, ὑδροχοῦς (as the constellation
Aquarius or as month name = Φαρμοῦθι) has the following forms:

---

[1] χρυσοχόος is usu. uncontr. in Att., but contr. forms occur in Att. and other inscrr.
(*LSJ*, s.v.; *MS*, 127).

ὑδρ⟦ὖ⟧χώς, ὑδροχόου, ὑδροχόωι, ὑδροχόον *PMich.* 149 xii.22; xiv.27-28; xii.23-24; xvi.19; etc. (2nd cent.)

ὑδρυχώου *sic PMich.* 153.7 (A.D. 431)

ὑδροχόῳ *POxy.* 235.14 (A.D. 20-50); *POxy.* 465.11 (late 2nd cent.); *POxy.* 2790 i.4 (A.D. 257); *PHarris* 53.6 (4th cent.); etc.

ὑδρηχόῳ *POxy.* 1476.4 (A.D. 260)

but ὑδροχῷ *PPar.* 19b.8,10 (A.D. 138)

e. φλοῦς follows either the contract second declension or the third declension:[1]

φλοῦν *BGU* 1122.17,20 (13 B.C.); *PMed.* 6.8 (A.D. 26)

φλοῦῳν *POxy.* 1692.17 (A.D. 188)

φλοός (gen.) *PMich.* 313.13, with φλώς (gen.) 26 (A.D. 37); *BGU* 1894.15,59 (A.D. 157)

φλωός *PMich.* 123 R V.14; X.29 (A.D. 45-47)

φλόα (acc.) *PGissBibl.* 12.6 (A.D. 87/88)

f. χλοῦς is attested in the acc. pl. χλοῦς *PMich.* 496.17 (2nd cent.).[2]

g. ἀδελφιδοῦς is usually declined according to the contract second declension, but heteroclitic third declension forms are sometimes found in the oblique cases of the singular (as also in θυγατριδοῦς), and an anomalous *o*-stem form also occurs.[3]

1) Contracted forms:

ἀδελφιδοῦς *PSI* 294.15 (3rd cent.); *SB* 7449.5 part. rest. (2nd half 5th cent.)

ἀδελφιδοῦ *POslo* 43.4,6 (A.D. 140/1); *SB* 8780.9 (A.D. 170); sim. *PGiss.* 33.3, so duplic. *PFlor.* 48.2 part. rest. (A.D. 222); *POxy.* 2711.4-5 (ca. A.D. 268-71); etc.

ἀδελφιδῷ *POxy.* 2351.12 (A.D. 112); *PFlor.* 319.3 (A.D. 132-7); *POxy.* 509.8-9 (late 2nd cent.)

ἀδελφιδοῦ(ν) *PSI* 164.9-10 (A.D. 287)

ἀδελφιδοῖ, -οῖς, -ῶν *SB* 7996 = *PSI* 1239.2,21,30 (A.D. 430)

ἀδελφιδῶν *POxy.* 727.16 (A.D. 154); *POxy.* 888 = *MChr.* 329.11 (A.D. 287); *PHermRees* 31.17 (6th cent.); etc.

ἀδελφιδοῖς *POxy.* 1269.7,17 (early 2nd cent.); *PGrenf.* i, 47.6: *BL* i, 182 (A.D. 148)

ἀδελφιδοῦς *POxy.* 2708.7-8 (A.D. 169?)

2) Open form:

ἀδελφιδέος *PCornell* 45 = *SB* 9833.4 (A.D. 299)

---

[1] This rarer form of φλοιός has a 3rd decl. acc. φλόα in Nic. (*LSJ*, s.v.).

[2] Contr. χλοῦς elsewh. only in Hp. ap. Gal. (*LSJ*, s.v.).

[3] Cf. τῷ ἀδελφιδεῖ (Nachmanson, 123, n. 1), and ἀδελφιδός LXX (*LSJ*, s.v.).

3) Heteroclitic forms:

τοῦ ... ἀδελφιδοῦς *POxy.* 1282.6-7 (A.D. 83); sim. *PSI* 772.2 (1st/2nd cent.); *PMerton* 68.4 (A.D. 137); etc.

τοῦ θυγατριδοῦς *POxy.* 45 = *MChr.* 222.6 (A.D. 95); cf. τῆς ... θυγατρι-δοῦς (for θυγατριδῆς) *BGU* 300 = *MChr.* 345.16-17 (A.D. 148)

τῷ ... ἀδελφιδῇ (= ἀδελφιδεῖ?) *SB* 9265 = *PMilVogl.* 53.3 (A.D. 152/3); *PFlor.* 36 = *MChr.* 64.25 (A.D. 312)

4) *o*-stem form:

ὁ ... ἀδελφιδός *PLond.* 1707.3 (A.D. 566)

h. The post-classical occupational designation λαξός (for λᾱοξόος)[1] has simple *o*-stem forms apparently based on the only nom. attested, λαξός, until the Byzantine period when open forms occur:

λαξός *PTebt.* 401.8 (early 1st cent.); *PBon.* 30.5 abbrev. (A.D. 42/43); *PMich.* 123 R XXI.11 (A.D. 45-47); *POxy.* 1547.16,17,20, etc. (A.D. 119); *StudPal.* xxii, 2.6 (2nd cent.); *PGen.* 37 = *WChr.* 400.18 (A.D. 186); *PLond.* 370 (ii, 251).8 (2nd/3rd cent.); *BGU* 392.46: *BL* i, 43 (A.D. 208); etc.

λαξοῦ *SB* 7260 = *PMich.* 121 R II ii.6 (A.D. 42); *POxy.* 2272.12 (2nd cent.); *BGU* 426 i.15 (ca. A.D. 200); *PGen.* 16 = *WChr.* 354.2 (A.D. 207); etc.

λαοξοῦ *SB* 9445 = *PMed.* 56.7 (6th cent.)

λαξῶι *PTebt.* 410.3 (A.D. 16); sim. *SB* 9494.19 (2nd cent.); *PAntin.* 46.41 (4th cent.); etc.

λαξοί *WO* 1485.11,15,19 (prob. 3rd cent.: *BL* ii, 1, 114); cf. *SB* 8805.4, inscr. (A.D. 80/81)

λαξῶν *BGU* 1028.13 (2nd cent.)

λαξοῖς *POxy.* 806 descr. (21/20 B.C.)

λαοξόου *POxy.* 2041.1 (6th/7th cent.)

λαοξόῳ *PSI* 955.17 (6th cent.)

i. Both contracted and open forms of ὀστοῦν/ὀστέον occur in documentary and more frequently in magical papyri:[2]

ὀστῶν *SB* 9025.6,28 (2nd cent.)

but [ὁ]στ[έ]ω[ν] *PSI* 1419.2: *BL* iv, 92 (3rd cent.)

cf. ὀστοῦν *PGM* 12.411,426 (A.D. 300-350)

ὀστᾶ *PGM* 4.1530; 5.270,460 (4th cent.)

but ὀστέον, ὀστέῳ, ὀστέα *PGM* 4.1886,2413,2994 (4th cent.)

ὀστέα *PGM* 1.244 (late 4th/5th cent.)

---

[1] This word, exc. in pass. sense "hewn from stone" used in S., is first attested in the Ptol. papp., declined as a simple *o*-stem (Mayser i², 2, 13), and later in Ptol. etc. (*LSJ*, s.vv.).

[2] Cf. gen. pl. ὀστέων Trag. Com., and uncontr. forms generally in later prose, as in Arist. (*LSJ*, s.v.). See further Schwyzer i, 518, 562.

5. Gender.

a. Feminine nouns of the second declension.

Nouns of the second declension in -ος which are feminine elsewhere in Greek are generally feminine in the papyri, but some are exclusively masculine, while others fluctuate in gender and/or show heteroclitic forms of the first or third declensions.[1] Many other traditionally feminine nouns are used without indication of gender.

1) The following nouns (and adjectives used substantively) are exclusively feminine:[2]

τὴν Αἴγυπτον *POxy.* 1681.19 (3rd cent.)
  τῇ Αἰγύπτῳ *PBouriant* 20 = *MChr.* 96 ii.9,14 (A.D. 350+)
τῆς ἄμμου *BGU* 530.20 (1st cent.); *POxy.* 2272.28, sim. 30,32 (2nd cent.)
  ἄμμου ἐξυσμένη[ς] *SB* 7991 = *PSI* 1330.8-9 (2nd half 3rd cent.: *BL* v, 127); *PFlor.* 157.5 (3rd cent.); etc.
  τὴν ἄμμον *PRyl.* 153.5 (A.D. 138-61)
τὴν ἄμπελον *POxy.* 729.18 (A.D. 137)
  τῆς ἀμπέλου *POxy.* 1631.29, sim. 21 (A.D. 280)
βίβλου ἱερατικῆς *PTebt.* 291 = *WChr.* 137.34 (A.D. 162)
  μίᾳ βίβλῳ *PSI* 98.4 (6th cent.); cf. *SB* 3919.8, inscr. (A.D. 111)
τῇ ... διαλ[έ]κτῳ *PCairMasp.* 31.16 (ca. A.D. 547)
ἡ διάμετρος *PSI* 186.11, sim. 13 (4th cent.?)
δοκόν τὴν ὑπὲρ τ[ὴ]ν μηχανήν *PLond.* 280 = *WChr.* 312.11 (A.D. 55)[3]
τῆ(ς) σῆς ἠπίρου (for ἠπείρου) *WO* 865.4 (A.D. 140); sim. *StudPal.* xx, 121.37 (A.D. 438)
τὰς κράνους *PMich.* 421.20 (A.D. 41-54)[4]
λήκυθο(ς) ἐν ᾗ ... *PRyl.* 127.33 (A.D. 29)
  λήκυθος ὑαλῆ *PRossGeorg.* ii, 29.1 (2nd cent.)
  λήκυθον [κα]σσιτερίνην *BGU* 717.13 (A.D. 149); sim. *PHamb.* 10.37 (2nd cent.); *PSI* 1115.11 (A.D. 153)

---

[1] Most fem. nouns of the class. 2nd decl. follow other decl. types in MGr., e.g., ἡ παρθένα (1st decl.), τὸ βάσανο (2nd decl. neut.), τὸ ἀμπέλι, τὸ ραβδί (neut. dimin. decl.), or have been replaced by other words, e.g., ὁδός by δρόμος, etc.; the ones wh. remain 2nd decl. fem. normally appear wo. -ς, as ἡ ἄμμο (Thumb, *Handbook*, § 63; Jannaris, § 292). This reflects the transition from inflectional distinctions betw. animate-inanimate to distinctions betw. masc.-fem. (cf. Chantraine[2], § 6-8). The basis of the MGr. system is the pattern: masc. nom. = stem + -ς, gen. = stem; fem. nom. = stem, gen. = stem + -ς (cf. Schwyzer i, 585).

[2] Cf. also from the mag. papp. ἡ ἄβυσσος *PGM* 4. 3064, w. τὴν ἄβυσσον 1148 (4th cent.); τῆς ἀβύσσου *PGM* 36.217 (4th cent.): etc.; ἡ δρόσος, τῆς δρόσου *PGM* 4.2982 (4th cent.); and from inscrr. οἶμον τριτάτην *SB* 7953.5-6 (early 3rd cent.); sim. *SB* 8071.20 (Rom.); πλείστης ψάμμου *SB* 8303.27 (A.D. 41-54).

[3] A heteroclitic 3rd decl. gen. δοκοῦς occurs in *SB* 9494.25 (2nd cent.). This word is masc. in Luc. (*LSJ*, s.v.).

[4] Later form for τὸ κράνον = κράνεια (*LSJ*, s.v.).

τῆς ληνοῦ *PAberd.* 66.4 part. rest., 6 (A.D. 21); *PSI* 918.4 (A.D. 38/39); *PMerton* 79.17 (2nd cent.); *OTait* 2467.4 (2nd cent.?); *PRein.* 54 = *PFlor.* 227.14-15 (A.D. 257); etc.

τὴν ληνόν *PFlor.* 139.2,7-8 (A.D. 264); *PSI* 50.17 (4th/5th cent.) τὰς ... ληνούς *POxy.* 502.36-37 (A.D. 164)

τῆς λίμνου (for λίμνης?) *POxy.* 103.18 (A.D. 316)

τῆς νήσου *BGU* 1031.12 (2nd cent.); *PCairMasp.* 313.44 (6th cent.); *StudPal.* iii, 132 = *WChr.* 7.4,9 (prob. 6th cent.); etc.

τῇ ... νήσῳ *PGrenf.* i, 59.6 (5th/6th cent.) τὴν νῆσον *BGU* 37 V (A.D. 51); *PMichael.* 62 ii.20 (Byz.) αἱ ... νῆσοι *PGiss.* 82.22 (A.D. 117)

τὴν νόσον *PStrassb.* 73.14 (3rd cent.) τῇ νόσῳ *PLond.* 982 (iii, 242-3).9 (A.D. 350-75: *BL* v, 54) νόσῳ βαρυτάτῃ *PLond.* 1676.15 (A.D. 566-73)

[τ]ῆς ὁδοῦ *PMich.* 465.20-21 (A.D. 107); etc. ἡ ... ἔφοδος *PStrassb.* 238.18 (A.D. 177/8); etc.

τῆς ... παρθένου *SB* 9230.9 (late 3rd cent.); *StudPal.* viii, 1069.2 (5th/6th cent.)

τῇ παρθένῳ *PFlor.* 309.3 (4th cent.); *PLond.* 983 (iii, 229).4 (4th cent.); etc.

τὴν ῥάβδον *PCairMasp.* 352 V.9 (6th cent.)

ἡ σύγκλητος *POxy.* 33 V = *WChr.* 20 iv.7-8 (late 2nd cent.) ἱερᾶς συγκλήτου *PBaden* 89.13,32 (A.D. 222-35)

[σ]υκαμείνου ἐκκεκομμένης *StudPal.* v, 28.14, sim. 6 (3rd cent.) [π]ροκειμένη συκαμείνῳ *BGU* 492.7 (A.D. 148/9) ἄλλας συκαμείνους *PJand.* 139.19-20 (A.D. 148?)[1]

τὴν πρώτην τετράμηνον *PRyl.* 695.6 (late 3rd cent.); etc. τῆς δευτέρας τετραμήνου *PLond.* 1663.21 (6th cent.); sim. *PLips.* 97 i.11, etc. (A.D. 338)

τὴν ὕαλον *PFay.* 134.4 (early 4th cent.)[2]

τὴν ψῆφον *PLips.* 105 = *WChr.* 237.19 (1st/2nd cent.) ταῖς ... ψήφοις *SB* 8444.13 (A.D. 98-138); *PLips.* 64 = *WChr.* 281.38 (A.D. 368/9); sim. *BGU* 1563.35-36 (A.D. 68)

τῆς ψιάθου *PLond.* 928 (iii, 190-1).10 (3rd cent.: *BL* 1, 288) τὰς ψιέθους[3] *PGiss.* 70.6 (ca. A.D. 117); sim. *PTaitPetr.* 257.6 (ca. A.D. 37-41)

2) The following nouns, attested as feminine elsewhere in Greek, are always masculine in the papyri:

[ἑ]κάστου βύσσου *SB* 9346.24 (ca. A.D. 156-70) τοῦ βώλ(ου) *POxy.* 2580.11 (early 3rd cent.)[4]

---

[1] This word is masc. rarely (*LSJ*, s.v.).
[2] This word is masc. in Thphr. (*LSJ*, s.v.).
[3] For the fluctuation in spelling, see Vol. i, 281-2.
[4] Fem. E. X. Mosch. (so Phryn., Moer.); masc. Arist. D.C. (*LSJ*, s.v.).

οὓς εὗρον γεράνους δύο *PFlor.* 167 R.13 (3rd cent.)[1]

[τρ]ίτου θόλου *POxy.* 2145.12 (A.D. 186)

ἐμβατικοῦ [θ]όλου *POxy.* 896 = *WChr.* 48.12-13 (A.D. 316)[2]

τὸν λίθον *OTait* 1997.5 (2nd/3rd cent.?); *BGU* 405.9 (A.D. 348)

   τοῦ λίθου *PMerton* 39.2, etc. (late 4th/5th cent.)

   λίθου αἱματίτου *SB* 10753.11 (mid 2nd cent.)

   λίθους μεγάλους *POxy.* 134.26 (A.D. 569)[3]

γυναικεῖος στάμνος *PLond.* 191 (ii, 264-5).7 (A.D. 103-17)

   στάμνον ἐν ᾧ *Archiv* v, p. 381, #56.5 (prob. late 1st cent.)

   στάμνον ἕνα *Archiv* iv, p. 130.33-34 part. rest. (A.D. 168); *SB* 9589.16
   (6th/7th cent.)[4]

3) The following nouns (and adjectives used substantively), feminine else-where in Greek except where noted, fluctuate in gender or have heteroclitic first or third declension forms:

   ἐν τῷ ἅλῳ *PHarris* 96.32 (1st/2nd cent.)[5]

   τὰς βασάνους *PAntin.* 87.14,17 (late 3rd cent.)

   but οὐκ ἐπτόησαν βάσανα *PCairMasp.* 24 V.8-9 (ca. A.D. 551)

   τὴν γύψον *BGU* 952.4 (ca. 2nd/3rd cent.)

      τῆι γύψου *sic SB* 8973.10 (6th/7th cent.)

   but τὸν γύψον *POxy.* 2272.15 (2nd cent.)[6]

   and τὸ γύπσος *SB* 8030 = *PMich.* 245.11, sim. 19,31-32 (A.D. 47)

   δέλτον χαλκῆν *PHamb.* 31.9 part. rest. (A.D. 117-38); *BGU* 265 = *WChr.*
      459.21 (A.D. 148); *BGU* 780.15 (A.D. 154-9); *SB* 4224.26-27, with
      τῆς δέλτο(υ) 32 (A.D. 161-80)[7]

   but ἐν ξυλίνοις δέλτοις *PLips.* 64.43 = *WChr.* 281.44 (A.D. 368/9)

   τῆς καμεί[ν]ου *POxy.* 2272.18,24 abbrev. (2nd cent.)

      τὴν κάμειν[ον] *OStrassb.* 736.2 (prob. 2nd cent.)

      μεγάλην κάμεινον *PCairMasp.* 21 V.23 (A.D. 567: *BL* i, 103)

   but [σ]ὺν ... καμίνη *PLond.* 994 (iii, 259).11 (A.D. 517)

   κειβωτὸς μεγάλη *StudPal.* xx, 46 R.22, sim. 26 (2nd/3rd cent.)

      τῆι κειβωτῶι *PFay.* 121.8 (ca. A.D. 100)

      ξυλίνην κιβωτόν *Archiv* iv, p. 130.38-39 (A.D. 168)

   but κυβοτὸν (for κιβωτὸν) κυπαρίσσινον *PMich.* 343.5 (A.D. 54/55)

---

[1] Masc. also Thphr. (*LSJ*, s.v.).

[2] Always masc. in the meaning "vaulted vapor bath," as in the papp. of all periods (*LSJ*, s.v. II; Nachmanson, 128, w. lit.; Mayser i², 2, 18).

[3] Always masc. in the meaning of ordinary stone/millstone, as in the papp. of all periods; fem. of precious stone Hp. Att. inscrr. Herc. and mag. papp.; fem. of marble Theoc. Luc. (*LSJ*, s.v.; *MS*, 129; Crönert, 177 & n. 2; Mayser i², 2, 18). It is also masc. in the mag. papp. in the meaning "magnet," e.g., μάγ[ν]ητον λίθον *PGM* 3.188-9 (A.D. 300).

[4] Fem. Hermipp. NT, Eratosth. ap. Ath. (*LSJ*, s.v.; *BDF*, § 49.1); always masc. in the Ptol. papp. (Mayser i², 2, 18-19).

[5] For fem. forms, see above, pp. 29-30. A masc. is found in the LXX, e.g., Ruth **3.2,3**.

[6] See further below, p. 101.

[7] Cf. also in the mag. papp. δέλτος ἀποκρουστική *PGM* 4.2241 (4th cent.).

τὴν κόπρον *PFlor.* 361.6 (A.D. 82/83); *POxy.* 729.10 (A.D. 137); *PRoss-Georg.* ii, 19.28 part. rest. (A.D. 141); *PJand.* 9.18-19,23 (2nd cent.); *POxy.* 934.9-10 (3rd cent.)

τῆς κόπρου *BGU* 393.17 part. rest. (A.D. 168); *SB* 7814.15,18 (A.D. 256); cf. *SB* 7475.6, inscr. (6th/7th cent.)

but τοῦ κόπρου *PMerton* 79.6-7 (2nd cent.); *OStrassb.* 718.6 (2nd cent.)

τῇ λαγύνου (for λαγύνῳ) *BGU* 1095.19 (A.D. 57)

αἱ ... λάγυνοι *PSAAthen.* 64.13-14 (2nd cent.); sim. *POxy.* 1294.6 (late 2nd/early 3rd cent.)

λαγύν[ο]υς Μασσαλιτινάς *PMich.* 501.19 (2nd cent.)

but ἐν τῷ λακ(ύνῳ) (for λαγύνῳ) *BGU* 972.7 (6th/7th cent.)[1]

τῇ λιμῷ *PLond.* 982 (iii, 242-3).7 (A.D. 350-75: *BL* v, 54); *POxy.* 902 = *MChr.* 72.9 (ca. A.D. 465); *PCairMasp.* 20 R.12 (6th cent.)

but λειμοῦ γεν[ομ]ένου *PFlor.* 61 — *MChr.* 80.54 (A.D. 85)

τῷ ... λιμῷ *PLond.* 1729.19-20 (A.D. 584)[2]

τῆς παρορίου *PFlor.* 50.9 part. rest., 86 (A.D. 268)

but τῷ παρορίῳ *PMerton* 34.11 (A.D. 346/7)

and τὰ παρόρια *OTait* 2149.4 (3rd/4th cent.); sim. *POxy.* 1475.22 (A.D. 267)

τοῖς παρορ[ίο]ις *POxy.* 1113 i.16-17 (A.D. 203)

ὀπτῆς πλίνθου *PAmh.* 99a.9 (A.D. 179); sim. *PFlor.* 50.58,63 (A.D. 268); *PSI* 712.5 (A.D. 295); *CPR* 19a.16 (early 4th cent.)

πλίν[θ]ου ὠμῆς *BGU* 362 = *WChr.* 96 viii.9 (A.D. 215)[3]

τῆς πλίνθου *PMerton* 44.2 (5th cent.)

but τοὺς πλίνθους *BGU* 625 = *WChr.* 21.10 (early 3rd cent.)

b. Other fluctuations in gender.

1) Epicene nouns, when used of women, are normally feminine; but the masculine is sometimes used and heteroclitic forms occur:

τῆι ἀντιδίκωι *POxy.* 37 = *MChr.* 79 i.8 (A.D. 49)

but ταῖς ἀντιδίκαις *SB* 8246.14 (A.D. 335: *BL* v, 102) perh. through influence of -αις endings in context

τῇ γεούχῳ *POxy.* 2144.6 (late 3rd cent.); etc.

but τῷ γεούχῳ *POxy.* 1653.19, with [τ]ῆς γεούχου for same person **3** (A.D. 306)

τῆς ἐνγύου *BGU* 1051.25, sim. 10 (30 B.C. - A.D. 14)

τὴν ... σύνευνον *BGU* 1080 = *WChr.* 478.22 (3rd cent.)

(ἡ) τροφός *BGU* 297.7, sim. 14 (A.D. 50); *BGU* 332.9 (2nd/3rd cent.); *POxy.* 1288.11 (4th cent.); *POxy.* 1107.1 (5th/6th cent.); etc.

---

[1] Normally masc.; fem. in Thessaly, Arist. Plu. etc. (*LSJ*, s.v.).

[2] Fem. Dor. according to Phryn., also *h.Cer.* Call. Plb. etc. (*LSJ*, s.v.; cf. Crönert, 177, n. 1). The gender also fluctuates in the Ptol. papp. (Mayser i, 8; i², 2, 18) and in the NT (*BDF*, § 49.1).

[3] Cf. also from the mag. papp. πλίνθον ὠμήν *PGM* 8.104 (4th/5th cent.); πλίνθους ὠμάς *PGM* 12.29 (A.D. 300-50); *PGM* 4.900-1, w. ταῖς πλίνθοις 912 (4th cent.).

τῇ συμβίῳ *PRossGeorg.* ii, 26.2-3,3-4 (A.D. 160); sim. *PLond.* 983 (iii,
     229).3-4 (4th cent.); etc.
τὴν ... σύμβιον *PLips.* 29 = *MChr.* 318.9 (A.D. 295); *PLond.* 409 =
     PAbinn. 10.28 (ca. A.D. 346); etc.
but τῇ συμβίᾳ *PLond.* 978 (iii, 232-4).19 (A.D. 331)

2) Epicene nouns designating animals, when used of the female, are regularly
feminine, but a first declension by-form also occurs for ὄνος:

ἵππον θήλειαν *PSI* 1031.17 (A.D. 134)
κάμηλον θήλειαν *PGen.* 29.6-7 part. rest. (A.D. 137); *StudPal.* xxii,
     30.5 (A.D. 138-61); *BGU* 100.3 (A.D. 159); etc.
ἡ κάμηλος *POxy.* 1164.5 (6th/7th cent.)
ὄνον θήλειαν *SB* 4322.8 (A.D. 84-96); *POxy.* 1707.5 (A.D. 204); *PCornell*
     13.11, sim. 28 (A.D. 288); etc.
τὴν ὄνον *PMerton* 120.5-6 (late 1st/early 2nd cent.); *PMilVogl.* 82.15,
     sim. 5-6 (A.D. 133?); *PTebt.* 419.4, sim. 12,13 (3rd cent.); etc.
but ὄνην θήλειαν *BGU* 228.3-4 (2nd/3rd cent.)

3) The following masculine nouns appear anomalously as feminine:

τὴν ... ἀμπελῶνα *PMich.* 266.8-10 (A.D. 38) perh. on the analogy of
     ἡ ἄμπελος; elsewh. masc., e.g., τοῦ ... ἀμπελῶνος *SB* 7742.8-9 (A.D.
     57); *PJand.* 9.9-10,17-18 (2nd cent.); etc.
γόμ(ον) μίαν *OTait* 1644.4 (A.D. 107?); 1655.5 (1st/2nd cent.)
but τὸν γόμον *PLond.* 301 (ii, 256-7).12 (A.D. 138-61); etc.
πολλὴν σῖτον *PCairMasp.* 75.3 (Byz.) perh. through bilingual interference
     from Copt. masc. ⲉⲃⲣⲁ and ⲉⲃⲣⲓ[1]
τὴν ταρσόν *PRyl.* 695.12 (late 3rd cent.)
but ταρσῷ δεξιῷ *PMich.* 241.8,17 (A.D. 16); sim. *PMich.* 337.6-7 (A.D.
     24); *SB* 7260 = *PMich.* 121 R III i.3 (A.D. 42)

Note. There are other sporadic anomalies involving the gender and form
of nouns of the second declension, such as the following.

1) Masc. > neut.:

τὸ ... χρόνον *PMich.* 263.25, corr. 39 (A.D. 35/36); sim. *PLond.* 1877.3
     (6th cent.)
κλάδον μέγα *SB* 8002.19 (prob. 3rd cent.)
τὸ βίον *PCairIsidor.* 62.9 (A.D. 296)
τὸ ... τόκον *PBaden* 27.5-6 (A.D. 316)

---

[1] See Vergote, "Grec biblique," col. 1359.

τὸ μέγα οἶκος *SB* 8000 = *PMed.* 81.18 (4th cent.)
τὸ ... ποταμόν *POxy.* 1929.6 (late 4th/5th cent.)
τὸ ὅρκον *PSI* 973.5 (6th cent.)
τὸ τοιοῦτο οἶνον *PApoll.* 10 i.k.; ii.8 (A.D. 704)
τὸ ... κάματον *PApoll.* 26.10 (A.D. 713)

2) Neut. > masc.:

τὸν χειρόγραφον *PBon.* 21.20-21 part. rest. (1st cent.); *PLBat.* xvi, 16.7
(A.D. 140)
[ὄρ]γανον ... αὐτόν *PSI* 1030.6, sim. 22 (A.D. 109)
τόν σου πρόσουπον (for πρόσωπον) *PJand.* 101.3 (5th/6th cent.); sim.
SB 5314.5 (Byz.)

3) Neut. > fem.:

ἰκονίδια δύ[ο], μίαν μὲν ἔχουσ(αν) ... τὴν δὲ ἄλλην ... *POxy.* 1925.6-7
(7th cent.)

C. THE THIRD DECLENSION

1. General features.

a. The gen. sg. sometimes ends in -ου, especially in s-stems.[1]

1) s-stems:

ἔτου *SB* 9109.18, corr. 4,5 (A.D. 31); *PMich.* 229.36 (A.D. 48); *SB* 7742.11
(A.D. 57); *CPR* 1 = *StudPal.* xx, 1.33, corr. 32 (Λ.D. 83/84); *PFouad*
22 ii.11, corr. 19 (A.D. 125); *SB* 10268.1 (A.D. 140); *PMilVogl.* 257.7
(2nd cent.); etc.
μέρου *PSI* 907.15 (A.D. 42); *PMich.* 583.35 (A.D. 78); *PHibeh* 220.5:
BL iv, 40 (A.D. 335)
γλεύκου *StudPal.* xxii, 4 ii.12 (A.D. 127/8)
ὄξου *PMich.* 123 V XII (a).3 (A.D. 45-47); *OTaitPetr.* 295.8 (ca. A.D.
6-50); *PLond.* 1159 = *WChr.* 415.49 (A.D. 145-7); *PMich.* 390.4 (A.D.
215); *PGen.* 71.8,12,15,17,22, with ὄξους 1,9,14,19,23 (3rd cent.: *BL*
i, 166)
ὕψου *SB* 5175.19 (A.D. 513)

---

[1] For Ἡρακλήου, etc., in s-stem names, see below, pp. 71-72. An s-stem gen. in -ου
also occurs in the Ptol. papp. (Mayser i², 2, 36).

Omission of final -ς[1] may underlie these forms, especially when the correct form -ους is written elsewhere in the same document, but analogy with -ος, -ου nouns of the second declension would have been strong, e.g., ἐνιαυτός: ἐνιαυτοῦ :: ἔτος: ἔτου.

2) Other stems:

με[ρ]ίδου *PSI* 1051.4 (A.D. 26)

σφυρίδου *PRyl.* 382.3,4 (early 2nd cent.)

[περισ]τερεώνου *PMich.* 554.31, with -ών 11, -ῶνι 23, -ῶνα 16,25 (A.D. 81-96)

ποταμοφυλακίδου *OBrüss-Berl.* 34.5-6 (A.D. 116)

γενημάτου *BGU* 61 i.8 (A.D. 199/200)

λιμένου *BGU* 1594.2 (3rd cent.)

διορύγου *BGU* 818.1 (Byz.); sim. *PThead.* 24.8-9; 25.10 (A.D. 334)

κωμογραμματέου *POxy.* 1835.4 (late 5th/early 6th cent.)

γραμματέου *PCairMasp.* 234.6 (6th cent.?)

cf. ἀλεκτόρου *PGM* 12.313 (A.D. 300-50)

In Modern Greek, -μάτου is an alternative gen. for -ματος, e.g., πρα(γ)-μάτου/πρά(γ)ματος.[2]

A nom. in -ος is also attested in διόρυκος (for διῶρυξ) *PMich.* 256.3-4,4 (A.D. 29/30); 263.28,30 (A.D. 35/36); διόρυγος *PMich.* 258.4 (A.D. 32/33); 263.10 (A.D. 35/36); cf. ὁ βασιλός *SB* 8177.2, inscr. (4th/5th cent.).

b. *o*-stem endings are sometimes found in other cases.

1) Dat. sg.:

ὀφρύῳ (analogy with μεσοφρύῳ?) *SB* 5110 = *PRyl.* 160d, ii.23 (A.D. 42); sim. *BGU* 2044.8,29 (A.D. 46)

2) Acc. sg.:

ἀμπελῶνον (for ἀμπελῶνα) *PMich.* 274.4 (A.D. 46/47)

μέρον *PLond.* 163 (ii, 182-3).14-15 (A.D. 88)

πόδον *POxy.* 1928.11, amulet (5th/early 6th cent.)

ποιμένον *PSI* 932.7 (A.D. 518/27)

ἄξονον *POxy.* 2779.13 (A.D. 530)

μῆνον *SB* 10269.6 (6th cent.)

---

[1] See Vol. i, 124-6.

[2] Thumb, *Handbook*, § 102-3; Mirambel, *Langue grecque*, 109; Jannaris, § 369; Hatzidakis, *Einl.*, 383-4; Kapsomenakis, 94-95, 126; Maspero, 48-49.

3) Acc. pl.:

χιϑώνους (for χίτωνας) *PRyl.* 189.3-4 (A.D. 128)

These *o*-stem endings reflect a preference for the vocalic declensional types over the consonantal, which led to the transfer of most ancient Greek nouns of the third declension to the first or second declension in Modern Greek.[1]

c. The acc. sg. of consonant stems very frequently ends in -αν (before words beginning with a vowel or consonant without distinction).

1) Stems in stops:

αἶγαν *PIFAO* i, 5.5 (8/7 B.C.); *SB* 7344.6 (A.D. 8/9)

μερίδαν *PAberd.* 53 i.2 (A.D. 10/11); *POxy.* 1482.21 (2nd cent.); *BGU* 603.13-14 (A.D. 168); *PAlex.* 14.4 (2nd/3rd cent.)

γυναῖκαν *PMich.* 276.24 (A.D. 47); *SB* 7356 = *PMich.* 203.37 (A.D. 98-117); *PCornell* 16.30 (A.D. 146/7); *BGU* 93.26-27 (2nd/3rd cent.); *POxy.* 1067.7-8 (3rd cent.); *SB* 9441 = *PMed.* 84.7 (4th cent.); *PCair-Preis.* 2.6; 3.6 part. rest. (A.D. 362); etc.

σφραγεῖδαν *PLBat.* vi, 3.12 (A.D. 92); *PMilVogl.* 25 v.2 (A.D. 126/7); sim. *BGU* 15 ii.21-22 (A.D. 197?)

παῖδαν *PGrenf.* ii, 59.7,18 (A.D. 189); *PJand.* 20.7 (6th/7th cent.)

μυριάδαν *POxy.* 1700.7 (late 3rd cent.); sim. *POxy.* 43 R iii.13 (A.D. 295)

νύκταν *PTebt.* 419.18 (3rd cent.); *POxy.* 2729.18 (4th cent.); *SB* 9135.4 (4th cent.); *PSI* 165.4 (6th cent.); *PMeyer* 24.5 (6th cent.)

2) *r*-stems:

ϑυγατέραν *PMich.* 587.9,17-18 (A.D. 24/25); *PMich.* 266.23 (A.D. 38); *PMich.* 482.10-11 (A.D. 133); *POxy.* 237 vii.5, corr. 22, etc. (A.D. 186); *BGU* 148.3 (2nd/3rd cent.); *POxy.* 1273.3 (A.D. 260); *PSI* 236. 36-37 (3rd/4th cent.); etc.; cf. *PColt* 131.3 (6th/7th cent.)

πατέραν *PMich.* 353.16, corr. 8 (A.D. 48); *PCornell* 16.16 (A.D. 146/7); *PStrassb.* 284.22 twice (A.D. 176-80); *BGU* 623.8 (2nd/3rd cent.); *PMich.* 514.31 (3rd cent.); *PThead.* 19.15 (A.D. 316-20: *JJP* ii, 60); *PCairGoodsp.* 15.21 (A.D. 362); etc.

μητέραν *SB* 7356 = *PMich.* 203.26 (A.D. 98-117); *PJand.* 9.37 (2nd cent.); *PMich.* 425.14 (A.D. 198); *BGU* 247.8-9 (2nd/3rd cent.); *PLBat.* xvii, 16 b.18 (2nd/3rd cent.); *POxy.* 123.22 (3rd/4th cent.); *PLond.* 404 = *PAbinn.* 25.12 (ca. A.D. 346); *PFouad* 82.3-4 (4th/5th cent.); *POxy.* 1300.8 (5th cent.); etc.

ἄνδραν *SB* 7356 = *PMich.* 203.31 (A.D. 98-117)

---

[1] See further Dieterich, 158-62; Thumb, *Handbook*, § 98-105.

χεῖραν *POxy.* 119.7 (2nd/3rd cent.); *POxy.* 2235.20 (ca. A.D. 346); *PLBat.*
   xi, 15.13-14 (4th cent.: *BL* v, 62); *PLips.* 39 = *MChr.* 127.13 (A.D.
   390); *PLond.* 991 (iii, 257-8).13 (6th cent.); etc.
σωτῆραν *PGrenf.* i, 61.9 (6th cent.)

3) *n*-stems:

μῆναν *PSI* 908.18 (A.D. 42/43); *PGissBibl.* 28.17: *BL* ii, 2, 68 (3rd cent.);
   SB 4294.7 (Rom.); *StudPal.* xx, 75 ii.12 (3rd/4th cent.); *POxy.* 903.36
   (4th cent.); *POxy.* 1862.19 (7th cent.); etc.
σιαγόναν *PSI* 903.4 (A.D. 47)
χειμῶναν *PMich.* 476.29-30 (early 2nd cent.); sim. *SB* 7662.7-8 (late
   2nd cent.)
λεγιῶναν *POxy.* 1665.6, corr. 5 (3rd cent.)

4) Diphthongal stems:

κωμογρ[α]μματέαν *POxy.* 1480.8-9 (A.D. 32)

The acc. ending -αν, found in some classical dialects,[1] appears earlier and
more frequently in the Greek of Egypt than elsewhere in the Koine,[2] where it
is not an inherited dialectal form but a new morpheme based on the analogy of
the acc. sg. in -ν of all vowel stem nouns. In the papyri, the analogy was strength-
ened by phonetic developments; the loss of quantitative distinction and the
partial loss of final /n/ made this -αν ending identical to the acc. -αν of first
declension nouns.[3] This led eventually to the back-formation of a nom. sg. in
in -α (e.g., ἡ μητέρα[4]) and to the transfer of these nouns to the first declension
in Modern Greek.

d. The nom. pl. -ες is occasionally used for the acc. pl. of masculine and
feminine nouns of the third declension.

1) Stems in stops:

π[έ]μσ[ις] ... θρ[ί]νακες ... καὶ λικμητρίδες *PFay.* 120.3-5 (ca. A.D. 100)
[ἐλέσθαι] γυναῖκες *BGU* 114 = *MChr.* 372 ii.1-2, corr. 20-21 (2nd cent.)
   τὰς γυναῖκες *POxy.* 465.146,153, astrol. (late 2nd cent.)
   τὰς δύω μαγίδες *PTebt.* 414.16 (2nd cent.)

---

[1] Cypr. Thess. El. and late inscrr. of various dialects (Buck, *GD*, § 107.1; Schwyzer i,
563).
   [2] It appears sporadically in the Ptol. papp. from the 3rd cent. B.C. on (Mayser i², 1, 172;
2, 46), in Asia Minor inscrr. from the 1st cent. B.C. on (Schweizer, 156-7; Nachmanson, 133),
and in Att. inscrr. in late Rom. times (*MS*, 130). It is also found in the mag. papp., e.g.,
νύκταν *PGMOstr.* 1.10-11 (late Rom.); στροφέαν *PGM* 36.136 (4th cent.). See further
Crönert, 169 & n. 4; Psaltes, 153-4; Dieterich, 159-60; Jannaris, § 330 & App. iii, esp. § 3-6.
   [3] So also Schwyzer i, 563; see Vol. i, 111-14, 325.
   [4] See below, p. 63.

ἀρτάβας ... χοίνικες *PStrassb.* 54.9, sim. 10 (A.D. 153/4)
τὰς ... [σ]φραγ[ί]δες *PGen.* 3 = *MChr.* 122.16-17 (A.D. 175-80)
αἴγες τρι[ά]κοντα (acc.) *PAlex.* 12 = *PAlexGiss.* 5.6 (A.D. 215)
μυριάδες ἑξακοσίας *StudPal.* viii, 1161.2 (5th cent.); sim. 1070.4 (5th/6th
    cent.)
cf. ἱέρακες *PGM* 36.182 (4th cent.)

2) Others:

τοὺς δέκα στατῆρες *PSI* 1432.5-6 (1st half 1st cent.); sim. *PFay.* 109.3
    (early 1st cent.); *PMich.* 202.11 (A.D. 105); *BGU* 38.25-26 (2nd/3rd
    cent.: *BL* i, 10); *BGU* 814.5 (3rd cent.)
τοὺς πράκτορες *BGU* 530.39-40 (1st cent.)
ἔχων κωπίωνες *PLBat.* xvii, 1 ii.6 (A.D. 138-61)
ἰς μακροὺς ἐῶνες (for εἰς ... αἰῶνας) *PWürzb.* 21 B.20-21 (2nd cent.)
θυγατέραις (= -ες for -ας) *PRyl.* 111.20 (A.D. 161)
εἰς ἄνδρες *PErl.* 43.5 part. rest., 8,11 (2nd cent.)
    ἄνδρες θέλομεν *PGrenf.* i, 53 = *WChr.* 131.25 (4th cent.)
τὰς χέρες (for χεῖρας) *BGU* 261.10, with acc. στατῆρες 15 (ca. A.D. 105:
    cf. *PMich.* 202)
μῆναις (= -ες for -ας) *StudPal.* xxii, 40.11 (A.D. 150); sim. *PGrenf.* ii,
    59.10-11 (A.D. 189)
τοὺς τέκτονες *POxy.* 121.25 (3rd cent.)
τὰς ... βόες *PGen.* 48 = *PAbinn.* 60.5-6, sim. 18-19, corr. 32 (A.D. 346)

This use of the nom. pl. -ες for the acc. in these nouns of the third declension
reflects a middle stage in the process by which the nominative supplanted the
accusative in the plural. The process began in *i*-stems in early Attic, spread to
diphthongal stems in -ευς and then to some consonantal stems in the Koine.
It resulted eventually in the adoption of -ες as the nom.-acc. pl. ending of the
first declension in Modern Greek with the shift of consonantal stems to the *a*-stem
declension.[1] Many of the above examples are found in connection with numerals
and designations of quantity, in which the nom. -ες first came to be used for
the acc. -ας in various ancient dialects.[2]

e. A dat. pl. -εσι is found in χοίνικεσι *CPR* 242 = *StudPal.* xxii, 173.10
(A.D. 40) and ἐσθήσεσι *BGU* 16 = *WChr.* 114.12 (A.D. 159/60); *PLond.* 77 =
MChr. 319.20 (late 6th cent.).[3] Cf. also τοῖς ... βλάβεσσι *BGU* 1103.28 (13 B.C.);
εἴδεσσι *PCairMasp.* 6 V.45 (ca. A.D. 567); *PMon.* 4-5 v.15 (A.D. 581); μ[έ]-

---

[1] Cf. Schwyzer i, 563-4, w. lit.; for MGr. (ἡ)μέρες, etc., see Thumb, *Handbook*, § 80-90;
Mirambel, *Langue grecque*, 112; *Gram.*, 48-60.
[2] Cf. 5th cent. B.C. Delph. δεκατέτορες, Phth. τοὺς δεκαπέντε στατῆρες, etc.; acc.
γυναῖκες also occurs in late Lesb. (Schwyzer i, 563; Buck, *GD*, § 107.4).
[3] ἐσθήσεσι also codd. LXX, NT, Str. J. etc. (*BDF*, § 47.4; Crönert, 173, n. 1).

ρεσσει *PMon.* 10.13: *BL* i, 310 (A.D. 586). This is not a survival of the -εσ(σ)ι ending characteristic of Aeolic dialects, Boeotian, etc.,[1] but an analogical formation following *s*-stems and *i*-stems (cf. the converse κτῆσι for κτήνεσι below, p. 67).

f. There is some anomalous fluctuation in the gender of nouns of the third declension such as the following:

πήχει ἀριστερᾷ *PMich.* 322a.22, corr. 35 (A.D. 46)
τὸν ... μέρος (cf. Copt. masc. ϲⲁ) *CPR* 4 = *MChr.* 159.7 (A.D. 51/53);
    POxy. 1208.28 (A.D. 291); *SB* 7997 = *PSI* 1239.7 (A.D. 430)
διῶρυξ εἰς ὅν *PRyl.* 154.18 (A.D. 66)
τὸ ἀνάπαυσιν *BGU* 644.32 (A.D. 69)
τὸ εὐσχήμονα *PMich.* 620.41 (A.D. 239/40)
εἰς τὸ λίβυς *POxy.* 2719.6 (3rd cent.)
δρυὸς ἑνός *POxy.* 2113.18 (A.D. 316)[2]
ποδὸς δεξειᾶς *PGen.* 64 = *PAbinn.* 67 V.10 (ca. A.D. 346)
τὴν ... στῆνος (for σθένος) *PCairGoodsp.* 15.23-24: *BL* i, 174 (A.D. 362)
τὸ τρίχα *POxy.* 1944.2 (6th/7th cent.)
cf. τοῦ ἐπιημερινοῦ φρικός *PGMXtn.* 5a.2-3, sim. 3-4,4-5 (4th cent.)

g. Some loanwords of the Latin third declension are declined according to the Greek third declension, but others fluctuate between the third and the other declensions or follow the first or second declension exclusively, usually through the addition of the suffixes -ιος or -ιον.

1) Nouns in -(*i*)*ō*, -(*i*)*ōnis* are normally declined -ιών, -ιῶνος, as λεγιών, λεγιῶνος;[3] *indictio* fluctuates between ἰνδικτίωνος and ἰνδικτίονος.[4] A few have by-forms of the first or second declension: τιρόναις *tiro* *BGU* 21 ii.11; iii.14 part. rest. (A.D. 340); ἐμτίου *emptio* *PVars.* 28.2 (6th cent.), but κουηεμπτίωνα *coemptio* *BGU* 1210 (33).93 (mid 2nd cent.); σιλίγ[ν]ων *siligo* *StudPal.* xx, 233.1 (6th/7th cent.).

2) Nouns in -*ōr*, -*ōris* are normally declined -ωρ, -ορος (no -ωρος in Greek), e.g., ἀδιούτορος *adiutor* *PRossGeorg.* ii, 26.8 (A.D. 160), ἀδιούτορι *StudPal.* iii, 315 V.1 (5th/6th cent.); κουράτορος *curator* *BGU* 705.4,6 (A.D. 206); κουράτορι *SB* 9118.2 (2nd half 3rd cent.); ἰουρατόρων *iurator* *SB* 7669 = *PCairIsidor.* 3.9 (A.D. 299); etc. But several are inflected according to the first declension masc. through the addition of the suffix -ης, as τρακτευτής *tractator*, ἐξπελλευτής *expellator* passim, ἐξάκτη *exactor* *BGU* 849.2 (4th cent.), with ἐξάκτωρ elsewhere, ἐ[ξ]κουβίτου *excubitor* *StudPal.* viii, 1089.2 (7th cent.), with ἐξκουβίτωρ elsewhere.

---

[1] Buck, *GD*, § 107.3; Schwyzer i, 564 & n. 1.
[2] Masc. also Pelop. according to Sch.Ar., inscr. Thyrrheum (*LSJ*, s.v.).
[3] For the spelling variation λεγιῶνος/λεγεῶνος, see Vol. i, 253.
[4] See Vol. i, 224.

3) Κέλερ *Celer WO* 1271.1 (A.D. 122), *BGU* 615.15 (2nd cent.), etc., also Κέλερος *StudPal.* iv, p. 68.323 (A.D. 72/73), has gen. Κέλερος *POxy.* 276.8 (A.D. 77), *BGU* 567 ii.29 (prob. 2nd cent.), etc., and Κελέρου *OMich.* 989.4 (A.D. 277), dat. Κέλερι *StudPal.* xx, 13.27 (2nd cent.), acc. Κέλεραν *BGU* 1897.144 (A.D. 166).

4) Κλήμης *Clemens POxy.* 241.1 (ca. A.D. 98), *SB* 9017 (12).6 (1st/2nd cent.), *PBerlLeihg.* 8.13 (ca. A.D. 162), etc., has gen. Κλήμεντος *BGU* 832.23 (A.D. 113), *BGU* 558 ii.23 (early 3rd cent.), etc., dat. Κλήμεντι *SB* 4576.8 part. rest., inscr. (Rom.), but dat. Κλήμηστ(ι) (1st hand), acc. Κλήμεντα (2nd hand) *BGU* 300 = *MChr.* 345.2,21, with Κλήμης 22 (3rd hand) (A.D. 148)

5) Nouns in *-es, -itis*: κόμες *comes POxy.* 1949.1 (A.D. 481), etc., also κόμις *BGU* 1027 xxvi = *WChr.* 424 i.9 (4th cent.), fluctuates between κόμετος/κόμιτος, etc.,[1] as well as the heteroclitic κομίτου *PLips.* 85.3 (A.D. 372), cf. Κομέτου *SB* 5560.3 (8th cent.), etc.; *limes* occurs only as a heteroclitic *o*-stem in λιμήτ[ο]υ *StudPal.* xx, 143.2: *BL* iv, 96 (5th/6th cent.), λιμίτου *SB* 9598.3 (5th cent.), *PCairMasp.* 76.13 (6th cent.), cf. Λιμίτου *BGU* 670.4: *BL* i, 439 (Byz.) and λιμέτου *SB* 7433 = *PRossGeorg.* v, 30 R.1 (A.D. 449-64).

6) Nouns in *-eps, -ipis* form the nom. in *-ιψ*, e.g., πρίγκιψ, μάγκιψ,[2] stem usually πριγκιπ-, but πριγκεπ- appears as a variant,[3] as well as the heteroclitic πρινκίπῳ *OTheb.* 143.8 (3rd cent.).

7) Nouns in *-is (-e), -is* fluctuate between the second and third declensions or are replaced by exclusively first or second declension formations.[4]

a) Second and third declension.

i. *principalis*:

     nom. πριγκ[ι]πᾶλις *PMich.* 465.16 (A.D. 107)
         πριγκιπᾶρις *SB* 8088.5 (2nd cent.)
     dat. πρινκιπαλίῳ *PFlor.* 278 iv.12-13: *BL* i, 156, with πρινκιπαλίων, -οις iii.8,14 (ca. A.D. 248)
         πρινκιπαρίῳ *BGU* 931.1 (prob. 3rd/4th cent.)

ii. *Cerealis*:

     nom. Κελεᾶρις (with transposition of λ and ρ[5]) *POxy.* 1102.4 (ca. A.D. 146); *PRossGeorg.* ii, 20.5 (ca. A.D. 146)

---

1 For exx., see Vol. i, 255.
2 For exx., see Vol. i, 251.
3 See Vol. i, 255.
4 For *classis* and *cohors* declined according to the 1st decl., see above, pp. 7, 8.
5 See Vol. i, 104.

Κερεᾶλις *PLBat.* xiii, 11.28 (A.D. 138); *SB* 9545 (23).1 (A.D. 164);
  sim. (24).1 (A.D. 180)
Κελεάριος *PPar.* 11 (p. 432).1 (A.D. 160)
gen. Κερεαλίου *PLond.* 1651.19 (A.D. 363)
dat. Κ[ε]ριάλει *BGU* 1036 = *MChr.* 118.1 (A.D. 108)
  Κερεᾶλι *PGrenf.* ii, 46a = *WChr.* 431.1,18 (A.D. 139)
  Κερεαλίῳ *SB* 9017 (14).10 (1st/2nd cent.)
    Κελεαρίῳ *Archiv* v, p. 178, #33.3 (n.d.)
acc. Κερεᾶλιν *PAberd.* 30.12 (ca. A.D. 139)

iii. *Liberalis*:

nom. Λιβελᾶρις *sic OMich.* 1038.4 (A.D. 233/64?)
gen. Λιβεραλίου *BGU* 780.4,12 part. rest., cf. 1 (A.D. 154-9); *BGU*
  613 = *MChr.* 89.41 (A.D. 138-61); etc.

b) Second declension only:

i. With the suffixes -ιος/-ιον, e.g., ἰλλούστριος *illustris*, κοντουβερνάλιος
contubernalis, ὀφφικιάλιος *officialis*, σιγγουλάριος *singularis*; βρέουιον *breve*,
βικεννάλιον *vicennale*, μαφόρ(τ)ιον *maforte*, φακιάλιον *faciale*.

ii. As a simple *o*-stem: κορτιανούς *cohortialis POxy.* 1253.4 (4th cent.).

8) Declined according to the consonantal third declension is the Latin fourth
declension noun *magistratus* with the addition of the suffix -ότης:[1] τῆς μαγιστρότητος *PAmh.* 138 = *MChr.* 342.10-11 (A.D. 326); sim. *PLond.* 1105 descr.
(iii, p. lvii) (4th cent.).

2. Stems ending in a stop.[2]

a. Velar stems.

1) διῶρυξ usually has the late Greek stem διωρυγ-, but the Attic διωρυχ-
is found occasionally.[3]

a) διωρυγ-:

διώρυγος *PMich.* 337.11 (A.D. 24); *PJand.* 52.21 (A.D. 96); *PRossGeorg.*
  ii, 19.25, etc. (A.D. 141); *POxy.* 2853.3,7,11 (ca. A.D. 245/6); *SB*

---

[1] Cf. Palmer, 115-16.
[2] Schwyzer i, 562-7, cf. 496-9, 507-8; Chantraine², § 62-66; Buck, *GD*, § 107; *MS*, 129-30;
Schweizer, 151-2; Nachmanson, 133-4; Hauser, 88-91; Mayser i², 2, 30-36; Crönert, 167-74;
BDF, § 46-48.
[3] διωρυχ- Th. Pl., διωρυγ- Hp. Plb. Diod. Str. Paus. (Mayser i², 1, 17). The Ptol. papp.
have διωρυγ- exclusively (Mayser, *ibid.* & i², 2, 30, *pace LSJ*, s.v.).

7756.1 (A.D. 359); *PLBat.* xi, 11.11,16 (A.D. 453); *PSI* 1056.7 (5th/6th cent.); *PHamb.* 56 vi.15 (7th cent.: *BL* v, 40); *PLond.* 1353.11 (A.D. 710); etc.

διώρυγι *PStrassb.* 193.14-15, prob. also 7-8 (A.D. 128); *PSI* 1036.4 (A.D. 192)

διώρυγα *PMich.* 556.15 (A.D. 107); *PGiss.* 15.5 (ca. A.D. 117); *PThead.* 14.26 (4th cent.); *PCairMasp.* 2 ii.21 (A.D. 567: *BL* i, 100); *PApoll.* 26.2 (A.D. 713)

διώρυγες *BGU* 543.7 part. rest. (27 B.C.); *PSI* 1143.15 (A.D. 164); *SB* 4325 ii.3, xi.5, with διωρύχων vi.10 (3rd cent.); *PFlor.* 153.9 (A.D. 268)

διωρύγων *PAmh.* 68 = *WChr.* 374.9 (A.D. 81-96); sim. *SB* 9340.17 (A.D. 198); *PRyl.* 172.23 (A.D. 208); *SB* 4774.9 (Byz.); *PLond.* 1456.4 (8th cent.)

διόρυγας *SB* 10535.27 (ca. A.D. 30)

cf. the dimin. διωρύγι(ον) *PLond.* 131 = *SB* 9699.633 (A.D. 78/79)
   διορυγίου *SB* 4755.11 (Byz.)

cf. ἀπώρυγες *PBerlLeihg.* 23.14 (A.D. 252)
   ἀπωρύγων, ἀπωρυγισμός *POxy.* 1631.10 (A.D. 280)
   ἀναρυγῆς (for ἀνορυγῆς) *PRyl.* 95.8 (A.D. 71/72)

b) διωρυχ-:

διώρυχος *PBerlLeihg.* 13.9,15 (ca. A.D. 117); *CPR* 189.6 (2nd cent.); *POxy.* 918 ii.3, v.15 abbrev. (2nd cent.); *SB* 5124.468 part. rest., etc., with διώρυγ(ος) 268 (A.D. 193: *BL* v, 94); *PSI* 87.5,7 (A.D. 423); *PSI* 689.36, etc. (5th cent.); *StudPal.* xx, 224.1 (6th/7th cent.); etc.

διώρυχι *PFlor.* 223.6 (A.D. 257); *PRein.* 115.4,12 (A.D. 261?)

διώρυχα *SB* 9415 (31).5 (3rd cent.); *PRyl.* 653.4, cf. 10 (A.D. 321)

διωρύχων *POxy.* 57.15 (A.D. 195/6: *BL* iv, 58); *PRyl.* 90.20 part. rest., sim. 33 (early 3rd cent.); *SB* 7361.7 (A.D. 210/11); *POxy.* 2847 i.27 (1st half 3rd cent.); *PSI* 460.11-12 (3rd/4th cent.); *PBeattyPanop.* 2.223 (A.D. 300); etc.

διώρυχας *POxy.* 1409.17, cf. διωρύχων 8 (A.D. 278)

cf. ἀνορυχαί *PCairMasp.* 295 ii.5 (6th cent.)
   ἀν[ορ]υχαῖς *PCairMasp.* 283 i.16 (before A.D. 548)

The fluctuation in the stem of this word is not phonological because γ and χ rarely interchange.[1] The common late Greek stem was διωρυγ-, perhaps formed from the second aorist passive ὠρύγην;[2] διωρυχ- may have been reintroduced through the Atticistic influence of the schools.[3]

---

[1] See Vol. i, 96.
[2] So Mayser, i², 2, 30.
[3] Phryn. 210 (Rutherford, 309-10) recommends διωρυχ-.

2) Peculiarities in the declension of γυνή may reflect the heteroclitic first declension γυνή, γυνῆς, used in Byzantine Greek[1] or may be interpreted as the nom. used indeclinably for other cases:[2]

gen. δ(ιὰ) γυνή, (ὑπὲρ) γυνή *PLond.* 1419.80,334,402,403,539 (A.D. 716+)
dat. γυνῇ (or γυνή) *PMich.* 507.7 (2nd/3rd cent.); *POxy.* 992 descr. (A.D. 413)

b. Dental stems.

1) Barytone -ιτ- and -ιδ- stems.[3]

a) The acc. sg. of χάρις fluctuates between χάρις and the Poetic-Ionic χάριτα.[4]

i. χάριν:

'favor': *PTebt.* 410.4 (A.D. 16); *PHamb.* 88.17 (mid 2nd cent.); *PBaden* 33.9 (2nd cent.); *POslo* 61.4 (3rd cent.); *POxy.* 941.6 (6th cent.); etc.
'thanks': *PBrem.* 52.6; 63.34 (ca. A.D. 117); *POxy.* 113.13 (2nd cent.); *POxy.* 963 descr. (2nd/3rd cent.); *PMichael.* 26.11 (ca. A.D. 300); *PHarris* 109.9 (3rd/4th cent.); *PCairMasp.* 151-2.260 (A.D. 570); etc.
'gift': *POxy.* 273 = *MChr.* 221.14 (A.D. 95); *PGrenf.* ii, 70 = *MChr.* 191.5 (A.D. 270); *PCairMasp.* 151-2.125,127 (A.D. 570); etc.
'pleasure': *PLond.* 409 = *PAbinn.* 10.19 (ca. A.D. 346)

ii. χάριτα:

'favor': *SB* 7615 = *PBon.* 43.11 (1st cent.); *PStrassb.* 117.9 (1st cent.); *PPrinc.* 162.12 (A.D. 89/90); *PGiss.* 40 ii = *MChr.* 378.6,7 (A.D. 215); *BGU* 48.7, with χάριν 14 (2nd/3rd cent.?: *BL* i, 11); *PFlor.* 128.4: *BL* i, 149 (A.D. 256); *SB* 9468.11 (A.D. 266); etc.
χάριταν *BGU* 596.13 (A.D. 84); *PLBat.* iii, 19.3 (after A.D. 208)
'thanks': *PHarris* 152.4 (3rd cent.?); *PThead.* 24.17, so duplic. 25.20 (A.D. 334); 22.18 (A.D. 342); *PLond.* 245 = *PAbinn.* 45.20 (A.D. 343); *PGen.* 47 = *PAbinn.* 47.17-18 (A.D. 346); etc.
'gift': *PGrenf.* ii, 71 = *MChr.* 190 ii.18 (A.D. 244-8)

---

[1] So already Com.: Pherecr. Philippid. Men. *Com.Adesp.* (*LSJ*, s.v.); see further Schwyzer i, 582-3; Dieterich, 161-2, Anm.; Psaltes, 153. The MGr. form is ἡ γυναῖκα (1st decl.), w. stereotyped survivals of τῆς γυνῆς (Thumb, *Handbook*, § 84; Jannaris, § 433.4).
[2] So Mayser i², 2, 30-31.
[3] Generally orig. *i*-stems (Schwyzer i, 464).
[4] The prepos. of course is always χάριν. χάριτα is found in Hdt. E. X. Phylarch. etc. (*LSJ*, s.v.). In the Att. inscrr., the acc. χάριν occurs in prose, but χάριτα is found in poetry (*MS*, 129). Only χάριν occurs at Perg., Lycia, and elsewh. in Asia Minor inscrr. (Schweizer, 151; Nachmanson, 133; Hauser, 88) and in the Ptol. papp. (Mayser i², 2, 31) and is usual in the NT (*BDF*, § 47.3) and in the mag. papp. (χάριτα only *PGM* 35.22, w. χάριταν 16 [5th cent.] & χάριταν *PGM* 71.4 [late 2nd/early 3rd cent.]). See further Crönert, 170, n. 6.

The absence of χάριτα in inscriptions from Ionic areas in Asia Minor suggests that this form, as well as the parallel κλεῖδα, ἰδρῶτα, etc., is not an Ionic element in the Koine but reflects an independent tendency to extend the dental stem throughout the paradigm.[1]

b) The acc. sg. of κλείς is normally κλεῖδα, rarely the Attic κλεῖν:[2]

κλεῖδα *POxy.* 2342.9 part. rest. (A.D. 102); *SB* 9484.3-4 (2nd cent.); *POxy.* 113.3 (2nd cent.); *PMilVogl.* 60.8 (2nd cent.); *PJand.* 95.5 (2nd/3rd cent.)
κλεῖδαν *POxy.* 1641.19 (A.D. 68); *BGU* 1036 = *MChr.* 118.25 (A.D. 108); *PMerton* 76.26 (A.D. 181); *PSI* 1562.18 (4th cent.)
κλεῖν *PMilVogl.* 25 v.2 (A.D. 126/7); *POxy.* 1127.25 (A.D. 183)

c) In the plural of κλείς, the dental stem fluctuates in the nom. and acc. with κλεῖς, an extension of the *i*-stem to the plural.[3]

i. Nom.:

κλεῖδες *POxy.* 2146.5 (3rd cent.)
κλεῖς (if pl.) *PErl.* 21.57 (ca. A.D. 195)

ii. Acc.:

κλεῖδας *PLond.* 1177 (iii, 180-90).291 (A.D. 113); sim. *PMilVogl.* 77.17 (2nd cent.); *PRyl.* 77.30 (A.D. 192); *PYale* 69.27 (A.D. 214); *POxy.* 912.28 (A.D. 235); *BGU* 253.18 (A.D. 244-9); *POxy.* 2284.10 (A.D. 258); *POxy.* 2109.47 (A.D. 261); etc.
κλεῖς *POxy.* 729.23 (A.D. 137); *BGU* 75 i.13, with [κλ]εῖδας i.6, κλεῖδες ii.24 (2nd cent.: *BL* i, 15); *POxy.* 502.34 (A.D. 164); *POxy.* 1128.27 (A.D. 173); *SB* 7444.13 (late 3rd/early 4th cent.); *PHarris* 82.29 (A.D. 345); *POxy.* 903.16,18 (4th cent.)

Note. The other forms of κλείς are regular; the old Attic spellings κλῄς, etc., do not appear in the papyri.

---

[1] So Schweizer, 151; cf. Introd. above, p. XX.

[2] κλεῖν Lys. And. Pl., Ion. κληΐδα; κλεῖδα in later Gr., incl. Aristo, Plu. (*LSJ*, s.v.). κλεῖν is the only acc. sg. in the Ptol. papp. (Mayser i², 2, 31); both forms appear in the NT (*BDF*, § 47.3). Only κλεῖδα is found in the mag. papp.: *PGM* 4.2293, w. κατακλεῖδα 301 (4th cent.).

[3] Acc. κλεῖς is cited by *LSJ*, s.v., only as a v.l. in Arist. It is also found along with κλεῖδας in the NT (*BDF*, § 47.3). κλεῖδας is alone attested in the mag. papp. in *PGM* 4.341, w. κατακλεῖδας *PGM* 2.72 (both 4th cent.).

d) ὄρνις 'hen' is usually inflected as a dental stem, but the velar stem is attested; the by-form ὄρνεον 'bird' also occurs.

i. Dental stem:[1]

ὄρνις *POxy.* 738.9 (ca. A.D. 1)
  cf. ὄρνις δύο *sic PColt* 133.4 (6th cent.)
ὄρνειθος *PMilVogl.* 238.21 part. rest. (A.D. 143/4); *PSI* 1124.21 (A.D. 150)
ὄρνιθα *SB* 9649 = *PMilVogl.* 220.20 (A.D. 133/4)
  ὄρνιθαν *PMilVogl.* 241.7 (2nd cent.); *PMerton* 107.21 (2nd cent.)
ὄρνιθες *SB* 10270 (40).6 (A.D. 226/7-9); *POxy.* 2797.6 (3rd/4th cent.); *SB* 5301.1, etc., abbrev. (Byz.)
ὀρνίθων *PAberd.* 66.7 (A.D. 21); *PLond.* 1159 = *WChr.* 415.73 abbrev. (A.D. 145-7); *SB* 9348 i.14 (A.D. 169/70); *PStrassb.* 67.6 (A.D. 228); *PPrinc.* 62.4 (3rd cent.); *POxy.* 1913.28 abbrev. (ca. A.D. 555?); etc.
ὄρνεισι *SB* 4630 = *PBrem.* 56 Anh. (p. 130).17 (ca. A.D. 117)
ὄρνιθας *SB* 9465 = *PMilVogl.* 145.6,9,22 (A.D. 174); sim. *PLond.* 335 = *WChr.* 323.18 (A.D. 166/7 or 198/9)

The dental stem is also the normal formative for derivatives:

ὀρνιθίου *PStrassb.* 368.9 (mid 2nd cent.)
  ὀρνίθια *SB* 9013 = *PMed.* 83.7 part. rest. (4th cent.); *POxy.* 2046.5 abbrev., etc. (late 6th cent.); *BGU* 725.24 (A.D. 618: *BL* i, 63); etc.
  ὀρνίθεια *POxy.* 1862.12,35 (7th cent.)
  ὀρνιθίων *POxy.* 1729.4 (4th cent.); *PLond.* 1259 (iii, 239-40).5 abbrev. (4th cent.); *PCairMasp.* 212.5 (6th cent.); *PAntin.* 202a.13 (6th/7th cent.); etc.
  ὀρνιτίοις (for ὀρνιθίοις) *PMichael.* 80.2; 81.1; 82.1; 83.1-2 (1st half 3rd cent.)
ὀρνιθοτροφῖον *SB* 9348 i.15 (A.D. 169/70); sim. *POxy.* 2424.15 (2nd/3rd cent.)
ὀρνιθοτρόπον *PStrassb.* 129 = *SB* 7685.12, sim. 8 (A.D. 331); *PStrassb.* 149 = *SB* 8753.9 part. rest., 13-14 (4th cent.)
ὀρνιθοπ[ωλῶ]ν *SB* 9245.2 (2nd/3rd cent.)
ὀρνιθοπούλλ(ια) *StudPal.* viii, 1329.1 (6th/7th cent.)
ὀρνιθάρια *PFay.* 118.16 (A.D. 110); sim. *PGiss.* 80.6 part. rest. (ca. A.D. 117)
ὀρνειθῶνα *POxy.* 1207.4 (A.D. 175/6?)
ὀρνιθᾶς *SB* 7527.5 (prob. 3rd cent.); etc.; see above, p. 19

---

[1] The Att. acc. sg. ὄρνιν (*LSJ*, s.v.; Schwyzer i, 573) does not occur in the papp.; only ὄρνιθα is found in the Ptol. papp. (Mayser, i², 2, 31) and at Lycia (Hauser, 90). The mag. papp. have only ὄρνιθος *PGM* 63.10 (2nd/3rd cent.); *PGM* 12.100 (A.D. 300-50); ὄρνιθες *PGM* 3.199 (A.D. 300 +).

ii. Velar stem (from by-form ὄρνιξ[1]) only in dat. pl.:

ὄρνιξι *PLond.* 131 R = *SB* 9699.67,125, etc. (A.D. 78/79)

iii. By-form ὄρνεον:[2]

ὄρνεον (acc.) *PSI* 458.9 (A.D. 155)

ὄρνεα *PLond.* 1259 (iii, 239-40).16 (4th cent.); *SB* 7536 = *PLBat.* i, 7.9 (4th cent.); *StudPal.* xx, 107.4 (4th cent.); *POxy.* 2047.4; 2048.4 (5th cent.); *POxy.* 1923.23 (5th/early 6th cent.); *POxy.* 1890.12 (A.D. 508)

ὀρνέων *PCairGoodsp.* 30, xviii.6 (A.D. 191-2)

ὀρνέοι[ς] *PCairMasp.* 141 v R.25 (6th cent.)

This by-form is also used as the formative in derivatives:

ὀρνεοτρόφ(ος) *BGU* 725.7, sim. 29, with ὀρνίθια 24 (A.D. 618: *BL* i, 63)

ὀρνηοτρόφῳ *PBaden* 95.428, sim. 455 (7th cent.)

2) Names.

a) Greek names in -ις are inflected according to a mixed dental and *i*-stem declension, with the oblique cases fluctuating between the regular -ιδ- and the peculiarly Egyptian -ιτ-:[3]

Ἄρτεμις *BGU* 1897.17 (A.D. 166)

Ἀρτέμιδος *PFlor.* 71.142 (4th cent.)

Ἀρτέμειτος *StudPal.* xx, 12.4,21 (2nd cent.); *BGU* 1891.104 abbrev. (A.D. 134)

Ἀρτέμιτος *POxy.* 1645.6 (A.D. 308)

Ἄρτεμιν *BGU* 1896.277 (A.D. 166); 1899.78 abbrev. (after A.D. 172)

Ἀχιλλίς *BGU* 1893.434 (A.D. 149)

Ἀχιλλίδος *BGU* 1896.271 (A.D. 166); 1898.356 (A.D. 172); *PMich.* 223.129,343,561 (A.D. 171-2); *PGiss.* 51.3 (A.D. 202); etc.

Ἀχιλλεῖτ(ος) *SB* 7460 = *PLBat.* v, x.38 (A.D. 174)

Ἀχιλλίδι *SB* 9495 (2a) = *PMilVogl.* 194.15 (A.D. 146/7)

Ἀχιλλῖτι *POxy.* 1142.1,18 (late 3rd cent.)

---

[1] Oblique cases of Dor. ὄρνιξ are found in Alcm. B. Pi. Theoc. etc. (*LSJ*, s.v. ὄρνις; cf. Schwyzer i, 496, 510). ὄρνιξ (nom.) occurs twice in the Ptol. papp. (Mayser i[2], 2, 31) and is found in codd. of Babr. and Simplic. (Crönert, 174(-5), n. 5). ὄρνιξ also occurs as a v.l. in the NT (*BDF*, § 47.4).

[2] ὄρνεον *Il.* Cratin. Th. Ar. Pl. Arist. (*LSJ*, s.v.). It is used in the Ptol. papp. and the NT for 'bird' (Mayser i[2], 2, 31; *BDF*, § 47.4) but only once in the Atticists (Philostr. Jun.: Schmid, iii, 26, 142; iv, 22). In MGr., τὸ ὄρνεον = 'vulture,' 'bird of prey'; ἡ ὀρνίθα and ἡ ὄρνις = 'hen,' 'fowl' (Kykkotis, s.vv.).

[3] The -ιτ- stem predominates in Eg. names in the Ptol. papp. but is found in only one Gr. name (Mayser i[2], 2, 32).

Ἀχιλλίδα *SB* 9495 (2a) = *PMilVogl.* 194.11 (A.D. 146/7)

Ἀχιλλίδαν *POxy.* 1494.12 (early 4th cent.)

[Εὐδ]αιμονίς *PAlex.* 24.1 (2nd cent.)

Εὐδαιμονίδος *PMich.* 121 V vi.18 abbrev. (A.D. 42); *POxy.* 2134.8 (ca. A.D. 170); *PBerlLeihg.* 14.32 (2nd cent.)

Εὐδαιμονίδα *PSI* 1062.12 (A.D. 104/5); *PBerlLeihg.* 15.20 (A.D. 189)

Ἡρατδος (gen.) *StudPal.* iv, pp. 58-78, lines 306,467 abbrev., 530 (A.D. 72/73); *StudPal.* xx, 19.22 (A.D. 211-17); sim. *PLond.* 1003 (iii, 259-60).3 (A.D. 562)

Ἡραεῖτος *StudPal.* xx, 137.8 (A.D. 522)

Ἡρατδι *CPR* 21 = *StudPal.* xx, 31.6 (A.D. 230); *CPR* 38 = *StudPal.* xx, 57.1-2 part. rest. (A.D. 263)

Ἡραεῖδι *PCairMasp.* 300.2 (A.D. 527: *BL* iii, 36)

Ἡρατν *PCairMasp.* 312.43 (A.D. 567)

Πάρις *PHeid.* 234.8 (1st/2nd cent.); *OHeid.* 288.2 (Rom.); *PLBat.* xi, 15.1,12,20,V (4th cent.: *BL* v, 62)

Πάριδος *PPar.* 17.4 (A.D. 154); *POxy.* 970 descr. (early 3rd cent.); *PGiss.* 117 η.6 (mid 4th cent.); *PFlor.* 71.47 (4th cent.); etc.

Πάριτο(ς) *PMich.* 124 R II.17 (A.D. 46-49)

Πάριδι, Πάριν *PJand.* 94.9,4 (late 2nd/early 3rd cent.)

b) The Egyptian names Ἶσις and Σάραπις form their oblique cases in -ιδ-; the *i*-stem declension is rarely retained.[1] When used as a feminine personal name, Ἶσις (Ἶσεις) fluctuates between -ιδ- and -ιτ-, and the dental stem is sometimes extended to the acc. A short gen. in -(ε)ι is also found:[2]

Ἶσις (goddess) *POxy.* 492.16 (A.D. 130); etc.

Ἴσιδος *POxy.* 525.10 (early 2nd cent.); *POxy.* 490.22 (A.D. 124); etc.

Ἶσεις (Ἶσεις) (personal name):

Ἴσιδος *BGU* 1621 iii.15 abbrev. (2nd cent.); *PMich.* 225.3189 (A.D. 173-4); *PPrinc.* 87.9,11 (A.D. 612); etc.

Ἴσιτος *PLond.* 257 (ii, 19-28).218 (A.D. 94); *PMich.* 223.982 (A.D. 171-2); *PMich.* 224.197,293,528 (A.D. 172-3); *PSI* 713.10 (3rd cent.); etc.

Ἴσειτος *BGU* 1891.37, etc. (A.D. 134); *PCol.* 1 R 1a, vii.31; 1b, iii.5 (A.D. 134/5); 1 V 3.30 (A.D. 155); *POxy.* 1446.57 (A.D. 161-210); *POxy.* 1463.24 (A.D. 215); *POxy.* 1208.9, sim. 10 (A.D. 291); etc.

Εἴσιτος *BGU* 1614 B.5 (A.D. 69/70)

Ἴσει (gen.) *OMich.* 248.6 (late 3rd/early 4th cent.)

Εἴσι (gen.) *OMich.* 106.14 (late 3rd/early 4th cent.)

Ἶσι (gen.) *OMich.* 351.6 (late 3rd/early 4th cent.)

---

[1] The *i*-stem declension is still common in these names in the Ptol. papp. (Mayser i[2], 2, 22-23).

[2] Cf. the short gen. in *i*-stem names below, p. 79.

Ἴσιδι *PPrinc.* 129.14 (A.D. 188/9); *PPrinc.* 96.32,69 (2nd half 6th cent.)

Ἴσιτι *PIFAO* ii, 28.1 (1st cent.); *PStrassb.* 233 V (2nd half 3rd cent.)

Ἴσειν *SB* 7195 = *PBerlLeihg.* 3 i.2 (A.D. 182/3); *POxy.* 1637.22 (A.D. 257-9)

Ἴσιδα *PFouad* 15.24 (A.D. 119)

Σάραπις:

Σαράπιδος *PTebt.* 298 = *WChr.* 90.70 (A.D. 107/8); sim. *PMich.* 514.30 (3rd cent.); *PSI* 68.2 (6th cent.); etc.

Σαράπιδι *PMich.* 475.8; sim. 476.5 (early 2nd cent.); etc.

Σαράπι (dat.) *BGU* 338.8 (2nd/3rd cent.); *StudPal.* viii, 968.1 (4th cent.)

Σάραπιν *PMich.* 466.18 (A.D. 107); etc.

c) Other Egyptian names in -ις, apart from those declined as *i*-stems,[1] usually form their oblique cases in -ιτ-, but -ιδ- is sometimes found, as well as various heteroclitic forms and a short gen. in -(ε)ι, as in the following examples:[2]

Ἀμόιν Ἀμόιτος *PMilVogl.* 211 b.5 (2nd cent.)

Ἀμόιτος *PSI* 878.1 (2nd cent.); *POxy.* 2134.9,34 (ca. A.D. 170); *PLeit.* 15.1,9 (late 2nd/early 3rd cent.)

Ἀμόι (gen.) *PFouad* 32.19, with acc. Ἀμόιν 18 (A.D. 174)

Ἆπις *BGU* 1615.11 (A.D. 84); etc.

Ἄπεις *BGU* 1900.37,44 (ca. A.D. 196); *PBon.* 28.24 (A.D. 220/4); etc.

Ἄπιτος *PMich.* 123 V III.33-36; V.28-29 (A.D. 45-47); *BGU* 95.10 (A.D. 145/6)

Ἄπειτος *PCol.* 1 V 2.89 abbrev. (ca. A.D. 160); *PMich.* 223.2020 (A.D. 171-2); *POxy.* 76.2 (A.D. 179); *PSI* 468.3-4,42-43 (A.D. 200); *OMich.* 85.6 (3rd/early 4th cent.); etc.

Ἄπιδος *PCol.* 1 R 3 vii.4 (A.D. 135-45?)

Ἆπις Ἆπι *BGU* 1616.4,15 (A.D. 118/19 or 139/40)

Ἄπει (gen.) *POxy.* 530.14 (2nd cent.); *BGU* 1897.30 (A.D. 166); *PMich.* 224.4248a, with Ἄπιτος 4252a (A.D. 172-3); *BGU* 1900.68 (ca. A.D. 196); *PGen.* 77.2: *BL* i, 167 (A.D. 211); etc.

Ἄπιος (gen.) *POxy.* 476.13 (ca. A.D. 159: *BL* i, 323)

Ἄπιτι *PMich.* 123 V v.29 (A.D. 45-47); *PGron.* 15 R A 1; V A 1 (prob. 2nd cent.)

Ἁρμάεις Ἁρμάειος *PMich.* 244.37 (A.D. 43)

Ἁρμάιτος *PGiss.* 43.5 (A.D. 118/19)

Ἁρμάειτο(ς), Ἁρμάειν *PMich.* 238.11,25 (A.D. 46)

---

[1] See below, pp. 78-79.

[2] In the Ptol. papp., Ἆπις and Ἁρμάις are inflected predominantly according to the *i*-stem decl. (Mayser i², 2, 21).

ʽΑρμάειν _PMich._ 240.62 (A.D. 46/47)
ʽΑρσεῖς (fem.) _PBrem._ 57.1 (ca. A.D. 117)
    ʽΑρσείους _BGU_ 1891.26,31 abbrev., 153, with ʽΑρσεῖτ[(ος)] 556 (A.D.
        134); _PCol._ 1 R 1a vii.26 abbrev. (A.D. 134/5)
    ʽΑρσεῖτος _POxy._ 728.2 part. rest., 29 (A.D. 142); _PTebt._ 355.4 abbrev.
        (ca. A.D. 145); _PSI_ 1034.6 (2nd/3rd cent.); _PFlor._ 4 = _WChr._
        206.11-12 (A.D. 245)
    ʽΑρσῖτος _PGiss._ 68.27 (ca. A.D. 117)
    ʽΑρσεῖτι _PLond._ 310 = _MChr._ 334.8 (A.D. 146)

d) Other names, mostly Egyptian, inflected according to the dental stem declension fall into the following ten sub-types.[1]

i. -ᾶς, -ᾶ/-ᾶτος, -ᾷ/-ᾶτι, -ᾶν (masc.), see above, pp. 16-18.

ii. -άς, -άδος (-άτος), -άδι (-άτι), -άδα(ν) (Greek fem., also masc.), e.g., ʼΑπιάς, ʼΑσκληπιάς, Διονυσιάς:

    ʼΑπιάδος _PRyl._ 81.17 part. rest. (ca. A.D. 104); 102.19 (2nd half 2nd
        cent.); _CPR_ 218.4 part. rest. (A.D. 180-93?); _PCornell_ 18.4 (A.D.
        291); _POxy._ 2146.8 (3rd cent.)
    ʼΑσκληπιάς _PLond._ 1217a (iii, 61).4 (A.D. 246); cf. _SB_ 7334.1-2, inscr.
        (2nd/3rd cent.)
    ʼΑσκληπιάδος _PLond._ 604 B (iii, 76-87).119 (ca. A.D. 47)
    ʼΑσκληπιάδι _POxy._ 498.1 (2nd cent.)
    Διονυσιάς, Διονυσιάδα _POxy._ 1278.3,16 (A.D. 214)
    Διονυσιάδος _POxy._ 715 = _MChr._ 212.4-5 (A.D. 131)
    Διονυσιάτι _PHamb._ 5.13 (A.D. 89)
    Διονυσιάδα _PRyl._ 102.32 (2nd half 2nd cent.); _POxy._ 1278.16 (A.D. 214)
    Διονυσιάδαν _PJand._ 96.7 (3rd cent.)

iii. -ᾶς, -ᾶντος, e.g., ʼΑκαμᾶντος _OTheb._ 87.1 (A.D. 133); _PRossGeorg._ ii, 21.4 (ca. A.D. 154/5).

iv. -αῦς, -αῦτος (-αοῦτος, -αῦ, -αοῦ), -αῦτι, -αῦν, e.g., Νααραῦς, Νεκφεραῦς, Παλλαῦς:

    Νααραῦς Νααραῦτος _PPrinc._ 8 vii.7,8 (ca. A.D. 27-32)
    Νααραῦς _SB_ 5124.340,407 (A.D. 192)
    Νααραῦτος _PRyl._ 133.4 (A.D. 33); _PChic._ 89.3 abbrev. (A.D. 158/9?);
        PMich. 223.235, etc., abbrev. (A.D. 171-2); _PMich._ 224.22,330

---

[1] Cf. the same types in the Ptol. papp. (Mayser i², 2, 33-36). For names like ʼΑκῆς, ʽΑτρῆς, inflected predominantly according to the s-stem decl., with heteroclitic dental stems in -ητ-, see below, pp. 72-74.

(A.D. 172-3); *PSI* 1229.7 (A.D. 217); *PLond.* 1170 (iii, 92-103).117, 132 (3rd cent.); etc.

Ναραῦτος *BGU* 607.10 (A.D. 163)

Νααραῦ (gen.) *StudPal.* iii, 550.2; 601.2 (6th cent.); *StudPal.* viii, 835.2 (6th cent.); *SB* 4497.9 (A.D. 616); *SB* 4672.7 (Arab.); etc.

Νααραοῦ (gen.) *SB* 5174.7 (A.D. 512); *SB* 5175.7 (A.D. 513); *StudPal.* x, 234.3 (6th cent.); 268.2 (7th/8th cent.); *PRossGeorg.* v, 70.5 (8th cent.); etc.

Νααραῦτι *PTebt.* 609 descr. (2nd cent.)

Νααραῦν *PMich.* 121 V X.1, with Νααραῦτ(ος) XI.12 (A.D. 42)

Νεκφεραῦς *PMich.* 223.625,824 (A.D. 172-3); *PMich.* 359 A.151 (A.D. 174-5); etc.

Νεκφεραῦτος *PMich.* 121 V XI.15 abbrev. (A.D. 42); *PMich.* 123 R IV.5 (A.D. 45-47); *PMilVogl.* 105.15 (before A.D. 132/3); *PSI* 1031.6 (A.D. 134); *BGU* 441.4 (A.D. 158/9); etc.

Νεκφεραοῦτος *PMich.* 123 R VIII.36 (A.D. 45-47)

Παλλαῦς, Παλλαῦτος *POxy.* 2412.50,144,155 (A.D. 28/29); sim. *PMich.* 121 R II x.1 (A.D. 42); *PFouad* 70.16 abbrev. (2nd/3rd cent.)

v. -εῦς, -εῦτος, -εῦτι, -εῦν, e.g., Εῦς, Χεῦς:

Εῦτος *PMich.* 123 R IV.16,17; V I.2 abbrev. (A.D. 45-47)

Ε[ὔ]τι *PRyl.* 244.1 (3rd cent.)

Χεῦς, Χεῦτος, Χεῦτι, Χεῦν *PTebt.* 376 = *WChr.* 350.1,21,26,32 (A.D. 162)

Χεῦτος *PLond.* 258 (ii, 28-36).85 (A.D. 94)

cf. Μιεῦτος *PMich.* 259.19,21,35, with Μιέους 2 (A.D. 33)

vi. -ῆς, -ῆτος (-ῆ, -ιους, -εῖος, -ῆς, -ήτου), -ῆτι, -ῆν, e.g., Κιαλῆς, Κοπρῆς, Μουσῆς:

Κιαλῆς *BGU* 659 ii.22 (A.D. 229)

Κιαλῆτος *BGU* 852.10 (A.D. 143/4); *BGU* 358 = *WChr.* 246.7 (A.D. 151); *PMich.* 614.11, with gen. Κια[λ]ῆ 2 (ca. A.D. 256); etc.

Κιαλῆ (gen.) *PMich.* 224.1792,4167 (A.D. 172-3); *BGU* 2 = *MChr.* 113.8 (A.D. 209); *SB* 4439.4 (A.D. 250); *POxy.* 2155.13 (4th cent.); *StudPal.* x, 79.11 (7th/8th cent.); etc.

Κιαλίους *SB* 8070 = *PFouad* 14.3 (after 7 B.C.)

Κιαλεῖος *PBouriant* 42.567, with nom. Κιαλῆ 577 (A.D. 167)

Κιαλῆτει *BGU* 824.1: *BL* i, 70 (A.D. 55/56)

Κοπρῆς *BGU* 1608.4 (A.D. 188); 1617.9 (prob. A.D. 198); 1634 ii.41, etc. (A.D. 229/30); etc.

Κοπρῆτος *BGU* 835.4 (A.D. 217)

Κοπρῆ (gen.) *PLond.* 188 (ii, 141-6).92 (3rd cent.?); *PGen.* 63 = *PAbinn.* 66.54; *PLond.* 252 = *PAbinn.* 72.9; *PAbinn.* 73.33, etc. (ca. A.D. 346); etc.

Μουσῆς *BGU* 343.3 (2nd/3rd cent.?); etc.

    Μουσῆτος, Μουσῆν *PCairMasp.* 296.7,16,18 (A.D. 535); *POxy.* 1917.10 (6th cent.)

    Μουσῆ (gen.) *PLond.* 410 = *PAbinn.* 34.3 (ca. A.D. 346); *SB* 5354.17 (5th cent.); *StudPal.* x, 54.10 (8th cent.); etc.

    Μουσῆτι *PErl.* 106.81 (early 4th cent.)

    Μουσῆν *PAntin.* 96.5 (6th cent.)

cf. Ταβῆς (nom. fem.) *SB* 3872; 4197; mummy labels (n.d.)

    Ταβῆτος *BGU* 1891.393 (A.D. 134); *BGU* 392.11 (A.D. 208: *BL* i, 43); *PRyl.* 388 V.1 (3rd cent.?)

    Θαβῆτ(ος) *BGU* 639 ii.32 (A.D. 208)

    Ταβῆς (gen.) *POxy.* 996 descr. (A.D. 584); *SB* 9561.15 (A.D. 590)

cf. also Χάρητος (gen.) *PFay.* 97 = *MChr.* 315.25 (1st hand), with Χαρήτου 38 (2nd hand) (A.D. 78); *POxy.* 520.1 abbrev., 3 (A.D. 143); *PLond.* 267 (ii, 129-41).326,327 (A.D. 114: *BL* i, 253); etc.

    Χάρητι *PHamb.* 4.13 (A.D. 87)

vii. -οῦς, -οῦτος, -οῦτι, -οῦν, e.g., Ἀμμωνοῦς, Κρονοῦς, Σαταβοῦς, Φηοῦς, Φιλοῦς:

    Ἀμμωνοῦς *PMich.* 223.1449,1512 (A.D. 171-2); *PMich.* 224.1381,1489 (A.D. 172-3); etc.

    Ἀμμωνοῦτος *PRyl.* 597.4 (A.D. 90); *PBrem.* 44.4 (ca. A.D. 117); *PMich.* 224.1856,3553 (A.D. 172-3); *PMich.* 381.6, sim. 12 (2nd half 2nd cent.); *SB* 8032 = *PRyl.* 599.6-7 (A.D. 226); etc.

    Κρονοῦς, Κρονοῦτι, Κρονοῦν *PPhil.* 11.5,6,7,17, etc. (A.D. 141)

    Κρονοῦτος *PTebt.* 327 = *WChr.* 394.3 part. rest. (late 2nd cent.); *SB* 5124.133,296 abbrev. (A.D. 193: *BL* v, 94); *POxy.* 1725.8 abbrev. (A.D. 229+); *SB* 7634.27 (A.D. 249); etc.

    Κρονοῦτι *PFouad* 77.7-8 (2nd cent.); *PStrassb.* 284.7 part. rest. (A.D. 176-80); etc.

    Κρονοῦν *BGU* 361 iii.18 (A.D. 184); *PTebt.* 366 = *WChr.* 371.9 (A.D. 188); etc.

    Σαταβοῦς, Σαταβοῦτος, Σαταβοῦ[τι], Σαταβοῦν *BGU* 153 = *MChr.* 263.9,11,13,18,21,25,39 (A.D. 152)

    Φηοῦς *BGU* 608 i.7 (Arab.)

    Φηοῦτος *PAmh.* 155.4 (5th cent.); *PLond.* 1701.5 (6th cent.); *PAlex.* 38.7 (6th/7th cent.)

    Φηοῦν *PCairMasp.* 328 i.6,22 (A.D. 521)

    Φιλοῦς *POslo* 110.8 (A.D. 131/2+)

    Φιλοῦτος *PMich.* 123 R IX.7 abbrev., etc. (A.D. 45-47); *PPhil.* 5.4 (mid 1st cent.); *PHarris* 138 iii.2 (1st cent.); *StudPal.* iv, pp. 58-83, lines 452,475 (A.D. 72/73); *BGU* 1891.38,119,182 (A.D. 134); *PSI* 229.25 (2nd cent.); etc.

    Φιλοῦν *POxy.* 1296.10 (3rd cent.)

viii. -ῦς, -ῦτος, -ῦτι, -ῦν, e.g., Κραμβῦν (acc.) *PFay.* 161 descr. = *PCair-Preis.* 5.5 (2nd/3rd cent.); Νειχῦτος *POxy.* 520.6 (A.D. 143); sim. *PRein.* 101.2 (A.D. 198-209); etc.

ix. -ῶν, -ῶντος, -ῶντι, -ῶντα, e.g., 'Εξακῶν: 'Εξακῶντος *POxy.* 506 = *MChr.* 248.3 part. rest. (A.D. 143); *PAmh.* 99a.4,27 (A.D. 179); 'Εξακῶντι *PAmh.* 128.118 (A.D. 128); 'Εξακῶντ(α) *PAmh.* 135 = *PSarap.* 96.21 (A.D. 129?).

x. -ῶς, -ῶτος (-ῶ), -ῶτι (-ῷ), -ῶν, e.g., Απολλῶς:

'Απολλῶς *PCornell* 22.6,80,128,129 (early 1st cent.); *PAberd.* 22.8 (2nd cent.); *PMerton* 83.15 (late 2nd cent.); *PGen.* 42.13 (A.D. 224); *StudPal.* iii, 95.1,9 (6th cent.); etc.
'Απολλῶ (nom.) *PFouad* 82.13-14 (4th/5th cent.); *StudPal.* viii, 813.1 (6th cent.); *SB* 4674.11 (Byz.); *StudPal.* x, 115.5 (7th cent.); etc.
'Απολλῶτος *PPrinc.* 152 ii.10 (A.D. 55-60); *PBrem.* 48.8 (A.D. 118); *OTait* 1380.3; 1389.5 (A.D. 147); *PMich.* 223.1901 abbrev. (A.D. 171-2); *PMarmarica* v.10; x.2 abbrev. (A.D. 190/1?); *PSI* 66.41 (5th cent.?); *PMerton* 97.14 (6th cent.); *PCairMasp.* 49.13 (6th cent.); etc.
'Απολλῶ (gen.) *PGen.* 61 = *PAbinn.* 23 V (ca. A.D. 346); *PAlex.* 40.7 (4th/5th cent.); *PGron.* 6.6 (5th cent.?); *PSI* 80.7,12,18,24 (6th cent.); *PCairMasp.* 26.2 (ca. A.D. 551); *POxy.* 1913.8 (ca. A.D. 555?); *StudPal.* iii, 38.1; 56.1; etc. (6th cent.); *PCairMasp.* 359 ii V.1, etc. (Arab.); etc.
'Απολλῶτι *OTaitPetr.* 244.1 (A.D. 36); *PMich.* 123 V, II.28 (A.D. 45-47); *PFay.* 129.2 (3rd cent.); *PCairMasp.* 138 ii R.27; 139 iii R.19; v R.10; vi V.15 (6th cent.); *PSI* 70.1 (6th cent.?); etc.
'Απολλῷ *StudPal.* viii, 1069.1; 1070.1 (5th/6th cent.); *StudPal.* iii, 207.2 (6th cent.); 344.2 (6th/7th cent.); *SB* 4909.1 (Byz.); etc.
'Απολλών *PMich.* 514.23 (3rd cent.)
cf. also Φασῶς Φασῶτος *PMich.* 300.1 (1st cent.); Σεναπολλῶς *SB* 1670.2 (A.D. 189/90); Σεναπολλῶτο(ς) *OStrassb.* 527.4 (2nd cent.); *WO* 938.4 (A.D. 174); Τααπολλῶτος *POxy.* 1444.9 (A.D. 248/9); etc.

3. Liquid stems.[1]

a. *l*-stems:

ἄλς (masc.) usually follows the classical liquid stem declension, but anomalous forms are found, and a neuter by-form ἄλας, the Modern Greek form presumably derived from the acc. pl. on the analogy of κρέας,[2] is also used.

---

[1] Schwyzer i, 562-5, 567-9, cf. 480-1; Chantraine², § 72-76; *MS*, 131; Schweizer, 156-7; Hauser, 95-96; Mayser i², 2, 42-43; *BDF*, § 46-47.
[2] Schwyzer i, 518, n. 3. ἄλας is found already in Arist., and occurs in the Ptol. papp.

ἁλός *POxy.* 736.7,74; 1143.5,7 (ca. A.D. 1); *PAmh.* 126 = *PSarap.* 55.31
(A.D. 128); *PLond.* 1169 (iii, 43-47).27,28,30 (2nd cent.); *BGU* 731
ii.8,11 (A.D. 180); *POxy.* 1731.16 (3rd cent.); *PLips.* 97 xxxiv.11,21
(A.D. 338); *PCairMasp.* 141 i V.19 (late 6th cent.?); etc.
ἁλεί *BGU* 246.9 (2nd/3rd cent.)
ἅλα *SB* 4425 iv.34, with ἁλός ii.17 (2nd cent.)
ἅλαες (for ἅλες *BL* i, 176) *PCairGoodsp.* 30 xv.19, xxii.4 part. rest.,
  xxix.14, xxxiii.7, with ἅλα xiv.20 (A.D. 191-2)
ἁλῶν *PBeattyPanop.* 2.248 (A.D. 300)
τὸ ἅλα *SB* 8030 = *PMich.* 245.10,21, with ἁλ{λ}ός 28 (A.D. 47)
τὸ ἅλας *PRyl.* 692.5; 695.12; 696.6 (late 3rd cent.); *POxy.* 1222.2 (4th
  cent.); *PSI* 1061.15,17 (6th cent.)
ἅλατος *PAntin.* 190 (a).23 (6th/7th cent.); *PApoll.* 93 B.3, etc. (A.D.
  703-15); etc.
ἁλάτων *PGissBibl.* 25.20 (3rd cent.)

b. *r*-stems.

1) πατήρ, μήτηρ, θυγάτηρ.[1]

a) The voc. sg. πάτερ, μῆτερ, θύγατερ tends to be replaced by the nom.:
πατήρ used as voc.: *PMich.* 476.5; 477.23 part. rest.; 480.5; 481.33 (all
  early 2nd cent.); *BGU* 423 = *WChr.* 480.11; *PAberd.* 71.4; *PWürzb.*
  21 A.12 part. emended, 19 (all 2nd cent.); *PRein.* 55 = *PFlor.* 180*.
  11 (A.D. 253); *PGen.* 75.17 (3rd cent.: *BL* i, 167); etc.
μήτηρ used as voc.: *BGU* 846.10 (2nd cent.); *SB* 7353 = *PMich.* 491.5,9
  (2nd cent.); *BGU* 814.12,26,33 (3rd cent.); *BGU* 1043.3 (3rd cent.);
  PRossGeorg. iii, 2.6,27 (A.D. 270: *BL* iii, 156); *PBerlZill.* 12.4-5 (3rd/
  4th cent.); etc.
θυγάτηρ used as voc.: *PLBat.* xvi, 30 iii.6 (3rd cent.)
cf. also voc. σωτήρ *PGM* 81.3, gnostic invocation (4th cent.)

This substitution of the nom. for the voc. reflects the general tendency to
eliminate the voc. case in the history of Greek,[2] furthered in *r*-stems by the
resultant simplification of a complex declensional type based on IE vowel gradation and by the identification of ε and η before /r/.[3]

b) Conversely, the voc. spelling is found sporadically for the nom.:

ἡ μήτερ *PMich.* 274-5.1 (A.D. 46/47); *PLond.* 154 (ii, 178-80).25 (A.D. 68)
ἡ θυγάτερ *SB* 8092.2 (ca. A.D. 500)

---

along with ἅλς from the 3rd cent. B.C. on, and in Gal. LXX, NT (*LSJ*, s.v.; Mayser i[2], 2,
45; *BDF*, § 47.4). ἅλατος is read in *PGM* 63.2 (2nd/3rd cent.); elsewh. the mag. papp. have
only forms of ἅλς.
  [1] For the freq. acc. sg. πατέραν, μητέραν, θυγατέραν, see above, p. 45.
  [2] Cf. Chantraine[2], § 13, 29, 50.
  [3] See Vol. i, 262.

c) Other anomalous spellings occur in the nom. and voc.:

μήτρη (voc.) *POxy.* 1678.4,8, with acc. μητέραν 20,23,25 (3rd cent.)
θυγάτρι (nom. and gen.) *StudPal.* iii, 99.1,2 (6th cent.)
θηγάτρι (nom.) *StudPal.* iii, 127.1 (6th cent.)

d) The dat. pl. θυγατρέσι *BGU* 1013.8 (A.D. 41-68) may be an instance of the interchange of stressed α and ε,[1] but the s-stem ending -εσι is found with other stems of the third declension.[2]

e) Evidence for the transfer of these nouns to the *a*-stem declension as in Modern Greek[3] is found in a few late forms:

εἰ μητέρα (for ἡ μητέρα) σου *PMichael.* 39.9, sim. 12-13 (Byz.)
ταῖς κυρίαις μου μητέραις *PBerlZill.* 12.1 (3rd/4th cent.)
ταῖς ... θυγάτ[ρ]αις *PCairMasp.* 300.2 (A.D. 527: *BL* iii, 36; iv, 14)

2) μάρτυς usually follows the *r*-stem declension, with the Attic nom. sg. μάρτυς,[4] and acc. sg. μάρτυρα (μάρτυν once[5]); but a few examples of an *o*-stem by-form also occur:[6]

μάρτυς *PLond.* 1912.26 (A.D. 41); *PCairIsidor.* 79.16 (early 4th cent.); *POxy.* 2603.8 (4th cent.); *PHermRees* 59.7 (late 4th cent.); *PLips.* 40 iii.6 (late 4th/early 5th cent.); *PGen.* 14.9 part. rest. (Byz.); *PAlex.* 38.6 (6th/7th cent.)
ὁ μεταξυμάρτυς *CPR* 19 = *StudPal.* xx, 86.14 (A.D. 330)
μάρτυν *PLips.* 40 ii.8, with μάρτυρα 9 (late 4th/early 5th cent.)
μάρτυρα *PSI* 893.20 (A.D. 315)
μάρτυρες *PSI* 36a.24: *BL* i, 390 (A.D. 11-19); *PSI* 1248.3 (A.D. 235); sim. *SB* 7559.15 (A.D. 118: *BL* iii, 189); etc.
μαρτύρων *PMichael.* 40.20,53 (mid 6th cent.); *PPrinc.* 78.5 (6th cent.); sim. *SB* 9525.15 (6th cent.); etc.
μάρτυσι *PRyl.* 160a.6 (A.D. 14-37); *PMich.* 287.15 (1st cent.); *PStrassb.* 241.13 (1st half 2nd cent.); etc.
μάρτυρας *PTouad* 32.17 (A.D. 174); *PHermRees* 31.4 (6th cent.); *PSI* 1267 = *PApoll.* 24.5 (A.D. 710); etc.

---

[1] See Vol. i, 281.
[2] See above, pp. 47-48.
[3] See above, p. XX; Thumb, *Handbook*, § 83; Mirambel, *Gram.*, 54-55.
[4] μάρτυς (by dissimilation from *μαρτυρς) (Schwyzer i, 260, 569; Lejeune, § 110) is likewise the form used in the Ptol. and Herc. papp. (Mayser i², 2, 43; Crönert, 167), but the Aeol.-Dor. μάρτυρ (*LSJ*, s.v.), orig. read but corrected to μάρτυρες in *PSI* 36a.24, recurs in late Byz. (see Crönert, 167, n. 1), prob. under the influence of Lat. *martyr*.
[5] μάρτυν Simon. Men. Plu. (7 times); μάρτυρα E. Pl. Plu. (6 times) (*LSJ*, s.v.; Crönert, 167, n. 1). μάρτυρα occurs twice in the Ptol. papp., never μάρτυν (Mayser i², 2, 43).
[6] The *o*-stem μάρτυρος is Ep. (*Il.* 2.302, etc.; *Od.* 16.423) and is found in inscrr. from central Greece (*LSJ*, s.v. μάρτυρος; Schwyzer i, 435, n. 5). It is also one form of this Gr. loanword in Copt. (Böhlig, 118).

μάρτυρος (nom.) *PGen.* 54 = *PAbinn.* 35.6 (ca. A.D. 346)
μάρτυρων (for μάρτυρον acc.) *POxy.* 1683.14 (late 4th cent.)
μαρτύροις *SB* 5108 = *PRyl.* 160.6 (A.D. 28/29)

3) χείρ sometimes has the stem χερ- in cases other than the dat. pl. χερσί, e.g., χερός, χερί, χέρα(ν), χέρας, also χεροναξίου, χερογραφ[ίαν], χερικήν; for examples, see Vol. i, 259.[1] The distinction between χειρ- and χερ- is purely orthographic.[2]

4) Fluctuations between ο and ω in the spelling of nouns in -ωρ, -ορος, e.g., κ[τ]ήτωρ and κτ[η̃]τορ (both nom. sg.) *PCairMasp.* 283 ii.23 (before A.D. 548), κτητόρον (gen. pl.) *PCairMasp.* 286.14 (A.D. 527/8), are likewise purely orthographic.[3]

5) Names in -ωρ, regularly declined -ωρ, -ωρος, etc., also have variants in -ορος:

'Αντήνωρος *PMich.* 310.8 (A.D. 26/27)
but 'Αντήνορος *PSAAthen.* 43 R.11 (A.D. 131/32?); *BGU* 558 i.15 (early 3rd cent.); etc.
Εὐφράνωρος *PMich.* 312.8, with Εὐφράνορ(ος) 46 (A.D. 34)
but Εὐφράνωρ Εὐφράνορος *POxy.* 2349.20-21 (A.D. 70); etc.

4. Nasal stems.[4]

a. κύων is the only *n*-stem with full vowel gradation which occurs; it is found only in the following forms:

κύων *BGU* 814.19 (3rd cent.); clearly *SB* 9321.3 (n.d.)
κυνί *StudPal.* xxii, 56.22 (2nd/3rd cent.)
cf. κυνός *PLBat.* i, 21.44, mag. (3rd cent.)
κυνόσβοραν *PCairMasp.* 141 i V.14 (late 6th cent.?)
κυνοβοσκός *SB* 5796.3, inscr. (n.d.)

b. Masc. and fem. stems with lengthened grade -ων/-ην in the nom. and normal grade -ον-/-εν- elsewhere are declined regularly, including εἰκών, which shows no trace of the Poetic-Ionic *s*-stem inflection:[5]

---

[1] Cf. Crönert, 115, n. 3; Mayser i², 1, 55; i², 2, 42-43.

[2] See Vol. i, 262.

[3] For the identification of ο and ω, see Vol. i, 275-7.

[4] Schwyzer i, 562-5, 567-9, cf. 485-8; Chantraine², § 77-81; *MS*, 131; Schweizer, 157; Nachmanson, 134; Hauser, 96; Mayser i², 2, 43-44.

[5] Gen. εἰκοῦς (from nom. *εἰκώ?) is attested in E., acc. εἰκώ A. E. Hdt. (also εἰκόνα) Pl. (both), and acc. pl. εἰκούς E. Ar. (*LSJ*, s.v.; cf. Chantraine², § 69). The oblique cases are formed on the stem εἰκον- in Att. inscrr. until Rom. times, when an acc. εἰκώ is also found (*MS*, 131). Only εἰκον- is found at Perg. and Magn. and in the Ptol. papp. (Schweizer, 157; Nachmanson, 134; Mayser i², 2, 43).

ἰκόνος *PSI* 784.3 (A.D. 362)

εἰκόνα *PBouriant* 1.175 (4th cent.); *StudPal.* viii, 1160 = xx, 196.2 (5th/
6th cent.); *SB* 5297.2 (Byz.); cf. *SB* 4243.2, inscr. (n.d.); etc.

εἰκόνες *PStrassb.* 79.10 (16/15 B.C.); *SB* 9213 i.6,7,8 (A.D. 215); sim.
SB 4292.7 (Rom.); etc.

ἰκόνων *BGU* 1127.36 (18 B.C.)

εἰκόνας *POxy.* 2349.23 (A.D. 70); *PBon.* 15.4 part. rest. (A.D. 215/16);
sim. *POxy.* 2476.2 (A.D. 288: *BL* v, 82)

c. The lengthened grade nom. ἀρήν/ἄρης[1] does not occur. The oblique
cases have the usual zero grade:

ἄρνες, ἄρνας *POxy.* 246 = *WChr.* 247.23;17,22 (A.D. 66)
   ἄρνες *PSI* 56.8,15 (A.D. 107)
ἀρνῶν *PMich.* 123 R IX.42 abbrev. (A.D. 45-47); *PRossGeorg.* ii, 18.50
   (A.D. 140); *PStrassb.* 300.9 (2nd cent.)
ἄρνασι *POxy.* 245.12 (A.D. 26)
ἄρνας *SB* 7344.13-14 (A.D. 8/9); *PCornell* 15.11, etc. (A.D. 128/9); *PSI*
   40.3 (A.D. 129); etc.

d. The nom. ῥίς/ῥίν does not occur, except in the derivative adjective εὐθύριν
(see below, p. 141).[2]

e. The original s-stem μείς/μήν[3] has the Epic-Ionic-Old Attic nom. μείς[4]
in *SB* 9309.10 (3rd cent.) and *POxy.* 465.11, astrol. (late 2nd cent.); cf. (for
acc.) *SB* 1191.5, mummy label (n.d.).

f. Most *n*-stem names, including Ἄμμων, Ἀπίων, Ἀπόλλων, Ἁρποκρα-
τίων, Βίων, Ἥρων, Θέων, Νειλάμμων, Σαραπίων, Φοιβάμμων, etc., are declined
-ωνος, -ωνι, -ωνα, with only occasional variant spellings in -ονος, -ονι, -ονα.
But Εὐδαίμων and Χαιρήμων are usually declined -ονος, -ονι, -ονα, with occasional variants in -ωνος, etc., e.g., Εὐδαίμονος *PCairIsidor.* 9.107, etc. (ca. A.D.
310), Εὐδαίμωνι *PPrinc.* 187.4 (1st cent.); Χαι[ρή]μωνος *SB* 7623 = *PCair-
Isidor.* 2.4 (A.D. 298), Χαι[ρ]ήμωνι *PCairMasp.* 141 v V.12 (late 6th cent.?).

---

[1] Nom. ἀρήν is found in an Att. inscr. of 1st half 5th cent. B.C. (*MS*, 142), in inscrr.
from Delos, Cos, and Gortyn (*LSJ*, s.v.), and in the Ptol. papp., along w. ἄρης and ἄρνον
(Mayser i², 2, 46).

[2] Nom. ῥίς X. Arist. Theoc. Philostr. (Stephanus, *Thesaurus*, s.v.) occurs in an Att.
inscr. of 320/17 B.C. (*MS*, 144); nom. ῥίν is found in Hp. (prob. f.l.) Aret. Luc. Sor. (*LSJ*,
s.v.; cf. Schwyzer i, 569, n. 4). The nom. is not attested in the Ptol. papp., but Mayser i²,
2, 43-44 suggests ῥίν in view of the ad⸴s.

[3] Cf. Lat. *mensis*, and see Schwyzer i, 515, n. 1.

[4] μείς *Il.* Hes. Anacr. Pi. Hdt. Hp. Pl. Arist. Thphr. Call. etc.; μήν Hes. Th. X. Thphr.
etc. (*LSJ*, s.v.; cf. Schwyzer i, 569; Chantraine², § 69).

These variations are not significant for morphology, because ο and ω represent the same sound /o/.[1]

5. *s*-stems.[2]

a. Neuter stems in -ος show the following peculiarities.

1) The gen. sg. sometimes appears in -ου because of the similarity of the nom. sg. to that of the second declension.[3]

2) The nom. is sometimes used for the gen.:[4]

τοῦ ... βλάβος *SB* 7174 = *PMich.* 233.20 (A.D. 24: *BL* v, 69)
τοῦ τέλος *WO* 1551.2-3 (A.D. 34); sim. *WO* 1330.3 (A.D. 160); *PMich.* 377.1 (mid/late 4th cent.)
τοῦ ... μέρος *PMich.* 252.2 (A.D. 26/27); *PMich.* 554.58 (A.D. 81-96); *SB* 10722.4 (2nd cent.); *PPar.* 17.8 (A.D. 154); *SB* 9881.8 (A.D. 315); *POslo* 138.7 (A.D. 323); *PCairMasp.* 327.39, sim. 40 (prob. A.D. 539); *SB* 4755.6, sim. 26 (Byz.); *POxy.* 1939.3 (6th/7th cent.); *SB* 9586.17 (A.D. 600); etc.
ἑβδόμου ἔτος *PMich.* 274-5.11 (A.D. 46/47); sim. *SB* 7340.21 (A.D. 540)
λόγος ὄξος (gen.) *OMich.* 248.1 (late 3rd/early 4th cent.)
τοῦ τεῖχος *SB* 7800.6 (6th/7th cent.: *BL* iii, 195)

Various factors may account for these spellings, including simple failure to decline, the analogy of other third declension genitives in -ος, and the partial identification of ο and ου.[5] No permanent declensional shift is involved: cf. Modern Greek μέρο(ς), μέρους, etc.[6]

3) Conversely, the gen. is used sporadically for the nom./acc.:

τῶι (for τὸ) ... μέρους *PMich.* 318-20.5 (A.D. 40); sim. *PMich.* 276.29 (4th hand), with μέρος for gen. μέρους 38 (5th hand) (A.D. 47); *POxy.* 1638.7 (A.D. 282)
τὸ ὄρους *PCairMasp.* 139 iii R.1, clearly iv V.9 (6th cent.)

4) The nom.-acc. pl. ends regularly in -η; uncontracted -εα forms appear

---

[1] See Vol. i, 275-7. Thumb's suggestion (*Hell.*, 143, n. 2), supported by Mayser i[2], 2, 44, of analogical formation of the stem vowel is valid only on the orthographic level.
[2] Schwyzer i, 570, 578-80, cf. 511-13; Chantraine[2], § 67-71; Buck, *GD*, § 108; *MS*, 131-7; Schweizer, 152-6; Nachmanson, 134-8; Hauser, 91-95; Mayser i[2], 2, 36-42; *BDF*, § 46-48.
[3] See above, pp. 43-44.
[4] Three exx. of nom. for gen. in *s*-stems also occur in the Ptol. papp. (Mayser i[2], 2, 37).
[5] See Vol. i, pp. 213-14.
[6] Thumb, *Handbook*, § 99; Mirambel, *Gram.*, 62.

only in the magical papyri.[1] The analogous τὰ μέρα is read in *BGU* 592 ii.6: *BL* i, 55 (2nd cent.).

5) The gen. pl. is regularly -ῶν, only sporadically the uncontracted -έων:[2]

ὀρέων *PGrenf.* ii, 84.5-6, schoolboy's exercise (5th/6th cent.); cf. *SB* 1521.2-3, inscr. (Byz.)

cf. also ἐτιῶν (for ἐτῶν) *PCairMasp.* 301.28 (A.D. 530: *BL* iv, 15)

6) A short dat. pl. κτῆσι (for κτήνεσι from κτῆνος) occurs in *PStrassb.* 299 V.17: *BL* v, 141 (2nd cent.); *OTait* 1826.2,5,7 (2nd/3rd cent.); *PRossGeorg.* v, 56.2 (3rd cent.); *PFlor.* 249 b.7 (A.D. 257); 267.5 (3rd cent.); 321.47 (3rd cent.); *PSI* 808.17 (3rd cent.?); *PCornell* 39.7: *BL* ii, 2, 49 (3rd/4th cent.); *SB* 9024.17 (late 3rd/early 4th cent.); *PLips.* 97 xxii.9 (A.D. 338); *PSI* 711.2 (A.D. 360); *PCairGoodsp.* 15.10 part. rest. (A.D. 362); etc.; κτήνεσι occurs in *BGU* 757.20 (A.D. 12); etc.

7) χρέος, which in Attic has a nom.-acc. sg. χρέως by quantitative metathesis from χρῆος (Homeric χρεῖος),[3] appears in both spellings:

χρέος *PStrassb.* 33.5 (1st cent.); *PLond.* 1158 = *MChr.* 256.15 (A.D. 226/7); *PLips.* 3 i.14 (A.D. 256); *CPR* 10 = *MChr.* 145.10 (A.D. 322/3); *PSI* 898.8 (4th cent.?); *POxy.* 128.13 (6th/7th cent.); etc.

χρέως *PLond.* 289 (ii, 184-5).21 (A.D. 91); *PLBat.* xvi, 32.8 (A.D. 305); *PGen.* 56 = *PAbinn.* 37.19 (ca. A.D. 346); *PLond.* 240 = *PAbinn.* 51.7 (A.D. 346); *PLond.* 241 = *PAbinn.* 52.9 (A.D. 346); *SB* 9444 = *PMed.* 61.4 (4th cent.); etc.

The gen. sg. is regularly χρέους,[4] nom.-acc. pl. χρέα:[5]

χρέους *POxy.* 2237.14 (A.D. 498); *PGrenf.* ii, 86.16 (A.D. 595); *PPar.* 21b.24 (A.D. 592); 21.43 (A.D. 616); etc.

χρέα *PSI* 1100.23 (A.D. 161); *BGU* 1027 xxvi = *WChr.* 424 i.21 (late 4th cent.: *BL* i, 88); etc.

---

[1] Cf. χείλεα *PGM* 4.401, w. χείλη 1338 (4th cent.); χείλη also *PGM* 2.19 (4th cent.).

[2] The uncontr. gen. pl. is fairly common in Trag. and X. (cf. Schwyzer i, 579; Chantraine², § 67). It is found 3 times in the Ptol. papp. (Mayser i², 2, 37) and is used in ὀρέων and χειλέων in the NT (*BDF*, § 48).

[3] χρέως is found in codd. of D. but χρέος in Pl. (*LSJ*, s.v.). Phryn., 370, gives χρέως as Att., w. χρέος only Ar. *Nu.* 30, an inserted choric frag. (Rutherford, *Phryn.*, 48; cf. 482, where he thinks that χρέος ought prob. to be regarded as a copyist's error when encountered in Att. texts). The Herc. papp. have χρέως, but χρέος *Iatrica* (Crönert, 167; cf. n. 3 for further citations from Koine and Byz. authors).

[4] Gen. χρείους E., χρέους codd. Lys., χρέως codd. opt. D. 49.18, but the spelling seems spurious (*LSJ*, s.v.; Rutherford, *Phryn.*, 482).

[5] χρέα Ar. Isoc. Pl., χρήατα (dbtfl.) Arc. inscr. (*LSJ*, s.v.).

b. Neuter stems in -ας.

1) κρέας follows the regular Attic *s*-stem declension, with heteroclitic *o*-stem forms also occurring:[1]

> κρέως *POxy.* 108 i.2, etc. (A.D. 183/215); *PCairGoodsp.* 30 ii.10, etc.
> (A.D. 191/2); *PGiss.* 49.15,23 (3rd cent.); *POxy.* 1194.24 (ca. A.D.
> 265); *PLips.* 84 vii.4,10 (A.D. 284-305); *PBeattyPanop.* 1.276, etc.
> (A.D. 298); 2.231 (A.D. 300); *POxy.* 1056.2 (A.D. 360); *POxy.* 1893.12
> (A.D. 535); etc.
>
> κρέα *PJand.* 93.14 (2nd cent.); *PFlor.* 31.10 (A.D. 312); etc.[2]
> κρεῶν *POxy.* 1545.1 (4th cent.)
> κρέος (nom.) *POslo* 44.6 (A.D. 324-5)
> κρέου (gen.) *PApoll.* 63.6 (A.D. 703-15)

2) κέρας is declined almost without exception according to the dental stem inflection in the sg. as well as in the pl.:[3]

> gen. κέρως *PBeattyPanop.* 2.82 (A.D. 300)
> but κέρατος *PCairMasp.* 141 ii R.26 (late 6th cent.?); cf. *SB* 8904.29,
> inscr. (A.D. 90)
> κέρατι *PLond.* 1164 (ii, 154-67) h.7 (A.D. 212); *PLond.* 1714.31 (A.D.
> 570); *PMon.* 4-5 V.12 (A.D. 581)
> κ[έρ]ασι *POxy.* 2136.6 (A.D. 291)

3) γῆρας has a gen. γήρους as well as γήρως and anomalous forms of the dat.:

> gen. γήρους *POslo* 124.13 (late 1st cent.); *PRyl.* 659.8 (A.D. 320: *BL*
> iii, 163)[4]
> γήρως *PFlor.* 382.36 (A.D. 222/3); *PLond.* 1827 descr. (early 4th
> cent.)
> dat. γήρᾳ *PFlor.* 382.65 (A.D. 222/3)
> γῆρι *PSI* 685.8 (A.D. 324-7: *BL* v, 123)
> γήρῳ *PCairMasp.* 154 V.20 (A.D. 527-65)

---

[1] Gen. κρέατος is found in an Att. inscr. of 338 B.C., elsewh. κρέα, κρεῶν (*MS*, 143). The dental inflection is also attested elsewh. in codd. of classical authors and in Koine and Byz. Gr. (Crönert, 172, n. 1). Only κρέα is found in the LXX & NT (*BDF*, § 47.1).

[2] Cf. Schwyzer i, 516; 579, n. 4; 581 & n. 5. κρέη Gal. codd. Euseb. etc. (Crönert, 172, n. 1).

[3] For the dental stem inflection, see Schwyzer i, 515 & n. 3. κέρως Th. X. Eub., κέρατος Hermipp. X., κέρατι S. Arist. Poll., κέρατα E., κεράτων prob. S., κέρασι A. (*LSJ*, s.v.), [κέρ]ατε δύο & [κέ]ρατ[α] δύο Att. inscrr. (*MS* 143), κέρατα and κεράτων NT (*BDF* § 47.1).

[4] γήρους is found in codd. Arist. Agatharch. J. Phot. etc., and γήρους and γήρει are used in the LXX, NT, and Byz. authors (Crönert, 168, n. 4; 169, n. 2; *BDF*, § 47.1; Psaltes, 154-5; Jannaris, § 421).

4) γέρας has a gen. pl. γερῶν *PMich.* 224.38 (A.D. 172-3); 225.1137 (A.D. 173-4), and an acc. pl. γέρα *POxy.* 1408.16 (ca. A.D. 210-14).

c. αἰδώς is declined regularly as in Attic:

αἰδοῦς *PCairMasp.* 295 iii.22 (6th cent.)
αἰδοῖ *PSI* 1178.6, hieroscopia manual (2nd cent.)
αἰδῶ *PUppsala* 8.5 [= G. Björck, *Der Fluch des Christen Sabinus* (Uppsala 1938), 6-7] (6th cent.)

d. γέλως is inflected exclusively according to the dental stem declension:[1]

γέλωτα *BGU* 1141.13 (14 B.C.); *POxy.* 471.85 (2nd cent.)
γέλωσι *PGiss.* 3 = *WChr.* 491.8 (A.D. 117)

e. *s*-stem names.

1) Greek names in ᾿ης tend to fluctuate between the *s*-stem and *a*-stem declensions, as already in late Attic, on the analogy of masc. nouns of the first declension in ᾿ης:[2]

Ἀριστοφάνους *PCairMasp.* 86.4 (6th cent.); *SB* 8988.112 (A.D. 647); *SB* 5123; 5564 (8th cent.)
but Ἀριστοφάνου *SB* 5560 B R.1; *SB* 5563; 5568; etc. (8th cent.)
Ἀριστοφάνην *PApoll.* 11.6,8 (A.D. 705)
Ἁρποκράτει *PGron.* 11 i.12 (2nd cent.)
but Ἁρποκράτου *PFlor.* 333 = *PBrem.* 23.16 (A.D. 116)
Δημοκράτους *SB* 6951 R.55 (A.D. 138-61); *BGU* 1898.26 part. rest. (A.D. 172), *BGU* 1900.35-36,43 (ca. A.D. 196)
but Δημοκράτου *PPrinc.* 131.9 (A.D. 197)
Δημοσθένους *PPrinc.* 126.7 part. rest. (ca. A.D. 150); *BGU* 913.7 (A.D. 206); *PBeattyPanop.* 1.308 (A.D. 298); *PFlor.* 71.674 (4th cent.); *PLond.* 1679.6 (1st half 6th cent.)

---

[1] Cf. Att. gen. γέλω, Ep. dat. γέλω/γέλῳ, poet. & late prose acc. γέλων (*LSJ* s.v.). See further Schwyzer i, 514; Chantraine[2], § 64, 68.

[2] Schwyzer, 579; Chantraine[2], § 67. In Att. inscrr., gen. -ου is very freq. from 350 B.C. on., w. -ους in wider scope in Rom. times; dat. -η appears only twice, prob. as an orthographic variant; acc. -ην is usu. from the 4th cent. B.C. on, but -η appears sporadically in Rom. inscrr. (*MS*, 134-6). On the Att. curse tablets, acc. -η is freq. along w. -ην (Schwyzer, "Vulg.," 256). At Perg., gen. -ους is freq. throughout the period of the inscrr. both in official and private inscrr., but the popular gen. -ου is also attested from the mid 3rd cent. B.C. on; acc. -η and -ην are both found (Schweizer, 154-5). In Magn. inscrr., gen. -ου is more freq. in B.C. inscrr., w. -ους used almost excl. in Rom. times; the dat. is always -η(ι); acc. -η is found only once (Augustus), elsewh. -ην in both Magn. and foreign inscrr. (Nachmanson, 135-7). At Lycia, the gen. is -ους or -ου, dat. is -ει or -η(ι), acc. invariably -ην (Hauser, 93-94). In the Ptol. papp., gen. -ους predominates in the 3rd cent. B.C., -ου in the 2nd-1st cent.; the dat. is reg. -ει, but -ηι is freq., esp. in the 2nd-1st cent.; the old acc. -η is found only sporadically; the normal acc. is -ην (Mayser i[2], 2, 37-40). See further Crönert, 160-1; Schmid iv, 582-3; Dieterich, 158-9, 170-1.

but Δημοσθένη *SB* 9202.2 (1st half 3rd cent.)

Διευχους *PSI* 281.29 (2nd cent.); *SB* 9190.6 (A.D. 131)

but Διευχου *PLond.* 604 A (iii, 70-76).113 (A.D. 47)

Διογένους *SB* 6995.10-11 (A.D. 124); *PAmh.* 115.2 (A.D. 137); *WO* 956.4 (A.D. 187); *PStrassb.* 2.2 (A.D. 217); *PSI* 295.3 (A.D. 235/8?); *BGU* 1093.17 (A.D. 265); *PErl.* 109.19 (early 4th cent.); etc.

    Διογένει *BGU* 842 iv.1; v.1; vi.1 part. rest. (A.D. 187); *PSI* 303.1 (3rd cent.?); *PSI* 316.1 (4th cent.?); sim. *PFay.* 32.3 (A.D. 131); *BGU* 1665.3 (A.D. 248); etc.

but Διογένου *BGU* 287 = *WChr.* 124.3 (A.D. 250)

    Διογένη *BGU* 1658.4 (A.D. 234); 1659.3 (3rd cent.)

    Διογένην *POxy.* 1032.28,36 part. rest. (A.D. 162); sim. *BGU* 1043.15 (3rd cent.); *SB* 10297.18 (3rd cent.)

Ἑρμογένους *PSI* 897.60,86 (A.D. 93); *PFouad* 73.9 (4th cent.)

but Ἑρμογένου *PColt* 37.29 (A.D. 560-80?)

    Ἑρμογένην *POxy.* 1480.8, with Ἑρμογένει 16 (A.D. 32)

Θε(α)γένους *PAmh.* 124 = *WChr.* 152.7 (2nd cent.)

but Θεογένου *POslo* 137.7 (3rd cent.)

Παγκράτους *PMich.* 223.1341 (A.D. 171-2); 224.2827,3820, sim. 4689, 6189,6193, but Πανκράτου 6082 (A.D. 172-3)

Πολυκράτους *PMich.* 238.77 (A.D. 46)

but Πολυκράτην *PMich.* 240.20 (A.D. 46/47)

Σωκράτους *PMich.* 267-8.14 (A.D. 41/42); *PFay.* 31 = *MChr.* 201.12, with Σωκράτηι 17 (ca. A.D. 129)

    Σωκράτει *PMich.* 505 V part. rest., with Σωκράτη 1 (diff. hands) (2nd/3rd cent.); *PMich.* 506.1,14 part. rest. (2nd/3rd cent.)

but Σωκάρτου *sic OMich.* 374.5 (late 3rd cent.)

    Σωκράτηι *PLond.* 163 (ii, 182-3).1 (A.D. 88); sim. *SB* 7352 = *PMich.* 490.15 (2nd cent.); *PFay.* 28.1 (A.D. 150/1); *PMich.* 505.1 (2nd/3rd cent.)

    Σωκρ[ά]την *BGU* 384 betw. 9-10 (2nd/3rd cent.)

    cf. Σωκράτος (nom.) *OMich.* 627.7-8 (early 4th cent.)

Ὠριγένους *OMich.* 1072.2 (late 3rd/early 4th cent.)

but Ὀριγένη (gen.) *PCairMasp.* 287 iv.8,16 (6th cent.?)

    Ὠριγένην *POxy.* 1670.27 (3rd cent.); 1642.12 (A.D. 289)

Because of the partial loss of final /n/ and /s/ and the probable identification of final -η(ι) and -ει, the distinction between declensional types in these names may have been mainly orthographic.

2) Greek names in -κλῆς also fluctuate among declensional types.[1]

---

[1] In the Att. inscrr., gen. -κλέου is found sporadically from 350 B.C. on, but -κλέως/-κλεος more commonly in Rom. times; acc. -κλέα is found until 300 B.C., then -κλῆν until Rom. times, when -κλέα and -κλῆν fluctuate (*MS*, 133-4). At Perg., only gen. -κλέους appears (Schweizer, 155). At Magn., gen. -κλέους (w. orthographic variants) and acc. -κλέα occur

a) Ἡρακλῆς fluctuates between s-stem forms and heteroclitic a-stem or o-stem forms as well as rare i-stem and dental stem forms. The o-stem forms seem to be heteroclitic (cf. Ἡρακλῆς, Ἡρακλήῳ *SB* 4322.2,6 [A.D. 84-96] and Ἡρακλῆς, -κλήου, -κλήῳ, -κλῆν *PTebt.* 317 = *MChr.* 348 passim [A.D. 174/5]) rather than deriving from a by-form Ἡράκλειος (-ιος, -ηος), found rarely in the nom. and acc. (cf. Ἡράκλειον *PMich.* 259.12, with Ἡρακλῆς 21, Ἡρακλῆν 13,14 [A.D. 33]; Ἡρά[κλε]ιος, Ἡ[ρ]άκλ[ειο]ν *POxy.* 278 = *MChr.* 165. 30,42 [A.D. 17]).

i. The gen. is less frequently the s-stem -έους (with orthographic variants -είους, -ήους) than the a-stem (o-stem) -έου (-είου, -ήου); an i-/eu-stem -έως (-έος) and dental stem -ῆτος also appear:

Ἡρακλέους *POxy.* 1261.4 (A.D. 325); *BGU* 941.5 (A.D. 376)
Ἡρακλείους *BGU* 757.2 (A.D. 12); *PAmh.* 151.2 (A.D. 610-40)
Ἡρακλήους *PRein.* 135.1 (A.D. 129); *OHeid.* 272.5 (A.D. 182); 280.4 (A.D. 189); etc.
Ἡρακλέου *PTebt.* 397 = *MChr.* 321.7,23 (A.D. 198); *PSI* 1126.13 (3rd cent.); *PFlor.* 211.3-4 (A.D. 255)
Ἡρακλείου *BGU* 60.6 (A.D. 187/8)
Ἡρακλήου (freq.) *PSI* 1129.1 (24 B.C.); *Archiv* v, p. 396 i,6 (early 1st cent.); *PCornell* 22.12,27,32, etc. (early 1st cent.); *PRyl.* 138.6 (A.D. 34); 141.4 (A.D. 37); *PMich.* 237.6, with Ἡρακλῆν 7,13 (A.D. 43); 238.25,35,43, etc. (A.D. 46); 306.8, with Ἡρακλῆ(ν) 16,36,47, etc. (1st cent.); *POxy.* 272.14,16 (A.D. 66); *PGrenf.* ii, 46 = *MChr.* 259.8 (A.D. 87); *PTebt.* 331.2, with Ἡρακλῆν 16 (ca. A.D. 131); *PFay.* 62.5-6 (A.D. 134); *PCol.* 1 R 1 b iii.10 (A.D. 134/5); *PFlor.* 23.4-5 (A.D. 145); *PStrassb.* 284.5 twice (A.D. 176-80); *PSI* 1106.5 (A.D. 336); etc.
Ἡρακλέως *PFouad* 55.1 (A.D. 128); *PSI* 1039.6 (3rd cent.)
Ἡρακλέος (πόλις) *PLBat.* xi, 13.5 (A.D. 372); *POxy.* 1133.3 (A.D. 396)
Ἡρακλῆτος *PFlor.* 43.5 (A.D. 370)

ii. The dat. appears in the o-stem form -έῳ (with orthographic variants -(ε)ίω(ι), -ή(ῳ)) or the dental stem form -ῆτι:

Ἡρακλέῳ *PTebt.* 640 R descr. (late 2nd cent.); *POslo* 146.1 (4th cent.)
Ἡρακλείωι *PGron.* 17 V, with voc. Ἡράκλειε 2 (3rd/4th cent.)
Ἡρακλίῳ *StudPal.* xxii, 4 iii.10 (A.D. 127/8)
Ἡρακλήῳ *PFay.* 109.1, sim. 15 (early 1st cent.); *SB* 4322.2 (A.D. 84-96); *PTebt.* 317 = *MChr.* 348.25 (A.D. 174/5)
Ἡρακλῆτι *WO* 1251.2 (A.D. 152)

(Nachmanson, 137-8). At Lycia, -κλέου appears twice in Rom. times along w. the usu. gen. -κλέους; both -κλέα and -κλῆν are found in the acc. (Hauser, 94-95). In the Ptol. papp., the gen. is reg. -κλέους (w. orthographic variants), rarely -κλέως or -κλέου; the acc. is normally -κλῆν, but twice -κλῆ (Mayser i², 2, 40-41). See further **Crönert, 162 & nn. 2-3**.

iii. The acc. appears in the *a*-stem form -ῆν or the *o*-stem form -ειον:

> 'Ηρακλῆν *PMich.* 237.7,13 (A.D. 43); *SB* 9484.8 (2nd cent.); *BGU* 166.12
> (A.D. 157); *PTebt.* 376 = *WChr.* 350.10-11,29 (A.D. 162)
> 'Ηράκλειον *PMich.* 259.12, with 'Ηρακλῆς 21, 'Ηρακλῆν 13,14 (A.D. 33)

b) Other names in -κλῆς normally follow the *s*-stem declension (with orthographic variants), but a late *a*-stem gen. in -ῆ is attested, as well as the acc. -ῆν:

> 'Αριστοκλέους *PRyl.* 598.10 (A.D. 73): *POxy.* 2190.8 (late 1st cent.);
> *PSI* 1119.15 (A.D. 156); *POxy.* 1113 i.7 (A.D. 203); etc.
> Διοκλέους *POxy.* 2242.3,37 (3rd cent.); *SB* 7633.2 (prob. 3rd cent.);
> cf. *SB* 7084.2, mummy label (n.d.); *PDura* 18.6,24, with Διοκλεῖ
> 3,17 (A.D. 87); 25.3,19 (A.D. 180)
> Διοκλήους *OTait* 1004.3 (A.D. 149)
> Διοκλῆ (gen.) *PLBat.* ii, 15 i.15; ii.21 (3rd/4th cent.)
> dat. Διοκλεῖ *PErl.* 97.18 (2nd cent.)
> 'Ερμοκλείους, 'Ερμοκλεῖ, 'Ερμοκλέα *PSI* 1228.15;7,12,30;26,42 (A.D.
> 188)
> 'Ερμοκλῆν *POxy.* 300.8 (late 1st cent.)

3) Names in -ῆς (mostly Egyptian) fluctuate principally between *s*-stem
and dental stem forms in the gen. and dat., but a short gen. in -ῆ is frequent,
while an *o*-stem gen. -ήου and an *i*-/*eu*-stem gen. -έως occur; an *a*-stem dat.
-ῆ is also found.[1]

'Ακῆς:

> gen. 'Ακήους *PMich.* 352.1 (A.D. 46); *PSI* 901.2,8,17 (A.D. 46); *PMich.*
> 344.4 (1st cent.); *POslo* 24.3-4 (A.D. 131?); *SB* 7515.695,703 (A.D.
> 155)
> 'Ακείους *PSI* 879.4,19,24 (A.D. 98/99); *PLond.* 266 (ii, 233-44).295,
> etc. (1st/2nd cent.); *PSI* 1405.5, with 'Ακίους 20 (A.D. 134); *BGU*
> 471.1: *BL* i, 47; 474 i.10 (2nd cent.); *PVars.* 9.4 (A.D. 160); *PLond.*
> 1170 (iii, 92-103).117, etc. (3rd cent.)
> 'Ακῆ *PFlor.* 226.3 (3rd cent.); *PRyl.* 236.6 (A.D. 256); *PFlor.* 222.12
> (A.D. 256)
> 'Ακῆτος *PMich.* 305.7 (1st cent.); *PFlor.* 132.5 (A.D. 257); *PCair-
> Goodsp.* 13.1 (A.D. 341); *PFlor.* 297.295 (6th cent.)
> dat. 'Ακῖ *PFlor.* 247.13 (A.D. 256)
> 'Ακίη *PFlor.* 272.4-5: *BL* i, 155 (A.D. 258)
> acc. 'Ακῆν *PFlor.* 226.21 (3rd cent.)

---

[1] See also above, pp. 59-60. Cf. Mayser i², 1, 41-42: nom. -ῆς, gen. -έους (-είους, -ήους)
or -ῆτος or -έως, dat. -εῖ (-ῆι) or -ῆτι, acc. -ῆν.

'Αμφιθαλῆς:

> gen. 'Αμφιθαλοῦς *PAmh.* 108.7-8 (A.D. 185/6)
> 'Αμφιθαλέος *POxy.* 928.4 (2nd/3rd cent.)

'Αννῆς:

> gen. 'Αννέους *PFlor.* 366.3 (2nd/3rd cent.)
> 'Αννῆτος *PFlor.* 313.9 (A.D. 449)

'Απελλῆς:

> gen. 'Απελλείους *PRyl.* 188.17 (early 2nd cent.)
> 'Απελλέω(ς) *PJand.* 136.17,18 (A.D. 135/6)
> 'Απελλῆτος *PPrinc.* 10 viii.23 abbrev. (A.D. 34); *POxy.* 53.3 (A.D. 316)

'Ατρῆς:

> gen. 'Ατρήους *PRyl.* 128.2 (ca. A.D. 30); *PMich.* 264-5.19 (A.D. 37);
> *PRyl.* 595.100 (A.D. 57); *OROM* 19.2 (A.D. 113); etc.
> 'Ατρείους *PMich.* 351.7,8 (A.D. 44); *PMeyer* 7.4,29 (A.D. 95: *BL*
> iii, 106); *BGU* 330.13 (A.D. 153); *BGU* 342.5 (A.D. 181); etc.
> 'Ατρήου *PSI* 907.10 (A.D. 42)
> 'Αθρείου *PRossGeorg.* ii, 36 A.2 (2nd cent.)
> 'Ατρῆ *PCairGoodsp.* 30 ii.14; iii.17,19; iv.1; etc. (A.D. 191-2); *PSI*
> 796.1 (A.D. 222/3); *PSI* 1037.12,16,26,41 (A.D. 301); *PLond.* 408 =
> *PAbinn.* 18.8 (ca. A.D. 346); *PGen.* 64 = *PAbinn.* 67 R.17 (ca.
> A.D. 346); *PMerton* 37.3 (A.D. 373); *POslo* 38.4 (A.D. 374/5);
> *PApoll.* 77 A.18; B.14,21 (A.D. 703-15); etc.
> 'Ατρῆτος *PMich.* 238.7, with acc. 'Ατρην 121 (A.D. 46); *PRyl.* 243.14
> part. rest. (2nd cent.); *OTaitPetr.* 320.6 (2nd/3rd cent.); *CPR*
> 6 = *MChr.* 158.11 twice (A.D. 238); *PSI* 699.2 (3rd cent.);
> *PRyl.* 640.15 (4th cent.); *BGU* 1094.7 (A.D. 525); etc.
> 'Ατρῆς (indecl.) *PBaden* 23.8 (A.D. 189/90)
> dat. 'Ατρῆ *BGU* 858.4 (A.D. 295: *BL* i, 74); *BGU* 984.16 (4th cent.);
> *PApoll.* 92.8 (A.D. 703-15)
> 'Ατρῆτι *PRyl.* 244.15 part. rest. (3rd cent.); *OTaitPetr.* 365.4,5,6
> (Rom.)
> acc. 'Ατρῆν *PMich.* 238.121, with 'Ατρῆτος 7 (A.D. 46)

Αὐνῆς:

> gen. Αὐνείους *BGU* 1891.157 (A.D. 134); *PJand.* 56.43 (2nd cent.); *BGU*
> 11 = *WChr.* 239.1,4 (2nd cent.); *BGU* 657 ii.7 (2nd cent.); *BGU*
> 204.2 (A.D. 158/9); 283.8 (A.D. 161-9); 198.4 (A.D. 162/3); etc.
> Αὐνίους *PChic.* 59.5 (A.D. 158/9)
> Αὐνήους *PRyl.* 140.3 (A.D. 36); *PMich.* 269-71.10 (A.D. 42)
> Αὐνήιους *PRyl.* 131.25 (A.D. 31)
> Αὐνῆτ(ος) *SB* 5124.118 (A.D. 193; *BL* v, 94)

Αὐνῇ *PFlor.* 19.6 (A.D. 248); *PLond.* 188 (ii, 141-6).97 (3rd cent.?); *PHamb.* 20.2 (A.D. 258); *PFlor.* 54.4 (A.D. 314); *PThead.* 30.16,17 (A.D. 322?); *PLond.* 113 (10) (i, 222-3).7 = *WChr.* 8.9 (A.D. 639/40)

dat. Αὐνῆτι *PMilVogl.* 52.25 (A.D. 138)

acc. Αὐνῆν *BGU* 815.12 (2nd cent.)

Μαρρῆς:

gen. Μαρρήους *PMerton* 8.2 (A.D. 3/4); *PMed.* 5.4 (A.D. 8/9); *PMich.* 247.7,8 (early 1st cent.); *PLond.* 139a (ii, 200-1).3 (A.D. 48); etc.
Μαρρείους *PMerton* 9.5 (A.D. 12); *PMed.* 9.2 (A.D. 13/14); 6.4 (A.D. 26); *PMich.* 238.129 (A.D. 46); *PRossGeorg.* ii, 12 iii.10,12 (A.D. 48); *PLips.* 16.4 (A.D. 138); *PMerton* 77.5 (A.D. 182); etc.
Μαρρέους *SB* 9479a = *PMilVogl.* 156.3 (A.D. 134/5)
Μαρρήου *POslo* 32.6 (1st hand), with Μαρρείους 3 (2nd hand) (A.D. 1)

dat. Μαρῆτι *PMich.* 257.2, with gen. Μαρήους 7 (A.D. 30)

acc. Μαρρῆν *PMich.* 238.160 (A.D. 46)

Πανῆς:

gen. Πανήους *OTait* 1970.2 (A.D. 14-37); *OTaitPetr.* 228.2 (A.D. 26); 234.2 (A.D. 30); 237.2 (A.D. 33); etc.
Πανήου *OTaitPetr.* 247.2 (ca. A.D. 14-37); 244.2 (A.D. 36)
Πανεύους *OTaitPetr.* 271.2 (A.D. 43/44); 269.1 (A.D. 44)
Πανῆτος *OTaitPetr.* 225.2 (A.D. 19); 227.1 (A.D. 26); 230.1 (A.D. 28); sim. *OTait* 1969.2 (A.D. 33)
Πανήτου *OTaitPetr.* 256.2 (A.D. 40)

Τεσῆς:

gen. Τεσήους *SB* 5235.4 (A.D. 12); *BGU* 226 = *MChr.* 50.3,15-16 part. rest. (A.D. 99)
Τεσείους *SB* 5236.2 (ca. A.D. 14); *PRyl.* 161.27 (A.D. 71); *PAmh.* 110.12 (A.D. 75); *BGU* 627.20 (prob. 2nd/early 3rd cent.); etc.
Τεσῆτο(ς) *SB* 5233.4 (ca. A.D. 14)

Φατρῆς:

gen. Φατρήους *PPrinc.* 10 v.9 (A.D. 34); 14 iii.7 (ca. A.D. 23-40); *WO* 165.1 (A.D. 136/7); *OTaitPetr.* 163.4 (A.D. 184); *OWilb-Brk.* 75.2 (late 2nd cent.); cf. *SB* 8580.17, inscr. (A.D. 18)
Φατρέους *SB* 9025.16,33 (2nd cent.)
Φατρέως *PPrinc.* 13 xi.10,26 abbrev. (ca. A.D. 35); *POxy.* 2351.23,49 (A.D. 112); *SB* 9317a.3,5,31; b.6,44 (A.D. 148); etc.
Φατρῆτο(ς) *Archiv* vi, p. 427 = *PBrem.* 21.32 (A.D. 116); *OHeid.* 268.4 (A.D. 179)

dat. Φατρῆτι *POxy.* 2351.27,44, with Φατρῇ 54 part. rest., 60, and gen. Φατρέως 23,49 (A.D. 112)

4) Εὐτυχής, derived from the s-stem adjective, appears in s-stem, o-stem, a-stem, and dental stem forms, listed separately in Preisigke, *NB*, under Εὐτύχης and Εὐτυχῆς:

> gen. Εὐτυχοῦς *SB* 8252 = *PFouad* 26.3,30 (A.D. 157-9); *BGU* 1899.34
> (after A.D. 172); 1900.79,89,92 (ca. A.D. 196); *SB* 9355 (4).2; (5).2
> (ca. A.D. 187-91)
> Εὐτυχοῦ *OTait* 862.4 (A.D. 152)
> Εὐτυχῆτος *PLond.* 190 (ii, 253-5).29 (2nd cent.: *BL* iii, 92); *BGU*
> 1896.124, with Εὐτυχοῦς (diff. person) 239 (A.D. 166); *BGU* 1589.
> 8-9 part. rest. (A.D. 166/7); *PSI* 164.6,26 (A.D. 287)
> Εὐτυχεῖτ(ος) *PBouriant* 42.524: *BL* ii, 2, 38 (A.D. 167)
> dat. Εὐτυχῆ *PRein.* 117 V (late 3rd cent.)

6. *i*-stems.[1]

a. The gen. sg., regularly -εως, has occasional orthographic variations, all representing the one morpheme {-ιος}.[2]

1) Gen. -ιος:[3]

> πράσιο(ς) *PMich.* 123 R V.19, with πράσεω(ς) 31 (A.D. 45-47)
> κτήσιος *POxy.* 1902.3 (early 6th cent.)
> πόλιος *PCairMasp.* 298.38 (6th cent.)
> cf. κολάσιος *PGM* 70.4 (late 3rd/early 4th cent.)

2) Gen. -εος:[4]

> προκηρύξεος *CPR* 1 = *StudPal.* xx, 1.5 (A.D. 83/84)
> Σενοκώμεος, μεγαλωπόλεος, πράξεος *POxy.* 1130.4-5,6,24 (A.D. 484)

b. The nom. -ις is also sometimes used for the gen.:

> πράσις (for πράσιος) *SB* 6705 = *PMich.* 121 V 1.4, etc. (A.D. 42); 122
> I.10,29 (A.D. 49); etc.
> τῆς πόλις *PGen.* 56 = *PAbinn.* 37.12 (ca. A.D. 346)
> cf. τῆς ... βεβεωσης (= βεβαίωσις) *PMich.* 276.19 (A.D. 47)

---

[1] Schwyzer i, 570-4, cf. 462-5, 495, 504-6; Chantraine[2], § 82-88; Buck, *GD*, § 109; *MS*, 137-8; Schweizer, 145-6; Nachmanson, 129; Hauser, 83-85; Mayser i[2], 2, 21-24.

[2] For the identification of ε and (ε)ι before a back vowel, see Vol. i, 261-2; for the identification of ο and ω, see Vol. i, 275-7.

[3] Gen. -ιος is attested in the Perg. inscrr. (called an Aeolicism or Ionicism by Schweizer, 145-6), and in the Ptol. papp., usu. alternating w. -εως in the same word (Mayser i[2], 2, 23).

[4] Gen. -εος is attested in Hom. Trag. Ion. and Att. inscrr. (Schwyzer i, 572, n. 3; *LSJ*, s.v. πόλις, etc.), and once at Magnesia in a Cret. copy, which also has -εως 5 times (Nachmanson, 129).

c. The acc. sg. appears sporadically as -ην, an orthographic variant of -ιν:[1]

τὴν πίστην *PFlor.* 86 = *MChr.* 247.11, corr. 3 (late 1st cent.); sim.
PFay. 122.22 (ca. A.D. 100)
τὴν αὐτὴν ἔπαυλην *PAmh.* 152.20 (5th/early 6th cent.)

d. The Egyptian loanword βάϊς is declined exclusively as an *i*-stem:[2]

nom. pl. βάϊς *POxy.* 1211.8 (2nd cent.)
βάεις *PLond.* 131 R = *SB* 9699.384-6, with βατῶν 390 (A.D. 78-79)
gen. pl. βατῶν *BGU* 1094.12 (A.D. 525)
acc. pl. βάϊς *BGU* 362 part. = *WChr.* 96, vii.13; x.14; xii.19 (A.D. 215);
SB 5637.5 (ca. A.D. 215)
cf. βάϊς, βατῶν *PGM* 12.277,228 (A.D. 300-50); βάϊν *PGM* 13.262 (A.D. 346)
βάϊν *SB* 6584.8, mag. (4th/5th cent.)
and βάϊα (linear measure, nom. pl.) *PBaden* 92.1, etc. (5th/6th cent.)
βάϊαι *PLBat.* xiii, 6.7 (1st cent.)

e. The earlier loanword πέπερι is likewise declined as an -*i*-stem throughout:[3]

πέπερ (gen.) μου *PPrinc.* 155 V.2, with πίπερ (nom.) R.10 (2nd/3rd cent.)
πεπέρεως *PTebt.* 273.19, med. prescriptions (late 2nd/early 3rd cent.);
PSI 1264.13,16 (4th cent.); *PLips.* 102 i.11 (late 4th cent.); cf. *PGM*
7.184, with πέπερι 185 (3rd cent.); *PGM* 4.1309-10 (4th cent.)
πιπέρεος *PSI* 1180.94,102 abbrev., med. prescriptions (2nd cent.)
πιπέρεως *PHarris* 98 i.2 (4th cent.); *PRossGeorg.* iii, 9.15-16 (4th cent.)

f. ἔπαυλις is usually inflected as an *i*-stem, but a dental stem form appears
once in the dat. sg.:[4]

ἔπαυλις *PHamb.* 15.9 (A.D. 209)
ἐπαύλεως *POxy.* 248.28 (A.D. 80); *PLond.* 901 (iii, 23-24).16,18 (late 1st/
early 2nd cent.); *PErl.* 60.5,7 (2nd cent.); *PSI* 184.8 (A.D. 292);
PLond. 113 (5a) (i, 210-11).15: *BL* i, 237 (A.D. 498); *PStrassb.* 15.2
(5th/6th cent.); *PLond.* 1691.10 (A.D. 532); *PCairMasp.* 109.23,26,30;
110.25; 111.16; 313.58 (6th cent.); *PBaden* 95.27, etc., with ἐπαύλος
(gen.) 102 (7th cent.)
ἐπαύλι *PSarap.* 76.15-16 (ca. A.D. 125)
ἐπαύλει *BGU* 3.24, with ἐπαύλεως 20 (A.D. 605)
but ἐπαυλίδι *PHamb.* 23.18 (A.D. 569)

---

[1] For the interchange of ι and η, see Vol. i, 235-9.
[2] Cf. Mayser i², 2, 31-32, where only the acc. βάειν occurs. βάϊν is also found in Horap.
(*LSJ*, s.v.). It renders Copt. ⲃⲁ (S ⲃⲁⲉ, ⲃⲁⲉⲓ, ⲃⲟⲓ; B ⲃⲁⲓ, F ⲃⲁ(ⲉ)ⲓ (Crum, s.v.). Cf. ⲛⲃⲁ
Bell and Crum, *Aegyptus* 6 (1925), 216, line 371, w. ⲃⲁⲓⲁ p. 196, line 370.
[3] There is no trace of the dental stem inflection of this word attested in Eub. Nic. Ael.
Ath. Philostr. (*LSJ*, s.v.).
[4] For τὴν ἔπαυλην, see **c.** above.

ἔπαυλιν *PMilVogl.* 150.12-13 (2nd cent.); *CPR* 73.17 (A.D. 222-35); *SB* 5344.14 (n.d.); *PCairGoodsp.* 15.5, with ἐπαύλεως 6,7,18 (A.D. 362); *CPR* 19a.14,19 (early 4th cent.); *SB* 4492.4 (6th cent.); sim. *POxy.* 1959.11,16 (A.D. 499)

ἐπαύλεων *SB* 6000 R.9 (6th cent.); *PCairMasp.* 151.117 (A.D. 570)

g. The Egyptian word λεσῶνις, usually declined as an *i*-stem in the Ptolemaic papyri,[1] normally appears as an *a*-stem masc. of the first declension in Roman papyri:

[λ]εσώνης *PTebt.* 313 = *WChr.* 86.6 (A.D. 210/11)
λεσώνου *PMich.* 349.14 (A.D. 30); 322a.13 (A.D. 46); 326.14 (A.D. 48); 314.5 (1st cent.)
λαισώνου *StudPal.* v, 127 = xx, 68 II R iii.16 (3rd cent.)
λεσώνῃ *BGU* 37 V: *BL* i, 10 (A.D. 51)
λεσῶναι *SB* 5252.7 (A.D. 65)
but λεσῶνες *BGU* 916.9 (nom.), 25 (acc.) (A.D. 69-79)

h. δάμαλις is normally declined as an *i*-stem, but an *a*-stem by-form is also found:[2]

δ[ά]μαλις *PPrinc.* 151.8 (A.D. 341 +)
δάμαλιν *PSarap.* 10. between 3 & 4 (A.D. 124)
δαμάλει[ς] *PCairMasp.* 4.11 (ca. A.D. 552: *BL* i, 100)
δαμάλις (acc. pl.), δαλῖν, δάμαλλιν *PAbinn.* 80 V.7,8;9;21 (ca. A.D. 346)
but δαμάλην *PSarap.* 8.4 (A.D. 103)
cf. δαμάλ(αι) *POxy.* 1734.2 (late 2nd/3rd cent.)

i. The neut. σίναπι has an *i*-stem gen. in -εως as well as in -ις; the nom. is once used indeclinably for the dat.:[3]

nom.-acc. τὸ σίναπι *PFay.* 122.3-4 part. rest., 12 (ca. A.D. 100)
σίναπ(ι) *StudPal.* x, 1.3-6 (7th cent.)
σίν(α)π(ι) *PLond.* 1414.50 (7th/8th cent.)
gen. σινάπεως *PFay.* 165 descr., part. rest. (2nd cent.); *POxy.* 920.2 (late 2nd/early 3rd cent.); *POxy.* 936.7 (3rd cent.); *POxy.* 2614.3 part. rest. (3rd cent.); *PSAAthen.* 66.16 part. rest. (3rd cent.)
σινάπε(ως) *POxy.* 1088.16, med. prescriptions (early 1st cent.); *PApoll.* 95 A.9 (A.D. 703-15)
σινήπεως *PLips.* 97 xxxiii.4 (A.D. 338)

---

[1] Mayser i², 1, 28; i², 2, 24; λεσώνου is found once.
[2] An *a*-stem by-form δαμάλη is attested in E. Theoc. (*LSJ*, s.v.).
[3] This loanword (Schwyzer i, 308), first attested in Anaxipp., has gen. in -εως and -ιος in the Ptol. papp. (Mayser i², 2, 24), excl. in -εως in the NT. The *u*-stem σίναπυ is also found in the Ptol. papp. (Mayser, *ibid.*), Diocl. Soc. etc. (*LSJ*, s.v.).

cf. σινάπεος *PSI* 1180.45, sim. 51, med. prescriptions (2nd cent.)
but σίναπις *SB* 9017 (12).10 (1st/2nd cent.); *PLond.* 453 (ii, 319-20).6-7
(early 4th cent.)
dat. σίναπι *PFlor.* 20 = *WChr.* 359.21 (A.D. 127)

j. σεμίδαλις has the gen. only in -εως, acc. -ιν:[1]

σεμιδάρεως (for σεμιδάλεως) *POxy.* 736.82 (ca. A.D. 1)
  σεμιδάλεως *BGU* 1067.15 abbrev. (A.D. 101/2); *PRossGeorg.* ii, 33
    ii.2 part. rest. (2nd cent.); *PMerton* 113.4 abbrev. (2nd cent.);
    POxy. 1655.4,10, sim. 6 (3rd cent.)
  σιμιδάλ(εως) *POxy.* 1921.15 (A.D. 621)
  σεμίδ[αλ]ιν *POxy.* 2148.3-4 (A.D. 27); sim. *PLond.* 190 (ii, 253-5).45-46
    (3rd cent.?)
cf. σιμιδαλίῳ *PAmh.* 148.3: *BL* iii, 5 (A.D. 487)

k. *i*-stem names.[2]

1) Place names in -ις are declined regularly, e.g., Μέμφις, Μέμφεως, Μέμφει,
Μέμφιν passim.

2) Personal names in -ις (mostly Egyptian) are usually declined -ιος, -(ε)ι-,
-ιν, but -εως or the undeclined -ις[3] and other anomalous forms are used frequently for the gen., e.g.:

Ἀκιᾶρις *BGU* 1893.162,371 (A.D. 149)
gen. Ἀκιάριος *PMilVogl.* 28.56,78 (A.D. 162-3)
  Ἀκιάρεω[ς] *BGU* 454.2 (A.D. 193)
  Ἀκιᾶρ *StudPal.* xx, 115.4 (A.D. 409); *POxy.* 1911.118,128,134 (A.D.
    557)
dat. Ἀκιᾶρι *PLond.* 379 (ii, 162).3-4: *BL* i, 256 (3rd cent.?)
Ἀνοῦφις *OFay.* 39.3 (3rd cent.); *CPR* 41.2-3 (A.D. 305)
dat. Ἀνούφει *PGiss.* 102.5 (A.D. 317)
Ἁρμᾶχις *SB* 748.1, mummy label (3rd cent.)
gen. Ἁρμάχιος *PLond.* 320 = *MChr.* 177.8 (A.D. 157/8); *PJand.* 33.3-4
    (A.D. 180-92); *PRossGeorg.* v, 15-16 ii.6 (2nd/3rd cent.)
  Ἁρμά[χ]εως *BGU* 217 i.10 (2nd/3rd cent.)
Λαβῆσις, with gen. Λαβήσιος and Λαβήσεως *PMich.* 244.31,36 (A.D. 43)
  Λαβῆσις Λαβήσιος *PMich.* 306.2,11 (1st cent.)
but τοῦ Λαβῆσις *PMich.* 332.22 (A.D. 48)

---

[1] Gen. -ιος found in the Ptol. papp. (Mayser i², 2, 23) and elsewh. (*LSJ*, s.v.) is unattested
later; σεμιδάλ(ιος) *PErl.* 111.16 (5th/6th cent.) should be -(εως).
[2] For the decl. of Ἶσις and Σάραπις, see above, pp. 56-57. For mixed *i*- and dental stem
decl. of Eg. names, see above, pp. 55-56, 57-61. For the decl. of *i*-stem names in the Ptol.
papp., see Mayser i², 2, 21-23.
[3] For freq. gen. -ις, see, e.g., *PMich.* 226-356 (cf. *PMich.* v, p. 13).

Μαρεψῆμις *PTebt.* 309.24,32 (A.D. 116/17)

gen. Μαρεψήμιος *PTebt.* 298 = *WChr.* 90.2 (A.D. 107/8)

   Μαρεψήμεως *PTebt.* 295.7 (A.D. 126-38); 293 = *WChr.* 75.4,8-9 (ca.
     A.D. 187); 292 = *WChr.* 74.11,23 (A.D. 189/90)

Μέρσις, gen. Μέρσιος *BGU* 1638 A.2, sim. 5,8 (2nd cent.)

gen. Μέρσιος *PMich.* 306.15 (1st cent.); *PLond.* 173 (ii, 66-67).7 (A.D.
   101); *PBrem.* 40.8 (ca. A.D. 117); etc.

   Μέρσεω(ς) *PMich.* 224.6223,6224, with Μέρσιος 2135 (A.D. 173-4)

   Μέρσις *SB* 771, mummy label (2nd/3rd cent.); *SB* 8478.1, inscr.
     (A.D. 223)

   Μέρσι *SB* 4388, inscr. (n.d.)

dat. Μέρσει *OStrassb.* 182.2 (A.D. 62)

Παχοῦμις *PBrem.* 32.15 (A.D. 119); *PBon.* 35.7 (2nd cent.)

   Παχῦμις *OMich.* 83.1,5 (3rd cent.); *SB* 9149.4 (4th cent.)

gen. Παχύμιος *BGU* 892.18 (2nd cent.: *BL* i, 78); *PLeit.* 4.4 (ca. A.D.
   161); *PLond.* 1649.6 (A.D. 373)

   Παχούμιος *PAchmim* 6.30 part. rest. (late 2nd cent.); *PPrinc.*
     130.9 (A.D. 198-209); *PBeattyPanop.* 1.188 (A.D. 298); *PGiss.* 9.2
     part. rest. (ca. A.D. 117); 10.19 abbrev. (A.D. 118)

   Παχοῦμις *POxy.* 65.3 (3rd/early 4th cent.); *OStrassb.* 287.4-5 (prob.
     4th cent.)

acc. Παχοῦμιν *PBrem.* 33.16, with Παχούμιος 26, cf. Παχομε 27 (A.D.
   119)

   Παχῦμιν *PLips.* 64.52,57 (ca. A.D. 368)

cf. Παχῦμι *SB* 7751.2, inscr. (2nd/3rd cent.)

7. *u*-stems.[1]

a. Nouns inflected according to the long *u*-stem declension are declined
regularly, except for orthographic variations and an acc. pl. in -ας.

1) An anomalous nom. sg. formed on the analogy of the *o*-stem declension
is found in στάχος *OTait* 2153.2 (4th cent.).

2) The gen. sg. is regular in -υος, but an ending in -εως, on the analogy
of short *u*-stems, e.g., πήχεως, also occurs:

   ἰχθύος *POxy.* 2234.23 (A.D. 31); *PGot.* 3.8 (A.D. 215/16); *PGiss.* 93.4
     (n.d.)

   δρυός *POxy.* 2113.18 (A.D. 316)

   ὀφρύος *PLond.* 143 (ii, 204-5).5 (A.D. 97)

   but ὀφ[ρ]έως *PLips.* 40 ii.25 (late 4th/early 5th cent.)

---

[1] Schwyzer i, 570-4, cf. 462-5, 506-7; Chantraine[2], § 89-95; Buck, *GD* § 110; *MS*, 138-9;
Schweizer, 146-7; Nachmanson, 129; Hauser, 85; Mayser i[2], 2, 24-26.

3) The dat. sg., regularly -ι, often with a diaeresis over the -ι, e.g., ὀφρύϊ *BGU* 2120.6 (2nd cent.), is frequently spelled -ει, e.g., ὀφρύει *BGU* 197.4 (A.D. 17), etc.,[1] but the ending is also omitted sporadically, e.g., οὐλ(ὴ) ὀφρῦ ἐξ ἀρι- στερῶν *SB* 4284.19, sim. 20-21 (A.D. 207). This last spelling is not an orthographic equivalent of υι[2] because in this case the {-i} represented an independent mor- pheme and was pronounced as a distinct vowel, as indicated also by the diaeresis above.

4) τὸ μεσόφρυον,[3] found frequently in the dat. sg. μεσοφρύῳ *PSI* 1144.3 (A.D. 100?), etc., appears in a *u*-stem by-form in the acc. sg. and in the dat. pl.:

μεσόφρυν *PMich.* 244.31 (A.D. 43); 246.16 (mid 1st cent.); *PSI* 1140.12 (A.D. 139)
μεσόφρυσι *PSI* 907.21 (A.D. 42); *SB* 7664 = *PLBat.* i, 9.9 (A.D. 109)
cf. [οὐ]λὴ μεσόφρυες (dat. sg./pl.) *PLBat.* iii, 11.7 (A.D. 151)

5) The dat. pl. δάκρυσιν appears in *PMilVogl.* 24.22 (A.D. 117) as well as the regular ἰχθύσιν *PGiss.* 93.1 (n.d.), etc.

6) The acc. pl. is normally -υας, an ending derived from consonantal stems and attested already in Homer:[4]

βότρυας *BGU* 1118.14 (22 B.C.); 1120.16 (5 B.C.); *PHarris* 137.28 (2nd cent.); *PLips.* 30 = *WChr.* 500.4 (3rd cent.)
εἰχθύας (for ἰχθύας) *PFay.* 113.13 (ca. A.D. 100)
ἰχθύας *SB* 9025.18-19 (2nd cent.)

b. Nouns inflected according to the short *u*-stem declension are also declined regularly except for orthographic variations in several cases and alternate forms in the gen. sg., acc. sg., and gen. pl.

1) A nom. ὁ πῆχις (for πῆχυς) appears in *POxy.* 9 V.11, with acc. τὼν πῆχων (for τὸν πῆχυν) 13 (3rd/early 4th cent.). An acc. πῆχιν also occurs in *PFlor.* 262.14 (3rd cent.), and γένι (for γένυν) in *PMich.* 322a.37 (A.D. 46). These forms, oc- curring in very incorrectly written documents, reflect a phonological confusion of vowels[5] rather than competing inflections on the analogy of *i*- or *o*-stems.

---

[1] For the interchange of ι and ει, see Vol. i, 189-91.
[2] See Vol. i, 202-7.
[3] Ptol. papp. *Placit.* Aret. Gal. Ruf. Opp. (*LSJ*, s.v.).
[4] Schwyzer i, 571; Chantraine[2], § 92. Acc. -υας is not found in the Perg. inscrr. nor often elsewh. (Schweizer, 146; Crönert, 174, n. 1). There are two exx. of βότρυας in the Ptol. papp. (Mayser i[2], 2, 25). βότρυας and ἰχθύας appear in the NT (*BDF*, § 46.2). Cf. also from the mag. papp. νέκυας *PGM* 4.227 (4th cent.) and ἰχθύας *PGM* 5.280 (4th cent.).
[5] For the interchange of υ and ι, see Vol. i, 267-71; for the interchange of υ and ω, see Vol. i, 294.

2) The gen. sg. πήχυος *POxy.* 242.15 (A.D. 77) reflects the analogy of the long *u*-stem declension.[1]

3) The acc. sg. of πρέσβυς appears as πρέσβεα in *BGU* 511 = *WChr.* 14 iii.1: *BL* iii, 257 (ca. A.D. 200+).[2]

4) The gen. pl. is usually -ῶν, but the uncontracted -εων appears exclusively in πρέσβυς and sometimes in πῆχυς:[3]

> πρέσβεων *POxy.* 1102.16-17,22 (ca. A.D. 146); *PSI* 1357.7 (A.D. 197-9)
> πήχεων *BGU* 1094.12 (A.D. 525)
> but πηχῶν *PMich.* 305.6,10,11,15 (1st cent.); *POxy.* 243 = *MChr.* 182.22
>   (A.D. 79); *PLond.* 191 (ii, 264-5).19 (A.D. 103-17); *BGU* 1663.8
>   (3rd cent.); *BGU* 456.11,12 (A.D. 348); *PFlor.* 310.8,15,18 (A.D.
>   425/35?); etc.

8. Diphthongal stems.[4]

a. Stems in *-ōi*.

The only word attested is πειθώ, which occurs in the regular dat. sg. πειθοῖ in *POxy.* 471.37 (A.D. 184?).

b. Stems in *-āu*.

1) γραῦς is declined regularly, with the following forms attested:

> γραῦς *BGU* 1024 vii.9 (late 4th cent.: *BL* i, 88); *POxy.* 2193.17 (5th/6th
>   cent.)
> γραός *POxy.* 67 = *MChr.* 56.18 (A.D. 338)
> γραῦν *StudPal.* xx, 283.2 (n.d.)
> γραῶν *PMich.* 126.34 (A.D. 46-49)

The poetic γραῖα seems to occur in the spelling γρέα in *POxy.* 2860.11 (2nd cent.).[5]

---

[1] Cf. πήχεος Hdt. Hp. Pl. Arist. LXX, Plb. Ph., πήχεως Arist. (*LSJ*, s.v.). The Ptol. papp. have πήχεως, with πήχεος once (Mayser i[2], 2, 25).

[2] For diphthongal stem forms of πρέσβυς, see now J.-L. Perpillou, *Les Substantifs grecs en* -εύς, § 182-6. See further exx. under Metaplasm below, p. 93.

[3] The mag. papp. have excl. πηχῶν *PGM* 4.63 (4th cent.); 36.274 (4th cent.). The open πήχεων (Att. according to Phryn. 222 [Rutherford, 318]) is alone found in Att. inscrr. (*MS*, 138). The later πηχῶν read in codd. of X. Arist. Phld. (*LSJ*, s.v.) is usual in the Ptol. papp., but πήχεων is found 3 times in the 3rd cent. B.C. (Mayser i[2], 2, 25). πηχῶν (w. v. ll.) is the only form in the NT (*BDF*, § 48) and in the Herc. papp. (Crönert, 172, where n. 3 describes the papyri data erroneously).

[4] Schwyzer i, 570, 574-8, cf. 476-80; Chantraine[2], § 96-102; Buck, *GD*, § 111; *MS*, 139-42; Schweizer, 147-51; Nachmanson, 129-32; Hauser, 85-88; Mayser i[2], 2, 26-30.

[5] γραῖα Hom. Hes. A. S. E. Theocr. etc. (*LSJ*, s.v.).

2) ναῦς appears only in the acc. sg. ναῦν in *PStrassb.* 276.12 (early 3rd cent.).[1]

c. Stems in *-ōu.*[2]

1) ἥρως is found mainly in inscriptions and magical papyri. It is inflected throughout according to the diphthongal stem declension. Attic second declension forms do not occur.

> ἥρως *SB* 5887.2, inscr. (n.d.)
> ἥρωος *PCairMasp.* 295 i.26 (2nd half 6th cent.)
> ἥρωες *PGM* 4.1393,1408,1420,1446 (4th cent.)
> ἡρώων *PGM* 4.1390,2732 (4th cent.)
> ἥρωας *SB* 1155.4, inscr. (n.d.)

2) For μήτρως, see above p. 32.

d. Stems in *-ou.*

1) βοῦς is declined as in Attic prose[3] (with orthographic variants in the gen. pl.), except for alternate forms in the dat. and acc. pl.[4] In the dat. pl., τοῖς βόες/βόας are nom./acc. for dat., and βοσί is probably an orthographic variant of βουσ(ε)ί,[5] but βόεσιν represents a sporadic alternate form;[6] in the acc., βόας, identical with a Homeric by-form, arose independently in the Koine on the analogy of the -ας ending of consonantal stems (and other diphthongal stems, see below).[7]

> βοός *SB* 9415 (3).5 part. rest. (3rd cent.); *PCairIsidor.* 41.11 (A.D. 303)
> βοῦν *PBaden* 19.4 (A.D. 110); *PJand.* 35.5 (late 2nd/early 3rd cent.);
>   *POxy.* 1905.19 (late 4th/early 5th cent.); *PSI* 920.8 (6th cent.)
> βόες *SB* 8750.25 (A.D. 98); *PRossGeorg.* ii, 29.7 (2nd cent.); *OStrassb.*
>   759.6 (prob. 2nd cent.)

---

[1] The formative ναο- in ναοπηγός *SB* 3506.23, mummy label (n.d.), has been shown by L. C. Youtie, *ZPE* 14 (1974), 178, to be a printing error.

[2] Chantraine[2], § 69, questions the diphthongal stem etymology of at least ἥρως on grounds of the absence of *u* in this word in Linear B.

[3] The gen. βοός is likewise the only form attested in the Att. inscrr. (*MS*, 139) and the Ptol. papp. (w. orthographic var. βοώς) (Mayser i[2], 2, 27); the poet. βοῦ is found in fragg. of A. and S. Nor does the nom. pl. βοῦς in Ar. Plu. appear (*LSJ*, s.v.).

[4] In addition, three amulets (n.d.) have the foll. forms: βοῦς, βουαι, βόα, βοῦς (*SB* 970.1-3); βοῦς, βοαι, βουα, βοῦς (*SB* 2021.1-4); βοῦς, βος, βοαι, βόα, βοῦς (*SB* 3573 R.1-4, V.1). Cf. also the combinative forms βοωτρόφοις *PLond.* 1654.2 part. rest., 3 (4th cent.) and βούδια, βουδίω[ν] *PFlor.* 150.2,11 (A.D. 267); τὰ βούδια *OMich.* 91.4 (late 3rd cent.), w. βοίδια *POxy.* 139.20 (A.D. 612); βοείδια *POxy.* 1867.4,8, sim. 9,11 (7th cent.); etc.

[5] For the interchange of ου and ο, see Vol. i, 211-14.

[6] βόεσιν corresponds to the Ep. βόεσσι. βούεσσι is attested in *IG* 7.317.38, a Boeot. inscr. (*LSJ*, s.v.).

[7] Both βόας and βοῦς are found in *Il.* (*LSJ*, s.v.). βοῦς is the only form in the Att. inscrr. (*MS*, 139) and is attested in Asia Minor (Schweizer, 147). In the Ptol. papp., βοῦς occurs 3 times in the 3rd cent., βόας once in the 2nd, as well as the anomalous βόιες twice (Mayser i[2], 2, 27). βόας also occurs excl. in the LXX and NT (cf. *BDF*, § 46.2).

βοῶν *PHamb.* 64.26 (A.D. 104); *PAlexGiss.* 44.5 (ca. A.D. 120); *PWürzb.* 22 = *PSarap.* 97.17 (A.D. 117-38); *PStrassb.* 513.7 (1st half 2nd cent.); *PCairGoodsp.* 30 ii.2,8 (A.D. 191-2); *PSI* 683.7 (A.D. 199); *POxy.* 1734.1 (late 2nd/3rd cent.); *PTebt.* 423.7 (early 3rd cent.); *BGU* 606.5 (A.D. 306); *PLBat.* xi, 10.16 (6th cent.); etc.

βωῶν *POxy.* 901 = *MChr.* 70.15 (A.D. 336)

βουῶν *PPrinc.* 66.6-7 (1st cent.)

βουσί *PHamb.* 86.13,16 (2nd cent.)

βουσεί *POxy.* 2986.6 (2nd/3rd cent.)

βοσί *SB* 9406.146, etc. (A.D. 246); 9408 (2).81 (A.D. 253/6)

cf. βόεσιν *SB* 6949 = *SB* 8546.15, inscr. (before A.D. 356)

τοῖς βόες *PAmh.* 143.5-6 (4th cent.)

τοῖς βόας *OTait* 1739.6 (2nd cent.)

βοῦς *PStrassb.* 221.3 (mid 2nd cent.); *PSI* 1526.11-12 (A.D. 160); *PBeatty-Panop.* 2.153,154 (A.D. 300); *POxy.* 71 ii.15: *BL* i, 314 (A.D. 303); *PMerton* 92.9,13 (A.D. 324); *SB* 4481.19 (A.D. 486)

but βόας *PSarap.* 10.3 (A.D. 124); *POxy.* 729.16 (A.D. 137); *PMich.* 503.12,21 (late 2nd cent.); *SB* 10567.34 (3rd cent.); *SB* 9415 (1).2 (A.D. 266)

cf. nom. for acc. τὰς βόες, τὰς ... βόαις[1] *PGen.* 48 = *PAbinn.* 60.5-6,18-19 (1st hand), with τὰς βόας 32 (2nd hand) (A.D. 346)

2) χοῦς, the measure of capacity,[2] is usually inflected on the model of βοῦς,[3] but *eu*-stem forms derived from χοεύς are also found.[4] The derivative τὸ ἡμίχοον usually follows the contract second declension, with an open form in the dat. sg.[5] τετράχοος (adj. and subst.) has open second declension and *eu*-stem third declension forms.

a) χοῦς declined like βοῦς:

χοῦς *POxy.* 739.11 (ca. A.D. 1); *PMich.* 510.31 (2nd/3rd cent.)

χοός *PMich.* 322a.7,24 (A.D. 46); *PMich.* 274-5.6 (A.D. 46/47); *POxy.* 529.7 (for acc.) (2nd cent.); *PPrinc.* 163.3 (2nd cent.)

χοῦν *SB* 8030 = *PMich.* 245.35 (A.D. 47); *BGU* 1097 R.13 (A.D. 41-68); *PAmh.* 126 = *PSarap.* 55.46 (A.D. 128); *PLond.* 190 (ii, 253-5).41 (2nd cent.: *BL* iii, 92); *OTait* 1723 ii.1, etc.; 1733.4,11 (2nd cent.); *PHamb.* 192.20 (1st half 3rd cent.); etc.

---

[1] For the interchange of ε and αι, see Vol. i, 192-3.

[2] For the decl. of χοῦς, 'excavated earth,' see above, pp. 34-35.

[3] Schwyzer i, 582.

[4] Forms of χοῦς on the analogy of βοῦς are found in Ar. D. Pl. etc.; forms from χοεύς in Hp. Ar. etc. (*LSJ*, s.v. χοῦς). χοῦς is declined like βοῦς in the Att. inscrr. (*MS*, 139). In the Ptol. papp., acc. sg. χοῦν and χόα are found, acc. pl. χοῦς, χόας, and nom. χοεῖς (Mayser i², 2, 27 & n. 2). For the χοεύς formation, see Perpillou, § 187-8.

[5] In Arist. and inscrr., ἡμίχοον follows the open or contr. 2nd decl., but ἡμιχόεα appears in Hp. (*LSJ*, s.v.). In the Att. inscrr., the pl. of ἡμίχοον is ἡμίχοα (*MS*, 127).

χό(ες) *PMich.* 322b.5, etc. (A.D. 51)
χόε(ς) *PGiss.* 10.17 (A.D. 118)
χόε[ς] *BGU* 14 iv.12 (A.D. 255)
χῶες *BGU* 765.4: *BL* i, 65 (A.D. 166?)

b) *eu*-stem forms of χοῦς:

χοέως *PMichael.* 18 B iv.12 (mid 3rd cent.: *BL* iv, 51)
χοεῖς *PAberd.* 181.13, with χοέων 12 (A.D. 41-68); *PLond.* 1170 (iii, 92-103).6 (3rd cent.)
χοέων *POxy.* 2190.60 (late 1st cent.); *PSI* 1030.15, with χοῦν 11 (A.D. 109)
χοέσι *WChr.* 176.7 (mid 1st cent.)
χοεῖς (acc.) *SB* 9025.26 (2nd cent.); *PFay.* 95.14, with χω[ῶ]ν 18, acc. χοῖς 24 (2nd cent.)
χωεῖς *POxy.* 9 V.13, with nom. χόος 14 (3rd/early 4th cent.)
but χοέας *PRyl.* 627.92-94,221-2 (A.D. 317-23)

c) τὸ ἡμίχοον:

ἡμιχόῳ *POxy.* 1070.30-31 (3rd cent.)
ἡμίχουν *POxy.* 1153.5 part. rest. (1st cent.); *PAmh.* 93 = *WChr.* 314.12, with χοῦν also 12 (A.D. 181); *POxy.* 936.7,9 (3rd cent.); *POxy.* 2728.34 (3rd/4th cent.); *SB* 1160.8 (n.d.)
ἱμίχουν *SB* 9017 (21).9 (1st/2nd cent.)

d) τετράχοος:

[τ]ετράχοον *POxy.* 2996.26 (2nd cent.?)
and τετράχοα (acc. sg.) *PSI* 1252.10 (3rd cent.)
τετραχόων *SB* 9569.14,19 part. rest. (A.D. 91); *POslo* 43.1 (A.D. 140/1); *PSI* 1249.20 (A.D. 265)

e. ἁλιεύς has open endings exclusively:[1]

ἁλιέως, ἁλιέα *PGot.* 3.3,6 (A.D. 215/16)
ἁλιέων *POxy.* 294.6 (A.D. 22); *PSI* 901.7, etc. (A.D. 46); *PLeit.* 14.21 (A.D. 148); *WO* 1330.3 (A.D. 160); *BGU* 756.6-7 (A.D. 199); *PSI* 737.6 (2nd/3rd cent.?); *PRein.* 54.22 (3rd/4th cent.); *StudPal.* x, 77.1 (6th/7th cent.); *PRossGeorg.* iii, 53.7 (A.D. 674/5); etc.

---

[1] In the Att. inscrr., stems ending in -ι- contracted the endings of the gen. and acc. sg. and pl. reg. in the 5th cent. B.C., but the contr. forms become less freq. and cease entirely ca. 200 B.C. (*MS*, 141-2). ἁλιῶς is also found in Pherecr. (*LSJ*, s.v.). For the rare assimilation of -ι- to -ε- in the acc. pl., see Vol. i, 250-1.

f. Other *eu*-stems.

1) The gen. sg. is normally the regular -εως, but -εος and -εους also occur. These are purely orthographic variants because of the interchange of ω with ο[1] and ου:[2]

ἱερέος *POxy.* 254.2, with Ἀδελφῶν 3 (ca. A.D. 20); *SB* 6611 = *PLBat.* vi, 20.5 (A.D. 120/1); *PMich.* 618.5-6 (ca. A.D. 166/9)
γναφέος *PMich.* 294.6 (1st cent.)
γραμματέος *PJand.* 8.5 (3rd cent.: *BL* i, 197); *StudPal.* iii, 40.2 (6th cent.)
ἀρχιερέος *BGU* 913.5, with πράξεος 10 (A.D. 206)
γραμματέους *PMich.* 226.5,10 (for nom.) (A.D. 37); *StudPal.* iii, 607 = xx, 202.3 (6th cent.)
ἱερέους *POxy.* 1297.3 (4th cent.)

2) The dat. sg. sometimes appears in the orthographic variant -ι for the regular -ει,[3] e.g., βαφῖ *OMich.* 174.2 (4th cent.); κεραμῖ *POxy.* 1754.5 (late 4th/5th cent.).

3) The acc. sg. is exclusively -εα,[4] e.g., ἱερέα *SB* 5233.7; 5234.1 (ca. A.D. 14); γραμματέα *PGiss.* 45.4 (A.D. 117-38); γναφέα *PJand.* 94.17 (late 2nd/early 3rd cent.).

4) The gen. pl. is normally the regular -έων. The contracted form -ῶν occurs only rarely,[5] and orthographic variants of -έων are also found.

a) -έων:

ἱερέων *SB* 7174 = *PMich.* 233.8,11 (A.D. 24: *BL* v, 69); *BGU* 2059 i.2 (1st cent.); *PMich.* 322b.4 (A.D. 51); *POxy.* 1072.14 (5th/6th cent.); etc.
ἱππέων *PMich.* 259.3,21 (A.D. 33); 303.1 (1st cent.); 185.2 (A.D. 122); etc.

---

[1] See Vol. i, 275-7. The -εος ending is found in the Lycian inscrr. in the ratio -εως: -εος:: 15:18 (Hauser, 87), but is not found at Perg. (Schweizer, 148). At Magn., the gen. is normally -εως, but from the reign of Nerva to the 3rd cent. incl., -εος appears almost as freq. as -εως (Nachmanson, 130-1). If -εος were a reflection of Ion. influence in Asia Minor, forms in -εος should occur freq. earlier rather than begin in the Rom. period. See further Crönert, 168, n. 2, w. exx. from Ptol. inscrr. and codd. of Koine and Byz. authors. In the Ptol. papp., -εος is sts. found in pers. names, rarely in common nouns (Mayser i², 2, 28-29).

[2] See Vol. i, 208-11.

[3] For the interchange of ει and ι, see Vol. i, 189-91.

[4] The contr. acc. -η is found freq. in Asia Minor (although not at Perg.), perh. as a Dor. residue (Schweizer, 148-9). Two exx. of -η are also found in a Magn. inscr. of A.D. 117-38 in wh. -εα occurs (Nachmanson, 132). In the Ptol. papp., the acc. is excl. -εα, w. orthographic variants (Mayser i², 2, 29).

[5] There is one dbtfl. ex. of ἱερῶν in the Ptol. papp. (Mayser i², 2, 29).

γονέων *PSI* 904.9, so duplic. *PMich.* 341.8 (A.D. 47); *PMich.* 465.8
(A.D. 107); *PLond.* 324 = *WChr.* 208.9 (A.D. 161); *PTebt.* 334.10
(A.D. 200/1); *PGrenf.* ii, 78 = *MChr.* 63.5 (A.D. 307); *CPR* 19 =
StudPal. xx, 86.19 (A.D. 330); *PCairMasp.* 6 R.5 (ca. A.D. 567); etc.
ἐγδοχέων *POxy.* 1673.7-8 (2nd cent.)
γναφέων *PTebt.* 287 = *WChr.* 251.4,15 (A.D. 161-9)
βασιλέων *POxy.* 2267.9 (A.D. 360)

b) -ῶν:

εἱαιρῶν (for ἱερέων) *PMich.* 226.23, with εἱαιρέων 11 (A.D. 37)

c) Orthographic variants of -έων:

γωιναίων (for γονέων) *PMich.* 339.5 (A.D. 46)
    γοναίων *POxy.* 1704.9 (A.D. 298); *PJand.* 128.10, with γονέων 17
    (5th cent.)

5) A relic of the dual is found in ἀμφοῖν τοῖν γονέοιν *PLips.* 41 R = *MChr.*
300.2 (2nd half 4th cent.).

6) The dat. pl. is the regular -εῦσι, e.g., τοῖς μου γονεῦσι *PRossGeorg.* iii,
1.2 (A.D. 270: *BL* iii, 156).[1]

7) The acc. pl. is usually the late Attic -εῖς, but -έας is also found.

a) -εῖς:

γονεῖς *PMich.* 202.17 (A.D. 105); *StudPal.* xx, 9.9 (A.D. 158); *BGU*
    385 = *WChr.* 100.7 (2nd/3rd cent.); cf. *SB* 5071.4, inscr. (n.d.)
ἀλεεῖς *PSAAthen.* 35.18 (A.D. 153/4); *PFlor.* 127.15 (A.D. 256); sim.
    PSI 160.21 (A.D. 149); *BGU* 1035 = *WChr.* 23.6 (5th cent.)
γραμματεῖς *PSI* 158.53, astrol. (3rd cent.?)
ἐγδοχεῖς *POxy.* 1669.2 (3rd cent.)

b) -έας:

[ἱ]ερέας *BGU* 176 = *WChr.* 83.9 (2nd cent.)
γονέας *PJand.* 97.8 (mid 3rd cent.)
ἀλιέας *PFlor.* 201.8 (A.D. 259)

This partial replacement of the acc. pl. morpheme by the nom.[2] reflects a
common development of Greek attested earlier in *i*-stems. It is striking that

---

[1] There is one ex. of -εῖσι in the Ptol. papp. in one copy of an official document (Mayser
i², 2, 29). For exx. of -εῖσι(ν) in Asia Minor, see Nachmanson, 132, Anm. (Magn. only -εῦσι(ν)).
[2] Schwyzer i, 575; cf. 563, n. 2.

the proper acc. pl. ending -έας is retained so long in the papyri, contrasted with its virtual extinction in contemporary inscriptions and literature.[1]

g. Diphthongal stem names.[2]

1) Names in -ω usually have the gen. in -οῦς, but an anomalous form in -ῶς occurs, as well as a dental stem inflection -οῦτος/-ῶτος; undeclined forms are also found in all cases:

('Ηδυτώ), 'Ηδυτοῦς *PCairMasp.* 175.4 (6th cent.)

'Ακουσώ *BGU* 1897a.49 part. rest. (prob. A.D. 166); *BGU* 558 iii.12 (early 3rd cent.)

(gen.) 'Ακουσῶς *PLond.* 259 (ii, 36-42).32 (A.D. 94)

Θεανώ *PPrinc.* 67.1 (1st/2nd cent.); *BGU* 1654.15,19 part. rest. (A.D. 98-117); 1893.76 (A.D. 149); 1896.160,323 (A.D. 166); 1898.323 (A.D. 172); etc.

Θεανοῦς (nom.) *BGU* 1893.282 (A.D. 149)

(gen.) Θεανοῦς *BGU* 1654.8 (A.D. 98-117); *BGU* 324 = *WChr.* 219.4 (A.D. 166/7)

Θεανώ *PMich.* 374 i.14 (mid 2nd cent.), *BGU* 124.6-7 (A.D. 186/7); *BGU* 193 = *MChr.* 268 ii.14 (A.D. 136); *SB* 4299.13 (A.D. 245)

Θεανοῦτος *BGU* 560 i.10 (2nd cent.); *BGU* 291 = *WChr.* 364.3 (ca. A.D. 170)

Θεανῶτος *BGU* 198.1 (A.D. 162/3); 1898.194 (A.D. 172)

(indecl.) Θεανώ (dat.) *BGU* 193 = *MChr.* 268 ii.10 part. rest., 25 (A.D. 136); *PFlor.* 24.20 (mid 3rd cent.: *BL* iii, 55); (acc.) *BGU* 1897a.3 (prob. A.D. 166); *BGU* 193 = *MChr.* 268.22 (A.D. 136); (voc.) *SB* 5961.1, inscr. (n.d.).

2) Names in -ευς either have the gen. regularly in -εως or fluctuate between diphthongal, dental, or o-stem declensions.

a) Declined regularly:

'Αμεννεύς *BGU* 425.6 (2nd/3rd cent.)

'Αμεννέως (gen.) *BGU* 1614 B.4 (A.D. 69/70); *POxy.* 505.1 (2nd cent.); *POslo* 107.16 part. rest. (early 2nd cent.); *PLBat.* v, xvii.3, etc. (A.D. 174); *PTebt.* 342.13 (late 2nd cent.); sim. *CPR* 64.10 (A.D. 227); *PSI* 1039.22-23,29, with acc. -έα 43,46 (3rd cent.)

'Αχιλλεύς, -έως, -έα *PRyl.* 77.34,42,42-43, etc. (A.D. 192)

---

[1] Acc. pl. -εῖς is found in Att. inscrr. from 307 B.C. on (*MS*, 141). At Perg., -έας is found only once on a late tombstone; elsewh. in Asia Minor, as well as in foreign inscrr. at Perg., -εῖς is freq., but -έας is found once in Rom. times (Schweizer, 150). At Lycia, the acc. pl. is always -εῖς (Hauser, 88). In the Ptol. papp., there are only two exx. of -έας next to the freq. -εῖς (Mayser i², 2, 29-30). Acc. -έας is rare even among the Atticists (Schmid, iii, 22-23; iv, 587). The LXX and NT have -εῖς excl. (*BDF*, § 46.2). See further Crönert, 173, n. 2.

[2] Cf. Mayser i², 2, 33.

Ἀχιλλέως *PLBat.* vi, 2.20; 3.16 (A.D. 92); 4.24,31-32 (A.D. 94); *BGU* 1896.274 abbrev.; 1897.129 (A.D. 166); 1898.283 (A.D. 172)

Ἐριεύς, Ἐριέως, -έος, etc., see Vol. i, 73.

(Κελλεύς) Κελλέως *PFlor.* 385.37 (2nd/3rd cent.)

Παμιεύς *BGU* 392.51 (A.D. 208: *BL* i, 43)

Παμιέως *PLond.* 1170 (iii, 92-103).336 (3rd cent.)

b) Fluctuating between diphthongal, dental, and *o*-stem declensions:

(Ἀρμιεύς) Ἀρμιέως *BGU* 1891.472 (A.D. 134); *POxy.* 918 iii.9 part. rest. (2nd cent.); *PCairPreis.* 36.4 (2nd/3rd cent.); *SB* 9009 = *PMed.* 68.6 (3rd cent.); *PLond.* 1170 (iii, 92-103).26, etc. (3rd cent.)

but Ἀρμιεῦτ(ος) *PLond.* 266 (ii, 233-44).161, etc. (1st/2nd cent.)

(Θοτεύς) Θοτέως *PMich.* 285-6.1 (1st cent.); *PMilVogl.* 98.39 part. rest. (A.D. 138/9?); *PBon.* 34.11 abbrev. (2nd cent.); *PMich.* 223.497,845 (A.D. 171-2); *PSI* 1112.20 (A.D. 231); etc.

but Θοτέου *PMich.* 224.142,735,836,2708 (A.D. 172-3); 225.112, with Θοτέως 1037,1374 (A.D. 173-4)

Ὀρσεύς *PBerlLeihg.* 6.35,71 (A.D. 166/7)

Ὀρσέως *PStrassb.* 185.2,3 (A.D. 55); *PSI* 1136.7 (A.D. 104/5); *PTebt.* 323 = *MChr.* 208.12 (A.D. 127); *PMilVogl.* 98.37,40 part. rest. (A.D. 138/9?); *PBerlLeihg.* 15.5 (A.D. 189); *MChr.* 200.3 (A.D. 224); etc.

but Ὀρσεῦτος *PSI* 1028.8 (A.D. 15); *SB* 6705 = *PMich.* 121 V i.7 abbrev. (A.D. 42); *PTebt.* 380.11,36 (A.D. 67); etc.

and Ὀρσέου *PMich.* 259.11,29 (A.D. 33)

Ὀρσεῦτι *PSI* 1028.5 (A.D. 15); *PMilVogl.* 52.33, etc. (A.D. 138); etc.

9. Heteroclitic neuters.[1]

a. Neuter stems in -μα, -ματος.

These substantives, originally qualitative abstracts with -α (for syllabic $n̥$[2]) in the nom.-acc. sg. and -ατ- in the oblique cases, with the suffix becoming stereotyped and very productive in the papyri,[3] are declined regularly, but there are tendencies towards indeclinability and analogical formation on the model of the *o*-stem second declension.

1) Indeclinable usage.

a) Many of these nouns appear with the nom.-acc. sg. used instead of the nom.-acc. pl., presumably because of the similarity of this form with that of the neut. pl. of the second declension. Many examples are ambiguous and could

---

[1] Schwyzer i, 580-1, cf. 491, 517-21, 522-4.

[2] Schwyzer i, 524.

[3] Palmer, 93-98.

represent the use of a sg. with the force of a pl., but the phenomenon is dispro-
portionately frequent in nouns of this sub-type:

> διὰ τὸ μὴ [εἰδέν]αι αὐτὸν γράμμα (for γράμματα) *PLond.* 256a = *WChr.*
> 443.18-19 (A.D. 15); sim. *POxy.* 278 = *MChr.* 165.39 (A.D. 17); *PMich.*
> 351.33 (A.D. 44); 314.5 (1st cent.); 196.30 (A.D. 122); *PCairMasp.*
> 95.21 (A.D. 548); *PLond.* 1395.6 (early 8th cent.); etc.
>
> τὰ κέρμα (for κέρματα) μιᾷ *BGU* 1078 = *WChr.* 59.6: Kapsomenos,
> "'Έρευναι," 336-7 (A.D. 39); sim. *POxy.* 1160.16, with τὰ ὑπομνήματα
> 17-18 (late 3rd/early 4th cent.); *PAmh.* 143.6-7 (4th cent.)
>
> τὰ βλάβη καὶ δαπάνημα (for δαπανήματα) διπλᾶ *CPR* 4 = *MChr.* 159.27
> (A.D. 51/53); sim. *PSI* 66.31 (5th cent.?)
>
> τὰ κυριακὰ πράγμα‛τα′ (τα added by 2nd hand) *PBrem.* 37.9-10 (ca. A.D.
> 117); sim. *PCairMasp.* 139, fol. v R.1 (6th cent.)
>
> πέμψαι ὑπόδημα (for ὑποδήματα) *PMich.* 477.27 (early 2nd cent.)
>
> χάλκωμα (for χαλκώματα) χαλκᾶ *PMerton* 71.2 (A.D. 160-3)
>
> εἰς τὰ ἀνάλωμα (for ἀναλώματα) ἡμῶν *StudPal.* xx, 96.14 (4th cent.)
>
> πέντε νόμισμα (for νομίσματα) *PLBat.* xi, 28.6 (twice), with τὸ ... νομι-
> σμάτων (for τὰ ... νομίσματα) 9 (4th/5th cent.: *BL* v, 63); sim. *PHamb.*
> 23.37 (A.D. 569); *PCairMasp.* 309.18, with νομισμάτων 32, sim. 43
> (A.D. 569)
>
> σάγμα (for σάγματα) τῶν ἀλόγων *StudPal.* iii, 204.4: *BL* iii, 234 (7th
> cent.)

b) The nom.-acc. sg. is also sometimes found for other cases of the sg.:

> εἰδὲ ἐὰν χρείαν ἔχῃς κέρμα (for κέρματος) *PRein.* 117.5-6 (late 2nd cent.)
>
> περί τινες πρᾶγμα (for τινος πράγματος?) *SB* 4317.19-20 (ca. A.D. 200)
>
> ἐν παντὶ πρᾶγμα μᾶλον (for πράγματι μᾶλλον) *POxy.* 2730.16-17
> (4th cent.)
>
> σὺ δὲ ἐπεβούλευσας σῶμα (for σώματι) ἀλλοτρ[ι]ωθέντι *BGU* 1024
> iv.9-10 (late 4th cent.: *BL* i, 88)
>
> χρῆμα ῥόδινον (for χρήματι ῥοδίνῳ) *PPar.* 18 bis = *WChr.* 499.11-12:
> Kapsomenos, "'Έρευναι," 362-3 (2nd/3rd cent.)

c) Conversely, the nom.-acc. pl. is sometimes used for the sg.:

> νομίσματα (for νόμισμα) ἕν *PLips.* 90.4, corr. 6 (Byz.)
>
> χρυσοῦ γράμματα (for γράμμα) ἕν *PMerton* 35.3-4 (A.D. 348)
>
> κατὰ τὸ ὀνόματα (for ὄνομα) *PSI* 836.15 (6th cent.)

The tendency of neuters in -μα to be used indeclinably did not survive into
Modern Greek, where most are inflected according to the *o*-stem declension with
the nom.-acc. pl. ordinarily -ματα, gen. -μάτω(ν).[1] But some dialectal plurals
in -μα are found.[2]

---

[1] Thumb, *Handbook* § 102-3; Jannaris, § 373b; Mirambel, *Gram.*, 63-64; Maspero, 48-49.
[2] Kapsomenakis, 94(-95), & n. 1.

2) Anomalous forms occur sporadically which might represent analogical *o*-stem formations or a scribal omission of -ατ-:[1]

 ὑποδήμον λευκὸν (for ὑποδημάτων λευκῶν) *PRossGeorg.* ii, 41.15: *BL* iii, 156, with ὑπόδημα πορφυρᾶ 32 (2nd cent.)

 τῶν ἐλαχίστων αὐτοῦ πράγμων (for πραγμάτων) *PLond.* 1676.20, with πράγματα 7,9, πραγμάτων 50, etc. (A.D. 566-73)

 cf. the adj. ἔγραψα καὶ ὑπὲρ αὐτοῦ ἀγρά|μου (for ἀγραμμάτου) *PMeyer* 13.24-25 (A.D. 141)

3) A new addition to this type is πίαρ, used in classical Greek only in the nom.-acc.[2] The gen. sg. πιάρματος occurs in *PPrinc.* 155 V.5 (2nd/3rd cent.).

b. Neuter stems with -αρ or -ωρ in the nom.-acc. sg. and -ατ- in the oblique cases.[3]

1) φρέαρ (and στέαρ[4]) are uncontracted:[5]

 φρέαρ *POxy.* 243 = *MChr.* 182.18,28 (A.D. 79); *PAmh.* 99a.9 (A.D. 179); *PGiss.* 49.11 (3rd cent.); *SB* 5344.15 (n.d.); etc.; cf. *PGM* 5.346 (4th cent.)
 nom. φρέαν *SB* 9931.11 (A.D. 330)

 φρέατος *POxy.* 502.35, with φρέαρ 18 (A.D. 164); *BGU* 940.10 (A.D. 398); *PLond.* 1023 (iii, 267-8).18 (5th/6th cent.); *POxy.* 2037.31 (late 6th cent.); *SB* 5295 = 9462.15 (6th/7th cent.); etc.; cf. φρέαθος *PMich.* 322a.7,24 (A.D. 46); φρέατρος *POxy.* 1105.10 (A.D. 81-96)[6]

 φρέατι *PTebt.* 342.19 (late 2nd cent.); *PStrassb.* 248.8 (A.D. 561: *BL* v, 140)

 φρέατρα (for φρέατα) *PCairPreis.* 12.15 (2nd cent.)

2) ὕδωρ is normally declined regularly, but a gen. sg. in -ους and indeclinable usages are found sporadically:[7]

 ὑδάτους *PMich.* 421.11 (A.D. 41-54); *PMich.* 322a.7,24 part. rest. (A.D. 46); *PRyl.* 81.7,10; 13,21 part. rest. (ca. A.D. 104)

 τοῦ ὕδωρ *PLond.* 1247 (iii, 225-6).24-25, so duplic. (A.D. 345)

---

 [1] For the sporadic gen. sg. in -μάτου, see above p. 44.

 [2] *LSJ*, s.v. An *r*-stem dat. πίαρι is noted from Suid.

 [3] Stems in -αρ, -ατ- are from (ϝ)ῃ̥ + *t*, the Att. long -ᾱρ by quant. metath.; stems in -ωρ, -ατ- are from -*or* + *t* (Schwyzer i, 518 & fn. 6; 519).

 [4] στέαρ occurs only in mag. papp., e.g., *PGM* 4.1332,1333, etc., w. στέασι 1339 (4th cent.). Contr. forms are also found in στῆρ *PGM* 4.2459 and {ἀ}στῆρ *PGM* 12.442 (A.D. 300-50).

 [5] In the Ptol. papp., στέαρ and φρέαρ are found mainly uncontr., but στῆρ, στῆτος, and φρῆτα are attested (all 3rd cent.) (Mayser i², 2. 33).

 [6] See Vol. i, 108. Cf. also φρέατος *PGM* 2.36-37 (4th cent.)

 [7] Other poss. indecl. occurrences are *PHamb.* 12 = *WChr.* 235.12-13, and again 13 (A.D. 209/10), and *StudPal.* v, 46.11 part. rest. (3rd cent.) if ἐφύδωρ is not to be read.

c. Neuter stems with -ι in the nom.-acc. sg. and -ιτ- in the oblique cases. Only μέλι occurs; the following forms are noteworthy.

1) The nom.-acc. sg., usually the regular μέλι, e.g., *POxy.* 2797.11 (3rd/4th cent.), appears as μέλιν in *PJand.* 18.1 part. rest., 7 (twice), 8 (6th/7th cent.) and as μέλ (= Lat. *mel?*) *SB* 5304.1,2 (Byz.).

2) The gen. sg. is regularly μέλιτος, e.g., *PLond.* 1171 V (iii, 105-7) a.8; b.6 abbrev. (A.D. 42); *POxy.* 936.9 (3rd cent.); *PAntin.* 96.6 (6th cent.); cf. *PGM* 36.284 (4th cent.); etc.[1]

3) An anomalous μέλεει (for μέλι?) occurs in *StudPal.* xxii, 56.7 (2nd/3rd cent.), in which most entries are in the gen., but others in the nom., dat., or acc.

d. Neuter stems with -υ in the nom. sg. and -ατ- in the oblique cases. Only γόνυ appears, normally inflected according to the dental stem declension γόνατος, etc., e.g., γόνατι *PPrinc.* 142.2 (ca. A.D. 23), but κουνα (for γο(ύ)νατι) is read in *PGen.* 64 = *PAbinn.* 67 V.4, with [γ]ούνατι 6, but cf. μετόπου μέσῳ with ω > ου 7 (ca. A.D. 346).[2]

e. οὖς fluctuates in the nom.-acc. sg. between οὖς and ὦς:[3]

οὖς *PMich.* 570.5 (A.D. 105/6); *POxy.* 234.24,27,40 part. rest., med. prescriptions (late 2nd/early 3rd cent.)

ὦς *PMich.* 121 R II vi.1 (A.D. 42)

The spelling ὦς may have arisen through back-formation from the oblique cases in ὠτ- or may be the result of phonological confusion of ου and ω.[4]

The acc. pl. is regular in ὦτα in *SB* 9641 V ii.15 (mid 2nd cent.) and *POxy.* 237 vi.22 (A.D. 186); cf. also *PGM* 7.329 (3rd cent.).

---

[1] In *PAntin.* 46.5 (4th cent.), ὑπὲρ τιμῆς μέλι τῆς[is read, w. μέλι used indecl. (or = μελίτης?).

[2] Att. γόνατος, Ep.-Ion. γούνατος, etc., cf. also Ep. γουνός, Aeol. pl. γόνα; E. has γουνάτων, γούνασι, but γουνός (*LSJ*, s.v.).

[3] Hom. Ion. Att. οὖς, Dor. ὦς, are derived from *ōus (Att. *ousos?) or *ὄϝος (Schwyzer i, 348, 520). The circumflex accent of the nom.-acc. sg. is secondary and its transfer to the ultima in the oblique cases analogous (*ibid.*, 377, 379). Dor. ὦς is found in Koine inscrr. from Oropos and Delos (2nd cent. B.C.) (*LSJ*, s.v. οὖς), and is the only form attested in the Herc. papp. (Crönert, 167). In the Ptol. papp., ὦς and οὖς both appear, as well as a masc. acc. sg. ὦτα (Mayser i², 2, 48). Only οὖς occurs in mag. papp., e.g., *PGM* 2.39; 4.909,916,2165 (4th cent.). A dimin. ὠτάριον also occurs in inscrr. (Crönert, 167, n. 4) and in the papp., as well as ὠτίον (Palmer, 85, 88). A Hell. dat. pl. ὤτοις after ὦτα, ὤτων, is condemned by Phryn. (Rutherford, 291).

[4] See Vol. i, 208-11.

D. FLUCTUATION OF DECLENSION (METAPLASM)[1]

1. *a*-stems and by-forms.

a. *a*-stems with by-forms of the second declension.

1) μύλη is the only first declension noun which has predominantly metaplastic *o*-stem forms; μύλος "millstone" is used, rarely the classical μύλη:[2]

μύλος *BGU* 251.17 part. rest. (A.D. 81)

ὁ μύλ[ος], τοῦ μύλου, τὸν μύλον *POxy.* 278 = *MChr.* 165.10,13,15, etc. (A.D. 17)

μύλου *SB* 5109 = *PRyl.* 160d, i.4 (A.D. 42)

μύλῳ *PFuadCrawford* 27.2,4 (1st half 3rd cent.)

μύλον *SB* 8255 = *PSAAthen.* 25.8,18 (A.D. 61); *BGU* 183 = *MChr.* 313.19,43, etc. (A.D. 85)

μύλοι *PRyl.* 167.10-11 (A.D. 39); *BGU* 1067.5 (A.D. 101/2)

but μύλη *StudPal.* xxii, 60.14 (2nd/3rd cent.)

2) For *o*-stem variants of the Latin loanwords κέλλα and τάβλα, see above, pp. 7-8.

3) κοίτη is used exclusively in the papyri, never κοῖτος:[3]

κοίτη *PFlor.* 50.37, etc. (A.D. 268)

κοίτης, κοίταις *PAmh.* 99a.14; b.8; b.14 (A.D. 179); sim. *PLips.* 8 = *MChr.* 210.9 (A.D. 220); *PLips.* 9 = *MChr.* 211.20 (A.D. 233); etc.

κοίτης *PLips.* 10 i.29 (A.D. 240); *PCairPreis.* 8 = *WChr.* 240.12 part. rest. (A.D. 322); *POxy.* 1161.10 (4th cent.); etc.

κοίτην *PRyl.* 168.9 (A.D. 120); *PLips.* 118.15 (A.D. 160/1)

κοίταις *PAmh.* 88 = *MChr.* 150.9-10 (A.D. 128); *PStrassb.* 2.7 (A.D. 217); *PFlor.* 50.4 (A.D. 268); etc.

b. *a*-stems with by-forms of the third declension.

1) πρεσβευτής, a secondary sg. to πρέσβεις,[4] is confined to the sg. as in early classical Greek,[5] with the third declension *u*-stem used also in the sg. and exclusively in the pl.

---

[1] Schwyzer i, 582-5; Buck, *GD*, § 112; Mayser i[2], 2, 45-50; Crönert, 175-6; *BDF*, § 49-52.

[2] μύλη Hom. Pherecr. Ar. Arist. Poll. as "mill(-stone)," Hp. LXX, Gal. Paus. etc. w. other meanings. μύλος first occurs relative to a mill(-stone) in LXX, Str. NT, Plu.; it is found in Hp. Artem. etc. w. other meanings (*LSJ*, s.vv.). Only μύλος occurs in the Ptol. papp. (Mayser i[2], 2, 50).

[3] κοῖτος is the normal form in *Od.*, but κοίτη is more widely used by other authors, incl. Trag. Pi. Pl. X. Arist. in the meaning "bed" (concretely and metaphorically); the meanings "lot" and "pen" are new in Rom. papp. (*LSJ*, s.vv.). Likewise, only κοίτη occurs in the Ptol. papp. (Mayser i[2], 2, 49-50).

[4] Cf. Schwyzer i, 584.

[5] The pl. of πρεσβευτής is attested in Aud. (and Alciphr.), but forms of πρέσβεις are used by D. Ar. X. etc. (*LSJ*, s.vv.). In the Att. inscrr., πρέσβεις is used until 250 B.C., then

a) Sg.:

πρεσβευτής *PSI* 1255.7 (3rd cent.)
    πρεσβευτοῦ *SB* 7944.2, inscr. (13 B.C.); *POxy.* 1560.11 (A.D. 209);
        SB 4101.1 part. rest. (n.d.); *BGU* 932.2 part. rest. (prob. Byz.)
    πρεσβευτῇ *POxy.* 933.31 (late 2nd cent.)
    πρεσβευτήν *SB* 8300.3, inscr. (A.D. 41-54); *POxy.* 33 = *WChr.* 20
        iii.11 part. rest. (late 2nd cent.)
πραίσβυς (for πρέσβυς) *PCairIsidor.* 138 descr. (n.d.)
    πρέσβεα *BGU* 511 = *WChr.* 14 iii.1 (ca. A.D. 200: *BL* iii, 257)

b) Pl.:

πρέσβεις (nom.) *PLond.* 1912.20, with πρέβεων *sic* 75 (A.D. 41); *BGU*
    511 = *WChr.* 14 i.17 part. rest., with πρέσβεα iii.1 (ca. A.D. 200: *BL*
    iii, 257); *BGU* 1074.2 part. rest. (A.D. 275); *POxy.* 2476.3 (A.D. 288:
    BL v, 82)
πρέσβεων *POxy.* 1102.16-17,22 (ca. A.D. 146); *PSI* 1357.7 (A.D. 197-9)
πρέσβεις (acc.) *SB* 9488.10,16 part. rest. (2nd cent.)

Note. πρεσβύτης, derived from πρέσβυς, occurs with the meaning "old
man:"[1]

πρεσβύτης *BGU* 180 = *WChr.* 396.22 part. rest. (A.D. 172); *PStrassb.*
    128 = *SB* 7684.7 (A.D. 186); *PStrassb.* 5.8, with -ην 16, -η 17 part.
    rest. (A.D. 262); *PStrassb.* 41.38,40 (ca. A.D. 250)
πρεσβύτην *PRein.* 113.8 (ca. A.D. 263); *PFlor.* 50.62,95 (A.D. 268)

2) Other nouns for which metaplastic inflections of the first and third declensions are attested elsewhere in Greek are found only in the first declension.

a) ἡ σκέκη, never τὸ σκέπας:[2]

σκέπης *BGU* 1054.15; 1055 = *MChr.* 104.40; 1056.26; etc. (all 13 B.C.);
    POxy. 785 descr. (ca. A.D. 1); *PSI* 1337.7 (3rd cent.); *PLond.* 391
    (ii, 329-30).15 (6th cent.?); etc.
σκέπη *PPhil.* 1.16 (ca. A.D. 103-24); cf. *SB* 1579.4, inscr. (Byz.)
    σκέπι (for σκέπη) *PPrinc.* 107.10-11, amulet (4th/5th cent.); cf. *SB*
    1572.6-8, inscr. (Byz.)
σκέπην *PLond.* 897 (iii, 206-7).6 (A.D. 84)

πρεσβευταί excl. (*MS.* 144). At Perg. and Magn., πρεσβευταί is found (incl. in an Eg. letter
at Magn.), but πρέσβεις is found once at Magn. and elsewh. in Asia Minor (Schweizer, 141;
Nachmanson, 121; Hauser, 79). In the Ptol. papp., πρεσβευτοῦ is found in 154 B.C. and
πρέσβεις in an inscr. of 29 B.C. (Mayser i², 2, 10 & 25). For the formation of πρέσβευς, see
J.-L. Perpillou, *Les Substantifs grecs en -εύς*, § 181-8.
[1] πρεσβύτης is the normal prose form of πρέσβυς (*LSJ*, s.v.).
[2] τὸ σκέπας *Od.* Hes. Lyc. *AP*, E. Porph. etc., but the prose form is more commonly
σκέπη (or σκέπασμα), as in Hdt. Hp. Pi. X. Arist. Plb. D.S. Ael. inscrr. etc. (*LSJ*, s.vv.).
Only σκέπη occurs in the Ptol. papp. (Mayser i², 2, 50). MGr. ἡ σκέπη.

b) ἡ στέγη, never τὸ στέγος:¹

στέγης *POxy.* 2146.1 (3rd cent.); *POxy.* 2581 i.30 (3rd cent.).
στέγῃ *CPR* 95.14 (early 3rd cent.); *PLips.* 17.15 (A.D. 377); *PBerlZill.*
    5.13 (A.D. 417); *PFlor.* 285.12 (A.D. 552); *PErl.* 73.21 (A.D. 604);
    PRossGeorg. v, **43.3** (7th cent.); *PRossGeorg.* iii, **56.7,8** (A.D. 707); etc.
στέγην *POxy.* 1701.9 (3rd cent.); *StudPal.* xx, 230.10 (4th cent.)

c) ἡ δίψα, never τὸ δίψος:²

δίψης *PFlor.* 176.12 (A.D. 256)
δίψαν *PCairMasp.* 2 ii.26 (A.D. 567: *BL* i, 100); *PLond.* 1674.65 (ca.
    A.D. 570)

d) ἡ νίκη, never the Hellenistic τὸ νῖκος:³

νείκης *PGiss.* 27 = *WChr.* 17.6 (A.D. 115: *BL* v, 34); sim. *POxy.* 1265.10
    (A.D. 336); *POxy.* 138.34 (A.D. 610/11)
νίκη *StudPal.* v, 121 = xx, 69.16 (A.D. 260-8)
νίκην *PFlor.* 284.5 (A.D. 538); cf. *PGM* 27.3 (late 3rd/early 4th cent.)

c. *a*-stems with by-forms of the second and third declensions.

ὁ γύης has by-forms in each declension.⁴ Many forms, such as γύου, γυῶν,
γύας are ambiguous.

1) The regular ὁ γύης is found frequently:

γύης (nom.) *PRyl.* 166.11 (A.D. 26); *SB* 7260 = *PMich.* 121 R II ii.2
    (A.D. 42); *PMich.* 272.4,5 (A.D. 45/46); *POxy.* 373 descr. (A.D. 79/
    80); *PHamb.* 62 = *PLBat.* vi, 23.10 (A.D. 123); *POxy.* 1279.12 (A.D.
    139); *POxy.* 2134.17 (ca. A.D. 170); *PRyl.* 87.7 (early 3rd cent.);
    POxy. 1636.14 (A.D. 249); *PFuadCrawf.* 21.11 (A.D. 253-60); *CPR*
    10 = *StudPal.*xx, 80.3 (A.D. 322); etc.

2) The second declension *o*-stem ὁ γύος is also found:

γύῳ BGU 1132.13,15, with γύου 10 (14 B.C.); (clearly) *PTebt.* 373.6-7

---

¹ τὸ στέγος A. S. LXX, D.S. Poll. Lib. Man.; ἡ στέγη A. Hdt. X. Arist. etc. (*LSJ*, s.v.),
as excl. in the NT (*BDF*, § 51.1).
² ἡ δίψα *Il.* Antiph. Pi. Th. Pl. Arist.; τὸ δίψος Th. Pl. X. Nic. Luc. and v.l. for δίψα
Ar.; both forms occur in the LXX (*LSJ*, s.vv.). Only the neut. is used in the NT, w. v.l.
δίψῃ (*BDF*, § 51.1). δίψη, a back-formation from διψῆν (Schwyzer i, 476), is attested in codd.
of A. and in Opp. (Schwyzer, *ibid.*; *LSJ*, s.v. δίψα). MGr. ἡ δίψα.
³ τὸ νῖκος Orph. LXX, Ptol. papp. NT (also ἡ νίκη once), Vett.Val. inscrr. (*LSJ*, s.v.;
Mayser i², 2, 47; i, 93, n. 8; *BDF*, § 51.1). MGr. uses only ἡ νίκη.
⁴ γύης is the only class. masc. form attested, but fem. forms are found in codd. of E.;
the other by-forms are found only in the papp. (*LSJ*, s.vv.). The Ptol. papp. have ὁ γύης,
w. one poss. ex. of ἡ γύη (Mayser i², 1, 19; i², 2, 10).

(A.D. 110/11); *PSI* 1143.13, sim. 28 (A.D. 164); sim. *PTebt.* 311.17-18
(A.D. 134); 390.13-14 (A.D. 167?)

γύον *PLips.* 106.16 (A.D. 98); *SB* 9619.14 (A.D. 184)

3) Athematic third declension forms also appear:

τῷ ... γύει *PRyl.* 207a.3, etc., with γύου 8, etc. (2nd cent.); *POxy.* 2098
V.2 (A.D. 267/8?)

τὸν γῦν *PLond.* 131 R = *SB* 9699.82,90,99,239, with γῆν (for γύην)
190,252, and τοῦ γύοου *sic* 231 (A.D. 78/79)

These examples may be phonological rather than morphological variants,
with γύει representing γύη,[1] and γῦν (γῆν) representing γύην with contraction
of similar or identical vowels.[2]

4) There is no unambiguous example of ἡ γύη.[3]

2. *o*-stems and by-forms.[4]

a. No nouns of the second declension masculine have an unambiguous
heteroclitic plural of the second declension neuter.

1) Plural forms of κέραμος could be masc. or neut., e.g., κερά[μο]ις, [τῶν
κερ]άμων *CPR* 232.16,17 (2nd/3rd cent.).[5]

2) The plural of σῖτος is not attested.[6]

b. No nouns of the second declension neuter have an unambiguous heteroclitic plural of the second declension masculine.

1) Masculine plural forms of στάδιον are partially restored in σταδ[ίου]ς
SB 4019, inscr. (A.D. 10/11) and σταδίου[ς] *POxy.* 1873.12 (late 5th cent.).[7]

---

[1] For the interchange of ει and η(ι), see Vol. i, 239-42.
[2] Cf. *BL* i, 230, and the parallel omission of η after οι (υ) in forms of ποιῶ, Vol. i, 298-9.
[3] ἐγ γύης *CPR* 111.9 is more likely nom. for gen./dat.; γύας in *PFlor.* 296.46, could be
acc. pl. of ὁ γύης. Cf. Preisigke, *WB*, s.v.
[4] For compds. w. suffixes in -ης wh. fluctuate w. by-forms in -ος, e.g., -άρχης/-αρχος,
-μάχης/-μαχος, -νόμης/-νομος, -ποιής/-ποιός, see Palmer, 66-69.
[5] The pl. of κέραμος is rare, e.g., κεράμων *Il.* 9.469 (*LSJ*, s.v.). κέραμα is read in one
Ptol. pap., but it may represent the omission of prevocalic ι in the usual κεράμια (Mayser
i², 1, 126; i², 2, 47).
[6] τὰ σῖτα Xenoph. Hdt. (*LSJ*, s.v.) is restored in a Ptol. pap. of the 3rd cent. (Mayser
i², 2, 48).
[7] For στάδιοι and στάδια (both used by Hdt. Th. Ar. Pl.), see *LSJ*, s.v., and Crönert,
175, n. 4. Mayser (i², 2, 47) cites 4 reff. to neut. pl., 1 to masc. pl. in the Ptol. papp.

2) θεμέλιος is properly an adjective (λίθος understood). The masculine plural θεμελίοις occurs in *PStrassb.* 9.8 (A.D. 352: *BL* iii, 230).[1]

c. Nouns of the second declension metaplastic according to the masculine and neuter declensions in the singular as well as the plural elsewhere in Greek follow one declensional type throughout. In the few forms which are distinguishable, δεῖπνον and ἔσοπτρον are neuter, σταθμός is masculine.

1) δεῖπνον:[2]

δῖπνον *SB* 4630 = *PBrem.* 56 Anh. (p. 130).14-15 part. rest. (ca. A.D. 117); *PMich.* 508.14 (2nd/3rd cent.); *PLond.* 1259 (iii, 239-40).34 (4th cent.)

2) ἔσοπτρον.[3] For examples, see Vol. i, 292.

3) σταθμός:[4]

σταθμός *PBeattyPanop.* 2.217 (A.D. 300)

d. Nouns of the second declension with by-forms of the first declension.

1) ὁ δεσμός has by-forms of the first declension.[5]

a) ὁ δεσμός.

i. Bundle:

δεσμ[ό]ς *PSarap.* 79 f (pp. 309-13) i.3 (ca. A.D. 125)
δεσμόν *PMich.* 508.5 (2nd/3rd cent.)
δυσμοί (for δεσμοί) *SB* 9379 iii.18, etc. = *PMilVogl.* 69 A.149, etc. (2nd cent.); sim. *POxy.* 2424.16 part. rest. (2nd/3rd cent.)
δεσμούς *BGU* 1120.14 part. rest. (5 B.C.); *PSarap.* 50.9 (A.D. 124); 51.19 (A.D. 125)

---

[1] For the uses of masc. and neut., see *LSJ*, s.v., and Crönert, 175, n. 5. Mayser (i[2], 2, 49) cites only the neut. pl. for the Ptol. papp.

[2] Only δεῖπνον is used in class. Gr. δεῖπνος first occurs as a v.l. in D.S., in a Sch.Ar. (*LSJ*, s.v.), and as a v.l. in the NT; it may have arisen on the analogy of σῖτος (*BDF*, § 49.2).

[3] ἔσοπτρος once Ptol. papp. and Clem.Alex. (Mayser i[2], 2, 20).

[4] The masc. sg. and pl. are much more common than the neut. in class. Gr. (*LSJ*, s.vv.); the masc. is normal in the Ptol. papp., but a neut. sg. occurs once (Mayser i[2], 2, 20, 48). See also J. Gagnepain, *Les Noms grecs en -ος et en -α*, 86-87.

[5] The neut. pl., orig. a collective fem. sg. (Chantraine[2], § 8), is found in *L.Merc.* Thgn. Hdt. Fl. and usu. in Trag., but the masc. pl. is found in A. E. and usu. in Pl. (*LSJ*, s.v. δεσμός). Both the masc. and neut. pl. occur in Att. inscrr. (*MS*, 143) and in the NT (*BDF*, § 49.3). The neut. pl. is preferred by the Atticists Aristid. Hermog. D.C. Philostr. (Schmid i, 84, iv, 584; Crönert, 175, n. 3). Only the sg. (o- and a-stems) is attested in the Ptol. papp. (Mayser i[2], 2, 45). Only pl. forms are used in mag. papp.; the neut. predominates (*PGM* iii, Indices). See also J. Gagnepain, 85.

ii. Shackle:

δεσμῷ *PSI* 452.28 (4th cent.)
δεσμοῖς *BGU* 1210 (20).62 (mid 2nd cent.)

b) ἡ δέσμη (bundle or measure):

δέσμην *PMich.* 496.16 (2nd cent.)
δέσμαι *OTheb.* 144.3,7 abbrev. (1st cent.)
δέσμες (for δέσμαις) *PFlor.* 322.31,37,50 (A.D. 258?)
δέσμας *PRyl.* 183.7; 183a.7 (A.D. 16); *PLond.* 892 (iii, 168-9).7-8: *BL*
    i, 286 (A.D. 16); *PRyl.* 129.12 (A.D. 30); *BGU* 544.5 (A.D. 138-61);
    PMich. 494.14-15 (2nd cent.); *PRyl.* 392.3 (2nd/3rd cent.); *PBerlLeihg.*
    9.7 (A.D. 240/1); *PFlor.* 127.17 (A.D. 256); *PSI* 1049.10 (A.D. 260?);
    PGen. 59 = *PAbinn.* 27.21 (ca. A.D. 346); *PSI* 711.5 (A.D. 360)

2) ὁ ζυγός/τὸ ζυγόν is metaplastic throughout according to the masculine and
neuter declensions, with by-forms of the first declension in Byzantine papyri.[1]

a) ὁ ζυγός (yoke/pair or balance):

τὸν ζυγόν *PFay.* 121.4-6 (ca. A.D. 100); sim. *PStrassb.* 32 = *PFlor.*
    134**.12 (A.D. 261)
τοὺς ζ[υ]γούς *PBon.* 22a¹.7 (6th/7th cent.)

b) τὸ ζυγόν (yoke/pair):

ζυγά *PRyl.* 393 V iii.6 (2nd/3rd cent.); *PThead.* 6.10 part. rest. (A.D.
    322); *SB* 5302.7 (Byz.)

c) ἡ ζυγή (pair):

ζυγήν *PAntin.* 44.12 (late 4th/5th cent.); *PSI* 183.6 (A.D. 484); *PSI*
    225.4 (6th cent.); *POxy.* 1843.19 (6th/7th cent.)
τὰς ζυγάς *PSI* 481.6 (5th/6th cent.)
cf. ζυγί (for ζυγή) *PColt* 95.42 (late 6th/early 7th cent.)

3) ἡ θεά is usually used rather than ἡ θεός:[2]

---

[1] ὁ ζυγός is found in various senses in *L.Cer.* Pl. Theoc. Plb. Jul. etc., rarely in the pl.,
but τὸ ζυγόν is usu. in Att. (*LSJ*, s.v.). The masc. predominates in Hell. Gr., is usu. in
the LXX, and is the only form in the NT (*BDF*, § 49.2) and MGr. (Chantraine², § 9). In
the Ptol. papp., the masc. sg. is alone attested once (Mayser i², 2, 20). The neut. pl. ζυγά
may represent an orig. collective (Schwyzer i, 581). First decl. by-forms are unattested
elsewh. (*LSJ*, s.v. ζυγή).
[2] The class. usage after Hom., who uses θεά, was ἡ θεός, exc. in Trag. Com. and Att.
prose in set phrases (*LSJ*, s.vv.). In the Att. inscrr. ἡ θεός is used in class. times exc. in
antitheses; ἡ θεά is first found in other instances from 282 B.C. on (*MS*, 125). ἡ θεός is also
used at Perg., but ἡ θεά and αἱ θεαί appear from ca. 165 B.C. on (Schweizer, 144-5). At
Magn., Artemis is always ἡ θεός, but Drusilla and Rom. women are θεά (Nachmanson, 126).

θεᾶς *PMed.* 3.4 part. rest. (A.D. 1-14); *SB* 5252.7 (A.D. 65); *POslo* 77.12
part. rest. (A.D. 169-76); *POxy.* 1117.2 (ca. A.D. 178); *SB* 421.11
(3rd cent.); *PLBat.* xvi, 12.4 & V (A.D. 345); etc.

θεᾷ *SB* 4650.4 (n.d.); *PRossGeorg.* iii, 4.4 (3rd cent.); cf. *SB* 436.1, inscr.
(A.D. 80/81); *SB* 604.1, inscr. (2nd/3rd cent.); etc.

θεοὶ θεαί τε *PRossGeorg.* ii, 26.4 (A.D. 160)

e. Some nouns of the second declension have by-forms of the third declension
(usually *s*-stem neuters).

1) ὁ ἄρακος fluctuates from the second century on with ὁ ἄραξ.[1]

a) ὁ ἄρακος:

ἀράκου *PLond.* 1171 (iii, 177-80).36,62 (8 B.C.); *PMich.* 121 R IV v.2
(A.D. 42); *PFlor.* 194.32 (A.D. 259); *PMeyer* 21.17 (3rd/4th cent.);
PCairPreis. 38.7 part. rest. (4th cent.); *PGiss.* 105.17 (5th cent.);
PFlor. 281.16 (A.D. 517); etc.

ἀράκῳ *PSI* 1029.12,17-18 (A.D. 52/53)

b) ὁ ἄραξ:

ἄρακος (gen.) *PMilVogl.* 212 ii R.12, etc. (A.D. 109); *PBrem.* 11.10
part. rest., 19 (ca. A.D. 117); *PSarap.* 25.5 (A.D. 124); *PMichael.*
63.3 (3rd cent.); *PLips.* 97 xxviii.1 (A.D. 338); *PSI* 34.13 (A.D.
397); *PLBat.* xiii, 15.11 part. rest., 22, with ἀράκου 12 (?) (A.D. 435);
POxy. 2032.75 (6th cent.); etc.

ἄρακι *POxy.* 2351.16 (A.D. 112); *PMichael.* 13.11,18 part. rest. (A.D.
160/1: *BL* iv, 50)

ἄρακει *PMeyer* 12.23 (A.D. 115)

ἄρακα *PSarap.* 79 f (pp. 309-13) i.19; ii.11 (ca. A.D. 125); *PTebt.* 423.4,
with gen. ἄρακος 6 (early 3rd cent.); *StudPal.* v, 8 = xx, 58 #8
ii.6 (ca. A.D. 265/6); *BGU* 938.10, with ἄρακος 5,9 part. rest.
(4th cent.); etc.

2) ὁ γάρος/τὸ γάρον are usual, but τὸ γάρος is found in documents of the
third and fourth centuries.[2] A diminutive τὸ γάριον also occurs.

At Lycia, ἡ θεός is used into the 3rd cent. A.D., but Artemis is usu. ἡ θεός (Hauser, 81-82).
In the Ptol. papp., θεά is normally used, w. ἡ θεός occurring only in the sg. and rarely; both
θεοί and θεαί are used in the pl. (Mayser i², 2, 8-9). In the NT, ἡ θεός (v.l. θεά) is used,
but Artemis is ἡ θεά (*BDF*, § 44.2, w. lit.).

[1] ὁ ἄρακος is attested only in Ar. Thphr. Gal. and the papp., ὁ ἄραξ only in the papp.
(*LSJ*, s.vv.). For ἄραξ as a back-formation from dimin. ἀράκιον, see Palmer, 51.

[2] ὁ γάρος A. Cratin. Pherecr. S. Pl. Com. Alciphr. Ruf.; τὸ γάρον Str. (*LSJ*, s.v.); τὸ
γάρος papp. & *Gp.* 20.46, ed. Basil., *EM* (*POxy.* 937.27, n. ad loc.).

a) ὁ γάρος/τὸ γάρον:

γάρος *BGU* 377.2 (7th/8th cent.)
γάρου *POxy.* 1760.14 (2nd cent.); 2983.9 (2nd/3rd cent.); *PGot.* 3.7 (A.D.
   215/16); *PSI* 890.48 (3rd cent.); *PLond.* 239 = *PAbinn.* 31.12 (ca.
   A.D. 346); *PHermRees* 23.5 (4th cent.); *PErl.* 111.14,15 (5th/6th cent.);
   POslo 147.4 (5th/6th cent.); cf. *PColt* 87.4,5 (7th cent.); etc.
γάρον *PFlor.* 334.5 (2nd cent.)

b) τὸ γάρος:

γάρους *POxy.* 937.27 (3rd cent.); *POxy.* 1770.27 (late 3rd cent.); *POslo*
   161.5 (late 3rd cent.); *PRyl.* 627.76; 629.88 (A.D. 317-23)
γάρος (acc.) *PGissBibl.* 25.12 (3rd cent.)

c) τὸ γάριον:

γάριον *PAlex.* 21.4 (2nd/3rd cent.)
γαρίου *POxy.* 1759.9 (2nd cent.)
γάρια *PJand.* 8.10 (3rd cent.: *BL* i, 197)

3) ὁ ἔλεος is used less frequently than the Hellenistic τὸ ἔλεος,[1] which
may have become popular to distinguish ἔλεος from ἔλαιον, identical in pronunciation in the oblique cases.[2] The word occurs, except for one inscription,
only in Byzantine papyri.

a) ὁ ἔλεος·

ὁ ἔλεος *POxy.* 130.16 (6th cent.); *PAberd.* 4.10 (6th cent.?)
ἐλαίῳ (for ἐλέῳ, not ἐλέει with ed.) *POxy.* 1989.27 (A.D. 590)
τὸν | [ἔλ]εον *SB* 8092.14-15 (ca. A.D. 500)

b) τὸ ἔλεος:

τὸ ὑμέτερον ἔλεος *PLond.* 1675.6 (A.D. 566-73)
τὸ ἔλεος *PAntin.* 198.5 (6th/7th cent.)
ἐλέους *SB* 6650.5, inscr. (1st cent. B.C./1st cent. A.D.: *BL* iii, 178); *POxy.*
   2479.23 (6th cent.); *PGen.* 14.5 (Byz.)

---

[1] τὸ ἔλεος Plb. LXX, NT (w. v.l. masc.), etc., but ὁ ἔλεος is also found in the LXX,
Agatharch. Phld. codd. Ph. etc. (*LSJ*, s.v.; Crönert, 176 & n. 1; *BDF*, § 51.2). Only ἐλέου
occurs in the Ptol. papp. (Mayser i², 2, 37).

[2] Several misspellings of forms of ἔλαιον have in fact found their way into grammars
and dictionaries as forms of ἔλεος, e.g., ἐλέου κοτύλας δύο *BGU* 86 = *MChr.* 306.37 (A.D.
155), cited by Crönert as gen. of ὁ ἔλεος (!) (176, n. 1), and ὑπ(ὲρ) ἐλέ(ου) ξ(εστῶν) *PBaden*
95.472 (7th cent.), listed under ἔλεος in Daris, *Spoglio*. The existence of the ancient derivative ἐλεεινός and the compd. νηλεής suggest that the *s*-stem may be orig. (*BDF*, § 51.2).

ἐλέει *POxy.* 1951.4 (5th cent.); *PCairMasp.* 126.1,43 part. rest. (A.D. 541); *PErl.* 120.12 (6th/7th cent.); *StudPal.* iii, 46.5 (6th/7th cent.); cf. *PColt* 107.3 (6th/7th cent.); 50.10; 51.1 part. rest. (early 7th cent.); 57.1,2,24,26,27 (A.D. 689)

4) ὁ πλοῦτος is normally used, but a form of τὸ πλοῦτος occurs once:[1]

a) ὁ πλοῦτος:

πλούτου *PFay.* 20.13 (late 3rd/early 4th cent.); *PCairGoodsp.* 15.20 (for dat.: *BL* i, 174) (A.D. 362)
πλούτῳ *PFlor.* 367.11 (3rd cent.); *PAmh.* 142 = *MChr.* 65.15 (A.D. 341+)
πλοῦτον *SB* 7518.14 (4th/5th cent.)

b) τὸ πλοῦτος:

πλοῦτος (prob. acc.) *SB* 7205.15 (late 3rd cent.)
πλούτει *PCairIsidor.* 75.10 (A.D. 316)

5) ὁ φόβος is normally used, but τὸ φόβος appears once:[2]

a) ὁ φόβος:

μέγας φόβος *BGU* 547.1 (Byz.)
    φόβος ... βασιλικός *PCairMasp.* 89 R b.19, with τὸν φόβον 20 (Byz.)
τὸν φόβον *PCairIsidor.* 69.22 (A.D. 310); *PAbinn.* 50.17 (A.D. 346); *PMerton* 38.12 (mid 4th cent.); *PLips.* 36 = *MChr.* 77.6 (A.D. 376/8); *PHermRees* 19.3 (A.D. 392); *PLBat.* xiii, 8.6 (A.D. 421); *WChr.* 470 = *PMon.* 2.13 (A.D. 578); *PLond.* 1356 = *WChr.* 254.33 (A.D. 710); cf. *PGM* 70.4 (late 3rd/early 4th cent.)

b) τὸ φόβος:

ἵνα περισσεύῃ τὸ φόβο[ς] τοῦ θεοῦ, διὰ τὸ φόβος γὰρ πάντα γίνετε (for γίνεται) *PLond.* 418 = *PAbinn.* 7.4-5 (ca. A.D. 346)

---

[1] τὸ πλοῦτος occurs 8 times in the NT in nom.-acc. sg., w. ὁ πλοῦτος and τὸν πλοῦτον 3 times each; the gen. is always πλούτου (cf. *BDF*, § 51.2). The neut. τὸ πλοῦτος is also found in Pastor Hermas (*POxy.* 1172.25,38, w. τὸν πλοῦτον 6, τῷ πλούτῳ 28 [4th cent.]) and in Hermog. Orig. (Crönert, 176, n. 4), and is used in MGr. (Thumb, *Handbook*, § 100).

[2] The neut. is not attested elsewh. in Gr. The corresp. Copt. word ⲉⲟⲧⲉ is fem.

6) ὁ υἱός occurs regularly as an *o*-stem; third declension forms are extremely rare.[1] Emended forms are to be rejected,[2] but a feminine υἱή is found in *SB* 7728.1, mummy label (2nd/3rd cent.).[3]

a) ὁ υἱός passim

b) ὁ υἱύς:

τοῦ ὑέος (foɪ υἱέος[4]) *BGU* 646 = *WChr.* 490.17 (A.D. 193)
οἱ υἱεῖς[5] *PAberd.* 53 ii.16 (A.D. 10/11)
τοὺς υεἱ[ῖ]ς *SB* 8091.32 (3rd cent.)
τοὺς ἐ[αυτο]ῦ υἱέας *PRyl.* 109.8 (A.D. 235)
[το]ὺς ὑέας *POxy.* 2711.4 (ca. A.D. 268-71)

7) ὁ διάκονος occurs occasionally as an *n*-stem of the third declension διάκων:[6]

διάκων *PMich.* 224.1546 (A.D. 172-3); *SB* 5124.207,208,209,283 (A.D. 193: *BL* v, 94); *OMich.* 1046.1 (3rd cent.); *PGiss.* 54.26 (4th/5th cent.); *SB* 4936.2 (Byz.); etc.
διάκονος *SB* 9653 = *PMilVogl.* 188 i.11, with διάκονι 15 (A.D. 127?); *PLond.* 1913.10 (A.D. 334); *BGU* 874.2 (Byz.); etc.
διάκονι *PGiss.* 101.10 (3rd cent.); *CPR* 227.4 (4th cent.); *PJand.* 103.1,2 (6th cent.)
διάκωνι *BGU* 597.3-4 (A.D. 75); *PMich.* 473.12 part. rest. (early 2nd cent.)
διάκονα *PStrassb.* 154 = *SB* 8944.1 (4th/5th cent.)
διάκωνα *PLond.* 1914.44,53 (A.D. 335?)

8) ὁ γύψος, normally an *o*-stem, as γύψου, τὸν γύψον *POxy.* 2272.13,15, etc. (2nd cent.), occurs ɪn the acc. neut. τὸ γύπσος *SB* 8030 = *PMich.* 245.11,

---

[1] Iɴ ᴛʜe Att. inscrr., athematic υἱύς, etc., are used, along with nom. υἱός & acc. pl. υἱούς exc. in the acc. sg. till 350 B.C., then excl. forms of υἱός (*MS*, 144). At Perg., the *o*-stem is used exc. in one poet. inscr. (Schweizer, 85, 145). At Magn., only *o*-stem forms occur (Nachmanson, 126). In the Ptol. papp., υ(ἱ)ός is ɪnflected according to the *o*-stem decl. exc. in the Ioɴ. Aɪᴛemisia pap. and one doc. wh. also has *o*-stem forms (Mayser i², 2, 20-21). In the NT, only *o*-stem forms are used (*BDF*, § 52, n. ad fin.). Athematic forms are found in codd. of Str. Plu. and in the more ornate style of Byz. authors (Crönert, 175, n. 1). See further *LSJ*, s.v.

[2] τ[ο]ῦ υ|ἱός *SB* 9194.17-18 (late 3rd cent.) is better understood as nom. for gen. as in τοῦ ἑαυτῆς υἱὸς Ὧρος *CPR* 4 = *MChr.* 159.30-31 (A.D. 51/53), etc., than emended to υἱ<έ>ος w. ed.

[3] L. C. Youtie suggests that Τερεῦ|ς Θορτ|ᾶις υἱή| L *SB* 101.3, inscr. (Rom.) would be better read Τερεῦ|ς Θορτ|αίου ῑη| L; τῆς υἱῆς *PGiss.* 34.13 (A.D. 265/6) is corr. emended to υἱ<δ>ῆς in *MChr.* 75. Cf. υἱήν· τὴν ἄμπελον, ἢ υἱόν Hsch. (*LSJ*, s.v.).

[4] For the interchange of υɪ w. υ, etc., in forms of this word, see Vol. i, 202-8.

[5] Dbtfl. reading; the υ is more like τ (ed., n. ad loc.).

[6] Cf. also ⲛⲁⲓⲁⲕⲱⲛ *PLond.* 1709.3 part. rest. 18 (before ca. A.D. 570?).

sim. 19,31-32 (A.D. 47) and in the gen. γύψιος in *POxy.* 1851.3 (6th/7th cent.). This latter form is presumably an error for γυψίου, gen. of the diminutive τὸ γυψίον which occurs in *StudPal.* x, 259.12 (6th cent.).[1]

f. The following nouns for which metaplastic inflections of the third declension are attested elsewhere in Greek appear only as *o*-stems in forms that can be distinguished.

1) ὁ ζῦτος:[2]

> ζύτου *POxy.* 736.27,60 (ca. A.D. 1); *PTebt.* 401.38 (early 1st cent.); *SB* 8030 = *PMich.* 245.35 (A.D. 47); *PSI* 181.4 (A.D. 91); *PStrassb.* 185 V.3 (A.D. 118); *BGU* 1069 V.8,9,10 (A.D. 243/4); *PFay.* 104.12 (late 3rd cent.); *POxy.* 1513.7 (4th cent.); etc.
> ζύτῳ *SB* 6949 = *SB* 8546.16, inscr. (shortly before A.D. 356)
> ζῦτον *PLond.* 131 R = *SB* 9699.262, etc. (A.D. 78/79); *PTebt.* 331.13 (ca. A.D. 131); *PMilVogl.* 28.46, etc. (A.D. 162-3); *OBruss-Berl.* 95.2 (2nd/3rd cent.)
> cf. also ζῦτα *PAlex.* 239 (p. 42).2 (6th/7th cent.)

2) ὁ ἦχος (inscriptions and magical papyri only):[3]

> ἦχος *PGM* 7.777 (3rd cent.)
> τὸν ἦχον *SB* 8339.8, inscr. (A.D. 123)

3) τὸ δένδρον:[4]

> τὸ δέ|δρον *sic PGrenf.* ii, 84.13-14 (5th/6th cent.)
> ὑπὸ δένδρα *SB* 5637.5 (ca. A.D. 215); *BGU* 362 part. = *WChr.* 96 i.6; vii.2; etc. (A.D. 215)

3. Athematic stems and by-forms.

a. τὸ ἔρεγμα has an *o*-stem masculine by-form ἐρεγμός in τὸν ἐρεγμόν *PTebt.* 417.17 (3rd cent.).[5]

---

[1] So ed. (n. ad loc.).

[2] ζῦτος, the Eg.-Gr. spelling of ζῦθος, occurs as masc. and neut. in the Ptol. papp. (Mayser i², 2, 20, 45). Elsewh. ὁ ζῦθος is usu., but τὸ ζῦθος is found in Thphr. and D.S. (*LSJ*, s.v.). For the formation, see Schwyzer i, 330, 512.

[3] τὸ ἦχος LXX, ἤχους once dbtfl. NT w. ἤχῳ once (*LSJ*, s.v.; cf. *BDF*, § 50, 51.2).

[4] τὸ δένδρος E. Hdt. Hp. Pherecr. Meno, Arr. inscrr., etc., dat. pl. δένδρεσι usu. in Att. prose; τὸ δένδρον first in Hdt. (Ep. δένδρεον, Aeol. δένδριον), reg. in Att. and later Gr. exc. in dat. pl.; ὁ δένδρος Ath. Med. ap. Orib. (*LSJ*, s.v.; see further Crönert, 174, & n. 4). In the Ptol. papp., only 3rd decl. and ambiguous forms occur (Mayser i², 2, 47).

[5] τὸ ἔρεγμα Thphr. Erot.; ὁ ἐρεγμός Gal. etc. (*LSJ*, s.v.). The Ptol. papp. have the *o*-stem masc. excl. (Mayser i², 2, 20).

b. Neuters of the third declension in -ος with by-forms of the first declension feminine in -η, as βλάβος/βλάβη, σκεῦος/σκευή, are treated under word formation.[1]

E. INDECLINABLE NOUNS[2]

Besides nouns which are occasionally used indeclinably, such as third declension neuters in -μα[3] and *i*-stem names,[4] some nouns are regularly used indeclinably.

1. Names for letters of the Greek alphabet are always used indeclinably, e.g., καὶ εἰμὶ ... ἀστῆς ἄλφα Ἡφ[αισ]τίωνος *PTebt*. 316 = *WChr*. 148.87-89 (A.D. 99), including δέλτα when used as a geographical designation for the quarter of Alexandria, e.g., τὴν [ἐ]πὶ τοῦ Δέλτα χαριτοδώτειραν *POxy*. 1380.9-10 (early 2nd cent.), or the Nile estuary, e.g., οἱ ἐν τῶι Δέλτα τῆς Αἰγύπτου ... οἰκοῦντες Ἕλληνες *SB* 8276.5-9, inscr. (A.D. 149-54). Their gender is neuter, as in the last examples and in τὸ ζῆτα (= sixth book of the *Iliad*) *POxy*. 930 = *WChr*. 138.15 (2nd/3rd cent.).

2. Some Egyptian loanwords are always used indeclinably, e.g., κοῦρι δέκα ἑπτά *StudPal*. iii, 135.5 (5th/6th cent.); λὰκ ἕν *SB* 5297.3 (Byz.). Likewise uninflected are the Egyptian month-names Θώθ, etc.

3. Names.

a. Egyptian names.

Very many Egyptian names are used indeclinably especially in papyri of the Byzantine period, but most have alternate formations which fit into Greek declensional types, e.g., παρὰ Ἀμοῦν *StudPal*. iii, 76 i.4 (5th/6th cent.), dat. Ἀμοῦν *StudPal*. viii, 1005.2 (5th cent.), Ἀμούνεως *PLond*. 350 = *WChr*. 353.4, with nom. Ἀμοῦνις 19 (A.D. 212), Ἀμοῦνιν *PGiss*. 77.11 (ca. A.D. 117); cf. also Ἄμμωνος *PLips*. 65 = *WChr*. 404.7,18 (A.D. 390), Ἄμμωνα *PThead*. 17.9-10 (A.D. 332), and Ἀμμωνίου *PRyl*. 115.3 (A.D. 156), Ἀμμωνίῳ *PTebt*. 308 = *WChr*. 319.3 (A.D. 174); gen. Φίβ *StudPal*. iii, 123.1; 261.6 (6th cent.), 418.5 (7th cent.), but Φιβίου *StudPal*. xx, 221.66,67 (6th cent.); *PGrenf*. i, 57.18 (A.D. 561); *PHamb*. 23.8 (A.D. 569); gen. Ὧρ *PGen*. 66 = *WChr*. 381.6 (A.D. 374); *POxy*. 139.14,30,34 (A.D. 612), acc. *PThead*. 17.9 (A.D. 332), but Ὥρου *POxy*. 485 = *MChr*. 246.15 (A.D. 178), Ὥρου, Ὥρῳ, Ὧρον *POxy*. 491 = *MChr*. 304.5, etc. (A.D. 126).

---

[1] See Palmer, 63-64.
[2] Schwyzer i, 585; Mayser i², 2, 1.
[3] See above, pp. 88-89.
[4] See above, pp. 78-79.

b. Semitic names.[1]

1) Many Semitic names are always used indeclinably in the papyri, e.g., gen. 'Ααρών *PLond.* 1420.78 (A.D. 706), 'Αδάμ *POxy.* 2244.78 (6th/7th cent.), Δαυείδ *PCairMasp.* 303.22 (A.D. 553); dat. 'Ελισάβετ *POxy.* 131.25 (6th/7th cent.); gen. 'Ιώβ *PAmh.* 150.11 (A.D. 592); gen. 'Ραχήλ *PMon.* 13.73 (A.D. 594); etc.

2) A few Semitic names are always inflected according to the Greek declensional types into which they fit, e.g., 'Ιωάννῃ *POxy.* 1841.6 (6th cent.), 'Ρεβέκκας *PLond.* 77 = *MChr.* 319.77 (8th cent.).

3) Most Semitic names, like Egyptian names, are used indeclinably but have alternate formations which fit into a Greek declensional type, e.g., gen. 'Αβραάμ *PCairMasp.* 330 ii.13 (2nd half 6th cent.), but 'Αβρααμίου *SB* 7519.2 (A.D. 510), 'Αβρααμίῳ *PLond.* 113 (11a) (i, 223-4).2 (6th/7th cent.); gen. Δανιήλ *PSI* 316.2 (4th cent.), *PPrinc.* 140 II V ii.23 (6th/7th cent.), but Δανιηλίου *SB* 7033.23 = *PPrinc.* 82.17 (A.D. 481), Δανιηλίῳ *PFouad* 74.1 (late 5th cent.: *BL* iii, 61); gen. 'Ενώχ *PAmh.* 155.2 (5th cent.), *PLond.* 1673.417, with nom. 'Ενώχις 231,265, 'Ενωχίο(υ) 13, etc. (6th cent.), 'Ενῶχις *SB* 4669.5 (A.D. 614); 'Ιακώβ, 'Ιάκουβος 'Ιακύβιος etc. (see Vol. i, 223); 'Ισαάκ, 'Ισαάκις, 'Ισάκιος, etc. (see Vol. i, 299); gen. 'Ιωσήφ *PGiss.* 121.6 (A.D. 534), dat. *POxy.* 1841.6 (6th cent.), acc. *POxy.* 1856.3 (6th/7th cent.), but 'Ιωσηφίο(υ) *PCairMasp.* 1.9, etc. (A.D. 514), 'Ιωσηφίῳ *PLond.* 1075 (iii, 281-2).16 (7th cent.); gen. Μαριάμ *PCairMasp.* 110.10 (A.D. 565), dat. *PHermRees* 31.5 (6th cent.), acc. *PJand.* 100.5 (2nd half 4th cent.), but Μαρία *OEdfou* 156.1 (A.D. 114), Μαρίας *PErl.* 53.14 (4th cent.), Μαρίᾳ *PHarris* 107.2 (3rd cent.?).

c. Arabic names are normally used indeclinably, e.g., gen. 'Αβδέλλ(α) *PLond.* 116a = *StudPal.* viii, 740.4 (7th cent.), 'Αειάν *PLond.* 1379.8 (A.D. 711), 'Ασσάν *PLond.* 1447.39 (A.D. 685-705), Ζώρα *PLond.* 1457.26 (A.D. 706-9), Καεῖς *PLond.* 1441.82 (A.D. 706), Μααμήτ *PLond.* 1434.93 (A.D. 714-15: *BL* v, 56), 'Ομάρ *PLond.* 1447.117 (A.D. 685-705), Χαλέδ *StudPal.* x, 197.4 (7th/8th cent.); but cf. gen. Ζιαδᾶ *PGrenf.* ii, 105.1; 106.1 = *StudPal.* iii, 258.3; 259.3 part. rest. (A.D. 719), Καρκάρο(υ) *PCairMasp.* 319.20 (6th cent.), *PLond.* 1419.826 (after A.D. 716).

---

[1] For lists of Semitic names in the papyri, see Heinz Wuthnow, *Die semitischen Menschennamen in griechischen Inschriften und Papyri des vorderen Orients* (Studien zur Epigraphik und Papyruskunde, hg. Fr. Bilabel) (Leipzig, 1930), and S. M. Ruozzi Sala, *Lexicon Nominum Semiticorum quae in papyris Graecis in Aegypto repertis ab anno 323 a. Chr.n. usque ad annum 70 p.Chr.n. laudata reperiuntur.* Testi e documenti per lo studio dell'antichità 46 (Milano, 1974).

II. THE DECLENSION OF ADJECTIVES[1]

A. ADJECTIVES OF THE FIRST AND SECOND DECLENSIONS (VOWEL STEMS)

1. Formation of gender.

Many adjectives which elsewhere in Greek are adjectives of only two terminations -ος, -ον, or fluctuate between two and three terminations, tend to have a
distinct feminine. The contrary tendency is observed in a few adjectives.

a. Adjectives which normally have three terminations elsewhere in Greek
usually have three terminations in the papyri. Included here are not only root
adjectives with three terminations, as ἀγαθός, -ή, -όν, and denominatives in
-κός,[2] which always occur with a distinct feminine in the papyri, but also derivative adjectives of types which sometimes have only two terminations in classical Greek.

1) Adjectives in -ιος.[3]

a) ἄθλιος:[4]

    ἀθλίας (gen. sg.) *PLond.* 1674.76 (A.D. 570)
    ἀθλίαν *PRyl.* 617.13 (A.D. 317?); *PCairMasp.* 4.3 (ca. A.D. 552: *BL* i,
    100); 10.9: *BL* i, 102 (6th cent.); 2 iii.17 (A.D. 567: *BL* i, 100); 279.9
    (ca. A.D. 570); etc.
    cf. πανταθλίας *PCairMasp.* 2.2 (A.D. 567: *BL* i, 100)
    πανταθλίας, -αν *PCairMasp.* 5.4,5 (6th cent.)
    πανταθλίᾳ *PCairMasp.* 9 R.2 (6th cent.)

---

[1] Schwyzer i, 465-8, 470-2, 480-3, 489-91, 494-5, 501-4, 513-17, 524-30, 533-9; Chantraine[2],
§ 103-26; Buck, *GD*, § 113; *MS*, 148-52; Schweizer, 158-61; Nachmanson, 140-3; Hauser,
96-100; Mayser i[2], 2, 50-62; Crönert, 178-92; *BDF*, § 59-62.

[2] Palmer, 34-39.

[3] Palmer, 30-34. Adjs. in -ιος wh. reg. have a distinct fem. in class. Gr. preserve it in
the papp., e.g., ἄξιος (-ος, -ον Nonn.: *LSJ*, s.v.), γνήσιος.

[4] ἄθλιος, -ον E. (*LSJ*, s.v.).

b) δημόσιος:[1]

δημοσία (nom. sg.) *POslo* 31.17 (A.D. 138-61); *PRossGeorg.* ii, 28.34
(A.D. 163/4+); *PLips.* 10 i.17 (A.D. 240); *BGU* 1623.12 (3rd cent.);
StudPal. xx, 121.14,15 (A.D. 438); *PRossGeorg.* iii, 49.7 (A.D. 604/5)
δημοσίας (gen. sg.) *PRyl.* 122.3 part. rest. (A.D. 127); *POxy.* 1123.12,
13,15 (A.D. 158/9); *SB* 7475.14 (6th/7th cent.); sim. *StudPal.* xxii,
92.6 (3rd cent.)
δημοσίαι (dat. sg.) *PAmh.* 70 = *WChr.* 149.5 (A.D. 114-17); sim. *BGU*
813.12 (2nd cent.); 1086 ii.3 (2nd/3rd cent.); *POxy.* 2109.11 (A.D.
261); *BGU* 1024 iv.4 (late 4th cent.: *BL* i, 88); *PStrassb.* 46.6 (A.D.
566); etc.
δημοσίαν *PGen.* 4 = *WChr.* 351.8 (A.D. 118); *POxy.* 899 = *WChr.* 361.22
part. rest. (A.D. 200); *POxy.* 2131.11 (A.D. 207)
δημοσίας (acc. pl.) *BGU* 661.11 (A.D. 140/1)

c) μακάριος:[2]

μακαρίας (gen. sg.) *PCairMasp.* 151-2.5 (A.D. 570); *PLond.* 1676.2-3
(A.D. 566-73)

d) μέτριος:[3]

μετρίας (gen. sg.) *PApoll.* 66.11 (ca. A.D. 710/11)
μετρίαν *PSI* 481.12 (5th/6th cent.)

e) νήπιος:[4]

νηπίας (gen. sg.) *PFlor.* 36 = *MChr.* 64.5 (A.D. 312)
νηπίαν *PTebt.* 326 = *MChr.* 325.6 (A.D. 266)
but νήπιος ... καταλειφθῖσα *PCairIsidor.* 63.7 (A.D. 296)

f) ὁμοπάτριος/ὁμομήτριος:[5]

ὁμοπατρίαι (dat. sg.) *BGU* 644.9 (A.D. 69)
    ὁμοπατρίαις καὶ ὁμομ[η]τρίαις *StudPal.* xxii, 43.6-7 (A.D. 151)
but ὁμοπατρίου καὶ ὁμομητρίου ἀδελφῆς *PLond.* 299 = *MChr.* 204.10-11
(A.D. 128)
[ὁ]μοπάτριοι καὶ ὁμομήτριοι ἀδελφαί *PMich.* 554.3 (A.D. 81-96);
sim. *PLond.* 289 (ii, 184-5).8-9 (A.D. 91)

---

[1] δημόσιος, -ον Hp. (*LSJ*, s.v.) & codd.J. Plu. etc. (Crönert, 183, n. 10).
[2] μακάριος, -ον Pl. (*LSJ*, s.v.).
[3] μέτριος, -ον Pl. (*LSJ*, s.v.), Ptol. papp. (Mayser i², 2, 51), and codd. Str. Plu. (Crönert,
186 & n. 2).
[4] νήπιος, -ον Lyc. (*LSJ*, s.v.).
[5] ὁμοπάτριος, -ον A.; ὁμομήτριος, -ον Lys. (*LSJ*. s.vv.).

g) ὅσιος:[1]

ὁσίας (gen. sg.) *PBerlZill.* 14.1 (6th cent.); *PMon.* 8.14,23 (late 6th cent.); *SB* 6249.5-6 (A.D. 601)

h) πατρῷος:[2]

[π]ατρῴας (gen. sg.) *PCol.* 123 = *SB* 9526.53 (A.D. 200); *PSI* 940.23 part. rest. (A.D. 266); *PLips.* 28 = *MChr.* 363.14, with -αν 27 (A.D. 381); *PGrenf.* ii, 82.11-12 (ca. A.D. 400)
πατρῴᾳ *POxy.* 1025 = *WChr.* 493.13 (late 3rd cent.)
πατρῴαν *SB* 7339.6 (A.D. 69-79); *PWürzb.* 9.49-50 part. rest. (A.D. 161-90); *POxy.* 1473.36 (A.D. 201)
πατρῴας (acc. pl.) *PBerlZill.* 4.19 (4th cent.)

i) μητρῷος:

μητρῴας (gen. sg.) *POxy.* 237 v.33; vi.24: *BL* i, 318 (A.D. 186)

2) Adjectives in -αιος.[3]

a) ἀναγκαῖος:[4]

ἀναγκαίας (gen. sg.) *WChr.* 461.20 (early 3rd cent.); *PFlor.* 158.4 part. rest. (3rd cent.); *PLond.* 1676.18 (A.D. 566-73); *PLond.* 1674.19 (ca. A.D. 570)
ἀναγκαίαν *PLBat.* xvi, 5.28 (A.D. 186); 10.8 (Λ.D. 468); 11.13, etc. (7th cent.); *PGrenf.* ii, 90.7 (6th cent.); *PCairMasp.* 2 iii.10 (A.D. 567: *BL* i, 100); *PMon.* 9.66 (A.D. 585); etc.
ἀναγκαίας (acc. pl.) *BGU* 98.13 (A.D. 211); *POxy.* 56 = *MChr.* 320.6-7 (A.D. 211); etc.

b) δίκαιος:[5]

δικαία *PRossGeorg.* ii, 19.32 (A.D. 141)
δικαίας (gen. sg.) *PGrenf.* ii, 71 i.14 part. rest. (A.D. 244-8); *POxy.* 899 (introd.) V i B.21 (3rd cent.); *PCairMasp.* 151-2.71 (A.D. 570); *PMon.* 8.17 (late 6th cent.)
δικαίαν *PLond.* 1912.81 (A.D. 41); *BGU* 180 = *WChr.* 396.17 (A.D. 172); *BGU* 267.8 part. rest. (A.D. 199); *PCairMasp.* 151-2.9, with gen. -ας 71, -ᾳ 221 (A.D. 570); etc.

---

[1] ὅσιος, -ον Pl. D.H. (*LSJ*, s.v.).
[2] πατρῷος, -ον A. E. etc. (*LSJ*, s.v.), Str. codd.J. Plu. (Crönert, 187 & n. 3).
[3] Palmer, 19-20. Ad᾽s. in -αιος wh. reg. have a distinct fem. in class. Gr. preserve it in the papp., e.g., ἀρχαῖος, περαῖος, τελευταῖος, etc.
[4] ἀναγκαῖος, -ον Th. Pl. etc. (*LSJ*, s.v.). A distinct fem. occurs in the Ptol. papp. (Mayser i², 2, 51).
[5] δίκαιος, -ον E. D.S. (*LSJ*, s.v.).

3) Adjectives in -ειος.[1]

a) τέλειος:[2]

τελείας (gen. sg.) *PLond.* 1717.11 (ca. A.D. 560-73); *BGU* 317.2,7 (A.D. 580/1); *PMon.* 6.77 (A.D. 583); sim. *SB* 4669.10 (A.D. 614)

τελείαν *PTebt.* 335.8 (ca. A.D. 165: *BL* iii, 242); *PGrenf.* ii, 76 = *MChr.* 295.19 (A.D. 305/6); *PCairMasp.* 2 i.15; ii.20; iii.14 (A.D. 567: *BL* i, 100); *PLond.* 1708.248 (A.D. 567?); *PMon.* 9.83,100 (A.D. 585); 13.34 (A.D. 594); etc.

τελείας (acc. pl.) *PHamb.* 10.14 (2nd cent.); *SB* 5277.5,8 (A.D. 238) but [τ]έλιον (acc. sg. fem.) *BGU* 1100.10 (30 B.C.-A.D. 14)

b) οἰκεῖος:[3]

οἰκείας (gen. sg.) *PCairMasp.* 320 A.2 (A.D. 541?); *PCairMasp.* 131.5 part. rest. (6th cent.); *PMon.* 13.10,14 (A.D. 594); *PLond.* 77 = *MChr.* 319.8 part. rest. (late 6th cent.)

οἰκείᾳ *BGU* 372 = *WChr.* 19 ii.14-15 (A.D. 154); *PLond.* 1107 (iii, 47-48).30 (3rd cent.); *PFlor.* 304.6 (6th cent.)

οἰκείαν *BGU* 372 = *WChr.* 19 i.4 (A.D. 154); *CPR* 30 = *MChr.* 290 ii.35 (6th cent.); *PCairMasp.* 24 R.32; 26.1 (ca. A.D. 551); 312.81 (A.D. 567); *PSI* 76.11 (A.D. 574-8)

οἰκείαις *PMon.* 6.53 (A.D. 583)

4) Adjectives in -ιμος (χρήσιμος):[4]

χρησίμην *PAntin.* 44.12 (late 4th/5th cent.)

b. Adjectives which usually have two terminations in classical Greek frequently have a distinct feminine.

1) Adjectives in -ιος (αἰώνιος):[5]

[αἰω]γία *BGU* 531 ii.20: *BL* i, 50 (A.D. 70-80: Olsson, 43, p. 128)

αἰωνίας (gen. sg.) *PBaden* 89.16, etc. (A.D. 222-35); *PPar.* 21b.5 (A.D. 592); sim. 21.8,18 (A.D. 616)

αἰωνίᾳ *PGrenf.* ii, 71 = *MChr.* 190 i.11 (A.D. 244-8); *PMon.* 9.27 (A.D. 585); cf. *SB* 6311.1, inscr. (5th cent.)

---

1 Palmer, 21-22.

2 τέλειος, -ον A. Pl. Arist. inscr. (*LSJ*, s.v.).

3 οἰκεῖος, -ον E. (*LSJ*, s.v.).

4 Palmer, 26-28. χρήσιμος, -ον X. Pl. (*LSJ*, s.v.).

5 αἰώνιος, -ον usu. in class. Gr., but αἰωνία Pl. αἰωνίη Aret. (*LSJ*, s.v.); -ος, -ον excl. Magn. inscrr. & Ptol. papp. (Nachmanson, 140; Mayser i², 2, 50); -ος, -ον & -ος, -α, -ον NT (*BDF*, § 59.2). Among Koine authors, -ος, -ον codd. Phld., -ος, -α, -ον Epict. (Crönert, 182 & n. 6).

αἰωνίαν *PColt* 21.15 (A.D. 562)
but αἰωνίου διαμογῆς *PSI* 1422.14 (3rd cent.)
προσφορᾶς αἰωνίου *PCairMasp.* 151-2.134, with -ον acc. sg. fem. 123
    (A.D. 570)
αἰώνιον συνήθε[ι]αν *BGU* 1563.41 (A.D. 68); sim. *PHarris* 107.12
    (3rd cent.?); *PPar.* 20.4 (A.D. 600)

2) Adjectives in -αιος (βέβαιος):[1]

βεβαία *PAmh.* 85 = *MChr.* 274.21 (A.D. 78); *PGrenf.* ii, 68.11 (A.D.
    247); 74.19 (A.D. 302); 75.15 (A.D. 305); *StudPal.* xx, 110.26 (5th
    cent.); *PGen.* 10.20 (prob. 6th cent.: *BL* v. 39)
βεβαίαν *PMon.* 9.88 (A.D. 585); *StudPal.* xx, 227.5 (6th/7th cent.); cf.
    PColt 22.16 (A.D. 566)
βεβαίας (acc. pl.) *POxy.* 270 = *MChr.* 236.41 (A.D. 94); *POxy.* 2134.22
    (ca. A.D. 170)

3) Adjectives in -ιμος.[2]

a) ἀρόσιμος:[3]

ἀροσίμην γῆν *SB* 9503 — *PMed.* 64.6 (A.D. 440/1); *POxy.* 2724.9 (A.D.
    469); *POxy.* 137.14 (A.D. 584)
but ἀρόσιμον γῆν *POxy.* 1899.11 (A.D. 476); 1900.13-14 (A.D. 528);
    sim. 2779.11 (A.D. 530); *PLond.* 776 (iii, 278-9).9 (A.D. 552); *PSI*
    60.16 (A.D. 595); *PLBat.* xiii, 20.8 (6th/7th cent.); etc.

b) γνώριμος:[4]

γνωρίμην *PTebt.* 286 = *MChr.* 83.5-6 (A.D. 121-38)

c) σπόριμος:[5]

σπορίμη *POxy.* 1915.4 (ca. A.D. 560)
σπορίμης *PAmh.* 68 = *WChr.* 374.8 (A.D. 81-96); *PVars.* 21 b.2 (2nd
    cent.); *SB* 4325 ii.8, iv.5, vi.12 (3rd cent.); *PCornell* 19.8,19 (A.D.
    298); *PRyl.* 656.11,13,18 (A.D. 300); *PLond.* 1313 (iii, 256).16,18
    (A.D. 507); *PFlor.* 323.4,7 (A.D. 525); *PMichael.* 34.3 (6th cent.):
    PHermRees 34.11 (7th cent.); *PWürzb.* 19.8 (A.D. 652?); etc.

---

[1] βέβαιος, -ον Th. Pl. etc.; -ος, -α, -ον E. Isoc.; S. fluctuates betw. two and three terminations (*LSJ*, s.v.). A distinct fem. occurs in the Ptol. papp. (Mayser i², 2, 51) & reg. in the NT (*BDF*, § 59.1).

[2] Palmer, 26-28.

[3] ἡ ἀρόσιμος Str. Hld. Ph. Byz. (*LSJ*, s.v.).

[4] γνώριμος, -ον, rarely -η, -ον, Pl. Luc. cod.Str. Plu. (*LSJ*, s.v.; Crönert, 183 & n. 8).

[5] σπόριμος, -ον X. Thphr. Theoc. Ptol. papp.; -α *Hymn.Is.*, -η Vett.Val. Paul.Al. (*LSJ*, s.v.; Mayser i², 2, 51).

σπορίμη *PLond.* 1007bc (iii, 264-5).13 (ca. A.D. 558)
σπορίμην *PLips.* 6 ii.6 (A.D. 306)
σπορίμαις *PBrem.* 68.6 (A.D. 99)
σπορίμας *PGiss.* 28.4 (A.D. 142/3); *PRyl.* 164.5 (A.D. 171); *SB* 4298.11
    (A.D. 204); *PAmh.* 96.3 (A.D. 213); *PLBat.* ii, 6.12 (A.D. 250)
but γῆς σειτοφόρου σπορίμου *POxy.* 45 = *MChr.* 222.11 (A.D. 95); *POxy.*
    46.23-24 (A.D. 100); sim. *POxy.* 1270.25-26 part. rest. (A.D. 159);
    POxy. 2134.14 (ca. A.D. 170)

d) φόριμος:[1]

ἀμπέλου φορίμης *StudPal.* v, 120 R iii.19 (3rd cent.)
but γῆς φορίμου *PCairMasp.* 151-2.115, with ἀμπελοφορίμου γῆς 105
    (A.D. 570)

e) φρόνιμος:[2]

φρονίμη γυνή *PRossGeorg.* iii, 2.27 (A.D. 270: *BL* iii, 156)
but θυγάτηρ ... φρόνιμος (or φρονίμη? ed., n. ad loc.) *PMich.* 474.7
    (early 2nd cent.)

f) τρόφιμος:[3]

τροφίμης *CPR* 95.8 (early 3rd cent.)
τροφίμην *PBerlLeihg.* 23.13 (A.D. 252)

4) χέρσος:[4]

ἀρούρας ... χέρσας *PLond.* 1003 (iii, 259-60).6-7 (A.D. 562)
but γῆ χ[έ]ρσος *SB* 7670 = *PCairIsidor.* 4.11 (A.D. 299)
    τῆς χέρσου *PAberd.* 66.5 (A.D. 21); sim. *BGU* 915.20 (1st/2nd cent.:
        BL i, 83); *PLond.* 350 = *WChr.* 353.6 (A.D. 212); *PBaden* 90.24,
        etc. (3rd cent.); *PLond.* 483 (ii, 323-9).14,26,40,56 (A.D. 616)
    τὴν πᾶσαν χέρσον *CPR* 19 = *StudPal.* xx, 86.6 (A.D. 330)

c. Other adjectives which usually have two terminations in classical Greek
generally preserve this usage. They include simple adjectives in -μος as well

---

[1] φόριμος, -ον *AP*, *Cat.Cod.Astr.* Hsch., but ἡ φορίμη = a kind of astringent substance
Dsc. Orib. (*LSJ*, s.v.).

[2] φρόνιμος, -ον exc. Plu. (*LSJ*, s.v.).

[3] τρόφιμος, -ον, but ἡ τροφίμη Poll. (*LSJ*. s.v.).

[4] χέρσος, -ον (adj. after Hom.) always, incl. in the Ptol. papp. (*LSJ*, s.v.; Mayser i²,
2, 50).

as compound adjectives of all types, inherited and new,[1] as ἄκυρος,[2] ἔγκυος,[3] ἔρημος,[4] and ἕτοιμος.[5]

d. New formations of adjectives in -ιος, -αιος, etc., or those of which a feminine usage is not attested elsewhere in Greek, generally have a distinct feminine, as ὁμογνήσιος[6] and ἡμεραῖος.[7]

e. Some few adjectives which usually have three terminations elsewhere in Greek or fluctuate between two and three terminations appear occasionally as adjectives of two terminations.

1) Adjectives in -ιος.

a) ἑκούσιος:[8]

ἑκουσίου ἀπαλλα[γῆς] *CPR* 127 = *StudPal.* xx, 15.19 (A.D. 190)
ἑκουσίῳ γνώμῃ *PMon.* 1.29 (A.D. 574); *PLond.* 1733.14 (A.D. 594)
ἐκ[ο]ύσιον κατ[ο]χήν *PRyl.* 174.23 (A.D. 112); sim. *POxy.* 473 = *WChr.* 33.3 (A.D. 138-60); *PGrenf.* ii, 112.8-9 (A.D. 577?)
but ἑκουσίᾳ γνώμῃ *StudPal.* xx, 121.6 (A.D. 438); *StudPal.* iii, 237.5 (6th cent.); *PRossGeorg.* iii, 52.9 (A.D. 674); *BGU* 320.11-12 (Byz./Arab.); cf. *PColt* 15.2 (A.D. 512)

---

[1] I have analyzed the formation of compds. in the papyri of the Rom. and Byz. periods along the lines set out by Palmer, as a sequel to his Vol. i: *Accidence and Word-Formation*; Part i: *The Suffixes*. This material will be published in a separate monograph.

[2] E.g., ἀκύρου οὔσης *BGU* 415 = *MChr.* 178.20,31 (A.D. 102: *BL* i, 44), but cf. ἀκύρας οὔσης *PPanop.* 22.12: *ZPE* 10:2 (1973), 110 (A.D. 336). One ex. of a distinct fem. occurs in the Ptol. papp., elsewh. -ος, -ον (Mayser i², 2, 53).

[3] E.g., ἐνκύου (for ἐγκύου) οὔση[ς] *POxy.* 267 = *MChr.* 281.20 (A.D. 36).

[4] E.g., ἔρημον κώμην *PThead.* 16.12 (A.D. 307). Usu. ἔρημος, -ον, but ἐρήμη *Od.* S. and in the meaning "undefended action" in Att. prose: Antiph. Lys. Th. Pl. D. (*LSJ*, s.v.). Scyl. Str. fluctuate betw. two and three terminations in the Herc. papp. (Crönert, 184). It is excl. of two terminations in the Ptol. papp. (Mayser i², 2, 50).

[5] E.g., ἡ ὑπηρεσία ... ἕ[το]ιμος ἔστω *PFlor.* 267.3-4 (3rd cent.), but cf. ἐὰν μὲν ἑτοίμη ἦν ἡ θυγάτηρ μου *PTebt.* 419.9-11 (3rd cent.). In class. Gr., usu. ἑτοῖμος, -ον (ἕτοιμος from 5th cent. B.C. on), but ἑτοίμη *Il.* Hp., ἑτοίμα S. (*LSJ*, s.v.). Distinct fem. forms are used in the Ptol. papp. (Mayser i², 2, 52). In the NT, αἱ ἕτοιμοι Mt 25.10, but ἑτοίμην 2 Cor 9.5, 1 Pet 1.5 (cf. *BDF*, § 59.2).

[6] E.g., ὁμ[ο]γνησία ... ἀδελφή *PLond.* 1008 (iii, 265).8 (A.D. 561). Cf. also gen. sg. ὁμογνησίας *POxy.* 2858.6,33 (A.D. 171); *PCairMasp.* 110.11 (A.D. 565); but ὁμογνησίης *SB* 9317 b.9 (A.D. 148).

[7] E.g., ἡμεραίας (gen. sg.) *PLips.* 40 iii.5 (late 4th/early 5th cent.).

[8] ἑκούσιος, -α, -ον S. etc., but also -ος, -ον Antiph. E. S. Th. etc. (*LSJ*, s.v.).

b) ἐνιαύσιος:[1]

ἐνιαυσίου ἀποχῇ[ς] *PRossGeorg.* v, 25.12 (3rd cent.)
ἐνι[α]ύσιον ... λιτουργίαν *PSI* 86.10-11 (A.D. 367/75)
ἐνιαυσίου[ς] καταβολάς *SB* 6944.18 (edict of Hadrian)

c) οὐράνιος:[2]

οὐρανίου ... τύχης *PSI* 1422.31 (3rd cent.); *PStrassb.* 42 = *WChr.* 210.6
(A.D. 310); *PLips.* 34.17; 35.20 (ca. A.D. 375); sim. *PThead.* 49.3
(A.D. 307-24?); etc.
οὐράνιον τύχην *PLBat.* xi, 1 i.7; ii.6 (A.D. 338); *PStrassb.* 149 = *SB*
8753.11 (4th cent.); *PLips.* 46.6 (A.D. 371); *PLips.* 54 = *WChr.*
467.5-6 (ca. A.D. 376); *PFlor.* 75 = *WChr.* 433.9 (A.D. 380);
WChr. 434.10 (A.D. 390); *PSI* 185.6 (A.D. 425/55); *PCairMasp.*
328 ix.7 part. rest.; xii.6-7 (A.D. 521); 115.9 part. rest. (Byz.); etc.
but [ο]ὐρανίας ν[ί]κης *PCairMasp.* 295 ii.16 (6th cent.)
οὐρανίαν τύχην *PFlor.* 34.8 (A.D. 342); *PLips.* 52.6 part. rest. (A.D.
372); *PLond.* 483 (ii, 323-9).82 (A.D. 616); etc.

2) Adjectives in -ειος (ἐπιτήδειος):

ξενίαν ἐπιτήδειον *PGen.* 73 = *WChr.* 496.13 (prob. 2nd/3rd cent.)
but ἐπιτηδίαν *POxy.* 1899.15 (A.D. 476)

3) Adjectives in -ιμος (νόμιμος):[3]

νομίμου ἐπαύξεως *PCairMasp.* 26.16-17 (ca. A.D. 551)
νομίμου παραγραφῆς *PLond.* 483 (ii, 323-9).19-20 (A.D. 616); sim.
PColt 26.21 (A.D. 570)
νόμιμον ἀποταγήν *PCairMasp.* 97 V d.53-54 (Byz.)
but νομίμη *BGU* 1210 (19).60, with νομίμην (19).59, (56).146 (mid 2nd
cent.)
νομίμην *SB* 9770.6 (6th cent.); *POxy.* 1895.10 (A.D. 554); *CPR* 30 =
MChr. 290 ii.16 (6th cent.)

f. Only rarely is the masculine form of an adjective used for the feminine
when the adjective invariably occurs with three terminations elsewhere, e.g.,
σφραγ(ῖδα) ἀργυροῦν *POxy.* 113.23-24 (2nd cent.); κριθῆς ῥυπαροῦ *POxy.*
1542.7,10-11 (A.D. 307).

---

[1] ἐνιαύσιος, -α, -ον E. Hdt. X. inscrr. etc.; -ος, -ον Th. codd.Arist. and Ptol. papp.
(*LSJ*, s.v.; Mayser i², 2, 51; Crönert, 184 & n. 5).
[2] οὐράνιος, -α, -ον, but -ος, -ον sts. E. Pl. Ion. inscrr. Ptol. papp. & NT (*LSJ*, s.v.; Mayser
i², 2, 51; *BDF*, § 59.2).
[3] νόμιμος, -η, -ον, but -ος, -ον Isoc. Arist. (*LSJ*, s.v.).

But the use of the masculine for the feminine is especially frequent in participles, e.g., αὐτὴ ἀμοιβόμενος (for ἀμειβομένη) *MChr.* 361.17, with ἑκών (for ἑκοῦσα) same line (A.D. 360).[1]

The above evidence of the preference for a distinct feminine form reflects a general tendency which reached its final stage in Modern Greek, in which all adjectives have three terminations.[2] Greek adjectives of the first and second declensions adopted as loanwords in Coptic tended to retain their distinction of gender while losing their case and number, but the feminine occurs less frequently and is often replaced by the masculine and sometimes also by the neuter.[3]

2. Formation of case.

a. Adjectives of the first and second declensions with the feminine in -ᾱ (normally only after ε, ι, or ρ as in Attic) occasionally have forms in -η, parallel to the phenomenon observed in corresponding first declension nouns.[4] The converse substitution of -α for -η occurs sporadically.

1) Simple adjectives.

a) μικρός appears in the feminine as μικρά in Roman papyri but sometimes as μικρή in Byzantine; a by-form μικ(κ)ός, -ή, -όν also occurs.[5]

i. μικρά:

μικρά *PGiss.* 78.7 (ca. A.D. 117); *BGU* 615.10 (2nd cent.); sim. *PBrem.* 50.6; 63.24 (ca. A.D. 117); etc.

μικρᾶς *POxy.* 485 = *MChr.* 246.16 part. rest. (A.D. 178); *PSI* 50.16 (4th/5th cent.); *PLond.* 1708.170 (A.D. 567?); sim. *BGU* 697 = *WChr.* 321.10-11 (A.D. 145)

---

[1] For sim. exx. of lack of agreement in dental stem adjs., see below, pp. 130-1.

[2] Thumb, *Handbook*, § 108. See further Jannaris, § 308-10; Dieterich, 178-9. Contrary to the general tendency, some Koine authors, incl. Ph. Plu. Hippol. Dam. and Phlp., preferred the two termination use of those adjs. wh. fluctuated in class. Gr. (Crönert, 181(-2), n. 2). See further W. Kastner, *Die griechischen Adjective zweier Endungen auf* -ος (Heidelberg, 1967).

[3] For exx., see Böhlig, 123-8. There are comparatively few true adjs. native to Copt.; adj. relationship is normally expressed by an adnominal gen. Copt. adjs. are usu. used wo. distinction of gender and indeclinably.

[4] See above, pp. 3-4.

[5] μικκός is Dor. Boeot. Ion. (*LSJ*, s.v.). It is found in Att. inscrr. as a foreign proper name and sporadically (in the spelling μικά, etc.) as an adj. from 390 B.C. on (*MS*, 83). See further Thumb, *Hell.*, 56, 60, 65; Hatzidakis, *Einl.*, 157-8; Crönert, 297, n. 1; Palmer, 39. By the Rom. and Byz. periods, there was no distinction in speech betw. the -κ- and -κκ- spellings (see Vol. i, 154-65).

μικράν *BGU* 811.7 (A.D. 98-103); *SB* 7741.14 (1st half 2nd cent.?); *BGU* 2129.23 (2nd cent.); *BGU* 33.18 (2nd/3rd cent.: *BL* i, 10); sim. *SB* 9001 = *PMed.* 76.11 (2nd/3rd cent.)

ii. μικρή:

μικρῆς *POxy.* 1917.55,59,117 (6th cent.); *PMon.* 9.42 (A.D. 585)
Μικρῇ *BGU* 749.3 (Byz./Arab.)
μικρήν *POxy.* 1931.6-7 (5th cent.); *PCairMasp.* 2 iii.9 (A.D. 567: *BL* i, 100); *PLond.* 1676.4 (A.D. 566-73); *SB* 8987.13, with μικρᾶς **28,33** (A.D. 644/5); *PApoll.* 44.7 part. rest., 9; 45.6,14 (A.D. 703-15)

iii. μικ(κ)ός:

μικκή *PRyl.* 382.4 (early 2nd cent.); *SB* 9441 = *PMed.* 84.3 (4th cent.)
    μική *POxy.* 2153.18,25, with μικρόν 23 (3rd cent.); sim. *PSI* 831.7 (4th cent.: *BL* vi, 180)
μικκοῦ *SB* 9017 (11).3 (1st/2nd cent.)
μικῷ *PFay.* 127.13, with μικόν 12 (2nd/3rd cent.)
μικῇ *PMichael.* 100.1; 101.2 (1st half 3rd cent.)
    μεικκῇ *PMich.* 514.13 (3rd cent.)
Μικκήν *BGU* 906.8 (A.D. 34/35); sim. *SB* 7449.6: *BL* ii, 2, 136 (2nd half 5th cent.)
μικκόν *PMich.* 510.23 (2nd/3rd cent.); *PGissBibl.* 25.12 (3rd cent.); *POxy.* 2599.33 (3rd/4th cent.); *SB* 5747.10 (n.d.)
    μικόν *SB* 9524.14 (3rd cent.)
Μικκέ *SB* 6239.2: *BL* ii, 2, 136, inscr. (Gr.-Rom.)
μικκά (neut. pl.) *PJand.* 96.11 (3rd cent.)
μικῶν *POxy.* 1655.9 (3rd cent.)

b) Others:

παλαιῇ *PGrenf.* ii, 83.3 (5th cent.)
φανερῆς *PSI* 872.6 (6th cent.)
δευτέρης *SB* 10612.3 (7th/8th cent.)
cf. [ἡ]μετέρην *SB* 3980.4, inscr. (n.d.)

c) η > α:

προτεταγμένας (for -μένης) *PCairMasp.* 159-60.17-18, with παρούσης 19, etc. (A.D. 568)

2) Contracted adjectives.

a) α > η:

στολὴν πορφυρῆν *PLBat.* vi, 21.20 part. rest., 32 (A.D. 122)
φιάλη ἀργυρῆ (nom. sg.) *BGU* 388 = *MChr.* 91 ii.22 (2nd half 2nd cent.)
ἀργυρῆν *PSI* 240.12 (2nd cent.); cf. *PGM* 13.1001 (A.D. 346)

b) η > α:

λινᾶ (for λινῆ) *POxy.* 1051.16 (3rd cent.)
λάμναν χρυσᾶν ἢ ἀργυρᾶν *PGM* 10.26 (4th/5th cent.)

The tendency to substitute -η for -α after ρ, supported in some instances by preceding -η endings and in μικρή by the by-form μικκή, led to the complete shift of adjectives in -ρα, -ρας to -ρη, -ρης in Modern Greek.[1]

b. Adjectives of the first and second declensions sometimes occur with masculine or neuter forms in -ις/-ιν for -ιος/-ιον as observed very frequently in diminutives and related nouns of the second declension.[2]

δημόσις (for δημόσιος) *PMed.* 3.3 part. rest. (A.D. 1-14); *PMich.* 272.4,5 (A.D. 45/46)
δημόσιν (for δημόσιον) *PMich.* 331.4 (A.D. 41); sim. *PMich.* 345.17 (A.D. 52); *BGU* 1097.20 (A.D. 41-68); *PStrassb.* 21 = *PSarap.* 61.12 (ca. A.D. 125); *PHamb.* 80.5 (3rd cent.)
ἄξιν (for ἄξιον) *POxy.* 285.12 (ca. A.D. 50)

This phenomenon occurs much less frequently in adjectives than in the corresponding nouns because the new forms reflect a tendency toward shortened formations rather than the effect of phonological causes.[3] The analogy of other adjectives in -ος, -α, -ον may have been a factor in retaining the -o- in the masculine and neuter.[4]

c. Adjectives of the first and second declensions occur sporadically with endings of the third declension, usually in connection with nouns of the third declension, e.g., πέμπτους ἔτους *OBrüss Berl.* 28.2 (A.D. 73), sim. *PStrassb.* 141 = *SB* 8023.4-5 (A.D. 300/1); δεῖγμα λευκόινα (for λευκόινον) *POxy.* 113.5 (2nd cent.), or where homoioteleuton is possible, e.g., ἐνάτους (with the following ἔτους omitted) *PTebt.* 312.22 (A.D. 123/4), but cf. also τοῦ ἀληθινοῦς φιλοσόφου *PHamb.* 37.5-6 (2nd cent.).

d. Other irregularities in forms of adjectives of the first and second declensions consist mainly of orthographic variations of the same morpheme, e.g.,

---

[1] Jannaris, § 442; Thumb, *Handbook*, § 108.
[2] See above, pp. 25-27.
[3] See above, pp. 28-29.
[4] Cf. Georgacas, *CP* **43** (1948), 243-60.

nom. sg. γλυκυτάτηι (with false -ι adscript) *POxy.* 1767.26-27 (3rd cent.), or are due to scribal error by anticipation or repetition, e.g., ἡ πρᾶσις κυρίας (with final -ς added to the nom. sg.) *PCairIsidor.* 86.9 (A.D. 309).[1]

3. Contract adjectives.

a. Adjectives in -εος/-οῦς.

These material adjectives are usually contracted, but open forms sometimes occur in ἀργύρεος, χάλκεος, and χρύσεος, as well as in the new σμάλλεος. The following forms occur.

1) ἀργύρεος/-οῦς.[2]

a) Contracted:

ἀργυροῦς *PMur.* 89.6 part. rest., 9,11,16 (2nd cent.)
ἀργυρᾶ (nom. sg.) *StudPal.* xx, 60.6 (A.D. 243-9)
ἀργυρῆ (for ἀργυρᾶ) *BGU* 388 = *MChr.* 91 ii.22 (2nd half 2nd cent.)
ἀργυρᾶς (gen. sg.) *SB* 7398.3-4 (A.D. 118); cf. *Archiv* vi, p. 219, #4.3 (A.D. 117/18)
ἀργυρῷ *POxy.* 1449.44 (A.D. 213-17); *BGU* 75 ii.14 (2nd cent.: *BL* i, 15)
ἀργυροῦν *PStrassb.* 216.9 (A.D. 126/7); *BGU* 590 i.20, with ἀργυρᾶ 21 (A.D. 177/8); *BGU* 162 = *WChr.* 91.7,12 (A.D. 180-93); *POxy.* 113.23-24 (2nd cent.); *PFuadCrawford* 8.8 part. rest., 12 (2nd cent.?); *SB* 8384.10 (A.D. 260-8); *SB* 6222.33 (late 3rd cent.)
ἀργυρῆν *PSI* 240.12 (2nd cent.)
ἀργυρᾶν *SB* 8384.12 (A.D. 260-8)
ἀργυρᾶ (neut. pl.) *BGU* 1101.8 (13 B.C.); *BGU* 1036 = *MChr.* 118.14 (A.D. 108); *PCairPreis.* 31.80 = *PRossGeorg.* ii, 18.318 (A.D. 140); *BGU* 162 = *WChr.* 91.10 (A.D. 180-93); *POxy.* 1051.19 (3rd cent.); *PBaden* 54.4 (5th cent.); *PRein.* 108.9 (6th cent.); etc.
ἀργυρῶν *PRyl.* 125.18 (A.D. 28/29); *BGU* 22.32 (A.D. 114); *POxy.* 1272.11 (A.D. 144); *SB* 9372.17 part. rest. (2nd cent.); *PHamb.* 10.45-46 (2nd cent.)
ἀργυροῖς *SB* 9159 = *PMilVogl.* 102.6 (2nd cent.); *PLond.* 1727.33 (A.D. 583/4)

b) Open:

ἀργύραιον (for ἀργύρεον[3]) *POxy.* 2419.9, sim. 10 (6th cent.)
ἀργύρε[ο]ν *PCairMasp.* 167.11 (6th cent.)

---

[1] See Introd. above, p. XIX.
[2] This adj. is usu. contr. in the mag. papp., but open forms occur: ἀργυρέου *PGM* 7.581 (3rd cent.); ἀργυρέαν *PGM* 4.826 (4th cent.).
[3] For the interchange of αι and ε, see Vol. i, 191-3.

ἀργύρεα, ἀργύρεον, ἀργυρέων *PLond.* 1007 (iii, 262-4).3,4,7, etc., with
    ἀργυρᾶ (neut. pl.) 26 (ca. A.D. 558)
    ἀργύρεα *SB* 9754.3 (A.D. 647)
ἀργυρίων (for ἀργυρέων) *PMich.* 343.4, with ἀργυροῦν also 4 (twice)
    (A.D. 54/55)

2) ἐρεοῦς/ἐριοῦς (contracted forms only):[1]

    ἐρεᾶ (nom. sg.) *POxy.* 2474.3 (3rd cent.)
    ἐρεᾶς *POxy.* 2110.5, etc. (A.D. 370)
    ἐρεᾷ *BGU* 1210 (71).182; (75).187; (76).188 (mid 2nd cent.)
    ἐριοῦν *BGU* 816.18-19 (3rd cent.); sim. *PGissBibl.* 32.18 (3rd/4th cent.)
        ἐραιοῦν *PRossGeorg.* iii, 1.9 (A.D. 270: *BL* iii, 156)
        ἐρεοῦν *BGU* 928.21 (A.D. 311: *BL* iii,15); *PRossGeorg.* iii, 12.6 (6th cent.)
        αἰραιοῦν (for ἐρεοῦν) *PSI* 1082.13 (4th cent.)
        αἰριῶν (for ἐρεοῦν) *PMilVogl.* 256.20-21 (2nd/3rd cent.)
    ἐρεᾶ (neut. pl.) *POxy.* 921.2,9 (3rd cent.)
        ἐρᾶ *PVars.* 26.17: *BL* iii, 254 (4th/5th cent.)
    ἐρεῶν *POxy.* 2593.12 (2nd cent.); *SB* 9305.7 (4th cent.)
    ἐρεαῖς *BGU* 16 = *WChr.* 114.12 (A.D. 159/60)
    ἐρεᾶς *PFouad* 10.8 (A.D. 120)
    cf. ἐρεινᾶ (neut. pl.) *PGrenf.* ii, 111 = *WChr.* 135.13 (5th/6th cent.)

3) ἠλεκτροῦς (contracted only):[2]

    ἠλεκτροῦν *PCairMasp.* 340 V.32, with διαχρυσᾶ 31, ἀργυροῦν 36, χαλκοῦν
    77,78 (6th cent.)

4) λινοῦς (contracted forms only):

    λινῆ (nom. sg.) *POxy.* 2474.3 (3rd cent.)
        λινᾶ (for λινῆ) *POxy.* 1051.16 (3rd cent.)
    λινοῦ *SB* 7536 = *PLBat.* i, 7.9 (4th cent.); *StudPal.* x, 188.3 part. rest.
    (4th cent.)
    λινοῦν *PTebt.* 406.17,18 (ca. A.D. 266); *PSI* 287.15 (A.D. 377); *POxy.*
    1905.6 (late 4th/early 5th cent.); cf. *PColt* 20.27 (A.D. 558); etc.
        λεινοῦν *POxy.* 285.11 (ca. A.D. 50); *BGU* 1036 = *MChr.* 118.14 (A.D.
        108)
    λινῆν *BGU* 93.7-8: *BL* i, 18 (2nd/3rd cent.)
        λεινῆν *PSI* 1117.13 (2nd cent.)
    λινᾶ *POxy.* 921.9 (3rd cent.); *POxy.* 1277.9, with λινῶν 7 (A.D. 255);
    PGrenf. ii, 111 = *WChr.* 135.12 (5th/6th cent.); *PCairMasp.* 6 V.88
    (ca. A.D. 567); etc.
    λινοῦς *POslo* 56.4 (2nd cent.)

---

[1] For the variation in spelling, see Vol. i, 253.
[2] This adj. is new; ἠλέκτρινος Call. Luc. Hld.; ἠλεκτρώδης Hp. Philostr. Cf. Palmer, 23.

5) μολιβοῦς/μολυβοῦς (contracted forms only):[1]

μολιβῇ *PLond.* 1823.9 (4th cent.)
μολυβοῦν *PAberd.* 181.10 (A.D. 41-69); *POxy.* 1648.62 (late 2nd cent.);
    PTebt. 406.22 (ca. A.D. 266)
μολιβᾶ *PMich.* 312.13 (A.D. 34)

6) πορφυροῦς (contracted forms only):

πορφυροῦς *PTebt.* 405.9, with φορφυροῦ[ν] *sic* 4 (3rd cent.)
πορφυρᾶ *OTait* 1948.1 (3rd cent.)
πορφυροῦν *PRyl.* 151.14 (A.D. 40); *POxy.* 1153.14 (1st cent.); *SB* 9158.18
    (5th cent.); *PCairMasp.* 6 V.81 (ca. A.D. 567); cf. *PDura* 30.17,19
    part. rest. (A.D. 232); 33.4-5 (A.D. 240-50)
πορφυρῆν *PLBat.* vi, 21.20,32 (A.D. 122)
πορφυρῶν *POxy.* 531 = *WChr.* 482.14 (2nd cent.); *PHamb.* 10.21, with
    πορφυροῦν 31 (2nd cent.)
cf. φόρφυρεν (for πόρφυρον) *PRyl.* 242.9 (3rd cent.)

7) σιδηροῦς (contracted forms only):[2]

[σι]δηρᾶ *PRyl.* 110.19 (A.D. 259)
σιδηρᾶς (gen. sg.) *PMichael.* 18 iii.3 (mid 3rd cent.: *BL* iv, 51)
σιδηροῦν *POxy.* 1035.13 (A.D. 143); sim. *PCairMasp.* 6 V.47 (ca. A.D.
    567)
[σ]ιδηρᾶν *SB* 9294.18 (6th cent.)
σιδηροῖ[ς] *PCairMasp.* 303.14 (A.D. 553)
σιδηραῖς *PLond.* 1164 (iii, 154-67) h.9 (A.D. 212)
σιδηρᾶς (acc. pl.) *BGU* 544.8 (A.D. 138-61)

8) σμάλλεος (open only):[3]

σμάλλεα (neut. pl.) *POxy.* 921.6 (3rd cent.)

9) ὑαλοῦς/ὑελοῦς (contracted forms only):[4]

ὑαλῇ *PRossGeorg.* ii, 29.1 (2nd cent.)

---

[1] For the variation in spelling, see Vol. i, 271.

[2] Dbtfl. σιδηραίου (for σιδηρέου, or σιτηραίου w. *BL* ii, 2, 165?) *StudPal.* xx, 217.9 (A.D. 580). Only contr. forms occur in mag. papp., e.g., σιδηροῦ *PGM* 7.631 (3rd cent.); σιδηρᾶς *PGM* **61.**12, w. σιδηρόν (for -οῦν) 31 (late 3rd cent.); etc.

[3] A new adj. formation connected w. μαλλός & equiv. to μαλλοειδής (Palmer, 23).

[4] For the variation in spelling, see Vol. i, 282.

ὑα[λ]οῦν *SB* 9238.19 (A.D. 198-211)
   ὑελοῦν *PLBat.* vi, 49a ii.3 (prob. A.D. 205)
ὑαλαῖ *POxy.* 1294.6 (late 2nd/early 3rd cent.)
   ὑελᾶ (for ὑελαῖ) *POxy.* 741.15 (2nd cent.)
ὑελᾶ *PLond.* 191 (ii, 264-5).16 (A.D. 103-17)
ὑαλῶν *POxy.* 2058.34 (6th cent.)
   ὑελῶν *PFay.* 104.1,2 (late 3rd cent.)
   prob. also ὑαιλῶν *PLBat.* vi, 49b ii.8 (prob. A.D. 205)

10) χάλκεος/χαλκοῦς.[1]

a) Contracted:

χαλκοῦς *POxy.* 1269.22-23,36 (early 2nd cent.); *PLBat.* xvii, 1 i.1, with
   χαλκαῖ 16, etc. (A.D. 138-61)
χαλκοῦν *PRyl.* 124.36 (1st cent.); *BGU* 1036 = *MChr.* 118.16 (A.D. 108);
   PRossGeorg. ii, 25.8 part. rest., 10 (ca. A.D. 159); *PStrassb.* 225.4 (2nd
   half 2nd cent.); *PErl.* 21.10 (ca. A.D. 195); *BGU* 338.1-5 (2nd/3rd
   cent.); *PStrassb.* 131 = *SB* 8013.9 (A.D. 363); etc.
χαλκῆν *BGU* 265 = *WChr.* 459.21 (A.D. 148)
χαλκοῖ *POxy.* 109.21 (late 3rd/4th cent.)
χαλκαῖ *POxy.* 2146.5 (3rd cent.)
χαλκᾶ *PMich.* 343.5 (A.D. 54/55); *BGU* 590 i.13 (A.D. 180-93)
cf. ὀριχαλκοῖς *PLond.* 1727.34 (A.D. 583/4)
   ὀρευχαλκοῦν *sic* *PColt* 176.7 (6th/7th cent.)[2]

b) Open:

χάλκεος *PRyl.* 110.15, with [χα]λκῆ 16, χαλκῆ 17, χαλκοῦν 18 (A.D. 259)
χάλκεον *CPR* 232.12 (2nd/3rd cent.)

11) χλωροῦς (contracted only):

χλωρᾶς (acc. pl.) *POxy.* 1211.8 (2nd cent.)

12) χρύσεος/χρυσοῦς.

a) Contracted:

χρυσοῦς (nom. sg.) *PLond.* 198 (ii, 172-3).10 (A.D. 169-77)
χρυσοῦ *POslo* 130.15 (2nd half 1st cent.); *POxy.* 1117.1 (ca. A.D. 178);
   POxy. 1413.25 (A.D. 270-5)

---

[1] Open forms are also found rarely in Trag. & codd. Pl. (*LSJ*, s.v.). Only contr. forms occur in mag. papp., e.g., χαλκῆ *PGM* 7.442 (3rd cent.).

[2] ὀρειχάλκινος Pl. The noun is ὀρείχαλκος, Lat. *orichalcum* (*LSJ*, s.v.). Cf. Palmer, **23**.

χρυσοῦ⟦ν⟧ *POxy.* 259 = *MChr.* 101.11 (A.D. 23)

χρυσῶ (for χρυσοῦν) *CPR* 19 = *StudPal.* xx, 86.10 (A.D. 330)

χρυσοῦν *SB* 7260 ii b.8 = *PMich.* 121 R II ii.8 (A.D. 42); *PSI* 1116.5
(2nd cent.); *PLond.* 1178 = *WChr.* 156.12-13 (A.D. 194); *PAntin.*
93.34 (4th cent.); *PSI* 216.2 (A.D. 534); etc.

χρυσõ(ν) *PRyl.* 125.16, with χρυσο(ῦν) 17 (A.D. 28/29)

χρεσόν (for χρυσοῦν) *SB* 6024.7, sim. 9 (Byz.)

χρυσῆν, χρυσοῦν *PMich.* 343.2,3 twice (A.D. 54/55)

χρυσᾶ *BGU* 729 = *MChr.* 167.12 (A.D. 144); *PCornell* 9.13 (A.D. 206);
PCairMasp. 4.17 (ca. A.D. 567); *PPar.* 21b.28 (A.D. 592); etc.

χρυσῶν *BGU* 1103.13 (13 B.C.); *POxy.* 267 = *MChr.* 281.6 (A.D. 36);
POxy. 265.3 part. rest. (A.D. 81-95); *POxy.* 1272.9 (A.D. 144); *SB*
7816 = *PSI* 1263.19 (2nd cent.); *PFay.* 20.12 (late 3rd/early 4th
cent.); etc.

χρυσοῖς *POxy.* 1274.17 (3rd cent.); *PLond.* 1727.33 (A.D. 583/4)

b) Open:[1]

χρυσέας (gen. sg.) *PMon.* 7.74 (A.D. 583)

χρύσια *PCairPreis.* 31.80 = *PRossGeorg.* ii, 18.318 (A.D. 140)

χρύσεα, χρυσέων *SB* 9763.6,16 (A.D. 457-74)

The open forms of these adjectives found occasionally along with the more
common contracted forms in the papyri and elsewhere in the Koine[2] could be
an Ionic legacy.[3] Neither the contracted nor the open forms have survived in
Modern Greek. Most ancient contract adjectives of the first and second declensions
have shifted to the simple *o-* and *a-*stem declensions, as χρυσός.[4] This shift was
facilitated by the identity of the contract declension with the simple declension
of *o-* and *a-*stems in all cases except the nom. and acc. sg. masc. and neut.

---

[1] Dbtfl. χρύσ[ε]α *PCairMasp.* 167.11: *BL* i, 448, w. ἀργύρε[ο]ν also 11 (6th cent.?).
Open forms sts. occur in Trag. dialogue and in prose: codd.X. Plu. Apollod. Ant.Lib. (*LSJ*,
s.v.). Both contr. and open forms occur freq. in the mag. papp., e.g., χρυσοῦν, χρυσοῦ *PGM*
4.825,941 (4th cent.); χρυσῶ *PGM* 12.207 (A.D. 300-350); χρυσᾶ *PGM* 7.168 (3rd cent.);
but χρυσέου *PGM* 7.580 (3rd cent.); χρύσεον *PGM* 70.11 (late 3rd/early 4th cent.); *PGM*
4.699,700,1027-8,2842-3 (4th cent.); χρύσεα *PGM* 4.665,675-6 (4th cent.).

[2] Adjs. in -εος are always contr. in Att. inscrr. (*MS*, 149). At Perg., χρυσοῦς and χρυσέα
occur (Schweizer, 141-2). Contr. and open forms are also found elsewh. in Asia Minor, w.
open forms prevailing at Magn. (Nachmanson, 123). In the Ptol. papp., only contr. forms
occur, exc. in poetry (Mayser i², 2, 53-54). Open forms of χρύσεος are found in codd. of
the NT (*BDF* § 45). Koine authors prefer contr. forms, but open forms are found even
in the Atticists (Crönert, 178 & nn. 3-4; Schmid iii, 19-20; iv, 580).

[3] So Kretschmer, *Entst.*, 22-25.

[4] Thumb, *Handbook*, § 109a; Jannaris, § 320-1; Schwyzer i, 586, n. 1. Other ancient
contr. adjs. appear in MGr. w. a diff. suffix, as χάλκινος (Thumb, *ibid.*).

b. Adjectives in -οος/-οῦς.

Considerable variation is found in the use of contracted and open forms and heteroclitic by-forms.

1) ἀθρόος is normally uncontracted in both the adjective and the adverb:[1]

ἀθρόον *PAmh.* 79.64 (A.D. 186)
ἀθρώων (for ἀθρόων) *WChr.* 16 = *PBrem.* 1.3 (ca. A.D. 115: *BL* v, 19)
ἀθρόως *POxy.* 1117.23 (ca. A.D. 178); *PLeit.* 8.9 (ca. A.D. 250); *PLips.*
119 V ii.2 (A.D. 274); *POxy.* 1252 V.31 (A.D. 288-95)
but cf. ἀθρός (for ἀθρόος) *SB* 8316.3, inscr. (Rom.)

2) εὔνους is normally contracted:

εὔνου *StudPal.* v, 125 — xx, 61 ii.7 (3rd cent.)
cf. εὔνουν *SB* 7871.19, inscr. (Rom.)
εὐνουστερ[*POxy.* 2611.7 (A.D. 192/3)
εὐνουστάτη *PLond.* 1724.7 (A.D. 578-82); sim. *POxy.* 2474.5, etc. (3rd cent.)
but εὐνόους *PMilVogl.* 73.7 (2nd cent.)

3) ἐπίπλοος is normally uncontracted:

ἐπίπλοα *BGU* 183 = *MChr.* 313.19 (A.D. 85); *CPR* 28 = *MChr.* 312.12
(A.D. 110)
ἐπιπλόων *BGU* 86 = *MChr.* 306.8,14 (A.D. 155)

4) Multiplicatives in -πλοῦς are contracted regularly, e.g., ἁπλοῦν *BGU* 2117.10 (late 2nd cent.); διπλοῦν *POxy.* 1752.3 (A.D. 378); τριπλοῦν *BGU* 159 = *WChr.* 408.9 (A.D. 216); τετραπλοῦ *PSI* 1055.13 (A.D. 265).

Note. The ordinal ὄγδοος appears in various forms, including ὄγδους and ὄγδον. See below, pp. 200-201.

5) Adjectival compounds in -χοος indicating capacity have open forms, but ἡμίχοον used substantively appears often in the contracted form ἡμίχουν.[2] See above, p. 84.

6) Compounds in -χροος designating color are usually inflected according to the contract declension, but open forms are found occasionally in several

---

[1] ἀθρόος/ἁθρόος Hom. Att., but contr. ἄθρους Ar. D. Hyp. (*LSJ*, s.v.). ἀθροῦν is the only form attested in the Ptol. papp. (Mayser i², 2, 54, w. lit.). Koine authors tend to prefer open forms (Crönert, 166(-7), n. 6; Schmid i, 104; ii, 72; iii, 98; iv, 120).

[2] The Ptol. papp. have ἡμίχουν and δωδεκάχου contr., but open forms w. other numerals (Mayser i², 2, 54).

adjectives as well as forms of the Attic second declension in μελίχρως;[1] some heteroclitic dental and *s*-stem forms also occur as well as by-forms in -χρωμος.

a) ἰδιόχρωμος:[2]

ἰδιόχρωμον *BGU* 327.5 = *MChr.* 61.6 (A.D. 176: *BL* i, 38); *POxy.* 109.7, with ἰδιόχρωμα 4 (late 3rd/4th cent.); *POxy.* 1645.10 (A.D. 308)

b) λευκομυόχρους:

λευκομυόχρουν *BGU* 1066.6 (A.D. 98); *PLond.* 303 = *MChr.* 160.16 (A.D. 142); *BGU* 228.4 abbrev. (2nd/3rd cent.)

λευκομυώχρουν *PIFAO* i, 11.11 (A.D. 123)

c) λευκόχρους.[3]

i. Contracted:

λευκόχρου[ς] *CPR* 57.5 (A.D. 211-17)

λευκόχρῳ *PMich.* 262.2 (A.D. 35/36)

λευκόχρουν *BGU* 912.10, etc., with μυούχρουν 40: *BL* i, 82 (A.D. 33); *POxy.* 1463.10 (A.D. 215); *BGU* 316 = *MChr.* 271.14 (A.D. 359)

ii. Open:

λευκοχρόαι̣ (for -χρόας, gen. sg. fem.) *PLond.* 333 = *MChr.* 176.22 (A.D. 166)

[λευκ]οχρόῳ *CPR* 55.6 (A.D. 193-211); sim. *StudPal.* xx, 29.12-13 (A.D. 226)

λευκοχρόη *CPR* 64.9 (A.D. 227)

λευκόχροον *POslo* 134.12 (4th cent.)

iii. By-form in -χρωμος:

λευκόχρωμο[ν] *POxy.* 1708.10 (A.D. 311)

---

[1] Forms of μελίχρως are 3 times more freq. than forms of μελίχρους; many occurrences of the word are abbrev. μελιχ( ). Besides μελίχρως, the Ptol. papp. also have λευκόχρως and μελάγχρως alternating w. μελίχρους/-χροος, λευκόχρους, and μελάγχρους/-χροος/-χρης as well as αὐτόχρους/-χροος and λευκομυόχρους (Mayser i², 2, 57-58). For the formation of these adjs., not widely attested outside the papp., see Schwyzer i, 450, 453.

[2] ἰδιόχρωμος Artem. (*LSJ*, s.v.).

[3] λευκόχρους E. Arist. Aret. Ptol.; λευκόχρως Arist. Eub. Theoc. Alex. (*LSJ*, s.v.).

d) μελάγχρους.[1]

i. Contracted:

μελάγχρους *SB* 9146.4 (6th/7th cent.)

ii. s-stem:

μελανχρής *PGrenf.* i, 45 = *WChr.* 200 A.4 (19 B.C.)

e) μελανόχρους.[2]

i. Contracted:

μελανόχρου *PLond.* 333 = *MChr.* 176.23 (A.D. 166)
μελανόχρουν *BGU* 2040.11 (2nd cent.)

ii. Open:

μελανόχροον *POxy.* 2998.6-7 (late 3rd cent.)

iii. Dental stem:

μελανόχρωτα *SB* 9214.12 (A.D. 311)

f) μελιτόχροος:[3]

μελιτοχρώου *PGrenf.* ii, 100.13 (A.D. 683)

g) μελίχρους.[4]

i. Contracted:

μελίχρους *PMich.* 281.2 (for acc.) (1st cent.); *CPR* 59.6 (A.D. 218-21);
    SB 5274 = *PLBat.* ii, 7.5, with μελιχρόου 8 (A.D. 225); *CPR* 73.8
    (A.D. 222-35); *CPR* 87.5; 88.3; 91.4; etc. (1st half 3rd cent.)
μελίχρο(υν) *POxy.* 1209.15 (A.D. 251-3)
cf. μελίχρος *POxy.* 2349.2 (A.D. 70); *CPR* 95.6 (early 3rd cent.)

ii. Open:

μ[ελί?]χρωος *PMich.* 264-5.17-18 (A.D. 37)
μελιχρόου *SB* 5274 = *PLBat.* ii, 7.8 (A.D. 225)
μελιχρόωι *PSI* 1131.11, with μελίχρωι 4, [μ]ελίχρως 29 (A.D. 41/44)

---

[1] μελάγχρους Hdt. Hp. Plu. etc.; μελαγχρής Cratin. Eup. Antiph. Men. etc. (*LSJ*, s.v.); also Ptol. papp. (Mayser i², 2, 58).
[2] μελανόχρως E. Arist. Theoc. (*LSJ*, s.v.).
[3] μελιτόχρους Sch.Nic. (*LSJ*, s.v.).
[4] μελίχρους *AP*; μελίχρως *AP*, Ptol. Q.S. Tryph. (*LSJ*, s.v.).

iii. Attic second declension:

μελίχρως *BGU* 1059.19 (30 B.C.-A.D. 14); *PSI* 1130.5,7 part. rest., with
μελίχρωι 9 (A.D. 25); *PMich.* 230.32 (A.D. 48); *PMilVogl.* 235.4 (1st
cent.); *POxy.* 722 = *MChr.* 358.7 (A.D. 91/107); *PFlor.* 81.2 (A.D.
103); *BGU* 2053.1 (early 2nd cent.); *PRyl.* 153.46 (A.D. 138-61); etc.
μελίχρω (gen.) *POxy.* 99.4, with [μ]ελίχρως 3 (A.D. 55); *POxy.* 2843.10,
(acc.) 12-13, with μελίχρως 7,18 (A.D. 86)
μελίχρωι (gen.) *POxy.* 2720.15 (A.D. 41-54)
μελίχρωι (dat.) *PSI* 1130.9 (A.D. 25); 1131.4, with [μ]ελίχρως 29 (A.D.
41/44); *BGU* 177 = *MChr.* 253.3, with μελίχρως 2 (A.D. 46/47); *CPR*
1 = *StudPal.* xx, 1.4, with μελίχρως 2 part. rest., 3 (A.D. 83/84);
PLond. 141 (ii, 181-2).4, with μελίχρως 3 (A.D. 88)
μελίχρω (acc.) *SB* 7555.12 (A.D. 154)

iv. Dental stem:

μελίχρωτ[α] (for -τος) *POxy.* 73.28, with μελίχρως 13, μελίχρω 20
(all 1st hand) (A.D. 94)

h) μυόχρους.

i. Contracted:

μυόχρους *BGU* 1568.4 (A.D. 261)
μυόχρουν *StudPal.* xxii, 20.29, sim. 5 (A.D. 4); *PMich.* 121 R I iii, xiii
(A.D. 42); *PGen.* 23 = *MChr.* 264.4 (A.D. 70); *PMich.* 551.18-19 (A.D.
103); *PSI* 1405.10 (A.D. 134); *PLond.* 313 (ii, 197-8).17 (A.D. 148); etc.
μυούχρουν *BGU* 912.40 (A.D. 33); *PLond.* 282 (ii, 194).12 (A.D.
69); *PSI* 38.6 (A.D. 101)
cf. μυόχρον *BGU* 584.4 (A.D. 44)

ii. Open:

μυόχροον *PSI* 1417.8 (A.D. 290/1)
μυόχροο(ι) *SB* 7365.114 (A.D. 114: *BL* v, 100)

iii. By-form:

μυόχρωμ(ον) *StudPal.* xxii, 101.7 (2nd cent.); *PMerton* 20.3 (A.D. 184?)
μυόχρωμον *POxy.* 1707.6 (A.D. 204); *PLBat.* xvi, 15.6 (A.D. 236);
PCornell 13.12 (A.D. 288)
μυόχρομον *PBerlLeihg.* 21.7 (A.D. 309)

i) μυρόχροος:

μυρό[χρ]οος *SB* 3912.3-4, inscr. (Xtn.)

j) πυροσιτόχροος:

πυροσειτόχρο�[ς] *SB* 7365.110 (A.D. 114: *BL* v, 100)

k) πυρρόχρους.

i. Contracted:

πυρρόχρους *PRyl.* 134.16 (A.D. 34); 140.12 (A.D. 36)

ii. By-form:

πυρρόχρωμον *PSarap.* 10.4 (A.D. 124)
φυρόχρωμον *PBaden* 19.5 (A.D. 110)

l) σιτόχρους.

i. Contracted:

σιτόχρουν *PSI* 1031.17-18 (A.D. 134); *PFlor.* 51 = *MChr.* 186.12 (A.D. 138-61)

ii. Open·

σιτοχρόου *BGU* 986.10-11 (A.D. 117-38)
σιτοχρόους *PFay.* 301 descr. (A.D. 167)

iii. By-form:

σειτόχρωμο[ς] *PMich.* 527.8-9 (A.D. 186-8)

m) χρυσόχροος:

χρυσωχρόων *PColt* 18.27 (A.D. 537)

4. Adjectives of the Attic second declension in -ως, -ων.

Besides the heteroclitic μελίχρως immediately above, adjectives belonging to this declensional type are ἵλεως, αἰγόκερως (used exclusively as a substantive in horoscopes: see above, p. 32), ἀγήρως, and ὑπεργήρως. ὑπόχρεως has generally shifted to the regular uncontracted second declension, while ἀξιόχρεος is alone attested (with ἀξιόχρον once).

a. ἵλεως:[1]

ἵλεως *POxy.* 939 = *WChr.* 128.7 (4th cent.); cf. *SB* 8687.1, inscr. (n.d.)

b. ἀγήρως:[2]

ἀγέρον (for ἀγήρων acc. sg. masc., with ω > ο 6 other times) *POxy.* 1871.2 (late 5th cent.)

c. ὑπέργηρως:[3]

ὑπέργηρως *PGiss.* 59 iv.14 (A.D. 119/20)

d. ὑπόχρεως/ὑπόχρεος.[4]

1) ὑπόχρεως:

ὑπόχρεως *PLips.* 10 = *MChr.* 189 ii.29 (A.D. 240)
[ὑπο]χρέω *BGU* 239.5-6: *BL* i, 29 (A.D. 159/60)
   [ὑ]πο[χρέ]ω *PFlor.* 86 = *MChr.* 247.13, with dat. ὑποχρέῳ 20 (late
   1st cent.)

2) ὑπόχρεος:

ὑπόχρεος *SB* 4415.11 part. rest., with -χρέου 8 (A.D. 144); *PCairIsidor.*
   68.16 (prob. A.D. 309/10)
ὑποχρέου *MChr.* 88 iii.23-24 (A.D. 141+); *BGU* 741 = *MChr.* 244.31
   part. rest. (A.D. 143/4); *PFlor.* 97.4 (2nd cent.); *BGU* 907.9,13 (A.D.
   180-93); *BGU* 118 i.11 (A.D. 188/9); *POxy.* 1538.9 abbrev. (early
   3rd cent.); *PLips.* 9 = *MChr.* 211.32 (A.D. 233); *SB* 5341 = *PLBat.*
   vi, 29.22,36,46 (A.D. 133); *PFlor.* 56 = *MChr.*24 1.11 (A.D. 234); etc.
ὑπόχρεον *BGU* 114 = *MChr.* 372 ii.18 (2nd cent.)
ὑπόχρεοι *BGU* 1053 = *MChr.* 105 ii.16 (13 B.C.); *PLBat.* vi, 19.25, with
   ὑποχρέου 22 (A.D. 118)
   ὑπόχριοι *PMich.* 333-4.23 (A.D. 52)
ὑποχρέοις *BGU* 362 xi.21 (A.D. 215)

3) Ambiguous forms:

ὑποχρέῳ *SB* 7817 = *PSI* 1328.24, with ὑπ[ο]χρέου 63 (A.D. 201); *BGU*
   362 xv.3; frag. iv.5 (A.D. 215)

---

[1] ἵλεως is also found in the Ptol. papp. (Mayser i², 2, 55).
[2] Cf. also ἀγή[ρ]ως in a citation from Hom. in *PCairMasp.* 295 iii.2 (late 6th cent.).
ἀγήρως, Hom. and Att. contr. of ἀγήραος, is attested in *Il. Od.* (also ἀγήραος) Hes. Pi. S. E.
Th. Ar. Pl. Jul. (*LSJ*, s.v.).
[3] ὑπέργηρως A. Ph. Babr. Luc.; ὑπέργηρος codd.*Gloss.* Vett.Val. (*LSJ*, s.v.).
[4] ὑπόχρεος inscrr. Plb. D.H. (*LSJ*, s.v.).

ὑποχρέωι *PBrem.* 68.9 (A.D. 99)
ὑποχρέων *POxy.* 1027 = *MChr.* 199a.1-2 part. rest., 8 (mid 1st cent.);
  PCairIsidor. 76.15 (A.D. 318)

e. ἀξιόχρεος:[1]

ἀξιοχρέου *PBeattyPanop.* 2.115,282 (A.D. 300); cf. *PMur.* 115.15 (A.D.
  124)
ἀξιόχρεον *PHarris* 67 ii.8 (ca. A.D. 150?)
but ἀξιώχρον *PGrenf.* ii, 41 = *MChr.* 183.22 (A.D. 46)
ἀξιόχρεοι SB 7350.24 (late 3rd/early 4th cent.)
ἀξιόχρεα *BGU* 909 = *WChr.* 382.25 (A.D. 359)
ἀξιοχρέων SB 8038.9 (prob. 1st cent.: *BL* iii, 199); *BGU* 747 = *WChr.*
  35 i.6 part. rest. (A.D. 139); *PSI* 1125.4 (A.D. 302)
ἀξιοχρέους SB 7558.34 (A.D. 172/3?); *PBeattyPanop.* 1.369,402 part.
  rest. (A.D. 298)

B. ADJECTIVES OF THE FIRST AND THIRD DECLENSIONS

1. *u*-stem adjectives.

a. Heteroclitic *o*-stem forms appear occasionally in the gen. and dat. sg.,
but the gen. sg. is usually the *i*-stem form -εως.

1) Gen. -ου (often through associative force of context):

παχήου (for παχέος) *POxy.* 1535 V.9-10, with παχήων (for παχέων) 4
  (A.D. 249/59: *BL* iv, 62)
τοῦ ὀξέου δρόμου *POxy.* 2115.6-7 (before A.D. 346: *BL* iii, 141); *PSI*
  1108.9 (A.D. 381); *PLond.* 1798.2 (A.D. 470)
κλυκύου (for γλυκέος) *PSI* 831.26 (4th cent.: *BL* vi, 180)

2) Gen. -εως (phonetically equivalent to -εος):[2]

τοῦ ὀξέως δρόμου *POxy.* 1913.10,41,57 (ca. A.D. 555?); *PGot.* 9.5-6,15
  (A.D. 564: *BL* v, 36); *POxy.* 2024.11 (late 6th cent.)
cf. also τοῦ ὀξεύρ(ς) δρούμου *sic POxy.* 2032.55 (6th cent.)

---

[1] ἀξιόχρεως Att., -χρεος Ion.: Hdt. (v.l. -χρεως) Hp.; Boeot. acc. pl. -χρειας prob. rest.
in an inscr.; neut. pl. -χρεα Hdt. (*LSJ*, s.v.). In the Ptol. papp., the forms ἀξιοχρείωι, -χρέους,
ἀξιόχρον, & nom. -χρους appear, as well as ἰδιόχρεα (Mayser i², 2, 55).

[2] For the interchange of o and ω, see Vol. i, 275-7.

3) Dat. -είῳ:

ὀξείῳ νοσήμ[ατι] *PRein.* 92.12 (A.D. 392)

b. The acc. sg. neut. appears as παχήν in *POxy.* 1300.9 (5th cent.). This spelling represents the interchange of η and υ,[1] and the erroneous addition of final -ν.[2]

c. ἥμισυς has the following inflectional variations in the papyri.[3]

1) The nom.-acc. neut. ἥμισυ is sometimes used indeclinably, e.g., ἀρτάβης ἥμισυ (for ἡμίσεως) *PSI* 33.17 (A.D. 266/7).[4]

2) A nom.-acc. neut. ἥμισον (with orthographic variations) is also found:

ἥμυσον μέρος *PMich.* 296.2; 297.1 (1st cent.); 322a.10,11 (A.D. 46); etc.
ἥμεσον μέρος *PMich.* 354.6 (A.D. 52)
ἥμισον μέρος *BGU* 183 = *MChr.* 313.41 (A.D. 85)
πῆχις εἴκοσι ἒξ ἥμυσον *PMich.* 308.2 (1st cent.); sim. *SB* 7260 = *PMich.*
121 R II ii.5 (A.D. 42); *PMich.* 294.3 (1st cent.)

This form, attested in dialectal inscriptions and elsewhere in the Koine,[5] may represent the beginning of the transfer of ἥμισυς to an adjective of the first and second declensions. The Modern Greek form is ordinarily μέσος, -η, -ο, but the *u*-stem neut. is preserved in fractions, as πεντέ 'μισυ.[6]

3) The gen. appears in various forms:

a) the contracted form ἡμίσους common in the Koine,[7] e.g., τῆς μιᾶς ἡμίσους ἀρούρης *PTebt.* 310.5 (A.D. 186);

---

[1] See Vol. i, 262-7.

[2] See Vol. i, 112-14.

[3] For orthographic variations of this adj., see ἥμισυς in Index to Vol. i, p. 348.

[4] Indecl. ἥμισυ v.l. LXX and NT (Schwyzer i, 599; *BDF*, § 48).

[5] ἥμισον inscrr. Locr., 5th cent. B.C., Chalcedon, 3rd/2nd cent. B.C., and Delph., 2nd cent. B.C.; pl. ἥμισα Argos, 5th cent. B.C.; also ἥμισσον Arc., 4th cent. B.C., Ephesus, 3rd/2nd cent. B.C., pl. ἥμισσα Delph., 4th cent. B.C. (*LSJ*, s.v.). See further Dieterich, 177.

[6] Thumb, *Handbook*, § 110; Jannaris, § 401b. Many *u*-stem adjs. have survived in MGr., as βαθύς, -(ε)ιά, -ύ, but others have transferred to the *o*-stem decl., as γλυκός (also γλυκύς); conversely, a few adjs. of the 1st and 2nd decl. have developed *u*-stem by-forms, as μακρύς (Thumb, *Handbook*, § 110; Mirambel, *Gram.*, 79-80).

[7] The non-Att.-Ion. ἡμίσους is the normal form in the Ptol. papp. (w. ἡμίσεος once 3rd cent.) (Mayser i², 2, 55) and in the NT (*BDF*, § 48). It is also found in D.H. Plu. and LXX as fem. (*LSJ*, s.v.). In the Att. inscrr., the gen. sg. is invariably ἡμίσεος, although contr. forms are found in the neut. pl. from 2nd half 4th cent. B.C. on (*MS*, 150).

b) ἡμίσεως, presumably an orthographic variant of the regular ending -εος,[1] e.g., *PLond.* 1227 (iii, 143).5 (A.D. 152); *PBouriant* 20 = *PAbinn.* 63.5 (A.D. 350);

c) an apparent *o*-stem form ἡμίσου, e.g., *PPrinc.* 144.10,22, with ἡμίσους 15 (early 3rd cent.); *PMerton* 91.8 (A.D. 316), which may simply reflect the loss of final -ς[2] or represent the indeclinable ἥμισυ (the copies of *PMerton* 91 have ἥμισυ in line 5).[3]

2. *n*-stem adjectives.

μέλας[4] fluctuates between regular third declension forms and a new first and second declension formation μελανός, -ή, -όν (best accented oxytone).[5]

a. Regular forms.

1) Masc.:

  [μέ]λας *PCairIsidor.* 93.9 (A.D. 282)
  [πε]ρ[ιμ]έλας *BGU* 806.4: *BL* i, 68 (A.D. 1)
  μέλανα *POxy.* 2846.8 (2nd half 1st cent.); *PCairIsidor.* 84.8 (A.D. 267)
  λευκομέλανα *PMerton* 106.9-10 (late 3rd cent.)
  μέλανας *SB* 10573.6 (10/9 B.C.); *BGU* 46 = *MChr.* 112.13 (A.D. 193)

2) Fem.:

  μελαίνης *PRossGeorg.* ii, 19.15 (A.D. 141); *PPhil.* 12.16, sim. duplic.
    PSI 33.16-17 (A.D. 266/7); *SB* 7054.3,11 abbrev. (n.d.)
  μέλαιναν *PMilVogl.* 82.6 part. rest. (A.D. 133?); *StudPal.* xxii, 170.17-18
    (A.D. 145); *PSI* 79.8 (A.D. 216-17); *SB* 8071.10, with μελάντερος
    5, poet. inscr. (early 3rd cent.); *PFlor.* 9.13 (A.D. 255)
  μέλεναν *StudPal.* xxii, 16.1 (A.D. 217)
  cf. μελαίνην *BGU* 153 = *MChr.* 261.15, with μέλειναν *sic* 33 (2nd
    hand) (A.D. 152)

3) Neut.:

  μέλανος (gen. sg.) *POxy.* 326 descr. = *SB* 10241 R.10 (A.D. 45); *PSI*
    1264.21 part. rest. (4th cent.)
  μέλαν *SB* 9221.8 (A.D. 261); *PFouad* 74.9 (late 5th cent.: *BL* iii, 61)
  μελάν[ων] *OMich.* 89.3 (4th cent.)

---

[1] ἡμίσεως also v.l. Th. & Dsc. (*LSJ*, s.v.).
[2] See Vol. i, 124-6.
[3] Ed., n. ad loc. For the interchange of ου and υ, see Vol. i, 214-16.
[4] For the orig. -ς in the nom. as χέρς, cf. Schwyzer i, 569. μελαν- represents a nasal suffix (*ibid.*, 490 & n. 2).
[5] *o*-stem forms are also attested in *Gp. Stad.* (*LSJ*, s.v. μελανός).

b. *o*- and *a*-stem forms.[1]

1) Masc.:

μελανόν *PMich.* 552.7 (A.D. 131); *POxy.* 2593.23 (2nd cent.); *POxy.* 922.12 (late 6th/early 7th cent.)

2) Fem.:

μελανήν *PJand.* 35.5-6 part. rest. (late 2nd/early 3rd cent.); *PLBat.* i, 18.13 (3rd cent.); *PStrassb.* 139 = *SB* 8021.8 (A.D. 277); *PGen.* 48 = *PAbinn.* 60.7 (A.D. 346)
μελανῶν *PLBat.* ii, 9ac.11 (A.D. 331?)

3) Neut.:

μελανοῦ (used subst.) *SB* 2251 (4th cent.)

This analogical formation shows a tendency towards regularization of the paradigm in this adjective. μέλας has generally been replaced by μαῦρος in Modern Greek.[2]

3. Dental stem adjectives.

a. Participles.

1) Concord.[3]

Participles violate agreement with their antecedents very frequently, mainly in gender and case.

a) Gender.

i. The masculine is frequently used for the feminine, not only through association in contexts in which the masculine is more common, but also when there are no such predominant contextual influences:

ἡ ὁμολογῶν *BGU* 1013.15 (A.D. 41-68)
Ἡραῒς ... εἰσελθὼν ... καὶ ... συνλαβών *PRyl.* 151.5-12 (A.D. 40)
τῆς Ταμάρωνος ἐλαττουμένου *PMich.* 276.12-13 (A.D. 47)
τῆς ἐνεστῶτος ἡμέρας *PSI* 903.19: ed., n. ad loc. (A.D. 47)[4]
διὰ μέσον ὄντες εἴσοδος καὶ ἔξοδος *PMich.* 305.9 (1st cent.)

---

[1] Cf. also from the mag. papp. μελανοῦ *PGM* 7.301, w. μελανῆς 652 (3rd cent.); μελανῆς *PGM* 4.800 (4th cent.); *PGM* 36.239 (4th cent.).

[2] Jannaris, § 447.

[3] Lack of agreement will be treated in full under Concord in Vol. iii. See further esp. Kapsomenakis, 40(-42), n. 2.

[4] But for poss. Copt. interference, see Introd., p. XXI.

τὴν πειπτοκότα μ[ο]ι ... [οἰκίαν] *BGU* 251.11 (A.D. 81)
παραθέσεων ἐπειδιχθέντων *PAmh.* 79.29-30 (ca. A.D. 186)
εἴδαμέν σε θυσιάζοντα (of a woman) *PRyl.* 112c.14 (A.D. 250)
ἀπὸ τῶν ὑπαρχόντων αὐτῇ ... ἀρουρῶν *POxy.* 1691.6 (A.D. 291)
ἔγραψα ὑπὲρ αὐτῆς γ[ράμ]ματα μὴ ἰδότος (= εἰδότος) *PGrenf.* ii, 75.28-29
    (A.D. 308: *BL* i, 191); sim. 97.9 (6th cent.)
ἀδελφαὶ ... κατοικοῦντα[ς] *PGen.* 11 = *PAbinn.* 62.2-3 (A.D. 350)
τὴν ἐλευθεροῦντα *MChr.* 361.11 (A.D. 360)
αἱ πεπρακότες *PMon.* 13.51 (A.D. 594)

ii. The feminine is only rarely used for the masculine or neuter, e.g., [τῶ]ν ὑπαρχουσῶν σοι ἐδαφῶν *PLond.* 1223 = *WChr.* 370.5 (A.D. 121), and the neuter for the masculine or feminine, e.g., ὄνον ... ἔχον *PMerton* 106.8-10 (late 3rd cent.).

b) Case.

Besides a rare use of the nom. sg. or pl. for an oblique case, e.g., τοῦ ἐνεστὸς η (ἔτους) *BGU* 61 i.7-8 (A.D. 200); ἡμεῖν τοῖς μετρί[ο]ις καὶ καλῶς εὖ βιοῦντες (for βιοῦσι) *PMerton* 91.6 (A.D. 316); *PCairIsidor.* 74.3 part. rest. (A.D. 315), the nom. pl. masc. is occasionally used for the acc., parallel to the use of nom. for acc. in nouns of the third declension:[1]

τοὺς τὸ τοιοῦτο διαπράξαντες *PRyl.* 139.21-22 (A.D. 34)
τοὺς ὁμολογοῦντες *PAmh.* 110.22-23 part. rest., corr. 17-18 (A.D. 75); *BGU*
    526.10 part. rest., 18 (A.D. 86); *SB* 7663 = *PLBat.* i, 8.8 (A.D. 86); etc.
ἕκαστον ... ἀνοικοδομοῦντες, etc. *PMich.* 584.24-27 (A.D. 84)
(τοὺς) ὑπο[μένον]τες *BGU* 136 = *MChr.* 86.17-18 (A.D. 135)
τοὺς φιλοῦντες *PLBat.* i, 18.29-30 (3rd cent.); etc.
ἡμᾶς ὑγιαίνοντες *BGU* 332.5 (2nd/3rd cent.)

Conversely, the acc. pl. is sometimes used for the nom.:[2]

οἱ ὁμολογοῦντας *PIFAO* i, 29.11 (1st half 2nd cent.)
ἐνεδείξαντο ... πανηγυρίζοντας ... μεταδόντας *POxy.* 705 = *WChr.* 153.
    32-38 (A.D. 199/200?: *BL* ii, 2, 96)

2) Formation of case.

Participles have analogical forms similar to those observed in the corresponding classes of nouns.

a) *o*-stem forms are found sporadically in the masc. and neut.:[3]

τοῦ ἐνεστώτου ἔτους *POxy.* 1130.15-16 (A.D. 484)
τὸν ὁμολογοῦντον (for τὴν ὁμολογοῦσαν!) *PNYU* 24.4-5 (A.D. 373)

---

[1] See above, pp. 46-47.
[2] For the interchange of α and ε in sim. phonetic environments, see Vol. i, 278-86.
[3] Cf. *o*-stem forms in 3rd decl. nouns above, pp. 43-45.

b) The fem. of mixed dental stem participles sporadically retains the -α of the nom. sg. in the oblique cases:[1]

τῇ ... γνώσει φερούσᾳ *PMerton* 125.3 (6th cent.)
βεβαίᾳ μενούσᾳ *PMichael.* 42 B.17 (A.D. 566)
παρούσᾳ *PCairMasp.* 151-2.66,100,221 (A.D. 570); *PCairMasp.* 311.29 part. rest. (A.D. 569/70?)

c) The fem. of mixed dental stem perfect active participles very frequently forms the gen. sg. and sometimes also the other cases of the singular in -ης, etc.[2] These endings are found regardless of the orthographic variants of the preceding diphthong.

i. Gen. sg.:

εἰδυίης *PMich.* 253.12 (A.D. 30); *PSI* 30.13 (A.D. 82); *PAmh.* 104 = *PSarap.* 36.16 (A.D. 125); *POxy.* 76.36 (A.D. 179); *PAntin.* 37.10 (A.D. 209/10); 39.17 (A.D. 324); *PLips.* 28 = *MChr.* 363.5 (A.D. 381); *PGrenf.* i, 60.57 (A.D. 581); etc.
εἰδυέης *PMich.* 258.17 (A.D. 32/33)
εἰδυείης *PMich.* 254-5.9 (A.D. 30/31); *POxy.* 485 = *MChr.* 246.48 (A.D. 178); etc.; cf. esp. *PMich.* v, p. 14
ἰδυίης *PMich.* 563.33 (A.D. 128/9); *BGU* 187.8 (A.D. 159); *BGU* 648 = *WChr.* 360.24 (A.D. 164/96); *BGU* 327.11 = *MChr.* 61.12 part. rest. (A.D. 176: *BL* i, 38)
εἰδύης *PMich.* 250.7 (A.D. 18); *PMich.* 305.19 (1st cent.); etc.
εἰδύεις *PMich.* 269-71.6 (A.D. 42)
ἰδύης *PRein.* 43.24 (A.D. 102)
ἐδύης *PLond.* 289 (ii, 184-5).37 (A.D. 91)
εἰδηείης *MChr.* 361.22 (A.D. 360)
εἰδηεῖος *SB* 8952 = *PSI* 1319.76 (A.D. 76)[3]
μετηλλαχυίης *PLond.* 289 (ii, 184-5).10 (1st hand), with ἐδύης 37 (2nd hand) (A.D. 91); *PRyl.* 108.9-10 (A.D. 110/11); *BGU* 55 ii.1 (A.D. 175); *PSI* 1040.9 (3rd cent.); etc.
συνπεπτωκυίης *PMich.* 307.4; -οιης duplic. *PSI* 914.5 (1st cent.); *POxy.* 510.13 (A.D. 101); etc.
ὑπογεγραφυίης *BGU* 832.23 (A.D. 113)
τετελευτηκυίης *SB* 9317 a.7; b.11,19-20, with γεγονυίης a.22 (A.D. 148); *POxy.* 2231.21, with εἰδυίης 46 (A.D. 241); etc.
ἠβροχηκυίης *PFay.* 33.13-14 (A.D. 163); *PMich.* 369.11-12 (A.D. 171)
γεγονυείης *POxy.* 712 = *MChr.* 231.16 (late 2nd cent.)

---

[1] Cf. the corresp. phenomenon in 1st decl. nouns in -ᾰ above, p. 6.
[2] Cf. ἄρουρα, ἀρούρης, etc., above, pp. 4-6.
[3] Anomalous fem. forms also occur sporadically, e.g., εἰδούσης *POxy.* 1957.22 (A.D. 430); εἰδύδες *StudPal.* xxii, 46.11 (1st cent.).

συμπεπρακυίης καὶ ἐσχη[κ]υίης ... μὴ εἰδυίης *SB* 4298.21 (A.D. 204)
κατηντηκυίης *SB* 4654.7 (A.D. 244: *BL* v, 93)

ii. Dat. sg.:

τετελευτηκυείη *PMich.* 226.15 (A.D. 37)
μετηλλαχυίη *POxy.* 2852.20 (A.D. 104/5)
μεμίσθωκυίη *POxy.* 101.45,47, sim. 31-32, with μεμισθωκυίας (gen.)
   41 (A.D. 142); *POxy.* 502.26,41 (A.D. 164)
γεγονυίη *PMed.* 51.7 (2nd cent.)
δεδανικυίη *PFlor.* 1 = *MChr.* 243.5, with -υίης 3, -υίη 6 (A.D. 153)

iii. Acc. sg.:

προγεγονυίην *PMich.* 353.7-8 (A.D. 48)
τετελε[υτη]κυίην *CPR* 63.17 (A.D. 161-80)

This late Greek development, attested frequently elsewhere in the Koine,[1] parallels the morphemic shift observed above in nouns of the first declension in -ρᾰ, -ρης, explained as a result of levelling of the inflectional system on the analogy of other nouns in -ᾰ whose stem ends in a consonant.[2] This parallel development of participles in -υια follows the pronunciation of the second element of the υι diphthong as a consonant [j].[3] This destroyed the *ratio* of the analogy between these feminine participles and nouns of the first declension in -ᾱ and assimilated them to nouns of the first declension ending in a consonant (including ρ) + ᾰ, as γλῶσσα, γλώσσης; ἄρουρα, ἀρούρης; etc.[4]

b. πᾶς, πᾶσα, πᾶν.[5]

---

[1] Cf. Mayser i², 1, 11-12 (an Ionicism in the Koine). In the NT, ptcs. in -υια form the gen. and dat. predominantly in ης, η in the early mss. (*BDF*, § 43 1). See also Debrunner, *Geschichte*, 109.

[2] See above, pp. 4-5.

[3] See Vol. i, 202-7. Note that several of the examples of -ης, -η follow υι with a diacritical mark over the ι, emphasizing its consonantal quality (i, 200-7). The consonantal quality of the -ι- in this position is also supported by such syllabications as ἠβρυχηκυ|ίης *PFay.* 33.13-14 (A.D. 163).

[4] On this hypothesis, the sporadic exx. above of the extension of the -η to the acc. would represent a further levelling of the inflectional system.

[5] There is some fluctuation in the use of πᾶς and ἅπας (w. copulative or intensive ἀ-: cf. Schwyzer i, 433). ἅπας is generally restricted to stereotyped phrases in wh. it perh. originated for the sake of euphony, as εἰς τὸν ἅπαντα χρόνον, e.g., *PMich.* 254-5.1,8 (A.D. 30-31) and ἐν ἅπασι, e.g., *PCairMasp.* 279.11 (ca. A.D. 570). Sometimes it seems to be used for emphasis, e.g., μουσικὴν ἅπασαν *PMed.* 47.6-7 (3rd cent.); ἅπαντα τὰ κατέλιψεν *PCairIsidor.* 64.6 (ca. A.D. 298); θεοὺς ἅπαντας *SB* 7673 = *PCairIsidor.* 8.12 (A.D. 309); τὰ εἰωθότα ἅπαντα ἀνεπλήρωσα *PFlor.* 36 = *MChr.* 64.9 (A.D. 312); ἀνεφάνη ἅπασιν ἡμῖν *POxy.* 939 = *WChr.* 128.4 (4th cent.); ἅπαντα ἡμῶν τὰ ὑπάρχοντα *POxy.* 1890.16 (A.D. 508); ἐφ' ἅπασιν τοῖς προγεγραμμένοις *PCairMasp.* 298.29 (6th cent.), without regard for the class. Att. rule of ἅπας after a consonant and πᾶς after a vowel. In other contexts, πᾶς and ἅπας appear to be used in parallel structure, e.g., περὶ πάντων λόγων τῆς περὶ ἁπάσης πίστεως

1) The acc. sg. masc. sporadically ends in -αν as in dental stem nouns,[1] e.g., ἄπανταν (corrected from -ον: ed., n. ad loc.) [χρ]όνο[ν] *BGU* 666.23 (A.D. 177); (in full) *SB* 6258.3 (5th/6th cent.).

2) The nom.-acc. sg. neut. is sometimes used for the acc. sg. masc. or fem.:[2]

τὴν ... τιμὴν ἄπαν ἐκ πλήρους *CPR* 4 = *MChr.* 159.14-15 (A.D. 51/53)
[τι]μὴν ... πᾶν ἐκ πλήρους *PRyl.* 161.12 (A.D. 71)
πᾶν τὸν νόμον *PMich.* 617.7 (A.D. 145/6)
τὸν δὲ καὶ ἐπ[ελ]ευσόμεν[ο]ν πᾶν *PTebt.* 397.17-18 (A.D. 198)

3) The nom.-acc. sg. neut. is sporadically used indeclinably for other cases in the singular or plural, e.g., πρὸ μὲν πᾶν σε εὔχομαι *SB* 9251.2 (2nd/3rd cent.).[3]

4) The acc. sg. fem. appears sporadically as πάσην, e.g., πάσην χάριν *PMich.* 499.9 (2nd cent.).

5) The acc. pl. masc. is frequently replaced by the -ες ending of the nom. as in dental stem nouns of the third declension:[4]

ἐπισκόπ(ου) τοὺς σοὺς πάντε(ς) *POxy.* 743.43 (2 B.C.)
ἀσπάζου ... τοὺς ἐν οἴκῳ πάντες *PCornell* 49.12-13 (1st cent.); sim. *PFay.* 112.23 (A.D. 99); 115.12 (A.D. 101); *BGU* 814.36,38 (3rd cent.); *BGU* 816.25 (3rd cent.); *SB* 9683.27 (late 4th cent.); etc.
ἀσπάζου πάντες τοὺς φίλους *POxy.* 1155.9-10 (A.D. 104); sim. *PMich.* 209.25 (late 2nd/early 3rd cent.); *PMich.* 476.23,31 (early 2nd cent.); etc.

BGU 86 = *MChr.* 306.23 (A.D. 155) and πάντας τ[ο]ὺ[ς] ἐν τῷ οἴκῳ σου ἄπαντ[ας] προσαγόρευε *POxy.* 1492.15-17 (late 3rd/early 4th cent.). But some contrast may be indicated by the deletion in τοῦτο δῆλον ἄπασιν, [[ἅ]]πᾶσα γὰρ ἡμῶν ἡ ἡλικία *POxy.* 1664.5-7 (prob. A.D. 196-8: *BL* iv, 62).

Also lexicographical is the freq. use of ὅλος, properly "whole, entire, complete in all its parts" (*LSJ*, s.v.), for πᾶς in the general sense of "all." This usage, attested already in S. Men. LXX, etc. (*ibid.*), is found in phrases in wh. πᾶς is more common, as πρὸ τῶν ὅλ[ων εὔχομ]αί σε ἐρρῶσθαι *PMich.* 466.3 (A.D. 107); πρὸ τῶν ὅλων ἀσπάζομαί σε *PAmh.* 133 = *PSarap.* 92.2 (early 2nd cent.); τούτων τοίνυν ὅλων *PCairMasp.* 295 ii.7 (6th cent.); ὅλας πεδιάδας *PCairMasp.* 1.18 (A.D. 514); etc. ὅλος is also used with πᾶς in such exx. as ἀσπάζομαι ... πάντας τοὺς ἐν τῇ οἰκίᾳ ὅλους κατ' ὄνομα *PLond.* 404 = *PAbinn.* 25.13-15 (ca. A.D. 346); καὶ πάντες οἱ ἀδελφοί σου κατ' ὄνομα ὅλ[οι] *PJand.* 13.20 (4th cent.).

[1] See above, pp. 45-46.
[2] Cf. sim. occurrences in the mag. papp., e.g., εἰς πᾶν τόπον *PGM* 36.354, w. poss. partial haplography (cf. Schwyzer i, 262-3, 585 & n. 3); cf. ἄπαντα χρόνον 48 (4th cent.). Sim. exx. of πᾶν/ἄπαν for the acc. sg. masc. in the Ptol. papp. (Mayser i², 2, 32) may also be the result of haplography.
[3] In MGr., πᾶς is preserved only in the indecl. form πᾶσα "every," e.g., πᾶσα εἷς "every one," πᾶσα 'μέρα "every day," and in the adv. πάντα "always" (Jannaris, § 449). Poss. traces of this indecl. use of πᾶσα are suspected in the NT (*BDF*, § 56.4).
[4] See above, pp. 46-47.

ἄσπασαι τοὺς ἡμῶν πάντες SB 9524.16 (3rd cent.); sim. *PBaden* 35.26 (A.D. 87); *PMich.* 475.18 (early 2nd cent.); *POxy.* 1160.3-6 (late 3rd/early 4th cent.); etc.

ἀσπάζετε (for -ται) ὑμᾶς πάντες *PWürzb.* 21 B.12-13, sim. 11 (2nd cent.); sim. *BGU* 276.25,26 (2nd/3rd cent.?); *POxy.* 1296.17,18 (3rd cent.); etc.

Conversely, the acc. pl. -ας is used sporadically for the nom.:

οἱ αὐτοῦ πάντας *BGU* 615.15-16 (2nd cent.); sim. *PMed.* 74.11-12 (2nd cent.); *SB* 7357 = *PMich.* 206.22 (2nd cent.)
ἡμῖς πάντας *PSI* 212.4 (6th cent.?)

6) There are sporadic instances of the nom. or acc. used for oblique cases in the plural:

μετὰ τῶν ἡμῶν πάντες (for πάντων) *POxy.* 2596.4 (3rd cent.)
ἵνα κἀγὼ ἴσος πάντας γένομαι (for πᾶσι γένωμαι) *POxy.* 2154.24 (4th cent.)

7) A heteroclitic *o*-stem dat. pl. masc. is found in αἱρῶσθαί σαι (for ἐρρῶσθαί σε) εὔχομαι σὺν πάντοις *POxy.* 2274.14 (3rd cent.).[1]

8) The adjective is doubled for emphasis in προσκύνησον τὴν Σάραν ... καὶ πάντας πάντας *PApoll.* 62.4 (A.D. 703-15).

C. ADJECTIVES OF THE THIRD DECLENSION

1. *s*-stem adjectives.

a. The acc. sg. masc.-fem. occasionally ends in -ν:[2]

ἀσφαλῆν SB 7600.9-10: *BL* iii, 190 (A.D. 16); *POxy.* 269 ii.10-11 (A.D. 57); *POxy.* 2721.28 (A.D. 234); *PSI* 1418.12 part. rest. (3rd cent.); *PSI* 900.6 (3rd/4th cent.); *POxy.* 1298.7-8 (4th cent.)
κατακλεινῆν *PMich.* 228.22-23, with οὔ{ν}τος 14 and Τανοὺ{ν}ρι 18 (A.D. 47); 229.28 (no other erroneous insertion or addition of ν) (A.D. 48)
οἰκογενῆν *POxy.* 2582.6 (A.D. 49); *PStrassb.* 505.13 (A.D. 108-16); *PLBat.* vi, 27.13 (A.D. 132); *PSI* 710.13 (2nd cent.); *PSI* 1248.24 (A.D. 235)
ὑγιῆν *PSI* 921 R.23 (A.D. 143/4); *BGU* 13 = *MChr.* 265.8 (A.D. 289)
συνγενῆν *PMich.* 498.15-16 (2nd cent.)
ἀτελῆν SB 4226, inscr. (prob. 2nd cent.)
ἀβλαβῆν *POslo* 61.4 (3rd cent.)

---

[1] The dat. pl. πάντοις is a dialectal characteristic of NWGr. (Schwyzer i, 92, 564; Buck, *GD*, § 107.3, 226). It is also found in a Delph. inscr. of the 2nd cent. B.C. through the influence of the NWGr. Koine, and in a late Att. inscr. (*LSJ*, s.v.; *MS*, 130).
[2] Cf. also εὐπρ[ε]πῆν *POxy.* 1380.130, Gr.-Eg. lit. papp.: invocation of Isis (early 2nd cent.).

συνήϑην *PFlor*. 203.6 (A.D. 264)
εὐμενῆν *POxy*. 925 = *WChr*. 132.7 (5th/6th cent.)
αὐϑάδην *PCairMasp*. 97 V d.43 (above line) (6th cent.)

This acc. in -ν, attested already in ancient Cyprian in ἀτελέν[1] and elsewhere in the Koine,[2] seems to have arisen on the analogy of other adjectives whose acc., especially of the fem., ended in -ν, supported by the analogy of *a*-stem substantives, both masculines in -ης and feminines in -η, which formed the acc. in -ην. This formation of the acc. sg. in -ν in adjectives of the third declension is parallel to that observed frequently in third declension nouns of various inflectional types.[3] It represents an initial stage in the process by which most *s*-stem adjectives were lost or transformed in the transition from ancient to Modern Greek. They developed into adjectives of the first and second declensions, e.g., ἀκριβός, -ή, -ό,[4] or were replaced by different formations, e.g., ὑγιηρός for ὑγιής.[5]

b. After a vowel, the acc. sg. masc.-fem. and the nom.-acc. pl. neut. normally end in -η (sg. -ην) with orthographic variations. This occurs not only after ι and υ, as in classical Attic, but also after ε.

1) After ι (with orthographic variations):[6]

ὑγιῆι, ὑγιῆ *POxy*. 278 = *MChr*. 165.18 (1st hand), 35 (2nd hand) (A.D. 17)
ὑγῆ *BGU* 912.13-14 part. rest., sim. 25 (A.D. 33); *PMich*. 312.32 (A.D. 34); *PSI* 1030.22 (A.D. 109); *POxy*. 530.20 (2nd cent.); etc.
ὑιῆ (for ὑγιῆ) *POxy*. 729.23 (A.D. 137); *PCornell* 45 = *SB* 9833.21 (A.D. 299)
but οἰγιᾶν *PMich*. 343.7 (A.D. 54/55)

---

[1] Schwyzer i, 563; Buck, *GD*, § 108.2. Like the corresp. acc. ending in -ν of 3rd decl. nouns, this ending in the Koine does not seem to be connected with the earlier dialectal ending (see above, p. 46).

[2] There is only one ex. in the Ptol. papp. (Mayser i[2], 2, 57), but ἀτελῆν is found in the Herc. papp. of Epicur. (Crönert, 178), and sim. acc. forms in -ην are attested occ. in the NT (*BDF*, § 46.1). See further Crönert 178(-9), n. 5, for exx. in -ην from codd. of Koine authors, and Dieterich, 175.

[3] See above, pp. 45-46.

[4] Thumb, *Handbook*, § 115; Mirambel, *Langue grecque*, 114. See further Kapsomenakis, 55-56; Jannaris, § 430.

[5] Thumb, *ibid*. In MGr., the *s*-stem decl. is retained in only a few adjs., as εὐλαβής, and in some others restricted to the *kathareuousa*. The modern inflection of these *s*-stem adjs. is masc. -ης (pl. -ηδες), fem. -ισσα, neut. -ικο (Chantraine[2], § 108; Mirambel, *Gram*., 83-84).

[6] Cf. Vol. i, 71. Class. Att. fluctuates in ὑγιής: acc. sg. ὑγιᾶ Th. Pl. X., ὑγιῆ Pl. inscrr.; neut. pl. ὑγιῆ Pl. and freq. inscrr., but ὑγιᾶ once in an inscr. 357-4 B.C. (*LSJ*, s.v.; *MS*, 150). No exx. are attested at Perg., but forms in -η are found elsewh. in Asia Minor (Schweizer, 153). ὑγιῆ(ι) alone occurs in the Herc. papp. of Phld. (Crönert, 179) and in the NT (*BDF*, § 48). The -η seems to have been introduced by analogy w. other adjs. of this class (Schwyzer i, 189).

2) After υ:

μεγαλοφυῆ (acc. pl. neut.) *PSI* 684.3 part. rest., 12 (4th/5th cent.)
ὑπερφυῆ (acc. sg. fem.) *PCairMasp.* 4.6 (ca. A.D. 552: *BL* i, 100); *PLond.*
1676.55 (A.D. 556-73); *PCairMasp.* 2.2, part. rest. (A.D. 567: *BL* i,
100); (acc. pl. neut.) *PCairMasp.* 295 i.3 part. rest. (6th cent.)[1]
[ε]ὐφυῆ (acc. sg. fem.) *PLond.* 1678.3 (A.D. 566-73)

3) After ε:

ἐνδεῆ (acc. sg. fem.) *POxy.* 281 = *MChr.* 66.20 (A.D. 20-50)
ἀποδεῆ (nom. pl. neut.) *PLBat.* xiii, 6.6 (1st cent.)
εὐκλεῆ (acc. sg. fem.) *PCairMasp.* 5.5 (6th cent.)

c. The corresponding derivative substantive is erroneously used for the adjective in τὴν συνήθειαν δαπάνην *PFlor.* 248.14-15 (A.D. 257). The correct συνήθη is used frequently, including by the same author in the same phrase in *PFlor.* 251.6-7 (A.D. 257).

d. The acc. sg. masc.-fem. is used sporadically for the neuter:

τὸ αὐτάρκη (for αὐτάρκες) ἄχυρον *PMich.* 312.20 (A.D. 34)
τὸ δὲ αὐτάρκη δῖγμα (for αὐτάρκες δεῖγμα) *PHibeh* 275.3-4 (2nd half
1st cent.)
but τὸ αὐτάρκες ὕδωρ *PWürzb.* 22 = *PSarap.* 97.10-11 (A.D. 117-38); etc.
αὐτὸ ὑγειῆν (for ὑγιές) *PThead.* 14.30 (4th cent.)

Conversely, the acc. sg. neut. is used for the fem. in ἀβλαβές *POxy.* 125.15 (A.D. 560).

e. The voc. sg. masc.-fem. sporadically ends in -η instead of the classical -ες:

εὐγενῆ σύνδικε *POxy.* 2407.3,11 part. rest., 18,26 (late 3rd cent.)
εὐτυχῆ [ἡγεμ]ών *POxy.* 41 = *WChr.* 45.3, sim. 13-14,21 (ca. A.D. 300)

f. The acc. pl. masc.-fem. is regularly -εῖς, even in ὑγιής:[2]

τοὺς συνγενεῖς μου *PLond.* 342 (ii, 173-4).8 (A.D. 185)
τὰς αἰσθήσεις ὑγιεῖς *PLond.* 1727.19 (A.D. 583/4)
cf. also σφραγεῖδες ὑγιαῖς (= nom. for acc., or dat. with *BL* iii, 21?)
BGU 1655.62 (A.D. 169)
τὰς βόας τρῖς ὑγειῆς *PMichael.* 22.19 (A.D. 291: *BL* iv, 51)

---

[1] Att. acc. sg. & neut. pl. ὑπερφυᾶ Ar., neut. pl. -φυῆ Pl. (*LSJ*, s.v.). Cf. εὐφυῆι and κακοφυῆι (w. false -ι adscript) in the Ptol. papp. (Mayser i², 2, 56).
[2] Acc. pl. masc. ὑγιᾶς is attested in an Att. inscr., but ὑγιεῖς occurs in inscrr. from Epidaurus and Cos and (as fem.) in E. (*LSJ*, s.v.).

g. There is some evidence for the transfer of these s-stem adjectives to the o- and a-stem declensions:

ἀβαρός (for ἀβαρές) *POxy.* 1757.14,18 (A.D. 138+)[1]
ὑγιοῦ *PMich.* 122 i.27 (A.D. 49)
  θειουστεφοῦ *SB* 4669.2 (A.D. 614)[2]
εὐσεβόν *PCairMasp.* 333.19 (6th cent.)
  ἀληθόν *SB* 5314.18 (Byz.)
  cf. μακροφυοῦ[ν] *PAmh.* 150.25 (A.D. 592)
ὑγειαί (or ὕγειαι) *POxy.* 1294.6 (late 2nd/early 3rd cent.)[3]
τοὺς ἐνγενούς *CPR* 4 = *MChr.* 159.16 (A.D. 51/53)

The acc. sg. of the adjective ἐπανάγκης, used only in the neuter, appears adverbially in -ον approximately as frequently as in -ες:[4]

ἐπάναγκον *PRyl.* 94.11 (A.D. 14-37); *BGU* 190 ii.12-13 (A.D. 81-96);
  PTebt. 376 = *WChr.* 350.26 (A.D. 162); *PSI* 961.21 (A.D. 176);
  POxy. 2134.22 (late 3rd cent.); *PSI* 42.7 part. rest. (4th cent.); etc.
  cf. ἐπάναγκα *PMich.* 349.1 (A.D. 30)
ἐπάναγκες *PMich.* 348.25 (A.D. 27);[5] *PSI* 465.21 part. rest. (A.D. 265?);
  SB 7175 = *PMed.* 52 i.10 (A.D. 303); *PMerton* 36.13 (A.D. 360);
  PAmh. 147.8 (4th/early 5th cent.); *PMon.* 13.63; 14.91 (A.D. 594); etc.

h. πλήρης has the following peculiarities.

1) The nom. sg. masc.-fem. πλήρης is frequently used indeclinably, especially in apposition to the object of payments *in full*:[6]

---

[1] Cf. also nom. εὐλαβούς *SB* 6186.3-4, inscr. (Xtn.).

[2] An i- or diphthongal stem gen. is read in [τ]οῦ συνγενέως (for συνγενοῦς) by R. G. Böhm in *PVars.* 10 iii.26: *BL* iv, 102 (A.D. 156). The regular gen. in -ους is normal, e.g., καταδεοῦς *PTebt.* 326 = *MChr.* 325.3 (A.D. 266); εὐκλέους *POxy.* 1976.5 (A.D. 582).

[3] The form ὕγιος is cited in Stephanus from a glossary (ed. n. ad loc.).

[4] See further exx. in Preisigke *WB* i & iv, and Daris, *Spoglio* s. vv. ἐπάναγκον is not a new formation but is found in the Cret. *Leg. Gort.* and in other inscrr. and in the Ptol. papp. (*LSJ*, s.v.). A nom. sg. masc. ἐπάναγκος is also found in the mag. papp., e.g., *PGM* 4.1036,2915 (4th cent.); *PGM* 5.435 (4th cent.); etc.

[5] This is, however, the only occurrence of this form in *PMich.* v (Tebtunis) as opposed to 9 occurrences of ἐπάναγκον.

[6] πλήρης is freq. used indecl. in the LXX and occ. in the NT, but always w. decl. variants, when modifying an acc., usu. w. foll. gen. (*LSJ*, s.v. sub IV; *BDF*, § 137.1). In the Ptol. papp., πλήρης is used indecl. once in connection w. a payment (160 B.C.), and twice more in inscrr. (Mayser, i², 1, 40; i², 2, 58, Anm. 7). For the freq. interpolation of this form in codd. of Arist. Plb. Phld. Diod. Str. etc. see Crönert, 179, n. 2. This indecl. use of πλήρης seems to be a feature of Egyptian Greek. Other adjs. in -ης are only appar. used indecl. in instances where the context can have misled the scribe, e.g., ἀτελής (for ἀτελοῦς) γῆς *SB* 9193.11 (A.D. 527-65), wh. also shows other errors in agreement.

γ(ίνονται) η πλήρης *BGU* 1660.9 (A.D. 41); sim. *PFlor.* 211.6-8 (A.D. 255); *POxy.* 1836.4 (5th/6th cent.); etc.

δραχμὰς ... πλήρης *POxy.* 513 = *WChr.* 183.54-55 (A.D. 184); *BGU* 1658.7-8 (A.D. 234); *PCairIsidor.* 83.16-17 (2nd half 3rd cent.); etc.

τοῦ ναύλου δοθέντος ὑπ' ἐμοῦ πλήρης *PPar.* 18 *bis* = *WChr.* 499.8-9 (2nd/3rd cent.)

ἐκφόριον ... πλήρης *BGU* 2038.4-7 (2nd cent.); 2040.4-9 (A.D. 223); *PFay.* 88.3-8 (3rd cent.); *PPrinc.* 37.6-8 (A.D. 255); *SB* 7624 = *PCairIsidor.* 111.6-10 (A.D. 298); etc.

ὀβολὸν ἕνα πλήρης *SB* 7181 A.12-13 (A.D. 220)

ἅπερ ... ἀπέσ[χ]αμεν παρὰ σοῦ πλήρης *BGU* 13 = *MChr.* 265.6-7 (A.D. 289)

ἔσχον τὴν τιμὴν πλήρης *BGU* 373.20-21, sim. 11-13 (A.D. 298); sim. *SB* 7175 = *PMed.* 52 i.19; ii.20 (2nd hand), with τιμὴν πλήρη i.7-8; ii.7-8 part. rest. (1st hand) (A.D. 303); *PLond.* 251 = *PAbinn.* 64.16-17 (ca. A.D. 346); *PMich.* 608.20 (6th cent.); etc.

ταλάντων ἓξ πλήρης *POxy.* 1715.11-12 (A.D. 292)

τοὺς μισθοὺς πλήρης *SB* 5615.18-19, sim. 6-11 (A.D. 324)

εἰς πλήρης *POxy.* 1933.14 (6th cent.); *PBas.* 19.7,8 (6th/7th cent.); *SB* 9011 = *PMed.* 48.12 (5th/6th cent.); *PLond.* 392 (ii, 332-3).8 (6th/7th cent.); *SB* 4502.8 (Byz.); *BGU* 371.20 (Arab.: *BL* i, 42); etc.

[εἰς] πλήρις (prob. for πλήρης) *PJand.* 35.8 (late 2nd/early 3rd cent.)

2) Classically correct forms also occur:

δραχμαὶ ... πλήρεις *POxy.* 2962.15-16 (A.D. 154); sim. *POxy.* 2967.16-17 (1st hand), with τὰς δραχμὰς ... πλήρης 23-26 (2nd hand) (A.D. 154)

τὰ ἄλλα πάντα πλήρη *POxy.* 530.6 (2nd cent.); sim. *PBeattyPanop.* 2.123 (A.D. 300); *POxy.* 84 = *WChr.* 197.17,23-24 (A.D. 316); *POxy.* 1261.10 (A.D. 325); *PMon.* 4-5 V.24 (A.D. 581); 9.70 (A.D. 585); etc.

ἀρούρ(αις) πλήρεσι σπορίμαις *PBrem.* 68.6 (A.D. 99)

εἰς πλῆρες *POxy.* 136 = *WChr.* 383.26 (A.D. 583); *PApoll.* 29.6-7 (ca. A.D. 713)

3) There is an occasional lack of agreement, especially with the neuter used for the feminine:[1]

ἃς ... πλήρη *POxy.* 2125.28-29 (A.D. 220/1)

[δραχμὰς διακοσίας] πλήρη *POxy.* 1697.44 (A.D. 242)

τὴν ... τιμὴν πλῆρες *PFlor.* 65.5-6 (A.D. 570/1?)

---

[1] These exx. may be orthographic variants of the indecl. πλήρης. For the omission of final -ς, see Vol. i, 124-29; for the interchange of ε and η, incl. before -ς, see Vol. i, 242-9.

4) *o*-stem forms are found sporadically in the gen. sg., as well as an anomalous form in -ος:[1]

ἐκ πλήρου *PMich*. 281.5 (1st cent.); *PGen*. 48 = *PAbinn*. 60.33 (2nd hand), with πλήρους 14-15 (1st hand) (A.D. 346)
ἐκ πλήρος *PMich*. 263.14 (1st hand), corr. 33 (2nd hand) (A.D. 35/36); *PMich*. 297.7 (1st cent.)

The regular genitive also occurs:

ἐκ πλήρους *PMich*. 241.6 (A.D. 16); *POxy*. 95 = *MChr*. 267.24 (A.D. 129); *PLond*. 1178 = *WChr*. 156.6,43 (A.D. 194); *BGU* 409.9 (A.D. 313); *PCairMasp*. 154 R.14 (A.D. 527-65); 163.25 (A.D. 569); 151-2.105,273 part. rest. (A.D. 570); etc.; cf. *PMur*. 114.17 (A.D. 171?)

5) An *o*-stem form is also found in the acc. pl. fem. in πλαγὰς πλήρους *PMich*. 228.19 (A.D. 47); 229.23-24 (A.D. 48).

6) There are also other sporadic analogical formations.

a) The neut. pl. appears as πλῆρα in κεράτια ὀκτὼ ἥμισυ ὄγδον (for ὄγδοον) πλῆρα *POxy*. 1887.10 (A.D. 538).

b) Dental stem formations are found in the following cases:

τοῦ νομίσμ(ατος) ἑνὸς πληράτου *BGU* 367.14-15 (Arab.: *BL* i, 42)
νομισμάτια πεντήκοντα δυγῶ (for ζυγῷ) Ἀλε[ξ]ανδρίας πλήρατα *SB* 9011 = *PMed*. 48.9-10, with πλήρατ(α) also 10 and πλήρα(τα) 19 (same hand), and πλήρης indecl. for acc. sg. neut. 12 (5th/6th cent.)

2. *n*-stem adjectives.

a. ἄρσην, -εν is found with occasional *o*-stem forms in the acc. sg. masc. and neut. and in the dat. and acc. pl. masc.[2]

1) Acc. sg.:[3]

ἄρσενον *POxy*. 744.9-10 (1 B.C.); *StudPal*. xxii, 20.29 (A.D. 4); *PMich*. 121 R I.iii (A.D. 42); *SB* 7356 = *PMich*. 203.6 (A.D. 98-117); sim. *PSI* 785.8,16 (A.D. 93)

---

[1] For the interchange of ο and ου, see Vol. i, 211-14.
[2] For the fluctuation betw. Att. -ρρ- and Ion. etc. -ρσ- and reg. *n*-stem forms, see Vol. i, 143-4.
[3] ἀρσένιν in τέκνον ἀρσένιν ... θῆλιν (for θῆλυν) *BGU* 1668.12 (early Rom.) is prob. for ἀρσένιον = ἀρσενικόν. Cf. Palmer, 32, 85. ἀρσένιος = ἀρσενικός occurs in a 3rd cent. A.D. inscr. from Teuthis (*LSJ*, s.v.). For -ιον > -ιν, see above, p. 115; cf. pp. 25-29.

ἄρσηνον *PLond.* 909a (iii, 170-1).5 (A.D. 136)
ἄρρενον (neut.) *PSAAthen.* 20.14 (A.D. 111); (masc.) *BGU* 88.6 (A.D. 147)
ἄρενον *SB* 9214.12 (A.D. 311)

2) Dat. pl.:

τοῖς ... ἀδελφοῖς ἀρσένοις *PMich.* 326.49 (A.D. 48)

3) Acc. pl.:

καμήλους ἀρσένους *PPetaus* 85.6-7 (A.D. 185)

These heteroclitic *o*-stem forms were supported by the influence of other *o*-stem forms in the contexts in which they occur, but the original *n*-stem genitive ἄρρενος seems to have been adopted as a late *o*-stem nominative elsewhere in Greek.[1]

b. εὐθύριν is found as well as an *o*-stem by-form εὐθύρινος:[2]

εὐθύριν (nom.) *PSI* 1131.3, with dat. εὐθύρινι 6,9 (A.D. 41/44); *BGU*
177 — *MChr.* 253.2 part. rest. (A.D. 46/47); *POxy.* 2349.3 (A.D. 70);
PLond. 141 (ii, 181-2).3, sim. also 3, with dat. εὐθύρινι 4 (A.D. 88);
PRyl. 153.46-50 (6 times) (A.D. 138-61)
εὐθύρρειν (nom.) *BGU* 1059.20 (30 B.C.-A.D. 14)
εὐθύρρεινι, εὐθύρρεινος *SB* 8256 = *PSAAthen.* 26.5,7 (A.D. 41-68)
εὐθύρεινα *SB* 7555.13 (A.D. 154)
εὐθύρινος (nom.) *PMich.* 264-5.18 (A.D. 37)
εὐθυρίνου (gen. sg. fem.) *PLips.* 5 = *MChr.* 171 ii.7 (A.D. 293)
εὐθυρίνην *PMich.* 281.4 (1st cent.)

3. *r*-stem adjectives.

a. Adjectives of this type are sporadically used indeclinably, e.g., τὴν γυναῖκά μου Ἰσάριον ἀπάτωρ *BGU* 225.11-12 (A.D. 161).

b. Fluctuation in the stem vowel, e.g., ἀπάτωρος *PMich.* 359 A.116 (A.D. 174-5), ἀπάτορι *PMich.* 370.9 (A.D. 189), is not significant for morphology in light of the identification of ο and ω.[3]

---

[1] Schwyzer i, 582.

[2] εὐθύρ(ρ)ιν, ὀξύριν, etc. are declined as *n*-stems in the Ptol. papp., w. 3 exx. of the *o*-stem gen. εὐθυρίνου (Mayser i, 213; i², 2, 56, 57). A nom. εὐθύρρις is attested in Poll. (v.l. -ριν) (*LSJ*, s.v.). ὀξύριν occurs in the Rom.-Byz. papp. only once, misspelled ὀξύριζ *SB* 4668.6 (A.D. 678).

[3] See Vol. i, 275-7, and Introd. to Morphology above, p. XIX.

c. The acc. sg. sporadically ends in -ν, e.g., παντοκράτοραν θεόν *BGU* 948.3 (prob. 4th/5th cent.).[1]

d. The voc. is the same as the nom., e.g., παντοκράτωρ *PGMXtn.* 8a.1 (6th cent.).[2]

4. Adjectives of one termination. ἀφῆλιξ, πένης, and φυγάς occur.[3]

a. ἀφῆλιξ is normally inflected according to the velar stem declension, but ο-stem forms derived from the gen. sg. ἀφήλικος are also found:[4]

ἀφήλικος (gen.) *SB* 9049.5 (A.D. 212-17)
    ἀφήλικι *PGrenf.* i, 49 = *WChr.* 248.12 (A.D. 220/1)
    ἀφήλικα *PMich.* 172.8 (A.D. 62)
    ἀφήλιξι *PGrenf.* i, 47.6 (A.D. 148)
but ἀφήλικος (nom.) *PMich.* 538.6 (A.D. 126); *POxy.* 2134.31 (ca. A.D. 170)
    ἀφηλίκους υἱούς *PCairMasp.* 6 R.2 (ca. A.D. 567)

b. πένης is found in the following forms:[5]

πένης *PBrem.* 38.21 (A.D. 118); *POxy.* 471.95 (2nd cent.); *PSI* 1243.18 (A.D. 208); (fem.) *BGU* 1024 vii.9 (late 4th cent.: *BL* i, 88)
πένητι *PRein.* 47.11 (2nd cent.); *PFlor.* 296.18 part. rest. (6th cent.); *PCairMasp.* 20 R.13 (Byz.)
πενήτων *POxy.* 2193.14 abbrev. (5th/6th cent.); *PLond.* 77 = *MChr.* 319.38,74 (late 6th cent.); *PCairMasp.* 20 R.11 (6th cent.); *PCairMasp.* 295 iii.9 (6th cent.)
πένησι *PCairMasp.* 9 V.24 (6th cent.)
cf. πένητας *SB* 6133.8-9, inscr. (prob. 7th/8th cent.)

---

[1] Cf. the acc. in -ν of *r*-stem nouns above, pp. 45-46.

[2] Cf. voc. πατήρ, μήτηρ, θυγάτηρ for πάτερ, μῆτερ, θύγατερ above, p. 62.

[3] μάκαρ is also found in Ζεῦ μάκαρ ἀθανάτων in a 2nd hand in the blank space between the columns of a taxing list in *POxy.* 832 (16/15 B.C.) and also in a poet. inscr., *SB* 4229.4,8 (3rd/4th cent.). μάκαρ is also found in the mag. papp., e.g., voc. in *PGM* 4.445,1966 (4th cent.); etc. It is generally replaced by the *o*- and *a*-stem derivative μακάριος (cf. Palmer, 32). τρίσμακαρ is also found in *SB* 2040.2, inscr. (Xtn.); cf. below, p. 158.

[4] In the Ptol. papp., *o*-stem forms of ἀφήλικος (and ἐνήλικος) are normal, w. ἀφῆλιξ attested only once (1st cent. B.C.) (Mayser i², 2, 57). ἀφήλικος does not occur outside of the papp., but ἐνήλικος is found in an inscr. and Plu. (*LSJ*, s.vv.). Both the velar and vowel stem formations are found in MGr. ἀνῆλιξ/ἀνήλικος, w. ἀφῆλιξ and ἐνήλικος (Kykkotis, s.vv.).

[5] πένης occurs as a masc. subst. in Democr. Hdt. Lys. S. Ar. X. Archyt. etc. and as an adj. in E. Fl. Luc., w. the compar. in X. and the superl. in D. (*LSJ*, s.v.). Although ἡ πένησσα is attested as a fem. of πένης in Hsch. (*LSJ*, s.v.), the one termination use of the adj. reflects its origin (as of most adjs.) as a subst. (Schwyzer ii, 134; cf. i, 543, n. 1).

c. φυγάς is used substantively in the following regular forms:[1]

φυγάς *PLond.* 1343.21, with φυγάδων 16,36, φυγάδας 29 (A.D. 709) and
sim freq. in the Aphrodito papyri in *PLond.* iv.
φυγάδων *PLond.* 1332.5,16 (A.D. 708); *PLond.* 1382 = *PRossGeorg.* iv,
1.4,10,14, etc. (A.D. 710); etc.
φυγ[ά]δας *POxy.* 44 = *WChr.* 275.15 (late 1st cent.)

D. ADJECTIVES WITH MIXED STEMS

1. μέγας, μεγάλη, μέγα is declined regularly, with only isolated abnormalities
arising mainly from confusion of gender and case.[2]

a. The acc. sg. neut. used sporadically for other cases may reflect the development of an indeclinable form:

ἐν τῷ ἐποίκῳ (for ἐποικίῳ) τῷ μέγα *SB* 4755.5-6 (Byz.)
ἐν τῷ μέγα ὑδροφόρ(ῳ) *POxy.* 1925.33 (7th cent.)

b. The acc. sg. neut. ends in -ν, identical in form with the masc., in τὸ μέγαν
προάστιον *PBas.* 19.6: *BL* iii, 7 (6th/7th cent.).[3] Conversely, the masc. is written
without the final -ν in the name τὸν Μέγα *PJand.* 21.4 (6th/7th cent.).[4]

c. The gen. is erroneously used for the acc. sg. masc. in εἰς τὸ μεγάλου (for
τὸν μέγαν) ποταμόν *POxy.* 1929.6 (late 4th/5th cent.).

2. πολύς, πολλή, πολύ is also declined regularly except for sporadic analogical forms and orthographic variants.[5]

a. The acc. sg. neut. ends in ν in πολὺν μέτρον *PLond.* 1404.4 (early 8th cent.).

---

[1] The origin of φυγάς is obscure. It may represent a dental stem formation from the
verb stem in -α- or perh. an ancient type of formation based on IE *-a-, -ad-*, as -ῐ(ς), -ῐδ-,
etc. (Schwyzer i, 508). In MGr., it is decl. as a vocalic stem subst. (cf. Jannaris, § 478).

[2] For the origin of the *l*-stem forms, see Schwyzer i, 584, & nn. 1, 3. The *l*-stem forms
are also Celtic and Germanic, but *n*-stem forms appear in Celtic and Latin (*magnus*). The *l*-stem
forms have been extended to all cases in MGr., so that the adj. has been transformed into
an adj. of the 1st and 2nd decl. throughout (μεγάλος, -η, -ο), although an indecl. μέγα is
found occasionally (Schwyzer, *ibid.*; Thumb, *Handbook*, § 108.2; Jannaris, § 482).

[3] Cf. also from the mag. papp. ὅ ἐστιν μέγαν καὶ θαυμαστόν *PGM* 13.738 (A.D. 346).

[4] For the freq. omission and addition of -ν, see Vol. i, 111-14.

[5] For the origin of this *-u-* suffix formation and its archaic inflection, see Schwyzer i,
463, 584; Chantraine[2], § 110.

b. The dat. pl. masc. appears anomalously as πολλοῖσιν χρόνοις in *PGen.*
53 = *PAbinn.* 36.23 (ca. A.D. 346).

c. The nom. and acc. sg. masc. and neut. sporadically have the stem πολλ-:

πολλύς *SB* 9139.7, with ἄλως for ἄλλως 15 (6th cent.)
πολλύν *POxy.* 1869.4 (6th/7th cent.)
πολλύ *POxy.* 1874.9 (6th cent.)

This is an orthographic variant involving the identification of single and
double consonants rather than a new formation. In Modern Greek, the stem
πολλ- is used throughout the paradigm *except* in these cases.[1]

3. πρᾶος, πραεῖα, πρᾶον occurs in the following forms:[2]

παρᾶος (for πρᾶος) *SB* 9125.10, amulet (n.d.)
πρᾶον (acc. sg. neut.) *SB* 8028.7 (6th cent.); *PLond.* 1663.9 (6th cent.);
    PCairMasp. 321 A.7 (A.D. 548/63)
cf. adv. πράως *SB* 5314.16 (Byz.)

4. The defective adjective σῶς/σῶος has the forms σῶς and σῶν, along with
σῶον, σῶα, and σώους:[3]

---

[1] πολύς, πολλή, πολύ; πολλοῦ, πολλῆς, πολλοῦ; πολύ(ν), πολλή(ν), πολύ; pl. πολλοί,
πολλές, πολλά, etc. (Thumb, *Handbook*, § 112; Mirambel, *Langue grecque*, 114; *Gram.*, 80-81;
Maspero, 60). For the interchange of λ and λλ in other words, as well as the converse λλ >
λ in πολοῖς, etc., see Vol. i, 155-6.

[2] πρᾶος supplies the sg. in Att. Trag. Com. exc. that the fem. is always πραεῖα (πρᾶος
is attested as fem. only in Plu.), but a sg. πραΰς (Ion. πρηΰς), formed by the addition of the
suffix -*ju*- (Schwyzer, i, 480), is used in Ep. Lyr. (also S. and usu. LXX, Plb. etc.). In the pl.,
forms of πρᾶοι are found in Isoc. Pl. while forms of πραεῖς are used by X. Arist. (*LSJ*, s.v.;
Schwyzer i, 574; Chantraine[2], § 109). The -ε/-ο stem is secondary in Att. (Schwyzer and
Chantraine, *ibidd.*). The *u*-stem inflection is found elsewh. in the Koine. It is used excl. in
the NT (*BDF*, § 26, 47.4), and the mag. papp.: πραΰς, πραΰν *PGM* 4.451,1042,1046,1972
(4th cent.), w. the Ion. πρηΰν *PGM* 1.321 (late 4th/5th cent.). See further Crönert, 50, n.
7; 187, n. 7; 290, n. 2. This *u*-stem form has survived in MGr. in the modification πραγύς,
πραγειά, πραγύ (Jannaris, § 480), along with the vocalic πρᾶος (Kykkotis, s.v.).

[3] σῶς represents a root formation in the strict sense w. extension of one vowel grade
throughout (Schwyzer i, 424). The stem σωο- never appears in Hom. or early poetry, only
σῶς for σόος. In Att., the nom. is σῶς, σῶν Th. D., w. fem. σῶς E. Ar. Pl. Call., fem. σᾶ Ar.
inscrr.; acc. σῶν Th. D.; nom. pl. σῶ Th. (according to Ael. Dion., codd. σῶοι); neut. σᾶ
E. Pl. inscr., σόα Hdt.; gen. pl. σόων (v.l. σώων) Hdt.; acc. pl. masc. σῶς D. Luc.; Hdt.
has nom. sg. σῶς, σῶν, acc. σόον (v.l. σῶον), nom. pl. masc., σόοι, fem. σόαι, neut. σόα,
gen. pl. σόων (v.l. σώων). The stem σωο- is attested in nom. σῶος X. Luc., fem. σώα D. X.
Aristid., neut. σῶον Lys. Arist. Plu. Aristid. Sor. Lib.; gen. sg. fem. σώας D. inscr. (Didymia);
acc. σώαν D. Aristid.; nom. pl. masc. σῶοι D. X.; acc. pl. masc. σώους Luc. Aristid.; neut. σῶα
X. Arist. (*LSJ*, s.v.; cf. Schwyzer, i, 558, n. 1). Att. prose inscrr. have part. rest. fem. σ[ᾶ],
neut. σῶν and σῶον, neut. pl. σῶ[α] (*MS*, 149). The neut. pl. σῶα is attested in Asia Minor
inscrr. from the Rom. period (Schweizer, 142). The LXX has acc. sg. masc. σῶον, nom.
pl. fem. σῶαι (v.l. σῶοι) (Theodotion), acc. pl. masc. σώους, neut. σῶα; the adj. is not
found in the NT; cf. also σώην Babr., σῶον *AP* (Phld.) (*LSJ*, *ibid.*).

σῶς (nom. sg. fem.) *POxy.* 2835.19 (mid 1st cent.)

σῶν *BGU* 1058 = *MChr.* 170.32 (13 B.C.)[1]

but σῶον *PMich.* 587.22,31 (A.D. 24/25); *PLond.* 301 = *MChr.* 340.13
(A.D. 138-61); *SB* 7534 = *PLBat.* i, 5.9 (A.D. 154); *PMeyer* 14.8
(A.D. 159/60); *BGU* 64 = *WChr.* 281.23 (A.D. 368/9)

σῶων (acc. sg.) *PLBat.* vi, 15.103 (ca. A.D. 114)

σῶα *BGU* 1106 = *MChr.* 108.31 (13 B.C.); *POslo* 52.7 (2nd cent.);
SB 6945.14 (A.D. 206); *PLond.* 948 = *MChr.* 341.8 (A.D. 236);
POxy. 903.11 (4th cent.); etc.

σώους *PCairPreis.* 31.11,89 = *PRossGeorg.* ii, 18.303, with σῶα 129,192
(A.D. 140)

E. COMPARISON OF ADJECTIVES[2]

Despite the simplification of comparison and the gradual decline of the superlative in Koine Greek,[3] the formation of the comparative and superlative
degrees of adjectives is still very much a living feature of the language of the
whole period of the papyri. Seventy-five formations of the superlative alone,
which occurs considerably less frequently than the comparative grade, are listed
in Gradenwitz for papyri of the Roman and Byzantine periods. These comprise
only those superlatives listed as independent entries by Preisigke, *WB*, and do
not include superlative degrees of common adjectives, as γλυκύτατος, ἥδιστος,
κάλλιστος, etc. It was in fact the too frequent use of the superlative, especially
in titles of respect in Byzantine documents, which eventually weakened its
force to that of a simple elative.[4]

1. Comparison by means of the suffixes -τερος and -τατος.

The suffix -τερος, originally denoting a contrasting situation, as δεξιτερός:
ἀριστερός, which led to πρότερος: ὕστερος, etc.,[5] became the normal comparative
formation in derivatives and compounds in Greek, especially in *o-* and *a* stem
adjectives. The suffix -τατος, derived from the ordinal suffix in δέκατος, etc.,
which led to ἔσχατος, became associated with -τερος as the superlative grade.[6]

---

[1] In σῶς οὖσα *PMon.* 8.8 (late 6th cent.), σῶς is prob. a pers. name. The reading οὔπω
ωμ σῶς ἔσχον *PStrassb.* 73.16 (3rd cent.) prob. represents οὔπω κομψῶς ἔσχον (cf. *BL* iii, 231).

[2] See esp. Schwyzer i, 533-9; Chantraine[2], § 111-26; Buck, *GD*, § 113; Thumb, *Handbook*, § 116-20; Jannaris, § 483-515; Mirambel, *Gram.*, 88-91; Maspero, 60-63.

[3] See esp. *BDF*, § 60.

[4] This development will be analyzed more fully in Vol. iii, *Syntax*.

[5] Schwyzer i, 533-4; Chantraine[2], § 119.

[6] Schwyzer i, 534; Chantraine[2], § 120.

In the papyri, these formations remained unaltered except for some few irregularities, and extended their scope to other adjectives normally developed by means of the primary comparative suffixes -ίων, -ιστος.

a. In adjectives of the first and second declensions, the lengthening of the thematic vowel before the comparative suffixes if the preceding syllable is short[1] is merely an orthographic device during the Roman and Byzantine periods, in view of the complete identification of o and ω in pronunciation.[2]

b. Several adjectives whose comparative and superlative were usually formed by means of the primary comparatives suffixes -ίων, -ιστος in earlier Greek have competing forms in -τερος, -τατος in the papyri of the Roman and Byzantine periods.

1) The comparative of ὀλίγος is still normally the suppletive ἥσσων or ἐλάσσων,[3] but [ὀ]λιγωτέρας is used in *PSI* 1422.7 (3rd cent.).[4]

2) The comparative of μικρός is likewise normally the suppletive ἐλάσσων, but μικρότερος occurs in the following forms:[5]

μεικρότερος *MChr.* 372 v.17 (2nd cent.)
μεικροτέρα *BGU* 781 vi.4 (1st cent.)
μικρότερον *POxy.* 131.7 (6th/7th cent.)

3) The Epic κρατερός (for usual κρείσσων[6]) is used in *SB* 5632.4, inscr. (3rd/4th cent.).

4) A comparative is formed from a participle in ἠγαπημενότ[ερον] *PApoll.* 72.4 (A.D. 703-15).

5) The superlative ἀγαθώτατος[7] is as common as βέλτιστος:[8]

ἀγαθωτάτῳ *PMich.* 498.8-9 (2nd cent.)
ἀγαθότατον (acc. sg. masc.) *PPar.* 18.3 (3rd cent.: *BL* iv, 67); *PLond.*
981 = *WChr.* 130.8 (4th cent.)

---

[1] Schwyzer i, 534-5; Chantraine[2], § 121. This distribution is generally maintained in the orthography of Att. and Koine inscrr. (*MS*, 151; Schweizer, 159; Nachmanson, 142-3).
[2] See Vol. i, 275-7.
[3] See exx. below, p. 152.
[4] ὀλιγώτερος Hp. App. S.E. Ael.; ὀλίγιστος *Il.* Hes. inscr. Ar. Pl. etc. (*LSJ*, s.v. ὀλίγος).
[5] μικρότερος, -τατος Ar. D. (*LSJ*, s.v. μικρός).
[6] See exx. below, pp. 152-3.
[7] ἀγαθώτερος is found in the LXX, D.S. Diod. Plot. & Rh., and ἀγαθώτατος in D.S. Hld. etc. (*LSJ*, s.v. ἀγαθός) and in the Lycian inscrr. (Hauser, 99).
[8] See exx. below, p. 155.

ἀγαθώτατον (acc. sg. masc.) *PMich.* 244.4 (A.D. 43); *PBaden* 37 = *PSarap.* 90.4 (prob. A.D. 108); *PBrem.* 5.6-7 (A.D. 117-19) ἀγαθοτάτην *POxy.* 1757.26 (A.D. 138+); sim. *PRyl.* 691.18 (late 3rd cent.)

c. Secondary formations in -ύτερος, -ύτατος[1] are found not only in those adjectives in which this formation was regular, but also in some adjectives in which the primary comparative suffixes were sometimes used elsewhere in Greek.[2]

1) Regular:

βαρυτάτης *WChr.* 6.12 (A.D. 425-50)
    βαρυτάτη *PLond.* 1676.15 (A.D. 566-73)
    βαρυτάτην *POxy.* 2131.12 (A.D. 207); *BGU* 159 = *WChr.* 408.4 (A.D. 216)
ὀξυτάτην, ὀξύτατος *PMilVogl.* 24.49,58-59 (A.D. 117)
πλατύτερον *POxy.* 2190.56 (late 1st cent.)
πρεσβύτερος *PPhil.* 1.49, with -ον 39 (ca. A.D. 103-24)
    πρεσβυτέρου *SB* 7339.2 (A.D. 69-79); *POslo* 111.188 abbrev. (A.D. 235); *PFlor.* 33.16 (early 4th cent.); etc.
    πρεσβυτέραν *PCornell* 40.23 (A.D. 105)

2) Others attested with primary suffixes elsewhere in Greek:

βαθύτερον *PLond.* 899 (iii, 208-9).4 (2nd cent.)[3]
βραδύτερον *PMich.* 252.9 (A.D. 26/27); *PMich.* 273.10 (A.D. 46); *PRyl.* 81.27 (ca. A.D. 104); etc.
    βραδύτερα *PSI* 905.16 (A.D. 26/27); *PMich.* 278-9.6-7 (ca. A.D. 30); *BGU* 69 = *MChr.* 142.19-20 part. rest. (A.D. 120); etc.[4]
βραχύτατον *PFlor.* 176.2 (A.D. 256)
    βραχυτάτων *PFlor.* 268.11 (3rd cent.); *BGU* 1027 xxvii.13 (4th/5th cent.)
    βραχυτάτας *PSAAthen.* 53 R.3 (3rd cent.)[5]
γλυκυτάτη *PLBat.* xvi, 30 iii.7 (3rd cent.)
    γλυκυτάτης *POxy.* 33 V = *WChr.* 20 i.13 (late 2nd cent.)

---

[1] Cf. Schwyzer i, 534; Mayser i², 2, 59.

[2] The form -ύτερος developed eventually into a productive stereotyped suffix and forms the MGr. compar. (freq. also written -ήτερος) even of some *o*- and *a*-stem ad:s., as μεγαλύτερος, μακρύτερος, etc., from wh. a positive by-form μακρύς developed (Schwyzer i, 534-5; Thumb, *Handbook*, § 116-17; Jannaris, § 496; Mirambel, *Gram.*, 88, Maspero, **61**).

[3] βαθύτερος Pl. X., βαθύτατος Hdt. Ar. Ael.; poet. βαθίων, βάθιστος; Dor. βάσσων (*LSJ*, s.v.).

[4] βραδύτερος Th. Theocr., βραδύτατος Ar., w. βραδίων Artem., βράδιστος *Il.* (βαρδ-), Aret. etc.; hybrid βραδίστατος Ael. (*LSJ*, s.v.).

[5] βραχύτερον Pl. X. Plb., βραχύτατος Lys. D., w. βράσσων Hom., βράχιστος Antiph. Pi. (*LSJ*, s.v.).

γλυκυτάτοις *PMich.* 207.2, with -ον 3, -οι 13 (2nd cent.)[1]

ἡδύτερον *POslo* 54.9 (2nd/3rd cent.)[2]

ταχύτερον (adv.) frequent in letters, e.g., *PTebt.* 410.11 (A.D. 16); *SB* 9120.12 (1st cent.); *PMich.* 479.9,13 (early 2nd cent.); *SB* 7529.6 (2nd/3rd cent.); *BGU* 816.14 (3rd cent.); etc.

cf. [ταχ]υτέρου (prob. for -ῳ) *PAmh.* 145 = *WChr.* 53.19 (ca. A.D. 400)[3]

d. The suffixes -έστερος, -έστατος, originating in Homeric ὀρέστερος, χαριέστερος, etc.,[4] are the regular comparative formation for *s*-stem adjectives, as in the following examples (with orthographic and analogical variants):[5]

ἀληθέστερον, θεοφιλεστάτου *PAntin.* 188.16,18 (6th/7th cent.)

ἀμεθέστατον *PSarap.* 22.9-10 part. rest. (A.D. 114/15); 48a (pp. 287-8).5-6 (A.D. 123); *PAmh.* 87 = *PSarap.* 27.26-27 (A.D. 125)

    ἀμεθεστάτους *PAmh.* 85 = *MChr.* 274.22 (A.D. 78); *PSarap.* 28 *bis* (pp. 277-8).8 (A.D. 122)

ἀφιδέτερα (for ἀφειδέστερα) *PMich.* 228.19 (A.D. 47)

    ἀφιδέστερα *PMich.* 229.23 (A.D. 48)

εὐτυχέστερον *PCairMasp.* 151.20 (A.D. 570)

    εὐτυχεστάτωι *POxy.* 2976.2 (2nd cent.)

    εὐτυχέστατον *PRossGeorg.* ii, 26.4 (A.D. 160)

καταδεέστεροι *PMich.* 532.7 (A.D. 181/2)

    ὑποδεέστερα *SB* 9518 = *PMed.* 72.2 (3rd cent.)

μεγαλοπρεπεστάτου *POxy.* 1829.2 part. rest., 5,12 part. rest. (ca. A.D. 577-9?)

πληρεστάτῳ *PFlor.* 66.3 (A.D. 398); *SB* 7996 = *PSI* 1239.6 (A.D. 430); *Archiv* iii, p. 418.18 (late 6th cent.); *PLond.* 77 = *MChr.* 319.9,39 (late 6th cent.)

προσεχέστερον *PMich.* 486.13 (2nd cent.)

προσφιλεστάτην *PRossGeorg.* ii, 43.25 (2nd/3rd cent.)

σαφέστερον *POxy.* 471.12-13 (2nd cent.)

σεμνοπρεπεστάτης *PCairMasp.* 279.7 (ca. A.D. 570)

    σεμνοπρεπεστάτη (for -ην) *POxy.* 1872.7 (late 5th/early 6th cent.)

φρικωδέστατον *PStrassb.* 48.6 (A.D. 566)

---

[1] γλυκύτερος, -τατος Pi.; γλυκίων *Od.* (also γλυκερώτατος, never γλυκύτερος *metri causa*: Schwyzer i, 534, n. 11), γλύσσων X., γλύκιστος B. Ael. (*LSJ*, s.v.). γλύσσων is the orig. formation, the -ίων suffix secondary (Schwyzer i, 536, 538).

[2] Cf. ἥδιστα below. ἡδύτερος Thphr. Ps.-Proc. *Anthol.*, ἡδύτατος Plu. *Anthol.*; ἡδίων *Od.* Lys. Pherecr. etc., ἥδιστα *Od.* Pl. etc. (*LSJ*, s.v.).

[3] Cf. θάσσων, τάχιστος below. ταχύτερος Hdt. Arist. Aret. etc. but not good Att., ταχύτατος (rare) adj. Pi., neut. pl. as adv. Antiph. codd.X.; θάσσων/θάττων Hom. Pi. S. Ar. Pl. X. Arist. D. Men. Theoc. Plb. Aristid.; ταχίων Hp. Men. LXX, D.H. D.S. Gem. NT, J. Ph. Plu. etc. (*LSJ*, s.v.) but condemned by Phyrn. 58 (Rutherford, 149-51).

[4] Schwyzer i, 535.

[5] MGr. retains the compar. suffix -έστερος (& superl. -έστατος) for adjs. in -ης, although later adjs. have only a periphrastic formation (Mirambel, *Gram.*, 88, n. 4; 91, n. 14).

e. The suffix -τατος added to the final consonant of the adjectival stem is preserved in the superlative φίλτατος, but a competing formation φιλαίτατος is found in Byzantine times:[1]

φίλτατε *PRossGeorg.* ii, 43.26 (2nd/3rd cent.)
> φίλτατα *PAmh.* 145 = *WChr.* 53.23 (ca. A.D. 400)
> φιλτάτων *PLips.* 34.16; 35.17 (both ca. A.D. 375); *PMerton* 98.4 (late 6th cent.)
> cf. τõ φιλτο (for τῷ φιλτάτῳ) *PLBat.* xiii, 19.1 (3rd cent.)
φιλαιτάτοις *PCairMasp.* 151-2.61 (A.D. 570)
>   αι
> φιλ ε [τά]τους *PCairMasp.* 310 R.17 (6th cent.); sim. *PCairMasp.* 97 V (d).38 part. rest. (2nd half 6th cent.)
cf. also γερα(ίτερος) *PLond.* 1164 (iii, 154-67) f.38; sim. i.22; k.27 (A.D. 212) and περαιτέρω, etc., below, p. 150.

f. The suffixes -τερος, -τατος are also added to adverbs, not only to form comparative and superlative adverbs, but to form adjectives as well:

ἀνωτέραν *PHermRees* 32.2 part. rest. (6th cent.); *PMichael.* 40.42 (mid 6th cent.); *POxy.* 1892.41 part. rest. (A.D. 581); *PMon.* 7.47 (A.D. 583); *POxy.* 2420.21 (A.D. 610)
> cf. ἀνώτερον *PColt* 16.38 (A.D. 512); sim. *PColt* 31.48,52 (6th cent.)
ἀνωτέρων *PDura* 31.41 (A.D. 204)
ἀνωτέρω *PGiss.* 48 = *WChr.* 171.24 (A.D. 202/3); *PBeattyPanop.* 1.9, etc. (A.D. 298); 2.115, etc. (A.D. 300); *PLond.* 483 (ii, 323-9). 40,68 (A.D. 616); etc.; cf. *PColt* 31.14 (6th cent.); etc.
ἀνωτάτωι *PLond.* 1912.103 (A.D. 41)
> ἀνωτάτῳ *PLond.* 1711 = *WChr.* 439 V c.11 (A.D. 42); *BGU* 1027 xxvii = *WChr.* 424 ii.16 (late 4th cent.: *BL* i, 88)
ἀνωτάτην *SB* 9458.16 (2nd half 2nd cent.); *BGU* 242 = *MChr.* 116. 15 (A.D. 186-8: *BL* i, 434); *PMich.* 175.19-20 (A.D. 193)[2]
ἐνδότερον *PLond.* 1768.2 (6th cent.)
> ἐντοτέρω (for ἐνδοτέρω[3]) *PSarap.* 96.14: *BL* vi, 172 (A.D. 129)
ἐξωτέρου *POxy.* 896 = *WChr.* 48.14 (A.D. 316); cf. *PColt* 98.9 (6th cent.)

---

[1] For φιλαίτερος, see Schwyzer i, 534. φιλίων *Od.*, φίλιστος interpolated in S.; φίλτερος Ep. Lyr. Trag. and late prose, φίλτατος Ar. Pl. X. Aeschin.; φιλαίτερος X. Call., φιλαίτατος X. Theoc.; φιλώτερος codd. X. Call.; periphrastic μᾶλλον φίλος A. S. Thpbr., μάλιστα φίλος X. (*LSJ*, s.v. φίλος sub fin., φίλτερος, φίλτατος). φίλτατος is preserved in MGr. although the normal mode of compar. is periphrastic (Mirambel, *Gram.*, 91).

[2] ἀνώτερος Arist. etc.; ἀνώτατος Hdt. etc.; ἀνωτέρω, ἀνωτάτω class. (*LSJ*, s.v.).

[3] See Vol. i, 81. Cf. ἐνδοτέρω Hp. J. Plu. D.L., ἐνδότατος Hsch. Just., ἐνδοτάτω Plu. Hdn. Luc. Procl. (*LSJ*, s.v. ἐνδοτέρω).

ἐξωτέραν *PStrassb.* 296 V.8 (A.D. 326)

ἐξώτερον *PFlor.* 100.11 (A.D. 231/2?)

ἐξοτέρων *SB* 6944.13 (prob. A.D. 136)

ἐξωτέρω *POxy.* 498.12 (2nd cent.)[1]

ἐσωτέρα(ς) *POxy.* 2195.164 (6th cent.)

ἠσωτέρα *SB* 4755.23 (Byz.)[2]

κατωτέρω *PBeattyPanop.* 1.25,30, etc. (A.D. 298); 2.1, etc. (A.D. 300);
   cf. *PDura* 43.35 (A.D. 238-44)

κατωτέρου *SB* 5164 (n.d.)
   cf. κατωτέρα *PColt* 105.3 (6th/7th cent.)[3]

περαιτέρω *BGU* 372 = *WChr.* 19 ii.12 (A.D. 154); *PCairMasp.* 97 R.52
   (6th cent.); 151-2.172; 156.22 part. rest. (A.D. 570); *PLond.* 483 (ii,
   323-9).62 (A.D. 616); *PApoll.* 29.5 part. rest. (ca. A.D. 713)

περετέρω *PLond.* 1674.45 (ca. A.D. 570); 113 (2) (i, 204-7).49 (6th/
   7th cent.); *PApoll.* 69.6 part. rest. (A.D. 703-15)

περαίτερον *PCairMasp.* 97 V d.73 (6th cent.)[4]

ὑπέρτερον *PCairMasp.* 2 i.7 (A.D. 567: *BL* i, 100)

ὑπ[ερ]τάτης *PStrassb.* 40.41 (A.D. 569)[5]

cf. also ὑστέρου *PFlor.* 86 = *MChr.* 247.25 (late 1st cent.); *POxy.* 1118.12
   (late 1st/early 2nd cent.); *PFlor.* 1 = *MChr.* 243.8 (A.D. 153); *PLond.*
   113 (i, 199-204) i.42 (6th cent.); etc.

ὕστερον *PJand.* 27.8-9: *BL* i, 198 (A.D. 100/1): *SB* 7352 = *PMich.*
   490.22 (2nd cent.)

ὕστατον *SB* 5223.13 (n.d.)[6]

g. Adverbial formations are also found in ὀρθρίτερον and ὀψίτερον:

ὀρθρίτερον *BGU* 1201.4 (A.D. 2); *SB* 7374 = *POslo* 21.9 (A.D. 71)

ὀρθρέτερον *PStrassb.* 37.14 (3rd cent.)[7]

---

[1] ἐξωτάτω Pl. Arist. Ph., ἐξώτατος LXX, Ph. (*LSJ*, s.v.).

[2] Cf. also ὁ ἐσώτερος *PGM* 7.558 (3rd cent.). ἐσωτέρω Hdt., ἐσωτάτω Hp., ἐσώτερος Ptol. papp. and NT (Mayser i², 2, 62; *BDF*, § 62), ἐσώτατος Ph. Sch.Pi. (*LSJ*, s.vv.).

[3] κατωτέρω Hdt. Ar. Alex., κατωτάτω Hdt. Phld., κατώτερος Hp. Call. LXX, NT, Vett.Val., κατώτατος X. LXX, w. neut. pl. as adv. Hdt. (*LSJ*, s.vv.; *BDF*, § 62). κατώτερος and κατώτατος are preserved in MGr. (Mirambel, *Gram.*, 88, n. 6; 91, n. 5).

[4] περαιτέρω A. Antiph. E. Th. Ar. Pl. X. etc., περαίτερος Pi. (*LSJ*, s.v.).

[5] ὑπέρτερος and ὑπέρτατος are common in poetry from Hom. on, and the superl. is also found in late prose (*LSJ*, s.vv.); ὑπέρτατος also Ptol. papp. (Mayser, i², 2, 62). ὑπέρτατος is preserved in MGr. (Mirambel, *Gram.*, 91).

[6] This is an ancient Gr. formation (cf. Schwyzer i, 533). ἔσχατος, representing the orig. ordinal suffix -to-, is retained in τῷ δὲ ἐσχάτῳ ἔτει *BGU* 918.19 (A.D. 111/12); τῷ δὲ ἐσχάτῳ ἐνιαυτῷ *POxy.* 101.13, sim. 16 (A.D. 142); τῆς ἐσχάτης ἐλπίδας (for ἐλπίδος) *BGU* 1024 iv.13 (late 4th cent.: *BL* i, 88); etc.

[7] ὀρθρίτερον also Ptol. papp. (Mayser i², 2, 58), ὀρθριαίτερος, ὀρθριαίτατος Hdn. (*LSJ*, s.v. ὄρθριος).

ὀψίτερον *BGU* 181.7 (A.D. 57); *POxy.* 2758.5 (ca. A.D. 110-12); *BGU* 759 = *PSarap.* 1.6 (A.D. 125)[1]
cf. ὀψιμώτερος *PFay.* 133 = *PFlor.* 134*.9 (A.D. 260)[2]

These forms may be based on the adverbs ὄρθρου and ὀψέ on the analogy of ὑψίτερος,[3] or they may be new comparative adjectival formations of ὄρθριος and ὄψιος with loss of the thematic vowel.

2. Comparison by means of the suffixes -ίων, -ιστος.

These suffixes, added directly mainly to monosyllabic roots, are primary, as opposed to the productive secondary suffixes -τερος, -τατος. The positive grade of these adjectives, where it exists, is secondary, formed from the same root by means of special suffixes.[4] Never as common in Greek as the secondary comparative suffixes -τερος, -τατος, these primary comparative suffixes are no longer productive in the Roman and Byzantine periods. But they are retained in the most common adjectives, though sometimes in competition with the secondary comparative suffixes.[5] Both long and short forms occur,[6] but the long forms predominate except in stereotyped expressions.[7]

a. Comparative formations in -(ί)ων are found in the following adjectives:[8]

---

[1] ὀψίτερον Pl. and Ptol. papp. (Mayser i[2], 2, 58), ὀψίτερα Pi., ὀψίτατον Poll.; Att. ὀψιαίτερος Arist. Thphr., ὀψιαίτατος X., w. neut. pl. as adv. Pl. Eub. Thphr. (*LSJ*, s.v. ὄψιος).

[2] For the formation of ὄψιμος, see Schwyzer i, 494.

[3] So Schwyzer i, 534, sub 1.

[4] Schwyzer i, 536.

[5] Comparatives in -ίων, -ιστος became rarer elsewh. in the Koine, as NT (*BDF*, § 61). In MGr., only κάλλιο is retained in certain usages (Schwyzer i, 537, n. 4; Mirambel, *Gram.*, 88).

[6] The compar. suffix originated in an *s*-stem suffix *-yes-/-yos-* (cf. Lat. *melioris* w. rhotacism) retained in the so called short forms in -ω and -ους. This *s*-stem suffix was further often expanded by the addition of a nasal suffix *-on-*, resulting in the -ίων, -ιονος, etc., formations existing as the normal long forms in most ad's. (Schwyzer i, 536-7; Chantraine[2], § 111-15).

[7] The short forms are particularly stable in Attic, used almost excl. in the inscrr. but in alternation with -ους, -ονας in lit., partly to avoid homophony. They are also Ion. (infreq. in Hom. but guaranteed by meter at end of line) and Dor. but -ω is always more freq. than -ονα (Schwyzer i, 536, n. 3; *MS*, 151-2). In the Perg. inscrr., however, only one very dbtfl. short form is found and none at Magn., although some appear elsewh. in Asia Minor (Schweizer, 159-60; Nachmanson, 134, 143). In the Ptol. papp., the short endings greatly predominate in both the sg. and pl. in the 3rd cent., while in the 2nd-1st cent. short and long endings are used in the sg. w. approx. equal frequency, while in the pl. the short forms are still more common (Mayser i[2], 2, 59-61). In the NT, the long forms predominate (*BDF*, § 47.2). Exx. of the -ω forms in phrases in wh. the neut. sg. is expected have been variously explained as adverbial formations on the analogy of advs. in -ω, as ἀνωτέρω, or as the acc. pl. neut. used adverbially (see the discussion betw. Crönert, 188, n. 5, and Mayser i[2], 2, 60-61, w. lit.). Mayser's suggestion (p. 61) that the neut. pl. adv. has become a stereotyped indecl. is supported by other evidence in the papp., e.g., πάντα used indecl. (see above, p. 135).

[8] μᾶλλον is not incl. here. Most of the ad's. listed here are also found in the Ptol. papp. (Mayser i[2], 2, 59).

ἀμείνονος *POxy.* 1469.17 (A.D. 298)

    ἀμείνονα *POxy.* 716 = *MChr.* 360.21 (A.D. 186); *PRyl.* 427, frag.
        11.6 (A.D. 198-209?); *PRossGeorg.* v, 25.10 (3rd cent.); *PCairMasp.*
        89 R b.4 (Byz.)

    but εἰς ἀμίνω αἵρεσιν *PLBat.* xiii, 18.37-38 (4th cent.)

    ἄμεινον *PBaden* 39 i = *PSarap.* 87.3 (ca. A.D. 117); *PAlexGiss.* 38.17
        (ca. A.D. 120); *BGU* 288.7 (A.D. 138-61); *POxy.* 2860.8 (2nd cent.);
        POxy. 471.11-12 (2nd cent.); *POxy.* 2276.8 (late 3rd/4th cent.);
        (ἄμινον) *PFay.* 136.8 (4th cent.)

    ἀμείνους αἱρέσεις διδόναι *POxy.* 2109.13-14 (A.D. 261)

βελτίου (for βελτίονι) *PAntin.* 42.21 (A.D. 542)

    βελτίονα *PCairMasp.* 299.21 (6th cent.); *POxy.* 2239.15 (A.D. 598);
        BGU 396.10 (Arab.: *BL* i, 44)

    βέλτειον *PGM* 31b.2-3 (1st cent.)

        βέλτιον *BGU* 1086 ii.2 (2nd/3rd cent.); *SB* 5174.10; 5175.12 (A.D.
            512)

[γλ]ύκιον *POxy.* 1142.16 (late 3rd cent.)[1]

ἐλάσσονος *PAmh.* 70 = *WChr.* 149.12 (A.D. 114-17); *PCairMasp.* 163.28
    (A.D. 569)

    ἐλάσσονι *BGU* 1047 iv.13 (A.D. 117-38)

    ἔλασσον *PGiss.* 61.18 (A.D. 119); *PMich.* 501.16 (2nd cent.); etc.[2]

    but [ἐλ]άσσω, ὁ ἐλάσσω *BGU* 977.10;12,19 (A.D. 162?)

        ἐλάττω φορτ[ία] *PFlor.* 278 ii.13, etc. (mid 3rd cent.)

        ἐλάσσω *PRyl.* 208.23,29 (2nd cent.)

        τῶν ἐλάσσω φανέντων *BGU* 145.5-6: *BL* i, 22 (A.D. 213)

ἥδιο[ν] *BGU* 372 = *WChr.* 19 i.14-15 (A.D. 154)

ἧσσον *CPR* 4 = *MChr.* 159.28 (A.D. 51/53); *CPR* 1 = *StudPal.* xx, 1.22
    (A.D. 83/84); *PLips.* 3 = *MChr.* 172.14 (A.D. 256); etc.

    ἧττον *BGU* 157.9 (2nd/3rd cent.); *PCairMasp.* 169.38 (6th cent.);
        PCairMasp. 97 R.66 (6th cent.); *PHermRees* 32.19 (6th cent.); etc.[3]

θᾶττον *POxy.* 2104.8 part. rest. (A.D. 241?); *POxy.* 122.6 (late 3rd/4th
    cent.)[4]

κρείττονος *PLond.* 1928.3 part. rest. (mid 4th cent.); sim. *SB* 8003.3
    (4th cent.); *PCairMasp.* 6 V.12 (ca. A.D. 567); 89 V.13 (ca. A.D.
    567); so duplic. 294.13 (6th cent.)

    κρείττονι *SB* 9218.18 part. rest., 21 κριτ- (A.D. 319/20 + ?); *PCair-*
        Masp. 151-2.67 (A.D. 570); *POxy.* 128.15 abbrev. (6th/7th cent.)

    κρείσσονα *POxy.* 1062.5 (2nd cent.)

---

[1] For forms of the superl. γλυκυτάτη, etc., see above, pp. 147-8 & Vol. i, Index, p. **341**.
[2] For additional forms, see Vol. i, **147, 159, 161, 164.**
[3] For additional forms, see Vol. i, **147, 158, 164.**
[4] Cf. Vol. i, 146. θᾶττον also occurs in the mag. papp. in *PGM* **2.87 (4th cent.)** and *PGM*
4.199,1467 (4th cent.).

κρείττονα *POxy.* 2680.24-25 (2nd/3rd cent.); *POxy.* 1676.15-16
(3rd cent.)[1]

πανκρείττονος *PCairMasp.* 151-2.35 (A.D. 570)

μείζονος *POxy.* 2416.4 (6th/7th cent.)

μίσονος *PAmh.* 130.16 (A.D. 70)

μίζονα *BGU* 2013.12 (mid 2nd cent.); *BGU* 326 = *MChr.* 316 i.4,
sim. 5 part. rest. (A.D. 189)

but μείζω (acc. sg. fem.) *POslo* 78.7 (A.D. 136); *PFay.* 20.2 (late
3rd/early 4th cent.); *PPhil.* 35.18 (late 2nd cent.); (acc. sg. neut.)
POslo 56.6 (2nd cent.)

μειζόνων *POxy.* 473 = *WChr.* 33.5 (A.D. 138-60)

μινζόνων *POxy.* 1033 = *WChr.* 476.9 (A.D. 392)[2]

τὰ μείζονα *SB* 7357 = *PMich.* 206.25 part. rest. (2nd cent.)

(as title) μείζων *POxy.* 1832.3 (5th/6th cent.)

μείζονος *PCairIsidor.* 62.6,28 (A.D. 296); *POxy.* 1626.5 (A.D. 325);
POxy. 2058.2, etc. (6th cent.)

μίσονος *POxy.* 1835.3,4 (late 5th/early 6th cent.)[3]

μείζονι *POxy.* 158.2 (6th/7th cent.); sim. *POxy.* 86 = *WChr.* 46.21
(A.D. 338); *POxy.* 2244.81, etc. (6th/7th cent.)

μίζοσιν *SB* 9558.14 (A.D. 325); sim. *POxy.* 1867.10 (7th cent.)

μείζονας *PRyl.* 245.12 (3rd cent.); *POxy.* 1853.8 (6th/7th cent.)

cf. also μειζότερος, etc., below, p. 158.

πλείονος *PMich.* 580.8 (ca. A.D. 19/20)

πλείονα *POxy.* 2190.52 (late 1st cent.); *PFlor.* 142.8 (A.D. 264);
PFlor. 150.10 (A.D. 267)

πλεῖον *POxy.* 279 = *WChr.* 348.3 (A.D. 44/45); *BGU* 2052.6 (2nd
cent.); *PCairMasp.* 20 R.2 (6th cent.); etc.

πλέον *BGU* 15 ii.16 (A.D. 197?); *POxy.* 41 = *WChr.* 45.5 (ca. A.D.
300); *PLBat.* xiii, 9.4 (early 4th cent.); *PCairMasp.* 2 ii.24,
with πλεῖον iii.14 (A.D. 567: *BL* i, 100); etc.[4]

πλῆον *PMich.* 309.4, so duplic. *PSI* 916.4 (1st cent.); sim. *PRyl.*
600.15,26 (8 B.C.)[5]

πλείονες *PErl.* 18.11 (A.D. 248); *POxy.* 122.7 (late 3rd/4th cent.)

but οἱ πλείους *SB* 9597.4 (late 4th cent.)

---

[1] Cf. Vol. i, 146-7, 164.

[2] For the insertion of the nasal, see Vol. i, 118-19.

[3] For the interchange of σ & ζ, see Vol. i, 123-4.

[4] πλεῖον/πλέον were used in Ep. according to the exigencies of the meter (*LSJ*, s.v.).
In the Att. inscrr., -ει- was written excl. before a long vowel, but either -ε- or -ει- before
a short vowel, although the neut. sg. was excl. πλέον in class. times (*MS*, 152; cf. further
Schwyzer i, 236). πλέον is the only form at Magn. wh. preserves the -ε- orthography. Much
fluctuation occurs in the use of these spellings and spellings w. ι, η, υ, etc., in the Ptol. papp.
(Mayser i², 2, 60-61); during the Rom.-Byz. periods, this variation is only orthographic:
there was only one spoken form [plio-].

[5] For the interchange of η and ε, see Vol. i, 242-9.

(αἱ) πλείους *PBerlZill.* 7.18 (A.D. 574)

πλείονα *PRyl.* 81.18 (ca. A.D. 104); *POxy.* 2708.10 (A.D. 200/1)

πλειόνων *POxy.* 2411.40 (prob. ca. A.D. 173)

πλείοσι *POxy.* 473 = *WChr.* 33.6 (A.D. 138-60)

πλείονας *POxy.* 2190.30 (late 1st cent.); *BGU* 48.6 (2nd/3rd cent.?:
  BL i, 11)

but τὰς πλείους ἡμέρας *PMich.* 493.6 (2nd cent.)

 πληγὰς πλείους *PRyl.* 141.19; 145.13; 151.12 part. rest. (A.D.
  37-40); *SB* 10244.3 (A.D. 50)

and πλείως (acc. pl. fem.) *PLBat.* xvi, 15.10 (A.D. 236)

πλείονα εὑρίσκῃ *POxy.* 2411.32-33, with πλέον εὑρίσκῃ 35 (prob. ca.
  A.D. 173)

 πλίονα γράψω *POxy.* 939 = *WChr.* 128.24 (4th cent.)

but τὰ πλείω *PLond.* 359 (ii, 150).3 (1st/2nd cent.); *PFuadCrawford*
 6.13 (3rd cent.?)

 πλείω *PMich.* 191-2.8 (A.D. 60); *POxy.* 274 = *MChr.* 193.6 (A.D.
  89-97); *PBaden* 21.4 (A.D. 117); *PMich.* 476.14 (early 2nd
  cent.); *BGU* 33.3 (2nd/3rd cent.: *BL* i, 10); *PSI* 1413.2 (2nd/
  3rd cent.); *PLeit.* 16.11 (A.D. 244-7); *PCairIsidor.* 81.22 (A.D.
  297); *SB* 7438.11, with πλείονα 12-13 (A.D. 527-65); etc.

  πλύωι, πλύω (for πλείω) *SB* 8030 = *PMich.* 245.27,29-30 (A.D.
   47); sim. *SB* 9017 (28).8,9 (1st/2nd cent.)[1]

cf. πλείω ἔλατ[το]ν *PLips.* 28 = *MChr.* 363.10 (A.D. 381)

 and stereotyped ἀρτάβων πεντακοσίων πλεοέλαττον *PMon.* 4-5
  V.10,48-49 (A.D. 581)

  πλέω ἔλαττον *PLond.* 1770.7 (6th cent.); *SB* 9396.5 (2nd half
   6th cent.); *PWürzb.* 19.8 (A.D. 652?); *PHermRees* 34.11
   (7th cent.); etc.

 cf. also πλεωτέραν and πλειοτέραν below, p. 158

το[ῦτ]ο ῥᾷον *POxy.* 1860.8 (6th/7th cent.)[2]

τάχιον *PPrinc.* 20.8 (2nd cent.); *PMich.* 209.9 (late 2nd/early 3rd cent.);
 PMich. 211.5-6 (2nd/3rd cent.); etc.

 τάχειον *POxy.* 113.24 (2nd cent.); *BGU* 417.28 (2nd/3rd cent.);
  PStrassb. 32.6 (A.D. 261); *PJand.* 13.17 (4th cent.); etc.[3]

χεῖρον *POxy.* 237 vii.43 (A.D. 186); *PSI* 1350 V.7 (6th cent.)

---

[1] For the interchange of ει and υ, see Vol. i, 272-3.

[2] ῥᾴων is more common: Th. etc., but ῥᾳδιέστερος Arist. Hyp. Plb. and as adv. Ph.;
Hyp. also ῥᾳδιώτερος (*LSJ*, s.v. ῥᾴδιος).

[3] Cf. the competing ταχύτερον above, p. 148.

χέρι[ο]ν *PStrassb.* 29.39: *WB* ii, s.v. χερείων (A.D. 289)[1]

χείρονα *BGU* 1120.34 (5 B.C.); *PFouad* 80.8 (4th cent.)

but χείρω *POslo* 56.8 (2nd cent.); *POxy.* 2783.13 (3rd cent.); *PRoss-Georg.* iv, 16.4 (A.D. 710)[2]

b. Superlative formations in -ιστος are found in the following adjectives:[3]

αἴσχιστον *PLBat.* xvi, 33.11 (A.D. 147?)

'Αρίστου (emperor) *BGU* 50 = *MChr.* 205.22 (A.D. 115)

    ἀρίστης *POxy.* 1891.2 (A.D. 495); 2237.3 (A.D. 498); 1959.3-4 (A.D. 499); 1960.4 (A.D. 511); *PCairMasp.* 167.2 (6th cent.?); 162.5 (A.D. 568)

    ἀρίσης (for ἀρίστης) *PCairMasp.* 23.5 (A.D. 569)

ἀρίστην *PCairMasp.* 21 R.1 (A.D. 567: *BL* i, 103)

ἄριστε *PCairIsidor.* 64.4 (A.D. 298); 65.3 (A.D. 298/9); *PLBat.* xvi, 32.7 (A.D. 305)

ἄριστα *POxy.* 292.12 (ca. A.D. 25)

ἀρίστοις *PGen.* 1.13 (A.D. 213: *BL* i, 156)[4]

cf. παναρίστης *PLond.* 1677.41 (A.D. 566/7)

    παναρίστῳ *POslo* 85.19 (A.D. 273?)

    πανάριστε *SB* 6649.8, inscr. (1st cent. B.C./1st cent. A.D.: *BL* iii, 178)

and πανταρίστου *PCairMasp.* 131 V A.4 (6th cent.)[5]

βελτίστου *PRyl.* 156.19 (1st cent.); *PCairMasp.* 2 i.1 (A.D. 567: *BL* i, 100)

    βελτίστη *POxy.* 2194.9 (5th/6th cent.)

    ⟦βέλτιστε⟧ *BGU* 1140 = *WChr.* 58.3 (5/4 B.C.)

βέλτιστα *BGU* 1118.11 (22 B.C.); 1120.11 (5 B.C.); *PStrassb.* 279.11 (6th cent.)

cf. βέλτιστον *PGM* 36.36,69 (4th cent.)

ἔγγιστος *POxy.* 496 = *MChr.* 287.12, sim. 13 part. rest. (A.D. 127)

ἐγγίστη (for -ης) *PAmh.* 142 = *MChr.* 65.16 (A.D. 341+)

ἔνγιστα *POxy.* 1258.7 (A.D. 45); *BGU* 1563.12 (A.D. 68); *BGU* 69 = *MChr.* 142.8 (A.D. 120); *PLond.* 1178 = *WChr.* 156.29 (A.D. 194)

    ἔγγιστα *PAntin.* 93.15 (4th cent.)

---

[1] A compar. χερείων is freq. in Hom. but rare in prose (*LSJ*, s.v.; cf. Schwyzer i, 539). The above form prob. represents a scribal anticipation of the -ιον ending.

[2] Cf. also in the mag. papp. χείρονας *PGM* 2.54 (4th cent.). χε(ι)ρότερος serves as the compar. of κακός in MGr. along w. κακύτερος and πιό κακός (Thumb, *Handbook*, § 117-18; Mirambel, *Gram.*, 88, & n. 1).

[3] μάλιστα is not incl. here. Most of these superl. adjs. are also found in the Ptol. papp. (Mayser i², 2, 59). μακάριστος might be added from *SB* 5765.4, inscr. (3rd/4th cent.), a new formation besides Hom. and Trag. μακάρτατος (*LSJ*, s.v.). Later, the reg. superl. is used, e.g., [μ]ακαριωτάτης *PCairMasp.* 6 V.1, etc. (ca. A.D. 567).

[4] ἄριστος is still used in MGr. (Mirambel, *Gram.*, 91).

[5] πανάριστος Hes. *Anthol.* Phld. Luc. inscr. (Amorgos); πανταάριστος was an honorary title in Sparta (inscr.) (*LSJ*, s.vv.).

ἐλάχιστος *PHermRees* 6.9 (4th cent.); *SB* 9566.16 (6th cent.); etc.

    ἐλαχίστου *BGU* 248.19 (1st cent.: *BL* i, 32); *PCairMasp.* 295 i. 29 (6th cent.); 312.47 (A.D. 567); *POxy.* 1901.30 (6th cent.); *PAntin.* 196.4 abbrev. (6th/7th cent.); etc.

    ἐλαχίστης *SB* 5230.28 (early 1st cent.); *PCairMasp.* 151-2.12, etc. (A.D. 570)

    ἐλαχίστων *PLond.* 1676.20 (A.D. 566-73); *SB* 9401.5 (6th/7th cent.); cf. *PColt* 148.1 (7th cent.)

ἥδιστα *POxy.* 1061.21 (22 B.C.); *SB* 7461.11 (A.D. 45); *PBrem.* 21.11; 22.11; 52.10-11 (ca. A.D. 117); *POxy.* 933.5 (late 2nd cent.); *POxy.* 1676.27-28 (3rd cent.); etc.

ἥκιστα *PAntin.* 100.5 (6th cent.)

κάκιστος *PCairMasp.* 5.24 (6th cent.)

    κακίστῳ *PCairMasp.* 97 V d.45 (6th cent.)

    κακίστην *SB* 7622 = *PCairIsidor.* 1.4 (A.D. 297)

καλλίστου *POxy.* 1024.8 (A.D. 129)

    καλίστης *POslo* 62.13 part. rest., 13-14 (1st half 4th cent.: *BL* iii, 123)

    κάλλιστον *PBrem.* 12.4-5 (ca. A.D. 117); *PFlor.* 228.21 part. rest. (3rd cent.); *PFlor.* 201.10 (A.D. 259)

    κάλλιστα *PPhil.* 34.8 (1st cent.); *PMich.* 212.5-6 (2nd/early 3rd cent.); *POslo* 159.4 (3rd cent.); *PSI* 1042.4 (3rd cent.); *PSI* 206.7 (3rd cent.); *PTebt.* 418.7 (3rd cent.); *POxy.* 1679.4 (3rd cent.); *SB* 6222.3 (late 3rd cent.)

    καλλίστοις *POxy.* 237 iv.37 part. rest.; sim. viii.8 (A.D. 186); *POxy.* 705 = *WChr.* 153.40 part. rest. (A.D. 199/200?: *BL* ii, 96)

    καλλίστους *BGU* 46 = *MChr.* 112.11 (A.D. 193)[1]

κράτιστος *PTebt.* 411.5 (2nd cent.); *PAberd.* 51 i.6 part. rest. (mid 2nd cent.); *PCairMasp.* 321 A.2 part. rest. (A.D. 548/63)

    κρατίστου *PAberd.* 147.8 (A.D. 117-38); *PMich.* 180.7; 181.8 (A.D. 131); *BGU* 43.1-2 (2nd/3rd cent.: *BL* i, 11); etc.

μεγίστη *PCairIsidor.* 77.18 (A.D. 320)

    μέγιστον *SB* 2266.27 (4th cent.)

    μέγιστε *BGU* 747 = *WChr.* 35 i.3 (A.D. 139); *BGU* 970 = *MChr.* 242.8 (A.D. 177)

    μεγίστων *PFlor.* 35.7 (A.D. 167)

    μεγίσ[τας] *PAmh.* 142 = *MChr.* 65.19 (A.D. 341+)[2]

    cf. τρισμέγιστος below, p. 158

μήκιστον *PLond.* 1923.23-24; 1929.19-20 part. rest. (mid 4th cent.); *PCairMasp.* 314 iii.14 (1st half 6th cent.); *PCairMasp.* 5.27 part. rest. (6th cent.); *POxy.* 1857.4 (6th/7th cent.); *PGrenf.* ii, 91.2 (6th/7th cent.); *POxy.* 1857.4 (6th/7th cent.); *SB* 9397.8 (6th/7th cent.)

---

[1] κάλλιστος is still used in MGr. as one superl. of καλός (Mirambel, *Gram.*, 91).

[2] Cf. additional citations of μέγιστος/μεγίστη in ref. to gods, goddesses, and emperors in Preisigke, *WB* ii, s.v.

μήκιστα *SB* 8000 = *PMed*. 81.6 (4th cent.)
ὀλιγίστους *PFlor*. 296.28 (6th cent.)
   cf. ὀλι[γ]ίσ[τ]ως *PFlor*. 295.4 (6th cent.)
πλείστου *PGiss*. 65.8-9 (ca. A.D. 117)
   πλεῖστον *BGU* 72.10 (A.D. 191)
   πλεῖστα χαίρειν *PTebt*. 408.2-3 (A.D. 3); 409.2 (A.D. 5); 410.2 (A.D.
      16); *PMich*. 466.2 (A.D. 107); *PFay*. 130.2 (3rd cent.); etc.
   πλεῖστα κτήνη ἔχομεν *PGiss*. 69.14 (A.D. 118/19)
   πλεῖστα ... προσκυνῶ *POxy*. 158.4 (6th/7th cent.)
   τὰ πλεῖστα *PFay*. 35 = *WChr*. i, 264.12 (A.D. 150/1)
   πλείστοις *PRyl*. 116.11 (A.D. 194); *POxy*. 939 = *WChr*. 128.3 (4th
      cent.)
πρώτιστα *BGU* 665 ii.16 part. rest. (1st cent.); *PMich*. 477.21 part.
   rest. (early 2nd cent.)[1]
τάχιστον *POxy*. 280.21 part. rest. (A.D. 88/89); *POxy*. 34 V = *MChr*.
   188 i.4 (A.D. 127)
   τὴν ταχίστην *PMich*. 602.13 (early 3rd cent.); *PStrassb*. 5.18 (A.D.
      262); *POxy*. 1412.14 (A.D. 284); *PAmh*. 137.5 (A.D. 288/9)[2]
   τάχιστα *PGiss*. 27 = *WChr*. 17.11 (A.D. 115: *BL* v, 34)
ὑψίστῳ (θεῷ) *SB* 1323.1, inscr. (2nd cent.); *PLBat*. xiii, 18.5 (4th cent.);
   PJand. 14.3 (4th cent.); *POxy*. 2194.7 (5th/6th cent.); etc.
   ὕψιστον (θεόν) *PHermRees* 9.21 (4th cent.); cf. *SB* 1572.4-6; 1574.6-7;
      1575; 1579.3; inscrr. (Byz.)[3]
πανϋψίστ[ῳ θεῷ] *PCairMasp*. 348.13 (6th cent.)

3. Double comparison.

a. Doubling of the -τερος suffix is found in ἡ δὲ πρεσβυτερωτέρα ἡμ[ῶν]
ἀδελφή *PLond*. 177 = *MChr*. 57.15 (A.D. 40/41).

b. Addition of the suffixes -τερος, -τατος to primary comparative formations
is found in the following adjectives.[4]

1) Comparative:

καλλιότεραι *POxy*. 1672.6,8 (A.D. 37-41)

---

[1] πρώτιστα, w. superl. suffix added for amplification, is attested in poetry from Hom.
on and in late prose, w. neut. sg. and pl. as adv. in class. Att. (*LSJ*, s.v.). Cf. MGr. πρωτύ-
τερος (Schwyzer i, 539).
[2] For the adverbial use of τὴν ταχίστην (sc. ὁδόν), see Schwyzer i, 621; ii, 69, 175.
[3] ὕψιστος A. Pi. S. Ar. LXX, NT, Paus. inscrr. (*LSJ*, s.v.). It is preserved in MGr. in
an elative sense (Mirambel, *Gram*., 91).
[4] Cf. MGr. π(λ)ειότερος, χε(ι)ρότερος, etc. (Thumb, *Handbook*, § 118).

perh. also καλλιόϙτερεν *sic BGU* 948.8 (4th/5th cent.)¹
μειζότερος *PLips.* 28 = *MChr.* 363.8-9 (A.D. 381)
    μ[ειζο]τέρᾳ *PLBat.* xiii, 14.3 (2nd cent.)
    μειζοτέρᾳ *POxy.* 131.25 (6th/7th cent.)
    μειζοτέραις *POxy.* 2416.10,14 (6th/7th cent.)²
As Byzantine title:³
    μειζότερος *POxy.* 943.3 (6th cent.); *PCairMasp.* 2 ii.9 (A.D. 567:
        BL i, 100)
    μειζοτέρου *PCairMasp.* 49.2 (6th cent.); *PStrassb.* 247.5 (A.D. 551);
        POxy. 922.21 abbrev. (late 6th/early 7th cent.)
    μειζοτέρ(ῳ) *POxy.* 2480.3, etc. (prob. A.D. 565/6); *PSI* 191.1 (A.D.
        566); *POxy.* 158.6 (6th/7th cent.)
    μειζότερον *PHarris* 160.5 (early 4th cent.); *SB* 9616 V.16 (A.D.
        550-8?); *POxy.* 1853.8, with τοὺς μείζονας 6 (6th/7th cent.)
πλεωτέραν *PLond.* 1722.27-28 (A.D. 573)
    πλειοτέραν *PMon.* 4.19 (A.D. 581)⁴

2) Superlative:

μεγιστότατος *PLond.* 130 (i, 132-9).49, horoscope (1st/2nd cent.)

c. Double comparison is also expressed by prefixing τρισ-, especially in reference to an attribute of a god:

τρισμεγάλου *PSI* 1438.4 (2nd/3rd cent.); *SB* 5659.6 (A.D. 201); *PFlor.*
    50.97 (A.D. 268)
τρισμέγιστος *PHermRees* 3.22 (4th cent.)
    τρισμεγίστου *StudPal.* v, 125 = xx, 61 ii.8 (3rd cent.); *WChr.* 470 =
        PMon. 2.11 (A.D. 578)
τρισμάκαρ *SB* 2040.2, inscr. (Xtn.)
τρισμακάριος *PLond.* 1927.46 (mid 4th cent.)
τρισμακαριωτάτῳ *PCairMasp.* 295 i.15 (6th cent.)⁵

---

¹ καλλίων, κάλλιστος are attested from Hom. on; καλλιώτερος also Sch.E., καλώτερος Hdn. (*LSJ*, s.v.). καλλιώτερον, read in Th. iv, 118, was condemned by Phryn. 111 (Rutherford, 209). The MGr. compar. is καλύτερος (cf. μακρύτερος, κακύτερος), also spelled καλήτερος (Schwyzer i, 535, n. 2; Chantraine², § 126, v; Jannaris, § 496b; Mirambel, *Gram.*, 88, n. 2).

² μειζότερος also NT (*BDF*, § 61.2). Cf. μειζονώτερος in a frag. of A. (*LSJ*, s.v. μέγας). See also Schwyzer i, 539.

³ Cf. additional reff. in Preisigke, *WB* iii, Abschn. 8, s.v., p. 133.

⁴ This compar. (of πλέως) is attested in *Od.* Arat. Call. etc. (*LSJ*, s.v.). It is the reg. MGr. compar. (sts. w. loss of the -λ-, as πιό < πλε(ῖ)ον or πιότερος) along w. περισσότερος (Schwyzer i, 539; Thumb, *Handbook*, § 118-19; Mirambel, *Gram.*, 88 & n. 1).

⁵ Cf. also the reg. superl. above, p. 155, n. 3.

d. A superlative is also expressed by repetition of the positive degree of the adjective, especially in reference to an attribute of a god:

Κρόνου κρατεοῦ θεοῦ μεγάλου μεγάλου *PMich.* 226.12,19-20 (A.D. 37); sim. *BGU* 86 = *MChr.* 306.4 (A.D. 155); *BGU* 28.6 (A.D. 183); *SB* 8067 = *PFouad* 11.6 (ca. A.D. 186); *BGU* 124.8 (A.D. 186/7); *SB* 8068 = *PFouad* 12.5 (A.D. 207)

Πετεσούχο(υ) θεοῦ μεγάλ(ου) μεγάλ(ου) *PMich.* 223.1250 (A.D. 171/2)

e. Periphrastic double comparison is also found in μᾶλλον λεπτοτέραν *POxy.* 1066.5 (3rd cent.).[1]

---

[1] Cf. μάλιστα ἀναγκαιοτάτοις in the Ptol. papp. (Mayser i², 2, 61-62). Periphrastic double comparison is normal for most adjs. in MGr., e.g., πιό καλός, ὁ πιό καλύτερος; the -τερος suffix (esp. -ύτερος, q.v. above, p. 147) is retained in many adj:s. (sts. supplemented by πιό), but the suffix -τατος is found only sporadically and mainly in an elative sense (Thumb, *Handbook*, § 116-19; Jannaris, § 491; Mirambel, *Gram.*, 88, 90-91).

III. THE DECLENSION OF PRONOUNS[1]

The declension of pronouns in the Roman and Byzantine papyri shows several morphological developments, especially in the first and second personal pronouns, which are further advanced than those observed in nouns and adjectives. Other deviations from the classical norm are not changes in form but extensions of usage, which pertain properly to syntax and will be treated in Volume III.

A. PERSONAL PRONOUNS

1. The first personal pronoun.

a. The disyllabic "emphatic" forms ἐμοῦ, ἐμοί, ἐμέ[2] are generally preferred to the enclitic forms after all prepositions including πρός and εἰς, where enclitic forms are also found occasionally. In other contexts, the forms vary according to word order and emphasis.

1) After prepositions (except πρός and εἰς):[3]

> ἀπ' ἐμοῦ *POxy.* 237 vi.21 (A.D. 186); *PMich.* 212.10,11 (2nd/early 3rd cent.)
> ἀντ' ἐμοῦ *PMich.* 485.9 (2nd cent.)
> δι' ἐμέ *BGU* 351.3 (Byz.)
> ἐπ' ἐμέ *PBeattyPanop.* 2.249,270,276, etc. (A.D. 300)
> κατ' ἐμέ *PAntin.* 188.17 (6th/7th cent.)
> μετ' ἐμέ *PSI* 696.5 (3rd cent.); *POxy.* 2283.9 (A.D. 586)

---

[1] Schwyzer i, 599-617; Chantraine[2], § 133-61; Buck, *GD*, § 118-31; *MS*, 152-7; Schweizer, 161-2; Nachmanson, 144-6; Hauser, 100-2; Mayser i[2], 2, 62-70; Crönert, 194-7; *BDF*, § 64; W. Dressler, "Vom altgriechischen zum neugriechischen System der Personalpronomina," *IF* 71 (1966), 39-63.

[2] The gen. & dat. appear to be formations within Greek based on ἐμέ on the model of the *o*-stem declension (Schwyzer i, 604; Chantraine[2], § 148).

[3] Cf. Schwyzer i, 600; Mayser i[2], 2, 62-63; Jannaris, § 528[b].

παρ' ἐμοῦ *PFay.* 109.2 (early 1st cent.); *SB* 7252 = *PMich.* 220.7 (A.D. 296)

ὑπ' ἐμοῦ *BGU* 115 = *WChr.* 203 ii.14 (A.D. 189)

ὑπ' ἐμέ *POxy.* 142.2 (A.D. 534)

ἕως ἐμοῦ *POxy.* 2275.10 (1st half 4th cent.)

2) After πρός and εἰς:

πρὸς ἐμέ *PSarap.* 35.8-9 (A.D. 124); *PMich.* 477.37 (early 2nd cent.); *POxy.* 2860.7 (2nd cent.); *BGU* 93.18 (2nd/3rd cent.); *POxy.* 2104.18 (A.D. 241?); *PLBat.* xiii, 19.2 (3rd cent.); *SB* 7249 = *PMich.* 217.21 (A.D. 296); *SB* 6096.2 (5th cent.); *PApoll.* 61.14 (A.D. 703-15); etc.

but πρός με *PBeattyPanop.* 2.218 (A.D. 300); *PLBat.* xiii, 18.14,21,23,33 (4th cent.); etc.

εἰς ἐμέ *POxy.* 237 vi.15 (A.D. 186); *PGrenf.* ii, 71 i.13 (A.D. 244-8); 69.40 (A.D. 265); *PBeattyPanop.* 2.241 (A.D. 300); *PCairGoodsp.* 15.4 (A.D. 362); *POxy.* 1965.14 (A.D. 553); *POxy.* 1860.9 (6th/7th cent.); etc.

but εἴς με *POxy.* 249.9, with πρός με 18-19 (A.D. 80); *POxy.* 481.11 (A.D. 99); 482.19 (A.D. 109); 75.6 (A.D. 129); *PWürzb.* 10 = *PSarap.* 1 *bis* (p. 275).15 (A.D. 130); etc.

cf. εἴς μοι *PMich.* 290.13 (ca. A.D. 37)

3) In other contexts:[1]

διὰ τὸ ἐμὲ καταλελοχίσθα‹ι› *PMich.* 338.9 (A.D. 45)

διὰ τὸ ἐμὲ ἐσχηκέναι *PTebt.* 392 = *MChr.* 338.34 (A.D. 134/5)

but ἐφ' ᾧ καὶ καρπίζεσθαί με *CPR* 27 = *MChr.* 289.27 (A.D. 190)

μηδὲ ἔχιν με ἀδελφὸν ἢ υἱόν *PTebt.* 397 = *MChr.* 321.26 (A.D. 198)

b. The acc. sg. occasionally ends in -ν. This is expanded sporadically by the addition of an -α and still further by a second -ν:

ἐμέν *PGen.* 25.8: *BL* i, 16 (A.D. 124); *PMerton* 24.11 (ca. A.D. 200); *PAlex.* 27.10 (2nd/3rd cent.); *SB* 9805.6 (2nd/3rd cent.); *PThead.* 25.16 (A.D. 334); *PGrenf.* i, 53 = *WChr.* 131.22 (4th cent.); *PGen.* 51 = *PAbinn.* 19.19 (ca. A.D. 346)

ἐμένα *PSI* 972.8-9,16 (4th cent.?)

ἐμέναν *POxy.* 1683.17 (late 4th cent.)

These forms illustrate the different stages of development of the ancient Greek (ἐ)μέ to the Modern Greek (ἐ)μένα(ν)(ε):[2] (1) ἐμέν = acc. sg. + -ν, as

---

[1] In MGr., the disyllabic forms continue to be used reg. w. prepos. and at the beg. of a phrase or preceding a verb as subject, while the enclitic forms are used when the pron. is the acc. object of the verb or a possessive gen., or when it follows the verb as subject (Mirambel, *Gram.*, 93-94).

[2] Jannaris, § 537; Mirambel, *Gram.*, 92.

frequently in the third declension;[1] (2) ἐμένα = ἐμέν + parasitic -α (perhaps on the analogy of τινα[2] and ἕνα) to preserve the preceding ν at a time when final -ν was frequently lost in pronunciation;[3] (3) ἐμέναν then results from the addition of a further analogous -ν.[4] In Modern Greek speech, (ἐ)μένα, ἐμέναν, and (ἐ)μένανε (with a further protective vowel) are all used.[5]

c. In the plural, the ἡ- is only rarely omitted:

τὴν γράσην μῶν (for γράστιν ἡμῶν) *PHamb.* 39 G ii.13 (A.D. 179)

τῶν κυρίων μῶν (for ἡμῶν) *PCairIsidor.* 101.17 (A.D. 300)

φιλανθρώπου μῶν δεσπό(του) *StudPal.* xx, 220 = *SB* 5269.4, corr. 3, etc. (A.D. 618)

cf. also ἐμᾶς *PSI* 742.2 (5th/6th cent.)

These isolated occurrences may be the result of scribal error rather than anticipations of the Modern Greek enclitic μας[6] in view of the very frequent ἡμῶν, etc.[7]

d. Other features of the inflection of the first personal pronoun are only sporadic and pertain properly to syntax, e.g., the use of the nom. for the acc., e.g., ἡμᾶς, ἐγώ τε καὶ Πατᾶν *POxy.* 1157.10 (late 3rd cent.); cf. the popular English "with John and I."

2. The second personal pronoun.

a. New disyllabic forms occur occasionally, especially in the gen. following a preposition, by analogy with the first personal pronoun ἐγώ, ἐμοῦ, etc., in the emphatic position:[8]

ἐσύ *PMich.* 518.19 (1st half 4th cent.)

παρ᾽ ἐσοῦ *OTaitPetr.* 245.4 (ca. A.D. 15-36); 240.3 (A.D. 34); *WO* 304.3

---

[1] See above, pp. 45-46, 135-6. ἐμέν is also found in inscrr. from Asia Minor and S. Italy (Dieterich, 190).

[2] τινα itself is an earlier analogical formation from *τιν (= Lat. *quem*?) on the model of ἕνα or of *n*-stems of the 3rd decl. (Schwyzer i, 616 & n. 6; Chantraine[2], § 143).

[3] See Vol. i, 111-14.

[4] Cf. Jannaris, § 535, 537-8, and App. iii, § 8-9 & esp. 30; Schwyzer i, 606; Chantraine[2], § 154.

[5] Mirambel, *Gram.*, 92; Thumb, *Handbook*, § 134. These forms serve equally for gen. & acc.

[6] Jannaris, § 538; Thumb, *Handbook*, § 134; Mirambel, *Gram.*, 92.

[7] Schwyzer, however, seemed to think these forms significant (i, 606). Cf. also <ὑ>μῶν below, p. 165, and the freq. interchange of ἡμεῖς and ὑμεῖς in all cases (Vol. i, 262, 264).

[8] Cf. Schwyzer i, 606; Jannaris, § 532; Hatzidakis, *Einl.*, 156; Dieterich, 190.

(A.D. 115); *PMich.* 473.31 (early 2nd cent.); *POxy.* 2793.8 (2nd/3rd cent.); *PGen.* 59 = *PAbinn.* 27.8 (ca. A.D. 346); *BGU* 899.7 (4th cent.?); *POxy.* 1683.23 (late 4th cent.); *POxy.* 1656.2 (late 4th/5th cent.); *StudPal.* xx, 255.7 (6th cent.); *StudPal.* iii, 337.3 (6th/7th cent.)

παρ' ἐσό *PHamb.* 39 G ii.13 (A.D. 179)

μετ' ἐσοῦ[1] *PFay.* 119.9: *BL* i, 131 (ca. A.D. 100); *SB* 8089.9 (early 2nd cent.); *PMich.* 482.15 (A.D. 133); *POxy.* 528.10 (2nd cent.); *POxy.* 531 = *WChr.* 482.4 (2nd cent.); *SB* 9484.8-9 part. rest. (2nd cent.); *POxy.* 119.2-3,3-4: *BL* i, 316 (2nd/3rd cent.); *PPar.* 18.10 (3rd cent.: *BL* iv, 67); *PCairIsidor.* 133.11-12 (late 3rd cent.); *PSI* 207.6 (3rd/4th cent.); *PGen.* 54 = *PAbinn.* 35.32 (ca. A.D. 346); *POxy.* 903.30 (4th cent.); *PLBat.* xi, 16.16-17: *BL* v, 62 (5th/6th cent.); cf. *PColt* 57.11 (A.D. 689)[2]

μετ' ἐσοί *PLond.* 239 = *PAbinn.* 31.17 (ca. A.D. 346)

κατ' ἐσοῦ *PLond.* 408 = *PAbinn.* 18.18 (ca. A.D. 346)

ἀπ' ἐσοῦ *PLond.* 404 = *PAbinn.* 25.5 (ca. A.D. 346); *POxy.* 1683.23, with ἐμέναν 17 (late 4th cent.)

παιρὶ (for περὶ) ἐσοῦ *PJand.* 128.21 (5th cent.)

πρὸς ἐσέ *PCairIsidor.* 123.8 (A.D. 317)

These new disyllabic forms of the second personal pronoun anticipate Modern Greek usage, which employs the long and short forms σύ/ἐσύ, etc., exactly as it employs those of the first personal pronoun, according to sentence stress.[3]

b. Parallel to ἐμέν, the acc. sg. of the second personal pronoun ends in an analogous -ν:

σέν *PMilVogl.* 24.4 (A.D. 117); *SB* 7242 = *PRossGeorg.* iii, 3.7 (3rd cent.); *POxy.* 1069.6,18 (3rd cent.); *POxy.* 1670.6 (3rd cent.); *SB* 7247 = *PMich.* 214.19 (A.D. 296); *PGen.* 13.7 (A.D. 310/11: *BL* i, 158); *BGU* 408.12 (prob. A.D. 312: *BL* i, 44); *BGU* 411.8 (A.D. 314); *PLond.* 417 = *PAbinn.* 32.10 (ca. A.D. 346)

ἐσέν *PJand.* 128.16,22 (5th cent.)

cf. σένε (for σοι = MGr. σένα?: *BL* v, 3) *PGen.* 46 = *PAbinn.* 59.24 (A.D. 345)

---

[1] In early editions, this phrase was printed μετεσου, e.g., *PPar.* 18, or divided μετὲ σοῦ, e.g., *PFay.* 119, *POxy.* 119, before ἐσοῦ was recognized as a late form of the pers. pron.

[2] Cf. also from the mag. papp. μετ' ἐσοῦ *PGM* 4.3165-6 (4th cent.).

[3] Mirambel, *Gram.*, 92-95.

Although σέν occurs more frequently than ἐμέν, the further developments (ἐ)σένα and (ἐ)σέναν[1] do not, perhaps because the acc. of the second personal pronoun remains predominantly the monosyllabic form; the disyllabic ἐσέ(ν) is quite rare.

c. In the plural, the ὑ- is omitted only sporadically, parallel to ἡμ- above, as in παρ᾽ μῶν (for παρ᾽ ὑμῶν) *PSI* 458.8 (A.D. 155).

d. In the plural, there is a very frequent confusion of ὑμεῖς, etc., with ἡμεῖς, etc. The explanation is phonological, in view of the frequent interchange and widespread identification of η and υ.[2] In actual speech, there was only one sound symbol for the two pronouns in each case: {imis, imon, imin, imas}.[3] This widespread confusion of ὑμεῖς with ἡμεῖς in all its cases provided the occasion for the later development of new forms in (ἐ)σεῖς, (ἐ)σᾶς on the model of the sg. (ἐ)σύ, etc., which, with (ἐ)μεῖς, (ἐ)μᾶς on the model of ἐγώ, ἐμοῦ, etc., form the plural of the personal pronouns in Modern Greek.[4] Perhaps an anticipation of the Modern Greek forms is found in ἡσῶν, ἡσῖν, ἡσᾶς *PRossGeorg.* iii, 10.16 & 25,26,23 (4th/5th cent.).

3. The third personal pronoun.

a. For spellings of αὐτοῦ in its various cases as ἀτοῦ, etc., see Vol. i, 227.

b. A further reduction of αὐτοῦ, etc., to simple του (the Modern Greek enclitic form[5]) occurs only rarely.[6] These forms might be substitutions of the definite article for the personal pronoun, and even on the hypothesis of a shortening of αὐτός, conformity with the corresponding forms of the article must have furthered the development.

---

[1] The MGr. forms are parallel to those of the 1st pers. pron., i.e., (ἐ)σένα, (ἐ)σέναν, and (ἐ)σέναvε (Thumb, *Handbook*, § 135; Mirambel, *Gram.*, 92).

[2] See Vol. i, 262-7.

[3] For the phonetic value of η and υ, see Vol. i, 266-7. For the loss of initial aspiration, see Vol. i, 133-8. For exx. of the interchange of ἡμεῖς & ὑμεῖς, etc., see Vol. i, 262, 264.

[4] Cf. Schwyzer i, 606; Chantraine[2], § 154; Jannaris, § 531-3; Thumb, *Handbook*, § 135; Mirambel, *Gram.*, 92-94. σᾶς is attested in the Byz.Chron. although no forms of the sg. ἐσοῦ, etc., occur (Psaltes, 193-4).

[5] τος, τη, το are used for αὐτός, -ή, -ό in MGr. in the same distribution as the enclitic forms of the 1st and 2nd pers. pronouns (Mirambel, *Gram.*, 93-95).

[6] An early instance of τας for αὐτάς is found in the Ptol. papp. (Mayser i[2], 2, 67(-68), Anm. 5). Further exx. are found in the mag. papp., e.g., τοῦ δὲ φανέντος *PGM* 13.536 (A.D. 346); sim. 22a.5 (4th/5th cent.), and in Byz. inscrr. and authors (Dieterich, 192; Psaltes, 194; Jannaris, § 530).

1) As a possessive:

ὡς οὖν διὰ τὴν πρόφασίν του οἶδες ... *PSI* 724.7: *BL* v 124, with ἐμᾶς for ἡμᾶς 1 and παρ' αὐτῆς 2 (5th/6th cent.)[1]

cf. ἐπίγραψ[ο]ν τὸ ὄνομά του *PGM* 70.22 (late 3rd/early 4th cent.)

2) As a substantive pronoun:

ἔγραψε ὑπὲρ τῶν (= τῶν for αὐτῶν) *PMich.* 282.8 (1st cent.)

συνκομιδὴν τῶν ἐν ταῖς (for αὐταῖς) σπαρησομένων *PHamb.* 62 = *PLBat.* vi, 23.9 (A.D. 123)

ἐχρῆν τοὺς (for αὐτοὺς) σ[υ]νεδρεύειν *POxy.* 2407.41 (late 3rd cent.)

c. Frequent indiscriminate use of the intensive αὐτός led to extensions of usage in which αὐτός seems to serve as the third personal pronoun in the nominative as well as in the oblique cases:

αὐτός μοι διαπέμπεται *SB* 7352 = *PMich.* 490.15-16 (2nd cent.)

αὐτὸς γὰρ οἶδεν *POxy.* 1671.7, sim. 15 (3rd cent.)

αὐτὸς ἔγραψέν μοι ἐπιστολήν *SB* 7655.23 (6th cent.)

Note 1. The intensive αὐτός is also used in conjunction with the first or second person, e.g., καὶ αὐτὸς κατέμεγον *POxy.* 1855.9 (6th/7th cent.); αὐτὸς οὖν ἀπόστιλον *POxy.* 2154.22 (4th cent.).

Note 2. When forms of αὐτός actually replace a first or second personal pronoun, contextual influence is usually operative, e.g., βούλομαι μισθώσασθαι παρὰ σοῦ ... τὰς ὑπαρχούσας αὐτῇ (for σοί) *PSI* 31.6, sim. 14 (A.D. 164); cf. the usual τὰς ὑπαρχούσας αὐτῇ (αὐτῷ) in similar constructions.[2]

B. REFLEXIVE PRONOUNS

1. First person.

a. ἐμαυτοῦ, etc., is the normal reflexive pronoun in the singular, declined regularly. For the occasional orthographic variants ἐματόν, etc., and also ματῇ, ματήν, see Vol. i, 187-8.

---

[1] Preferable to τοῦ = τίνος w. ed., wh. is not used in the papp.; moreover, τίνος occurs in l. 6.

[2] When αὐτῆς, etc., refers to the person addressed in the respectful manner in vogue in Byz. documents, it remains a 3rd pers. pron.

b. ἐμαυτοῦ is expanded to ἐμεαυτοῦ[1] and ἐμεαυτῶν (for -όν) in *StudPal.* xx, 128 = *SB* 5273.19 (A.D. 487).[2] An anomalous pl. occurs in τοὺς ἐμαυτούς (for ἐμαυτοῦ) in *PLBat.* xiii, 12.8 (A.D. 105).

c. ἑαυτοῦ, etc., is used for the reflexive of the first person normally in the plural and sometimes in the singular.[3]

1) In the plural:

ἑατούς ἀνασκευάζωμε[ν] *POxy.* 745.5 (ca. A.D. 1)

παρεξόμεθα ἑαυτούς *PMich.* 276.8 (A.D. 47)

ἵνα δυνηθῶμεν καὶ τῇ ἑαυτῶν γεωργίᾳ προσκαρτερεῖν *PAmh.* 65.2-3 (early 2nd cent.)

ἀπογραφόμεθα δηλοῦντες ἑαυτούς *POxy.* 2566 ii.10 (A.D. 225?)

ἑαυτούς παρηγ[ο]ροῦμεν *PStrassb.* 140 = *PSarap.* 100.10-11 (early 2nd cent.)

κατεπωλήσαμεν δὲ ἑαυτούς *PThead.* 16.18 (A.D. 307 +)

οὐδὲ οὕτω αἰαυτοῖς προσαίχομεν (for ἑαυτοῖς προσέχομεν) *POxy.* 120 R.8-9 (4th cent.)

ἑαυτούς ἀσφαλισζόμενοι τούσδε τοὺς λιβέλλους ἐπιδίδομεν *POxy.* 1033 = *WChr.* 476.13-14 (A.D. 392)

ἐθέλομεν ... [... ἐνεγκεῖν] μεθ' ἑατῶν *PJand.* 25.2-3 (6th/7th cent.)

Note. The simple ἡμᾶς is used for the reflexive pronoun in ὡς ... ἐχόντων ἐκ τούτου εἰς ἡμᾶς δαπανῆσαι *PAmh.* 131 = *PSarap.* 80.14-16 (early 2nd cent.).

---

[1] Cf. (ἑ)σεαυτοῦ below, p. 169.

[2] Att. ἐμαυτοῦ originated in a contraction of ἐμεαυτόν (cf. Ion. ἐμεωυτοῦ Hdt. etc.) (*LSJ*, s.v.; Schwyzer i, 607; Chantraine², § 159).

[3] ἑαυτοῦ, the 3rd pers. reflexive, developed from ἓ αὐτόν, etc., w. both elements decl. in Hom. (Schwyzer & Chantraine², *ibidd.*), to a proper compd. ἑαυτόν, etc. (Alc. Hdt. Att. prose: *LSJ*, s.v.), wh. supplanted the 3rd pers. reflex. pron. ἓ, σφᾶς, etc. (in Att. inscrr. from 395 B.C. on: *MS*, 153), and was sts. used for the 1st and 2nd pers. reflex. pron. as a simple reflex. wo. distinction of person, replacing ἡμᾶς αὐτούς, ὑμᾶς αὐτούς, etc., in the pl. and not infreq. in the sg., esp. in the 2nd pers. sg. 5 times A., as well as Isoc. Pl. X. Aeschin. etc. (*LSJ*, s.v.; Chantraine², § 159; *KB* i, 1, 599, Anm. 2; ii, 1, 572; Crönert, 196(-7), n. 1), while in the non-literary Koine, only its use in the pl. is common, where it is normal in the Ptol. papp. (w. 1 exc. of ἡμᾶς αὐτούς 3rd cent. B.C.) and found in the LXX and NT, but appearing in the sg. only once in the Lycian inscrr. and several times in the Ptol. papp., only dbtfl. in the NT (*LSJ*, s.v.; Hauser, 100; Mayser i², 2, 63-64; ii, 1, 66-67; *BDF*, § 64.1). It is not found at all in the Att. inscrr., not at Perg. or Magn. MGr. uses ὁ ἑαυτός μου, etc., or ἀτός μου, ἀπατός μου, or (rarely) ὁ ἐμαυτός (Thumb, *Handbook*, § 140; Jannaris, § 546-9; Mirambel, *Gram.*, 95-96).

2) In the singular:

μετὰ κυρίου ἐμοῦ τοῦ ἑαυτῆς υἱοῦ *PMich.* 253.1-2 (A.D. 30)
ἀπογράφομαι ἑαυτήν *BGU* 2019.10-11 (A.D. 188)
ὅ[τ]ε δὲ τὴν μητέρα μου εἶχα μεθ᾽ [ἑ]αυτῆς *PBouriant* 25.9: *BL* ii, 2,
   35 (5th cent.)
τὰ καθ᾽ ἑαυτὸν διανοηθεὶς ἐσκόπησα *PCairMasp.* 151-2.22 (A.D. 570)

2. Second person.

a. The singular reflexive pronoun σεαυτοῦ, etc., is found in three orthographies.

1) The usual spelling is σεαυτοῦ, etc., e.g., σεαυτοῦ *PLond.* 1393 = *SB* 7241.22 (A.D. 697/712); σεαυτῷ *PMich.* 464.18 (A.D. 99).

2) The spellings σαυτοῦ, etc., occur occasionally:

σαυτοῦ *BGU* 1095.22 (A.D. 57); *PMich.* 464.16, with σεαυτῷ 18 (A.D. 99);
   PAmh. 132 = *PSarap.* 81.4-5 (early 2nd cent.); *PTebt.* 315 = *WChr.*
   71.32 (2nd cent.); *POxy.* 1062.13 (2nd cent.); etc.
σαυτῆς *PIFAO* ii, 10.25 (1st/2nd cent.)
σαυτῷ *PRein.* 117.2 (late 3rd cent.); *POxy.* 1771.8 (late 3rd/early 4th
   cent.)
σαυτόν *PLond.* 356 (ii, 252).15 (1st cent.); *PHamb.* 87.10 (early 2nd
   cent.); *PCairMasp.* 281.6 (6th cent.?); *PApoll.* 59.4 (A.D. 703-15); etc.
σαυτήν *PSI* 1359.3 (2nd/3rd cent.)

The occasional recurrence of this form in papyri of the Roman and Byzantine periods after it had apparently dropped out of use in papyri subsequent to the second century B.C. may perhaps be attributed to Atticistic influence.[1]

3) Further shortened forms σατοῦ, etc., with loss of the υ in the ᾱυ diphthong parallel to ἐματοῦ, etc., are also sometimes found:[2]

σατοῦ *BGU* 1079 = *WChr.* 60.31, with σατόν 25 (A.D. 41); *PBaden*
   35.27 (A.D. 87); *PFay.* 119.24 (ca. A.D. 100); *PIFAO* ii, 16.6 (2nd cent.)
σατῷ *PMich.* 476.17 (early 2nd cent.); *BGU* 380.16 (3rd cent.)

---

[1] The shortened form σαυτοῦ, etc., was peculiar to Att., where even Trag. sts. uses the longer form (*LSJ*, s.v.; Schwyzer i, 607). σαυτῷ is also found in the Att. *Tab. Defix.* (Schwyzer, "Vulg.," 258). In the Ptol. papp., it is the more common form in the 3rd cent., less common in the 2nd, and appar. unattested in the 1st cent. (Mayser i², 2, 65; ii, 2, 71-72). It is found in the Herc. papp., w. 1 exc. of σεα[υτό]ν (Crönert, 196). It is not used in the NT (*BDF*, § 64.1).

[2] For the loss of the 2nd element of the long diphthong ᾱυ, see Vol. i, 187-8.

σατόν *PHamb.* 86.6 (2nd cent.)

σατέν *SB* 8027.9, with change of o > ε as in μετάμελες (for -ος) 5-6 and μικρές (for -ός) 10 (2nd/3rd cent.)[1]

cf. σατήν *PGM* 4.2322 (4th cent.)

4) An anomalous form, probably a scribal error, is σεαστῆς *POxy.* 1767.10 (3rd cent.).

5) A new form ἐσεαυτοῦ, with ἐ- (presumably false aspiration for ἐ-) prefixed parallel to ἐμαυτοῦ (cf. ἐσοῦ on the analogy of ἐμοῦ, etc., above, pp. 163-4) is found in εἰ δὲ ἀφ' ἐσεαυτοῦ ἐθελήσῃς ἀναχωρῆσαι *BGU* 3.20-21 (A.D. 605).

b. ἑαυτοῦ, etc., is sometimes used in the singular and normally in the plural for the second person reflexive pronoun parallel to its use in the first person.[2]

1) In the plural:

ἐπιμελέ̄σθε ἀτῶν (for ἑαυτῶν) *BGU* 1078 = *WChr.* 59.11-12: Kapsomenos, "Ἔρευναι," 339 (A.D. 39)

παρηγορεῖτε οὖν ἑαυτούς *POxy.* 115 — *WChr.* 479.11 (2nd cent.)

ἀπαντήσατε ἀπ' ἑαυτῶν *PFay.* 136.5-6 (4th cent.)

ἀνάγετε μεθ' ἑαυτῶν *PLips.* 64 = *WChr.* 281.4 (A.D. 368/9)

ὑμῶν ... τὰ ἐκφόρια ἑαυτῶν σπουδάσατε συντῖναι ἑαυτούς *PVindobWorp* 13.11-15 (5th/6th cent.)

2) In the singular:[3]

μὴ σκ{λ}ύλλε ἑατήν ἐνπῆναι (for ἐμβῆναι: *BL* v, 76) *POxy.* 295.5-6 (ca. A.D. 35)

μένε ἐπὶ ἑαυτοῦ *PGiss.* 21.13 (ca. A.D. 117)

ὅτι ... παρεμβάλλεις ἑαυτόν, σε παρεμβάλλοντα ἑαυτόν *POxy.* 129 = *MChr.* 296.4-5,7 (6th cent.)

Note 1. ὑμῶν αὐτῶν is preserved, not as a reflexive but as an emphatic pronoun,[4] in a quote from a letter of Hadrian to the city of Antinoopolis in *PWürzb.* 9.33 (A.D. 161-9).

Note 2. The simple ὑμᾶς stands for the reflexive (sg. or pl.?) in [ἐπ]ισκοπ[οῦ δ]ὲ ὑμᾶς καὶ [πά]ντας τοὺ[ς] ἐν οἴκῳ in *POxy.* 293.16-17 (A.D. 27).

---

[1] Cf. Vol. i, 290.

[2] See above, pp. 167-8.

[3] Cf. also from the mag. papp. ἐλθὼν πρὸς ἑαυτόν ... θές *PGM* 7.842-3 (3rd cent.).

[4] Ed., n. ad loc.

3. Third person.

a. The classical σφᾶς αὐτούς is read in an imperial rescript in *PCairMasp.* 24 R.7 (ca. A.D. 551).[1]

b. When αὐτός is used in reference to the subject of the phrase or sentence, it probably represents the personal pronoun (with a smooth breathing) rather than the Attic contracted form of the reflexive pronoun (αὑτοῦ for ἑαυτοῦ with a rough breathing)[2] even when used reflexively in the attributive position,[3] e.g., παραδοῦναι αὐτὸν τὸ αὐτοῦ πλοῖον *POxy.* 2347.10-11 (A.D. 362), or in contexts in which a form of ἑαυτοῦ is used elsewhere, e.g., καλεῖ σαι (for σε) Θέων εἰς [γ]άμους τῆς ἀδελφῆς αὐτοῦ *POxy.* 1580.1-2 (3rd cent.) compared with καλῖ σε Θέων ... εἰς τοὺς γάμους τῆς ἀδελφῆς ἑαυτοῦ *POxy.* 1487.1-4 (4th cent.). The contracted forms do not seem to have survived elsewhere in the Koine.[4] Further, there is evidence for a syntactical confusion of the reflexive and personal pronouns,[5] indicated by forms of ἑαυτ- used sometimes for the personal pronoun of the third person:[6]

ἔκραψεν ὑπὲρ ἑαυτῶν (for ἔγραψεν ὑπὲρ αὐτῆς) *PRyl.* 161.31 (A.D. 71)

---

[1] [σ]φέα[ς] is also read in the poet. *PCairMasp.* 97 V B.24 and σφῖσι in 120 V C.44 (6th cent.). ἐπὶ σφᾶς καί in *SB* 9007 = *PMed.* 78.33 (3rd cent.) has been corrected to ἐπεὶ φάσκει (*BL* vi, 77). σφεῖς, a formation within Gr. itself (Schwyzer i, 601, 604), served orig. as the pl. of the 3rd pers. pron. With the sg. οὗ, οἷ, ἕ, it came to be used generally in a reflex. sense by itself in a subordinate clause or construction to refer to the subj. of the principal verb, and in combinations w. αὐτῶν, etc., wo. this restriction (*LSJ*, s.v.; Schwyzer i, 606-7; Chantraine[2], § 155-9). It disappeared from use in Att. prose inscrr. ca. 395 B.C. and was replaced by ἑαυτῶν (αὑτῶν), etc., attested sporadically even earlier (*MS*, 153). But it is used by some Koine authors, as Agatharch. Str. Onos., along w. ἑαυτῶν, etc. (Crönert, 197, n. 2).

[2] The contr. αὑτοῦ, etc., like σαυτοῦ, was peculiarly Attic (*LSJ*, s.v.; Schwyzer i, 607). It represents a further contraction of the orig. ἑο(ι)αυτῶι, etc. (Schwyzer, *ibid.*; Chantraine[2], § 159).

[3] For the attributive position of the reflex. pron. used in the gen. as a possessive, see Mayser ii, 2, 68-73.

[4] In the Att. inscrr., both the contr. and uncontr. forms are found in approx. equal frequency in the 4th cent. B.C., but the forms in ἑαυτ- predominate from 300-30 B.C. in the ratio of 100:7 (*MS*, 153-4, contra *LSJ*, s.v., and Chantraine[2], § 159). At Perg., the forms in ἑαυτ- greatly predominate in both royal and Rom. times and are the only forms found in private inscrr. (Schweizer, 161-2). At Magn., the contr. forms are not attested beyond doubt; the uncontr. forms are freq. (Nachmanson, 144). At Lycia, the contr. forms are very infreq. in comparison w. the forms in ἑαυτ- (Hauser, 101). In the Ptol. papp., the contr. forms predominate over the uncontr. forms in the 3rd cent. by 4:1, but the relationship is reversed in the 2nd cent., while in the 1st cent. only ἑαυτ- is attested (Mayser i[2], 2, 65). In the NT, forms in ἑαυτ- are alone certain, w. forms in αὐτ- only as v.ll. (*BDF*, § 31.1; 64.1).

[5] The reflex. and pers. pronouns begin to interchange in Att. inscrr. from the 4th cent. B.C. on and do so freq. in Rom. times (*MS*, 154). Instances of the use of the reflex. for the pers. pron. are also found in the Ptol. papp. (Mayser i[2], 2, 64, Anm. 1).

[6] Sim. confusion is also found w. the 1st & 2nd persons, e.g., ἑαυτὸς το[ί]νυν ὀρφανὸς καταλελιμμένης (for -μένος) ... ἀδικοῦμαι *PThead.* 19.6-7 (A.D. 316-20; *JJP* ii, 60); ἀφῆκα τὰ ἐρίδια σεαυτῇ ἵνα ἢ τι θέλις ἀνηλώσῃς σεαυτῇ *SB* 7250 = *PMich.* 218.6-8 (A.D. 296).

παρ' αὐ[τ]ῆς Ἡροῦ[τ]ος φερνὴν ἐπὶ τῇ ἑαυτῆς θυγατρί *PMerton* 72.11 (A.D. 162)
καὶ ἐπιτελεῖν περὶ ἑαυτῶν *PTebt.* 319.20 (A.D. 248)
(γίνονται) ἐπὶ τὸ ἑαυτό *PFlor.* 322.16 (A.D. 258?)
οὐδένα λόγον ἔχω πρ[ὸ]ς ἑ[α]υτόν *POxy.* 1880.11 (A.D. 427)

There was probably no distinction between αὐτόν and αὑτόν in pronunciation because of the widespread loss of initial aspiration.[1] Thus, a form of αυτ- used reflexively has no aspiration in [ἀ]ντ' αὐτο[ῦ] in *POxy.* 2340.23 (A.D. 192) but does in καθ' αὑτόν *POxy.* 63.8 (2nd/3rd cent.).

c. Similar confusion of the personal and reflexive pronouns is reflected in the formation ἑαυταδέλφου (for αὐτ-) used reflexively in *CPR* 155.6 (2nd cent.?).

d. ἴδιος is occasionally used to strengthen the reflexive pronoun, e.g., τοῖς ἰδίοις ἑαυτῶν δαπανήμασιν *BGU* 13 = *MChr.* 265.15 (A.D. 289); φιλοπραγματίας ἕνεκα ἰδίας ἑαυτοῦ καὶ ἐσχροκερδίας (for αἰσχρο-) and ἰδίᾳ ἑαυτοῦ βουλήσι (for -σει) *POxy.* 2267.6-7,11 (A.D. 360). This usage led to the eventual replacement of ἑαυτοῦ, etc., by ἴδιος in Modern Greek.[2]

C. THE RECIPROCAL PRONOUN

1. The reciprocal pronoun ἀλλήλων, etc., is sometimes replaced by the reflexive ἑαυτῶν, etc., without distinction of person, e.g., ὁμολογοῦμεν ... διη-[ρ]ῆσθαι πρὸς [ἑ]αυτούς, συντεθεῖσθαι [πρ]ὸς ἑαυτούς *PLips.* 26.5-6 (early 4th cent.); διαιρήκαμεν πρὸς ἑαυ[το]ύς, σ[υ]νεπίσθημεν (for συνεπείσθημεν) πρὸς ἑαυτούς *PGen.* 11 = *PAbinn.* 62.5-6,8, with ὁμ[ο]λογοῦσιν πρὸς ἀλλήλους 1-2 (A.D. 350); τιμὴν ἣν συν[ε]φώνησαν πρὸς ἑαυτούς *PCairIsidor.* 91.6-7 (A.D. 309); sim. *PCairIsidor.* 92.6-7 (A.D. 314). This use of ἑαυτούς for ἀλλήλους is found already in classical Greek.[3]

2. The sporadic use of ἄλλος for ἀλλήλων, e.g., ἄλλων [ἔ]γγ[υο]ι{ς} εἰς ἔκτεισιν *PLBat.* vi, 6.10 (A.D. 99) and συμπεφωνημένην πρὸς ἄλλους *BGU*

---

[1] See Vol. i, 133-8. Mayser i², 2, 65, n. 1, suggests rightly that the loss of aspiration contributed to the predilection for the ἑαυτ- forms to avoid confusion w. those of the pers. pron. in αὐτ-.

[2] For the reflex. use of ἴδιος (and οἰκεῖος), see Vol. iii, *Syntax*. Exx. of this usage of ἴδιος are already found in the Ptol. papp. (Mayser i², 2, 65, Anm. 2; ii, 2, 73-74), in Att. inscrr. from 69 B.C. on (*MS*, 235), in the NT (*BDF*, § 286.1), and in Koine authors, incl. Gal. Ptol. (*LSJ*, s.v. ἴδιος, I, 6). See further Dieterich, 195, and for the use of οἰκεῖος as a reflex. in the papp., G. Kuhring, *De Praepositionum Graecarum in Chartis Aegyptiis Usu Quaestiones Selectae* (Bonn, 1906), 13.

[3] So Hdt. S. Th. Pl. D. etc. (*LSJ*, s.v. ἑαυτοῦ, III). The reflex. pron. is also found w. reciprocal force in the Ptol. papp. (Mayser i², 2, 64) and in the NT (*BDF*, § 287).

940.18-19 (A.D. 398), is probably the result of partial haplography[1] rather than an anticipation of Modern Greek usage.[2] The identical phenomenon occurs in the compound ἐξ ἀλλεγγύης (for ἀλληλεγγύης) *POxy*. 1881.15 (A.D. 427).

3. Sporadic examples of the reciprocal pronoun with only two terminations, e.g., ἀπὸ οἰκιῶν δύο συνηνωμένων ἀλλήλοις (for ἀλλήλαις) *POxy*. 1701.5 (3rd cent.), are best regarded as instances of lack of agreement in gender.

4. The anomalous gen. sg. read in ἀνὰ μέσον ἀλλήλου *PAntin*. 43.16-17, with ἀνὰ μέσο(ν) ἀλλήλους *sic* 3-4 (late 3rd/4th cent.), is best assumed to reflect a loss of final -ς,[3] and both spellings to represent the use of the acc. pl. ἀλλήλους for the gen. pl. ἀλλήλων after the prepositional phrase.

D. POSSESSIVE PRONOUNS

1. The possessive pronoun-adjectives of the first and second person are declined regularly, e.g., πάντες οἱ ἐμοί *POxy*. 115 = *WChr*. 479.6-7 (2nd cent.); ἡ σὴ ἀρετή *POxy*. 1834.3 (late 5th/early 6th cent.); μέτρῳ τῷ σῷ *BGU* 740.5 (Byz.); τὰ σὰ καὶ τὰ ἐμά *PMich*. 492.15-16 (2nd cent.); μετὰ τῶν σῶν πάντων *PFouad* 77.4 (2nd cent.).

2. A new form of the second person possessive pronoun ἐσός is formed on the analogy of ἐμός (cf. ἐσοῦ after ἐμοῦ, etc., above, pp. 163-4):

τοῦ ἐσο(ῦ) δούλου, τοῦ ἐσο(ῦ) μεγέθο(υ)[ς] *PLond*. 1786.5,13, with τὼ ἐσὼν (for τὸ ἐσὸν) μέγεθος 7 (5th cent.)[4]

πρὸς τὸν ἐσὸν τοῦλος καὶ υἱός (prob. for παρὰ τοῦ σοῦ δούλου καὶ υἱοῦ) *PLond*. 1887 descr. (6th cent.)

The possessive pronoun did not survive into Modern Greek. Its function is served by the genitive of the personal pronoun or by δικός μου, etc.[5]

---

[1] Cf. sim. exx. of the loss of a syllable in Vol. i, 312-13.

[2] In MGr., the reciprocal pron. is normally expressed by ὁ ἕνας ... ὁ ἄλλος (Thumb, *Handbook*, § 141; Jannaris, § 1413; Mirambel, *Gram.*, 96; Maspero, 76).

[3] For the freq. omission of -ς, see Vol. i, 124-6.

[4] This form seems more likely the gen. of the possessive pron. than of the pers. pron. because of its attributive position and the presence of ἐσών (for ἐσόν) in l. 7 and the reg. possessive τὼ πιττάκιόν σο(υ) in l. 9.

[5] δικός, perh. a contamination of ἴδιος 'one's own' and εἰδικός 'special' (Schwyzer ii, 205; cf. i, 608-9), seems to have developed from the gradual adoption of ἴδιος as a possessive pron., a usage known in class. Gr. (Schwyzer, *ibidd*.) and attested freq. in Rom. and Byz. papp. οἰκεῖος is also used as a possessive in the papp. See above, p. 171, n. 2.

E. DEMONSTRATIVE PRONOUNS

1. The definite article is declined regularly.[1] Variations which occur are mainly phonological.[2] In particular, the -ν is occasionally omitted in the acc. sg., e.g., ἀσπ[άζο]με (for -μαι) τὴ μητέραν *sic* μου ... τὴ ἀδε[λφή]ν μου *BGU* 843.10-11,14 (1st/2nd cent.). This loss of -ν occurs more often in the feminine, but is also found in the masculine.[3] It parallels the general loss of final -ν found frequently in many words in the papyri[4] and does not follow the Modern Greek pattern in which the final nasal of the article is written and pronounced only before a word beginning with a vowel or with a stop consonant (κ, π, τ, ξ, and ψ), when it is assimilated to the order of a labial or velar stop.[5] The nom. pl. masc. τοί in καὶ τοὶ τούτου ἀδελφοί *BGU* 581 = *WChr.* 354.22 (A.D. 207) is an isolated blunder in view of the very frequent οἱ.

Note. The Coptic article is used for the Greek in καρπῷ φχιρός and οὐλὴ φχιρός *PGen.* 64 = *PAbinn.* 67 V.13,14 (ca. A.D. 346).

2. ὅδε, ἥδε, τόδε is declined regularly.[6] Some purely orthographic variations occur, such as ἥδη (for ἥδε), τῆσθε (for τῆσδε), and τήντε (for τήνδε).[7]

a. It is used only rarely as a substantive pronoun, e.g., [μ]έχρι τοῦδ[ε] *BGU* 195.17 (A.D. 161); ἐς τώδε (for τόδε) *POxy.* 1216.10 (2nd/3rd cent.); ἡ δῖνα (for δεῖνα) ... θυγάτηρ ... τοῦδε, μητρὸς τῆσδε *SB* 6000 R.1, etc. (6th cent.).[8]

---

[1] The def. art. has retained its class. inflection in the cases still in use (nom. gen. acc.) in MGr., exc. for the phonologically conditioned variation of final -ν and for the fem. pl., wh. has nom. οἱ (as masc.), acc. τίς (Thumb, *Handbook*, § 55; Mirambel, *Gram.*, 40; Maspero, 29-30). The fem. has thus generalized the vowel [i], spelled variously η, οι, and ι, throughout the paradigm. Ancient forms of the fem. still survived dialectally at the beg. of the 20th cent. (Jannaris, § 560-1).

[2] For such orthographic variants as τώ (for τό), τõ (for τῷ), ὐ (for οἱ), ἐ (for αἱ), δάς (for τάς), etc., see Vol. i, Index, 354.

[3] See additional exx. in Vol. i, 111-12.

[4] See Vol. i, 111-14.

[5] Thumb, *Handbook*, § 34; Mirambel, *Gram.*, 21, 29; Maspero, 19-20.

[6] This demonstr. pron., formed by the addition of the enclitic -δε to the orig. weak demonstr. ὁ, ἡ, τό (later the def. art.), sim. to the colloquial English juxtaposition 'this here' (Schwyzer i, 611 & n. 2), was gradually lost in the Koine. It occurs freq. at Magn. until ca. 100 B.C., but later only rarely (Nachmanson, 145). In the Ptol. papp., it is freq. in the 3rd and 2nd cent., but no exx. of its substantival use are attested from the 1st cent. (Mayser i², 2, 66; cf. ii, 1, 73-74; ii, 2, 78-79). In the NT, ὅδε is practically limited to the formula τάδε λέγει (*BDF*, § 289). It has not survived in MGr. speech exc. in the stereotyped forms ὁ τάδες and τάδε (= δεῖνα) (Jannaris, § 564; Mirambel, *Gram.*, 103; Schwyzer i, 612), but it is retained in set phrases in the *kathareuousa* (cf. Kykkotis, s.v.). See further L. Rydbeck, *Fachprosa*, 88-97.

[7] See Vol. i, 81, 97, 245.

[8] See Vol. iii for a more detailed treatment of this and the foll. uses.

b. It occurs frequently as an attributive, generally limited to recurring formulae, e.g., τόδε τὸ βιβλείδιον *BGU* 2 = *MChr.* 113.16-17 (A.D. 209); τοῦδε τοῦ γραμματίου *PGen.* 46 = *PAbinn.* 59.6-7 (A.D. 345); τῇδε τῇ μισθ(ώσει) *StudPal.* iii, 411.6 (7th cent.).

c. It occurs rarely without the definite article, e.g., δραχμαὶ αἵδε *PMich.* 577.5-6 (A.D. 41-68); εἰς τάσδε μηνειαας (= fem. μηνιαίας for neut. -αῖα?) *PFlor.* 272.7 (A.D. 258).

d. A form of οὗτος is sometimes added to strengthen this demonstrative which was losing its force, e.g., κατὰ τήνδε τὴν πρᾶσιν ταύτην *PMich.* 277.1 (A.D. 48); κατὰ τήνδε τὴν ὁμολογείαν ταύτην *PMich.* 585.14-15 (A.D. 87).

3. οὗτος, αὕτη, τοῦτο is generally declined regularly, with only sporadic variants.

a. The acc. sg. neut. ends in -ον in ἠ (for εἰ) δὲ οὐδὲ τοῦτον θέλεις χρησειμεῦσέ (for χρησιμεῦσαί) μοι *PSI* 1426.6 (5th/6th cent.).

b. The masc.-neut. stem τουτ- is transferred to the fem. in the acc. sg. τούτην τὴν ὁμολογίαν *PLond.* 1730.26 (A.D. 585).[1]

c. The definite article is sometimes omitted with this demonstrative, probably through haplography, e.g., ταύ|την ἐπιστολήν *BGU* 801.13-14 (2nd cent.).

d. This demonstrative is sporadically replaced by the personal pronoun αὐτός, -ή, -ό, e.g., ὑπὲρ αὐτοῦ (for τούτου) τοῦ πράγματος *BGU* 1655.42 (A.D. 169).[2]

e. It is also sometimes replaced by the definite article, e.g., χω[ρ]ὶς τοῦ (for τούτου) *PMerton* 82.8 (late 2nd cent.); ἐπὶ τοῖς (for τούτοις) *POxy.* 2586.43 (A.D. 253); καὶ τὰ (for ταῦτα) μὲν πάντα *PCairIsidor.* 72.35 (A.D. 314).

4. τοσοῦτος, τοιοῦτος. The acc. sg. neut. fluctuates between -ον and -ο, with the -ον ending predominating in τοσοῦτος, the -ο ending in τοιοῦτος. Both endings occur in identical phrases, so that the initial sound of the following word does not seem to be a factor.

---

[1] In MGr., the fem. is formed on the stem τουτ- (Schwyzer i, 614; Chantraine[2], § 135, Remarque 1; Thumb, *Handbook*, § 145; Jannaris, § 566-7; Mirambel, *Gram.*, 98; Maspero, 77-78).

[2] See Vol. iii for a more detailed treatment. See also Thumb, *Handbook*, § 144, Maspero, 77, Mirambel, *Gram.*, 98, for the use of αὐτός as the equivalent of τοῦτος in MGr.

a. τοσοῦτος.

1) Acc. sg. neut. -ον:

ἐπὶ τοσοῦτον *BGU* 665 ii.6 (1st cent.); (-σσ-) *PTebt.* 304.9 (A.D. 167/8); *PSI* 1103.15,17 (2nd/3rd cent.: *BL* iii, 228); (τουσ-) *POxy.* 1165.2 (6th cent.); *PLond.* 1075 (iii, 281-2).19 (7th cent.); etc.

τοσοῦτον τέλεσμα *PGiss.* 6 ii.9, with τοσοῦτο τέλεσμα i.6 part. rest., iii.7 (each col. diff. hand) (A.D. 117)

τοσοῦτον also *PMilVogl.* 25 ii.26; iii.3 (A.D. 126/7); *PMilVogl.* 73.11 (2nd cent.); *PBeattyPanop.* 2.99,139,232, with τοιοῦτο 225 (A.D. 300); *PSI* 741.8-9 (4th cent.); *PLips.* 38 = *MChr.* 97 i.8 (A.D. 390); *SB* 7518.13 (4th/5th cent.); *POxy.* 1833.6 (late 5th cent.); *PMon.* 6.72 (A.D. 583); *POxy.* 1869.6 (6th/7th cent.)

2) Acc. sg. neut. -ο:

τοσοῦτο τέλεσμα *PBrem.* 34 = *WChr.* 352.9 (A.D. 117); *PRyl.* 96.7 (A.D. 117/18)

τοσοῦτο [πλῆ]θος *POxy.* 237 v.5 (A.D. 186)

τοσοῦτο ἀργύριον *POxy.* 2783.7 (3rd cent.)

τοσοῦτο μαρτυραμένη *PAmh.* 141 = *MChr.* 126.17 (A.D. 350)

b. τοιοῦτος.

1) Acc. sg. neut. -ον:

μηδὲν τοιοῦτον *PBrem.* 37.16 (ca. A.D. 117)

τοιοῦτόν τι *POxy.* 2182.15 (A.D. 166); *PSI* 285.11 (A.D. 294?); *PBouriant* 20 = *PAbinn.* 63.43 (A.D. 350)

τι τοιοῦτον *PTebt.* 335.15 (ca. A.D. 165: *BL* iii, 242)

τὸ δὲ πρᾶγμα τοιοῦτόν ἐστιν *BGU* 168 = *MChr.* 121.5 (ca. A.D. 169/70: *BL* v, 10)

τοιοῦτον also *PWürzb.* 9.70 part. rest. (A.D. 161-9)

2) Acc. sg. neut. -ο:

τὸ τοιοῦτο *PRyl.* 129.15 (A.D. 30); *PRyl.* 139.21, with τὸ τοιοῦτω (for τοιοῦτο) 15 (A.D. 34); *PFlor.* 241.5 (A.D. 254); *PFlor.* 36 = *MChr.* 64.23 (A.D. 312); *PLond.* 1363.6 (A.D. 710); etc.

τοιοῦτο τέλεσμα *PBrem.* 36.9 (A.D. 117)

τοιοῦτο ἀκήκοε *POslo* 17.9 (A.D. 136)

οὐδὲν τοιοῦτο *BGU* 1574.19 (A.D. 176/7)

μηδὲν τοιοῦτο *POxy.* 128.4, with ἐπὶ τοσοῦτον 7-8 (6th/7th cent.)

τοιοῦτό τι *PSI Omaggio* 12.6 (3rd cent.); *PLond.* 77 = *MChr.* 319.51 (late 6th cent.)

τι τοιοῦτο *POxy.* 2603.3 (4th cent.)

τὸ τοιοῦτο σιγέλλιν *PSI* 1266 = *PApoll.* 9.11 (before A.D. 704); sim. *SB* 7240.11,16 (A.D. 697/712)

τὸ τοιοῦτο οἶνον *PApoll.* 10 k (A.D. 704)

τὸ τοιοῦτο χρυσίον *PApoll.* 13.6 part. rest. (A.D. 706); 16.3 (ca. A.D. 705/6); *PLond.* 1387 = *PRossGeorg.* iv, 10.10 part. rest. (A.D. 710); *PLond.* 1365.2; sim. 1369.10 (A.D. 710)

τοιοῦτο also *POxy.* 237 viii.37 (A.D. 186); *POxy.* 1409.20 (A.D. 278); *SB* 6000 R.18 (6th cent.); *POxy.* 1854.6,8 (6th/7th cent.); *PLond.* 1356 = *WChr.* 254.22,31 (A.D. 710)

This fluctuation reflects an earlier morphemic variation, through which the apparently original and more common forms in -ον[1] were modified by the omission of the final -ν, on the analogy of τοῦτο. In Roman and Byzantine papyri, this variation appears to be mainly orthographic in view of the widespread loss of final -ν in pronunciation.[2]

5. αὐτός, αὐτή, αὐτό is declined regularly with only sporadic abnormalities.

a. The nom.-acc. sg. neut. is regularly -ο, not -ον, e.g., ἐπὶ τὸ αὐτό *PTebt.* 375.11 (A.D. 140); αὐτὸ μόνον *POxy.* 531 = *MChr.* 482.11 (2nd cent.); διὰ αὐτὸ τοῦτο *PGen.* 47 = *PAbinn.* 47.10 (A.D. 346); etc.[3]

b. The nom.-acc. pl. neut. αὐτά is sometimes used to refer to substantives of other genders or numbers, e.g., οὐδὲ αἱ ἐπιστολαὶ ἐξῆθαν· προσδέχομαι αὐτά (for αὐτάς) *PMich.* 492.7 (2nd cent.); δραχμὰς ... ἐὰν διδῇ αὐτά, δέξαι α[ὐτά] *PCairIsidor.* 132.4-5, sim. 7-8, with τὸ στιχάριν. καὶ ἐκτίναξον αὐτὰ μὴ ἀλόβροτα γένηται 13-14 (3rd cent.). These examples seem to be instances of lack of agreement or phonological variants rather than reflections of an indeclinable use of αὐτά.

---

[1] Only forms in -ον occur in Hom. and are best attested in Att.-Ion. (*LSJ*, s.vv.; *KB* i, 1, 606; Schwyzer i, 127, 406, 609(-10), n. 6; Chantraine[2], § 137). They are the only forms found in Att. and Magn. inscrr., but 1 ex. each of -ον and -ο occurs in the Lycian inscrr. (*MS*, 155; Nachmanson, 145; Hauser, 102). In the Ptol. papp., forms in -ον predominate before both vowels and consonants, w. forms in -ο also found in both positions (Mayser i[2], 2, 66). Both forms are also found in the Herc. papp. and in various Koine authors (Crönert, 195 & n. 1). In the NT, forms in -ον are found, w. v.ll. in -ο (*BDF*, § 64.4).

[2] See Vol. i, 111-14.

[3] Neut. αὐτόν is attested in the Cret. *Leg.Gort.* and in Att. inscrr. from 409 B.C. on (*LSJ*, s.v.; Schwyzer i, 609(-10), n. 6; Chantraine[2], § 139; *MS*, 155). At Perg. and Lycia, αὐτό is alone attested (Schweizer, 162; Hauser, 102), and is the usual form in Ptol. documentary papp., but τὸ αὐτόν or ταὐτόν is found in lit. texts (Mayser i, 158-9; i[2], 2, 67). Forms in both -ον and -ο are found in the Herc. papp. and in various Koine authors (Crönert, 194[-5], & n. 3). In MGr., the neut. is αὐτό (Mirambel, *Gram.*, 78, 97-98; Maspero, 77) when not expanded to αὐτόνος, -η, -ο (Thumb, *Handbook*, § 144; Jannaris, § 577).

c. Forms of αὐτός are frequently repeated redundantly, e.g., καὶ εἰ χρεία αὐτῷ γένηται | αὐτῷ *PAntin.* 92.21-22 (4th/5th cent.), or used resumptively, e.g., ἡ φερῥοῦσά σοι ... τοῦτο τὸ ἐπιστόλ[ιο]ν παράσχου αὐτῇ ... *PMerton* 23.3-5 (late 2nd cent.); sim. *PFay.* 127.5-8 (2nd/3rd cent.).[1]

6. ἐκεῖνος, ἐκείνη, ἐκεῖνο is declined regularly, including the nom.-acc. sg. neut. in -ο, e.g., κατ᾽ ἐκεῖνο *PStrassb.* 285.3 (ca. A.D. 200); παραπέμψατε ἐκεῖνο *WChr.* 469.6 (late 4th cent.); τὸ μέγα ἐκεῖνο δικαστήριον *SB* 7033 = *PPrinc.* 82.13 (A.D. 481). No forms of the Ionic-Poetic κεῖνος occur.[2]

7. ἕτερος, -η, -ον.

a. Forms of ἕτερος are sometimes used, mainly in Byzantine papyri, in crasis with the definite article in the forms θάτερον and θατέρου. These forms, which are not attested in the Ptolemaic papyri, occur mainly in the neuter, used substantively and attributively.[3]

1) Substantively:

δυοῖν θάτερον γενέσθαι *POxy.* 1119 = *WChr.* 397.20 (A.D. 253: *BL* i, 332)
ἵνα μὴ θάτερον εἴπω *SB* 7518.2 (4th/5th cent.)
ὑ[π]ὸ θατέρου (masc.) *SB* 8951 = *PSI* 1341.13 (5th cent.)

2) Attributively:

ὑπὸ θατέρου μέρους ... τοῦ ἑτέρου μέρους *PSI* 452.3 (4th cent.)
ἐκ δὲ θατέρου μέρους *PCairMasp.* 159-60.9 (A.D. 568); 156-7.5 (A.D. 570)
ἐκ μὲν τοῦ ἑνὸς μέρους ... ἐκ δὲ τοῦ θατέρου μέρους *PLond.* 1712.5-6 (A.D. 569); sim. *PLond.* 1713.12 (A.D. 569); *PFlor.* 93 = *MChr.* 297.6-8 (A.D. 569); *SB* 9278 = *PHermRees* 29.6 (A.D. 586)
ἐκ μὲν τ[ο]ῦ ἑνὸς μέρους ... ἐκ δὲ θατέρου *PLond.* 1707.2-3 (A.D. 566); *PMon.* 4.8-13 (A.D. 594); *PMon.* 7.10 (A.D. 583)

---

[1] See Vol. iii for a more detailed treatment. For Coptic interference underlying the resumptive use of the personal pron., see esp. Vergote, "Grec biblique," col. 1356.

[2] κεῖνος is found in Asia Minor inscrr. and sporadically in the Ptol. papp. (Schweizer, 162; Mayser i², 2, 67). Both forms, as well as a by-form ἐκειός, are used in MGr. (Mirambel, *Gram.*, 98; Thumb, *Handbook*, § 146; Jannaris, § 570-1).

[3] θάτερον is Att., based on the older ἅτερος, not ἕτερος, and attested in the neut. in Trag. and Att. prose, in the masc. and fem. in late Att. and Hell. as well as in Byz. authors (*LSJ*, s.v. ἕτερος; Schwyzer i, 401; Chantraine², § 140; Crönert, 196 & nn. 2-3; Psaltes, 199).

The recurrence of ϑάτερον, ϑατέρου, especially in Byzantine papyri, was probably the result of Atticistic influence.[1]

b. ἕτερος is still frequently used in its proper dual sense of "the other" (of two), but it more commonly refers to "another" (of more than two), even in the same document.[2]

1) "the other":

τὴν ἑτέραν οἰκίαν *PMich.* 554.21, sim. 17, with ἕτερον τόπον "another" 22 (A.D. 81-96)

ἐν μὲν ... τὸ δὲ ἕτερ[ον] *PMilVogl.* 25 ii.7, with ἕτερα πρόσ[ωπα] "others" 32 (A.D. 126/7)

αἴϑρα δύω, ὧν ἐν τῷ ἑτέρῳ ... *POxy.* 502.18, with ἕτερα "other" 20 (A.D. 164)

ἐ[π]ισταλμάτων δύο ... ἑνὸς μὲν ... τοῦ δὲ ἑτέρου *POxy.* 1415.4-5 (late 3rd cent.)

2) "another":

ἑτέρᾳ σφραγῖδι *SB* 7568 = *PMich.* 232.11 (A.D. 36)

ἐκδιῶξε (for -αι) ἕτερον *PMich.* 231.11 (A.D. 47/48)

ἕτερα χρηστήρια *POxy.* 250.20 (A.D. 61?); *POxy.* 248.30 (A.D. 80)

ἑτέροις πωλεῖν *POxy.* 242.22 (A.D. 77)

τοὺς ἀδελφοὺς καὶ ἑτέρους *POxy.* 249.19-20 (A.D. 80)

παρ' ἑτέρῳ αὐτῆς δανιστῇ *PLBat.* vi, 19.13 (A.D. 118)

μεϑ' ἕτερα *POxy.* 237 vii.42: *BL* i, 318 (A.D. 186); *PMich.* 529.26 (A.D. 232-6); *POxy.* 2187.24,27 (A.D. 304)

ἑτέρῳ τρόπῳ *PCairIsidor.* 62.16-17 (A.D. 296)

c. The pronoun ἕτερος is frequently replaced by ἄλλος, as elsewhere in the Koine,[3] e.g., τὸ ἄλλο μέρος *PMerton* 92.22 (A.D. 324); φοίνικας δύο, τὸν μὲν ἕνα ... καὶ τὸν ἄλλον *BGU* 456.10-12 (A.D. 348); ὁ εἷς ... ὁ ἄλλος *PLips.* 40 iii.3 (late 4th/early 5th cent.). Occasionally both pronouns are used together, e.g., περὶ ἑτέρου ἄλλου πράγματος *PMed.* 7.30-31 (A.D. 38).

ἕτερος did not survive into Modern Greek.[4]

---

[1] Cf. δυοῖν ϑάτερον (*POxy.* 1119) Herod.Att. Luc. Ael. & 22 times Aristid. (Schmid i, 197, 312; ii, 184; iii, 177).

[2] See further exx. and discussion in Vol. iii.

[3] See Mayser ii, 2, 87-90; *BDF*, § 306; Dieterich, 203; Schwyzer i, 614.

[4] *Ibidd.*

F. RELATIVE PRONOUNS

1. The definite relative ὅς, ἥ, ὅ is declined regularly.[1] It is frequently replaced, however, by the definite article, especially from the late third century A.D. on:[2]

τὰ πεπιάκαμεν δεδώκαμεν *SB* 9017 (14).9 (1st/2nd cent.)

τὸ οἰ[νάριο]ν? τὸ ἠγόρακα *PAberd.* 72.3-4 (2nd/3rd cent.)

τὰ χαλκώματα τὰ ἔχις παρὰ σοί, δὸς αὐτά ... *SB* 7253 = *PMich.* 221.8 (ca. A.D. 296)

τὸ πορφύρειν (for πορφύριον) τὸ ἔλεγες *POxy.* 2599.12, sim. 31,33-34, 34-35 (3rd/4th cent.)

περὶ τοῦ βρεουίου τό μοι δέδωκες *PLond.* 414 = *PAbinn.* 5.8-10; sim. *PLond.* 413 = *PAbinn.* 6.9,21; *PLond.* 418 = *PAbinn.* 7.14; etc. (all ca. A.D. 346)

τὴν χῖρα (for χεῖρα) τὴν δέδωκεν Ἰοᾶς *PLond.* 244 = *PAbinn.* 22.14 (ca. A.D. 346)

δὸς ἐμοὶ κέρμα ἀπὸ τῶν ἔχις *POxy.* 1683.20-21 (late 4th cent.)

καὶ τὴν [π]ροχρείαν τὴν ἔχει *PAntin.* 92.15 (4th/5th cent.)

καὶ τὰ ἐξ νομίσματα τὰ ἔπεμψες, καὶ τὸ ἀνάλομα (for -ωμα) τὸ ἔπεμψες *POxy.* 1862.26-27,43 (7th cent.)

The article served as a relative pronoun in many classical Greek dialects[3] as still in some dialects of Modern Greek. But the normal relative is now πού,[4] an indeclinable universal relative pronoun apparently simplified from the ancient adverb ὅπου, which served as a relative pronoun already in Aristophanes[5] and much more frequently in late Koine and Byzantine literature.[6]

2. The indefinite relative pronoun ὅστις[7] is generally declined with double

---

[1] In the Ptol. papp., the acc. sg. neut. sts. appears before vowels as ὅν, parallel to (τὸ) αὐτόν above, p. 176, n. 3 (Mayser i², 2, 68).

[2] Cf. also from the mag. papp. τὸ σῶμα ... τὸ ἔτεκεν *PGM* 36.249-50 (4th cent.).

[3] *LSJ*, s.v. ὁ, ἡ, τό sub C; Schwyzer i, 615; Chantraine², § 141; Buck, *GD*, § 126. This usage, unattested in Att. prose, is found sporadically in Att. inscrr., although never in decrees (*MS*, 156). See further P. Monteil, *La Phrase relative en grec ancien*, 21-97. In the Ptol. papp., the art. is also found used as a rel. (Mayser i², 2, 68-70). It is also, though only rarely, so used elsewh. in the Koine (Dieterich, 198-9; Psaltes, 197-8).

[4] Schwyzer i, 615; Chantraine², § 135, Remarque 2; Thumb, *Handbook*, § 149; Mirambel, *Gram.*, 104-5; Maspero, 79-80. See further Jannaris, § 606-8.

[5] *LSJ*, s.v.

[6] Cf. Jannaris, § 608; Psaltes, 197; Dieterich, 201. Exx. of a rel. ὅπου in the papp. are highly dbtfl., e.g., ἐνεβαλόμεθα εἰς τὸ πλοῖον ['Ι]έρακος ... ὅπου ἔμενες ἐνθάδε ἂν ἐν τῇ οἰκίᾳ αὐτοῦ *PBaden* 43.6-10: *BL* iii, 255 and Kapsomenakis, 99(-100), & Anm. 2 (3rd cent.), where ὅπου is prob. better construed as an adv. of place. πού also occurs as an adv. of place in τόπον δὲ αὐτοῖς παράσχες πού μίνωσιν *PGen.* 75.13-15 (3rd cent.: *BL* i, 167), and possibly in τὸ ὁ[σ]πί[τι]ν πού (or σου?) ἐμισθώσω *PBas.* 19.3: *BL* iii, 7 and Kapsomenakis, 99, & Anm. 1 (6th/7th cent.).

[7] The variant form ὅ τις is found in the mag. papp. in δεῦρό <μοι> ὅ τις θεός *PGM* 4.236,238, etc., w. ὅστις ποτ' εἶ 347, sim. 370, etc. (4th cent.). ὅ τις is a collateral form in

inflection, including cases in which the short forms with only the second element inflected, and that in a collateral form, were preferred in classical Greek.

a. Doubly inflected forms found already in Homer,[1] e.g., καθ᾽ ὁντιναοῦν τρόπο[ν] *PGiss.* 35.3 (ca. A.D. 285/6); ἥντινα *POxy.* 1899.16, with ἥτις 17 (A.D. 476); *POxy.* 2283.11 (A.D. 586); *PLond.* 77 = *MChr.* 319.65 (late 6th cent.); οἵτινες *POxy.* 40.6 (late 2nd/early 3rd cent.); οἵστισιν *PLBat.* xiii, 9.2 (early 4th cent.).

b. Gen. and dat. sg. masc. and fem., e.g., οὗτινος *POxy.* 237 vi.18: *BL* i, 318 (A.D. 186); *POxy.* 2983.15 (2nd/3rd cent.); οὗτινοσοῦν *POxy.* 100.15 (A.D. 133); *WChr.* 27.6-7 (2nd cent.); *POxy.* 2134.23-24 part. rest. (ca. A.D. 170); *PSI* 1035.15 (A.D. 179); *PLBat.* xvi, 9.27 (A.D. 183); *POxy.* 719.25 (A.D. 193); *POxy.* 1276.17 (A.D. 249); ᾧτινιοῦν *POxy.* 491 = *MChr.* 304.8 (A.D. 126); *PFlor.* 1 = *MChr.* 243.9 (A.D. 153); *PLips.* 29 = *MChr.* 318.10 (A.D. 295); ἥτινι *PCairMasp.* 89 V.26 (6th cent.); *PCairMasp.* 97 R.19 (6th cent.).

c. The short forms are found in set phrases like ἕως, ἐξ, and ὑφ᾽ ὅτου,[2] e.g., ὃς (= ὡς for ἕως) ὅτου *POxy.* 2353.14 (A.D. 32); ἕως ὅτου *BGU* 625 = *WChr.* 21.17 (early 3rd cent.); ὑφ᾽ ὅτου *PMilVogl.* 25 iv.4 (A.D. 126/7); ἐξ ὅτου *PLond.* 190 (ii, 253-5).14 (2nd cent.: *BL* iii, 92).

d. A hybrid dat. sg. form occurs in ἢ ἄλλῳ ὁτῳδήτινι τρόπῳ *PFay.* 21.11-12 (A.D. 134).

e. Anomalous nom. sg. fem. forms also occur, e.g., ἥτι (for ἥτις) *OTait* 2001.3-4 (2nd/3rd cent.); ἥτινα (for ἥτις) *PRyl.* 701.6 (A.D. 305).

f. The indefinite relative ὅστις, etc., is very frequently used for the definite relative ὅς, ἥ, ὅ, especially in the nom. sg. masc. and fem. (normally so in dating), and sometimes also in the pl. This use was probably introduced to avoid confusion with the definite article.[3] Some examples are: ὅστις *POxy.* 486 = *MChr.*

Ep. Ion. Arc. (*LSJ*, s.v. ὅστις; Schwyzer i, 617; Chantraine[2], § 145). In the mag. papp., however, it is either a new formation on the analogy of ὅ τι (so Jannaris, § 611; cf. Schwyzer i, 617, Zus.) or a scribal omission of σ. Gen. sg. ὅτινος and pl. ὅτινων are found dialectally in MGr. (Schwyzer & Jannaris, *ibidd.*).

[1] *LSJ*, s.v.

[2] In Att. inscrr., the gen. and dat. sg. masc. and neut. are invariably ὅτου, ὅτῳ, but the fem. is ἥστινος, ἥτινι (*MS*, 156). This rule holds w. few exceptions in Trag. & Att. prose before the 4th cent. (*LSJ*, s.v.). The short forms are found only sporadically in the Ptol. papp. (Mayser i[2], 2, 68).

[3] See Vol. iii for a detailed treatment, as well as for the partial replacement of the general rel. pron. by ὃς ἐάν, etc., e.g., ὃ ἐὰν προσοφείλ(η) *POxy.* 2188.10 (A.D. 107). See further Mayser ii, 1, 76-77; Dieterich, 199-200; Psaltes, 198; Chantraine[2], § 139, Remarque 2; *BDF*, § 64.3

59.4 (A.D. 131); ἥτις (very frequent) *POxy.* 489.7 (A.D. 117); *PCairIsidor.* 62.11 (A.D. 296); *POxy.* 896.27 (A.D. 316); *PCairMasp.* 328 ii.9; iv.12; v.11, etc. (A.D. 521); *PLBat.* xiii, 20.21 (6th/7th cent.); etc.; οἵτινες *PCairIsidor.* 63.27 (A.D. 296+); ἅτινα *PCairMasp.* 4.18 (ca. A.D. 552: *BL* i, 100); *PCairMasp.* 283 i.10 (before A.D. 548); cf. also from the mag. papp. ἐγώ εἰμι ὅστις σοι ἀπήντησα *PGM* 2.127 (4th cent.).

G. INTERROGATIVE AND INDEFINITE PRONOUNS

1. τίς, τί, both as interrogative and indefinite, is declined regularly, except that the acc. sg. masc. sometimes end in -ν, e.g., τίναν (probably interrog.) *POxy.* 1874.11 (6th cent.); sim. *PColt* 57.10,13 (A.D. 689); τιναν (indef.) *PGiss.* 90.2 (ca. A.D. 117); *PLond.* 1786.10,26 (5th cent.). The short forms of the indefinite του, τῳ are not used.[1]

2. The numeral εἷς is occasionally used as the indefinite pronoun as in Modern Greek (now ἕνας[2]), e.g., δι' ἑνὸς τῶν περὶ σὲ ὑπηρετῶν *POxy.* 1119 = *WChr.* 397.13 (A.D. 253: *BL* i, 332); ἕνα τῶν παρὰ σοὶ τεκτόνων *PFlor.* 185.10-11 (A.D. 254); εἷς ὢν ἐκ τῶν κδ Μακρόβιος *POxy.* 2110.23, sim. 27,31,36 (A.D. 370). It is also used in a negative context, e.g., καὶ οὐκέτι φόβος οὐδὲ εἷς ἔνει (for ἔνι) *POxy.* 1668.19-20 (3rd cent.). In some later documents, it is used as the equivalent of an indefinite article, e.g., ἐπιστολὴν μίαν *PBeattyPanop.* 1.378 (ca. A.D. 298); sim. *PApoll.* 46.8-9; 50.3 (A.D. 703-15); γέγραπται γὰρ ἐν μιᾷ βίβλῳ *PSI* 98.4 (6th cent.).[3]

3. The adjective φανερὸς is used as the equivalent of an indefinite pronoun in late Byzantine documents, e.g., φανερόν χρέος *PLond.* 1000 = *MChr.* 73.4 (A.D. 538); ἄνδρα φανερόν *PCairMasp.* 194.5 (6th cent.); φανερὰ πράγματα *PLond.* 1676.9 (A.D. 566-73); περὶ φανερῶν κεφαλαίων *PLond.* 992 = *MChr.* 365.11 (A.D. 507); etc.[4]

& 293. The indef. rel. ὅστις has been replaced in MGr. by ὅποιος (cf. MGr. ποιός for τίς below). ὅποιος is to be distinguished from ὁ ὁποῖος, etc., sts. used as a def. rel. pron. in the popular language, esp. after prepos. The ancient neut. ὅτι, however, has survived as an indecl. pron. and adj. in the sense of an indef. rel. (Mirambel, *Gram.*, 105; Thumb, *Handbook*, § 150; Jannaris, § 611).

[1] The gen. and dat. του, τῳ used in Trag. and Att. inscrr. (τῳ also Hom.) are rare after 300 B.C., and are never found in the LXX and NT. They were revived by the Atticists, as D.H. Plu. etc. τινος and τινι are found in Pi. Trag. (τινι also Hom.) as indef. and interrog. and in Att. Com. and prose as interrog. (*LSJ*, s.v.). In the Att. inscrr., του and τινος fluctuate in the 5th-4th cent., but after 300 B.C. the short forms of this pron. no longer occur (*MS*, 156-7). In the Ptol. papp., the short forms never appear in the interrog. pron., but the gen. του is found sporadically for the indef. τινος (Mayser i², 2, 70).

[2] Mirambel, *Gram.*, 99; Chantraine², § 137, Remarque 4; Hatzidakis, *Einl.*, 207; Jannaris, § 622-3. See further Dieterich, 202; Psaltes, 191.

[3] For the inflection of εἷς, see below, pp. 183-5.

[4] See further examples in Preisigke, *WB*, & Daris, *Spoglio*, s.v.

4. ὁ, ἡ, τὸ δεῖνα, normally declined as an *n*-stem in classical Greek,[1] is usually used indeclinably (with orthographic variations) in the magical papyri,[2] but fluctuates between a nasal and a dental stem inflection in documentary papyri, e.g., τοῦ δῖνος (15 times), τοῦ δ(ε)ίνατος (13 times), always in the order τοῦ δῖνος τοῦ δ(ε)ίνατος, ὁ δ(ε)ῖνα (2 times), τὸν δῖνα (9 times) *PMich.* 122 (A.D. 49); τῷ τῖνι (for δεῖνι) *PCairMasp.* 58 iii.6; vi.19 (6th cent.); τὴν δεῖνα *PCair-Masp.* 97 V d.57 (6th cent.).[3]

5. The interrogatives πόσος and ποῖος are declined regularly, e.g., πόσον *POxy.* 2150.7 (3rd cent.); πόσου *BGU* 248.25 (1st cent.: *BL* i, 32); ποῖον *BGU* 1047 ii.7 (A.D. 117-38); ποίου *PAmh.* 68 = *WChr.* 374.7 (A.D. 81-96); etc. Only orthographic variations occur, e.g., ἱς ποῖν (for εἰς ποῖον) *PPhil.* 35.25 (late 2nd cent.). Both of these pronouns have survived in Modern Greek. The latter, with change of accent to ποιός, has generally replaced the interrogative τίς, except for the indeclinable τί and the occasional τίνος.[4]

6. Interrogative adverbs interchange sporadically with correlatives, e.g., πόθεν (for ὅθεν) *PLBat.* xvi, 17.11 (A.D. 106); πῶς (for ὅπως) *PSarap.* 83a.8 (early 2nd cent.); (δραχμὰς) ποσ[άσδε] (for τοσάσδε) *PLond.* 1157. V = *MChr.* 119.5 (A.D. 246).

---

[1] Exc. Ar., who uses it indecl. (*LSJ*, s.v.; Chantraine[2], § 138, Remarque).

[2] E.g., τῆς δεῖνα, τοῦ δεῖνα, τῷ δεῖνα *PGM* 4.327,328 & 1330,1328 (4th cent.); τοῦ δῆνα (for δεῖνα) *PHarris* 55.22-23 (2nd cent.). But it is declined in τοῦδε τῖνος (for δεῖνος) *PGM* 70.24 (late 3rd/early 4th cent.).

[3] The dental stem inflection is known from A.D. *EM* (*LSJ*, s.v.), but only the *n*-stem inflection (w. a nom. sg. ὁ δεῖνας) is used in MGr. (Thumb, *Handbook*, § 157; Mirambel, *Gram.*, 103; Maspero, 84; Jannaris, § 600).

[4] Thumb, *Handbook*, § 151; Mirambel, *Gram.*, 103-4; Maspero, 84-85; Jannaris, § 589-93; Schwyzer i, 617, Zus.

IV. THE DECLENSION OF NUMERALS[1]

The declension of numerals, like that of pronouns, shows some morphological changes which are further advanced along the line of development from ancient to Modern Greek than those observed in the declension of nouns and adjectives. In particular, the formation of compound numerals, ordinals, and fractions anticipates the Modern Greek method of computation.

A. CARDINAL NUMBERS

1. εἷς, μία, ἕν shows the following irregularities in declension.

a. The acc. masc. ἕνα is sometimes used for the nom.-acc. neut. and sporadically for other cases.

1) Nom.-acc. neut.[2]

a) With a singular substantive:

σαργανίτιν (for -ίτην?: *BL* i, 96) ἕνα *BGU* 1095.21 (A.D. 57)
δοροδόκιον ἕνα *PMerton* 39.5 (late 4th/5th cent.)
[ζ]ῳίδιον ἕνα *PIFAO* ii, 12.12: *Aegyptus* 57 (1976), 97-98 (5th cent.)
ν(ομισμάτιον) α ἕνα μ(όνον) *StudPal.* iii, 127.5 (6th cent.)
γεμεῖσαι ἕνα κεράμιν *POxy.* 1851.3 (6th/7th cent.)
νο(μισμάτιον) α, ἕνα *PGrenf.* ii, 102 = *StudPal.* viii, 784.3 (7th cent.)

---

[1] Schwyzer i, 586-99; Chantraine[2], § 162-9; Buck, *GD*, § 114-17; *MS*, 157-64; Schweizer, 163-5; Nachmanson, 146-8; Hauser, 102-4; Mayser i[2], 2, 71-80; Crönert, 197-200; *BDF*, § 63.

[2] ἕνα appears once erroneously for the acc. fem. in the Ptol. papp., but never for the neut. (Mayser i[2], 2, 71). Exx. of neut. ἕνα are found in the later Koine and in the Byz.Chron. (Dieterich, 185; Psaltes, 191).

b) With a plural substantive:

κεράτια εἴκοσι ἕνα *PGrenf.* ii, 95 = *StudPal.* iii, 301.3, with κεράτια
εἴκοσι ἕν 4 (6th/7th cent.)

κερ(άτια) εἴκοσι ἕνα ὕμησῃ *StudPal.* viii, 706.4 (7th cent.)

2) Other cases:

ἐπὶ καμ(ήλῳ) ἕνα *PAlexGiss.* 9.4-5 (A.D. 172)

It is possible that the -α developed independently in the neut. sg. as an addition to preserve the pronunciation of the final -ν, which was frequently lost
in the pronunciation of other words at this period,[1] or represented a plural formation with a plural substantive, but the appearance of ἕνα (and of ἕναν immediately below) in other genders and cases points to the borrowing of the acc.
masc. In Modern Greek, ἕνα has become the regular nom.-acc. neut.[2]

b. The acc. masc. sometimes adds a -ν, parallel to the frequent addition
of -ν to consonantal stem nouns of the third declension.[3] This expanded form
also appears for the fem. and neut.

1) Masc.:

ἕναν *OTaitPetr.* 295.7 (ca. A.D. 6-50); *BGU* 2033.7 (A.D. 94); *SB* 10278.19
(A.D. 98-138); *PFlor.* 51 = *MChr.* 186.3 (A.D. 138-61); *PMich.* 507.5
(2nd/3rd cent.); *PGen.* 68.9 (A.D. 382); *PLond.* 1786.21 (5th cent.);
PAmh. 152.6 (5th/early 6th cent.); *POxy.* 1884.5 (A.D. 504); *PRoss-
Georg.* iii, 17.3,5 (6th/7th cent.)

2) Fem.:

ἕναν *POxy.* 1862.50 (7th cent.)

3) Neut.:

ἕναν *POxy.* 1683.12 & prob. 22 (late 4th cent.); *SB* 9395.8 (6th/7th
cent.); *SB* 5132 = *StudPal.* viii, 756.4 (7th cent.); *POxy.* 1862.18
(7th cent.)

4) Dbtfl. gender:

ἕναν *StudPal.* iii, 275.3,4 (5th/6th cent.)

---

[1] See Vol. i, 111-14.

[2] Thumb, *Handbook*, § 128; Mirambel, *Gram.* 41, 107; Maspero, 65.

[3] See above, pp. 45-46.

This form has survived in the Modern Greek nom. masc. ἕνας, acc. ἕνα(ν) or ἕνανε.[1]

c. An *o*-stem acc. masc. is found in ὄνον ἕνον *BGU* 806.3 (A.D. 1).

d. An anomalous plural may be represented by ἑκάτερος ἕνες *POxy.* 276.7-8 (A.D. 77), unless this form is an orthographic variant of ἕνας, the Modern Greek nom. sg. formed from the late acc. ἕναν.[2]

e. Other apparent plural formations probably represent a lack of agreement or orthographic variants, e.g., ἀργυρίου δραχμὰς ὀκτακοσίας ἴκοσι μίας (if not gen. sg. μιᾶς or = μίαν with ν > ς[3]) *SB* 7515.310 (A.D. 155); ἄμματα εἴκοσι μία τρίτον *SB* 9193.13 (A.D. 527-65).

f. Forms of οὐδείς and μηδείς parallel those of the simple numeral.

1) The acc. masc. sometimes adds a -ν:

οὐδέναν *SB* 9271.6 (1st/2nd cent.) ; *PGiss.* 14.8 (ca. A.D. 117); *POxy.* 2731.17 (4th/5th cent.)
[οὐ]δαίναν *PJand.* 128.16 (5th cent.)
οὐδίναν *PLond.* 410 = *PAbinn.* 34.7 (ca. A.D. 346)
μηδέναν *PAlexGiss.* 15.20 (A.D. 119); *BGU* 27 = *WChr.* 445.14 (2nd/3rd cent.); *PTebt.* 413.15 (2nd/3rd cent.)

οὐδείς and μηδείς have generally been replaced in Modern Greek by κανείς/κανένας, acc. masc. κανένα(ν)(ε), parallel to ἕνα(ν)(ε), etc.[4]

2) A plural form is attested in ἡμε[ῖς] αὐ|τῷ οὐδένες ἐσμέν *PSI* 1336.11-12 (2nd/3rd cent.).[5]

3) The nom.-acc. neut. οὐδέν and μηδέν are sometimes used for the masc. or fem. acc., e.g., ὅτι [ο]ὐδὲν ἔχωμεν μάρτυρων (for μάρτυρα) ε[ἰ] μὴ ὁ θε[ό]ς *POxy.* 1683.13-14 (late 4th cent.); μάλιστα μηδὲν δίκαιον λόγον ἔχειν *SB* 8988.36, with μηδένα λόγον 52 (A.D. 647). If not mere scribal errors, these examples may reflect the use of οὐδέν and μηδέν for the simple negatives οὐ and μή,[6]

---

[1] Thumb, Mirambel, Maspero, *ibidd.*
[2] For the interchange of α and ε, see Vol. i, 278-86. ἕναν itself occurs for the nom. masc. in the very illiterate ἀπέθανα ὁς ἕναν ἐκ τὸν μνιμίον *PRossGeorg.* iv, Anh. (p. 100).3 (A.D. 619-29).
[3] See Vol. i, 131-2.
[4] Thumb, *Handbook*, § 153; Mirambel, 99; Maspero, 81-82.
[5] The pl. of this word is found, although rarely, in class. Gr. in E. Hdt. S. X. D. and later in Paus. (*LSJ*, s.v.).
[6] Cf. Kapsomenakis, 71-72.

which led to the Modern Greek negative δέν with complete loss of the οὐ- and μη- elements. This Modern Greek form is anticipated in ὅμος δὲν ἐ ἁμαρτίε ὑμῶν ἐσίν (for ὅμως δὲν αἱ ἁμαρτίαι ὑμῶν εἰσίν) *POxy.* 1874.13 (6th cent.).

4) The more emphatic, unelided forms of οὐδείς, μηδείς are found occasionally, as in the following examples:

> σάκκους δύο ... οὐδὲ ἕνα ἔχομεν *PFlor.* 272.6 (A.D. 258)
> οὐδὲ ἕνα ἔχω [π]αῖδα *PSI* 41.6 (4th cent.)
> οὐδὲ ἓν | [γ]ράμα *PBerlZill.* 10.3-4 (1st/2nd cent.)
> οὐδὲ ἓν | τετέλεσται *PSI* 971.7-8 (3rd/4th cent.)
> μὴ αὐτῷ δὺ (for δός) μηδὲ ἕν *SB* 9017 (28).6-7 (1st/2nd cent.)
> βλάβος μηδὲ ἓν ποιῶν *CPR* 45 = *StudPal.* xx, 21.18 part. rest. (A.D. 214); *PCairIsidor.* 99.19 (A.D. 296); *SB* 7674 = *PCairIsidor.* 100.13 (A.D. 296)
> μηθὲ ἓν τῶν ... διδο[μέ]νων *PSI* 446.12-13 (A.D. 133/7)[1]

2. δύο is declined as follows.

a. The nominative-accusative.

1) The nom.-acc. for all genders is most often the regular δύο:

> οἱ δύο *PMich.* 241.25 (A.D. 16); *PMich.* 269-71.12, so duplic. *PSI* 907.8 (A.D. 42); etc.
> οἱ ἄλλοι δύο, δύο ψυχάς *PApoll.* 38.6,8 (ca. A.D. 708/9)
> αἱ δύο *PMich.* 282.10, so duplic. *PSI* 917.14 (1st cent.); *PMich.* 283-4.1 (1st cent.); etc.
> δουλικὰ σώματα δύο *PCairIsidor.* 64.21 (ca. A.D. 298)
> ἄρτους μεγάλους δύο *PMich.* 476.7 (early 2nd cent.)
> τὰς ἄλλας δύο μοι ἀρτάβας πέμψαι *BGU* 48.5-6 (2nd/3rd cent.?: *BL* i, 11)
> εἰς τὰς δύο ἡμέρας ταύτας *PSI* 1430.9 (7th cent.)
> cf. δοίο (for δύο) *SB* 7373 = *POslo* 33.13,17 (A.D. 29)

2) The spelling δύω occurs frequently, without distinction in usage from δύο:

> οἱ δύω *CPR* 242 = *StudPal.* xxii, 173.28 (A.D. 40)
> τάλαντα δύω *PLBat.* xvi, 27 C.13 (A.D. 78-79)
> κεράμια δύω *PMich.* 481.16-17 (early 2nd cent.)
> δραχμὰς δύω *WO* 577.4 (A.D. 137)
> δερματιναὶ δύω νευρεαί *BGU* 40.4 (2nd/3rd cent.: *BL* i, 11)
> σάκκια δύω *StudPal.* iii, 140 = xx, 167.4 (5th cent.)
> κεράτια δύω *StudPal.* iii, 596.4 (6th cent.)

---

[1] For the variants οὐθείς and μηθείς, see Vol. i, 97.

Mayser regards δύω as a by-form on the analogy of ἄμφω.[1] Such analogy could be operative only on the orthographic level. With the identification of ο and ω in /o/,[2] there was only the one morpheme {-o} and consequently the one spoken form [dyo], whether written δύω or δύο.

3) The spelling δύωι (an orthographic variant of δύω with the erroneous addition of -ι adscript[3]) occurs sporadically:

ὺ δύωι (for οἱ δύο) PMich. 304.2, with ῥύμηι βασιλικήι 7 (A.D. 42?)
οἱ δύωι PSI 909.1 (A.D. 44); StudPal. xxii, 35.7,17 (A.D. 50)
acc. δύωι PFay. 120.4 (ca. A.D. 100)

4) The spelling δύοι (presumably equivalent to δύωι) occurs in οἱ δύοι PMich. 586.20 (ca. A.D. 30).

5) An acc. fem. form is found sporadically:[4]

δούλας δύας PSI 903.32 (A.D. 47)
ἀρούρας δύας SB 10263.7 (A.D. 205)

6) An apparent neut. form occurs in τὰ δύα τύλαρα PSI 825.16-17,18 (4th/5th cent.). This isolated form is probably the result of scribal error through the associative influence of the -α context.[5]

b. The genitive.

1) The gen. is most often δύο (with orthographic variants) used indeclinably:

δύο ὑδάτων BGU 33.3 (2nd/3rd cent.. BL i, 10)
βωμῶν δύο BGU 337 = WChr. 92 i.3 (2nd/3rd cent.)
τῶν δύο OMich. 655.6 (late 3rd/early 4th cent.)
τῶν δύο μερῶν PCairIsidor. 13.19 (A.D. 314)
τῶν δύο αὐτῆ(ς) τέκνων PApoll. 79.6 (A.D. 703-15)
τῶν δύο ἐχθεγίων, δύω ἀπὸ ἑκάσ{σ}του τρημισείου (for τριμησίου) PSI 1426.2-3 (5th/6th cent.)
μηνῶν δύω PGrenf. i, 48 = WChr. 416.17-18 (A.D. 191)
cf. τῶν ἀλ[ο]υρων (for ἀλουργῶν?) τῶν δούω PMich. 201.6-7 (A.D. 99)[6]

---

[1] Mayser i², 2, 71-72. δύω is found in epic and elegiac poetry, but not in Trag. or Att. prose or inscrr. (LSJ, s.v.; MS, 157). It is found in the Koine in codd.NT, Plu. etc., and in the papp. and various inscrr. (Schweizer, 163; Crönert 197[-8], n. 3). In origin, it represents the lengthened dual ending; the origin of the -o of δύο is unclear (Chantraine², § 163).

[2] See Vol. i, 275-7.

[3] See Vol. i, 185-6. δύωι also occurs in a Ptol. pap. published subsequently to Mayser (PSI 1315.5 [127 B.C.]).

[4] Fem. acc. δύας is attested in a Thess. inscr. (LSJ, s.v.; Schwyzer i, 589; Buck, GD, § 114).

[5] See Introd. above, p. XX.

[6] For the interchange of ου and υ, see Vol. i, 214-15.

2) The classical dual δυοῖν occurs rarely:

ἀρουρῶν δυοῖν ἡμίσους τρίτου *PStrassb.* 52.33 (A.D. 151)
δυοῖν θάτερον *POxy.* 1119 = *WChr.* 397.20 (A.D. 253: *BL* i, 332)
τῶν δυοῖν *SB* 9616 V.24 (A.D. 550-8?)

3) The late Attic dual δυεῖν occurs sometimes:[1]

τῶν δυεῖν ἀρουρῶν *PSI* 905.7 (A.D. 26/27)
δυεῖν *PRyl.* 676.13 (A.D. 69-79?)
εἰς ὄνομα δυεῖν *BGU* 256.5 (A.D. 138-61)
ἐκ δυεῖν οἴκ[ω]ν *PRyl.* 269.5 (2nd cent.)
τῶν δυεῖν μερίδω[ν] *SB* 7515.379 (A.D. 155)
ἐκ δυεῖν ταλάντων *POxy.* 1117.16 (ca. A.D. 178)
[μετ]ὰ δυεῖν θυγατέρων *PLond.* 1178 = *WChr.* 156.30 (A.D. 194)
ἀρουρῶν δυεῖν *PRyl.* 357 descr. (A.D. 201-11)
τῶ[ν] δυεῖν ... ἀφηλίκων *PRyl.* 109.5-6 (A.D. 235)
τῶν δυεῖν μηχανῶν *PSI* 286.14 (3rd/4th cent.)
δυεῖν νομισμάτων *PCairMasp.* 307.13 (A.D. 524/39)[2]
cf. τῶν ... δυεῖν γυμνασίων *SB* 411.2, inscr. (3rd/4th cent.)

4) A late gen. δυῶν also occurs sporadically:[3]

τῶν δυῶν ἀρωνος (for ἀρουρῶν) *PMich.* 252.10 (A.D. 26/27)
ἀρουρῶν δυῶν *BGU* 282.25, with dat. δυσί 10 (A.D. 161-80)

c. The dative.

1) The dat. is most often the late δυσί(ν) (with orthographic variations):

τοῖ(ς) δυσί *PRyl.* 183.3 (A.D. 16); (in full) *PRyl.* 174a.9 (A.D. 139)
σὺν χοινίκεσιν δοισί *CPR* 242 = *StudPal.* xxii, 173.10, with δοιῶι (for
  δύο) 19 and οἱ δύω 28 (A.D. 40)
ἐν δυσί σφραγῖσι *BGU* 1037.7 (A.D. 48: *BL* i, 90); *PMich.* 545.16 (A.D.
  88/89); *PStrassb.* 284.7 part. rest., 11 (A.D. 176-80); etc.
ἔτεσιν δυσεῖν *POxy.* 68 = *MChr.* 228.14 (A.D. 131); sim. *POxy.* 2350.12
  (A.D. 223/4)
ἐν κλάσσαις δυσί *BGU* 113 = *WChr.* 458.2 (A.D. 140)
τοῖς δυσὶ Πέρσαις *PStrassb.* 209.11 (A.D. 152)
τ[ο]ῖς δυσί *PStrassb.* 204.14 (A.D. 161-9)
ἐπὶ ὄνοις δυσί *BGU* 1593.4,11-12 (late 2nd/early 3rd cent.); *BGU* 92 =
  WChr. 427.2-3 (A.D. 212); *BGU* 94.3-4 (3rd cent.); etc.

---

[1] δυεῖν is prob. also to be read for δυσίν in τῶν αὐτῶν δυσὶν κλήρων *PMich.* 262.8 (A.D.
35/36), where the ed. notes: 'It is also possible to read δυεῖν, but since this form is very rare
in the papyri, δυσίν for δυῶν is more probable.' δυσίν as gen. is to my knowledge unparalleled
in the papp., and δυεῖν is not as rare as the ed. suggests.
[2] 'l'ε est à peu près certain, quoique endommagé' (ed., n. ad loc.).
[3] δύων appears for the acc. in *OTait* 1643.4 (A.D. 97) and 1648.3 (A.D. 119?).

ἐν δυσὶ κοίταις *PLips.* 8 = *MChr.* 210.9 (A.D. 220)
ἐν δόσεσι δυσί *POxy.* 912.20 (A.D. 235); *POxy.* 1127.19 (A.D. 183)
[ἐ]ν ταλάντοις δυσί *PSI* 1037.20 (A.D. 301)
σὺν μυλῶσι δυσί *PAlex.* 32.10 (A.D. 448/63: *BL* v, 4)
ἐν δυσεὶ καταβολ(αῖς) *POxy.* 2002.9 (A.D. 579)

2) δύο used indeclinably also appears for the dat.:[1]

ἐπὶ καμή[λ]οις δύο *PLond.* 1266 b (iii, 38).4-5 (A.D. 180/212)
σὺν (ἑκατοσταῖς) [δ]έκα καὶ ἑκατοσταῖς δύο *PCairIsidor.* 47.43 (A.D. 309)
ταῖς δύο ταῖς μειζ[ο]τ[έ]ραις *POxy.* 2416.10 (6th/7th cent.)

In summary, the language of the Roman and Byzantine papyri usually has the indeclinable δύο in the genitive, sometimes δυεῖν, rarely δυοῖν or δυῶν, while in the dative it usually has δυσί(ν), occasionally δύο. In this distribution, it follows in general the usage of the Ionic and late Attic inscriptions and of the Ptolemaic papyri,[2] but also includes elements of classical Attic (gen. δυοῖν),[3] post-classical Attic (gen. δυεῖν),[4] and literary Ionic and Doric (δυῶν).[5] Without these elements, it parallels the usage of the NT,[6] but differs from the usage of early Koine authors, who generally prefer the genitive δυεῖν,[7] and of the Atticists, who prefer the genitive δυοῖν,[8] but dative δύο.[9] In Modern Greek, δύο (usually oxytone δυό) is used indeclinably in ordinary speech, but a pedantic genitive δυονῶ(ν)(ε) (or δυῶ(νε)) is sometimes used.[10]

---

[1] Cf. also from the mag. papp. τοῖς δύο ὀνόμασιν *PGM* 2.69-70 (4th cent.).

[2] Cf. Schweizer, 163; Hauser, 102; *MS*, 157; Mayser i², 2, 72-73. Indecl. δύο is also the usage of Hom. and Hdt. (*LSJ*, s.v.; Schwyzer i, 588).

[3] Class. Att. lit. uses δυοῖν in gen. and dat. appar. according to the rule that δύο may be attached to pl. substantives, but if δυοῖν is used, the subst. must have the dual inflection unless it is an abstract noun (cf. *Phryn.*, 185 [Rutherford, 290-1]). This rule is obviously not followed in the papp. δυοῖν is also used in Att. inscrr. in the gen. and dat. to 329 B.C., and is also found in Hp. (*LSJ*, s.v.; *MS*, 157).

[4] δυεῖν is used in Att. inscrr. from 329-229 B.C. (*MS*, 157), and is found in codd. of E. and cited from Th.; it is used esp. in the fem. gen. (*LSJ*, *ibid.*). There is one occurrence of δυεῖν in a lit. Ptol. pap. (Mayser i², 2, 73).

[5] δυῶν Hdt. *Leg.Gort.*, and other Att. and Dor. inscrr. The Ion. dat. (Hdt.) is similarly δυοῖσι (*LSJ*, *ibid.*; Schwyzer i, 589). δυῶν is sporadic and uncertain in the Ptol. papp., but is found in some Koine authors and more freq. in Byz. authors (Mayser i², 2, 72-73; Crönert, 198, n. 1).

[6] NT gen. δύο, dat. δυσίν (*BDF*, § 63.1).

[7] See Crönert, 198 & n. 1. δυεῖν is not found in the Byz.Chron.

[8] So J. Aristid. Herod.Att. Luc. Ael. Philostr.Jun. (Schmid i, 197, 312; ii, 184-5; iii, 177; iv, 23, 46). δύο is also used in the gen. by Ael. Philostr.Jun., as well as Apollon.Cit. Gem. Fhld. etc. (Schmid iii, 28; iv, 33; Crönert, 198 & n. 1).

[9] δυσί(ν), an analogical formation after τρισί(ν) (Schwyzer i, 589; Chantraine², § 163), is not commonly used by the Atticists (exc. D.C.), who prefer δύο. δυεῖν also dat. Aristid. Plb. (Schmid i, 226; ii, 17-18; iv, 23); δυσί(ν) codd.Th., v.l. Hp., Arist. etc. (*LSJ*, s.v.). δυσίν is alone attested in the Herc. papp. and predominates in Str. (Crönert, 199 & n. 1).

[10] Schwyzer i, 589; Chantraine², § 163; Jannaris, § 632; Thumb, *Handbook*, § 128; Mirambel, *Gram.*, 107, n. 3; Maspero, 66.

d. ἄμφω is sometimes still used in Roman and Byzantine documents in the genitive and dative, normally with the dual ending -οῖν:[1]

> ἡ πρὸς ἀλλήλους φιλ[ί]α φανερ[ά] ἐστιν ἀμφοῖν *PStrassb.* 169 = *PLBat.* xvii, 14.5-6 (2nd cent.)
> τὴν ἐξ ἀμφοῖν γενομένην θυγατέρα *PTebt.* 326 = *MChr.* 325.5-6 (A.D. 266)
> καὶ τ[οῦ ἐξ] ἀμφοῖν ἡμῶν υἱοῦ *PLBat.* ii, 4.7 (ca. A.D. 280)
> ἐφ' ὅλον τὸν τῆς ἐξ ἀμφοῖν ζωῆς χρόνον *PFlor.* 93 = *MChr.* 297.12; so copy *PLond.* 1713.18 part. rest. (A.D. 569); *PCairMasp.* 311.14 (A.D. 569/70?)[2]
> παρὰ τῶν ἀμφοῖν ἡμῶν τέκνων *PLond.* 1727.17 (A.D. 583/4)
> τοὺς ἐξ ἀμφοῖν κλ[ηρονόμους] *PLond.* 113 (2) (i, 204-7).10 (6th/7th cent.)
> ἐξ ἀμφοῖν τεχθησόμενα *SB* 8986.23 (A.D. 640/1)

e. ἀμφότεροι normally occurs only in the plural, e.g., ἐ[ξ ἀμ]φοτέρων *BGU* 115 = *WChr.* 203 i.7-8, sim. 19, with ἀμφοτέρους i.9, etc. (A.D. 189); sim. *BGU* 117.9-10 (A.D. 189); [ἀμ]φοτέροις (for -αις) *POxy.* 268 = *MChr.* 299.16 (A.D. 58); but an apparent dual form is read in an obscure phrase Ἡρακλείδῃ Πάγκτι καὶ Ἀνοῦφις φαλλ' ἀμφοτέροιν ... χαίρειν *CPR* 41.1-6 (A.D. 305).[3]

3. τρεῖς, τρία is declined regularly in the Roman and Byzantine papyri, as in the Ptolemaic papyri.[4] Orthographic variations occur frequently, including nom.-acc. masc.-fem. τρῖς *PMich.* 226.4 (A.D. 37); *PLBat.* xiii, 5.10 (3rd cent.); *PSI* 1082.10 (4th cent.?); etc.; neut. τρεία *PLBat.* xi, 10.5 (6th cent.); gen. τρειῶν *PMich.* 303.3 (1st cent.) and τρῶν[5] *PTebt.* 423.16 (early 3rd cent.). The neut. is used sporadically for the masc.-fem., e.g., ἀρτάβας τρία (for τρεῖς) *POxy.* 2007.8 (early 6th cent.).[6] τρεῖς preserves its classical Attic declension in Modern Greek, but the dative is generally not used, and the neuter is sometimes oxytone.[7]

4. τέσσαρες, τέσσαρα.

a. Stem variations.

---

[1] ἄμφω is used indecl. in *h.Cer.* Arist. A.R. Theocr. (*LSJ*, s.v.). The gen.-dat. dual ending -οῖν is generally retained in Koine authors (Crönert, 196 & n. 4). ἄμφω tended to be replaced by ἀμφότερος (cf. Schwyzer i, 589; Chantraine[2], § 163).

[2] *PCairMasp.* 311 reads ἐξαμφοιν, wh. led Preisigke, *WB*, and *LSJ* to list this ex. alone under a separate entry ἐξάμφω.

[3] ἀμφότεροι has been replaced in MGr. speech by κ' οἱ δυό and sim. phrases (Thumb, *Handbook*, § 128).

[4] Mayser i[2], 2, 73-74.

[5] For loss of unstressed prevocalic ι, see Vol. i, 304.

[6] There are a few indecl. forms in the Ptol. papp. (Mayser i[2], 2, 74).

[7] Schwyzer i, 589; Jannaris, § 635[b]; Thumb, *Handbook*, § 128; Mirambel, *Gram.*, 107; Maspero, 65.

1) For the spellings τέσσερες, τέσσερα, see Vol. i, 278. These spellings probably reflect the reduction of unstressed vowels at this period (Vol. i, 285).[1] They are less likely an Ionic legacy, since they occur only sporadically in the Ptolemaic papyri.[2] For [τέτ]ταρα, see Vol. i, 146.

2) A truncated form τέρας is read eight times in the phrase δραχμὰ τέρας (for δραχμαὶ τέσσαρες), which is further syncopated to δραχμτέρα and other unpronounceable forms, in *PFlor.* 363.3-10 (A.D. 184-6). These extraordinary forms are not morphologically significant.

b. The accusative.

1) The acc. masc. fem., regularly τέσσαρας, is very frequently replaced by the nom. τέσσαρες:

> δραχμὰς ... τέσσαρες *BGU* 1051.12-13 (30 B.C.-A.D. 14); sim. *PMed.* 6.15 (A.D. 26); *PMich.* 244.18 (A.D. 43); *WO* 16.3; 48.4; 102.4-6; 123.8 (A.D. 60); *POxy.* 1269.28 (early 2nd cent.); *BGU* 881.4,5,7,11 (A.D. 153); *OWilb-Brk.* 12.6 (late 2nd cent.); *PAlex.* 16.4, etc. (A.D. 222-3: *BL* v, 4); etc.
>
> βροχὰς τέσσαρες *POxy.* 280.5 (A.D. 88/89); *POxy.* 1686.5 (A.D. 165)
>
> ἀρούρας τέσσαρες *PSI* 875.13 (1st/2nd cent.); *PWürzb.* 12 = *PSarap.* 24.5 (A.D. 123); *PLBat.* iii, 11.15 (A.D. 151); *BGU* 301.10-11 (A.D. 157); *BGU* 1018.8 (3rd cent.); etc.
>
> ἀρτάβας τέσσερες *PBerlLeihg.* 20.5 (A.D. 149); sim. *SB* 9436 υ) 2-3 (4th cent.); *StudPal.* xx, 51.5-6,9-10 (A.D. 238); *POxy.* 1863.9 (7th cent.); etc.
>
> τοὺς τέσσαρες σάκκους *PFlor.* 184.17 (3rd cent.)
>
> σάκκους τέσσαρες *OMich.* 930.5 (A.D. 313)

This use of τέσσερες for the accusative, observed frequently also in the Ptolemaic papyri,[3] is parallel to the extension of the nominative ending -ες to the accusative in consonantal stem nouns of the third declension, but occurs

---

[1] Rare occurrences of the -ερ- spelling in accented syllables, e.g., τεσέρων *PSI* 66.11 (5th cent.), τεσσέρω(ν) *StudPal.* xx, 210.4 (7th cent.), are to be explained either in terms of the interchange of stressed α and ε through bilingual interference (Vol i, 285-6), or by analogy at least on the orthographic level with the nom. and acc.

[2] Mayser i², 1, 13, 34-35; i², 2, 74. Ion. influence prob. accounts for the appearance of these spellings in Asia Minor inscrr. (Schweizer, 163-4). They are also found in Att. inscrr. from the 5th cent. B.C. on (*LSJ*, s.v.; Schwyzer i, 589-90; cf. Buck, *GD*, § 114.4). The origin of the spellings in -ερ- is obscure; they may result from assimilation or dissimilation, or reflect IE vowel gradation (cf. Schwyzer, *ibid.*; Chantraine², § 163; Hatzidakis, *Einl.*, 149-50; Thumb, *Hell.*, 72).

[3] Mayser i², 1, 37; i², 2, 74.

earlier and more frequently.[1] It may have arisen on the analogy of δύο and τρεῖς, which had long had the same form for both nominative and accusative.

2) For the occasional orthographic variant τέσσαρος, see Vol. i, 286-7.

3) The neut. is sometimes used for the acc. masc.-fem. and vice versa, reflecting either the instability of final -ς[2] or syntactical confusion, e.g., ἀρούρας ε[ἰκοσι τ]έσσαρα ἥμισ[υ] *POxy.* 2349.32 (A.D. 70); ἀρτάβας τέσαρα *SB* 2093 (n.d.); conversely, ἐπὶ ... ἔτη τέσσαρες *PMich.* 314.3 (1st cent.); εἰς ἔτη τέσσαρας ἀπό ... *POxy.* 1688.7-8 (3rd cent.); σπατία τέσσερες *PLond.* 418 = *PAbinn.* 7.16 (ca. A.D. 341-4).

c. The genitive is regularly τεσσάρων, e.g., *PLond.* 140 (ii, 180-1).13 (A.D. 69-79); *PLond.* 363 (ii, 170-1).5 (1st/2nd cent.); *StudPal.* xx, 53.24 (A.D. 246); *StudPal.* iii, 429.3 (5th/6th cent.).

d. The dative is normally τέσσαρσι, but phonological and morphological variants occur.

1) The regular τέσσαρσι(ν) is found in such examples as ἀρτάβαις τέσσαρσι *PSAAthen.* 14.10 (A.D. 22); μησὶν τέσσαρσιν *POxy.* 1471.19 (A.D. 81); τέσσαρσι σφραγῖσι *PPhil.* 15.10 (A.D. 153/4).[3] Phonological variants are found in τοῖς τέσσαρεσι *PMich.* 321.5 (A.D. 42) and τοῖς τέρσαρσιν *BGU* 1049.3 (A.D. 342).

2) The Attic τέτταρσι[4] is read in *PLBat.* xvi, 14.18, with τεσσάρων 10 (A.D. 131). It also seems to appear in the spelling τέταρσι in *PSI* 1028.10 (A.D. 15).[5]

3) The poetic and late prose τέτρασι is read in *BGU* 2030.4 (2nd/3rd cent.), *SB* 4284.9 (A.D. 207), and *PSI* 1126.9 (3rd cent.).[6]

---

[1] It is in numerals and words signifying quantity that the use of the nom. -ες for acc. -ας is first found. [τέτορ]ες is restored in a 6th cent. B.C. El. inscr., and μνᾶς δεκατέτορες is read in a 5th cent. B.C. Delph. inscr. (Schwyzer i, 563; Buck, *GD*, § 107.4).

[2] See Vol. i, 124-6.

[3] τέσσαρσι(ν) Th. NT (*LSJ*, s.v.). It is the only dat. attested in the Ptol. papp. (Mayser i², 2, 74).

[4] τέτταρσι Isoc. etc. (*LSJ*, s.v.). For the fluctuation between -σσ- and -ττ- in the papyri, see Vol. i, 145-54.

[5] τέταρσι is attested elsewh. appar. only in a Delph. inscr. of the 1st cent. B.C. (*LSJ*, s.v.). For simplification and gemination in the papyri, see Vol. i, 154-62.

[6] τέτρασι, arising secondarily perh. from the ordinal τέτρα-τος (Schwyzer i, 590), is attested in Hes. Pi. LXX, Str. Hermog. Alex.Aph. and as a v.l. in codd. of Arist. and the NT (*LSJ*, s.v.). It is also found 3 times in the Byz.Chron. (Psaltes, 192).

4) The nom. is also sometimes used for the dat. through lack of concord, e.g., ἐν μη[σὶ] τέσσαρες *StudPal.* xxii, 4 iii.16-17 (A.D. 127/8); ἐν τοῖς εἰκοσιτέσσαρές εἰμι *POxy.* 2110.4 (A.D. 370).

5. The numerals for 5-10 are used indeclinably as generally elsewhere in Greek.[1] For the many phonological variants of πέντε and ὀκτώ, see Vol. i, Index of Greek Words and Forms, s.vv.

6. The numeral for 9 is also found in the variant spellings ἐνέα (see Vol. i, 158), ἐνήα, and ἐννήα (see Vol. i, 245), which along with the spelling ἐννηια *CPR* 41.13 (A.D. 305)[2] and the evidence of other words for the change of prevocalic stressed /i/ to /j/ with concomitant shift of the accent to the final syllable,[3] indicate the existence of the Modern Greek form now spelled ἐννιά (*kathareuousa* ἐννέα).[4]

7. Note on combinative forms. In composition, the numerals for **2** and **3** are regularly δι-, τρι-, as δίμηνος, τριετής, etc.[5] The numeral 4 normally appears in the form τετρα- before both consonants and vowels,[6] as τετράδραχμος, τετραετής. The -α of this combinative form contracts with ο in τετρώβολον (τετράβολος is also found). τεσσαρα- is rarely used in composition; cf. τεσσαράμηνος along with the usual τετράμηνος. The numerals 5-12 and 20 appear in combinative forms in -α: πεντα-, ἑξα-, ἑπτα-, ὀκτα-, ἐννεα-, (δω)δεκα-, εἰκοσα-. This -α, original in ἑπτα-, ἐννεα-, (δω)δεκα-, was extended by analogy to the other numerals.[7] These forms in -α are regular in the Roman and Byzantine papyri before consonants, as πεντάδραχμος, ἑξάμηνος, ὀκτάδραχμος, εἰκοσάδραχμος. They are normal before ε-, as πενταετής, etc., and usually contract with α- and ο-, as πεντάρουρος (but δωδεκααακτιονίκης) and πεντώβολον (but ἐννεόβολος). A double combinative formation is found in εἰκοσαπενταρούρων, e.g., *PMich.* 341.1-2, sim. 10, so duplic. *PSI* 904.2-3, sim. 11 (A.D. 47).

---

[1] The isolated μερῶν ὀκ[τ]ών *PSI* 914.2-3 (1st cent.) represents an erroneous addition of final -ν (see Vol. i, 112-14); duplic. *PMich.* 307 has οἰκοπέδων ὀκ[τ]ών. For the secondary gen. form of these numerals in Aeol., see Schwyzer i, 590.

[2] Ed., n. ad loc.: 'deutet auf die Aussprache [enjá] hin.'

[3] See Vol. i, 302-3.

[4] Thumb, *Handbook*, § 127; Mirambel, *Gram.*, 107; Maspero, 64.

[5] For reff., see Preisigke, *WB*, and Daris, *Spoglio*, s.vv.

[6] This combinative form is used excl. in the Ptol. papp. (Mayser i², 2, 74).

[7] Already in Hom.: cf. Schwyzer i, 591. But the combinative form of the numeral 5 in class. Att. inscrr. is πεντε-, w. elision of the -ε before vowels; πεντα- is first found at the end of 2nd or beg. of 1st cent. B.C. (*MS*, 158). Cf. *Phryn.*, 385 (Rutherford, 489-90). πεντα- is the combinative form in Ion. Asia Minor inscrr. (Schweizer, 164; Nachmanson, 147; Hauser, 103), while in the Ptol. papp., πεντα- is the preconsonantal form but πεντ- normally occurs before vowels (Mayser i², 2, 74-75).

8. Numerals above 10 in the Koine tend as a general rule to be so formed that the larger number precedes and the unit follows. Thus, the numerals 13-19 are normally δεκατρεῖς, etc., in place of the classical τρεῖς καὶ δέκα (or τρεισκαί-δεκα), on the model of εἰκοσιτρεῖς, etc. (see 13-19 below). The numeral 12 fluctuates between the classical δώδεκα and the Koine δεκαδύο, while the numeral 11 normally preserves its classical formation.

9. The numeral 11.

Contrary to the tendency for the larger number to precede the unit in numerals above 10, the numeral 11 is regularly ἕνδεκα in the Roman and Byzantine papyri; the form δεκαείς is found only rarely.

a. ἕνδεκα occurs passim, e.g., *PMich.* 347.6 (A.D. 21); *POxy.* 1447.5 (A.D. 44); *OHeid.* 284.5; 285.4 (A.D. 192?); *PRein.* 143.4 (A.D. 228/9); *OMich.* 480.5 (A.D. 300); *PStrassb.* 317.8 (A.D. 529); *PCairMasp.* 340 V.33 (6th cent.); *SB* 9154.17 (6th/7th cent.).

b. δεκαείς occurs in the following forms:

> δεκαέν *BGU* 1195.6 (ca. 11 B.C.); *PSI* 1063.25 (A.D. 117)
> δεκαμιᾶς *POxy.* 248.23 (A.D. 80); *PBeattyPanop.* 2.164,172,181,200,262 (A.D. 300)

The Roman and Byzantine papyri here differ remarkably from the Ptolemaic papyri, in which δεκαείς is the normal form, with ἕνδεκα found only twice.[1] The Modern Greek form is ἕντεκα (*kathareuousa* ἕνδεκα).[2]

10. The numeral 12 fluctuates in papyri of the Roman period between the classical δώδεκα and the later δεκαδύο, while in Byzantine papyri δώδεκα again becomes the normal form. This also represents a difference from the Ptolemaic papyri, in which δεκαδύο is alone used, except in traditional expressions like δώδεκα θεοί.[3] The Modern Greek form is δώδεκα.[4]

---

[1] Mayser i², 2, 75-76. δεκαείς is also found in an inscr. and in Plu. (*LSJ*, s.v.).

[2] Thumb, *Handbook*, § 127; Mirambel, *Gram.*, 107; Maspero, 64.

[3] Mayser i², 2, 75-76. δώδεκα is used excl. in Att. and Ion. inscrr. until ca. 100 B.C., when δεκαδύο also begins to appear (*MS*, 159; Schweizer, 164; Nachmanson, 147 & n. 1; Hauser, 103). δεκαδύο appears only as a v.l. in the LXX and NT (*BDF*, § 63.2). It is also attested in Ascl. Gem. Plu. Memno ap. Phot., and the Byz.Chron. (*LSJ*, s.v. δέκα; Crönert, 199, n. 3; Psaltes, 192-3).

[4] Thumb, Mirambel, Maspero, *ibidd.*

a. δώδεκα and variants:

δώδεκα *PBaden* 25.11 (1st cent.); *PMerton* 113.10 (2nd cent.); *BGU* 744.9,11 (A.D. 261/2); *PLBat.* xi, 21.3,4 (4th cent.); *POxy.* 994 descr. (A.D. 499); *PMon.* 6.77 (A.D. 583); *SB* 8988.89,106 (A.D. 647); *PApoll.* 66.8 part. rest. (A.D. 710/11); etc.
δυόδεκα (cf. Lat. *duodecim*) *OMeyer* 26.4 (A.D. 118); *SB* 9590.18 (7th cent.)
δωούδεκα *PLond.* 905 (iii, 219).4 (2nd cent.)[1]

b. δεκαδύο and variants:

δεκαδύο *SB* 7344.11 (A.D. 8/9); *PMed.* 10.4-5,6 (A.D. 45); *PSAAthen.* 51 R.5,21 (A.D. 75/76); *PLond.* 166a (ii, 116).5 (A.D. 129); *PMerton* 19.5-6 (A.D. 173); *PFlor.* 211.6 (A.D. 255); 202.13 (A.D. 264); *BGU* 316 = *MChr.* 271.29 (A.D. 359), *SB* 4755.29 (Byz.); etc.; cf. also *PDura* 17.5 (ca. A.D. 180); 23.8 (A.D. 134); 126.11 (A.D. 235)
δεκαδύω *WO* 23.4 (A.D. 72); *SB* 10069.19, inscr. (A.D. 89/90); *WO* 60.3 (A.D. 99/100); *WO* 80.4 (A.D. 107/8); *BGU* 535.18 (2nd cent.); *OMich.* 546.8 (early 4th cent.); cf. *PMur.* 114.11 part. rest. (A.D. 171?)
δεκαδίου *OBrüss-Berl.* 23.5-6 (A.D. 30)
ἀρτάβαις δεκαδυσί ἥμισι *PMilVogl.* 106.11 (A.D. 134)

Both forms are sometimes found in the same document, e.g., *BGU* 881 (A.D. 153), with δώδεκα 4, δεκαδύο 8; *POxy.* 1685 = *PMerton* 17 (A.D. 158), with δεκαδύο 11, δώδεκα 45, etc. Cf. δώδεκα *PMich.* 388.3 (A.D. 172/3?), the only occurrence of this form in *PMich.* vi, vs. fourteen occurrences of δεκαδύο.

11. The numerals 13-19.

These numerals rarely follow the classical formation, in which the unit precedes, followed by καί and δέκα, as πεντεκαίδεκα *POxy.* 1408.2,8 (ca. A.D. 210-14). The normal formation in Roman and Byzantine papyri, as in the Ptolemaic papyri and the New Testament,[2] is δέκα followed by the unit without an intervening καί,[3] e.g., δεκατρεῖς *PHamb.* 10.14 (2nd cent.); δεκατριῶν *BGU* 644.5 (A.D. 69); δεκατέσσαρες *PFlor.* 143.12 (A.D. 264); δεκατέσσαρα *POxy.* 1414.1 (A.D. 270-5); [δεκ]ατεσσάρων, δεκατέσσαρας, *PHamb.* 8.11,22 (A.D.

---

[1] δυόδεκο Arc.; δυώδεκα Ep. Ion. Lyr. (*LSJ*, s.v. δυώδεκα; Schwyzer i, 594; Chantraine², § 165).
[2] Mayser i², 2, 75-76; *BDF*, § 63.1. δεκατρεῖς is already found as part of a larger number in D. (*LSJ*, s.v. δέκα). This new method of formation is also normal elsewh. in the Koine (Schwyzer i, 594; Chantraine², § 165; Dieterich, 186-7; Thumb, *Hell.*, 82; Hatzidakis, *Einl.*, 151). These forms have survived in MGr. (Thumb, *Handbook*, § 127; Mirambel, *Gram.*, 107; Maspero, 64).
[3] The older formation is retained, however, in the combinative forms, as δωδεκα-, τρισκαιδεκα-, etc. For reff., see Preisigke, *WB*, and Daris, *Spoglio*, s.vv.

136); δεκαπέντε *PSI* 1324.9 (A.D. 173); δεκαέξ *PLond*. 140 (ii, 180-1).12 (A.D. 69/79); [δ]εκαεπτά *PCairIsidor*. 91.6 (A.D. 309); δεκαοκτώ *PSI* 1251.12 (A.D. 252); δεκαεννέα *POxy*. 1855.13 (6th/7th cent.); etc. Phonological and other variants occur, e.g., δεχοκτώ *PHamb*. 192.21-22 (1st half 3rd cent.).

This late mode of formation developed concomitantly with a change in the word order of substantive and numeral. The classical forms τρεῖς καὶ δέκα, etc., usually preceded the substantive, so that there was a logical progression from the smaller number to the larger and then to the substantive. With the change in the order of the formative elements of these numerals in later Greek, the place of the substantive is also changed so that the substantive is written first followed by the numeral, with the result that the larger number remains next to the substantive, and there is now a logical progression from the substantive to the larger number and then to the smaller. δεκατρεῖς and δεκαπέντε are already found following the substantive in Attic inscriptions from ca. 400 B.C. on.[1] In the Roman and Byzantine papyri, when the numeral does precede the substantive, as in the first attributive position, the newer forms are used, e.g., τῶν δεκαοκτὼ κερατίων *PCairMasp*. 70.3 (6th cent.).

12. The larger numbers.

The numbers from 20 on are similarly so formed that the larger number(s) precede(s) the smaller number(s), without an intervening καί; again the substantive normally precedes the entire numeral,[2] e.g., ἀρουρῶν εἴκοσι μιᾶς *PFlor*. 325.12 (A.D. 488); δραχμὰς εἴκοσι τέσσαρες *PGrenf*. ii, 63.5 (mid 2nd cent.: *BL* i, 189); ἐτῶν πεν[τ]ήκοντα δύο *BGU* 339 = *MChr*. 250.6 (A.D. 128); etc.

The older formation of the numeral is still also found, e.g., λιτρῶν πέντε καὶ εἴκοσι *PBeattyPanop*. 2.239 (A.D. 300).

13. The tens from 30-50 show rare and late morphological developments which anticipate the Modern Greek forms of these numerals.

a. τριάκοντα is found not only in orthographic variants like τριάκωντα *PStrassb*. 298.8,10 part. rest. (A.D. 65) and τριάκον *PLBat*. vi, 2.27 (A.D. 92), but also in the Modern Greek form τριάντα in *POxy*. 1874.7 (6th cent.). This syncopated form is also reflected in the spelling τρίαντων in *SB* 7536 = *PLBat*. i, 7.10 (4th cent.) and repeatedly in the fraction δυ(ο)τρίαντον (see below, p. 207).[3]

---

[1] *MS*, 160-1.

[2] In the Att. inscrr., the formation was ἑπτὰ καὶ εἴκοσι or εἴκοσι καὶ ἑπτά, or (mainly w. a preceding subst.) εἴκοσι ἑπτά (*MS*. 161). This last method is alone used at Magn. and Lycia, and predominates in the Ptol. papp. (Nachmanson, 147; Hauser, 103; Mayser i², 2, 76). It is used excl. in M.Gr. (Hatzidakis, *Einl*. 150-1; Jannaris, § 640; Thumb, *Handbook*, § 127; Mirambel, *Gram*., 107-8; Maspero, 66).

[3] The ed. of *POxy*. 1874 cites ⲧⲣⲓⲁⲛⲧⲉ in Coptic from Crum-Bell, *Wadi Sarga*, 358.5. τριάντα is also found in Rom. inscrr. from Argos and Amorgos (*LSJ*, s.v.; Schwyzer i, 592).

b. σαράκουντα (for σαράκοντα) is read in *POxy.* 1998.7 (6th cent.). A fraction σερακ(οσ)τ(όγδοον) is also found (see below, p. 207)[1]. For orthographic variants of the full form τεσσαράκοντα, see Vol. i, Index of Greek Words and Forms, p. 362.

c. πετήντα is read in one account on an ostracon, *SB* 1979 (6th cent.). Some few other variations occur which are purely orthographic, e.g., πεντάκοντα *PLBat.* xi, 16.11-12 (5th/6th cent.).[2]

Of these forms, τριάντα is the Modern Greek form, πετήντα reflects the same kind of syncope as the Modern Greek πενήντα, while σαράκο{υ}ντα represents a middle stage between the classical τεσσαράκοντα and the Modern Greek σαράντα, with the syllable -κο- not yet lost. Its eventual loss in all the -κοντα numbers for 30-90 (Modern Greek = simply -ντα[3]) was explained by Thumb, followed by Schwyzer,[4] as dissimilation before an intervening καί, as in τριάκοντα καὶ εἷς. But the evidence of the papyri indicates that καί had generally dropped out of use in compound numbers long before the forms in -ντα for -κοντα began to appear.[5] The syllable -κο- seems to have been lost through a type of syncope;[6] perhaps τριάντα arose first, and the rest followed by analogy. It seems doubtful whether even the initial syllable τεσ- of τεσσαράκοντα was lost by dissimilation, as in τὰ τεσσαράκοντα and similar phrases not common in the non-literary Koine.

14. The numerals for 60-80 appear in various anomalous forms and spellings.

a. The numeral for 60 is sporadically spelled ἑξῆκον, with loss of the final syllable -τα, e.g., *SB* 7619 = *PRein.* 103.13, corr. 11,15,33 (A.D. 26); *PMich.* 605.20 (A.D. 117); *PPhil.* 25.4 (A.D. 127/8). These spellings seem to be scribal errors; no pattern of influence of the following word emerges.

b. The numeral for 70 has many orthographic variants[7] and is sometimes confused with the numeral for 80, e.g., ὁδομήκοντα (for ἑβδο-) *POxy.* 728.32 (A.D. 142) and ὁδδομήκοντα (also for ἑβδο-) *POxy.* 1646.13-14 (A.D. 268/9); conversely, ἑυδεήκοντα appears for ὀγδο- in *PCairIsidor.* 50.23 (A.D. 310),

---

[1] σαράκοντα is also found once in the Byz.Chron. (Psaltes, 192).

[2] πεντέκοντα *PMed.* 48.10 (5th/6th cent.) is a misprint for πεντήκοντα (see Tavola XIX).

[3] Thumb, *Handbook*, § 127; Mirambel, *Gram.*, 107; Maspero, 64.

[4] Schwyzer i, 265.

[5] See above, p. 195. For further exx. of -ντα in Koine inscrr. and lit., see Dieterich, 186.

[6] So Hatzidakis, *Einl.*, 150; Jannaris, § 639.

[7] See Vol. i, Index, p. 343. Additional variants are ἐχδεμήκοντα *PAmh.* 79.58 (ca. A.D. 186) and ἑπτύκοντα *SB* 9593.17 (6th/7th cent.).

and the spelling ἐυδοήκοντα in *POxy.* 1655.12 (3rd cent.) could represent either 70 or 80.[1]

c. The numeral for 80 appears in the apocopated spelling ὀγδοῆκον in *Archiv* i, pp. 492-500 V.10, astrol. (early 7th cent.), and in many orthographic variants, including spellings on the analogy of the numeral ὀκτώ, e.g., ὀκτοήκοντα *PMich.* 571.24 (A.D. 96-98?); ὀκτωήκοντα *POxy.* 142.6 (A.D. 534); ὀκταήκοντα *PMich.* 588.3-4,5 (mid 3rd cent.), spellings reflecting assimilation of the consonant cluster, e.g., ὁδοήκοντα *PWürzb.* 22 = *PSarap.* 97.7 (early 2nd cent.), and spellings perhaps reflecting confusion with the numeral for 70, e.g., ἐγτήκοντ[α] *PSarap.* 49.6 (A.D. 123); ἐκδοήκοντα *PHamb.* 42.7 (A.D. 216); ἐγδόκοντα *PStrassb.* 395.3 (5th/6th cent.); ἐγδοήκοντα *POxy.* 2000.10 (6th/7th cent.).

15. 200-900.

a. Forms in -κόσιοι are declined regularly. These forms have survived, with phonetic changes, in Modern Greek, and are declined according to the Modern Greek declension for *o*- and *a*-stem adjectives.[2]

b. Isolated syncopated forms with loss of the syllable -κο- are read in τετρα-σίας and πεντασίας *PSI* 820.61,63-65 (3 times), with ἑπτακοσίας 56, etc. (A.D. 314).

c. The numeral for 400 seems to be τεσσαρακόσιοι in ἀρχυρίου (for ἀργυ-ρίου) δραχμὰ[ς τεσ]σαρακο[σίας ὀ]γδοήκοντα *PCornell* 6.16-17 (2nd hand) (A.D. 17).

d. The numeral for 900 is occasionally spelled ἐννα-, by gemination of -ν- or on the analogy of ἐννέα, e.g., ἐννακοσίας *BGU* 301.7 (A.D. 157); *PRyl.* 177.5 (A.D. 246); *PCairIsidor.* 49.6 (A.D. 309); 53.27 (A.D. 314); *PSI* 820.51 (A.D. 314). The Modern Greek form is ἐννιακόσιοι /enjakosi-/.[3]

e. There is occasional lack of agreement between these numerals and their substantives, e.g., μοδίους διακοσίας *POxy.* 2004.4, following ἀρτάβας ... μόνας 3-4 (5th cent.). This occurs most often with the nom.-acc. neut. used for other

---

[1] For ἐυ- representing ἐβ-, see Vol. i, 70. I have not yet found -ντα for -κοντα forms in this numeral. The spellings ἐβδομήτα -δύο, -έξ, -επτά listed in Gradenwitz rest on an error in the Index of *PSI* vii. The forms in question read ἐβδομήκοντα-δύο, -έξ, -επτά (*PSI* 738.8; 788.10-11; 820.51-52,70-71).

[2] Thumb, *Handbook*, § 127; Mirambel, *Gram.*, 107; Maspero, 65. For the spelling τρια-κόσαι in *PSI* 810, see Vol. i, 304.

[3] *Ibidd.*

genders and cases, e.g., ἄρουραι διακόσια ... χείλιαι διακόσια *SB* 4325 ii.5 (3rd cent.); ἀναλώματος μυ(ριάδας) διακόσια εἴκοσι *POxy.* 1729.5,6,8, sim. 7,9,10, corr. 3,13 (4th cent.); διακόσια εἴκοσι δύο ἀρτάβας *POxy.* 1862.5-6 (7th cent.).

16. 1,000-9,000.

a. 1,000 is expressed by χίλιοι (with orthographic variants),[1] declined regularly, e.g., δραχμὰς χιλείας ὀκτακοσίας *POxy.* 2134.11,31, sim. 14,19 (ca. A.D. 170).

b. Multiples of 1,000 are expressed regularly by a compound of the appropriate numerical adverb and χίλιοι, e.g., νομίσματα δισχίλια δεκαέξ *POxy.* 1843.4-5 (6th/7th cent.).[2]

17. 10,000 and its multiples are expressed by μύριοι and its compounds, especially modifying δραχμαί, or by the substantival numeral μυριάς.

a. μύριοι (additional thousands, if two or more thousand, follow directly without an intervening καί; if less than two thousand, sometimes after καί),[3] e.g.:

δ[ρ]αχ[μ]αὶ μύρ[ι]αι ἑπτακισχείλιαι *POxy.* 1473.34 (A.D. 201)
ν[ο]μίσματος δραχμὰς μυρίας δισχειλίας *PSI* 1253.6-7 (A.D. 186)
νομίσματος δραχμῶν μυρίων ὀκτακισχειλίων *POxy.* 1701.14 (3rd cent.)
but [νομίσματος δ]ραχμῶν δισμυρίων καὶ χειλίων ἑξακοσίων *POxy.*
  1634.9 (A.D. 222)

b. μυριάς:

πλίνθ(ου) μυριάδες δ'ΔΧ *PTebt.* 402.34-35, etc. (A.D. 172)
μυριάδες Ι', τῶν τριῶν μυριάδων[4] *POxy.* 2778.7,10 (2nd/3rd cent.)
ἀργυρίου δραχμῶν μυριάδων δύ[ο] κα[ὶ χιλί]ων *POxy.* 2136.6-7 (A.D. 291)
[ὠ]μοπλίνθων μυριάδων τριῶν *SB* 5270 = *StudPal.* xx, 209.15-16 (7th
  cent.)

In Byzantine documents, this substantival numeral is used in coinage to express 10,000 denarii; cf. [δηναρ]ίων μυριάδας ἑκατονεννέα *PBeattyPanop.*

---

[1] See Vol. i, 86, 238.

[2] For the numerals 2,000, etc., MGr. uses either the substantival numeral χιλιάς, as δύο χιλιάδες ἕνα, or δισχίλιοι, etc. (Thumb, *Handbook*, § 127; Mirambel, *Gram.*, 108-9; Maspero, 65-66).

[3] μυρίοι (for accent, see *LSJ*, s.v.) is also used as an indef. number 'innumerable,' e.g., μοιρίοις *sic* σὺν χρηματισμοῖς *Archiv* v, p. 383 R.12 (1st/2nd cent.); ἐν μυρίαις *PFlor.* 33.14 (early 4th cent.); τὰς μυρίας *POxy.* 1873.3 (late 5th cent.); μετὰ μυρίων κύκλων *POxy.* 1853.1 (6th/7th cent.).

[4] Or accent μυριαδῶν as in Att.? (cf. *LSJ*, s.v.; Schwyzer i, 383).

2.261-2,263 (A.D. 300); [ἀργυρίου δηναρίων μυ]ριάδαν μίαν *POxy.* 896 = *WChr.* 48.17 (A.D. 316):[1]

ἀργυρίου μυριάδας χιλίας διακοσίας *StudPal.* viii, 758.3 (4th/5th cent.); sim. 759.2; 761.2 (5th cent.); *POxy.* 1129.12 (A.D. 449)

[ἀρ]γυρίου μυριά[δ]ας διακοσίας *PSI* 1265.6 (A.D. 426/41)

Neither of these expressions for 10,000 has survived in Modern Greek, where 10,000 is now expressed by δέκα χιλιάδες.[2] But μυριάδες is retained, along with χιλιάδες, as an indefinite number 'thousands,' used always in apposition,[3] and μύριοι is retained in the compound numerals ἑκατομμύριο 1,000,000 and δισεκατομμύριο 1,000,000,000.[4]

B. ORDINAL NUMBERS

1. The ordinal numbers 1st to 12th are in general formed and declined regularly, but occasional orthographic and morphological variants occur in the ordinals 8th, 9th, and 12th.

a. The ordinal 8th usually appears as ὄγδοος both as an attributive and as a fraction, e.g., ἔτους ὀγδόου *SB* 7817 = *PSI* 1328.6 (A.D. 201); ἥμισυ ὄγδοον *SB* 7670 = *PCairIsidor.* 4.10 (A.D. 299); but many orthographic variants are found in the attributive ordinal, while contraction to ὄγδους is found in both functions, with occasional simplification to ὄγδον in the fraction.

1) Variants of ὄγδοος:[5]

ὄγδωον *POxy.* 1032.12 (A.D. 162)
 ὀγδώου *SB* 8030 = *PMich.* 245.6 (A.D. 47); *POxy.* 280.6 (A.D. 88/89); *PMich.* 537.14 (A.D. 104); *WO* 74.2; 75.2; 76.2 (A.D. 105); *PStrassb.* 230.17 (A.D. 143-4); etc.
 ὀγδώης *POxy.* 1130.16 (A.D. 484)
 ὠγδώου *Archiv* v, p. 170, #2.2 (A.D. 75); *WO* 26.2; 27.2: *BL* ii, 1,47 (A.D. 76)
 ἐγδόης *POxy.* 2007.6 (early 6th cent.)

---

[1] The substantival numeral is often abbrev. μ( ), μυ( ), or μυρ( ) (all, e.g., *POxy.* 1729.3-12 and 1730.4-7 [4th cent.]) or μο(ριάδες), w. change of υ > οι (see Vol. i, 198-9) *POxy.* 1656.2, etc. (late 4th/5th cent.).
[2] Thumb, *Handbook*, § 127; Mirambel, *Gram.*, 109; Maspero, 65-66.
[3] Mirambel, *Gram.*, 111.
[4] Thumb, *ibid.*; Mirambel, *Gram.*, 109; Maspero, *ibid.*
[5] For additional variants, see Vol. i, 162, 165, 239.

ὄκδο(ον) *SB* 10585.5 (1st/2nd cent.)
 ὀκδόου *PSI* 473.14 (A.D. 168/73)
 ὀκτώου *PMed.* 5.13 (A.D. 8/9)
 ὀκτόου *PAlex.* 35.4 (A.D. 618)
ὀδόῳ *SB* 10196.11 (ca. A.D. 180)
cf. also ὀκδόμου (= 8th?) *PLond.* 172 (ii, 205).5 (A.D. 105)

2) Contraction to ὄγδους:

 ὄγδουν *PMich.* 303.4,6,7 (1st cent.); *BGU* 1580.10 (A.D. 119); *POxy.*
 715 = *MChr.* 212.24 (A.D. 131); *OTait* 1444.7 (A.D. 159); *OTait*
 1490.5 (A.D. 176); etc.
 ὄγδου (gen.) *PMerton* 21.4 part. rest. (A.D. 188)
  (acc.) *WO* 866.4 (A.D. 141)
 ὄκδου *SB* 9545 (2).4 (A.D. 62)

3) Simplification to ὄγδον in the fraction:

 ὄγδον *PMich.* 554.10,20 (A.D. 81-96); *SB* 9647 = *PMilVogl.* 209 ii.16;
 iii.9 (A.D. 108); *WO* 824, between lines 4-5 (A.D. 127); 834.5 (A.D.
 131); *OStrassb.* 378.6 (A.D. 161); 419.5 (prob. 2nd cent.); *PMich.*
 395 i.17 (A.D. 183); *WO* 1164.4 (2nd/3rd cent.); *PTebt.* 367.15 (A.D.
 210); *POxy.* 1887.10 (A.D. 538); etc.
 ὄκτον *WO* 1546.6 (A.D. 16)
 ὄκτων *OEdfou* 322.4 (Byz.)

ὄγδοος[1] remained uncontracted in classical Greek, probably because it was parisyllabic with ἕβδομος, etc.[2] In the Ptolemaic papyri, contracted forms in ὄγδους fluctuate with open forms, as in some contract adjectives.[3] The simplification to ὄγδον in the fraction may represent an initial stage of the transfer of contract adjectives of the first and second declensions to the non-contract type.[4]

b. The ordinal 9th appears occasionally in the spelling ἐννάτου, ἐννάτης, with gemination of the -ν- (for examples, see Vol. i, 158). This is the converse of the simplification of ἐννέα to ἐνέα, etc. (see above, p. 193 and Vol. i, 158, 245). While analogical levelling with ἐννέα may have been operative on the orthographic level, there would have been no distinction in pronunciation between the two spellings during the Roman and Byzantine periods.[5]

---

[1] From ὄγδοϝος/-ωϝος to ὀκτώ[ϝ] as Lat. *octāvos* to *octō* (Schwyzer i, 595 & n. 3; Chantraine[2], § 169).
[2] Schwyzer i, 252.
[3] Mayser i[2], 2, 54-55.
[4] See above, pp. 116-20.
[5] For the identification of single and double consonants, see Vol. i, 154-65.

c. The ordinal 12th, regularly δωδέκατος, e.g., ἔτους δωδεκάτου *PMich.* 333-4.2 (A.D. 52), is also found in the variant forms δυωδέκατον *PMich.* 395 i.11 (A.D. 183) and δυοδέκατον *SB* 9198.5 (5th/6th cent.)[1] and in various orthographic variants, e.g., δωδεκάδου *PSarap.* 42.4 (A.D. 121?).[2]

d. The ordinal is replaced sporadically by the cardinal, e.g., πρὸς ὥραν δέκα (for δεκάτην) *PLond.* 241 = *PAbinn.* 52.7 (A.D. 346); τέταρτον ἕνδεκα *POxy.* 250.10 (A.D. 61?).

Only the ordinals 1st to 4th have survived in ordinary Modern Greek speech, with others preserved in particular uses, e.g., for days of the week. The ordinals above 4th tend to be replaced by the definite article and the corresponding cardinal number, as ὁ πέντε 'fifth.'[3]

2. The ordinals 13th-19th no longer have the double inflection τρίτος καὶ δέκατος, etc., of classical Greek; the first element is generally changed to the corresponding cardinal number (used indeclinably in the case of 13th and 14th), e.g., τρεισκαιδεκάτης *POxy.* 1855.4 (6th/7th cent.), but the double inflection may occur in ἀπὸ τρί[τ]ο[υ καὶ] δεκάτο[υ] (for τρίτης καὶ δεκάτης) τοῦ Παῦνι μηνός *PStrassb.* 185.15-16 (A.D. 55).[4] The alteration in the formation of these ordinals represents an adoption of Ionic forms.[5] The following variations occur.

a. The first element of the ordinal 13th frequently appears in the spelling τρισ-, e.g., τρισκαιδεκάτου *PMich.* 333-4.16 (A.D. 52); τρισκαιδεκάτῃ *PStrassb.* 250 f.6 (2nd cent.); and also as τρι-, e.g., τρικαιδεκάτου *PMich.* 310.6 (A.D. 26/27). Other isolated anomalous spellings occur, e.g., [τ]ρισκαιδε{και}κάτου *PStrassb.* 126 = *PSarap.* 41.7, corr. 13 (A.D. 129).

b. The first element of the ordinal 14th shows the following variations.

1) The nom. masc.-fem. is usually used, e.g., τεσσαρεσκαιδεκάτου *PLond.* 154 = *MChr.* 255.2 (A.D. 63); *PStrassb.* 218.5 (A.D. 150); τεσσαρεσκαιδεκάτης *PMich.* 412.1 (1st half 4th cent.); *POxy.* 1983.20 (A.D. 535); *POxy.* 140 = *WChr.* 438.11 (A.D. 550); *PCairMasp.* 46.2; 49.8; 56 iv.3 (6th cent.); etc.

---

[1] Cf. δυόδεκα (and δωούδεκα) above, p. 195.
[2] For additional orthographic variants, see Vol. i, 82, 186.
[3] Jannaris, § 647; Thumb, *Handbook*, § 130; Maspero, 66.
[4] Class. double inflection is also found in the mag. papp., e.g., τῇ τετάρτῃ καὶ δεκάτῃ, πέμπτον καὶ δέκατον ὄνομα *PGM* 3.435,436, etc. (after A.D. 300). τρίτον κ[αὶ] δέκατον, orig. read in *PMerton* 77.12-13 (A.D. 182), has been corr. to τρίτον δ[ω]δέκατον (cf. *BL* v, 66).
[5] Thumb, *Hell.*, 72-73; cf. Schwyzer i, 594. These forms are found even in Att. inscrr. in Rom. times (*MS*, 163). They are the sole forms found in doc. Ptol. papp., w. the older forms retained in some lit. papp. (Mayser i², 2, 77-78). They are normal in Ion. inscrr., the LXX and NT, and later Koine lit. (Schweizer, 165; *BDF*, § 63.2; Crönert, 199; Dieterich, 187).

2) The acc. masc.-fem. is also used occasionally,[1] e.g., τεσσαρασκαιδεκάτου *PSI* 878.14-15 (2nd cent.); τεσσαρασκαιδεκάτης *PSI* 78.3 (5th cent.); *PMerton* 124.8-9 part. rest. (A.D. 520); *POxy.* 1986.22 (A.D. 549); *StudPal.* iii, 119.4 (6th cent.); *PSI* 192.2 (A.D. 566); *PSI* 60.25-26 part. rest. (A.D. 595); *POxy.* 138.14,21,44 (A.D. 610/11); τεσσαρασκαιδεκάτη *PLond.* 1877.5 (6th cent.); *StudPal.* iii, 76 i.5 (5th/6th cent.).

3) The nom.-acc. neut. (or acc. masc.-fem. with loss of -ς?) is also sometimes found,[2] e.g., τεσσερακαιδεκάτης *PSI* 191.4 (A.D. 566); *StudPal.* viii, 797.5 (7th cent.); τεσσαρακαιδεκάτης *PLBat.* xi, 10.3 (6th cent.).

4) A spelling [τ]εσσαροσκαιδεκάτου, probably representing either the nom. or acc. masc.-fem.,[3] is read in *PTebt.* 373.1 (A.D. 110/11).

5) A spelling τεσσαρεισκαιδεκ[άτης] is found in *PCairMasp.* 32.5 (A.D. 551). This form, which appears in a document written outside Egypt, anticipates the Modern Greek form of the cardinal number τέσσερ(ε)ις.[4]

c. The first element of the ordinal 15th is spelled πεντη- in πεντηκαιδεκάτου *BGU* 68.7-8: *BL* i, 14 (A.D. 113/14); πεντηκαιδεκάτης *OMich.* 1021.4-5 abbrev. (early 4th cent.); *PNYU* 11a.105-6,127, etc., with πέντη 5 (1st half 4th cent.); *PBaden* 55.21 (6th cent.); *BGU* 972.7 part. rest. (6th/7th cent.); etc.[5]

d. The first element of the ordinal 16th is regularly ἑκ- as in ἑκκαιδεκάτου *PTebt.* 361.1 (A.D. 132); ἑκκαιδέκατον *SB* 7670 = *PCairIsidor.* 4.10 (A.D. 299), etc., but ἑξ- also occurs, e.g., ἑξκα[ι]δ[ε]κάτης (printed as three separate words) *BGU* 887.13 (A.D. 151); ἑξκαιδεκάτου *PHeid.* 247.2 (6th cent.); *BGU* 255.2 (A.D. 599); cf. ἑξκαιδεκάτη *PColt* 22.4 (A.D. 566). Spellings with ἑξ- are attested elsewhere in Greek.[6]

e. The first element of the ordinal 19th is regularly ἐννεα-, as in ἐννεακαιδεκάτου *PRyl.* 191.4; 192b.10; 194.1 (2nd cent.), but several orthographic variations occur, including ἐνηακαιδεκάτου{ς} *PHamb.* 31 A iii.22 (A.D. 179);[7] ἐννηκαιδεκάτου *PLBat.* i, 12.6-7 (A.D. 179); ἐννακαιδεκάτης *PTebt.* 367.20 (A.D. 210); ἐννα(και)δεκά[τη] *StudPal.* viii, 1079.6 (6th/7th cent.). These last forms

[1] This form is also attested in inscrr. (*LSJ*, s.v.).
[2] So also Str. Sch.Ar. etc. (*LSJ*, s.v.; Schwyzer i, 594).
[3] See above, pp. 191-2, and Vol. i, 286-7, 290-1.
[4] Thumb, *Handbook*, § 127; Mirambel, *Gram.*, 107, n. 1; Maspero, 64. τεσσαρισκαιδεκάτη is also found in the Byz.Chron. (Psaltes, 193).
[5] Cf. also the spellings πέντη and δεκαπέντη in Vol. i, 245.
[6] ἑξκαιδέκατος Hp., cardinal ἑξκαίδεκα Hp. codd.Str. etc. (*LSJ*, s.v.; Crönert, 200, n. 2).
[7] For the spelling ἐν(ν)ήα of the cardinal number, see above, p. 193, and Vol. i, 245.

probably reflect the omission in writing of a symbol representing [j][1] rather than actual morphemic variants on the analogy of ἔν(ν)ατος.

f. The cardinal is sometimes substituted for the corresponding ordinal, e.g., ἔτους ἑκκαίδεκα *PSI* 1059.1 (A.D. 112); [ὁ]κτωκαίδεκα | ἔτο[υς] *PHamb.* 67 = *PLBat.* vi, 36.17-18 (A.D. 156).

3. The ordinals 21st-99th are regularly so formed that the smaller number (normally the cardinal for the number 1, the ordinal for the other numbers) precedes καί followed by the larger.[2]

a. The ordinals 21st, 31st, etc., normally have the cardinal for the unit, e.g., ἔτους ἑνὸς καὶ τεσσερακοστοῦ *PLond.* 262 = *MChr.* 181.1 (A.D. 11); ἑνὸς καὶ εἰκοστοῦ ἔτους *PMich.* 260-1.20,21,39,40 (A.D. 35); but the ordinal is sometimes used, e.g., (ἔτους) πρώτου καὶ εἰκοστοῦ *PFay.* 68.3-4 (A.D. 158). In Modern Greek, the ordinal is used, following the decimal, e.g., εἰκοστὸς πρῶτος, but in ordinary speech, the cardinal preceded by the definite article is used, e.g., ὁ τριάντα ἕνας.[3]

b. In the other ordinals, the unit normally precedes καί followed by the larger number, e.g., ἐνάτου καὶ εἰκοστοῦ *BGU* 174.2,3 (A.D. 7); δευτέρας καὶ εἰκοστῆς *POxy.* 2349.2,27 (A.D. 70); τετάρτου καὶ εἰκοστοῦ, πέμπτου καὶ εἰκοστοῦ *PMich.* 385.22,33 (A.D. 182-5). But the καί is sometimes omitted, e.g., δευτέρου τριακο[σ]τοῦ *POxy.* 826 descr. (A.D. 3), or joined by crasis to the following number, e.g., δευτέρας κἰκοστῆς *PLond.* 256a = *WChr.* 443.3 (A.D. 15). The larger number precedes the unit only sporadically (without καί), e.g., εἰκοσεβδό-μωι, εἰκοσιεβδόμου *PMich.* 605.8 (1st hand), 22 (2nd hand) (A.D. 117). In Modern Greek speech, the cardinal preceded by the definite article has replaced the ordinal formation in these numbers, e.g., ὁ σαράντα ἔξι for τεσσαρακοστὸς ἕχτος.[4]

c. The ordinal 40th, normally τεσσαρακοστός, has the combinative prefix τετρα- as the first element in τὰ τετρακοσστὰ *PFay.* 113.14 (A.D. 100) in the meaning '(celebration of) the fortieth day (after birth).'[5] The ordinal 40th has survived in Modern Greek in a form derived from the regular τεσσαρακοστός in σαρακοστή 'Lent'; cf. πεντηκοστή 'Pentecost.'[6]

---

[1] Cf. the change of stressed /i/ > /j/ before a back vowel, w. concomitant shift of the accent to the final syllable, Vol. i, 302-3. For the poss. identification of front vowels before a back vowel, see Vol. i, 235-62, esp. 261-2. Cf. also ἐννέα = /enja/ above, p. 193.

[2] This is likewise the formation of these ordinals in the Att. inscrr. and the Ptol. papp., but the number 1 is always a cardinal (*MS*, 164; Mayser i², 2, 78).

[3] Mirambel, *Gram.*, 112-13; Maspero, 64, 66.

[4] *Ibidd.*

[5] See Olsson, # 55, n. ad loc. (pp. 163-4); *LSJ*, s.v. (w. τετρακοστός, -ή, -όν Tz.).

[6] Jannaris, § 647b; Thumb, *Handbook*, § 130; Mirambel, *Gram.*, 113; Maspero, 70.

4. Dates are expressed in one of the three following ways:[1]

a. By the ordinal in the feminine (sc. ἡμερα), e.g., μηνὸς Καισαρείου τρίτη *POxy.* 2349.4-5,19 (A.D. 70); Θὼθ τοῦ μηνὸς ἑβδόμη *PHamb.* 23.2 (A.D. 569).

b. By the use of a substantival numeral in -άς, e.g., μηνὶ Μεχεὶρ τ[ε]τράδι *PTebt.* 318 = *MChr.* 218.5 (A.D. 166); τὴν σήμερον ἡμέραν ἥτις ἐστὶν τριακὰς τοῦ παρόντος μηνός *POxy.* 2419.1 (6th cent.). The unit precedes, with an intervening καί, e.g., Φαρμοῦθι μία καὶ εἰκάς *POxy.* 2135.8-9 (A.D. 188). The unit is normally expressed by a cardinal number, e.g., ἐν τῇ πέντε καὶ εἰκάδι τοῦ Ἐπεὶφ μηνός *PLBat.* xiii, 16.13 (6th/7th cent.); but an ordinal is sometimes found, e.g., κατὰ τὴν [ἑβδό]μην καὶ εἰκάδα τοῦ Μεσορὴ μηνός *PCairIsidor.* 66.7-8 (A.D. 299).

c. By Latin forms of dating, e.g., τῇ πρὸ ι̅β̅ καλανδῶν Α[ὐγ]ούστων, τῇ πρὸ μιᾶς εἰδῶν Ὀκτωβρίων *POxy.* 2348.44-45,54 (A.D. 224); πρὸ μιᾶς καλανδῶν Σεπτεμβρίων *PLips.* 64 = *WChr.* 281.6 (A.D. 368/9).

Dates are expressed in Modern Greek by the cardinal number preceded by the definite article with or without the preposition (εἰ)ς, as (σ)τις εἴκοσι, but for the 1st, the ordinal is used, as (σ)τὴν πρώτη.[2]

C. FRACTIONS[3]

1. $^1/_2$ is normally expressed by the neuter ἥμισυ, which, like all fractions, follows the integer immediately without an intervening καί, e.g., ἀρτάβας πέντε ἥμισυ *POxy.* 2140.10-11 (3rd cent.).[4] It is normally used indeclinably, e.g., ἀρταβῶν ἓξ ἥμισυ *PLBat.* xiii, 15.10-11, sim. 11,21-22,22-23 (A.D. 435); but inflected forms are found occasionally, e.g., ἀρούρης μειᾶς ἡμείσους *PMich.* 266.11 (A.D. 38); ἀρουρῶν δύο ἡμίσεος τετάρτου *PLBat.* xvi, 13.5,10 (early 2nd cent.).

A heteroclitic *o*-stem form ἥμεσον (with orthographic variants) is also sometimes found.[5] $^1/_2$ can also be expressed by a compound of ἡμι-, e.g., ἡμιαρούριον, ἡμιαρταβία, etc.[6] In Modern Greek, $^1/_2$ is expressed by μισός, -ή, -ό.[7]

2. $1^1/_2$ is expressed by ἓν ἥμισυ, e.g., ἀρτάβην μίαν ἥμισυ *POxy.* 2140.8-9 (3rd cent.). But 'half as much again,' 'including 50 % interest,' is expressed by

---

[1] Cf. Preisigke, *WB* iii, Abschn. 7; Mayser i², 2, 78.
[2] Thumb, *Handbook*, § 131; Mirambel, *Gram.*, 110.
[3] Cf. Mayser i², 2, 78-80.
[4] For the many orthographic variants of ἥμισυ, see Vol. i, Index, p. 348.
[5] See above, p. 128.
[6] For reff., see Preisigke, *WB*, and Daris, *Spoglio*, s.vv.
[7] Thumb, *Handbook*, § 131; Mirambel, *Gram.*, 115.

the adjective ἡμιόλιος, e.g., ἀργύριον μεθ᾽ ἡμιολίας *PRein*. 103.27 = *PRyl*. 178.9 (A.D. 26); σίτου καθαροῦ σὺν ἡμιολίᾳ ἀρτάβας εἴκοσι ἑπτά *PMerton* 37.7, sim. 15 (A.D. 373); σὺν καὶ τῇ ἀνιλημμένῃ ἡμιολίᾳ, τὰς ὑπὲρ αὐτῶν ἡμιο-λείας *PAmh*. 147.7,15 (4th/early 5th cent.).[1] Interest of 50% is also expressed by the feminine ἡμίσεια, e.g., ἐκτείσω σοι ... διάφορον ἐξ ἡμισείας *POxy*. 1474.17-18 (A.D. 216). ἐφήμισυ is also used for 'half again as much' in τὸ ἐφήμισυ ἐδώ-καμεν τοῖς ἐργαζομένοις *POxy*. 1668.10-11 (3rd cent.). In Modern Greek, $1\frac{1}{2}$ is expressed by ἑνά 'μισυ/ἑνάμισι, etc.[2]

3. $1\frac{1}{3}$ (surtax of $\frac{1}{3}$) is expressed by ἐπίτριτος, e.g., ἐπιτρίτου *OTebt*. 6.3 (6/5 B.C.); *SB* 9620 = *PMilVogl*. 245 i.7; ii.8; iii.6; etc. (A.D. 106).

4. $\frac{2}{3}$ is expressed by the neuter δίμοιρον, both as a fraction and attributively with μέρος, e.g., ἀρούρας δεκαδύο δίμοιρον *PAmh*. 87 = *PSarap*. 27.9-10 (A.D. 125); τὸ ὑπάρχον αὐτοῖς ... δίμοιρον μέρος κλήρου *PTebt*. 318 = *MChr*. 218.10, sim. 15 (A.D. 166). This latter mode of expression is formed into a compound διμοιρόμερος in περὶ τοῦ διμοιρομέρους τῶν χρυσικῶν δημοσίων *PLond*. 1380 = *WChr*. 285.4,16-17,24-25 (A.D. 710/11). In Modern Greek, $\frac{2}{3}$ is expressed by τὰ δύο τρίτα.[3]

5. Proper fractions whose numerator is 1, as $\frac{1}{3}$, $\frac{1}{4}$, etc., are expressed by the neuter of the ordinal added directly and indeclinably to the cardinal integer without an intervening καί, e.g., ἀρούρα[ς] πέντε τέταρτον 5 $\frac{1}{4}$ *POxy*. 488.10-11 (late 2nd/3rd cent.).

6. Proper fractions whose numerator is other than 1 are formed by adding fractions in diminishing order from the highest to the lowest common denomina-tor, e.g., ἀρούρας τρεῖς ὄγδον τετρακαιεξηκοστόν 3 + $\frac{1}{8}$ + $\frac{1}{64}$ = 3 $\frac{9}{64}$ *PFlor*. 18.15-16 (A.D. 147/8); ἀρτάβας ὀγδοοίκοντα ἐννήα ἥμισυ τρίτον 89 + $\frac{1}{2}$ + $\frac{1}{3}$ = 89 $\frac{5}{6}$ *PCairIsidor*. 50.26-27 (A.D. 310); ἥμισυ τρίτον δωδέκατον τετρα-καιεικωστὸν τεσσαρακωστόγκτων ἐννηκωστέκτῳ(ν) $\frac{1}{2}$ + $\frac{1}{3}$ + $\frac{1}{12}$ + $\frac{1}{24}$ + $\frac{1}{48}$ + $\frac{1}{96}$ = $\frac{95}{96}$ *PBeattyPanop*., p. viii, 2-4 (A.D. 339-40).

7. Some ordinals used as fractions assume special forms, many of which are new to Greek.

a. The ordinal 8th appears frequently in the simplified spelling ὄγδον (for references, see above, p. 201).

---

[1] For additional reff., see Preisigke, *WB*, and Daris, *Spoglio*, s.v. See further N. Lewis, "The Meaning of σὺν ἡμιολίᾳ and Kindred Expressions in Loan Contracts," *TAPA* 76 (1945), 126-39.

[2] Thumb, *Handbook*, § 131; Mirambel, *Gram*., 115; Maspero, 67.

[3] Mirambel and Maspero, *ibidd.*

b. The ordinals 30th and 40th used as component elements of fractions sometimes appear in syncopated forms parallel to those found in the corresponding cardinal numbers.[1]

1) 30th as a fraction, regularly τριακοστόν as in δυοτριακοστόν *SB* 4325 ii.8,9; iv.2,4,8 part. rest.; v.7,10 (3rd cent.), or in an orthographic variation in δυοδριακοστόν, δυοδριακοστοῦ *PVindobWorp* 5.29,33 part. rest. (A.D. 169), is found also in the form -τρίαντον, with orthographic variants:[2]

> δυοτρίαντον *SB* 7669 = *PCairIsidor.* 3.12,16 part. rest.; *SB* 7671-2 = *PCairIsidor.* 5.26 (A.D. 299); *PThead.* 55.7 (A.D. 300: *BL* iii, 249); *PCornell* 20a.38 part. rest. (A.D. 303); *PCairMasp.* 118.21 (A.D. 547); *PCairMasp.* 243.10 (6th cent.)
> δυοτρείαντον *PCornell* 20.13,15,197 part. rest., 220 (A.D. 302)
> cf. ἐν δίμυρον τρίαντων (for δίμοιρον τρίαντον) *SB* 7536 = *PLBat.* i, 7.10 (4th cent.)

2) 40th as a fraction, regularly τεσσαρακοστ-, e.g., τεσσαρακοστόν *SB* 4325 v.13; vii.13; ix.7 (3rd cent.), and with phonetic changes, as in [τεσ]σορακοστόν *PLBat.* xiii, 11.11 (A.D. 138), appears as σερακοστ- in δωτέκ(α)τ(ον) σερακ(οσ)-τ(όγδοον) εἰκ(οσ)τ(οτέταρτον) σερακ(οσ)τ(όγδοον) *StudPal.* iii, 506 = *PGrenf.* ii, 104.3,4 (7th/8th cent.).

c. The number 2 (the cardinal δύο) used as the first element of a fraction is sometimes shortened to δυ-:

> δυτριακοστόν, δυτριακοστοῦ *PMich.* 322a.23;25,29 (A.D. 46)
>   δυτριακοστόν *PMich.* 539.17 part. rest. (A.D. 53); *PSarap.* 47 bis.7,9 (A.D. 131)
> δυδριακοστόν *PMilVogl.* 186.5,16 (A.D. 99); *PJand.* 28.7 (A.D. 104)
> δυτριακοστοῦ *PLBat.* vi, 1.21,24 (A.D. 89/90?)
>   δυδριακοστοῦ *BGU* 2050.8,9,14 all part. rest. (A.D. 107); *PMich.* 557.7 with -ον 12 (A.D. 116)

d. The number 4 used as the first element of a fraction appears in the combinative form τετρα-;[3] the intervening καί is sometimes joined by elision or crasis with the following ordinal or is lost completely, sometimes with subsequent further contraction.[4]

---

[1] See above, pp. 196-7.
[2] For these formations, see N. Lewis, "Two Terminological Novelties," *AJP* 81 (1960), 186-88.
[3] So also τετραεικοστόν in the Ptol. papp. (Mayser i², 2, 79).
[4] This mode of formation differs from another late formation found in Koine authors and mathematicians with the order of the composite elements reversed: εἰκοστοτέταρτος Plu., -τεταρταῖος Gal., ἑξηκοστοτέτταρτος Hero Nicom. (*LSJ*, s.vv.).

1) ¹/₂₄:

τετρακαιεικοστόν *OTait* 1973.6-7 (prob. 12 B.C.); *OTait* 1181.4 abbrev. (A.D. 88); *PRyl.* 156.10 (1st cent.); *PTebt.* 369.7 (A.D. 148); *OTaitAsh.* 55.3 abbrev. (A.D. 151); *PFay.* 83.10 (A.D. 163); *OHeid.* 272.6 (A.D. 182); *OTait* 1636.6 (A.D. 252/3); *PBeattyPanop.* 1.397,398 (A.D. 298); etc.

τετρακαιεικοστοῦ *PMich.* 238.139 abbrev. (A.D. 46); *PLBat.* xvi, 9.9 (A.D. 183)

τετρακαικοστόν *SB* 4252.7 abbrev. (2nd cent.); *PLips.* 87.5 (late 4th cent.)

τετρακικοστόν *SB* 4252 = *OMeyer* 56.7 abbrev. (2nd cent.); *WChr.* 236 v.9,12 (3rd cent.)

cf. *SB* 4325, with τετρακαιεικοστόν ix.8; x.3; τετρακαεικοστόν vii.6,9; τετρακικοστ(όν) iii.4; v.9,12; τετραεικοστόν xi.4; τετράκοστον vii.11 (3rd cent.)

2) ¹/₆₄:

τετρακαιεξηκοστόν *PHamb.* 62 = *PLBat.* vi, 23.6,24 part. rest., with -οῦ 23 (A.D. 123); *SB* 7671-2 = *PCairIsidor.* 5.26; *SB* 7669 = *PCairIsidor.* 3.16 part. rest. (A.D. 299); *PCornell* 20a.35,37,62 (A.D. 302); etc.

τετρακαιξηκοστόν *PMeyer* 12.20 (A.D. 115); *PMich.* 557.12 (A.D. 116)

τετρακαεξηκοστόν *PFlor.* 372.19 (3rd cent.); *PFlor.* 50.59,94 (A.D. 268)

τετραεξηκοστόν *PCornell* 20.15,155 part. rest., with τετρακαιεξηκοστόν 113 (A.D. 302); *PHermRees* 22.11-12 (A.D. 394)

τετραξηκοστοῦ *PErl.* 75.6 (A.D. 535-7)

cf. *WChr.* 236, with τετραεξηκοστόν iv.4-5,8,9; v.7,10-11; τετρακαξηκοστόν iv.2; τετρακαεξηστόν *sic* v.15; τετρακικοστόν v.9,12 (3rd cent.)

cf. *SB* 4325, with τετρακαεξηκοστόν i.9; ii.5,8; τετρακαξηκοστόν iv.2; τετραεξηκοστόν iv.8,9; v.7,10-11; vi.10,14; τετραξηκοστόν iii.3,11 part. rest., 14; vi.11-12; vii.5; etc. (3rd cent.)

e. The order of the composite elements of the fractions ¹/₂₈, ¹/₄₈, ¹/₇₂, and ¹/₉₆ are reversed, with false aspiration of the formative suffix -τ- before ὄγδο(ο)ν:[1]

¹/₂₈ εἰκοσθόγδ[οον] *PLBat.* xiii, 11.6 (A.D. 138)

¹/₄₈ τεσσερακοσθούγδουν *Archiv* v, p. 393, #308.12 (A.D. 131)

τεσσαρακοσθογδόου *PLBat.* xvi, 9.14-15 (A.D. 183)

τεσσερακοσθόγδον *SB* 4325 i.13 part. rest.; ii.10,11; iii.4,12; v.8-9,12; vii.6,7,9,10; x.3; xi.3 (3rd cent.)

---

[1] Sim. formations are attested elsewhere in the Koine: τριακοστόδυος, -ον Nicom., -πεμπτος Hero Tz.; τεσσαρακοστόγδοον Tz.; ἑβδομηκοστόδυος Plu., -μονος Archim., -τριτος and -πεμπτος Tz., but δυοκαιεβδομηκοστός in a 3rd/2nd cent. B.C. inscr. from Chalcedon (*LSJ*, s.vv.).

cf. εἰκοσιτοτα|σαρακοσογδ(οον) (= εἰκοσιτέταρτον τεσσαρακοστόγ-
δοον) *PLond.* 1751.3-4 (Arab.)

$^1/_{72}$ ἑβδομηκοστοδύο *POxy.* 46.25-26 (A.D. 100)

$^1/_{96}$ ἐνενηκόσεκτον (for ἐνενηκοστόεκτον) *PLBat.* xvi, 9.15-16,22,35-36
(A.D. 183)

These various new formations of fractions developed from the regular formation of compound ordinals in quite different ways. The classical compound ordinal
formation retained in the papyri consisted of ordinal + καί + ordinal (e.g.,
ὄγδοος καί τεσσαρακοστός). The new forms of ordinals used as fractions evolved
from the regular compound ordinals and became proper compounds, either by
transposing the composite elements and dropping καί, or by changing the first
element either to a combinative form (sometimes with subsequent loss of καί)
or to a cardinal with loss of καί and sometimes with transposition. The lines of
development may be illustrated by the following table. Hypothetical interme-
diate stages are marked with an asterisk; forms attested outside the papyri
are enclosed in parentheses.

Lines of Development in the Formation of Fractions

ordinal + καί + ordinal

(e.g., τέταρτος καί εἰκοστός)

either

changes first element
to combinative form
τετρακαιεικοστόν
τετρακαιεξηκοστόν

with subsequent
phonetic changes
τετρακαεικοστόν
τετρακαεξηκοστόν

or occasional elision
τετρακαικοστόν
τετρακαιξηκοστόν

or crasis
τετρακικοστόν
τετρακαξηκοστόν

or complete loss
of καί
τετρακεικοστόν
τετρακαεξηκοστόν

sometimes with
further contraction
τετρακοστόν
τετραξηκοστόν

transposes elements
with loss of καί
(τεσσαρακοστόγδοον)

with subsequent
phonetic change
εἰκοσθόγδοον
τεσσακοσθόγδοον
σερακ(οσ)τ(όγδοον)
ἐνενηκόσεκτον

changes first element to
corresponding cardinal
*δυοκαιτριακοστόν
(δυοκαιεβδομηκοστόν)

with subsequent
loss of καί
δυοτριακοστόν
*δυοεβδομηκοστόν

with subsequent
transposition
ἑβδομηκοστοδύο

with subsequent
phonetic change

of the first
element
δυτριακοστόν

of the second
element
δυοτρίαντον

of both elements
δυτρίαντον

D. MULTIPLICATIVES

1. Multiplicatives in -πλοῦς are contracted regularly, e.g., ἁπλοῖ *POxy.* 2145.6, etc. (A.D. 186); διπλᾶ *PTebt.* 393.24 (A.D. 150); τριπλοῦν *BGU* 159 = *WChr.* 408.9 (A.D. 216); etc.[1] These numeral adjectives, like all contract adjectives of the first and second declension,[2] have transferred in Modern Greek to the simple declension διπλός, etc.,[3] and are often replaced by equivalent expressions like δυὸ φορές with a comparative adjective.[4]

2. Proportionals.

a. Proportionals in -πλάσιος, -πλασίων are διπλάσιος, τριπλάσιος, μυριαντοπλάσιος; διπλασίων.[5] They have not survived in Modern Greek.[6]

b. Proportionals in -σσός are δισσός, τρισσός, τετρασσός, ἑξασσός, ὀκτασσός.[7] They are declined regularly.

3. Numerical adverbs in -άκις.

a. New members of this type have been formed by the addition of the suffix -άκις to the numerical adverbs δίς and τρίς in [δ]ισάκις and τρισάκις κατὰ μῆνα *PHamb.* 23.25 (A.D. 569). ἅπαξ δύο is also used for δίς in *SB* 8536.2, with ἐν ἅπαξ 17, inscr. (late 6th cent.).[8]

b. For movable -ς in these numerical adverbs, see Vol. i, 128.

4. Distribution is frequently indicated by repeating the numeral (or substantive or adverb). This is primarily the effect of bilingual interference from Coptic.[9]

a. Repetition of the numeral:

ἀνὰ ἓν ἕν *SB* 7660.31 (ca. A.D. 100)

---

[1] For additional exx., see above, p. 121, Preisigke, *WB*, and Daris, *Spoglio*, s.vv.
[2] See above, pp. 116-25.
[3] Cf. poet. διπλός Opp. etc.; ἁπλός *An.Ox.* (*LSJ*, s.v.).
[4] Jannaris, § 651, 653-4; Thumb, *Handbook*, § 132; Mirambel, *Gram.*, 114.
[5] For reff., see Preisigke, *WB*, and Daris, *Spoglio*, s.vv.
[6] Jannaris, § 655-7.
[7] For reff., see Preisigke, *WB*, and Daris, *Spoglio*, s.vv.
[8] But δίς is still found, e.g., δὶς δὶς τοῦτο κέκρικα *PSI* 281.18 (2nd cent.).
[9] Cf. ⲕⲁⲧⲁ ⲥⲛⲁⲧ ⲥⲛⲁⲧ 'two by two,' etc.

ἔχε ἐγγὺς σοῦ μίαν μίαν 'together' *POxy*. 940.6: *BL* iii, **133** (5th cent.)
ἔρε (for αἶρε) κατὰ δύο δύο *PGM* 24a.19-20 (3rd cent.)
εἶνα δήσῃ τρία τρία *POxy*. 121.19 (3rd cent.)

b. Repetition of the substantive:

περιποιῆσαί σοι γάμον γάμον *SB* 8003.4 (4th cent.)
κατὰ πρᾶγμα πρᾶγμα *PLond*. 1732.7: *BL* iii, 98 (A.D. 586?)

c. Repetition of the adverb:

πολλὰ πολλὰ πολλὰ προσαγορεύω *PFlor*. 303.8 (6th cent.)

SUMMARY OF DECLENSION

The above evidence for declension indicates a morphemic structure in the language of the papyri of the Roman and Byzantine periods different from that of classical Attic in the loss of certain forms, in the assimilation of some elements from other dialects, and in the analogical development of many forms which anticipate those of the Modern Greek inflectional system.

A. NOUNS OF THE FIRST DECLENSION

1. The dual has disappeared except for sporadic remnants (p. 1).

2. There is a limited interchange of endings between nouns in -η and -α in both Greek words and Latin loanwords (pp. 1-2). Analogical levelling is most frequent in nouns in -ρᾰ, which tend to form their gen. sg. in -ρης on the analogy of those in -σσα, -σσης, etc., in which consonants other than /r/ precede the /a/ (pp. 4-11).

3. Masc. nouns in -ας or -ης sometimes replace the anomalous gen. sg. -ου, borrowed earlier from the *o*-stem declension, by the stem vowel -α or -η (pp. 12-16). Masc. nouns in -ης have some heteroclitic plural forms of the more common masc. *o*-stem declension, especially in Byzantine times (pp. 14-15).

4. Names in -ας and -ης fluctuate among *a*-, *s*-, and dental stem types (pp. 12-22).

Classical Attic Greek		Roman-Byzantine Papyri		Modern Greek	
		Feminine Nouns			
-ρᾰ	{-ă}	-ρα	{-a}	-ρα {-a}	-ρη {-i}
					or
-ρας	{-ās}	-ρης	{-is}	-ρας {-as}	-ρης {-is}
but		and		and	
-σσα	{-ă}	-σσα	{-a}	-σσα	{-a}
-σσης	{-ēs}	-σσης	{-is}	-σσας	{-as}

Classical Attic Greek		Roman-Byzantine Papyri		Modern Greek	
		Masculine Nouns			
-ᾱς	{-ās}	-ας	{-as}	-ας	{-as}
-ου	{-ou}	-ου/-α	{-u/-a}	-α	{-a}
-ᾱι	{-āi}	-ᾳ	{-a}	—	
-ᾱν	{-ān}	-αν	{-an}	-α	{-a}
and		*and*		*and*	
-ης	{-ēs}	-ης	{-is}	-ης	{-is}
-ου	{-ou}	-ου/-η	{-u/-i}	-η	{-i}
-ηι	{-ēi}	-ῃ	{-i}	—	
-ην	{-ēn}	-ην	{-in}	-η	{-i}
		plural			
-αι	{-ai}	-αι/-οι	{-ε/-y}	-ες	{-es}
-ῶν	{-ōn}	-ῶν	{-on}	-ῶ(ν)(ε)	{-o(n)(e)}
-αις	{-ais}	-αις/-οις	{-es/-ys}	—	
-ᾱς	{-ās}	-ας	{-as}	-ες	{-es}

B. NOUNS OF THE SECOND DECLENSION

1. There is an occasional interchange of endings with nouns of the first and third declensions (pp. 23-25).

2. Nouns in -ιος and -ιον which tend to be readily abbreviated, including names, titles, and diminutives, occur frequently in -ις/-ι(ν), and apparently shift the accent to the final syllable in the gen. and dat. sg. (pp. 25-29).

3. Some nouns of the Attic second declension are replaced by non-Attic forms of another declensional type or show heteroclitic formations, leading to the elimination of this type in Modern Greek (pp. 29-32).

4. Some contract nouns have open forms and/or heteroclitic third declension forms; these nouns have either been replaced by other words or have changed to the simple *o*-stem declension in Modern Greek (pp. 33-37).

5. There is some fluctuation in gender of feminine nouns, most of which became extinct or transferred to other declensional types in Modern Greek (pp. 38-43).

Classical Attic Greek		Roman-Byzantine Papyri		Modern Greek	
-ιος/-ιον	{-ios/-ion}	-ι(ο)ς/-ι(ο)(ν)	{-is/-i(n)}	-ιος/-ι	{-ios/-i}
-ιου	{-iou}	-(ι)οῦ	{-ju}	-ιου	{-ju}
-ίωι	{-iōi}	-(ι)ῷ	{-jo}	—	
-ιον	{-ion}	-ι(ο)ν/-ι(ο)(ν)	{-i(n)}	-ιο/-ι	{-jo/-i}

C. NOUNS OF THE THIRD DECLENSION

1. The acc. sg. of consonantal stem nouns very frequently adds a final -ν on the analogy of vocalic stem nouns of all declensions, leading to the back-formation of the Modern Greek nom. in -α(ς) (pp. 45-46).

2. The nom. pl. is occasionally used for the acc. pl. in the masc. and fem., leading to the adoption of the nom.-acc. -ες as the ending for the plural of *a*-stems, with the transfer of most ancient consonantal stem nouns to the vocalic declension in Modern Greek (pp. 46-47). Analogous levelling of the acc. pl. of *u*- and *ou*-stem nouns with those of consonantal and *a*-stem nouns is also found (pp. 80, 83).

3. Occasional heteroclitic *a* and *o*-stem forms in consonantal stem nouns reflect the tendency toward a vocalic stem declension (pp. 43-45).

4. There is analogical levelling in mixed dental and *i*-stem nouns, which tend to extend the dental stem throughout the paradigm (pp. 52-55).

5. The nom. is occasionally used for the voc. sg., especially in *r*-stems (p. 62).

6. *s*-stem names have forms of the *a*-, *o*-, and dental stem declensions (pp. 69-75).

7. Some nouns and many names tend to be used indeclinably (pp. 87-90).

Classical Attic Greek		Roman-Byzantine Papyri		Modern Greek	
γυνή	{-φ}	γυνή	{-φ}	γυναῖκα	{-a}
γυναικός	{-os}	γυναικός	{-os}	γυναῖκας	{-as}
γυναικί	{-i}	γυναικί/γυνῇ	{-i/-φ}	—	
γυναῖκα	{-a}	γυναῖκα(ν)	{-a(n)}	γυναῖκα	{-a}
μήτηρ	{-ēr-φ}	μήτηρ/μητέρα	{-ir-φ/-ɛr-a}	μητέρα	{-er-a}
μητρός	{-r-os}	μητρός	{-r-os}	μητέρας	{-er-as}
μητρί	{-r-i}	μητρί	{-r-i}	—	
μητέρα	{-er-a}	μητέρα(ν)	{-ɛr-a(n)}	μητέρα	{-er-a}
μῆτερ	{-er-φ}	μῆτερ/μήτηρ	{-ɛr/ir-φ}	μητέρα	{-er-a}

plural		plural		plural	
μητέρες	{-er-es}	μητέρες	{-ɛr-ɛs}	μητέρες	{-er-es}
μητέρων	{-er-ōn}	μητέρων	{-ɛr-on}	μητέρω(ν)(ε)	{-er-o(n)(e)}
μητράσι	{-ra-si}	μητράσι/ μητέραις	{-ra-si/ -ɛr-ɛs}	—	
μητέρας	{-er-as}	μητέρας/-ες	{-as/-ɛs}	μητέρες	{-er-es}

Classical Attic Greek		*Roman-Byzantine Papyri*		*Modern Greek*	
τέλος	{-os}	τέλος	{-os}	τέλο(ς)	{-o(s)}
τέλους	{-ous}	τέλου(ς)	{-us/-u}	τέλου(ς)	{-us/-u}
τέλει	{-ei}	τέλει	{-i}	—	
Σωκράτης	{-ēs}	Σωκράτης	{-is}	-άτης	{-is}
Σωκράτους	{-ous}	Σωκράτου(ς)	{-us/-u}	-άτη	{-i}
Σωκράτει	{-ei}	Σωκράτει/-ηι	{-i}	—	
Σωκράτη	{-ē}	Σωκράτη(ν)	{-i(n)}	-άτη	{-i}
Ἡρακλῆς	{-ēs}	Ἡρακλῆς		-κλῆς	{-is}
Ἡρακλέους	{-eous}	Ἡρακλε(ί)ου(ς)/-ήου(ς)/-ῆτος	-κλῆ	{-i}	
Ἡρακλεῖ	{-ei}	Ἡρακλε(ί)ω(ι)/-ήῳ/-ῆτι		—	
Ἡρακλέα	{-ea}	Ἡρακλῆν/-εῖον		-κλῆ	{-i}
πόλις	{-is}	πόλις	{-is}	πόλη	{-i}
πόλεως	{-eōs}	πόλεως/-εος/-ιος{-ios}		πόλης	{-is}
πόλει	{-ei}	πόλ(ε)ι	{-i}	—	
πόλιν	{-in}	πόλιν/-ην	{-in}	πόλη	{-i}
πρᾶγμα	{-φ}	πρᾶ(γ)μα	{-φ}	πράμα	{-φ}
πράγματος	{-t-os}	πρᾶ(γ)ματος/ -άτου	{-t-os/-t-u}	πράματος/ -ατου	{-t-os/-t-u}
plural		*plural*		*plural*	
πράγματα	{-t-a}	πράγματα/ πρᾶγμα	{-t-a/-φ}	πράματα	{-t-a}
πραγμάτων	{-t-ōn}	πραγμάτων/ πράγμων	{-t-on/-on}	πραμάτω(ν)(ε)	{-t-o(n)(e)}

D. ADJECTIVES

1. Many adjectives of the first and second declension which elsewhere have only two terminations or fluctuate between two and three terminations tend to form a distinct feminine (pp. 105-13). This tendency reached its completion in Modern Greek, where all adjectives have three terminations.

2. Adjectives in -ρος sometimes have the feminine in -ρη, as in Modern Greek (pp. 113-15).

3. Contract adjectives sometimes have open or heteroclitic forms, leading to the elimination of this declension in Modern Greek, with the transfer of most of the adjectives of this type to the simple declension of *o*- and *a*-stems, a transfer facilitated by the identity of the contract declension with the simple in all cases except the nom. and acc. sg. masc. and neut. (pp. 116-25).

4. Some adjectives of the first and third declensions have heteroclitic *o*- and *a*-stem forms (pp. 127-30).

5. Perfect active participles tend to form the oblique cases of the feminine in -υίης, -υίῃ, parallel to the late declension of *a*-stem nouns in -ρᾰ (pp. 132-3).

6. *s*-stem adjectives occasionally have the acc. sg. masc.-fem. -ῆν, voc. -ῆ, as well as *a*-and *o*-stem forms, representing an early stage in the process by which most *s*-stem adjectives were lost or developed into adjectives of the first and second declensions in Modern Greek (pp. 135-40).

7. Comparison of adjectives shows a tendency towards regularization by extensions of the -τερος, -τατος formations to adjectives which form the comparative by means of a different stem in classical Greek, as well as to more *u*-stem adjectives and to adverbs (pp. 145-51).

8. These secondary comparative suffixes are also occasionally added pleonastically to the primary comparative formations, but the latter, although no longer productive, are retained in the most common adjectives (pp. 151-8).

Classical Attic Greek	*Roman-Byzantine Papyri*	*Modern Greek*
βέβαιος, -ον	βέβαιος, -α, -ον	βέβαιος, -η, -ο
μικρός, -ά, -όν	μικρός, μικρά/μικρή/ μικκή, μικρόν	μικρός, -ή, -ό
χρυσοῦς, -οῦ	χρυσοῖς, -εα/-ια, -έας	χρυσός, -οῦ
ὀξύς	ὀξύς	ὀξύς
ὀξέος	ὀξέου/ὀξέως	ὀξύ/ὀξιοῦ
ὀξεῖ	ὀξείῳ	—
εἰδυῖα, -ας, -ᾳ	εἰδυῖα, -ης, -η	—
εὐγενής	εὐγενής	εὐγενικός, -ή, -ό
εὐγενοῦς	εὐγενοῦς	
εὐγενεῖ	εὐγενεῖ	or συγγενής, -ισσα, -ικό
εὐγενῆ	εὐγενῆ/-ῆν	pl. συγγενῆδες, -ισσες, -ικά
voc. εὐγενές	εὐγενῆ	
acc. pl. εὐγενεῖς	εὐγενεῖς/-ούς	or ἀκριβός, -ή, -ό
ἐλάσσων	ἐλάσσων/μικρότερος	μικρότερος
καλλίων	καλλιότερος	κάλλιο/καλήτερος/πιό καλός
μείζων	μείζων/μειζότερος	μεγαλύτερος/πιό μεγάλος
μέγιστος	μέγιστος/μεγιστότατος	ὁ πιό μεγάλος/ ὁ μεγαλύτερος/ ὁ πιό μεγαλύτερος

E. PRONOUNS

1. The expanded acc. sg. in -ν(α) of the first and second personal pronouns, the emphatic ἐ- forms of the second personal pronoun, and unemphatic forms of the third personal pronoun are already the Modern Greek forms (pp. 162-6).

2. There are analogical formations in the singular of the reflexive pronouns, and the distinctive reflexives of the first and second persons are partially replaced by those of the third person, as attested already in classical Greek (pp. 166-9).

3. ἐ- is prefixed occasionally in Byzantine documents to the possessive pronominal adjective of the second person on the analogy of ἐμός (p. 172).

4. The occasional replacement of the definite relative pronoun by the article may have been inherited from ancient dialects and is paralleled elsewhere in the Koine (p. 179).

5. Analogical levelling has extended the double inflection of the general relative pronoun throughout the paradigm, except in stereotyped phrases (pp. 179-80).

6. The occasional replacement of the indefinite relative pronoun by the numeral εἷς led to the adoption of the numeral as the ordinary indefinite pronoun in Modern Greek (p. 181).

Classical Attic Greek		*Roman-Byzantine Papyri*		*Modern Greek*	
ἐγώ	{egō}	ἐγώ	{ɛgo}	(ἐ)γώ	{(e)go}
(ἐ)μοῦ	{(e)mou}	(ἐ)μοῦ	{(ɛ)mu}	(ἐ)μένα(ν)(ɛ)	{(e)mena(n)(e)}
(ἐ)μοί	{(e)moi}	(ἐ)μοί	{(ɛ)my}	—	
(ἐ)μέ	{(e)me}	(ἐ)μέ(ν)(α)(ν)	{(ɛ)mɛ(n)(a)(n)}	(ἐ)μένα(ν)(ɛ)	{(e)mena(n)(e)}
ἡμεῖς	{hēmeis}	ἡμεῖς	{(h)imis}	(ἐ)μεῖς	{(e)mis}
ἡμῶν	{hēmōn}	(ἡ)μῶν	{(h)(i)mon}	(ἐ)μᾶσ(ɛ)	{(e)mas(e)}
ἡμῖν	{hēmīn}	ἡμῖν	{(h)imin}	—	
ἡμᾶς	{hēmās}	ἡμᾶς	{(h)imas}	(ἐ)μᾶσ(ɛ)	{(e)mas(e)}
σύ	{sy}	(ἐ)σύ	{(ɛ)sy}	(ἐ)σύ	{(e)si}
σοῦ	{sou}	(ἐ)σοῦ	{(ɛ)su}	(ἐ)σένα(ν)(ɛ)	{(e)sena(n)(e)}
σοί	{soi}	σοι	{sy}	—	
σέ	{se}	(ἐ)σέ(ν)	{(ɛ)sɛ(n)}	(ἐ)σένα(ν)(ɛ)	{(e)sena(n)(e)}
ὑμεῖς	{hymeis}	ὑμεῖς	{(h)ymis}	(ἐ)σεῖς	{(e)sis}
ὑμῶν	{hymōn}	(ὑ)μῶν	{(h)(y)mon}	(ἐ)σᾶσ(ɛ)	{(e)sas(e)}
ὑμῖν	{hymīn}	ὑμῖν	{(h)ymin}	—	
ὑμᾶς	{hymās}	ὑμᾶς	{(h)ymas}	(ἐ)σᾶσ(ɛ)	{(e)sas(e)}

Classical Attic Greek		Roman-Byzantine Papyri		Modern Greek	
αὐτός	{autos}	α(ὐ)τός	{a(w)tos}	(αὐ)τός	{(af)tos}
αὐτοῦ	{autou}	(α)(ὐ)τοῦ	{(a)(w)tu}	(αὐ)τοῦ(νου)	{(af)tu(nu)}
ἐμαυτόν	{emāuton}	(ἐ)μ(ε)α(υ)τόν	{(ε)m(ε)a(w)ton}	ὁ ἑαυτός μου/ὁ ἐμαυτός	
σ(ε)αυτόν	{s(e)āuton}	(ἐ)σ(ε)α(υ)τόν	{(ε)s(ε)a(w)ton}	ὁ ἑαυτός σου	
ἑαυτόν	{heāuton}	ἑα(υ)τόν	{(h)ia(w)ton}	ὁ ἑαυτός του	
σός	{sos}	(ἐ)σός	{(ε)sos}	δικός σου	

F. NUMERALS

1. The transfer of the acc. masc. ἕνα, sometimes expanded by -ν, to the neut. led to its replacement of ἕν as the Modern Greek neut. and the back-formation of the Modern Greek nom. masc. ἕνας (pp. 183-5).

2. The use of the indeclinable δύο as the normal gen. and the late plural δυσί as the normal dat. parallels the use of Ionic and late Attic inscriptions. Remnants of the classical and post-classical dual and non-Attic plural formations are preserved in the gen. (pp. 186-9).

3. The nom. ending -ες is used frequently for the acc. in τέσσαρες, parallel to the same phenomenon in consonantal stem nouns (pp. 191-2).

4. The numerals above 10 are normally so formed that the larger number precedes the unit. This late mode of formation developed concomitantly with a transposition in the word order of numeral and substantive, which itself now generally precedes the entire numeral. But number 11 reverted to its classical form, and is followed in the Byzantine period by the number 12, which fluctuated between the two formations in the Roman period (pp. 194-5).

5. The numerals 30 50 show rare and late morphological developments which anticipate the Modern Greek forms (pp. 196-7).

6. The ordinals 13th-19th lost the separate inflection of their elements and changed the first element to the corresponding cardinal, an initial step in the process by which all ordinals above 4th are normally replaced by the cardinals in Modern Greek speech. But ordinals above 20th normally retained their classical formation in the papyri (pp. 202, 204).

7. Some ordinals used as fractions assumed special combinative forms, either by transposing the composite elements and dropping καί, or by changing the first element to a combinative form or to a cardinal, usually with loss of καί and sometimes with transposition (pp. 206-9).

Classical Attic Greek		*Roman-Byzantine Papyri*		*Modern Greek*	
εἷς	{heis}	εἷς	{(h)is}	ἕνας	{enas}
ἕνα	{hena}	ἕνα(ν)	{(h)ɛna(n)}	ἕνα(ν)(ε)	{ena(n)(e)}
μία	{miā}	μία	{mia}	μιά	{mja}
μίαν	{miān}	μία(ν)	{mia(n)}	μιά(ν)(α)	{mja(n)(a)}
ἕν	{hen}	ἕν(α)(ν)	{(h)ɛn(a)(n)}	ἕνα	{ena}
δύο	{dyo}	δύο	{dyo}	δυό	{ðjo}
δυοῖν	{dyoin}	δύο/δυοῖν/δυεῖν/δυῶν		δυό(νῶ)(ν)(ε)	{ðʲo(no)(n)(e)}
			{dyo/dyyn/dyin/dyon}		
δυοῖν	{dyoin}	δυσί(ν)/δύο	{dysi(n)/dyo}	—	
τέσσαρες	{tessares}	τέσσερες	{tɛsɛrɛs}	τέσσερ(ε)ις	{teseris}
τέσσαρας	{tessaras}	τέσσερας/-ες	{tɛseras/-ɛs}	τέσσερ(ε)ις	{teseris}
τριάκοντα	{triakonta}	τριά(κον)τα	{trja(ko)nda}	τριάντα	{trianda}
τεσσαράκοντα	{tessarakonta}	(τεσ)σαράκουντα	{(tɛ)sarakonda}	σαράντα	{saranda}
πεντήκοντα	{pentēkonta}	πε(ν)τή(κο)ντα	{pɛ(n)ti(ko)nda}	πενήτα	{peninda}
τρεῖς καὶ δέκα		δεκατρεῖς		δεκατρεία	
πέντε καὶ εἴκοσι		εἴκοσι πέντε		εἴκοσι πέντε	
τρίτος καὶ δέκατος		τρ(ε)ισκαιδέκατος		ὁ δεκατρεία	
δεύτερος καὶ εἰκοστός		δεύτερος καὶ εἰκοστός		ὁ εἴκοσι δύο	

SECTION TWO

CONJUGATION

V. AUGMENT AND REDUPLICATION[1]

The augment, both syllabic and temporal, is occasionally omitted in past tenses of the indicative or transferred to other moods and tenses. Reduplication is likewise occasionally omitted or replaced by the syllabic augment. There is some fluctuation in the place of the augment in compound verbs.

A. SYLLABIC AUGMENT

1. Syllabic augment in general.

The syllabic augment is occasionally omitted in compound verbs whose prefix ends in a vowel, but only rarely in compound verbs whose prefix ends in a consonant. In simple verbs, it is occasionally omitted in the pluperfect and sometimes in other tenses. Conversely, the syllabic augment sometimes appears in moods and tenses of both compounds and simples where no augment is required.

a. Omission of the syllabic augment.

1) In compounds.

a) Prefix ending in a vowel:

διασείσθην *POxy.* 284.5 (ca. A.D. 50)
 διάγραψεν *PSI* 181.3 (A.D. 91)
 διαπέμψετο (for -ατο) *POxy.* 1068.7 (3rd cent.)
  διαπεμψάμην *POxy.* 129 = *MChr.* 296.10,13 (1st hand), corr. 14 (2nd hand) (6th cent.)
 κατάγραψεν *POxy.* 327 (*BL* i, 321).2 (late 1st cent.)
 κατάλειψεν *PTebt.* 406.8 (ca. A.D. 266)

---

[1] Schwyzer i, 646-56; Chantraine[2], § 212-15; 356-8; Buck, *GD*, § 137; *MS*, 169-74; Schweizer, 169-74; Nachmanson, 150-3; Hauser, 105-6; Mayser i[2], 2, 92-113; Crönert, 202-9; *BDF*, § 66-69.

κατεφύτευσεν *PPrinc.* 119.11 (ca. A.D. 325: *ZPE* 8 [1971], 15)
κατάβαλαν *PCairGoodsp.* 15.17 (A.D. 362)
κατάμενων (for κατέμενον) *PLond.* 1332.9 (A.D. 708)
ἀπόστιλες *PBerlZill.* 10.1 (1st/2nd cent.)
ἀνάβη *PPrinc.* 70.9 (2nd/3rd cent.); *POxy.* 2154.21 (4th cent.)
    ἀνάγνω *SB* 7696.48, corr. 20,27, etc. (A.D. 250)
    ἀναδεξ[ά]μην *POxy.* 71 i = *MChr.* 62.16 (A.D. 303)
    cf. ἀνανεώθη *SB* 7475.10, inscr. (6th/7th cent.)
παραγεν[ό]μην *PMich.* 507.3 (2nd/3rd cent.)
    παραλάβαμεν *SB* 7621.3,38-39,86,97, etc. (A.D. 310-24)
    παρασκευάσατε *BGU* 1027 xxvi.16 (4th/5th cent.)
    παραδόθησαν *PApoll.* 21.2 (A.D. 710)
ἐπίστειλεν *POxy.* 1257.5 (3rd cent.)
ὑπώγραψα (= ὑπόγραψα) *SB* 4706.13 (Byz.)

b) Prefix ending in a consonant:

συνκομισά|μην *PMich.* 422.18-19 (A.D. 197)
    συνζεύχθημεν *PLond.* 1727.9 (A.D. 583/4)
ἐνβαλόμην *PLBat.* xi, 1 ii.20 (A.D. 338)
προσφων[ή]σατε *PThead.* 14.32 (4th cent.)
εἰσπράξαντο *PLips.* 64 = *WChr.* 281.32 (A.D. 368/9)

2) In simples.

a) Pluperfect:

γεγραφήκειν *BGU* 1141.28 (prob. 13 B.C.)
    γεγράφειν *POxy.* 113.19 (2nd cent.); *PJand.* 144.9 (A.D. 214?)
    γεγράφει *POxy.* 237 vi.39 (A.D. 186)
δεδώκειν *POxy.* 743.28 (2 B.C.); sim. *PHarris* 104.8: *BL* iii, 81 (2nd cent.?)
    δεδώκεις *PGiss.* 47 = *WChr.* 326.21 (A.D. 117-38)
    δεδώκεισαν *PLBat.* ii, 1.5 (after A.D. 87)
πεπυρέχειν *POslo* 152.4 (1st/2nd cent.)
γεγόνει *PMich.* 492.5 (2nd cent.)
μεμελήκι *PMich.* 498.8 (2nd cent.)
πεπόνφην *PTebt.* 414.9-10 (2nd cent.)
    πεπόμφειν *POxy.* 122.5 (late 3rd/4th cent.)
πεποιήκειν *PHarris* 104.6 (2nd cent.?)

b) Other tenses.

i) After the vowel /ε/ (usually aphaeresis after καί):

καὶ γράψεν *SB* 9122.8-9 (1st cent.)
καὶ λέγε *PMich.* 477.12-13 (early 2nd cent.)
καὶ μαχησάμην (for ἐμαχεσάμην) *PSI* 1430.6 (7th cent.)

ii) After other vowels and consonants:

ὡς γράψας *PAmh.* 133 = *PSarap.* 92.14 (early 2nd cent.); sim. *PGrenf.*
  i, 53 = *WChr.* 131.10 (4th cent.); *SB* 10476.5 (5th/6th cent.)
ἐν ἐμαυτῷ λέγον *SB* 4317.16 (ca. A.D. 200)
οὗ θέμεθα *PGiss.* 33.13 (A.D. 222)
ἃ πλήρωσεν *PGrenf.* ii, 75.7 (A.D. 308: *BL* i, 191)
οὐδὶς κόλυσεν *PAlex.ined.* 209 (p. 43).7 (5th cent.)
καθ᾽ ἃ κέλευσ[ε] *PAlex.ined.* 17 (p. 43).2 (6th cent.)
τ[ό]πων λεηλατήθησαν *PLond.* 1677.36 (A.D. 566/7)
ἀσφάλει[α]ν θέμ[η]ν *PCairMasp.* 309.50 (A.D. 569)
ταύτην τίθεντο *PPar.* 20.4 (A.D. 600)
cf. ἀπὸ Βομπαή, βίω(σεν)... *SB* 5999.5, mummy label (n.d.)

b. Transfer of the augment to other moods and tenses:

ἐδέδωκας *OTait* 2139.2 (5th/6th cent.)
  μετεβεβλ[ή]καμεν *SB* 7244.7 (mid 3rd cent.)
  παρεδεδώκαμεν *POxy.* 1855.7 (6th/7th cent.)
κατελείπειν *PMilVogl.* 59.15 (2nd cent.)
  παρεσχεῖν *SB* 4491.8 (6th/7th cent.)
παρεδεχομένης *PBrem.* 34 = *WChr.* 352.14-15 (A.D. 117)
  ἐποιήσας (ptc.) *PSI* 460.6 (3rd/4th cent.)
  ἐλαβότας (for λαβόντας) *PPrinc.* 100.4 (4th cent.)

This occasional loss and converse transfer of the syllabic augment, paralleled in great part elsewhere in the Koine,[1] is a step toward a more restricted use of the augment in Modern Greek. Since the past tenses of the indicative were already sufficiently characterized in most verbs by the endings and/or the stem, the augment was largely a superfluous morpheme,[2] making it particularly subject to phonological tendencies (e.g., inverse elision following /ε/) and levelling within the paradigm. In Modern Greek, the syllabic augment is used generally only when it bears the accent.[3] It has been incorporated into many verb stem classes, e.g., καταβαίνω, ξεφεύγω (from ἐξέφ(ε)υγον).[4]

---

[1] The syll. augm. is often om. in compds. (once in Att. inscrr., freq. in Asia Minor inscrr. and Ptol. papp.), less often in the ppf. of simple verbs (never in class. Att. inscrr., rarely in Asia Minor inscrr. and Ptol. papp., but normally in the ppf. act. in the NT, sts. in the Atticists, and freq. in the Byz.Chron.); it is also sts. transferred to other moods and tenses (*MS*, 170, 172-4; Schweizer, 169-70; Nachmanson, 151; Hauser, 105-6; Mayser i², 2, 98; Crönert, 209, n. 5; *BDF*, § 66.1; Schmid i, 229; ii, 21; iii, 34; iv, 28, 591; Psaltes, 200-1, 204, 207-8; Dieterich, 212-13; Kapsomenakis, 27-28).

[2] The augm., orig. facultative, remained largely optional in poetry but became regular in prose: so Att., incl. Trag. dialogue, and new Ion. from Hp. on, but still om. in Hdt. in iteratives and in some ppfs. (Schwyzer i, 651-2; Chantraine², § 358; *KB* ii, 1, 16-21).

[3] Therefore only in monosyllabic verb stems, and never in the 1 or 2 pers. pl. (Hatzidakis, *Einl.*, 69-71; Thumb, *Handbook*, § 182-3; Mirambel, *Gram.*, 125; Maspero, 119).

[4] Schwyzer i, 656; Hatzidakis, *Einl.*, 63-67; Thumb, *Handbook*, § 182.

2. Syllabic augment in particular verbs.

a. ἐχρῆν (contracted from χρὴ ἦν) has the augment:[1]

> ἐχρῆν *SB* 7741.7 (early 2nd cent.); *PMilVogl.* 27 iii.11 (A.D. 128/9);
> *POxy.* 2983.23 (2nd/3rd cent.); *PBeattyPanop.* 1.217 (A.D. 298);
> *PAntin.* 35 ii.6 (late 3rd cent.); *POxy.* 2407.31,41,43 (late 3rd cent.);
> *POxy.* 900 = *WChr.* 437.7 (A.D. 322); *PLips.* 39 = *MChr.* 127.5
> (A.D. 390); *POxy.* 1163.5 (5th cent.); *POxy.* 2039.17 (6th cent.);
> *PRossGeorg.* iii, 15.1 (6th cent.); *PLond.* 1708.224 (A.D. 567?); *PCair-
> Masp.* 353.32 (A.D. 569); etc.
> cf. also ἐ[χ]ρῆι (for ἐχρῆ) *PBaden* 39 ii = *PSarap.* 88.5 (A.D. 117?)
> ἐχρῆ *PMichael.* 16.3 (2nd/3rd cent.)
> but possibly χρῆν (if not χρή{ν} or χρῆν‹αι›) *POxy.* 2569.21 (A.D. 265)
> cf. ⟦ἐ⟧χρῆ[ν] *sic BGU* 614.27 (A.D. 217)

b. Verbs beginning with a vowel.[2]

1) ὠνέομαι normally has syllabic augment and reduplication with ἐ-, but the augment and reduplication are sometimes omitted or transferred to the substantive.[3]

a) With augment:

> ἐωνησάμην *PRyl.* 107.11-12 (ca. A.D. 84)
> ἐωνήσατο *PMilVogl.* 85.26 (A.D. 138)

b) With reduplication:

> ἐώνημαι *SB* 5232.5 (A.D. 14/15); *PMich.* 266.12 (A.D. 38); *PPar.* 17.21
> (A.D. 154); *POxy.* 1320 descr. (A.D. 497); etc.
> ἐώνησαι *BGU* 748 iii.6 (A.D. 62)
> ἐώνηται *PMich.* 583.18 (A.D. 78); *PFay.* 62.4-5 (A.D. 134); *PPrinc.*
> 119.10 (ca. A.D. 325: *ZPE* 8 [1971], 15); *POxy.* 1470.10 (A.D. 336);

---

[1] Att. authors, incl. A. S. Ar. Lys. Th. Pl. D., as also Pi., have exx. of both augm. and unaugm. forms, the latter being more freq. attested. χρῆν is unaugm. in the Att. inscrr. (Veitch & *LSJ*, s.v. χρή; *MS*, 173).

[2] To avoid repetition, the ἐ- redupl. of these verbs is included here. ἐ- redupl. also occurs in ἀνέῳγμαι, late impf. mid. corresp. to Att. aor. ἀνέῳξα (from *ἀν-η(ϝ)οι- or on analogy of ἀνέωσα, cf. Schwyzer i, 653, n. 10); for exx., see below, pp. 249-50.

[3] The prevocalic syll. augm., arising from loss of init. ϝ, and redupl. ἐ-, from *(ϝ)ε(ϝ)ω- (cf. Schwyzer i, 654; Chantraine², § 356), is normally om. in Ep. & Ion. (Hom. Hdt. Hp.) and in later authors (ὠνησάμην *AP*, Plu. Luc. Paus.). In class. Att., the augm. and redupl. are sts. om. in compds. (And. Aesch.), only dbtfl. in the simple verb (codd.Lys. Eup.). The augm. is sts. om. in Asia Minor inscrr., always in the NT, and freq. in later authors, but reg. retained in the Ptol. papp. (Veitch & *LSJ*, s.v.; Schweizer, 170; Hauser, 105; Mayser i², 2, 93; *BDF*, § 66.2; Crönert, 283 & n. 4; Psaltes, 203).

cf. *PDura* 26.2, sim. 9 (A.D. 227)

αἰώνηται *PLips.* 4 = *MChr.* 171 i.12 (A.D. 293)

ἐώνητο *PLBat.* ii, 3.11 (A.D. 279)

ἐωνῆσθαι *PMich.* 572.14-15 (A.D. 131); *PMilVogl.* 98.7-8,12-13 (A.D. 138/9?); *POxy.* 1508.5-6 (2nd cent.)

ἐωνημένη *PLond.* 251 = *PAbinn.* 64.6-7 (ca. A.D. 346)

ἠωνημέναι *PMich.* 259.25 (A.D. 33)

cf. ἐῳγημένου, -ῳ *PDura* 26.13,24 (A.D. 227)

c) Without augment:

ὠνήσατο *PRyl.* 617.7 (A.D. 317?)

συνωνήσατο *PFlor.* 165.7 (3rd cent.); *SB* 9470.7 (A.D. 265)

d) Without reduplication:

ὠνημένη *PMich.* 254-5.3 (A.D. 30/31)

ὠνημένης *POxy.* 270 = *MChr.* 236.18,21,25 (A.D. 94); *POxy.* 346 descr. (A.D. 100); *SB* 7817 = *PSI* 1328.50 (A.D. 201)

συνωνημένων *POxy.* 1288.3 (4th cent.)

e) With augment transferred to the substantive:

ἐωνή *PSI* 1443.6 (2nd half 3rd cent.)

2) ὠθέω usually has the syllabic augment.[1]

ἐξέωσε *PSI* 41.16 (4th cent.)

ἐξέωσαν *PFlor.* 58.9 (3rd cent.)

but ὤθησαν *SB* 9399.13 (6th cent.)

3) κατάγνυμι has syllabic augment and reduplication with ἐ- not only in the proper tenses, but also transferred to the participle and subjunctive and to the derived substantive, where it becomes part of the normal stem.[2]

---

[1] Syll. augm. and redupl., of same origin as in ὠνέομαι (cf. Schwyzer and Chantraine, *ibidd.*), is usu. om. in Ep. & Ion. and in the LXX (ὦσμαι) and Arr. Plot. (ὥσθην). In class. Att., the impf. is found wo. augm. in Pl. and a Trag. frag., aor. ἀπῶσε in S. (along with ἐξέασα), and ἀπωσάμην as a v.l. in Ar. The augm. is om. in most codd. of the NT (Veitch & *LSJ*, s.v.; *BDF*, § 66.2) and in the mag. papp.: ὦσεν *PGM* 4.2662 (4th cent.).

[2] The syll. augm. is Att. for *ἠ-Ϝαγ-, w. quant. metath. to ἐ-ᾱγ- (Schwyzer i, 653). The redupl. is om. once in a lit. Ptol. pap. (Mayser i², 2, 98). The augm. is already transferred to the aor. ptc. κατεάξαντες in codd. of Lys. (perh. to distinguish it from the 1st aor. of ἄγω), a form wh. is common in late Gr. (Luc. Ael. etc.), as late fut. κατεάξει in the NT (Veitch & *LSJ*, s.vv. ἄγνυμι & κατ-; *BDF*, § 66.2, 101 s.v. ἀγνύναι). The mag. papp. have only ptc. κατάξας *PGM* 7.523 (3rd cent.).

a) With augment and reduplication:

κατέαξαν *BGU* 908.25 (A.D. 101/2: *BL* i, 81)
κατέαγεν (3 sg. aor. indic. pass.) *PFlor.* 175.7 (A.D. 255)
κατεαγμένα *PFlor.* 185.7 (A.D. 254)

b) Transferred to the participle or subjunctive:

κατεάξαντες *PMich.* 421.20 (A.D. 41-54)
κατιακῇ (for κατεαγῇ) *PSI* 1030.16 (A.D. 109)

c) Transferred to the substantive:

κατέαγμα, κατεάγματα *BGU* 647.12,13,25-26 (A.D. 130)
καταιάγματος (for κατεάγματος) *PAmh.* 93 = *WChr.* 314.19-20 (A.D. 181)

4) ὁράω augments the imperfect regularly with ἑ-, e.g., ἑώρουν (for ἑώρων 1 sg.) *POxy.* 2667.9 (A.D. 309).[1]

5) ἁλίσκομαι has the form ἥάλω (η = ε before a back vowel[2]) *PAberd.* 177.6 (2nd cent.).[3]

c. Syllabic augment η-.[4]

θέλω (in which the augment derives from ἐθέλω[5]), normally retains the η- augment, as in ancient (except Epic and Lyric) and Modern Greek;[6] but βούλομαι, μέλλω, and δύναμαι, regularly augmented η- in the Ptolemaic papyri, show a reversion to the classical ε- augment in different degrees.[7]

1) θέλω is normally augmented η-:

ἤθελον *BGU* 1078 = *WChr.* 59.8 (A.D. 39); *PLond.* 897 (iii, 206-7).20 (A.D. 84); *PRyl.* 81.6 (ca. A.D. 104); etc.

---

[1] For redupl. ἑόρακα/ἑώρακα, see below, p. 247. The syll. augm. is Att. for *η-ϝορ-, w. init. aspiration on analogy of ὁρῶ (Schwyzer i, 653; Chantraine[2], § 356; *LSJ*, s.v.).

[2] See Vol. i, 242-62, esp. 261-2.

[3] *η-ϝαλ- became Att. ἑάλων by quant. metath., Ion. ἥλων (Schwyzer i, 653; *LSJ*, s.v.).

[4] This is diff. in origin from the syll. augm. η- before ϝ-, wh. changed to ε-; it developed by analogy through association in meaning with the prototype θέλω-ἤθελον (Schwyzer i, 654).

[5] For pres. θέλω, sts. ἐθέλω, see below, pp. 276-7.

[6] Veitch, s.vv. ἐθέλω & θέλω; *LSJ*, s.v. ἐθέλω; Thumb, *Handbook*, § 183; Mirambel, *Gram.*, 131-2, 163; Maspero, 119.

[7] This roughly parallels the practice of the NT, in wh. η- is always found in θέλω, but never in βούλομαι, while μέλλω and δύναμαι vacillate in the codd. between η- and ε- (*BDF*, § 66.3). The η- augm., exc. in θέλω, is rare in class. authors (Veitch & *LSJ*, s.vv.).

ἠθέλησα *PMich.* 465.17-18 (A.D. 107); *POslo* 126.5 (A.D. 161); *PApoll.* 39.3,4,6 (A.D. 708/9); etc.

ἠθέλησας *POxy.* 931.3 (2nd cent.); *POxy.* 602 descr. = *PCairPreis.* 48.5 (2nd cent.); *POxy.* 237 v.42; vi.2,40; viii.10,19 (A.D. 186); etc.

ἠθέλησεν *SB* 7404.42 = *PLBat.* vi, 24.85 (early 2nd cent.?); *CPR* 20 = *StudPal.* xx, 54 i.8 (A.D. 250); *PLond.* 1914.7 (A.D. 335?); etc.

but ἔθελεν *PIFAO* ii, 16.4 (2nd cent.)

ἐθέλατε *PAlex.* 27.24 (2nd/3rd cent.)[1]

The augment is transferred to the present in ἠθέλω *PLond.* 418 = *PAbinn.* 7.10 (ca. A.D. 346) and to the aorist subjunctive in ἠθελήσῃ *PAntin.* 92.10 (4th/5th cent.).

2) βούλομαι has the η- augment only sporadically and early; the ε- augment occurs very frequently.

a) With η- augment:

ἠβούλετο *POxy.* 281 = *MChr.* 66.16 (A.D. 20-50)

b) With ε- augment:

ἐβουλόμην *PBrem.* 61.9 (ca. A.D. 117); *PLond.* 479 (ii, 255-6).5 (3rd cent.?); *PPrinc.* 102.3 (4th cent.); *PSI* 825.5 (4th/5th cent.); *SB* 9399.2 (6th cent.); *PApoll.* 69.17 part. rest. (A.D. 703-15); etc.

ἐβουλόμεθα *PLond.* 1380 = *WChr.* 285.21 (A.D. 710/11)

ἐβουλήθην *PMich.* 486.6 (2nd cent.); *PTebt.* 407.3,14-15 part. rest. (A.D. 199?); *CPR* 19 = *StudPal.* xx, 86.3 (A.D. 330); etc.

ἐβουλήθη *SB* 7602 = *PLBat.* vi, 33.4 (A.D. 151); *BGU* 2071.13 (mid 2nd cent.); *PAlex.* 5 13 (2nd cent.); *PSI* 1258.15-16 (3rd cent.); *PBeattyPanop.* 2.213 (A.D. 300); *BGU* 909 = *WChr.* 382.7 (A.D. 359); *POxy.* 128.2 (6th/7th cent.); etc.

It first appears in the other verbs in Att. inscrr. ca. 300 B.C. (Schwyzer i, 654; *MS*, 169). It is freq. in Asia Minor inscr.. (Schweizer, 173, Anm. 2; Nachmanson, 150; Hauser, 105), and normal in the Ptol. papp., w. rare exceptions in the aor. of βούλομαι and δύναμαι. The η- augm. is extended to other verbs, incl. φέρω, ζημιόω, τυγχάνω, wo. this association in meaning, in Rom. inscrr. and the Ptol. papp. (Schwyzer i, 654; Mayser i², 2, 93-94). While η- forms are found in careful Atticists (Schmid iv, 590-1), Koine authors in general prefer the ε- augm., but ἠδυν- is attested freq. (Crönert, 202 & n. 3); in later Koine lit., the η- forms again become common (Psaltes, 203-4). In MGr., ἤπια (from ἔπιον), ἤφαγα (εἴφαγα), etc., are used, and dialectally many other η- forms (Schwyzer i, 656; Dieterich, 212 & Exkurs; Hatzidakis, *Einl.*, 72; Jannaris, § 720; Thumb, *Handbook*, § 183; Mirambel, *Gram.*, 163; Maspero, 119).

[1] αἰθέλαισαν, αἰθέλαισα *PSI* 831.5,12 (4th cent.: *BL* vi, 180) prob. represent ἠθέλησα with η > αι in both augm. and stem. For the occasional interchange of η and αι, see Vol. i, 247-9.

ἐβουλήθημεν *PLond.* 1359.8 (A.D. 710)
ἐβουλήθητε *PGiss.* 62.4 (ca. A.D. 117)
ἐβουλήθησαν *CPJ* 513.11 (A.D. 586)

3) μέλλω has the η- augment more often than βούλομαι, but the ε- augment is more common.

a) With η- augment:

ἤμελλον *SB* 4650.12 (n.d.); *PRossGeorg.* iii, 4.12 (3rd cent.); *PFlor.* 378.10 (5th cent.)
    ἤμελλα *PBouriant* 23.13 (late 2nd cent.); *POxy.* 1160.15 (late 3rd/ early 4th cent.)
ἤμελλες *PFouad* 85.1 (6th/7th cent.)
ἤμελλεν *PMich.* 492.15 (2nd cent.); *BGU* 1040.11 (2nd cent.); *PRyl.* 77.36 (A.D. 192)
    ἤμελλε *PSI* 842.14 (4th cent.?)

b) With ε- augment:

ἔμελλον *POxy.* 2339.11,17-18 (1st cent.); *PSarap.* 79a (p. 290) ii.3-4 (ca. A.D. 125); *POxy.* 1488.20-21 (2nd cent.); *PWürzb.* 21 A.8 (2nd cent.); *BGU* 276.14-15 (2nd/3rd cent.?); *PLond.* 411 = *PAbinn.* 28.20 (ca. A.D. 346); (ἔμελον) *PJand.* 15 iii.8 (4th cent.); etc.
ἔμελλες *BGU* 845.11 (2nd cent.); *PJand.* 97.22 (mid 3rd cent.); *PFlor.* 226.19 (3rd cent.)
ἔμελλεν *PLond.* 853a = *PSarap.* 98.13 (early 2nd cent.); *POxy.* 2954.38 (3rd cent.)
ἐμέλλησα *PFay.* 20.6, with ἔμελλον 4 (late 3rd/early 4th cent.)

4) δύναμαι sometimes has the η- augment, especially during the Roman period, but the ε- augment is always more common.

a) With η- augment:

ἠδυνάμην *POxy.* 2192.20 (2nd cent.); *PSI* 1103.15 (2nd/3rd cent.: *BL* iii, 228)
ἠδυνόμην *BGU* 625 = *WChr.* 21.6-7 (early 3rd cent.)
    εἰδυνόμην (more prob. = ἠ- than ἐ-[1]) *PMich.* 473.9 (early 2nd cent.)
ἠδύνατο *SB* 8246.15 (A.D. 335: *BL* v, 102)
ἠδυνήθην *PRein.* 44 = *MChr.* 82.33 (A.D. 117-38); *PFay.* 123.8 (after A.D. 110: *BL* iv, 29); *PMilVogl.* 59.15 part. rest. (2nd cent.); *PMich.*

---

[1] For the conditions and relative frequency of the interchanges of η with ει and ε, see Vol. i, 239-47.

486.5 (2nd cent.); *PLips.* 108.5 (2nd/3rd cent.); *PHarris* 153.11-12 part. rest. (3rd cent.); etc.

ἠδυνάσθην (see below, p. 319) *POxy.* 743.36 (2 B.C.)

ἠδυνάσθη *Archiv* v, p. 381, #56.4 (prob. late 1st cent.)

οἰδηνήθημεν (for ἠδυν- with η x υ/οι[1]) *PSI* 301.13 (5th cent.)

b) With ε- augment:

ἐδυνάμην *MChr.* 372 v.23 part. rest. (2nd cent.); *PAlex.* 28.16 (3rd cent.); *POxy.* 1165.8 (6th cent.); etc.

ἐδύνω *BGU* 892.10 (2nd cent.: *BL* i, 78)

ἐδύνατο *MChr.* 372 iv.13 (2nd cent.); *CPJ* 435 iii.26 (2nd cent.); *CPR* 19 = *StudPal.* xx, 86.16 (A.D. 330); etc.

ἐδυνάμεθα *PGiss.* 17 = *WChr.* 481.11 (A.D. 117-38)

ἐδυνήθην *PRyl.* 113.29 (A.D. 133); *PSI* 1335.22 (3rd cent.); *POxy.* 2788.16 (3rd cent.); *SB* 8003.4 (4th cent.); *PSI* 1075.5,7 (A.D. 458); *PSI* 1428.10 (6th cent.); *PCairMasp.* 96.34 (A.D. 573/4); etc.

ἐδυνήθη *POxy.* 2784.10 (3rd cent.); *PJand.* 8.8-9 part. rest. (3rd cent.: *BL* i, 197); *POxy.* 1495.12 (4th cent.); *PAntin.* 94.6,22 (6th cent.); etc.

ἐδυνήθημεν *POxy.* 128.5 (6th/7th cent.)

αἰδυνήθημεν *PGen.* 54 — *PAbinn.* 35.20 (ca. A.D. 346)

ἐδυνήθητε *PVars.* 28.3 (6th cent.)

ἐδυνήθησαν *PLips.* 33 ii = *MChr.* 55.12 (A.D. 368)

5) The second aorist active and middle of ἔχω has an η- augment very late:

ἤσχον *POxy.* 1863.12 (7th cent.)

ἤσχεν *SB* 9397.2 (6th/7th cent.)

παρήσχε(ν) *PLond.* 113 (9c) (i, 221).1; (9d).1 (7th cent.); *PLond.* 116a = *WChr.* 286.1 (7th cent.); *StudPal.* iii, 694.1; 699.1; viii, 708.1; 726.1; etc. (7th cent.); *BGU* 680.1; 682 = *StudPal.* viii, 783.1; etc. (Byz./Arab.)

ἤσχαμεν *StudPal.* iii, 66.2 (6th cent.)

παρησχόμην *StudPal.* iii, 351.3 (6th/7th cent.)

6) In other verbs, an η- augment (with orthographic variants) occurs sporadically. It probably represents a phonological interchange of η and its orthographic equivalents with ε:[2]

ἤγραψ[α] *PStrassb.* 208.19 (A.D. 75); (in full) *BGU* 667.24 (ca. A.D. 221/2)

ἴφερων (for ἔφερον) *PLBat.* xi, 28.4: *BL* v, 63 (4th/5th cent.)

εἰσωμάτισα (for ἐσωμάτισα) *PRossGeorg.* v, 41.9 (6th/7th cent.)

---

[1] For the freq. interchange of η with υ and οι, see Vol. i, 262-7.

[2] For the interchange of ε with η, ι, and ει, see Vol. i, 242-62, esp. 248-9, 261-2.

B. TEMPORAL AUGMENT[1]

Temporal augment and/or reduplication is omitted occasionally in both simple and compound verbs beginning with α-, ε-, αι-, or οι-, frequently in verbs beginning with ο-, usually in verbs beginning with ευ-, and normally in verbs beginning with ι-, ει-, and υ-.

Temporal augment is also sometimes transferred to moods and tenses other than past indicative.

1. Verbs beginning with a simple vowel.

a. Verbs beginning with ι or υ.

These verbs traditionally revealed augment only in meter, normally undergoing no change in orthography to indicate the length of the initial vowel. But during the time when ει was used as the orthographic representation of ι,[2] verbs beginning with ι- were sometimes augmented ει-, as in the Ptolemaic papyri.[3] This spelling is found only occasionally in Roman and Byzantine papyri, e.g., εἴσχυσε *POxy.* 396 descr. (late 1st cent.); εἴσχυσα *POxy.* 1666.14 (3rd cent.). With loss of all quantitative distinction,[4] there was no difference in pronunciation between ει and ι; ει and ι in fact are simply orthographic variants in εἴσχύει, ἴσχυκα *PRossGeorg.* iii, 1.4,13 (A.D. 270: *BL* iii, 156). In most forms of verbs beginning with ι-, the augment is not indicated, e.g., ἱκά-μ[ην] *BGU* 843.6 (1st/2nd cent.); ἀφίκοντο *PMon.* 14.58 (A.D. 594).

b. Verbs beginning with ο-.

The regular augment and reduplication to ω- is frequently omitted, since the augment became merely orthographic with the loss of quantitative distinction and the identification of ο and ω:[5]

ἀπόλε[σ]εν *POxy.* 743.22 (2 B.C.)
ὄφειλεν (impf.) *PMich.* 192.16 (A.D. 60)
    ὄφειλαν (for ὤφειλον) *PAmh.* 110.18 (A.D. 75)
ὄμοσα *BGU* 92 = *WChr.* 427.28 (A.D. 187); *POslo* 111.11,22 (A.D. 235);
    PMichael. 40.70 (mid 6th cent.)

---

[1] Temporal augm. and temporal redupl., although arising from diff. sources, are treated together because they follow parallel paths of development. Also treated here, for the same reason, are the augments in ει- of verbs beg. w. *s-, *w-, or *j. Cf. Schwyzer i, 650, Zus. **3**; 653-5; Chantraine², § 214, 356-7.

[2] See Vol. i, p. 191, n. 2.

[3] Cf. Mayser i², 2, 99.

[4] See Vol. i, 325.

[5] See Vol. i, 275-7, 325; cf. Introd. to Morphology above, p. XIX.

ὁμολόγησα *PMich.* 553.3 (A.D. 283/4); *PLBat.* xi, 13.23 (A.D. 372); *SB* 9189.16 (late 4th cent.); *PLond.* 113 (1) (i, 199-204).82 (6th cent.); etc.

ὀνομάσθης *PGiss.* 54 = *WChr.* 420.5-6 (4th/5th cent.)

ὀλιγώρησεν *PCairMasp.* 322.3 (6th cent.)

ὁμ[ί]λησα *PCairMasp.* 5.14 (6th cent.)

ὅρισαν *PMon.* 1.23 (A.D. 574)

ὁρίσθη *PMon.* 14.53 (A.D. 594)

ὀφθαλμίασα *PSI* 889.9 (6th/7th cent.)

Conversely, the phonetically equivalent ω is sometimes used in unaugmented tenses and moods, e.g., ὡμολογῶ *SB* 7742.5 (A.D. 57); ὠμνύω *PMed.* 3.13 (A.D. 1-14).

c. Verbs beginning with α-.

1) Augment and reduplication are occasionally omitted:

μεταλλαχέναι *SB* 6663.21 (prob. 6/5 B.C.)

ἀπαλλάχθαι *POxy.* 2768.23 (late 3rd cent.)

παραξίου *CPR* 18 = *MChr.* 84.13 (A.D. 124)

ἀνάγκασεν *MChr.* 88 vi.2 (after A.D. 141); *BGU* 378 = *MChr.* 60.20 (mid 2nd cent.)

παράγγειλα[ς] *POxy.* 2343.7 (ca. A.D. 288)

ἐπαρτημένῳ *PLond.* 1660.33 (ca. A.D. 553)

ἐξαρτισ(μένα) *SB* 10529 A.14-15 (n.d.)

ὑπαγόρευσα (α corr. from o !) *PCairMasp.* 312.21 (A.D. 567)

ἀγώρακαν (for ἠγόρακα) *BGU* 605.2 (7th/8th cent.)

2) The η- augment is sometimes replaced by ε-, especially in the Byzantine period, either through confusion with the syllabic augment or a phonological interchange of η and ε:[1]

ἐγόρακα *OTait* 2044.23 (2nd cent.)

παρέγγιλα (for παρήγγειλα) *PBeattyPanop.* 1.207 (A.D. 298)

παρεγγέλθην *PCairMasp.* 76.8 (6th cent.)

ἐξεσθενηκέναι *PThead.* 20 i.5 (4th cent.)

ὑπεγόρευσα *PCairMasp.* 324.10 (6th cent.)

ὑπεγορέσαμεν (for ὑπηγορεύσαμεν) *PMichael.* 45.35 (A.D. 540)

[ἐξ]ελλάχθαι *PCairMasp.* 121.13 (A.D. 573)

ἐφανίσθησαν (for ἠφ- from ἀφ-) *POxy.* 2732.5-6 (6th cent.?)

---

[1] See Vol. i, 242-9

3) The augment is only rarely transferred to other moods and **tenses**:

κατηντῆσαι *PBrem.* 37.6 (ca. A.D. 117)
ἀπηγορευομένου (if not pf.) *BGU* 114 = *MChr.* 372 ii.1 (2nd cent.)
εἰμὶ ἠναγ'κασθ[είς] *PMich.* 530.4 (3rd/4th cent.)

d. Verbs beginning with ε- (augment η-).

1) Augment and reduplication are occasionally omitted:

ἔγγισαν *POxy.* 2234.18 (A.D. 31)
ἀπέλθον *BGU* 824.7: *BL* i, 70 (A.D. 55/56)
    ἀνέλθεν *PSI* 836.1 (6th cent.)
    ἀπέρθαν (for ἀπῆλθον) *POxy.* 1874.16 (6th cent.)
ἐρώτησε *PFay.* 114.8 (A.D. 100)
    ἐρώτησα *PHermRees* 50.7 (6th cent.)
    ἐπερώτησα *PCairMasp.* 87.10 (A.D. 543)
ἐπένεγκα *PVars.* 10 iii.21 (A.D. 156)
    ἔ[ν]εγκα *PGen.* 51 = *PAbinn.* 19.28 (ca. A.D. 346)
    ἐνεν[έ]γκαμεν *SB* 5672.17 (A.D. 156/7)
    ἀπενεγκάμεθα *POxy.* 653 = *MChr.* 90.13 (A.D. 160-62)
ἐξέτασε *BGU* 380.5 (3rd cent.)
    ἐξέτακα *PLond.* 404 = *PAbinn.* 25.8 (ca. A.D. 346)
ἐρημώθη *PSI* 71.11 (6th cent.)
ἐτοιμάκιν (ppf.) *PTebt.* 592 descr. (3rd cent.)

2) The augment is sometimes transferred to other moods and tenses:

ἐξήλθης *PIFAO* ii, 2.4 (14 B.C.)
    ἔξηλθε (impt.) *POxy.* 1591.10 (4th cent.)
    ἠλθοῦσαν *PHermRees* 28.6 (A.D. 503)
ἀπηνεγκάμενος *SB* 7363 = *PLBat.* vi, 38.12 (A.D. 168)
    προηνεγκέσθαι *POxy.* 2110.38 (A.D. 370)
    ἠνεγκεῖν *PPrinc.* 106.6 (6th cent.)
        ἀπηνεγκεῖν *SB* 4683.6 (Byz.)
    ἀπηνηνεγμένης *PCairMasp.* 24 R.44 AB (ca. A.D. 551)
ἐπηρωτηθέντες *POxy.* 909.32-33 (A.D. 225)
εἰλάσθαι (for ἐλέσθαι) *PMon.* 8.7 (late 6th cent.)

3) A false de-augmentation is found in compounds of ἐνεγκ-, **indicating** that the initial ε- was sometimes mistaken for an augment:

ἀνανεγκῶ (fut.) *POxy.* 1757.9-10 (after A.D. 138)
ἀνανέγκης *PHamb.* 87.16 (early 2nd cent.)

ἀνανίκης *PLond.* 245 = *PAbinn.* 45.18 (A.D. 343); *PLond.* 407 = *PAbinn.* 53.15 (A.D. 346)

καταανίκη *BGU* 811.11: *BL* i, 68, with κατενέγκη 8 (A.D. 98-103)
ἀνανέγκωμεν *PLond.* 408 = *PAbinn.* 18.14 (A.D. 346)
προσανάνηνκον (impt.) *POxy.* 2732.17 (6th cent.?)
παρανεγκῖν *PGissBibl.* 53.10, with παρενεγκῖν 14 (A.D. 223)
ἀνανεγκῖν *SB* 8006.3-4, with impt. ἀνένεγκον 17 (3rd cent.?)
μετανίγκαι *PLond.* 236 = *PAbinn.* 4.12 (ca. A.D. 346)
ἀνανενκόντ[ο]ς *SB* 7404.46 = *PLBat.* vi, 24.89 (up to A.D. 124)
ἀνανηνυγμένη *PLond.* 1168 (iii, 135-8).28 (A.D. 44: *BL* i, 282)
μετανεχθέντω‹ν› *PFlor.* 222.3 (A.D. 256)

e. Verbs beginning with ε- (augment ει-).[1]

1) Augment or reduplication ει-, e.g., εἶχεν *PMich.* 340.91 (A.D. 45/46); ἐπεῖδον *PTebt.* 286 = *MChr.* 83.20 (A.D. 121-38), is sometimes replaced by the phonetically equivalent ι- (or η-):[2]

ἴχον *PFlor.* 59.6 (A.D. 225/41); *PLond.* 243 = *PAbinn.* 8.19 (ca. A.D. 346)
ἐπῖχο[ν] *BGU* 747 = *WChr.* 35 i.11 (A.D. 139)
διῖλον *POxy.* 2407.7 part. rest., 33 (late 3rd cent.)
συνῖδαν *PMon.* 1.20 (A.D. 574)
ἵρηχε *BGU* 597.23 (A.D. 75)
παρίληφα *PAlex.ined.* 159 (p. 24).17 (Rom.); *StudPal.* v, 119 R iii.23 (A.D. 266)
παρίληφεν *BGU* 986.11 (A.D. 117-38)
παριληφέναι, παρίληφεν, with εἰληφώς *SB* 7404.29,57,58 = *PLBat.* vi, 24.66,97,98 (up to A.D. 124)
παριληφένα[ι] *PRyl.* 657.5 (A.D. 323-4)
παρηλήφα[μεν] *SB* 7441.13 (A.D. 230)

2) The augment is only rarely omitted, e.g., ἔασα *BGU* 1035 — *WChr.* 23.11 (5th cent.) and ἔασε *PLBat.* xi, 28 i.8 (4th/5th cent.: *BL* v, 63), where ε = ει before a back vowel;[3] ἐσχήκειν (ppf.) *BGU* 465 i.6; ii.7 (A.D. 137); παρεχόμην *PSI* 50.14 (4th/5th cent.).

3) The augment is transferred in ἵνα μὴ εἰάσῃς *PApoll.* 61.14, with aor. indic. εἴασες 11 (A.D. 703-15).

---

[1] These verbs orig. began with *s-, *w-, rarely *j-: see above, pp. 232, n. 1.
[2] For the interchange of ει and ι, see Vol. i, 189-91; of ει and η, Vol. i, 239-42.
[3] See Vol. i, 256-62. The augm. is also om. in the mag. papp. in ἔασεν *PGMXtn.* 2a.4 (n.d.).

4) In ἐργάζομαι, ει- and η- fluctuate during the Roman period, not only in augmented tenses of the indicative, where both spellings have some historical justification (ει- from ε[ϝ]εργ-, η- from Attic *η-ϝεργ- as *η-ϝάγην, etc.[1]), but also in reduplicated tenses, in which only ει- (from [ϝ]ε-[ϝ]εργ-) is etymologically correct. Forms in ει- are normal in Byzantine papyri.

a) Augment.

i. Forms in ει-:

ἐξειργάζατο *PCairMasp.* 97 V d.43 (2nd half 6th cent.)
εἰργασάμην *PCairMasp.* 156-7.11 (A.D. 570)
    εἰργάσω, εἰργάσατο *PLips.* 40 ii.25; iii.1 (late 4th/early 5th cent.)
    εἰργάσατο *OMich.* 271.2 (A.D. 215?)
        ἐξειργάσατ[ο] *PCairMasp.* 4.12 (ca. A.D. 552: *BL* i, 100)
    εἰργάσαντο *PLBat.* xiii, 8.8 (A.D. 421)

ii. Forms in η-:

ἠργ(άσατο) *PLond.* 165 (ii, 103) a.2; b.2; c.2 (A.D. 49); *SB* 9567.3 (A.D. 51/52); *OMich.* 818.2 (A.D. 210?)
    συνηργάσατο *BGU* 530.15-16 (1st cent.)
ἠργάσαντο *PStrassb.* 518.5 (ca. A.D. 300)

b) Reduplication.

i. Forms in ει-:

εἴργ(ασται) *PStrassb.* 155.2; 157.2; etc. (A.D. 119-44); *PSorb.* 59.4 (A.D. 148); *PLond.* 321 (ii, 104-5) a.3; b.3; c.4 (A.D. 157-9); *PFay.* 77.3; 78.4; 79.3 (A.D. 147 & 197); *PMerton* 103.3 (A.D. 157/8); *PMich.* 418.3 (A.D. 157); 419.5 part. rest. (A.D. 162); 420.5 (A.D. 200); etc.
κατ᾽ε᾽ιργασμένη *PCairMasp.* 20 R.19 (6th cent.)

ii. Forms in η-:

ἠργασται *PMich.* 337.8 (A.D. 24); *PCornell* 50.15 (1st cent.); *PHarris* 76.1 (A.D. 88)
ἠργ(ασμένου) *POxy.* 520.14,15 (A.D. 143)

---

[1] Schwyzer i, 653-4; Chantraine[2], § 356. ἠργ- (impf.) Hyp.; (impf. & aor.) Ar. and inscrr., among which the Att. inscrr. have augm. η- almost excl. in class. times (w. redupl. ει-), while later this distribution is sts. reversed. In the Ptol. papp. and NT, η- is the usu. augm. (impf. & aor.), ει- the usu. redupl. (Chantraine[2], *ibid.*; Veitch & *LSJ*, s.v.; *MS*, 171; Schweizer, 170-1; Mayser i[2], Σ, 95, 97; *BDF*, § 67.3). The mag. papp. have ἠργάσατο *PGM* 74.10 (2nd/3rd cent.).

iii. Reduplication omitted:

ἐργασμένων *SB* 9868.2 (early 8th cent.)

The variation in the augment and reduplication of this verb is purely orthographic; η and ει (and ε) probably represent the same sound, at least before /r/.[1]

2. Verbs beginning with a diphthong.

a. Verbs beginning with ει- retain the ει- unaugmented, e.g., εἶξα *POxy.* 1642.17,47 (A.D. 289); καθεῖρξαν *PGrenf.* ii, 78 = *MChr.* 63.11 (A.D. 307).[2]

b. Verbs beginning with αι.

1) The augment is regularly η-:

ἠσχύνετο *POxy.* 2190.45 (late 1st cent.)
ἀπήτεις *PSI* 281.41 (2nd cent.)
　ᾔτει *POxy.* 1869.13 (6th/7th cent.)
　ᾔτησα *POxy.* 1673.22 (2nd cent.)
　　ἀπήτησα *PWürzb.* 22 = *PSarap.* 97.5 (A.D. 117-38)
　ἀπητήθην *SB* 7656.9 (Byz.)
ᾐκίσατο *SB* 7464.11 (A.D. 248)
　ᾐκίσαντο *POxy.* 2853.8 (ca. A.D. 245/6)
ᾐτιασάμην *POxy.* 1880.8 (A.D. 427); *PSI* 1114.6 (A.D. 454)

2) The augment or reduplication is sometimes omitted:

ἀνταναίρησαι *PTebt.* 394.5 (A.D. 149)
διαιρήκαμεν *PGen.* 11 = *PAbinn.* 62.5-6 (A.D. 350)
ἀναιλούμεθα (for ἀνῃρούμεθα) *PLond.* 412 = *PAbinn.* 55.6 (A.D. 351)
ἀπαιτήσαται (for ἀπῃτήσατε) *PSI* 93.8-9 (3rd cent.)
　ἀπαιτῆσθαι *BGU* 21 i.9 (A.D. 340)
　ἀπαίτησε *PHermRees* 7.8 (4th cent.)
　cf. also ἐτιάσατο (— αἰτιάσατο for ᾐ-) *POxy.* 52.11 (A.D. 325)

3) The augment is transferred only sporadically to other moods and tenses:

ἠτῖ (for αἰτεῖ) ... καὶ ἀξιοῖ *PLond.* 239 = *PAbinn.* 31.8-9 (ca. A.D. 346)
cf. also ἀπὸ κ[οι]νῶν καὶ <ἀ>διῃρέτων *POxy.* 47.19-20: *BL* i, 312 (late
1st cent.)

---

[1] See Vol. i, 239-49, 261-2; cf. the sim. fluctuation in forms of αἱρέω below, p. 238.
[2] ει- was augmented to ηι- in the class. Att. inscrr. (*MS*, 171), and to η- when augm. in the Ptol. papp. (Mayser i², 2, 101-2).

4) The reduplication of αἱρέω varies among η-, ει-, and ι-, all of which represent the same sound before /i/.[1] The spelling ει- (or- ι-) is more common in the early Roman period and in the Fayum; the spelling η- is found upriver and generally later.[2]

a) Reduplication ει-:

διείρημαι, συνδειείρημαι, συνδιείρημαι *PMich*. 318-20.1,3,5 (A.D. 40)
    συνδιείρημαι, συνδιειρημένων *BGU* 1037.40 (3rd hand), 10 (1st hand),
        with συνδιήρημαι 38 (2nd hand) (A.D. 48: *BL* i, 90)
    ἀνείρημαι *PStrassb*. 524.16 (A.D. 102/3); *PFlor*. 1 = *MChr*. 243.12
        (A.D. 153); *PLond*. 1164 (iii, 154-67) h.26 (A.D. 212); *PLips*.
        4-5 = *MChr*. 171 ii.4 (A.D. 293); etc.
ἀνείρηται *POxy*. 38 = *MChr*. 58.6 (A.D. 49/50); *PFlor*. 1 = *MChr*. 243.3
    (A.D. 153); *PLond*. 1164 (iii, 154-67) h.12 (A.D. 212); etc.
διειρῆσθαι *PMich*. 327.6 (early 1st cent.); *PMich*. 326.3 (A.D. 48); *PTebt*.
    391.4 (A.D. 99); *POslo* 31.7 (A.D. 138-61?); *PSI* 697.3 (2nd cent.);
    POxy. 1278.10 (A.D. 214); etc.
εἰρημένου *PMarmarica* vi, 28 (190/1?)
    ὑφιειρη(μένων) *POxy*. 282 = *MChr*. 117.22 (A.D. 30-35)
ὑφειρηκέναι *PMerton* 83.6 (late 2nd cent.)

b) Reduplication ι-:

συνδιίρη[μαι] *PTebt*. 383.48 (2nd hand), with ϲυνδιείρημε 54 (3rd hand)
    (A.D. 46)
    συνδιίρημε *PMich*. 323-5.29 (2nd hand), with συνδιείρημαι 31 (3rd
        hand) and 34 (4th hand), so copy *PSI* 903.27,29,31 (A.D. 47)
    ἀνίρημαι *PFay*. 100.19,26 (A.D. 99)
ἐπανίρηται *PFlor*. 51 = *MChr*. 186.22 (A.D. 138-61)
ἐπανιρήμεθα *PMich*. 554.56 (A.D. 81-96)
ἀνιρῆσθαι *SB* 6611 = *PLBat*. vi, 20.21, with [π]αριληφέναι 40 (A.D.
    120/1)

c) Reduplication η-:

συνδιήρημαι *BGU* 1037.38 (2nd hand), with συνδιείρημαι 40 (3rd hand)
    (A.D. 48: *BL* i, 90)
    διήρημαι *PFlor*. 50.118, etc. (A.D. 268); *PLond*. 978 (iii, 232-4).18,
        19,21 (3 diff. hands) (A.D. 331)

---

[1] See Vol. i, 235-42, 261-2; cf. augm. forms of ἐργάζομαι above, p. 236.
[2] αἱρέω is the only verb in the Ptol. papp. in wh. ει- (phonetic shortening of ηι) appeared almost wo. exception in the pf. system, while the impf. and aor. of this verb and all forms of other verbs had η(ι) (Mayser i, 127; i², 1, 100; i², 2, 100). The ει- spelling is found in Att. inscrr. from 378-100 B.C. (*MS*, 171).

ᾕρηται *PTebt.* 397 = *MChr.* 321.4 (A.D. 198)

προῃρήμεϑ[α] *PFlor.* 127.7-8 (A.D. 256)

διῃρῆσϑαι *POxy.* 503.5 (A.D. 118); *PHamb.* 65.2-3, with ἐπανειρῆσϑαι 10 part. rest., 25; [ἐπαν]είρημαι 27 (2nd hand) (A.D. 141/2); *PStrassb.* 29.4 part. rest. (A.D. 289); *PSI* 698.4 (A.D. 392); etc.

ᾑρῆσϑαι *POxy.* 653 = *MChr.* 90.7 (A.D. 160-2)

ἀνῃρῆσϑαι *PLond.* 1164 (iii, 154-67) c.17 (A.D. 212)

τοῖς ᾑρημένοις *BGU* 287 = *WChr.* 124.1-2 (A.D. 250) and virtually all libelli

c. Verbs beginning with οι-.

1) The augment or reduplication, normally ᾠ-, e.g., ᾤκει *POxy.* 1121.18 (A.D. 295); ᾠκοδόμει *PTebt.* 488 descr. (A.D. 121/2), is sometimes omitted in verbs in οἰκο-, where the retention of the unaugmented form was supported by the existence of the substantives οἰκία/οἶκος:[1]

οἴκουν (impf.) *PSI* 463.17,20 (ca. A.D. 157/60)

ἀνοικοδομημένος *POxy.* 986 iv (A.D. 131/2)

οἰκονομημένον *BGU* 832.27 (A.D. 113)

ἐξοικονομημέγα *BGU* 1047 iv.7 (A.D. 117-38)

οἰκοδομήϑησαν *PMich.* 620.11 (A.D. 239/40)

2) The augment is sometimes transferred to other moods and tenses and to the substantive:

διῳκεῖται *POxy.* 474.13 (A.D. 184?)

ᾠκοδομοῦντας *BGU* 901.4 (2nd/3rd cent.)

ᾠκονομήσας, ἐξῳκονομηκέν<αι> *MChr.* 88 iii.6; ii.32-iii.1 (after A.D. 141)

ἐξῳκονομήσαντα *POxy.* 2349.30 (A.D. 70)

ᾠκοδομήν *PFlor.* 384.69 (5th cent.?)

d. Verbs beginning with αυ- are regularly augmented ηυ-, as ηὐξάνοντο *PCairMasp.* 295 iii.15 (6th cent.); cf. διηύγαζεν *PLond.* 130 (i, 132-9).70, horoscope (1st/2nd cent.); διηύγασεν *PGM* 13.165 (A.D. 346); ηὐξήϑης *PGM* 4.2981 (4th cent.).[2] The augment ευ- does not occur.[3]

---

[1] Unaugm. forms of οἰκοδομέω are found in Att. inscrr. along w. forms in -ωι, even in compds. (*MS*, 172). The augm. is om. in some Koine inscrr. of Asia Minor, though not at Perg. or Magn. (Schweizer, 172; Nachmanson, 152; Hauser, 106). Unaugm. forms also appear in the Ptol. papp. and NT (Mayser i², 2, 102; cf. 100-1, w. exx. of ω- for ωι-; *BDF*, § 67.1).

[2] Cf. also ηὔξηκ[ε] *POxy.* 221.26 (Sch. Hom. *Od.* 21.65) (2nd cent.).

[3] For this spelling, see *BDF*, § 67.1.

e. Verbs beginning with ευ- usually retain the ευ- unaugmented, but the regular augmented forms in ηυ- are found increasingly frequently in later Roman and Byzantine documents.¹

1) Unaugmented forms:²

εὗρον *PMilVogl.* 50.13 (1st cent.); *POxy.* 1155.7 (A.D. 104); *PTebt.* 330 = *MChr.* 110.5 (2nd cent.); *BGU* 731 ii.9 (A.D. 180); *PLBat.* xi, 27.6 (3rd/4th cent.); *PStrassb.* 180.3 (4th cent.); *PLips.* 111.7 (4th cent.); etc.

εὗρεν *SB* 9120.9 (1st cent.); *PSI* 317.3 (A.D. 95); *BGU* 35.9 (A.D. 223); *POxy.* 1567.1 (4th cent.); etc.

εὕραμεν *PPrinc.* 67.3 (1st/2nd cent.); *PMich.* 512.2 (early 3rd cent.); *PSI* 1080.4 (3rd cent.?); *SB* 6222.12; 14,34 part. rest. (late 3rd cent.); *PLond.* 1359.6 (A.D. 710); etc.

εὕρηκα *SB* 7356 = *PMich.* 203.9 (A.D. 98-117); *POxy.* 2596.12 (3rd cent.); *PMed.* 80.12 (3rd cent.); *PLBat.* xi, 16.10 (5th/6th cent.); etc.

εὑρέθη *POxy.* 743.25-26 (2 B.C.); *PPar.* 19.12 (A.D. 138); *PPrinc.* 100.7 (4th cent.); *PGrenf.* i, 53 = *WChr.* 131.26 (4th cent.)

εὐεργετημένος *POxy.* 2234.24-25 (A.D. 31); *PLond.* 177 = *MChr.* 57.26 part. rest. (A.D. 40/41); *BGU* 46 = *WChr.* 112.20-21 (A.D. 193); etc. (for additional examples, see below, p. 306)

εὐχρήστησαν *PSI* 1235.17 (1st cent.); *POxy.* 241.30 (ca. A.D. 98)

εὐδόκηκα *PMich.* 473.14, sim. 20-21 (early 2nd cent.)

  εὐδόκηκας *PMich.* 474.14 (early 2nd cent.)

  εὐδοκηκέναι *PLond.* 77 (i, 231-6).39 (late 6th cent.)

  εὐδόκημαι *CPR* 154.16 (A.D. 180)

διευθύναμεν *PLond.* 924 = *WChr.* 355.8 (A.D. 187/8)

εὐθύμησα *POxy.* 1593.11 (4th cent.)

εὐσχόλησα *PSI* 842.5 (4th cent.?)

εὐπορήσαμεν *PCairMasp.* 9 R.9 (6th cent.)

εὐλόγησεν *PLond.* 1380 = *WChr.* 285.13, with ηὕραμεν 7 (A.D. 710/11)

---

¹ ευ- was reg. augm. to ηυ- in class. Att. inscrr., but unaugm. forms are found from the end of the 4th cent. on and after 300 B.C. excl. (*MS*, 171-2). Even in class. Att. lit. (Th. Isoc. Pl. X. etc.), ευ- was sts. left unaugm. and unredupl. (Veitch & *LSJ*, s.v. εὑρίσκω). Augm. forms are rare in Asia Minor inscrr., the Ptol. papp., and Koine and Byz. authors (Schweizer, 172-3; Nachmanson, 153; Hauser, 106; Mayser i², 2, 101, 103, 111-12; Crönert, 205 & nn. 1, 3; Psaltes, 203), but in the NT some augm. forms are well attested, and the augm. has survived in MGr. ηὕρα/ἤβρα (*BDF*, § 67.1; Schwyzer i, 656; Thumb, *Handbook*, § 183; Mirambel, *Gram.*, 163; Maspero, 119). For the origin of Att. ηὗρον (perh. from *ηϝρον), see Schwyzer i, 653, 709, n. 2.

² Cf. also from the mag. papp. εὗρον *PGM* 7.204 (3rd cent.); 2.50 (4th cent.); 4.776, 2432 (4th cent.); εὗρε *PGM* 12.245 (A.D. 300-50); εὑρέθη *PGM* 4.805 (4th cent.); 5.365 (4th cent.).

2) Augmented forms:[1]

ηὖρον *PSI* 1344.1 (6th cent.); *SB* 9396.5 (2nd half 6th cent.); *PCairMasp.* 78.7; 89 V.6, duplic. of 294.7 (6th cent.); *PSI* 1430.1 (7th cent.)

ηὖρεν *PAntin.* 188.2 (6th/7th cent.); *BGU* 728.4 (Byz.)

ηὕραμεν *PCairMasp.* 4.5 (ca. A.D. 552: *BL* i, 100); *PLond.* 1380.7 (A.D. 711)

ηὖραν *SB* 7520.17 (A.D. 710)

ηὕρηκα *PNYU* 25.15 (4th cent.)

ηὑρέθης *PHarris* 112.4 (5th cent.); *PCairMasp.* 97 V d.72 (6th cent.)

ηὑρέθη *POxy.* 1933.16 part. rest. (6th cent.); *PCairMasp.* 333.21 (6th cent.)

ηὑρέθησαν *PLond.* 1708.157,168 (A.D. 567?); *PCairMasp.* 70.2 (late 6th cent.)

ηὐτυχήσαμεν *POxy.* 1202.5 (A.D. 217)

ηὔφρανας *PFlor.* 154 R.12 (3rd cent.)

ηὐφράνθημεν *BGU* 1080 = *WChr.* 478.7-8 (3rd cent.)

ηὐφράνθησαν *POxy.* 1927.12, liturgical frag. (5th/6th cent.)

ηὐχόμην *PSI* 41.4 (4th cent.); *PSI* 1446.6 (4th cent.); *PHarris* 157.7 (5th/6th cent.)

ηὐλ[ο]γημένῳ *PAmh.* 145 = *WChr.* 53.1 (ca. A.D. 400)

ηὐεργέτησεν *PLond.* 1677.28 (A.D. 566/7)

ηὐχαρίστησα *POxy.* 1164.2 (6th/7th cent.); *POxy.* 1844.20 (6th/7th cent.)

3) A transferred augment is found in ηὑρεθῆγχι *PRossGeorg.* iv, 1.36 (A.D. 710).

The causes which led to the loss of temporal augment and reduplication[2] are (1) *morphological*:[3] (a) the tendency of later Greek to eliminate inessential morphemes; (b) the complementary tendency to regularize inflectional systems; and (2) *phonological*: (a) the shortening of the first element of the long diphthong ηι (possibly also of ωι and ηυ) in the early Koine,[4] which led to a loss of feeling for the temporal augment; and (b) the later elimination of the diphthongs by their reduction to simple vowels (αυ and ευ to a vowel + consonantal element),[5]

---

[1] Cf. also from the mag. papp. ηὑρέθη *PGM* 7.864 (3rd cent.); κατηυλόγησεν *PGM* 1.210 (4th/5th cent.); ηὐλογήθησαν *PGMXtn.* 13.12 (4th/5th cent.).

[2] Temporal augm. is still found in MGr. in some verbs in wh. it appears as an accented initial /i/, e.g., ηὖρα, ἦρθα, εἶδα εἶχα, εἶπα. The augm. is sts. incorporated into the stem, e.g., πῆρα < ἐπ-ῆρα, aor. of αἴρω (Schwyzer i, 656; Chantraine², § 358f; Jannaris, § 720; Thumb, *Handbook*, § 183; Mirambel, *Gram.*, 163; Maspero, 119). Reduplication was lost with the pf. system; it is not used even in the pf. pass. ptc. wh. alone has survived (Schwyzer i, 650, 779; Jannaris, § 737; Thumb, *Handbook*, § 184).

[3] See above, p. 225.

[4] Cf. ει for ηι not only in augm. forms of verbs in ει- and αι- (as οι- for ωι- and ευ- for ηυ- and αυ-), but also in the 2 pers. primary mid. ending and in the dat. sg. of the 1 decl. (Schwyzer i, 201-3, 655; Lejeune, § 210; *MS*, 36-39, 171; and above, p. 238, n. 2).

[5] See Vol. i, 183-234.

and the loss of all quantitative distinction.[1] Temporal augment and reduplication became solely a qualitative rather than a quantitative change, and so ceased to constitute lengthening.

C. REDUPLICATION[2]

1. Reduplication in general.

Reduplication is occasionally omitted in compounds and in simple verbs or is sometimes replaced by the syllabic augment. Conversely, reduplication is sometimes transferred to forms outside the perfect system.

a. Omission of reduplication.

1) Omission of full reduplication.[3]

a) In compounds:

διαπρακέναι (for διαπεπρακέναι) *PRyl.* 127.16 (A.D. 29)
ὑπολόγηκα (for ὑπολελόγηκα) *PMich.* 127 II.39 (A.D. 45-46)
ὑποχυμένος (for ὑποκεχυμένος) *POxy.* 39 = *WChr.* 456.9 (A.D. 52)
σωμφο[νημένην] (for συμπεφωνημένην) *SB* 7612 = *PMed.* 60.19 (2nd cent.)
ἐπίδωκα (for ἐπιδέδωκα) *WChr.* 26 ii.34 (A.D. 156); *PWürzb.* 9.72 (A.D. 161-9); *PRyl.* 104.16 (A.D. 167); *PCairMasp.* 283 iii.6 (before A.D. 548)
ἐμμενηκ[έ]ναι (for ἐμμεμενηκέναι) *POxy.* 237 iv.11 (A.D. 186)
ἀποδειγμένου (for ἀποδεδειγμένου) *SB* 6293.6 (A.D. 195/6)
ὑπόταχα (for ὑποτέταχα) *SB* 7817 = *PSI* 1328.54, with προστεταγμένοις 64-65, etc. (A.D. 201)
παραμετρήμεθα (for παραμεμετρήμεθα) *POxy.* 1040 ii.40 (2nd hand), corr. 7-8 & prob. 18-19 (1st hand) (A.D. 225)
ἐντυλιγμένα (for ἐντετυλιγμένα) *PSI* 1082.16-17 (4th cent.?)
ἀποτένεκα (for ἀποτετένεκα) *PHarris* 158.2 (n.d.)

b) In simple verbs:

γραμένος (for γεγραμμένον) *PMich.* 346a.7-8 (A.D. 13)
πτόκ(εν) (for πέπτωκεν) *PMich.* 235.3 (A.D. 41)
θηκότα (for τεθηκότα) *SB* 10575.7 (1st half 1st cent.)

---

[1] See Vol. i, 325.
[2] For temporal redupl., see the preceding section.
[3] Haplography may account for some instances: cf. the sim. phenomenon when **pf.** redupl. is not involved, e.g., βαιώση (for βεβαιώσει) *PMich.* 188.23 (A.D. 120); βαιώσω (for βεβαιώσω) *PMerton* 19.14 (A.D. 173); ἐμβάσαι (for ἐμβιβάσαι) *PSI* 282.16 (A.D. 183).

μίσθωκα (for μεμίσθωκα) *PAmh.* 87 = *PSarap.* 27.3 (A.D. 125)

μισθώκαμεν (for μεμισθώκαμεν) *PBerlLeihg.* 19.41 (A.D. 221/2-225/6)

κλοφέναι (for κεκλοφέναι) *PMich.* 581.15 (ca. A.D. 126/8)

καρπωνη[μ]ένον (for κεκαρπωνημένον) *POxy.* 728.10-11 (A.D. 142)

τελώνιται (for τετελώνηται) *PAlexGiss.* 13.1 (2nd/3rd cent.)

γεωργηκ[ότ]ων (for γεγεωργηκότων) *PTebt.* 288 = *WChr.* 266.6-7 (A.D. 226)

ποιηκώς (for πεποίηκα) *BGU* 1044.5 (4th cent.)

2) Omission of reduplication ε-.

a) In compounds whose preverb ends in a vowel:

ἐπισκεμμένας *PLond.* 276 (ii, 148-9).14 (A.D. 15)

ἐπισταλμένοις *POxy.* 504.17 (early 2nd cent.)

ἀποστάλκιται *PPrinc.* 183.18 (A.D. 345)

b) In simple verbs:

σφράκικα (for ἐσφράγικα) *SB* 9642 (6).29 (2nd cent.)

    σφραγισμέν[ο]ς *PHermRees* 7.20 (4th cent.)

σχῆκα (for ἔσχηκα) *PLBat.* xiii, 19.3 (3rd cent.)

b. Transfer of reduplication to forms outside the perfect system:[1]

διαγεγραφεῖσαι *OTait* 1950.3-4 (A.D. 112?)

προγεκιμένας (κ corr. from γ) *POxy.* 732.8 (A.D. 150)

γεγευσαμένους *POxy.* 2990.6-7 (3rd cent.)

συμπεφωνηθεῖσα[ν] *PGen.* 48 = *PAbinn.* 60.10 (A.D. 346)

c. Replacement of reduplication by the syllabic augment.

1) In simple verbs:

ἔμελκε *POxy.* 1155.5 (A.D. 104)

ἐκαρπονήκαμεν *POxy.* 728.29 (2nd hand), with καρπωνη[μ]ένον 10-11 (1st hand) (A.D. 142)

ἐτρήκατε (for ἐδρήκατε: *BL* iii, 10) *BGU* 246.7 (2nd/3rd cent.)

ἐπράκαται *POxy.* 1160.11 (late 3rd/early 4th cent.)

    cf. ἐπράχαμεν *SB* 4075.3-4, inscr. (n.d.)

ἐπαυμένην (for πεπαυμένοι) *POxy.* 1299.6, with ἐθύκαμεν (perh. for τεθύκαμεν) 7 (4th cent.)

ἐπλήρωκα *POxy.* 2729.21-22 (4th cent.)

    ἐπληρῶσθ[αι] *SB* 9593.13-14 (6th/7th cent.)

---

[1] Cf. also in a cognate adj. ἐγγέγραφον *PLond.* 978 (iii, 232-4).4 (A.D. 331).

ἐμισθώκαμεν *PGen.* 70 = *WChr.* 380.18-19 (A.D. 381)
ἐτόρμηκας (for τετόλμηκας¹) *BGU* 948.7 (prob. 4th/5th cent.)
αἰλάληκα (for λελάληκα) *PJand.* 128.8 (5th cent.)

2) In compounds:

παραεχώρημαι *PHamb.* 62 = *PLBat.* vi, 23.22, corr. 2, etc. (A.D. 123)
ἀνεπταμένην *PMich.* 425.16 (A.D. 198)
ἐνεγυήκα[μεν] *PCairIsidor.* 106.6 (A.D. 306/7)²

d. Converse replacement of syllabic augment by reduplication:

τεθεασάμεθα *SB* 7523 (A).3 (A.D. 153)
πεπλήρωσα *POxy.* 1489.5 (late 3rd cent.)

Similar loss of reduplication, at first almost exclusively in compounds, is found in some Koine inscriptions and in the Ptolemaic papyri.³ It is the result of simplification and regularization by elimination of a morpheme unnecessary for a system already sufficiently characterized in most verbs by a distinct perfect stem. Reduplication is not used in Modern Greek, even in the perfect passive participle, which alone has survived from the ancient perfect system.⁴

2. Reduplication in particular classes of verbs.

a. Verbs beginning with a single consonant (except ρ, for which see **d.** below) are reduplicated according to the Attic practice by prefixing the initial consonant + ε, or, in the case of an initial aspirate, by prefixing only the occlusive element, as τέθειμαι, τεθνάναι, etc. (Grassmann's Law). Abnormal reduplication of the aspirate, probably through scribal error, is found sporadically:

συγχεχορημένην *PMich.* 301-2.7 (1st cent.)
θέθει[τ]αι *POslo* 24.12 (A.D. 131?)
θεθνάναι *POxy.* 130.12 (6th cent.)
cf. also in the pres. καταθιθεμένης, καταθιθεμένων *PSI* 1338.6,13, with ποθισμού[ς] (for ποτισμούς) 10 (A.D. 299)

b. Verbs beginning with two or more consonants (except a stop + liquid), or with a double consonant, including ζ, which had been simplified to a sibilant,⁵

¹ For the interchange of λ and ρ, see Vol. i, 102-7.
² ἐγγυάω is often augm. and redupl. as a compd. (see below, p. 252 & n. 1).
³ Hauser, 106 (κατασκεύαστο); Mayser i², 2, 98, 106-7. Cf. further Crönert, 206 & n. 3; Dieterich, 213-16; Thumb, *Hell.*, 170; Psaltes, 206-7; Hatzidakis, *Einl.*, 74-75; Jannaris, § 736-8.
⁴ Schwyzer i, 650, 779; Jannaris, § 737; Thumb, *Handbook*, § 184.
⁵ See Vol. i, 120-4.

are reduplicated regularly by prefixing ε-, e.g., ἐστεγνωμένα *PSI* 315.25 (A.D. 137/8); ἐσκορπισμέναι *StudPal.* v, 7 = xx, 58 ii.17 (ca. A.D. 265/6); ἐσβέσθαι *PMon.* 1.43 (A.D. 574); ἐξηραμμέ(να) *POxy.* 1188.19, sim. 21,23 (A.D. 13); ἐψεῦσθαι *POxy.* 1266.32 (A.D. 98); ἐπεζηκέναι *POxy.* 68 = *MChr.* 228.13,17 (A.D. 131).

1) κτάομαι normally appears with full reduplication as κέκτημαι, only sporadically as ἔκτημαι:[1]

    κέκτημαι *POxy.* 2192.42 (2nd cent.); *PCairPreis.* 4 = *WChr.* 379.5-6 (A.D. 320); *PMerton* 92.2 (A.D. 324); *PAbinn.* 50.5,9,25 (A.D. 346); *PCairGoodsp.* 15.5 (A.D. 362); *PSI* 742.1 (5th/6th cent.)

    κεκτήμεθα *PCairMasp.* 21 R.18 (A.D. 567: *BL* i, 103)

    κεκτῆσθαι *PJand.* 144.5 (A.D. 214?); *BGU* 8 i.27 part. rest. (ca. A.D. 248)

    ἐνκεκτῆστε (for ἐγκεκτῆσθαι) *PMilVogl.* 98.27, sim. 47 (A.D. 138/9?)

    κεκτημένος *PPhil.* 1.13, etc. (ca. A.D. 103-24); *PFlor.* 382.35,57-58 (A.D. 222/3); *PCairMasp.* 24 R.3,25 part. rest. (ca. A.D. 551); etc.

    κεκτημένου *PCairMasp.* 117.12 abbrev. (A.D. 524); 297.3 abbrev. (A.D. 535); 89 R b.17 abbrev. (6th cent.); 111.4 (A.D. 585); etc.

but ἐκτημένος *BGU* 587.12 (A.D. 141)

cf. also complete loss of reduplication by haplography in καὶ κτηται (for κέκτηται) *SB* 8265.17 (A.D. 335-45)

2) μιμνήσκω is reduplicated regularly:

    μεμνηκέναι *SB* 4779.7 (Byz.)

    μέμνημαι *StudPal.* v, 25 ii.7 (3rd cent.); *PJand.* 23.9 (6th/7th cent.)

    ἐπιμέμνησμαι sic *POxy.* 791 descr. (ca. A.D. 1)

    μέμνησαι *PStrassb.* 41.41, with μέμνημαι 42 (ca. A.D. 250)

    μέμνηται *PSI* 76.3 (A.D. 574-8)

    μεμνήμεθα, μεμνημένη *POxy.* 1664.4,7-8 (3rd cent.)

    μέμνη[σ]ο *POxy.* 525.9 (early 2nd cent.)

c. Verbs beginning with a stop + liquid/nasal are reduplicated regularly:[2]

---

[1] ἔκτημαι is poet.-Ion., but is found in some Att. authors, notably Pl., esp. after a consonant, and sts. together w. κέκτημαι (Veitch & *LSJ*, s.v.). κέκτημαι is attested at Magn., but ἔκτημαι is usual in other Asia Minor inscrr. (Nachmanson, 152; Schweizer, 171; Hauser, 105; Dieterich, 214-15) and is found at least once in the Ptol. papp. along w. the usual κέκτημαι (Mayser i², 2, 107). ἔκτημαι may have arisen on the analogy of verbs in *s + cons. or *j-, in wh. the redupl. ε- arises from the loss of these consonants, e.g., ἔσπαρμαι < *se-sp-; dissimilatory loss of consonant or prothesis are also poss. (Schwyzer i, 649; Chantraine², § 214). It parallels the replacement of redupl. by the syll. augm., and the traditional fluctuation in these verbs may have furthered the general tendency.

[2] So also in the Ptol. papp., w. 3 exceptions (Mayser i², 2, 106-7). Redupl. ε- is largely dialectal, found in Ion. and other inscrr. (*MS*, 174 [inscr. from Ephesus]; Hauser, 105; Dieterich, 215). The origin of the ε- is prob. the same as in ἔκτημαι.

γέγραφα, γέγραμμαι passim[1]
βέβληκα *SB* 7572.19 (prob. 1st half 2nd cent.)
    παραβέβλη[κ]α *PFlor.* 312.8 (A.D. 91: *BL* i, 458)
    καταβέβληκεν *PFlor.* 323.5 (A.D. 525)
    ἐνβεβλῆσ[θ]αι *PLond.* 256a = *WChr.* 443.6 (A.D. 15)
        ἐμβεβλῆσθαι *PFlor.* 75 = *WChr.* 433.12 (A.D. 380)
καταβεβλαμένα *sic PFlor.* 384.82 (5th cent.?)
γεγλ[υμ]μένους *POxy.* 326 descr. = *SB* 10241 R.12-13 (A.D. 45)
κεκμηκόσιν *PFlor.* 57 = *Archiv* iv, pp. 437-8 (A.D. 223/5)
    περκέκμηκα (for περι-) *PFay.* 20.14 (late 3rd/early 4th cent.)
κεκράτηκεν *PCairMasp.* 283 i.2 (before A.D. 548)
πεπλήρωμαι *PFlor.* 360.1 (5th cent.)
    πεπληρῶσθαι *PFlor.* 314.7 (A.D. 428)

d. Verbs beginning with ῥ- are augmented and reduplicated as in classical Greek by prefixing ε-.[2]

1) In forms of ῥώννυμι, the initial ρ is usually doubled in writing:

ἔρρωσο and ἐρρῶσθαι passim[3]
ἔρρωται *PGiss.* 20 = *WChr.* 94.25 (early 2nd cent.)
ἔρρωνται *POxy.* 1252 V.37 (A.D. 288-95)
ἐρρωμένην *POxy.* 2276.29 (late 3rd/4th cent.); *PCairMasp.* 151-2.199
    (A.D. 570); *POxy.* 2283.8 (A.D. 586); etc.

2) In other verbs beginning with ῥ-, the ρ is usually not doubled:

ἔριψεν *PRyl.* 125.25 (A.D. 28/29); *PLips.* 40 i.17, but with ἐρριμμένας
    ii.20 (late 4th/early 5th cent.)
    ἀπέριψεν *PSI* 298.10 (early 4th cent.)
ἐράβδισαν *PRyl.* 148.20 (A.D. 40)
διέρηξεν *SB* 7449.11 (2nd half 5th cent.)
συνερευκώς *POxy.* 1475.16-17 (A.D. 267)
but κατέρρηχεν *Archiv* ii, p. 125 b.10 (ca. A.D. 125)

This variation is purely orthographic.[4]

---

[1] But in the mag. papp., γρ- is sts. redupl. ε-, e.g., ἐπεγραμμένῳ, ἐγραμμένον *PGM* 8.40,41 (4th/5th cent.). Sim. forms were used in Cret. and perh. El. (Buck, *GD* § 137; *LSJ*, s.v.), but the occurrences in the mag. papp. and in an ex. from the Lyc. inscrr. (Hauser, 105) are prob. independent developments.
[2] See Schwyzer i, 649; Chantraine[2], § 214. In the mag. papp., full redupl. of ῥ- is found, e.g., ῥέριμμαι, ἀπορέριπται *PGM* 4.194,2039 (4th cent.).
[3] But cf. also spellings ἐρῶσθαι, ἔρωσο, and ἐρωμένος, Vol. i, 156.
[4] For the identification of single and double consonants in pronunciation, see Vol. i, 154-62.

e. (ἐ)θέλω is fully reduplicated τεθ- instead of the regular ἠθ-:[1]

τεθελήκουσι (pf. w. pres. ending) *PAmh.* 130.16-17 (A.D. 70)
τεθελήκασι *POxy.* 237 vii.18 (A.D. 186)

f. Reduplicated middle-passive forms of λέγω formed on the stem λεγ- occur with full reduplication.[2]

1) In the sense of "collect," "select":

προαναλλελεγμέναι *sic* *SB* 4425 iii.10 (2nd cent.)
ἐπιλελεγμένων *POxy.* 1210.4 (late 1st cent. B.C./early 1st cent. A.D.)
καταλ[ε]λέχθαι *BGU* 1073 = *MChr.* 198.10 (A.D. 275)

2) In the sense of "say":

προλέλεκται *PFlor.* 295.6 (6th cent.)
λέλεκται *PLond.* 1338 = *WChr.* 255.15, with εἴρηται 33-34 (A.D. 709); *PLond.* 1343.12 (A.D. 709); *PLond.* 1344.15, with εἴρητ[αι] 14 (A.D. 709/10); *PRossGeorg.* iv, 1.28 part. rest. (A.D. 710); iv, 27e.4 (ca. A.D. 710); etc.
but διείλεκται *BGU* 1080 = *WChr.* 478.11 (3rd cent.)

g. The Attic ἑόρακα (for *Fε-Fόρακα) and the Hellenistic ἑώρακα (on the analogy of the imperfect ἑώρων from *η-Fόρων with quantitative metathesis) are both used:

ἑόρακας *PLips.* 40 ii.9 (late 4th/early 5th cent.)
ἑόρακεν, ἑορακέναι *POxy.* 471.57, sim. 59; 74 (2nd cent.)
ἑώρακα *PCairMasp.* 87.8 (A.D. 543)
ἑωράκαμεν *PCairMasp.* 2 iii.21 (A.D. 567: *BL* i, 100)
ἑωρακέναι *SB* 7368.27 (late 2nd/early 3rd cent.)

This fluctuation is not significant for morphology in view of the identification of o and ω.[3]

The reduplication ε- is itself omitted sporadically, e.g., ἰσώρακεν *BGU* 261.12-13 (ca. A.D. 105: cf. *PMich.* 202).

---

[1] ἠθέληκα was the Att. form (Aeschin. X. D.), τεθέληκα the predominant Koine form (LXX, Mosch. Phld. S.E. Or. etc.) (Veitch, s.vv. ἐθέλω & θέλω; *LSJ* s.v. ἐθέλω). τεθέληκα is said by Phryn. 307 (Rutherford, 415-16) to be the proper Alexandrian and Eg. form.

[2] The pf. mid.-pass. λέλεγμαι is rare in class. Gr. in the meaning "collect"; εἴλεγμαι is preferred. In the meaning "say," λέλεγμαι is reg. (when εἴρημαι is not used), exc. in the compd. δι- (Veitch & *LSJ*, s.v.). Sim. exx. are found in the Ptol. papp. (Mayser i², 2, 97). Full redupl. in place of class. Att. ει- is also found in the variant pf. λέλογχα for εἴληχα (see below, p. 301).

[3] See Vol. i, 275-7.

h. For the reduplication of ἐργάζομαι and αἱρέω, see above, pp. 236-7 and 238-9.

3. Attic reduplication is preserved in the perfects ἀκήκοα, ἀλήλιφα, ἐλήλυθα, ἐνήνοχα, (ἀπ-)όλωλα, ὀμώμοκα, and also ἀγείοχα (perfect of ἄγω). For examples, with phonological and morphological variants, see below, pp. 299-305.[1]

D. PLACE OF THE AUGMENT AND REDUPLICATION IN COMPOUND VERBS[2]

The normal position of the augment and reduplication in compound verbs remains after the prefix. In some few verbs, however, mainly those whose simple form was not in common use, the prefix is regularly augmented; in others, the position of the augment varies; in some others, double augment is found.

These variations arose for the most part in classical Greek. Prepositional as well as non-prepositional decomposita were properly augmented and reduplicated on the preverb, but analogy led to the increasingly frequent augment and reduplication after the preverb. Conversely, many verbal compounds whose simple forms were obsolete, or whose etymology was no longer known, came to be augmented and reduplicated on the preverb. These fluctuations in turn led to forms with double augment.[3] The Modern Greek augment, when used in compounds, always precedes the preverb.[4]

1. Single augment and reduplication (of the preverb or stem).

a. Some few verbs are regularly augmented and reduplicated on the preverb instead of the stem (temporal augment/reduplication to η- only):[5]

ἠμφισβήτησαν *PMich.* 340.86 (A.D. 45/46)

---

[1] Cf. also the aor. ἤγαγον (along w. ἦξα), ἤνεγκον/ἤνεγκα (w. orthographic variants), and less obviously ἑσπόμην (< *wekw-, dissimilated from *we-wkw-) and εἶπον (< *sesekw-) (Chantraine[2], § 198).

[2] Incl. here are both verbal compds. (paratheta) and compds. derived from prepositional compd. nouns and adjs. (parasyntheta). Parasyntheta derived from non-prepositional nominal compds., incl. those in δυσ- (before a consonant or long vowel) and εὐ-, have reg. init. augm. and redupl., e.g., ἐμαρτυροποιεῖτο *SB* 5217.20 (A.D. 148); *BGU* 1032.9 (A.D. 173); τεθηκοποτημένων *BGU* 757.15 (A.D. 12); sim. *PRyl.* 142.16 (A.D. 37); ἐφιλοπρ[αγμο]νήθημεν *PCairMasp.* 4.5 (ca. A.D. 552: *BL* i, 100); πεφιλοκαλημένον *PHamb.* 23.17 (A.D. 569); ἐδυσωπήσαμεν *POxy.* 128.4 (6th/7th cent.); ηὐτυχήσαμεν, etc., above, p. 241.

[3] Cf. Schwyzer i, 655-6; Chantraine[2], § 358; *KB* ii, 1, 32-37; Hatzidakis, *Einl.*, 65-67; Rutherford, *Phryn.*, 79-87.

[4] Cf. Thumb, *Handbook*, § 182.

[5] Cf. also from the mag. papp. the verbal compd. ἠμφιεσμένος *PGM* 4.933 (4th cent.) w. augm. on the preverb as in class. Gr. (Schwyzer i, 656; Chantraine[2], § 358b).

ἠμφισβήτησεν *MChr.* 88 i.18; sim. iv.16-17 (after A.D. 141)
    διημ[φ]ισβήτησεν *PLBat.* iii, 14.11 (2nd cent.)
ἠμφισβητήσαμεν *PLond.* 992 = *MChr.* 365.10 (A.D. 507)
    ἠμφισβ[ή]τησα *SB* 5941.10 (A.D. 509)[1]
ἠνεχυρασμένων *POxy.* 1027 = *WChr.* 199a.7 (mid 1st cent.)
ἠμφοδηκέναι *SB* 6265.7-8 (late 1st cent.)
ἠπίστατο *POxy.* 2111.8 (ca. A.D. 135)
ἠπειληκέναι *POxy.* 2182.19 (A.D. 166)
ἤπειξε *POxy.* 1681.13 (3rd cent.); (-εν) *PFlor.* 156.6 (3rd cent.)
    ἠπείχθην *POxy.* 161 = *POxy.* 938.5-6 (late 3rd/4th cent.); sim. *POxy.*
    900 = *WChr.* 437.14 (A.D. 322)

b. ἀνοίγω (ἀνοίγνυμι[2]) is normally augmented on the preverb but reduplicated on the stem (rarely both preverb and stem).[3]

1) Augment (of the preverb):[4]

ἤνυξα (for ἤνοιξα) *POxy.* 1288.12 (4th cent.)
ἠνύγη (for ἠνοίγη) *BGU* 1655.60 (A.D. 169); *BGU* 326 = *WChr.* 316
    ii.10 (A.D. 194); *POxy.* 2348.51 (A.D. 224)
ἠνοίχθη *PHamb.* 73.19 (2nd cent.)

2) Reduplication (of the stem):[5]

ἀνέῳκται *SB* 5112.37 (A.D. 618?); *SB* 5114.17 (A.D. 613-40)
ἀνεῳγμένον *StudPal.* xxii, 54.17-18 part. rest. (A.D. 210: *BL* iii, 238);
    PSI 1058.5 (5th/6th cent.); *PRossGeorg.* v, 39.7 (6th cent.); *SB* 4491.1
    (6th/7th cent.)
ἀνεῳγμένου *SB* 4706.1,3 (Byz.)
ἀνεῳγμένης, -μένον *SB* 9153.18,22 (A.D. 596)

---

[1] This verb took double augm, ἠμφεσ- in Att. lit. and inscrr., although forms w. augm. only on the preverb are common in codd. of the best Att. authors (Veitch & *LSJ,* s.v.; Schwyzer i, 656; Chantraine[2], § 358c; *MS,* 173; cf. Rutherford, *Phryn.,* 83). The double augm. is preserved in MGr. *kathareuousa* ἠμφεσβήτησε (Kapsomenos, "'Ερευναι," 363).

[2] For the thematic and athematic pres. formations, see below, p. 281.

[3] Double augm. is usual in the Ptol. papp., but redupl. of the stem alone, exc. redupl. of the preverb once (Mayser i[2], 2, 104, 108). NT codd. show all forms of the augm., but redupl. normally only of the stem (*BDF,* § 101 s.v.; cf. § 66.2).

[4] Cf. also from the mag. papp. ἠνοίγησαν, ἠνοίγη *PGM* 12.324,325 (A.D. 300-50); ἠνοίγησαν *PGM* 36.298 (4th cent.); ἠνύγη *PGM* 13.531 (ca. A.D. 346). The normal class. augm. is ἀνέῳγον and ἀνέῳξα; ἤνοιγον and ἤνοιξα are found in X. and late prose (Veitch & *LSJ,* s.v.).

[5] This form of redupl., for (ἀν-)εοιγ- from *Fε-Fοιγ- on the analogy of the class. augm. (ἀν-)έῳξα < *η-Fοιγ- (Schwyzer i, 653, n. 10) is Att., but ἤνοιγμαι is found in compds. in Hp. and later in Hld., and the simple in J. (Veitch & *LSJ,* s.v.). παρανεῳγμένη is found in the mag. papp. in *PGM* 7.524 (3rd cent.).

ἀνεῳγμένη *PLond.* 871 (iii, 269).16, sim. 17 (A.D. 603); *SB* 4492.4
(6th cent.)

ἀνεῳγμένην *SB* 4493.1 (Byz.); *PMon.* 16.8 (late 6th cent.); *SB*
5112.26 (A.D. 618?)

3) Reduplication of preverb and stem:[1]

ἠνέῳκται *PLond.* 1724.37 (A.D. 578-82)

{ἀν}ηνέῳκται *PMon.* 13.30 (A.D. 594)

ἠνεῳγμένο(υ) *PCairMasp.* 96.21 (A.D. 573/4)

ἠνεῳγμένης *PCairMasp.* 309.24; 313.55 part. rest. (6th cent.)

c. ἀναλίσκω is normally augmented and reduplicated on the verb stem,
but sporadically on the preverb or on both stem and preverb; the augment
(of the verb stem) is also frequently transferred to other moods and tenses and
to cognate substantives.

1) Augment and reduplication of the verb stem:

ἀνήλωσα *PMich.* 496.7 (2nd cent.); *PCairMasp.* 156-7.12 part. rest.
(A.D. 570); *PMon.* 9.65 (A.D. 585)

κατανήλωσεν *PPrinc.* 119.10-11 (ca. A.D. 325: *ZPE* 8 [1971], 15)

ἀνήλωκας *SB* 9643.5 (1st cent.)

ἀνηλωκώς, ἀνηλοκός *PMich.* 605.14,23 (A.D. 117)

ἀνηλωκυεῖα *PMich.* 188.16 (A.D. 120)

ἀνηλῶσθαι *BGU* 21 i.12 (A.D. 340)

ἀ[ν]ηλωμένα *BGU* 193 = *MChr.* 268 ii.26 (A.D. 136)

ἀνηλώθη *PLond.* 1177 = *WChr.* 193.60 (A.D. 113); *POxy.* 1288.8 (4th cent.)

ἀνηλώθησαν *PAmh.* 131 = *PSarap.* 80.19 (early 2nd cent.); *POxy.*
519 = *WChr.* 492.10 abbrev. (2nd cent.); *BGU* 81.15 abbrev.
(A.D. 189); *PMich.* 620.213, etc. (A.D. 239/40)

2) Augment and reduplication of the preverb:[2]

κατηνάλωσεν *PSI* 41.20 (4th cent.)

ἠ[ν]αλλω(μένων) *StudPal.* viii, 1111.3 (6th cent.)

3) Double augment:

κατηνήλωσεν *PSI* 944.13 (A.D. 364/6?)

---

[1] A double augm. is poss. reflected in ἠνύωγεν (for ἠνέῳγεν?) *PMich.* 583.10,31 (diff.
hands) (A.D. 78). The augm. is om. in the mag. papp. in ἀνύγησαν *PGMXtn.* 13.106
(4th/5th cent.).

[2] Augm. of the preverb is rare in class. Gr. and appar. only in the compd. κατ- (Hp.
Isoc.) (Veitch & *LSJ*, s.v.). In the Att. inscrr., augm. occurs invariably after the preverb
(*MS*, 173).

4) Transferred augment:[1]

ἀνηλοῦντι *POxy.* 1143.6 (ca. A.D. 1)
  ἀνηλώσης *SB* 7250 = *PMich.* 218.7 (A.D. 296)
  ἀνηλωθέντων *PMilVogl.* 151.1 (2nd cent.)
  cf. also ἀνηλογοῦσαν *PCairMasp.* 151-2.89, with ἀναλωμάτων 213
    (A.D. 570)
ἀνήλωσις *PPrinc.* 152 ii.5 (A.D. 55-60)
ἀνήλωμα *PAberd.* 66.1 abbrev. (A.D. 21); *SB* 9379 = *PMilVogl.* 69
    A.145, etc. (2nd cent.)
  ἀνηλώματα *PMich.* 350.20 (A.D. 37); *PMich.* 554.41 (A.D. 81-96);
    SB 9824.8 (A.D. 114/33); *PAmh.* 126 = *PSarap.* 55.15,47,50
    abbrev. (A.D. 128); etc.
  ἀνηλωμάτων *PLond.* 131 R = *SB* 9699.3, etc. (A.D. 78/79); *PMil-*
    Vogl. 52.13 abbrev. (A.D. 138); etc.
  ἀνηλώμασιν *PMich.* 346a.11 (A.D. 13); *PMich.* 350.15-16 (A.D. 37);
    PLond. 1166 (iii, 104-5).7 part. rest. (A.D. 42); etc.
but ἀνάλ(ωμα) *PPrinc.* 60.3 (2nd/3rd cent.)
  ἀναλόματ(α) *PSarap.* 65 i.2, with ἀνηλό(ματα) ii.1 (ca. A.D. 128)
  ἀναλωμάτων *PSI* 1152.6 (1st half 2nd cent.); *PHeid.* 236.8 abbrev.
    (2nd cent.); *PMilVogl.* 55 v.1 abbrev. (2nd cent.); *PPrinc.* 61.10
    abbrev. (A.D. 264); etc.
  cf. ἀνηλογίας *SB* 9154.12 (6th/7th cent.); *PLips.* 103 = *WChr.* 257.3
    abbrev., 7 part. rest. (Arab.)
    ἀνηλογίαν *PMichael.* 42 A.19 (A.D. 566); *PLond.* 1708.238,241 (A.D.
      567?); *PLond.* 1369.14 (A.D. 710)
but ἀναλογίαν *PLond.* 1733.44,62 (A.D. 594)

5) Augment omitted:[2]

ἀνάλωσα *POxy.* 1295.8 9 (2nd/early 3rd cent.)
  ἀνάλω[σ]εν *PCairGoodsp.* 30 xiv.12 (A.D. 191-2)
ἀναλώθη *BGU* 14 ii.17 (A.D. 255)
  ἀναλώθησαν *BGU* 362 = *WChr.* 96 iii.23 part. rest., vi.11 abbrev.,
    sim. x.2, frag. v.5 (A.D. 215)
[ἐ]παναλωσάμην *PFlor.* 305.4-5 (6th cent.)

d. Some other verbs are augmented and reduplicated on the preverb by
way of exception.

---

[1] ἀνηλίσκω became the normal pres. form in the Ptol. papp. and led to the transfer
of -η- to all moods and tenses and to cognate substantives; ἀναλίσκω is found only in the
earlier documents (Mayser i², 2, 112-13). ἀνήλωμα is also found in Asia Minor inscrr.
(Schweizer, 174; Anm. 3). Cf. further Crönert, 286(-7), nn. 2-4.
[2] This is hardly a relic of the class. variants ἀνᾱλωσα E., ἀνᾱλωκα codd.Th., ἀνᾱλώθην
(*LSJ*, s.v.).

1) Temporal augment and reduplication:

   ἠπάντηκα *POxy.* 1683.19 (late 4th cent.)
   ἠπαίτησας *PLond.* 1345.13 (A.D. 710)
       ἠπαιτήθησαν *PLond.* 1075 (iii, 281-2).13.24 (7th cent.)

2) Syllabic augment and reduplication:

   ἐκάθισα *PMeyer* 19.5 (2nd cent.)
       ἐκάθισεν *BGU* 511 = *WChr.* 14 i.16 (A.D. 200+)
   ἐκάθητο *PRossGeorg.* ii, 31.7 (2nd cent.)
   παρεσυνγραφῇ (false augm. = subj.) *PMerton* 109.18, corr. 21 (2nd cent.)
   ἐπροσφώνησεν, ἐκατέχιν (for κατεῖχε), ἐδιαληθῆναι (false augm. = infin.
       -λυθῆναι) *SB* 9683.11,24,25 (late 4th cent.)
   ἐπροσδόκων *SB* 10269.3 (6th cent.)
   σεσύλληχα (for συνείληχα) *POxy.* 1160.16, with ἐπράκαται (for πεπρά-
       κατε) 11 (late 3rd/early 4th cent.)

   e. Some denominatives whose form resembles a compound are sometimes
augmented or reduplicated with syllabic augment inserted between the supposed
preverb and the stem or with the supposed initial vowel of the stem augmented:

   ἐνεγύησας *POxy.* 2154.17 (4th cent.); *PSI* 841.10 (4th cent.)
       ἐγεγύησαν *PFlor.* 58.13 (3rd cent.)
   ἐνεγυησάμην *PCairIsidor.* 80.27 (A.D. 296); *PWürzb.* 16.16-17 part.
       rest. (A.D. 349)
   ἐνγεγύημαι *POxy.* 259 = *MChr.* 101.7 (A.D. 23)
   ἐγγεγυῆσθαι *PCairPreis.* 13.6; 15.6 (4th cent.); etc.[1]
but with the reduplication omitted in ἐγγυημένων *PFlor.* 314.9 (A.D.
   428)
   ἀνήνκακων (for ἠνάγκαζον) *PGissBibl.* 19.5 (A.D. 55)
       ἀ[ν]ή[γκ]αζε *BGU* 1042.5-6: *BL* iii, 16 (3rd cent.)
   ἀνήγκασεν *PBrem.* 38.11 (A.D. 118)
       ἀνήγκασαι (for ἠνάγκασε) *PMich.* 581.11 (ca. A.D. 126-8)
       ἀνήκασαι (for ἠνάγκασε) *POxy.* 2783.29 (3rd cent.)
       ἀνηκάσαμεν (for ἠναγκάσαμεν) *PAmh.* 133 = *PSarap.* 92.12 (early
       2nd cent.)
   ἀνήγκασαν *PMich.* 421.26 (A.D. 41-54)
   ἀνηγκάσθημεν *POxy.* 2861.11-12 (2nd cent.)

---

[1] This verb is so augm. and redupl. as a compd. freq. in codd. of D. Is. (Veitch & *LSJ*,
s.v.) and in the Ptol. papp. (Mayser i², 2, 110).

but κατηνάγκασεν *PCairMasp.* 76.6 (6th cent.)

κατηνάγκασαν *PAmh.* 84.8 (2nd/3rd cent.)

ἠναγκάσθην *WChr.* 176.9,14-15 (mid 1st cent.); *PLeit.* 5.6 (ca. A.D. 180); *PLeit.* 7.7 (prob. A.D. 219-24); *PCairMasp.* 62.2 (6th cent.)

cf. ἠνήνκασε *SB* 8252 == *PFouad* 26.44 (A.D. 157-9)

2. Double augment.

Double augment occurs sometimes in several verbs. It is found in the four possible variations.

a. Double syllabic augment:[1]

ἀπεκατέστησα *PTebt.* 413.4 (2nd/3rd cent.)

cf. ἀπεκατεστάθη *Archiv* ii, p. 436.31, inscr. (A.D. 80/81)

ἀπεκατέστησεν *PGM* 4.154-5 (4th cent.)

ἐπαρεκάλεσα *SB* 7168.2 (5th/6th cent.)

cf. ἐδιεκρίνατο *SB* 10709 G.4, inscr. (4th/5th cent.)

A type of double reduplication occurs in μεμισθοπεπρακέναι *POxy.* 2136.4 (A.D. 291).

b. Double temporal augment:[2]

ἠνώχλησεν *POxy.* 2788.4-5 (3rd cent.)

ἠνώχλησα *CPR* 19 — *StudPal.* xx, 86.10 (A.D. 330)

ἠνωχλούμην (with ω above ο deleted) *POxy.* 1588.5 (early 4th cent.)[3]

but cf. the augment omitted:

διενόχλησεν *SB* 9483.7 (2nd cent.)

]ενόχλησεν *PCairMasp.* 71.7 (Byz.)

c. Syllabic augment of the preverb and temporal augment of the stem:[4]

ἐδιώκησας, ἐδιώκησα *POxy.* 2407.3,48, sim. 11,27 (late 3rd cent.)

ἐδιόκαιτο (= ἐδιώκετο) *PGronf.* ii, 84.7, with διωκόμενος 8 9 (5th/6th cent.)

ἐπαρῆλθεν (or ἐπανῆλθεν?) *PCairMasp.* 68.2 (6th cent.)

---

[1] Double syll. augm. is not found in the Ptol. papp. (Mayser i², 2, 109), but occurs in ἀποκαθίστημι in the NT (*BDF*, § 69.3).

[2] See also κατηνήλωσεν above, p. 250.

[3] This verb has double augm. in the best mss. of class. authors (Veitch & *LSJ*, s.v.) and in the Ptol. papp. (Mayser i², 2, 109).

[4] Cf. also syll. redupl. of the preverb alone in δεδιοίκ(ηκα) *POxy.* 2409.4 (late 2nd cent.). Augm. + redupl. are found in this verb only in the pf. pass. in a frag. of Antiph. and in Macho ap. Ath. and Phld. (Veitch & *LSJ*, s.v.).

d. Temporal augment of the preverb and syllabic augment of the stem:[1]

ἠνεσχόμην *PSI* 1248.16 (A.D. 235); *POxy.* 903.36 (4th cent.); *BGU*
   1039.5 (Byz.); *PApoll.* 66.3 (ca. A.D. 710/11)
   ἠνέσχετο *PHermRees* 48.2 (5th cent.); *POxy.* 130.15 (6th cent.);
      SB 9616 V.25 (A.D. 550-8?); *PLond.* 1007 (iii, 262-4).22 (ca. A.D.
      558); *PCairMasp.* 75.5 (6th cent.); *PGrenf.* i, 64.2 (6th/7th cent.);
      PSI 1267 = *PApoll.* 24.3 (A.D. 710); *PApoll.* 32.10 (ca. A.D.
      713); 46.7 (A.D. 703-15); etc.
   ἠνέσχοντο *POxy.* 1877.7 (ca. A.D. 488); *PCairMasp.* 70.2 (6th cent.);
      PCairMasp. 24.35-36 part. rest. (ca. A.D. 551); *PLond.* 1708.109
      (A.D. 567?); etc.[2]
but cf. ἐνέσχετο *POxy.* 1931.4,6 (5th cent.)
ἠπέθανεν *POxy.* 922.24 (late 6th/early 7th cent.)

---

[1] See also forms of ἀνοίγω above, pp. 249-50, as well as ἠνήνκασε, p. 253, and ἀπηνη-
νεγμένας, p. 234.
[2] Double augm. is usual in the impf. and aor. of this verb in Att. authors, but in mosr
codd. of the NT, only the single augm. of the stem is found (Veitch & *LSJ*, s.v.; Schwyzet
i, 656; Chantraine², § 358c; *BDF*, § 69.2).

VI. FORMATION OF THE TENSE STEM

A. FORMATION OF THE TENSE STEM IN GENERAL[1]

Variations from classical usage in the formation of the stems of the different tense systems of verbs consist mainly in the extension by analogical levelling of a single stem vowel or a single stem consonant throughout the paradigm.

1. Modification of the stem vowel.

a. Vowel stems.

Vowel stems in -α- and -ε- regularly change the vowel preceding the tense suffix to η (= lengthening in classical Greek[2]), e.g., τιμάω, τιμήσω; ποιέω, ποιήσω; βάλλω, βέβληκα (a vowel stem by metathesis).[3] The following variations occur.

1) The -α- is normally retained in the *a*-pure verbs, according to Attic usage, after a vowel or ρ (= ᾱ before the loss of quantitative distinction), e.g., ἐᾶσαι *PLond.* 256e = *WChr.* 344.5 (A.D. 11); εἴασα *PLond.* 982 (iii, 242-3).15 (A.D. 350-75: *BL* v, 54); πειράσομαι *POxy.* 1666.16 (3rd cent.).

a) The (short) α is retained on the analogy of the present, as in Attic, in ἀποσπάσω *BGU* 1125.9 (13 B.C.); *POxy.* 1295.6 part. rest. (2nd/early 3rd cent.); etc.

---

[1] Schwyzer i, 737-9; Chantraine[2], § 170-7, 363-7; Buck, *GD*, § 141-2; Crönert, 224-31; *BDF*, § 70-72. The other authors treat the general variations under the individual tenses.

[2] More exactly, the η represents an independent suffix added to the stem of tenses other than the pres. to make the formation of these tenses more uniform; cf. Schwyzer i, 738; Chantraine[2], § 365-6.

[3] Vowel stems in -ο- similarly 'lengthen' this vowel to ω, as δηλόω, δηλώσω; but by the time of the Rom.-Byz. papp., after the loss of quant. distinction, this change is merely orthographic. Stems in -ι- and -υ-, lengthened to ῑ and ῡ in class. Gr., show neither a morphemic nor an orthographic change.

b) This same convention is also used in Hellenistic variants of verbs in
-έζω, as [π]επιάκαμ[εν] *PMich.* 473.27 (early 2nd cent.).

c) The athematic δύναμαι retains the -α- in its occasional Epic-Ionic-Lyric
sigmatic aorist passive ἐδυνάσθην.[1]

d) Other verbs retain the -α- sporadically, e.g., δαπανάσης *PAberd.* 72.5
(2nd/3rd cent.), but δαπανήσης *BGU* 424.7-8 (2nd/3rd cent.), etc.[2]

e) An anomalous tense formative -α- is found in an -έω contract verb ἠμέ-
λασα (for ἠμέλησα) *PYale* 79.12-13 (ca. A.D. 150).

2) The historically short -ε- is retained regularly in verbs like τελέω, e.g.,
τελέσειν *PStrassb.* 185.21 (A.D. 55); διετέλεσα *BGU* 287 = *WChr.* 124.7-8
(A.D. 250).[3] It is also found occasionally in the future and aorist of verbs in
which a tense formative -η- was used in classical Greek.[4]

a) στερέω/στερίσκω:[5]

    ἀπεστέρεσαν *BGU* 1200.26 (2/1 B.C.)
        στερέσε (for στερέσαι) *POxy.* 2133.23-24 (late 3rd cent.)
            ἀποστερέσαι *PMilVogl.* 229.15 (ca. A.D. 140); *PRyl.* 116.16
                (A.D. 194)
        cf. ἐπὶ ἀποστερέσι *POxy.* 71 i = *MChr.* 62.10-11 (A.D. 303)
    but ἐστέρησε *PGissBibl.* 30.9 (3rd/4th cent.)
        ἀποστερήσ⟦ιω⟧ωσι *PLond.* 1917.19 (ca. A.D. 330-40)
        στερῆσαι *POxy.* 237 vi.25 (A.D. 186)
            ἀποστερῆσαι *BGU* 1024 iv.13 part. rest., cf. vii.16; viii.15 (late
                4th cent.: *BL* i, 88); *PLond.* 1708.37 (A.D. 567?)
        στερηθείς *PThead.* 19.6 (A.D. 316-20: *JP* ii, 60)
        ἀποστερηθῆναι *PLond.* 1915.9-10 (ca. A.D. 330-40)
        στερηθήσεται *POxy.* 2954.22-23 (3rd cent.)
        cf. ἀποστερητῆι *POxy.* 745.7 (ca. A.D. 1)

---

[1] Cf. Veitch & *LSJ*, s.v. For exx., see below, pp. 318-19.

[2] Mayser (i², 2, 118) explains the sim. ἠρώτασα by postulating an unnecessary confusion
of -άω and -άζω pres. formations.

[3] The -ε- is retained because τελέω is not a denominative of the normal -έω type, but
an orig. *s*-stem (Chantraine², § 203). But by analogy τελήσασθαι occurs as a v.l. in Aristid.
and both ἐπετέλησεν and τετέληκα occur in inscrr. and in the Ptol. papp. (Veitch, s.v.;
Schweizer, 180; Mayser i², 2, 131, 148). ἐτέλησα is also found in *PColt* 15.18 (A.D. 512);
note that there is a freq. interchange of η and ε at Nessana (see Vol. i, 249, n. 1).

[4] The class. usage is maintained in Asia Minor inscrr. and in the Ptol. papp., w. only
occ. variations (Schweizer, 180; Nachmanson, 162; Hauser, 110-11; Mayser i², 2, 131, 148).

[5] Cf. στερέσαι *Od. AP*, inscrr., and v.l. LXX (Veitch & *LSJ*, s.v.; Schwyzer i, 709;
Crönert, 225, n. 1). Four occurrences of -ε- are found in this verb in the Ptol. papp. along
w. two of -η- (Mayser i², 2, 131). ἀπεστέρησε occurs in the mag. papp. in *PGM* 40.2 (4th
cent.). Cf. also κυέση *SB* 4324.3, love charm (n.d.), also connected w. an alternative pres.
formation in -σκω.

b) -οφείλω:[1]

προσοφειλέση in leases: *POxy.* 640 descr., part. rest. (A.D. 120/1); *POxy.* 730 = *MChr.* 273.25 (A.D. 130); *POxy.* 101.42-43 (A.D. 142); *POxy.* 502.39 (A.D. 164); *POxy.* 1127.26-27 (A.D. 183); *POxy.* 912.31 (A.D. 235); etc.

προσοφειλέσωσι *POxy.* 2351.52 (A.D. 112)

ἐνοφειλέσαντος *POxy.* 986 iii (A.D. 131/2)

but ἐπώφληται, ἐπωφληθέντος *PCairMasp.* 131.6,16 (6th cent.)

ἐποφληθέντα *PCairMasp.* 168.63 (6th cent.)

c) φορέω:[2]

φορέσεις *POxy.* 531 = *WChr.* 482.15 (2nd cent.)

ἐφόρεσα *PMeyer* 37.1 (5th cent.)

φορέσῃς *SB* 7247 = *PMich.* 214.33 (A.D. 296)

[π]ληροφορέσαι *PSI* 1345.4 (6th/7th cent.)

πιστοφορέθητι *PLond.* 1338 = *WChr.* 255.10 (A.D. 709)

but ἐκφορήσῃ, ἐξεφόρησεν *POxy.* 1642.22,33 (A.D. 289)

ἵνα ... πληροφορήσω *PAmh.* 66.42 (A.D. 124)

διαφορηθῇ *SB* 7448 = *PSI* 1160.11 (1st half 1st cent.: *BL* iii, 228)

ἀδιφορηθῆναι *PLond.* 144 (ii, 253).15 (2nd/3rd cent.: *BL* i, 266)

cf. φορήσε(ως) *StudPal.* viii, 854.2 (7th/8th cent.)

d) ὑστερέω:[3]

ὑστερέσῃς *PLond.* 1398.6 (A.D. 709?); *PLond.* 1359.14 part. rest. (A.D. 710); *PLond.* 1353.17 (A.D. 710)

ὑστερέσῃ *PFlor.* 278 iv.13, with ὑστερήσῃ ii.11; iii.16; etc. (A.D. 248)

ὑστερέσαι *PLond.* 1380 = *WChr.* 285.30 (A.D. 710/11)

ὑστερεθῇ *PLond.* 1393 = *SB* 7241.50 (A.D. 697/712)

cf. [ὑστ]ερείσι *POxy.* 1678.5-6 (3rd cent.)

but ὑστέρησα *PLond.* 1839.1 (1st half 6th cent.)

ὑστέρησες *PLond.* 1332.17 (A.D. 708)

ὑστέρησ[ας] *PLond.* 1358.8 (A.D. 710)

ὑστερήσῃς *PMerton* 83.24 (late 2nd cent.); *PLond.* 1399.12 (A.D. 709-14)

ὑστερήσῃ *PLond.* 1346.16 (A.D. 710)

---

[1] Class. Gr. has -η- in all tense stems of this verb exc. in the 2 aor. A fut. -έσω is first found in an Asia Minor inscr. (Veitch & *LSJ*, s.v.; Schweizer, 180; Hauser, 110; Crönert, 225, n. 3).

[2] Forms in -ε- are generally post-class. (Aristid. NT, and early Xtn. lit.) and have survived in MGr. (Veitch & *LSJ*, s.v.; *BDF*, § 70.1; Crönert, 225, n. 3; Psaltes, 27-28; Schwyzer i, 753; Thumb, *Handbook*, § 201; Mirambel, *Gram.*, 159; Maspero, 129). The -ε- may have been retained on the analogy of ἠμφίεσα (Hatzidakis, *Einl.*, 334).

[3] ὑστέρισα is a freq. v.l. (*LSJ*, s.v.).

ἀφυστερήσῃ *PFlor.* 34.11 (A.D. 342); *PAmh.* 139 = *WChr.* 406.19 (A.D. 350); *PHermRees* 55.2; 56.3 (4th cent.); *PLond.* 1648.23 part. rest.; 1649.19 (A.D. 373); *PSI* 86.14 (A.D. 367/75); *PLips.* 54 = *WChr.* 467.14 (ca. A.D. 376); *PLips.* 56.19 (A.D. 398); etc.

ἀφυστερή[σ]ωσι *PFlor.* 3 = *WChr.* 391.17 (A.D. 301)

ὑστερησάντων (for -τος sg.) *POxy.* 118.30-31 (late 3rd cent.)

ὑστερηθῆναι *PLond.* 1338 = *WChr.* 255.13 (A.D. 709)

ὑστερηθείς, ὑστερήθη *PLond.* 1708.85,209 (A.D. 567?)

cf. ὑστερησμῷ *PFlor.* 296.52 (6th cent.); *PCairMasp.* 19.13 part. rest. (A.D. 548-51)

e) Other verbs (only sporadically):

ἐπεζήτεσε *PMerton* 80.7 (2nd cent.)

but ἐζήτησα *PMerton* 79.7 (2nd cent.)

ἐπεζήτησας *PCairMasp.* 167.29 (6th cent.); etc.

φοβεθείς *PCairMasp.* 89 V.31 (Byz.)

but φοβηθείς *PGrenf.* ii, 84.3-4 (5th/6th cent.); *PCairMasp.* 294.28 (6th cent.); etc.

πωλέσῃ *PApoll.* 66.9 (ca. A.D. 710-11)

but πώλησον *PGiss.* 105.3 (5th cent.); etc.

f) The Hellenistic present βαρέω also sometimes retains the -ε-:[1]

ἐπιβαρέσε[ις] *PLond.* 1674.24 (ca. A.D. 570)

βαρέσαι *POxy.* 126 = *WChr.* 180.8 (A.D. 572)

βαρέσαντες, βαρεθέντ(ος) *PLond.* 1345.20,33; sim. 1356.25,38 (A.D. 710)

perh. also βαρεθἕναι (for -ῆναι: see below, p. 261, n. 2) *POxy.* 1872.4 (late 5th/early 6th cent.)

but βαρήσι̣[ς] *POxy.* 2596.10 (3rd cent.)

ἐβάρησα *BGU* 1674.9 (2nd cent.); *SB* 7993 = *PSI* 1333.7 (3rd cent.)

ἐπεβάρησα *PRossGeorg.* v, 4.10 (2nd cent.)

βαρήσω (aor. subj.) *POxy.* 1159.2-3 (late 3rd cent.)

ἵνα μὴ βαρήσεις *POxy.* 1677.8 (3rd cent.)

βεβαρημένη *PTebt.* 327 = *WChr.* 394.25-26 (A.D. 180+)

βεβαρημένου *SB* 7518.13 (4th/5th cent.)

βεβαρημένοι *Archiv* v, p. 245 = *PGiss.* i, p. 30.10 (ca. A.D. 117); *PCairIsidor.* 75.9 (A.D. 316)

βαρηθῶσιν *WChr.* 238 = *PBrem.* 2.5-6 (ca. A.D. 117)

καταβαρηθέ[ν]τος *POxy.* 487 = *MChr.* 322.10-11 (A.D. 156)

cf. also βαρῆσαι *PColt* 24.7 (A.D. 569), but ἐβάρεσαν *PColt* 75.4 (late 7th cent.)

---

[1] The MGr. form is normally βάρεσα (Mirambel, *Gram.*, 159; Maspero, 129), sts. βάρισα from βαρίσκω (Thumb, *Handbook*, § 201). In the Rom.-Byz. papp., the pres. is βαρύνω (see below, p. 280), but the other tenses are formed from βαρέω.

g) The -ε- is also retained in an early occurrence of the aorist passive participle ῥεθείς/ῥηθείς:[1]

ῥεθέ[ντω]ν *POxy.* 237 vii.40 (A.D. 186)
but ῥηθέντος *PAntin.* 97.6 (6th cent.)
ῥηθέντων *PLond.* 113 (1) (i, 199-204).26 (6th cent.); *BGU* 872.4 (Byz.)
προρηθεί[ς] *PCairMasp.* 158.11 (A.D. 568)
προρηθείσης, προρηθέντος *PMichael.* 41.8,69 (A.D. 539/54)
προρηθείσης *PCairMasp.* 279.11 (ca. A.D. 570)
προρηθέντι, προρηθέντος *PLond.* 1676.33,60 (A.D. 566-73)
προρηθέντων *PCairMasp.* 312.94 (A.D. 567)

h) But πονέω, in which the -ε- is sometimes retained in violation of the classical norm in other Koine documents and literature, rarely appears with -ε-:[2]

ἐκπονέσασιν *PPrinc.* 119.36 (ca. A.D. 325: *ZPE* 8 [1971], 15)
but ἐπόνη[σα] *PJand.* 21.3 (6th/7th cent.)
[πο]νήσαντι *PCairMasp.* 295 i.15 (6th cent.)
φιλοπονῆσε (for -σαι) *POxy.* 1069.23 (3rd cent.)
φιλοπονήσῃ *PGiss.* 80.12 (ca. A.D. 117)
καταπεπονῆσθαι *PSI* 767.46 (A.D. 331?)
καταπονηθῆναι *SB* 7656.5 (Byz.)

3) Conversely, some vowel stems in which the -ε- is regularly retained throughout or in which the stem vowel varies according to tense, sometimes have the -η- formative.

a) αἰνέω:[3]

συνήνησεν *PFlor.* 304.3 (6th cent.); *PMon.* 14.51 (A.D. 594)
but παραινέσαι *PJand.* 16.4 (5th/6th cent.)
[συ]ναινέσαντ[ο]ς *PCairMasp.* 89 R a.2 (Byz.)
ἐπαινεθήσει *PFlor.* 304.9 (6th cent.)

---

[1] The short vowel was retained in the aor. pass. in Arist. and later authors, but appar. only in the indic. (Veitch, s.v. ῥέω; *LSJ*, s.v. ἐρῶ). The short vowel indic. is also found as a v.l. in the NT, but the ptc. always has -η-, as in the Ptol. papp. (*BDF*, § 70.1; Mayser i², 2, 156); -ε- is found in the ptc. in Cyrill.Alex. (Crönert, 267, n. 7). Cf. also from the mag. papp. ῥηθέντα *PGM* 4.730-1 (4th cent.); *PGM* 1.193-4 (4th/5th cent.).

[2] Some gramm. say that the -ε- is retained when πονέω expresses bodily pain. Class. authors, however, seem to use it constantly with -η-, exc. Hp., who fluctuates betw. -η- and -ε- wo. observing this distinction. Forms in -ε- are common from Arist. on, incl. the LXX (Veitch & *LSJ*, s.v.). πονέσαι is attested once in the Ptol. papp. (Mayser i², 2, 131). The MGr. aor. is in -εσα (Thumb, *Handbook*, § 201).

[3] The -η- forms are Ep. and Lyr. (Veitch & *LSJ*, s.v.).

b) ἀρέσκω:

ἤρησα *POxy.* 1893.8 (A.D. 535)
συνήρησεν *PLBat.* xi, 10.14 (6th cent.); *StudPal.* xx, 217.17 (A.D. 580)
but ἤρεσεν *PSI* 82.3 (A.D. 65); *POxy.* 1870.3 (5th cent.); *PLond.* 1380 = *WChr.* 285.19 (A.D. 710/11)
ἤρεσε *PSI* 94.6 (2nd cent.)
ἀπαρέσῃ *PBaden* 19.10-11 (A.D. 110)
ἐὰν ... ἀρέσει *PAntin.* 188.9 (6th/7th cent.)
συναρέσαι *PLond.* 113 (1) (i, 199-204).43 (6th cent.)
συναρεσάσης *PPar.* 21.35 (A.D. 616)
ἀρέσαντα *POxy.* 2110.19 (A.D. 370)
συναρέσαντα *PHermRees* 30.14 (6th cent.)
ἀρέσασαν *PRein.* 102.2 (6th cent.)
συναρέσασαν *PLBat.* xiii, 2.6 (prob. late 4th cent.: *BL* v, 63); *SB* 5174.7 (A.D. 512); *SB* 5175.8 (A.D. 513); etc.

c) καλέω:[1]

παρεκάλησαν *PTebt.* 420.19-20 (3rd cent.)
καλήσω (subj.) *OTheb.* 133.6: *BL* ii, 1, 41 (prob. 3rd cent.)
παρακ[α]λήσω *PAmh.* 154.6 (late 6th/7th cent.)
also ἐγκαλῆσαι *POxy.* 1837.1, with σπουδὲς (for σπουδῆς) 10 (early 6th cent.)
but καλέσαι *POxy.* 1416.2 (ca. A.D. 298: *BL* v, 78)
φιλοκαλέσαι *PApoll.* 32.8 (ca. A.D. 713)
μετεκαλέσω (2 sg. aor. mid.) *POxy.* 1252 R.26 (A.D. 288-95)
φιλοκαλέσητε, φιλοκαλεθῆναι *PApoll.* 31.2,4 (ca. A.D. 713)
cf. also παρεκάλασα *PMich.* 500.7-8 (2nd cent.)

d) μάχομαι:[2]

μαχησάμην (for ἐμαχ-) *PSI* 1430.6 (7th cent.)
but μαχεσθῆναι *PFouad* 79.12-13 (3rd/4th cent.)

e) εὑρίσκω, in which tenses are formed by the addition of -ε/η-, sometimes has the aorist passive in -η- instead of the classical -ε-, especially in the Byzantine period:[3]

---

[1] Cf. ἐκάλησα Ps.-Callisth. (Veitch & *LSJ*, s.v.); ἐγκαλήσηις Ptol. papp. (Mayser i², 2, 131). The MGr. form is κάλεσα (Thumb, *Handbook*, § 120; Mirambel, *Gram.*, 159; Maspero, 129).

[2] The class. aor. is -εσ(σ)- w. fut. -ησ-; aor. -ησ- is late: D.S. Paus. (Veitch & *LSJ*, s.v.; Schwyzer i, 721).

[3] Only forms w. -ε- are found in Magn. inscrr. and in the Ptol. papp. (Nachmanson, 167; Mayser i², 2, 101, 103, 155); but -η- is found in the fut. pass. in Porph. *Gp.* (Veitch, s.v.). The MGr. aor. pass. is εὑρέθηκα/βρέθηκα (Thumb, *Handbook*, § 120; Maspero, 132).

εὑρήθη *PBeattyPanop.* 1.104, with εὑρεθέντα 195, εὑρέθειεν 386 (A.D. 298)

εὑρηθῇ *SB* 8030 = *PMich.* 245.27 (A.D. 47)

εὑρηθείη *PCairMasp.* 328 vii.18, corr. elsewh. (A.D. 521); *PBaden* 55.25 part. rest. (6th cent.); *PLond.* 483 (ii, 323-9).31 (A.D. 616); *StudPal.* iii, 134.5 (Byz.); etc.

cf. εὑριθείη *PMich.* 608.15 (6th cent.)

εὑρηθείησαν *PCairPreis.* 38.8 (4th cent.)

εὑρηθῆναι *PCairMasp.* 297, above line 10 (A.D. 535); *PCairMasp.* 94.12, part. rest., with ε[ὑρ]ηθ[εί]η 14 (A.D. 553)

εὑρηθείς *PCairMasp.* 161.17 (A.D. 566); *PLond.* 1716.15 (A.D. 570?)

εὑρηθέντος *PLBat.* xvii, 10.9 (A.D. 523)

but εὑρέθη *PPar.* 19.12 (A.D. 138); *SB* 7696.47 (A.D. 250); *POxy.* 43 R vi.23 (A.D. 295); *PGrenf.* i, 53 = *WChr.* 131.26 (4th cent.); *PPrinc.* 100.7 (4th cent.); etc.

εὑρεθῇ *POxy.* 36 = *WChr.* 273 ii.10 (2nd/early 3rd cent.)

ε[ὑ]ρεθείη *PSI* 684.13 (4th/5th cent.)

εὑρεθῆναι *StudPal.* iii, 244.2 (6th cent.); *PCairMasp.* 291.9 (6th cent.?)

συνευρεθῆναι *PSI* 98.1 (6th cent.); *PLond.* 1332.5; so duplic. 1333.6 (A.D. 708)

εὑρεθέντα *PCornell* 33.18 (3rd cent.)

εὑρεθη[σο]μένης *PFouad* 35.8 (A.D. 48)

The confusion and partial identification of the sounds represented by the letters ε and η in the speech of many writers of the papyri[1] facilitated the analogical influences at work in these verbs.[2]

b. Denominative -*jo*- stems and analogical formations in -ζω.[3]

1) Stems in -άζω sometimes have -η- instead of -α- for the stem vowel:[4]

ἠναγκήσθην *BGU* 180 = *WChr.* 396.16-17 (A.D. 172)

[ἀ]ναγκήσῃς *PLond.* 242 = *PAbinn.* 48.14-15 (A.D. 346)

ἀπηργήσατο *BGU* 163.9 (A.D. 108)

---

[1] See Vol. i, 242-9, cf. 261-2.

[2] Cf. esp. βαρεθῆναι (*POxy.* 1872.4, above, p. 258), w. η > ε in the ending as well as σε for σῇ also 4 and γεγράφεκα for -φηκα 5,6 part. rest. (late 5th/early 6th cent.), and ἐγκαλῆσαι (*POxy.* 1837.1, above, p. 260), w. η > ε in σπουδὲς for -ῆς 10, etc. (early 6th cent.).

[3] Cf. Palmer, 137-44.

[4] Mayser explains sim. changes of stem vowels in the Ptol. papp. as the result of a confusion of verbs in -ζω with contract verbs within the pres. system (i², 2, 118 and see above, p. 256, n. 2), but such confusion is less freq. in the pres. stem than in other tense stems. The relationship of pres. and aor. stem and their reciprocal analogical influence are discussed in detail by Hatzidakis in connection with the formation of the MGr. pres. (*Einl.*, 390-417 = Excurs ix, 'Zur Präsensbildung im Neugriechischen'; cf. also Jannaris, § 853^(b-c); Thumb, *Handbook*, § 204).

συνεργήσαντας *PLips.* 40 iii.24 (late 4th/early 5th cent.)

ἐ'σ'πούδησα, ἐξήτησα (perh. for ἐζήτησα: *BL* v, 1) *PLond.* 418 = *PAbinn.*
7.11,12 (ca. A.D. 346)

cf. also δοκιμείσας (w. η > ει?[1]) *PFay.* 20.17 (late 3rd/early 4th cent.)

2) Stems in -ίζω also have -η- in the aorist rarely:

κατεχώρησ(α) *SB* 10196.38 (ca. A.D. 180)

ἀπελογησά[μην] *BGU* 266 = *WChr.* 245.6 (A.D. 216/17)

ἐγέμησεν *SB* 1976 (5th cent.)

This is probably an orthographic variation, in view of the widespread identification of η and ι.[2]

c. Stems preserving IE vowel gradation.

The stem vowel of these verbs is modified for the most part as in classical
Greek, but some irregularities occur through levelling of the paradigm.[3]

1) The *e*-grade of the present is sometimes transferred to the second aorist
passive in κλέπτω:[4]

ἐκλέπη *PRyl.* 134.13; 137.11 (A.D. 34); 140.11 (A.D. 36); *PMich.* 581.3
(ca. A.D. 126-8); *POxy.* 2730.6 (4th cent.)

κλεπῇ *POxy.* 472.16 (ca. A.D. 130)

κλεπέντα *BGU* 454.19 part. rest. (A.D. 193)

κλεπέντων *BGU* 322 = *MChr.* 124.27; so duplic. *SB* 6.28 (A.D.
216)

but ἐκλάπη *SB* 7469.4 (A.D. 193)

αἰκλάπη *POxy.* 2274.4 (3rd cent.)

κλαπέ[ν] *SB* 9786.8 (4th cent.)

κλαπέντος *POxy.* 2238.13 (A.D. 551)

κλαπέντ(α) *PAntin.* 190 (b).5, sim. 7,15 (6th/7th cent.)

ἀποκλαπέντα *PAmst.* 1 = *PGron.*, p. 53.14 (A.D. 455)

κλαπ(έντων) *StudPal.* x, 252.14 (6th cent.); *PAntin.* 189.14 (6th/
7th cent.); sim. *BGU* 675 = *StudPal.* viii, 1139.7 (Byz./Arab.)

2) The *o*-grade of the perfect active of πέμπω, e.g., πεπόμφειν *POxy.* 122.5
(late 3rd/4th cent.), is sporadically transferred to the perfect middle, e.g.,

---

[1] δοκιμήσῃς is found in a 2nd cent. B.C. pap. (Mayser i², 2, 118).

[2] See Vol. i, 235-42.

[3] A sim. phenomenon is observed sporadically in denominatives, e.g., εὐτρεπίζω, wh.
shows aor. εὐτροπίσαι *POxy.* 1840.4 (6th cent.), on the analogy of the cognate noun τροπή
and ad'. εὔτροπος.

[4] Cf. from the Ptol. papp. ἐμπλεκείς, ἐκτρεπέντος, etc. (Mayser i², 2, 160-1). The *e*-grade
is used in 1 aor. ἐκλέφθην (Hdt. E.), κλεφ(θέν) *StudPal.* x, 252.10, w. κλαπ(έντων) 14 (6th
cent.).

[ἀν]απεπόμφθαι (or [δι]α-: *BL* i, 7) *BGU* 5 ii.19-20 (ca. A.D. 138); ἀναπεπομμένον *POxy.* 2349.3 (A.D. 70).¹ Conversely, the *e*-grade of the present is extended to the perfect in πέπεμφαν *SB* 3558.3, mummy label (n.d.).

3) Besides the Attic *a*-grade perfect of (δια)φθείρω, the poetic *o*-grade is also found in διεφθόροσι (for διεφθόρασι or διεφθορότα) *POxy.* 2190.11 (late 1st cent.), and διεφθορότα *PLBat.* vi, 15.36,95, with διεφθάρθαι 49-50 part. rest., 70; διεφθαρμένα 64 part. rest., 88,123, ων 83; διαφθαρέντα 49,91 (ca. A.D. 114).

d. Liquid stems.

1) σημαίνω usually has -α- in the aorist active instead of -η- according to classical Attic-Ionic usage, while other verbs in -αίνω, including φαίνω, have only -η-, as exclusively in Attic.² The aorist middle of all these verbs, including σημαίνω, is regular in -η-.

a) σημαίνω:

> ἐσήμανα *BGU* 1208.10 (27/26 B.C.); *BGU* 1097.17 (A.D. 41-68); *POxy.* 1844.12 (6th/7th cent.); *PApoll.* 46.10 (A.D. 703-15)
> [ἐσ]ήμανε *Archiv* v, pp. 381-2, #56.11 (prob. late 1st cent.)
> ἐσήμμανεν *PCairMasp.* 60 = *WChr.* 297.1 (6th cent.)
> σημάνω (subj.) *BGU* 1207.15 (28 B.C.); *PSI* 225.3 (6th cent.); *PLond.* 1791.5, with σημᾶναι 2 (7th cent.)
> σημάνῃς *SB* 7348.14 (A.D. 23)
> σήμανον *PMerton* 62.11 (A.D. 6); *PFay.* 119.20 (ca. A.D. 100); *PSI* 95.13 (3rd cent.)
> σημᾶναι *BGU* 1078 = *WChr.* 59.4-5 (A.D. 39); *PLBat.* i, 13.8 (2nd cent.); *WChr.* 72 = *StudPal.* xx, 33.7 (A.D. 234); *POxy.* 1855.2 (6th/7th cent.); *PGot.* 54.5 (6th/7th cent.); etc.
> σημάνας *PSI* 95.2-3 (3rd cent.)
> σημάνασα *POxy.* 162 = *POxy.* 942.5 (6th/7th cent.)
> but ἐσήμηνα *PLBat.* xvi, 16.3 (A.D. 140)
> σημῆναι *BGU* 1208.10 (27/26 B.C.); *PBeattyPanop.* 2.139 (A.D. 300)

---

¹ The *o*-grade of the pf. act. of τίκτω, e.g., τέτοκεν *PTebt.* 422.18 (3rd cent.), is transferred to the aor. act. in ἔτοκεν *PGM* 36.47,113 (4th cent.).

² In the Ptol. papp., σημαίνω and φαίνω fluctuate betw. -η- and -α- (Mayser i², 2, 132-3). In the NT, even σημαίνω and φαίνω are treated like other verbs in -αίνω w. the aor. act. in -α- (*BDF*, § 72). For the Att. usage, cf. Phryn. 16 & 17 (Rutherford, 76-78); *MS*, 182. ἐσήμανα is found in codd. of X. and in post-class. Gr.: LXX, Str. Arr. Polyaen. etc., while the class. forms in -ηνα are retained in Ion. inscrr. (Veitch & *LSJ*, s.v.; Schweizer, 180; Hauser, 111). The formation w. -α- was generalized in the Koine and is uniform in the Byz.Chron. (Psaltes, 223). ἀνέφηνεν occurs in the mag. papp. in *PGM* 2.82 (4th cent.). MGr. has the -α- formation more freq. than -η-, now -υ- (Thumb, *Handbook*, § 203; Mirambel, *Gram.*, 149; Maspero, 125-6).

ὑπεσημηνάμην *PSI* 471.3 (5th/6th cent.); *StudPal.* viii, 1112.4 part.
rest. (6th cent.)

προεσημηνάμην *PCairMasp.* 151-2.151 (A.D. 570)

ἐπεσημήνατο, ἐπεσημηνάμην *PBeattyPanop.* 2.61,70 (A.D. 300)

κατασημηνάμενος *BGU* 388 = *MChr.* 91 iii.9 (2nd half 2nd cent.)

b) φαίνω:

ἔφηνας *SB* 9399.4 (6th cent.)

ἔφηνεν *PLBat.* xiii, 21.8 (1st cent.)

ἀπέφηνεν *MChr.* 88 ii.15-16 (after A.D. 141); *BGU* 2012.25 (mid
2nd cent.); sim. (-ε) *SB* 7696.108: *BL* iv, 82, with ἀπεφήνα`ν´το
86 (A.D. 250)

ἀποφήνας *PRyl.* 109.7 (A.D. 235)

ἀπεφηνάμην *PRein.* 44 = *MChr.* 82.5 (A.D. 117-38); *PTebt.* 286 = *MChr.*
83.4 (A.D. 121-38); *WChr.* 81 = *PAchmim* 8.28 (A.D. 197)

ἀπεφήνω *POxy.* 1117.6 (ca. A.D. 178)

ἀπεφήνατο *PVindobWorp* 1.19 (A.D. 91-96); *PPhil.* 1.50 (ca. A.D. 103-
24); *POxy.* 706 = *MChr.* 81.6 (ca. A.D. 115); *PLBat.* vi, 24.75,78,
84,89 (up to A.D. 124); *SB* 7264.7 part. rest.: *BL* ii, 133 (2nd
cent.); *PBouriant* 20 = *PAbinn.* 63.25 (A.D. 350); etc.

ἀπεφήναντο *PMilVogl.* 251.4 (2nd cent.); *SB* 7696.86 (A.D. 250)

ἀποφήνη[τα]ι̣, ἀποφηνάσθω *POxy.* 2857.9; 7 part. rest., 14 (A.D. 134)

c) Other verbs:

ἐκοιλάνα̣τ̣[ε] *PTebt.* 484 descr. (ca. A.D. 14)

ἀναξηράναντα *SB* 4416.15 (ca. A.D. 157)[1]

ηὔφρανας *PFlor.* 154 R.12 (3rd cent.)

ἐμηνά[μ]ην *StudPal.* v, 7 i.18 (3rd cent.)

ὑγιανῶ (subj.) *BGU* 954 = *WChr.* 113.13,30 (prob. 6th cent.)

ἐδυσχέρανεν *PLond.* 1007 (iii, 262-4).20 (ca. A.D. 558)

2) αἴρω and its compounds have the aorist active in -α- (when not augmented), as in the Ptolemaic papyri and the New Testament,[2] whereas in classical
Attic the aorist active (except in unaugmented tenses of the simple αἴρω) is
formed in -η-:[3]

---

[1] Cf. also from the mag. papp. ἀνεξήρανας (not ἀνε<κ>ξήρανας w. ed.: *PGM* iii, Index, s.v., p. 56) *PGM* 36.109-10 (4th cent.); ξήρανον *PGM* 13.28 (ca. A.D. 346); κατα-
ξηρά[ναϲ] *PGM* 7.995-6 (3rd cent.).

[2] Mayser i², 2, 133; *BDF*, § 72. Cf. also from the mag. papp. ἄρης *PGM* 52.21 (3rd cent.);
ἄρον *PGM* 12.315 (A.D. 300-50); 61.3 (late 3rd cent.); 4.781 (4th cent.); ἔπαρον *PGM* 5.234
(4th cent.); ἄρας *PGM* 7.914 (3rd cent.); 12.77; 4.899; etc.

[3] Rutherford, *Phryn.*, 76. In the Att. inscrr., the simple αἴρω has -α- in the aor.; only
unaugm. moods are attested (*MS*, 182). -αρα, like -ανα-, is generalized i- the Koine. MGr.
has mainly -αρα (Mirambel, *Gram.*, 148).

ἄρης *PMich.* 202.6 (A.D. 105)
    ἄρη *PHamb.* 89.8 (2nd/3rd cent.)
    ἄρον *BGU* 388 = *MChr.* 91 ii.23 (2nd half 2nd cent.); *PTebt.* 417.34
        (3rd cent.); *PRossGeorg.* iii, 1.18 (3rd cent.); (-ρρ-) *POxy.* 119.10
        (2nd/3rd cent.)
    ἄραι *PJand.* 97.14 (mid 3rd cent.)
    ἄρας *BGU* 22.28 (A.D. 114); *PTebt.* 308 = *WChr.* 319.9 (A.D. 174);
        POxy. 2155.15 (4th cent.); etc.
ἐξᾶραι *PLond.* 177 = *MChr.* 57.21 (A.D. 40/41)

3) The occasional interchange of ει and ι in the aorist of other liquid stems, e.g., ἔκρεινεν *POxy.* 1102.7 (ca. A.D. 146); ἐπέστιλας *POxy.* 2118.2 (ca. A.D. 156), is purely orthographic.[1]

2. Modification of the stem consonant.

a. Velar stems which in classical Attic-Ionic, as opposed to West Greek, normally lost the velar in the formation of the sigmatic tenses,[2] occasionally appear with the velar in these tenses, earlier and much more frequently than the alternative -σ- formation in βαστάζω, later and less frequently than -σ- in ἁρπάζω.

1) βαστάζω.[3]

a) Future and aorist active with -ξ-:

    βαστάξεις *SB* 10278.4 part. rest. (A.D. 98-138); *POxy.* 1705.11 (A.D. 298)
        βαστάξει *POxy.* 1293.42 (A.D. 117-38)
        [β]αστάξετε *PApoll.* 49.4 (A.D. 703-15)
        βαστάξουσιν *PRossGeorg.* iii, 22.5, with aor. subj. βαστάξομεν (for
        -ωμεν) 6 (7th cent.)
    ἐβάσταξα *POxy.* 1973.9 (A.D. 420); *POxy.* 914.8 (A.D. 486)
        ἐβάσταξε *PMich.* 525.23 (A.D. 119-24); *POslo* 156.10 (2nd cent.);
        PMilVogl. 222.10 (A.D. 157-9)
        ἐβάσταξαν *BGU* 769.4 (A.D. 172); *SB* 6952.4 (A.D. 195); *SB* 9238.16
        (A.D. 198-211); *PMerton* 91.14 (A.D. 316)
        βαστάξῃ *PRossGeorg.* iii, 13.6 twice (6th cent.)
            cf. βαστάξουσιν (for -ωσι) *PColt* 134.2 (late 6th cent.)

---

[1] For the identification of ει and ι, see Vol. i, 189-91.

[2] Schwyzer i, 737; Chantraine[2], § 206, 297; Buck, *GD*, § 142.

[3] The mag. papp. have the -σ- formation only in βαστάσας *PGM* 13.24 (A.D. 346), w. 10 occurrences of the velar formation, incl. βαστάξει *PGM* 1.119 (late 4th/5th cent.); βάσταξον *PGM* 4.2487 (4th cent.); *PGM* 1.67; βαστάξας *PGM* 1.178-9, etc.; βαστάξαντες *PGM* 4.2082; ὑποβαστάξας *PGM* 7.526 (3rd cent.); etc.

βάσταξον *PJand.* 22.2 (A.D. 619-29)

βαστάξαι *PFay.* 122.6-7,11 (ca. A.D. 100); *BGU* 454.19 (A.D. 193); *SB* 9867.15 (3rd cent.); *POxy.* 1839.3 (6th cent.); *PLond.* 1346.19 (A.D. 710); cf. *PColt* 74.5 (ca. A.D. 685); 160.5, sim. 6 twice (6th/7th cent.); sim. 75.4 (late 7th cent.); etc.

βαστάξαντες *PBrem.* 40.15,20 (ca. A.D. 117); *PAmh.* 77 = *WChr.* 277.22 part. rest. (A.D. 139); *PGen.* 3 = *MChr.* 122.16 (A.D. 175-80); *PGen.* 47 = *PAbinn.* 47.8 (A.D. 346)

b) Aorist active with -σ-:

ἐβάστασε *PMich.* 423-4.8 (A.D. 197)

ἐβάστασεν *BGU* 195.32 part. rest. (A.D. 161); *PFlor.* 59.7 (A.D. 225/41)

βαστάσῃς *PSI Omaggio* 14.12 (A.D. 712)

βαστασάντων *PLond.* 1387 = *PRossGeorg.* iv, 10.5 (A.D. 710)

c) The aorist passive always has the velar formation:

ἐβαστάχθη *BGU* 46 = *MChr.* 112.10 (A.D. 193)

ἐβαστάχθησαν *PRyl.* 81.6 (ca. A.D. 104)

βασταχθῇ *PHamb.* 192.7-8 (1st half 3rd cent.)

βασταχθ(εισῶν) *POxy.* 522.4 (2nd cent.)

διαβασταγῆναι *PApoll.* 42.7 (A.D. 703-15)

2) ἁρπάζω.

a) Aorist active with -ξ-:

ἥρπαξας *PLond.* 408 = *PAbinn.* 18.11 (ca. A.D. 346)

ἀφήρπαξεν *SB* 9683.4,19 (late 4th cent.)

διήρπαξεν *SB* 9622.8 (A.D. 343); (clearly) *POxy.* 2479.22 (6th cent.)

ἁρπάξα[ι] *PCairMasp.* 205, above line 6 (6th cent.?)

ἀναρπάξαι, διαρπάξαι *PCairMasp.* 2 i.18; iii.20 (A.D. 567: *BL* i, 100)

ἁρπάξας *PFlor.* 36 = *MChr.* 64.11 (A.D. 312)

b) Aorist active with -σ-:

ἥρπασας, ἥρπασεν *PLips.* 40 iii.22,23 (late 4th/early 5th cent.)

ἥρπασεν *PThead.* 15.10,16 (A.D. 280/1); sim. *PStrassb.* 216.7 (A.D. 126/7)

ἀνήρπασεν *PRyl.* 145.15 (A.D. 38); *PRyl.* 119.25-26 (A.D. 54-67); *POslo* 18.3 (A.D. 162); *POxy.* 2187.10 (A.D. 304); *PThead.* 22.8-9 (A.D. 342)

ἀφήρπασεν *POxy.* 37 = *MChr.* 79 i.17 (A.D. 49); *POxy.* 285.10 (ca. A.D. 50); *PIFAO* i, 16.4 (2nd half 1st cent.?); *PLond.* 412 = *PAbinn.* 55.14 (A.D. 351); etc.

ἥρπασαν *BGU* 341.3 (2nd cent.)

ἥρπασαν, ἀφήρπασ[α]ν *PStrassb.* 5.13,15 (A.D. 262)

ἀνήρπασαν *PSI* 281.31 (2nd cent.)

διήρπασαν *PSI* 1102.14 (3rd cent.)

ἀφήρπασαν *PSI* 893.14 (A.D. 315)

    ἀφήρπασαν, ἀφαρπάσαι̣ *PCairGoodsp.* 15.16,17 (A.D. 362)

ἀφαρπάσαι *BGU* 1141.23 (prob. 13 B.C.)

ἁ[ν]αρπάσαι *BGU* 291 = *WChr.* 364.13 (ca. A.D. 170)

διαρπάσαι *PCairMasp.* 77.5 (Byz.)

ἀφαρπάσας *SB* 9150.19 (5th cent.)

    ἀφαρπάσαντες *POxy.* 71 ii.15 (A.D. 303)

c) The perfect middle-passive has the -σ- formation:[1]

συνηρπασμένοι *PRyl.* 119.28 (A.D. 54-67)

ἡρπασμένα *BGU* 759 = *PSarap.* 1.23 (A.D. 125)

d) The second aorist passive with the velar formation is found along with the first aorist passive -σ- formation:[2]

ἡρπάγησαν *BGU* 341.13: *BL* i, 40, with ἁρπασ[θέντας] 12, cf. ἥρπασαν 3 (2nd cent.)

ἁρπαγέντα *PLips.* 40 iii.7 (late 4th/early 5th cent.)

καθηρπασθέν[τα] *PThead.* 23 = *PAbinn.* 44.14 (A.D. 342)

The velar in the sigmatic tenses of βαστάζω and ἁρπάζω, unparalleled in the Ptolemaic papyri and Asia Minor inscriptions[3] but found in late prose,[4] was more likely a new formation rather than a Doric residue.[5] Further confusion of verbs in -ζω with those of other types, including contract verbs, led to a much wider extension of the velar aorist formation in Modern Greek.[6]

b. The velar is retained, as in classical Greek, in other velar stems:[7]

ὑπώρυξαν *PRyl.* 127.11-12 (A.D. 29)

---

[1] The velar form ἥρπαγμαι is found in Paus. (*LSJ*, s.v.). The MGr. pf. ptc. pass. is ἁρπαγμένος (Thumb, *Handbook*, § 210).

[2] The 1 aor. pass. (ἡρπάσθην Hdt., ἡρπάχθην Hdt. D.S.) is normal in class. Gr.; the 2 aor. is late: Lyc. Str. Apollod. NT (along w. 1 aor.) (Veitch & *LSJ*, s.v.; *BDF*, § 76.1).

[3] Mayser i², 2, 133-5; Schweizer, 181; Nachmanson, 163-4.

[4] See Veitch & *LSJ*, s.vv., for reff. to Apollod. J. Ps.-Callisth. etc. βαστάξαι is found in a NT cod. and other velar forms in Byz.Chron. (*BDF*, § 71; Psaltes, 224).

[5] Dor. influence was claimed by Kretschmer, *Entst.*, 117; contrast Hatzidakis, *Einl.*, 134-7.

[6] Cf. MGr. ἄρπαξα, βάσταξα, στήριξα, σπούδαξα, ἄλλαξα, etc. (Hatzidakis, *ibid.*, Thumb, *Handbook*, § 201; Mirambel, *Gram.*, 153-60; Maspero, 130).

[7] No aor. of σαλπίζω is attested. Cf. the variants in the noun σαλπιστής *SB* 4591.3, inscr. (n.d.); σαλπικτῇ *POxy.* 519 = *WChr.* 492.16 (2nd cent.); σαλπικτοῦ, σαλπικτής *BGU* 1074.17,23 (A.D. 275); σαλπιγκ[τοῦ] *StudPal.* xx, 69.1 (A.D. 253-60).

[δ]ιώρυξαν *PMich.* 421.6 (A.D. 41-54)
ὀρύξας, ὤρυξα *SB* 8384.6,13 (A.D. 260-68)
cf. ὠρύγη *SB* 8902.7, inscr. (A.D. 80/81); *SB* 8903.6, inscr. (A.D. 86/87)
καταρήξ[α]ντες *BGU* 36 = *MChr.* 125.11 (A.D. 98-117)
διέρηξεν *SB* 7449.11 (2nd half 5th cent.)
στηρίξαι *PSI* 452.3 (4th cent.)¹
[ἔ]σφαξε *POxy.* 259.33 (A.D. 23)
κατ[έ]σφαξα[ν] *PGiss.* 82.11 (A.D. 117)

3. Insertion of a consonant.

a. Insertion of σ.²

1) σ is inserted only rarely in tense stems in which it is not found in classical Greek.³

a) σ inserted in the future passive:⁴

κλησθήσετα[ι] *POxy.* 1100.10 (A.D. 206)
πιρασ[θ]ήσεσθαι (for πειρασθήσεσθε) *BGU* 1027 = *WChr.* 424 i.11 (late 4th cent.: *BL* i, 88)

b) σ inserted in the perfect middle-passive:⁵

ἐπιμέμνησμαι *POxy.* 791 descr. (ca. A.D. 1)
ἐμπέπρησται *BGU* 890 ii.11 (A.D. 138-61)

c) σ inserted in the perfect active:⁶

διαιγνωσκέναι (for διεγνωκέναι) *SB* 7601 C.12 (A.D. 135)
γεγόνασμεν *BGU* 1198 ii.13 (5/4 B.C.); *PRossGeorg.* iii, 4.18 (3rd cent.)

---

¹ Cf. late aor. ἐστήρισα LXX, *AP*, App.; mid. ἐστηρισάμην Plu. (Veitch & *LSJ*, s.v.).
² For the occasional loss and converse insertion of σ before a dental stop or μ, see Vol. i, 130-1.
³ For the tendency to extend σ throughout the paradigm, see Schwyzer i, 772-3; Chantraine², § 367.
⁴ Cf. the converse omission of σ in ἀποσπαθῆναι *POxy.* 275 = *WChr.* 324.28-29 (A.D. 66) and *PSI* 710.4 (2nd cent.).
⁵ See further below, pp. 305-6. Cf. also the converse omission of σ in πεπειμένοι *PLond.* 1727.22 (A.D. 583/4) and the assimilation of σ in σεσημαμμένης *PMerton* 109.15 (2nd cent.); σεσημαμμένοις *POxy.* 2349.22 (A.D. 70); and κατασεσημημμένα (w. -η- transferred from the aor. mid. or introduced on the analogy of vowel stems) *POxy.* 117.14-15 (2nd/3rd cent.). These forms reflect a tendency of liquid verbs in -ν- to form the pf. mid.-pass. in the Koine in -μμ- instead of the class. Att. -σμ- (*BDF*, § 72; for the Att. usage, cf. *MS*, 185).
⁶ Cf. Schwyzer i, 773; Kapsomenakis, 49.

2) σῴζω only sporadically and doubtfully has -σ- in the tense stems:[1]

σεσῶσ[μ]εϑα *PJand.* 13.7 (4th cent.)
but σέσωμαι *PMich.* 482.26 (A.D. 133); sim. *PMich.* 478.16 part. rest.
(early 2nd cent.)
διεσώϑης *BGU* 615.5,22 part. rest. (2nd cent.); *PMich.* 500.5 (2nd
cent.)
διεσώϑητε *BGU* 332.7 (2nd/3rd cent.)
διασωϑῇ *PMich.* 487.12 (2nd cent.)
σωϑῆγαι *PCairMasp.* 77.12 (6th cent.)
σωϑέντων *PLond.* 1674.58 (ca. A.D. 570)

b. Insertion of μ in tense stems of λαμβάνω.

The -μ- is normally transferred from the present to the future and to the
aorist passive. This represents analogical levelling at least on the orthographic
level,[2] and is paralleled in classical Ionic[3] and widely in the literary and non-
literary Koine:[4]

λήμψομαι *PMich.* 349.8 (A.D. 30); *BGU* 2123.13 (A.D. 85); *PMich.*
184.9 (A.D. 121); *PFlor.* 8 = *MChr.* 355.9 (A.D. 136/8); *POxy.* 1664.12
(prob. A.D. 196-8: *BL* iv, 62); etc.
but λήψομαι *PStrassb.* 218.16 (A.D. 150); etc.
λήμψεσϑαι *PMich.* 555-6.17 (A.D. 107); ἀντι- *POxy.* 1123.9 (A.D.
158/9)
μεταλημψομένοις *PAmh.* 68 — *WChr.* 374.23 part. rest. (A.D. 81-96);
PMich. 554.30 part. rest. (A.D. 81-96); *PLBat.* xvi, 9.23 (A.D.
183); etc.
ἐλήμφϑη *PStrassb.* 5.18 (A.D. 262)
λημφϑέντας *BGU* 372 = *WChr.* 19 ii.11, sim. 22 (A.D. 154)
καταλημφϑέντα *POxy.* 2228.41 (A.D. 285: *BL* v, 81)

4. Change of stem.

a. σκοπέω, used in the best classical authors only in the present and im-

---

[1] σῴζω has pf. pass. w. -σ- in Trag. Com. and Att. prose in general, but σέσωται Pl.;
the aor. pass. is always wo. -σ-, exc. in Hsch. (Veitch & *LSJ*, s.v.).
[2] There appears to have been no diff. in pronunciation betw. forms w. or wo. μ; see
Vol. i, 116-19.
[3] Cf. λάμψομαι and ἐλάμφϑην Hdt. (Veitch & *LSJ*, s.v.).
[4] *Ibidd.*; Schweizer, 179; Crönert, 65-68; Mayser i², 1, 116-17; cf. also λήμψεται *PDura*
19.10 (A.D. 88/89), but μεταληψομένοις *PDura* 18.27 (A.D. 87) and παρα[λ]ήπτου *PDura*
20.5 (A.D. 121).

perfect while forms of σκέπτομαι are used in the other tenses,[1] is sometimes extended to the aorist active and passive in Byzantine documents.

1) Forms of σκοπέω:

ἐσκόπησα *PCairMasp.* 151-2.22 (A.D. 570)
    ἐσκόπησα, σκοπήσας *PRyl.* 712.3,5, with σκ[ο]πεῖν 1 (6th cent.)
    σκοπῆσαι *SB* 9453.2 (5th/6th cent.); *PSI* 1428.2 (6th cent.)
    σκόπησον *PFouad* 85.16 (6th/7th cent.)
    σκοπήσας *PMon.* 6.54 (A.D. 583)
σκοπηθῆναι *PLond.* 1708.189 (A.D. 567?)

2) Forms of σκέπτομαι:[2]

σκέψομαι *POxy.* 602 descr. = *PCairPreis.* 48.6 (2nd cent.)
    σκέψη *PFay.* 116.3 (A.D. 104)
ἐσκεψάμην *POxy.* 1773.13 (3rd cent.); *PGron.* 16.8 part. rest. (2nd half
    3rd cent.); *POxy.* 2228.31 (A.D. 285: *BL* v, 81)
σκέψηται *PErl.* 18.15 (A.D. 248)
ἐπισκέψασθε *POxy.* 533.20 (late 2nd/early 3rd cent.)
ἐπισκέψασθαι *SB* 5232.32 part. rest. (A.D. 14/15); *PCairMasp.* 64.18
    (6th cent.)
σκεψάμενος *PCornell* 50.4 (1st cent.); *PPar.* 19.2 (A.D. 138); *PSI*
    1326.10 (A.D. 181/3); *SB* 7696.104 (A.D. 250); *SB* 8988.37 (A.D.
    647); etc.
ἐπεσκεμμένο[ν] *PLips.* 9 = *MChr.* 211.21 (A.D. 233)
    ἐπεσκεμμένου *PFlor.* 67.43 (A.D. 161/9)
    ἐπεσκεμμένη *PMilVogl.* 98.32 (A.D. 138/9?)

b. ἕλκω continues to form the aorist on the stem ἑλκυ-, as in classical Attic;[3] εἷλξα also occurs:

ἥλκυσα *SB* 8504.3, inscr. (A.D. 226)
ἥλκυσε *SB* 8474.7, inscr. (A.D. 217); *SB* 8487.1, inscr. (A.D. 244)
ἑλκύσῃ *BGU* 822.5 (ca. A.D. 105: cf. *PMich.* 202); *POxy.* 121.20
    (3rd cent.)
[ἑλκ]ύσαι *PLond.* 1260 (*PBeattyPanop.* App., pp. 153-6).14 (late
    3rd/early 4th cent.)

---

[1] So Pi. Trag. Att. prose; other tenses of σκοπέω are first found in Arist. (Veitch & *LSJ*, s.v.).

[2] Cf. also from the mag. papp. σκέψη, σκέψασθαι *PGM* 4.162,223 (4th cent.) and ἐπίσκεψαι *PGMXtn.* 5b.28 (5th cent.); no forms of σκοπέω occur.

[3] This aor. was prob. formed on the analogy of εἴρυσα (Schwyzer i, 721). εἷλξα and εἷλχθην, after the fut. ἕλξω, are found in late poetry and prose (Veitch & *LSJ*, s.v.). The mag. papp. have only ἑκκῦσαι (for ἑλκῦσαι) and ἐφελκυσάμενος *PGM* 13.944,640 (A.D. 346).

ἑλκύσεσθαι *PHermRees* 58.2 (4th cent.)
παρηλκύσθην *PMich.* 493.8-9 (2nd cent.)
[εἰλ]κύσθημεν *PLond.* 1674.15 (ca. A.D. 570)
παρελκυσθέντος *PLond.* 311 = *MChr.* 237.15 (A.D. 149)
but ἐφεῖλξαν *PLond.* 1356 = *WChr.* 254.36 (A.D. 710)
ἕλξω (subj.) *BGU* 1675.20 (prob. 2nd cent.)
ἕλκσετε (for ἕλξητε) *PRossGeorg.* iii, 10.26 (4th/5th cent.)

B. FORMATION OF THE PRESENT STEM[1]

The formation of the present stem by means of standard suffixes is analyzed by Palmer in *A Grammar of the Post-Ptolemaic Papyri*, pp. 122-49. This section will consider alternate thematic present formations based on the same root.

1. Phonetic or analogical variants of the same stem.[2]

a. ἁρμόζω and ἁρμόττω.

ἁρμόζω, a rare formation with the suffix -όζω (cf. δεσπόζω),[3] is the normal present in the Roman period and is still used in the Byzantine; but the Attic ἁρμόττω,[4] which may have arisen on the analogy of πλάττω,[5] predominates in the Byzantine period.

1) ἁρμόζω:

ἁρμόζι *SB* 7599.26 (A.D. 95)
ἁρμόζει *SB* 5673.19-20 (A.D. 147); *BGU* 93.16 (2nd/3rd cent.);
 PCairMasp. 28 = *MChr.* 382.15 (ca. A.D. 551)
ἥρμοζε *PBrem.* 37.9 (ca. A.D. 117)
ἁρμόζαι (for ἁρμόζειν) *PMon.* 1.43: *BL* i, 310 (A.D. 574)
ἐναρμόζοντος *PSI* 1117.38 (2nd cent.)

---

[1] Schwyzer i, 672-737 (mainly word-formation by suffixes); Chantraine[2], § 233-92 (same); Buck, *GD*, § 161-2; *MS*, 174-9; Schweizer, 174-9; Nachmanson, 153-8; Hauser, 107-9; Mayser i[2], 2, 113-20; Crönert, 242-83 passim; *BDF*, § 73. The actual transition of the various classes of athematic presents to the thematic is treated under -μι verbs below, pp. 375-85. Fluctuations betw. contracted and non-contracted pres. formations of the same stem is treated under contract verbs below, pp. 363-5.

[2] For βόλομαι, etc., see Vol. i, 212.

[3] Palmer, 144. Its origin in this word is uncertain (Schwyzer i, 734, n. 2).

[4] ἁρμόττω (Pl. Att. orat.) is the sole form in the Att. inscrr. and is more common in Koine authors; ἁρμόζω appears in Trag., the Perg. inscrr., and some later authors (Veitch & *LSJ*, s.v.; *MS*, 177; Schweizer, 176; Crönert, 135 & n. 3). συνήρ[μο]ζεν occurs in the mag. papp. in *PGM* 7.1002 (3rd cent.).

[5] Schwyzer i, 734, n. 1.

ἀρμοζούσης *PMich.* 231.31 (A.D. 47/48); *PMon.* 1.43 (A.D. 574)

ἀρμοζούσῃ *SB* 5763.48 (A.D. 647)

ἀρμόζοντα *PGiss.* 67.5 (ca. A.D. 117)

ἀρμόζουσαν *BGU* 1120.32 (5 B.C.); *PFlor.* 55.17 (prob. A.D. 88); *PBrem.* 49.4-5 (A.D. 117-38); *PHarris* 68 B.5 part. rest. (A.D. 225) (τοῖς) ἀρμόζουσι *PLond.* 256e = *WChr.* 344.5 (A.D. 11); *POxy.* 485 = *MChr.* 246.33 (A.D. 178); *PMich.* 615.30 (ca. A.D. 259)

ἀρμοζούσας *SB* 4284.16 (A.D. 207)

ἀρμόζεσθαι *PLips.* 27 = *MChr.* 293.26 part. rest. (A.D. 123); *POxy.* 906.7 part. rest. (2nd/early 3rd cent.); *POxy.* 2770.20 part. rest. (A.D. 304); etc.

συναρμόζεσθαι *BGU* 1103.23 (13 B.C.); 1104.24 part. rest. (8 B.C.); *PLips.* 27 = *MChr.* 293.25-26 part. rest. (A.D. 123); sim. *PSI* 921. 30 (A.D. 143/4)

ἀρμοζόμενος *CPR* 20 = *StudPal.* xx, 54 i.16 (A.D. 250); (-μένῳ) *PMich.* 530.24 (3rd/4th cent.)

συναρ[μ]οζόμενα *PLeit.* 12.7 (A.D. 210/11)

2) ἀρμόττω:

[ἀρμ]όττει *PLond.* 1349 = *WChr.* 284.9 (A.D. 710)

ἄρμοττον, ἀρμόττουσαν *PCairMasp.* 151-2.150,274 (A.D. 570)

ἀρμόττ[ουσ]αν *PHermRees* 2.13 (4th cent.)

ἀρμόττοντα *PCairMasp.* 159.23-24 (A.D. 568); *PCairMasp.* 294, above line 26 part. rest. (Byz.)

The reappearance of this Attic form, last attested in the papyri in a literary piece of the second century B.C.,[1] may be attributed to the Atticistic influence of the schools.[2]

b. An analogous fluctuation is found between τινάσσω and a new present formation τινάζω.

1) τινάζω:

ἐκτινάζουσι *SB* 9406.162 part. rest., 236, with τινάσ(σοντες) 264 (A.D. 246)

ἐκτινάζοντα *PBrem.* 61.28 (ca. A.D. 117)

ἐκτινάζοντες *SB* 9410 (3).6,18,21 (3rd cent.)

τινάζ(οντες) *SB* 9413.6 (n.d.)

---

[1] Mayser i², 2, 118.

[2] For the use of ἀρμόττω in the Atticists, see Schmid i, 52 (Polem.), 109 (D.C.); ii, 82 85 (Aristid.); iii, 18 (Phld.), 104 (Ael., both forms); iv, 137, 277 (Philostr.Jun.).

2) τινάσσω:[1]

ἐκτίνασσε *BGU* 827.22 (2nd cent.); *PMilVogl.* 77.13 (2nd cent.)
[τιν]άϛσοντ(ες) *SB* 9386.18 (2nd cent.)
ἐκτιννάϛοντες *PLond.* 1170 V (iii, 193-205).8 (A.D. 258-9)
τινασσό(ντων) *PFay.* 102.1 part. rest., 12 (ca. A.D. 105)

c. κα(ί)ω and κλα(ί)ω.[2]

1) καίω/κάω:

καίειν *OStrassb.* 675.11 (2nd cent.)
ὑποκαίειν *PGiss.* 40 ii = *WChr.* 22.19 (A.D. 215)
κατακαίε[ται] *SB* 9641 V i.12-13 (mid 2nd cent.)
cf. καιομένη *OTait* 2167.5, lit. (7th cent.)
but κάει *SB* 6264.5 (Rom.)
ὑποκαόντ(ων) *PHibeh* 282.13 (late 1st/early 2nd cent.)
καομένους *POxy.* 1453.18 (30/29 B.C.)

2) κλαίω only:

κλαίω *PMich.* 465.10 (A.D. 107)
ἔκλαιε *BGU* 1042.11 (3rd cent.)
κλέων (for κλαίων) *POxy.* 528.8 (2nd cent.); *PGissBibl.* 29.8 (3rd cent.);
 PLond. 1244 (iii, 244).6 (4th cent.); *SB* 9616 R.9 (A.D. 550-8?)
κλαίουσα *PAntin.* 95.10 (6th cent.)
κλαίοντα *PMilVogl.* 24.21 (A.D. 117)
κλέο[ντ]ες (?) *PAntin.* 198.3 (6th/7th cent.)
cf. κλαῖε *SB* 4313.15, inscr. (1st/2nd cent.)

d. σώ(ι)ζω, χρή(ι)ζω. The spellings σώζω and χρήζω (for the older σώιζω and χρήιζω) became normal with the reduction of the long diphthongs to their corresponding simple vowels.[3]

---

[1] Cf. from the mag. papp. τινάσσων *PGM* 6.9 (2nd/early 3rd cent.).

[2] For the interchange of αι and α, see Vol. i, 194-7. κα(ί)ω and κλα(ί)ω represent primary derivatives formed by means of the -*je-*/-*jo-* suffix as substitutions for ancient athematic presents (Schwyzer i, 714; Chantraine², § 268). The phonetic development of the orig. -αϝj- was probably -αϝϝ- > -ᾱ(ϝ)- in the Att. forms as opposed to the normal metath. -αιϝ- in the Ion. forms (Schwyzer i, 266, cf. 272-3). For the uncertainty and appar. fluctuation betw. these forms in Att. lit., see Veitch, s.vv. Only -αι- forms occur in the Att. inscrr. and in the NT, but -α- forms occur in the Ptol. and mag. papp. (κατακάω, παρακάεται, προσπαρακάεται *PGM* 4.1541,1219-20,3070 [4th cent.]; but κλαίοντα *PGMXtn.* 10.36 [6th cent.]) and in Koine authors (*MS*, 178; *BDF*, § 30.1; Crönert, 106-7; Mayser i², 1, 85; i², 2, 119).

[3] See Vol. i, 183-6, w. exx. of χρήζονται, etc.

e. οἶμαι/οἴομαι.

1) οἶμαι, which seems to have arisen from the thematic οἴομαι through lack of sentence stress in its common parenthetical usage,[1] is found considerably less frequently than οἴομαι, and only in the indicative:

a) οἶμαι + infin.: οὐκ οἶμαι ἀγνοεῖν *PBrem.* 6.3 (ca. A.D. 117); possibly also διαφέρειν οἶνται[2] *PCairMasp.* 312.50 (A.D. 567)

b) οἶμαι + acc. with infin.: *PTebt.* 286 = *MChr.* 83.5 (A.D. 121-38); *PMerton* 114.4 (late 2nd cent.); *PRossGeorg.* ii, 43.19 (2nd/3rd cent.); *PBeattyPanop.* 2.227 (A.D. 300); *POxy.* 1833.6 (late 5th cent.)

c) οἶμαι parenthetical: *POxy.* 471.3 (2nd cent.)

d) Other usages: *PSI* 683.17 (A.D. 199); *POxy.* 2597.11 (3rd/4th cent.); *SB* 5314.8 (Byz.)

e) impf. ᾤμην + acc. with infin.: *Archiv* v, pp. 383-4, #73.2 (early 2nd cent.?); *PBeattyPanop.* 2.229 (A.D. 300)

2) The thematic οἴομαι occurs in similar constructions, except parenthetically, and also in the infinitive and participle:

a) οἴομαι + infin.: *PGiss.* 41 = *WChr.* 18.7(-8) (A.D. 117)

b) οἴομαι + acc. with infin.: *BGU* 486.4 (2nd cent.); *POxy.* 1666.2 (3rd cent.); *PAmh.* i, 3a ii.8 = *SB* 9557.19 (A.D. 250-85)

c) οἴομαι + acc.: *PFay.* 20.9 (late 3rd/early 4th cent.)

d) impf. ᾤοντο + acc. with infin.: *PLips.* 41 R = *MChr.* 300.6-7 (2nd half 4th cent.)

e) οἴεσθαι + infin.: *POxy.* 2712.17 (A.D. 292/3)

f) οἰόμενος + acc. with infin.: *PCairMasp.* 97 V d.34 (6th cent.); (-μένων) *PLond.* 358 = *MChr.* 52.13 (ca. A.D. 150)

g) οἰόμενος + infin.: *BGU* 747 = *WChr.* 35 i.10-11 part. rest. (A.D. 139); *PFlor.* 332.8 (2nd cent.); *PCairMasp.* 153.10 (A.D. 568)

---

[1] Schwyzer i, 16, n. 1; 280; 619; 679, n. 7; ii, 534; etc. οἶμαι is usual in Trag. and prevails in Att. prose, excl. in parenthesis; it is common in the Ptol. papp. (incl. in the impf.) and Koine authors. οἴομαι is freq. in Ar., and is found in the Magn. inscrr. and in many Koine authors. Both forms occur in the NT (Veitch & *LSJ*, s.v.; Schweizer, 175; Nachmanson, 155; Mayser i², 2, 119-20; Crönert, 271 & n. 3; *BDF*, § 101, s.v.).

[2] Ὀινται semble avoir été écrit ensuite sur οιονται, ed., n. ad loc.

(-μένη) *POxy.* 898.24(-26) (A.D. 123); *CPR* 19 = *StudPal.* xx, 86.20 (A.D. 330)[1]

(-μενοι) *BGU* 1027 = *WChr.* 424 i.22 (late 4th cent.: *BL* i, 88); *PCair-Masp.* 353.9 (A.D. 569); *PFlor.* 93 = *MChr.* 297.11; so copy *PLond.* 1713.17 (A.D. 569); *PCairMasp.* 311.13 (A.D. 569/70?)

3) Both forms are found in *POxy.* 237 (A.D. 186), with οἶμαι + acc. v.8, οἰόμενος + acc. with infin. vi.14-15; οἰόμενοι + acc. with infin. viii.12.[2]

4) A hybrid form οἰήμην (unaugmented contamination of ᾤμην and ᾠήθην?[3]) is read in *PGot.* 12.7 (late 3rd/early 4th cent.).

f. ἐσθίω/ἔσθω.

1) The normal prose form ἐσθίω predominates:[4]

ἐσθίεις *PMerton* 81.36-37 (2nd cent.)
  ἐσθίει *PFlor.* 127.21-22 (A.D. 256)
  ἐσθίομεν *PCairMasp.* 2 iii.10 (A.D. 567: *BL* i, 100)
  κατεσθίομεν *PLond.* 1674.93 (ca. A.D. 570)
  ἐσθίουσι *POxy.* 1734.4 part. rest., 10 (late 2nd/3rd cent.)
ἐσθείωσιν *SB* 10564.19 (late 1st/early 2nd cent.)
ἐσθίειν (proverbial saying in writing exercise) *POxy.* 1185.10 (ca. A.D. 200)
  κατεστείειν, κατεστείουσιν (for -εσθι-) *POxy.* 58 = *WChr.* 378.6,10 (A.D. 288)
κατεσθιόμενα *PFlor.* 150.6 (A.D. 267)

2) The poetic ἔσθω is rare:[5]

ἔσθω *PMich.* 465.10 (A.D. 107)
  ἔσθουσιν *POslo* 153.15 (early 2nd cent.)
ἔσθειν *PGiss.* 80.6 (ca. A.D. 117)
cf. ἔσθοντα *SB* 5730.4, lit. (4th/5th cent.)

---

[1] Cf. also from the mag. papp. πάρεδρον οἰομένη τὰ σκεύη *PGM* 4.2109-10 (4th cent.).

[2] The first 2 exx. occur in parts of the petition, the third in part of a decree.

[3] So ed. (Zucker), n. ad loc.

[4] Note lack of Hell. contr. in ἐσθίει, ἐσθίειν, etc., opposed to πεῖν < πιεῖν (see Vol. i, 295).

[5] ἔσθω is found in Hom. Alcm. Trag. Com. and later poets and sts. in later prose, as LXX, NT, Plu. Aret. etc., in an inscr. from Cos, and appar. excl. in the Ptol. papp. ἐσθίω is also attested in the same sources as well as in Att. prose: Pl. X. etc., and predominates in the NT (Veitch & *LSJ*, s.vv.; Mayser i[2], 2, 178; Crönert, 255 & n. 3; *BDF*, § 101, s.v.). Both forms are found in the mag. papp.: ἐσθίεις, ἐσθίειν, ἐσθίοντα, ἐσθιέτω *PGM* 4.54; 73; 756-7; 1392,1516 (4th cent.); κατέσθεται *PGM* 5.279 (4th cent.). Both presents are back-formations from ἔσθι, impt. of Ep. pres. ἔδω, i.e., *ἔδ-θι (Schwyzer i, 421; 704, n. 1; 713, n. 6; Chantraine[2], § 265). Both forms have been replaced in MGr. by τρώγω, already used along w. ἐσθ(ί)ω in the NT (*BDF*, § 101, s.v.).

g. Variants of χέω.

χέω occurs both in contracted and uncontracted forms in compounds in the present system.[1] The following variants occur.

1) χύω[2] (a back-formation from κέχυκα, κέχυμαι, ἐχύθην[3] or an orthographic variant of χέω[4]?):

ἐκχύοντες *PMich.* 326.51 (A.D. 48)

2) χοίζω[5] (if related to χέω and not χόω, for which see below, p. 282):

[ἐ]κχοίζουσι *POxy.* 2272.66 (2nd cent.)
cf. ἐκχοεῖσαι *OStrassb.* 677.3,6 (2nd cent.)
]...ἐχοισμένης *SB* 5230.44 (early 1st cent.)

h. ἐθέλω/θέλω.

θέλω is the normal present, but forms of the older ἐθέλω[6] (with orthographic variants) are sometimes found in the Roman period and occasionally in the Byzantine; ἐ- forms also occur outside the present system:[7]

γινώσκιν ἐ[θ]έλω (if not <σ>ε θέλω) *BGU* 948.4 (prob. 4th/5th cent.)
ἠθέλω *PLond.* 418 = *PAbinn.* 7.10 (ca. A.D. 346)
ἐθέλεις *PMerton* 23.8-9 (late 2nd cent.)
οὐκ αἰθέλη (for ἐθέλει) *StudPal.* xx, 223.4-5: *BL* iii, 238 (6th/7th cent.)

---

[1] See below, p. 371.
[2] χύω Aret. Alex.Trall.; χεύω Nic. Opp. Q.S. Nonn. etc.; χύν(ν)ω LXX and usu. NT (Veitch & *LSJ*, s.v. χέω; *BDF*, § 73) and mag. papp.: ἐπίχυννε *PGM* 61.4 (late 3rd cent.); ἐπίχυνε *PGM* 13.369 (ca. A.D. 346). Cf. also the late fut. and aor. χύσω, ἔχυσα (Veitch, *ibid.*; Schwyzer i, 685; Jannaris, § 848). Only χύνω has survived in MGr.
[3] The υ in these systems is the reduced grade of the orig. pres. χέϝω reflected in the Ep. fut. χεύω (cf. Schwyzer i, 685, 740; Chantraine[2], § 244, 275).
[4] For the occ. interchange of ε and υ, see Vol. i, 273-4; cf. προσδυομένων (for προσδεομένων) from the same village archive in *PMich.* 322a.31,42 (A.D. 46).
[5] This same formation ἐκχοίζω is also found in the Ptol. papp. in the pass. 'to be decanted into jars (of wine),' in *PSI* 517.2 (251/50 B.C.) and Suid. (*LSJ*, s.v.).
[6] ἐθέλω is Ep. Ael. and the normal form in class. lit.; θέλω is found in Trag. and in Att. prose mainly after a long vowel (Veitch & *LSJ*, s.vv.). θέλω is found in Ion. inscrr. from the 5th cent. B.C. on (*LSJ*, s.v.; Nachmanson, 155, Anm. 3; Schweizer, 173, Anm. 2), in Att. inscrr. from 250 B.C. on (*MS*, 178), virtually wo. exception in the Ptol. and Herc. papp. (Mayser i[2], 2, 119; Crönert, 131), and invariably in the NT and MGr. (*BDF*, § 101 s.v.; Jannaris, § 722[b]). On the origin of the ἐ- in ἐθέλω and the causes of its loss, see Schwyzer i, 434, 648, n. 3; ii, 491; Jannaris, § 723; *BDF*, *ibid.*).
[7] Cf. also from the mag. papp. [ἐ]θέλεις *PGM* 17b.17 (n.d.); ἐθέλῃς *PGM* 7.407 (3rd cent.); *PGM* 3.190,263 part. rest. (A.D. 300+); 1.103 (4th/5th cent.); and ἐθέλοντα *PGM* 4.2934 (4th cent.), w. more than 60 occurrences of θέλω.

ἐθέλομεν *PJand.* 25.2 (6th/7th cent.)

ἐθέλουσιν *SB* 7436.2 (late 6th cent.)

ἂγ ἐθέλῃς *PMich.* 500.10 (2nd cent.); sim. *PLBat.* i, 20.4 (3rd cent.); *PAlex.* 34.9 (6th/7th cent.)

ἐθέλῃ *PLBat.* xvii, 14.28 (2nd cent.); *PRossGeorg.* ii, 43.21 (2nd/3rd cent.); *PGissBibl.* 30.24 (3rd/4th cent.)

ἐθέλοι *PRyl.* 691.9 (late 3rd cent.)

ἐθέλων *BGU* 1074 = *SB* 5225.6 (A.D. 275); *POxy.* 1469.16 (A.D. 298)

ἐθέλοντας *PCairMasp.* 29.10 (A.D. 548/9?)

cf. ἐθελήσομεν *PSI* 881.7 (6th cent.)

ἐθε[λήσ]ετε *PRein.* 57 = *WChr.* 390.9 (4th cent.)

ἐὰν ... ἐθελήσουσιν sic *PLond.* 971 = *MChr.* 95.12, with indic. ἠθέλησεν 9 (4th cent.)

ἐθελήσο[ντα] *PCairMasp.* 314 iii.5 (ca. A.D. 527)

ἐϑελήσῃς *BGU* 1024 viii.8 (late 4th cent.: *BL* i, 88); *BGU* 3.20-21 (A.D. 605)

ἐθελήσῃ *PAntin.* 92.6, with ἠθελήσῃ 10 (4th/5th cent.); *POxy.* 140 = *WChr.* 438.27 (A.D. 550)

ἐθελήσητε *PLond.* 1912.102 (A.D. 41)

ἐθελήσοις, ἐθελήσαντος *PMichael.* 41.42,62 (A.D. 539/54)

ἐθελήσοιμεν *PCairMasp.* 158.21 (A.D. 568)

ἐθελήσειεν *PLond.* 1727.47 (A.D. 583/4)

cf. also ἐθελοκακεῖν *PCairMasp.* 151-2.216 (A.D. 570)

2. Variants in the reduplication of the present stem.

a. μιμνήσκω appears in several present formations, including the regular μιμνήσκω, e.g., μιμνή[σκει] *PGiss.* 91.2 (ca. A.D. 117) and ὑπομιμνήσκ[ω] *POxy.* 1414.24 (A.D. 270-5); a possible orthographic variant ὑπομημνήκω *PBas.* 16.6 (1st half 3rd cent.);[1] an unreduplicated present middle μνήσκῃ (for μιμνήσκῃ) *PGissBibl.* 25.20: *BL* iii, 69 (3rd cent.),[2] cf. ὑπόμνησκεν *PSI* 1564.13 (4th cent.); a new formation μνημίσκομαι (from μνημ- as in μνήμη and ὑπόμνημα) in μνημίσκεσθαι *PHamb.* 37.4 (2nd cent.) and μνημισκομένην *BGU* 1578.13 (2nd/3rd cent.); and a hybrid ὑπομνημνίσκω *PFlor.* 189.3 (A.D. 257).

b. For the normal γίνομαι, γινώσκω in place of the classical γίγνομαι, γιγνώσκω through assimilation of the velar nasal, see Vol. i, 176.

3. Variants resulting from the addition of a nasal or dental suffix.

---

[1] For the interchange of η and ι, see Vol. i, 235-9; for the occ. loss of σ before a stop, see Vol. i, 130.

[2] Cf. μνήσκομαι in Anacr., a Lyc. inscr., codd. of class. and Koine authors and LXX; ὑπομνήσκω (act.) Orph. Hp. Byz.Chron. (Veitch & *LSJ*, s.vv.; Hauser, 107; Crönert, 269(-70), n. 4; Psaltes, 247). μ(ι)νήσκω is found in M.Gr. (Jannaris, § 996.166; Kykkotis, s.v.).

a. The following compounds of λ(ε)ιμπάνω,[1] without distinction in meaning or usage from corresponding compounds of λείπω, are found in late Roman and Byzantine papyri:[2]

παραλειμπά[ν]ω *PApoll.* 66.5 (ca. A.D. 710-11)

πα[ρ]αλίμπαναι (for -ε ımpt.), πα[ρ]αλιμπάνιν *POxy.* 1191.7-8,20-21 (A.D. 280)

καταλιμπάνειν *PGrenf.* i, 60.46 part. rest. (A.D. 581); *PMon.* 13.47 (A.D. 594); *SB* 5112.50 (A.D. 618?); 5113.16 (7th cent.); 5114.32 (A.D. 613-40); *SB* 5267.6 (Byz.)

παραλιμπάνον (for -ων ptc.) *POxy.* 1101.22 (A.D. 367-70)

ἀπολειμπάνεσθαι *PSI* 180.5 abbrev. (6th/7th cent.); *PSI* 52.21 abbrev. (6th/7th cent.); *PSI* 61.24 part. rest. (A.D. 609); *POxy.* 2420.14 (A.D. 610)

ἀπολειμπανόμενον *PHermRees* 55.2 (4th cent.); sim. *POxy.* 1426.12-13 part. rest. (A.D. 332); *SB* 9152.12-13 (A.D. 492)

καταλειμπανομένων *SB* 9402.8 (6th/7th cent.)

καταλιμπανομένοις *POxy.* 907 = *MChr.* 317.5 part. rest. (A.D. 276); *SB* 8265.4 (ca. A.D. 335-45)

ἀπολιμ[π]ανομένους *PFlor.* 3 = *WChr.* 391.15 (A.D. 301)

b. αὐξάνω/αὔξω.

The usual form in the documentary papyri is the primary present αὔξω, but forms of αὐξάνω appear rarely.[3] The late by-forms αὐξέω and αὐξύνω are not used.[4]

1) αὔξω:

ἐπαύξειν *PSI* 1422.16-17 (3rd cent.)

προσαύξειν *BGU* 1074 = *SB* 5225.6 (A.D. 275)

---

[1] λιμπάνω, formed by the suffix *-°*ne*/o- added directly to ancient presents w. nasal infix (Chantraine², § 254; Schwyzer i, 417, n. 1; 699; 701), is first attested (in compds.) in Sapph. Antiph. E. Hp. Th. etc. It is also found as a simple in Hp. (pass.) and act. in Arat. and Chrys. (impf.). It occurs in compds. in the Att. inscrr. and more freq. in later Gr.: D.H. Plu. Luc. LXX, NT, Ptol. papp., Byz.Chron. (Veitch & *LSJ*, s.vv. the indiv. compds.; *MS*, 176; Mayser i², 2, 185; Schwyzer i, 699; Psaltes, 242). It has not survived in MGr.

[2] Cf. also from the mag. papp. καταλιμπάνων *PGM* 4.55 (4th cent.).

[3] αὔξω is the more freq. form in class. lit., incl. Att. prose, but αὐξάνω is also found in A. E. Hdt. Pi. Ar. Isoc. D. etc. (Veitch & *LSJ*, s.v.). αὔξω is the sole form attested in Att. and Asia Minor inscrr., Herc. papp., Byz.Chron., and w. one exception in the Ptol. papp. (*MS*, 176; Schweizer, 175; Nachmanson, 154-5; Hauser, 107; Crönert, 223, Psaltes, 246; Mayser i², 2, 170). Both forms are found in the NT (*BDF*, § 101, s.v.) and in the mag. papp., e.g., αὔξων *PGM* 12.244 (A.D. 300-50); αὐξόμενος, αὔξεται *PGM* 4.719,2347 (4th cent.); αὐξανομένη *PGM* 7.763 (3rd cent.). αὐξα(ί)νω is used in MGr. (Mirambel, *Gram.* 150; Maspero, 137).

[4] For these by-forms, see Veitch & *LSJ*, s.v.; Crönert, 223, n. 3; Schwyzer i, 700; Psaltes, 246.

συναύξη (for -ειν) *PFay.* 20.16 (late 3rd/early 4th cent.)
αὔξοντα *PCairMasp.* 89 R b.16 (Byz.)
 cf. αὔξων *Archiv* iii, p. 138, #21.2, inscr. (n.d.)
αὔξεται *SB* 7696.105 (A.D. 250)
αὔξονται *POxy.* 1450.21, with αὔξᾳ[ς] 3 (A.D. 249/50)
 cf. ἐπαυξομένας *SB* 8303.9-10, inscr. (A.D. 41-54)

2) αὐξάνω:

αὐξάνε[ι] *PRyl.* 77.36 (A.D. 192)
ηὐξάνοντο *PCairMasp.* 295 iii.15 (6th cent.)

c. δύνω/δύομαι and related forms.

1) δύομαι is found in the documentary papyri in ἀναδύομᾳ[ι] *PLeit.* 5.47 (ca. A.D. 180); ἀνεδύετο *PGissBibl.* 32.6-7 (3rd/4th cent.).

2) The poetic δύνω[1] is found in horoscopes and magical papyri in δύνει *POxy.* 235.15 (A.D. 20-50); δύνων *PGM* 3.136 (A.D. 300+); 4.1645; 36.219; 38.17 (all 4th cent.); δύνοντος *PGM* 4.333; δύνοντα *PGM* 14.2 (2nd/3rd cent.); 4.997,1604-5; 8.74 (4th/5th cent.); 1.311 (late 4th/5th cent.); ἔνδυνε *PGM* 7.271 (3rd cent.).

3) A reduplicated διδύσκω is also found in ἐγδιδύσκειν *PLond.* 1711.27 (A.D. 566-73) and in its draft copy *PCairMasp.* 310 R.9: *BL* i, 449; it is also probably to be restored in the parallel *PCairMasp.* 305.10 (A.D. 568).[2] Palmer suggests that such formations reflect the process by which some verbs in -ύνω were replaced by those in -ύσκω in the transition from ancient to Modern Greek.[3]

d. The normal present is αἴσθομαι, but αἰσθάνομαι occurs twice:[4]

αἰσθέσθωσαν *PGot.* 12.18 (late 3rd/early 4th cent.)

---

[1] For the formation of δύνω by means of a nasal suffix and its partial replacement of δύω in poetry, see Schwyzer i, 696, 698; Veitch & *LSJ*, s.v. δύω. δύομαι is the only form in the Att. inscrr. and in doc. Ptol. papp., and act. & pass. forms of δύω are more common in Koine lit.; but δύνω is retained in several places in the lit. Eudoxus pap., is freq. in Str., and is found in the Byz.Chron. (*MS*, 178; Mayser i², 2, 119; Crönert, 252 & n. 4; Psaltes, 243). δύνω is the MGr. form (Jannaris, § 996.55).
[2] Cf. also from the mag. papp. the fut. pf. ἐνδεδύσ[ε]τε (for -ται) *PGM* 11a.19 (4th/ 5th cent.).
[3] p. 18. The NT ἐνδιδύσκειν (v.ll. -δυδισκ- after verbs in -ισκειν) may be a Doricism (*BDF*, § 73). Forms of -διδύσκειν also occur in the LXX, *Gp.* J. and the Shepherd of Hermas, and in the spelling -δυδισκόμενος in a Delph. inscr. (*ibid.* & *LSJ*, s.v. ἐνδιδύσκω).
[4] αἴσθομαι is rare and sts. dbtfl. in class. authors, as Th. Isoc. Pl. (Veitch & *LSJ*, s.v.), but αἰσθάνομαι, found in Trag. and Com. as well as Lys. Th. Isoc., seems to be of secondary origin (cf. Schwyzer i, 644(-5), n. 5; 700; 701, n. 4; Chantraine², § 255). Only αἰσθάνομαι

αἴσθεσθαι *POxy.* 472.3 (ca. A.D. 130)

αἰσθόμενος *BGU* 249.19 (1st cent.: *BL* i, 32); *BGU* 531 ii.19 part. rest. (both A.D. 70-80: Olsson, #42-43, pp. 125-33)

ἐσθόμενος *PLips.* 35.8 (ca. A.D. 375)

αἰσθόμενον *BGU* 248.17-18 (1st cent.: *BL* i, 32); *BGU* 417.4 abbrev., sim. 16-17 (2nd/3rd cent.)

αἰσθομένη *PMich.* 465.31 part. rest. (A.D. 107); *PRyl.* 114.3 (ca. A.D. 280)

αἰσθό[μενοι] *PLBat.* i, 19.5-6 (2nd cent.)

αἰσθομέγους *SB* 7518.5 (4th/5th cent.)

αἰσθάνομαι *PSI* 297.3 (5th cent.?)

ἐσθανομένοις *SB* 7529.18 (2nd/3rd cent.)

e. Only the classical βαρύνω is used; the Hellenistic βαρέω is not found:[1]

βαρύνηι *SB* 8444.18, with βαρυνομένην 5 (A.D. 98-138)

βαρύνειν *PSI* 1406.9-10 (A.D. 137/41)

βαρύνομαι *POxy.* 298.26-27 (1st cent.)

ἐϰβ[αρ]ύγεσθαι *PLBat.* vi, 15.65 (ca. A.D. 114)

βαρυνομέν[ην] *BGU* 1563.7 (A.D. 68)

f. The anomalous ἀγοράννο (for ἀγοράζω) *POxy.* 2599.13,33 (3rd/4th cent.) might reflect a confusion of the -άνω and -άζω suffixes.[2]

g. The Ionic-Hellenistic present ἀλήθω is alone attested: [ἀ]λήθειν, [ἀ]λήθοντας *POxy.* 908 = *WChr.* 426.26,34 (A.D. 199).[3]

4. Variants arising from late analogical formations connected with the transition of athematic presents to those of the thematic type.

a. μίσγω/μ(ε)ίγνυμι.

---

occurs in the Ptol. papp. (Mayser i², 2, 135), only αἴσθομαι in the mag. papp.: ἔσθη (for αἴσθη) *PGM* 2.58 (4th cent.). The MGr. present is αἰστάνομαι (Schwyzer i, 205).

[1] βαρύνω is used in the pres. and impf. act. in Ep. Lyr. and Att. prose; the pass. is used in Hom. Trag. Com. βαρέω, late exc. in pf., is attested in NT, App. Luc. Ath. (Veitch & *LSJ*, *BDF*, § 101, s.vv.).

[2] Cf. Palmer, 138, 146. The MGr. pres. is ἀγοράζω (Mirambel, *Gram.*, 156).

[3] Forms of ἀλέω are found in Hom. (ϰατ-), Hdt. Pherecr. Th. etc., while ἀλήθω is attested (mostly in the pres.) in Hp. Thphr. D.S. *AP* (Lucillus), etc. (*LSJ*, s.vv.). Only forms of ἀλήθω are found in the mag. papp.: ἄληθε, ἀλήθοντος, ἀληθομένου *PGM* 4.3088,3097,3110 (4th cent.). ἀλέω appears to be a thematic development of an orig. athematic pres. (Schwyzer i, 682), while ἀλήθω is formed by the addition of the suffix -θ-, perh. on the analogy of σήθω (*ibid.*, 703; Chantraine², § 265). The MGr. form is ἀλέθω (Mirambel, *Gram.*, 155).

Both the thematic μίσγω and the athematic μ(ε)ίγνυμι are found in the present:[1]

χαταμίσ[γ]ουσι *POxy.* 2272.30-31 (2nd cent.)

μί[σ]γεσθα[ι] *SB* 5235.12 (A.D. 12)

μιγνύναι *PAmh.* 67.9 (ca. A.D. 232)

μείγνυσθ[αι] *BGU* 372 = *WChr.* 19 ii.2-3 (A.D. 154)

μίσγω is the earlier form,[2] for which the athematic μ(ε)ίγνυμι was often substituted even in Attic prose.[3]

b. ἀνοίγω/ἀνοίγνυμι. ἀνοίγω alone occurs:[4]

[ἀνοί]γεται *POxy.* 1294.11 (late 2nd/early 3rd cent.)

ἀνύγεσθαι *PRossGeorg.* ii, 26.9 (A.D. 160)

This may have been the original form, from which the later Attic οἴγνυμι could be a back-formation.[5] It is likewise the only form found in the Ptolemaic papyri,[6] and is the Modern Greek form.[7]

c. τίνω appears in the regular form τίνω, e.g., ἐκτίνειν *POxy.* 1282.36-37 (A.D. 83); *PMilVogl.* 143.20 (A.D. 147/8); in the phonetically equivalent spelling with -νν-,[8] e.g., ἐκτίννειν *POxy.* 2973.27 (A.D. 103); *PBaden* 22.12 (A.D. 126); *BGU* 896.8 (A.D. 161-9); ἐκτίννιν *BGU* 282.40 (A.D. 161-80); and in the form τινύειν *CPR* 5 = *StudPal.* xx, 10.18 (A.D. 168). This last form, paralleled by

---

[1] Cf. also from the mag. papp. μίσγε, συμμίσγεται *PGM* 4.1910,1980-1;2102,2104,2106 (4th cent.); σμίγων *PGM* 2.83 (4th cent.); etc. This latter form, attested in Thphr. Nonn. and M.Gr. (Jannaris, § 996, s.v.), arose from metathesis (Schwyzer i, 311) rather than by syncope from συμμί(σ)γω (Jannaris, § 136).

[2] μίσγω is used excl. by Hom. and Hdt., and occurs once in Trag. and sts. in Att. and later prose (Veitch & *LSJ*, s.v.; Crönert, 270). Its form is the result of phonetic developments; it may represent a pres. w. the suffix -σκω (Chantraine², § 257; cf. Schwyzer i, 708), or a redupl. pres. *mi-msg-ō (Schwyzer i, 336, 690).

[3] μ(ε)ίγνυμι, found in Simon. Hp. Pi. Th. Ar. Pl. and later authors (Veitch & *LSJ*, s.v.), seems to be a back formation from the aor. ἔμειξα (Chantraine², § 251; Schwyzer i, 697). For the orthography μει-/μι-, of which the latter appears more orig., see *LSJ*, s.v. and Schwyzer i, 771. A later secondary thematic pres. μιγνύω, used by Pi. (impf.) Arist. Damox. etc. and in compds. by Hp. Ar. X. etc. (Veitch & *LSJ*, s.v.), is still used in MGr. (Kykkotis, s.v.). Cf. also from the mag. papp. ἐπιμιγνύων *PGM* 1.30 (4th/5th cent.); περιμίγνυται *PGM* 4.2921 (4th cent.).

[4] So also in the mag. papp., e.g., ἀνοίγει *PGM* 1.101 (4th/5th cent.).

[5] Chantraine², § 251. οἴγω is found in Hes. Hdt. Pi. Trag. etc. and excl. in Att. inscrr. to 347 B.C. It is also found in a Lycian inscr. οἴγνυμι first occurs in Lys. Ar. D. and Att. inscrr. after 347 B.C. (Veitch & *LSJ*, s.vv. οἴγω & ἀνοίγω; *MS*, 191; Hauser, 109).

[6] Mayser i², 2, 188.

[7] Thumb, *Handbook*, § 199; Jannaris, § 996.173.

[8] The orthography fluctuates betw. -νν- and -ν- in several late Gr. formations, incl. forms of τίνω and (ἀπο)κτείνω; cf. Schwyzer i, 697; *BDF*, § 73. For the identification of -νν- and -ν-, see Vol. i, 154-5, 158.

τιννύω in Plu. in the meaning 'pay the penalty,'[1] may represent a transfer of the athematic by-form τίνυμι[2] to the thematic conjugation, in common with the widespread transition of verbs in -νυμι to the thematic conjugation with forms in -νύω, as δεικνύω, ὀμνύω, etc.[3]

d. χόω and variants.

The compound προσχόω appears in the present formation προσχώνουσιν *PRyl.* 653.8, with aor. προσχώσαντας 10 (A.D. 321). This form may represent a similar transfer of the late athematic present προσχώννυμι[4] to the thematic type, either for -χωνύουσι in accordance with the ordinary development of verbs in -νυμι to -νύω,[5] or for -χώννουσι, paralleling the -νν-/-ν- orthographic variation noted above in τίνω.

But the late thematic form of this verb -χωννύω, attested elsewhere in Greek,[6] appears in χωννύ[οντ(ες)], χωννύοντ(ες) *PMilVogl.* 212 ii V.7; ix V.7 (A.D. 109).

For forms of χοίζω. see above, p. 276.

5. Other alternate present formations.

a. σκέπτομαι/σκοπέω.[7]

The present system is normally formed on the stem σκοπε- in the Roman and Byzantine papyri, but σκέπτομαι is also attested.

---

[1] *LSJ*, s.v.

[2] The act. τίνυμι is attested only in post-class. Gr.: D.S. (v.l.) Ps.-Callisth. Olymp., but the mid. τίνυμαι is found in Hom. Hes. E. Hdt. etc.; note also τιννύμενος in App. (Veitch & *LSJ*, s.v.). The compd. ἀποτιννύω is found in the LXX, Ph. etc.; ἀποτ(ε)ίνυμι is attested in inscrr. from Crete and Syros, w. ἀποτίννυμι in Them. J. and Att. inscrr. (*LSJ*, s.v. ἀποτίνυμι).

[3] See -μι Verbs below, pp. 375-8. The reg. τίνω itself prob. represents an earlier (perh. IE) transition of an athematic pres. τίνυμι to the thematic type via -νϝω > -νω (Chantraine[2], § 253; Schwyzer i, 642, 698).

[4] This form is attested in Plb. and J., w. the simple χώννυμι found in Arr. D.C. etc. (*LSJ*, s.vv.; Veitch, s.v. χόω).

[5] See -μι Verbs below, pp. 375-8.

[6] προσχωννύω Thphr., χωννύω Plb. D.S. *Geop.* (pres.) App. Arr. etc. (Veitch & *LSJ*, s.vv.).

[7] σκέπτομαι is rare in Att. in the pres. and impf.; these are supplied by σκοπῶ. It is found more freq. in Plb. and later Koine lit., and in the mag. papp.: σκέπτομαι, σκεπτό-μεν<ος> *PGM* 7.358,332 (3rd cent.), but is not found in the Ptol. papp. or NT (exc. ἐπι-σκέπτομαι, 'to visit') (Veitch & *LSJ*, s.vv.; Mayser i[2], 2, 120; *BDF*, § 101, s.v.; Psaltes, 243-4). σκοπέω may orig. have been an iterative of σκεπτ- (Chantraine[2], § 287). In MGr., σκέπτομαι (popular σκέφτομαι) is used in the meaning 'think,' and σκοπεύω in the meaning 'aim at,' 'intend' (Jannaris. § 875, 996; Kykkotis, s.vv.).

1) σκοπέω:

σκοπῶ *POxy.* 940.5 (5th cent.)
[ἐ]πισκο[ποῦσ]ι̣ν *PAmh.* 68 = *WChr.* 374.25 (A.D. 81-96)
σκόπει *POxy.* 471.142 (2nd cent.)
σκοπεῖν *SB* 9847.10 (2nd cent.); *PLips.* 38 = *MChr.* 97 ii.2 (A.D. 390)
σκοποῦσαν *PCairMasp.* 24 R.28 (ca. A.D. 551)
ἐπισκοποῦμαι *POxy.* 325 = *SB* 10240.14 (A.D. 41); *POslo* 153.26, sim.
16 (early 2nd cent.); *PGiss.* 12.7 (ca. A.D. 117); *PHarris* 106.9 part.
rest. (2nd cent.); *PIFAO* ii, 17.14 (1st half 3rd cent.)
ἐπεισκ[ο]πεῖτε, ἐπισκοπούμετα (for -ται, -μεθα) *SB* 9122.11,12-13
(1st cent.)
ἐπισκοποῦντε (for ἐπισκοπεῖται) *SB* 7660.31 (ca. A.D. 100)
ἐπισκωποῦ *POxy.* 294.31 (A.D. 22); sim. *POxy.* 293.16 part. rest. (A.D.
27); *PGissBibl.* 19.10, with [ἐπ]ισκοπῖτα‹ι› 11 (A.D. 55)

2) σκέπτομαι:

ἐπισκεπτόμενος *PLond.* 1361.3 (A.D. 710)

b. ἕλκω forms the present on the stem ἑλκ-, never ἑλκυ-, as in the following
examples:[1]

διέλκουσι̣ *SB* 7173.15 (2nd cent.)
ἑλκε (for εἷλκε impf. or ἕλκει) *POxy.* 259.28 (A.D. 23)
cf. εἷλκε *SB* 8071.8, poet. inscr. (early 3rd cent.)
παρέλκῃ *SB* 7404.48 = *PLBat.* vi, 24.90 (up to A.D. 124)
ἀνθέλκῃ *PStrassb.* 140 = *PSarap.* 100.9 (early 2nd cent.)
ἕλκε (impt.) *SB* 7452.22, love charm (not later than 3rd cent.)
διέλκειν *BGU* 1120.35 (5 B.C.)
ἕλκουσα *PSI* 909.16, sim. 5 (A.D. 44)
ἑλκ[ο]υσαν, ἑλκο[ύσης] *PTebt.* 383.31, sim. 33 (A.D. 46)
ἕλκοντες *PCairMasp.* 294.12, so duplic. 89 V.13, with ἕλ̣κ̣[εσ]θαι 89
R d.1 (6th cent.)
παρέλκομαι *POxy.* 120 R.15 (4th cent.)
παρέλκητα̣[ι] *MChr.* 88 v.30 (after A.D. 141)
ἕλκεσθαι *PSI* 292.11 (3rd cent.); *PCairMasp.* 283 i.2 part. rest. (before
A.D. 548); *PCairMasp.* 6 R.5 (ca. A.D. 567); etc.
ἐφελκόμενο[ς] *PLond.* 895 (iii, 129-30).11 (ca. A.D. 30: *BL* i, 281)
ἀνθελκόμενος *SB* 4518 = *PBrem.* 3.5 (ca. A.D. 117)
ἐνελκουμένου *PFlor.* 370.14 (A.D. 132)

---

[1] So also in the mag. papp., e.g., ἕλκε (impt.) *PGM* 4.376,537,628 (4th cent.). Cf. ἑλκυ-
as the stem for the formation of other tenses above, pp. 270-1. A later pres. ἑλκύω is found
in Philem. (v.l.) and Tz. (Veitch & *LSJ*, s.v.). In MGr., ἑλκύζω is found (Jannaris, § 868),
along w. ἑλκύω and ἕλκω (Kykkotis, s.vv.; Maspero, 119).

καθελκομένου *BGU* 762.16-17 (A.D. 162-3); *PLond.* 328 (ii, 74-76). 19-20: *BL* i, 247 (A.D. 163); etc.
cf. τῆς ἑλκίστης ἀμάξης (from ἕλκυστος < ἕλκειν) *PCairMasp.* 303.7, sim. 13 (A.D. 553)

c. The late present κρύβω, a back-formation from the second aorist passive ἐκρύβην,[1] is found in the participle κρύβων *PSI* 1266.7 = *PApoll.* 9.8 (before A.D. 704); cf. also εἰσκρύβωμεν *SB* 10709 G.3, inscr. (4th/5th cent.).[2]

d. A periphrastic present appears in εἰμὶ γράφων *PLBat.* xi, 27.13 (3rd/4th cent.).

e. A type of periphrasis for the imperfect occurs with the use of a form of ἔμελλον as an auxiliary followed by the present or aorist infinitive, e.g., ἤμελλα ... γράφειν (= ἔγραφον) *PBouriant* 23.13: *BL* iii, 32 (late 2nd cent.); ἔμελλον ... ἀναβῆναι *POxy.* 936.12-13 (3rd cent.); ἔμελλον ... κινδυνεύειν *PAmh.* 142 = *MChr.* 65.9 (4th cent.). See Kapsomenakis, 25, and Vol. iii, *Syntax*.

C. FORMATION OF THE FUTURE STEM[3]

The tendency towards regularization is reflected in the formation of sigmatic futures in many verbs which had only a contract future (Attic future) in classical Greek, and in the development of some new futures formed on stems of other tenses within the paradigm in verbs in which a future formed on a different stem was used. Some evidence of periphrastic future construction is also found.

1. Replacement of contract futures by sigmatic futures.

a. The contract presents καλέω and τελέω[4] have a sigmatic future formally distinct from the present καλῶ, τελῶ, as commonly elsewhere in post-classical

---

[1] See below, p. 315.

[2] Cf. also from the mag. papp. κρύβε *PGM* 1.146 (late 4th/5th cent.); 4.922,1251,2512 (4th cent.); etc., never κρύπτω in pres. (*PGM* iii, Indices); κρύβω is found mostly in compds. as a v.l. in Hp. and in *Gp.* Sch.E. Conon, LXX (pass.), NT, J. Phlp. Byz.Chron. etc. (Veitch & *LSJ*, s.v.; *BDF*, § 73; Dieterich, 233-4; Psaltes, 244). It is used in MGr. along w. κρύφτω (Kykkotis, s.v.; Thumb, *Handbook*, § 119; Mirambel, *Gram.*, 152; Maspero, 130).

[3] Schwyzer i, 779-89, Chantraine², § 293-301; Buck, *GD* 141-3; *MS*, 179-81; Schweizer, 178-80; Nachmanson, 158-9; Hauser, 109-10; Mayser i², 2, 128-30; Crönert, 225-6; *BDF*, § 74; Psaltes, 216-19; see also now B. Panzer, *Das Futurum des Griechischen: Ein Beitrag zur Struktur und Entwicklung des griechischen Verbalsystems* (Münchener Studien zur Sprachwissenschaft 16 [1964]), 55-73.

[4] These verbs followed parallel paths of development, although orig. of diff. types. καλέω, a disyllabic vowel stem, came to have a contr. fut. identified w. the pres. through

Greek,[1] e.g., καλέσωι *CPR* 12 = *StudPal*. xx, 2.19 (A.D. 93); προσεπιπαρα-
καλέσωι *sic BGU* 249.18 (A.D. 70-80: Olsson, #42, p. 125); ἐνκαλέσειν
POxy. 2349.12 (A.D. 70); τελέσω *PAmh*. 68 = *WChr*. 374.22 (A.D. 81-96);
συνεπιτελέσω *BGU* 237.14 (A.D. 164/5); τελέσομεν *POxy*. 1631.22 (A.D. 280);
ἐκτελέσειν *BGU* 194 = *WChr*. 84.12 (A.D. 177).

b. The sigmatic future is also found sporadically in other verbs of this type
which also form an aorist in -εσα, as ἀλέσω *BGU* 1067.13, sim. 15 (A.D. 101/2).[2]
But others, including ἀπόλλυμι and πίπτω, have only contract forms, e.g.,
ἀπολλῖ (for ἀπολεῖ) *PGen*. 51 = *PAbinn*. 19.10 (ca. A.D. 346);[3] ἐμπεσουμένοις
POxy. 243 = *MChr*. 182.26, sim. 33-34 (A.D. 79);[4] etc.

c. Liquid futures retain the regular contract formation, e.g., μεταβαλοῦμαι
POxy. 512.7-8 (A.D. 173); δεροῦσι *PMich*. 204.9-10 (A.D. 127); ἐρεῖ *BGU* 388
= *MChr*. 91 ii.40 (prob. 2nd half 2nd cent.); καθαρεῖ *PTebt*. 373.10 (A.D.
110/11); ὑπομενοῦμεν *PLond*. 1246 (iii, 224-5).21 (A.D. 345); ἀποφανοῦμαι *SB*
7696.79 (A.D. 250).[5] Only νέμω has a sigmatic future: νεμήσεται *POxy*. 245.10
(A.D. 26) and probably also ναμήσεται *PRossGeorg*. ii, 13.4 (A.D. 54-68).[6]

d. Some polysyllabic verbs in -ίζω also have a sigmatic future, but contract
futures are retained in others, and some verbs fluctuate between the two formations:[7]

---

loss of the intervocalic fut. suffix -σ-, and served as a model for the extension of the contr.
fut. to the *s*-stem denominative τελέω and other verbs, both primary and derivative
(Schwyzer i, 784-5; Chantraine[2], § 295-6; Buck, *CG*, § 127, 390-1).

[1] The sigm. fut. of τελέω is sts. retained in Hom. (-σσ-) and is found in Pi. X. Theocr.,
in codd. of El. D., and in post-class. authors; καλέσω is prob. post-class., but is found freq.
in codd. of Aeschin. D., esp. in compds. (Veitch & *LSJ*, s.vv.). The sigm. fut. of these verbs
is found in Att. inscrr. from the 2nd cent. B.C. on, and is normal in Asia Minor inscrr., the
Ptol. papp. (along w. some contr. forms of τελῶ), and NT (*MS*, 180; Schweizer, 179; Mayser
i[2], 2, 129; *BDF*, § 74.1). Cf. also ἐγκαλέσει[ν] *PDura* 32.13, sim. 14 (A.D. 254), etc., and
ἐγκαλλέσσειν *PDura* 31.12,37-38, w. ἐνκαλέσσῃ 45 (A.D. 204).

[2] For the pres. ἀλήθω, see above, p. 280.

[3] The sigm. fut. ἀπολέσω is Ep. but rare in Att. It begins to appear in the Ptol. papp.
and is used almost excl. in the NT (Veitch & *LSJ*, s.v.; Mayser i[2], 2, 129; *BDF*, § 74.1; 101,
s.v.).

[4] The contr. fut. of this verb originated in a disyllabic stem (Schwyzer i, 784; Chantraine[2], § 295).

[5] The contr. fut. was extended to all roots ending in a liquid or nasal presumably on
the model of the disyllabic roots in -ε preceded by a liquid, as καλε- (Schwyzer i, 784-5;
Chantraine[2], § 296). The contr. fut. of liquid verbs is generally preserved in the Koine
(Schweizer, 179; Nachmanson, 159, Anm. 1; Mayser i[2], 2, 129-30).

[6] The sigm. fut. of νέμω is late: (act.) Longus, (mid.) D.H. Plu. (Veitch & *LSJ*, s.v.).

[7] The contr. fut. of verbs in -ίζω, mostly derivative, was widespread in Att.-Ion. For
its origin and shift of accent, see Schwyzer i, 785; Chantraine[2], § 297. The contr. fut. is used
reg. in the Att. and Asia Minor inscrr. and, w. only dbtfl. exceptions, in the Ptol. papp.;
but the sigm. fut. is the prevailing form in the NT, and is also found in some Atticists (*MS*,
179; Schweizer, 178-9; Nachmanson, 158-9; Mayser i[2], 2, 128; *BDF*, § 74.1; Schmid iv, 595).

ἀπαρτίσω *SB* 4515 = *PBrem.* 63.27 (ca. A.D. 117)
but ἀπαρτειῶ *PHamb.* 70.23 (A.D. 144/5+)
  ἀπαρτιοῦσιν *MChr.* 88 iii.13 (A.D. 141+)
  καταρτιῶμαι (for -οῦμαι: cf. Olsson, #74, pp. 202-5) *POxy.* 1153.19-
    20 (1st cent.)
ἀσφαλίσομαι *PRyl.* 77.40 (A.D. 192)
γνωριεῖς *POxy.* 1024.18 (A.D. 129)
  γνωριεῖται (for -τε) *POxy.* 2185.10 (A.D. 92)
ἐλπίσω *SB* 10269.5 (6th cent.)
ἱματίζω (for -ίσω fut.[1]) *PLips.* 28 = *MChr.* 363.18 (A.D. 381)
καθαρίσομεν *PLips.* 111.12 (4th cent.)
καρπιεῖται (for καρπιεῖται) *POxy.* 265.6 (A.D. 81-95)
συγκομίσω *PTebt.* 591 descr. (late 2nd/early 3rd cent.)
  κομίσε[σ]θαι *PLond.* 445 (ii, 166-7).15 (ca. A.D. 14/15)
but [ἀνα]κομιούμενος *BGU* 179.27: *BL* i, 24 (A.D. 138-61)
μερίσω *BGU* 511 = *WChr.* 14 ii.12 (A.D. 200+)
[ὁ]ριεῖν *POxy.* 2712.16 (A.D. 292/3)
σφραγιῶ *BGU* 86 = *MChr.* 306.38, etc. (A.D. 155) and passim
φροντίσει *PDura* 128 e.1 (prob. ca. A.D. 245)
but φροντιεῖ *PAlex.ined.* 574 (p. 38).1 (Rom.); *POxy.* 1307 descr. (3rd
    cent.); *PBerlZill.* 4.17 (4th cent.)
  φροντιοῦμεν *PMichael.* 11.6 (1st/2nd cent.)
χαρίσομαι *POxy.* 1382.15, Greco-Egyptian literary papyrus (2nd cent.)
  χαρίσεται *PAntin.* 188.19 (6th/7th cent.)
but χαριῇ (2nd sg.) *PHermRees* 1.8 (1st cent.)
    χαριῇι *PBrem.* 9.20 (ca. A.D. 117)
    χαριεῖ *PBaden* 87.7: *BL* ii, 2, 183 (3rd cent.); *PAntin.* 44.13 (late
      4th/5th cent.)
    χαρειεῖς *PMich.* 506.10 (2nd/3rd cent.)
    cf. χαρίεσαι (2nd sg., with -σαι from the pf. mid.[2]) *POxy.* 292.9
      (ca. A.D. 25)
    χαριῖτε (for χαριεῖται) *POxy.* 2351.32-33 (1st hand), with χαρεῖτε 81
      (2nd hand) (A.D. 112)
    χαριεῖσθε *POxy.* 1869.14 (6th/7th cent.)
καταχορίζω (for -ίσω fut.[3]) *PGrenf.* ii, 41 = *MChr.* 183.16 (A.D. 46)
    κατα[χω]ρίσ(ω) *StudPal.* v, 94 = *WChr.* 194.23 (2nd hand), with
      καταχωριεῖ 9 (1st hand) (A.D. 267)
but καταχωριῶ *POxy.* 1420.7 (ca. A.D. 129); *SB* 9049.10 (A.D. 212-17);
    StudPal. v, 82.11 part. rest.; 83.14 part. rest.; 93.7 (3rd cent.);
    etc.

---

[1] For the interchange of σ and ζ, see Vol. i, 120-24.
[2] See below, p. 358.
[3] See fn. 1 above. This doc. has many misspellings wh. point to Eg. interference in
pronunciation.

[κ]αταχωρεῖ (for -χωριεῖ[1]) *PLond.* 306 = *WChr.* 263.15 (A.D. 145)
cf. [κατα]χωρῖν (for -χωριεῖν) *PLBat.* xiii, 22.10-11 (2nd cent.)

e. Verbs in -άζω have only the sigmatic future, including verbs which in Attic or in the Ptolemaic papyri had a contract future, e.g., προσαγο[ρ]άσωι *BGU* 112 = *MChr.* 214.24 (after A.D. 59/60); ἀπαναγκάσεις *PFay.* 122.18 (ca. A.D. 100); ἐκβιβάσω *PHamb.* 4.10 (A.D. 87); ἐργάσομαι *PLips.* 111.12 (4th cent.); ἐτυμάσο (for ἐτοιμάσω) *POxy.* 1299.9 (4th cent.).[2]

f. Conversely, the future of συγκλείω appears as συνκλειοῦμεν *PRyl.* 97.8 (A.D. 139).

2. Replacement of suppletive futures by futures formed on other stems within the paradigm, usually the aorist.[3]

a. The future of φέρω.

1) οἴσω continues to be the normal future, e.g., ἐποίσω *PHamb.* 8.27 (A.D. 136); ἐποίσεις *PLBat.* xi, 8.22 (A.D. 127); εἰσο[ἴσ]ει *PFay.* 124.24 (2nd cent.); οἴσομεν *PBas.* 2.11 (A.D. 190); εἰσοίσουσι *POxy.* 729.6 (A.D. 137); ἐποίσειν *POxy.* 2199.22 (A.D. 123?); διοίσοντος *PTebt.* 288 = *WChr.* 266.11 (A.D. 226).

2) A contract future formed on the reduplicated aorist stem ἐνεγκ- is found occasionally, including in persons in which a formal distinction between indicative and subjunctive exists.

ἐνεγκῶ *PMich.* 494.12 (2nd cent.); *Archiv* v, p. 177, #36.3 (Rom.)
ἐπενεγκῶ *SB* 9388a = *PMilVogl.* 191.14; *SB* 9388b = *PMilVogl.* 192.13 (A.D. 130/1), *PHamb.* 44.7; 45.8 (A.D. 215)
ἐπενεκκῶ *BGU* 223.9 (A.D. 210/11)[4]
ἀνανεγκῶ (for ἀνενεγκῶ[5]) *POxy.* 1757.9-10 (after A.D. 138)
ἀνενεγκῶ *PRyl.* 233.8 (2nd cent.)
κατενεγκῶ *POxy.* 1260.28 (2nd hand), with ἐποί[σ]ω 15 (1st hand) (A.D. 286)
ἐνεγκεῖς *POxy.* 1760.15 (2nd cent.)
ἐπενεγκεῖς *PHamb.* 67 = *PLBat.* vi, 36.9 (A.D. 155)

---

[1] For Hell. contr. of -ιει- to -(ε)ι-, see Vol. i, 295-8.
[2] The contr. fut. is used excl. in -άζω verbs, incl. ἀγοράζω and ἐργάζομαι, in the Ptol. papp. (Mayser i², 2, 128-9).
[3] An additional fut. formed on the aor. stem is found in the mag. papp. in ἀφελοῦμαι *PGM* 5.282 (4th cent.). This form is also attested in late inscrr. and authors, incl. D.H. and Byz.Chron. (Veitch & *LSJ*, s.v.; Psaltes, 218).
[4] For the occ. assimilation of -γκ- to -κκ- in this word, see Vol. i, 171-2.
[5] For false de-augmentation in this verb, see above, pp. 234-5.

κατενεγκεῖς *PMich.* 476.28: Kapsomenakis, 32; 477.42 part. rest.
(early 2nd cent.)
μετενεγκεῖς *POxy.* 1705.12 (A.D. 298)
ἐνεγκῖ *BGU* 822 V.29 (ca. A.D. 105: cf. *PMich.* 202)
ἐπενεγκοῦμε ‹ν› *PFay.* 64.7-8 (2nd cent.); sim. *PHamb.* 80.4-5 (early
3rd cent.)
εἰσενεγκοῦμεν *PFlor.* 21.14 (A.D. 239)
προσενεγκοῦμ[ε]ν *POxy.* 1414.10 (A.D. 270-5)
ἐνεγκοῦσιν *POxy.* 1867.10 (7th cent.)

3) A future built on the stem φερ- itself is found in μεθ᾽ ἡμέρας πλίονας
ἀποφέρωμεν parallel to μεθ᾽ ἡμέρας ὄψωμαι immediately preceding in *PAmh.*
130.13-14 (A.D. 70).

b. The future of ἔχω.

1) The regular ἕξω is normal, even in Byzantine papyri, e.g., ἕξω *PAmh.* 92
= *WChr.* 311.18 (A.D. 162/3); παρέξει *PRyl.* 157.17,19 part. rest., 21 (A.D. 135);
SB 6266 = 6704.19,21,27 (A.D. 538); ἕξειν *SB* 4652.3 (A.D. 305: *BL* v, 93);
PMon. 1.33 (A.D. 574); 7.47 (A.D. 583); ἀνθεξόμενοι *PCairMasp.* 26.23 (ca.
A.D. 551).

2) σχήσω occurs only sporadically: παρασχήσεις *POxy.* 937.24 (3rd cent.);
[π]αρ[ασχ]ήσεσ[θ]αι *PLips.* 41 R = *MChr.* 300.7 (2nd half 4th cent.).[1]

3) A late future σχῶ formed on the aorist stem may be indicated in παρασχῶ ἐνιαυσίως τὸν φόρον *BGU* 303.23 (A.D. 586); παρασχῶ [σοι] ὑπὲρ ἐ[ν]οι-
κίου *PLond.* 113 (6b) = *MChr.* 147.30-31 (A.D. 633); ὁμολογοῦμεν παρασχεῖν
PAmh. 150.26 (A.D. 592).

c. The future of ἔρχομαι.

1) ἐλεύσομαι is normally used, e.g., ἐλεύσομαι *PMich.* 485.17 (2nd cent.);
ἐπελευσόμεθα *BGU* 13 = *MChr.* 265.11 (A.D. 289); ἐπελεύσονται *PMich.*
305.17 (1st cent.); ἐλευσόμενα *POxy.* 489.10,19 (A.D. 117).

2) εἶμι[2] occurs very frequently, usually in the participle in such phrases as
τοῦ εἰσιόντος ἔτους, τῆς εἰσιούσης ἰνδικτίωνος, passim. The indicative also

---

[1] σχήσω was not used even in Att. inscrr. or in the non-literary Koine (*MS*, 180;
Schweizer, 179; Hauser, 109).

[2] The oblique moods of the pres. of ἔρχομαι, as well as the impf. and fut., were generally
replaced in Att. by forms of εἶμι, but ἐλεύσομαι was preferred in later Greek (Veitch &
LSJ, s.v.).

occurs, e.g., εἰς Κόπτον ... εἶμι (rather than εἰμί) *POxy*. 529.16-17 (2nd cent.). The two forms are contrasted in a single sentence in two instances: (συγχωρεῖ) μηδ' ἄλλον ὑπὲρ αὐτοῦ ἐνκαλεῖν μηδ' ἐνκαλέσειν μηδ' ἐπελεύσεσθαι τῷ Ἡρακλείδῃ μηδ' ἐπιέναι αὐτοῦ (for αὐτῷ) "... that neither he nor anyone else on his behalf is accusing or will accuse H. or is proceeding or will proceed against him..." *POxy*. 2349.12-13 (A.D. 70) and τοῖς ἀνιοῦσιν στρατιώταις εἰς Πεντάπολιν (cf. *BL* i, 210) ἀπελευσομένοις εἰς Ἀφρικήν "fur die in die [Pentapolis] marschierenden nach Afrika bestimmten Soldaten" *PLips*. 63.7 (A.D. 388).

3) ἐλθῶ also appears as a contract future in τάχα δὲ ἀξιώσω τὸν πατρῶνά μου ... καὶ ἐν τάχι ἐλθῶ (rather than ἔλθω) πρὸς ὑμᾶς *PLips*. 110.16-18 (prob. 3rd/4th cent.) and ἐὰν εὕρω πλοῖον, ἐλθ[ῶ] ἐν τάχι *PAmh*. 144.13 (5th cent.).

4) ἔρχομαι is also used in a futuristic sense, e.g., *SB* 7356 = *PMich*. 203.8,20 (A.D. 98-117).[1]

σχῶ and ἐλθῶ (and perhaps φέρω) in the examples above may represent the futuristic use of the aorist (and present) subjunctive,[2] connected with the confusion of future and aorist, indicative and subjunctive.[3] Cf. also the use of the subjunctive (present and aorist) with οὐ μή,[4] e.g., οὐ μὴ γράψω, λάβω χεῖραν, φάγω, πείνω *POxy*. 119.4,7,14-15,15 (2nd/3rd cent.).[5]

d. The future of ἐσθ(ί)ω[6] appears as φάγομαι, attested commonly in the Koine,[7] e.g., καταφάγονται *PJand*. 26.23-24,34 (A.D. 98), but the classical ἔδομαι is found again during the Byzantine period, e.g., ἐδόμενοι *PCairMasp*. 2 iii.11 (A.D. 567: *BL* i, 100).[8]

3. A periphrastic future construction by means of ἔχω and the aorist infinitive is found in the following instances:

οὐκ ἔχεις ... ἀκ[οῦ]σαι "You will not hear" *PMich*. 176.12 (early 2nd cent.)

---

[1] See further Vol. iii.
[2] Cf. Mayser ii, 1, 234-5; Ljungvik, *Syntax*, 69, 83, 87; Horn, 124; *BDF*, § 363-4; Jannaris, § 1922; Hatzidakis, 218; Psaltes, 217-18.
[3] See below, pp. 358-9; cf. Dieterich, 243-5; Hatzidakis, 190-3.
[4] Cf. Mayser ii, 1, 233; Horn, 92-93; *BDF*, § 365; Jannaris, § 1921.
[5] The sporadic occurrence of the pres. and aor. stem σπειρ- in the fut. for σπερ-, e.g., σπειρῶ (for σπερῶ) *PHamb*. 68.24 (A.D. 550+), may also reflect a syntactic confusion of aor. and fut. (so Kapsomenakis, 32), but phonological identification of ει and ε before ρ (see Vol. i, 256, 259, 261-2) is more probable.
[6] For the pres. ἐσθίω/ἔσθω, see above, p. 275.
[7] καταφάγομαι already D.; φάγομαι after ἔφαγον :: πίομαι : ἔπιον LXX (along w. ἔδομαι), NT (excl.); cf. also φαγοῦμαι LXX, φαγήσω (dbtfl.) Lib. (Veitch & *LSJ*, s.v. φαγεῖν; Schwyzer i, 780 & n. 9; Chantraine², § 293; *BDF*, § 74.2, 77).
[8] ἔδομαι (short vowel subj.: Schwyzer i, 791) *Il*. Ar.; cf. ἐδοῦμαι Luc. (*LSJ*, s.v. ἐσθίω).

ἐλπίζω ... ὅτι ἑκάτερον ἔχει προβῆναι "I hope ... that both will make
progress" *PGrenf.* i, 64.6-7 (6th/7th cent.)

ὁ θεὸς ἔχει βοηθῆσαι "God will [or "is able to"?] help" *PJand.* 19.4
(6th/7th cent.)

A periphrastic future construction by means of the future of εἰμί and the
present participle is found in ἔσει (for ἔσῃ) χαριζόμενος *PHermRees* 9.11-13
(4th cent.).

The increasingly frequent replacement of the future tense by periphrastic
constructions in the later Koine,[1] mainly by θέλω ἵνα and the subjunctive, led
to the elimination of the future as a morphemic system and its replacement in
Modern Greek by θά (syncopated from θέλω ἵνα) followed by either the present
or the aorist subjunctive,[2] thus introducing a distinction of aspect into the future.[3]

D. FORMATION OF THE AORIST STEM (ACTIVE AND MIDDLE)[4]

The tendency towards regularization is reflected in the use of many secondary sigmatic aorist formations along with the inherited root aorists. Stem
variation is also found in ὤμοσα and ἤνεγκον.

1. Sigmatic aorists are found along with the classical root aorists very frequently in ἄγω and -λείπω, and occasionally in other verbs.[5]

a. ἄγω:[6]

ἦξα *POxy.* 933.13 (late 2nd cent.)
κατῆξα *PLond.* 295 (ii, 99-100).6: *BL* i, 250 (A.D. 118); *PCol.* 1

---

[1] Replacement of the fut. by periphrasis is characteristic of the Byz.Chron. and later
authors (Dieterich, 246; Psaltes, 216-18; Jannaris, App. iv).

[2] Thumb, *Handbook*, § 225; Mirambel, *Gram.*, 120, 125-6; Maspero, 86, 96, etc.

[3] Cf. Chantraine[2], § 301. θέλω + aor. infin. in a fut. sense is found in ἀποθανῖν θέλι
(for ἀποθανεῖν θέλει) "he will die" *PMichael.* 39.10, sim. 13-14 (Byz.). See also P. Bur-
guière, *Histoire de l'infinitif en grec* (Etudes et Commentaires 33 [Paris, 1960]), 117-224,
229-30.

[4] Schwyzer i, 739-56, 763-4; Chantraine[2], § 178-84, 193-208; *MS*, 181-4; Schweizer,
180-84; Nachmanson, 162-7; Hauser, 111-15; Mayser i[2], 2, 131-45; Crönert, 231-6; *BDF*,
§ 75; Psaltes, 219-25.

[5] For the adoption of the athematic sigm. aor., orig. partly factative, as the 'normal'
formation of the Gr. aorist, and its extension throughout the Gr. language at the expense
of the thematic root aor., see Schwyzer i, 754; Chantraine[2], § 204-5.

[6] Cf. also from the mag. papp. ἦξας, ἦξεν *PGM* 4.2934;2449,2942 (4th cent.); ἄξῃς
PGM 4.400; 7.907,914 (3rd cent.); ἄξητε *PGM* 4.1457, etc.; ἄξατε (impt.) *PGM* 7.611;
but ἠγάγομεν *PGM* 12.406 (A.D. 300-50); ἀγάγῃς *PGM* 5.185 (4th cent.); 1.291 (4th/5th
cent.); ἄγαγε *PGM* 7.476 (3rd cent.); ἐξαγαγόντα *PGM* 4.3048 (4th cent.) The sigm. aor.
of ἄγω is found already in Hom. (thematic) and Hes., but is rare in class. Gr. (Veitch &
LSJ, s.v., & esp. Rutherford, *Phryn.*, 215-21). It is freq. in the Koine (Mayser i , 2, 144;
Crönert, 232, n. 2; *BDF*, § 75; Psaltes, 219).

R 4 iii.8, sim. vi.7 (A.D. 155); *SB* 7515.32, sim. 71,117, etc. (A.D. 155)

συνῆξας *PLond.* 1357 = *WChr.* 298.6 (A.D. 710)

ἦξεν *SB* 9066 i.22 (A.D. 138-61); *SB* 6222.32 (late 3rd cent.)

κατήξαμεν *BGU* 81.20-21 (A.D. 189)

διήξαμεν *PCairMasp.* 158.23 (A.D. 568)

κατῆξαν *PGrenf.* ii, 44.11 (A.D. 101); *BGU* 607.15 (A.D. 163)

ἄξω (subj.) *PGiss.* 27 = *WChr.* 17.9 (A.D. 115: *BL* v, 34)

διάξω *POxy.* 1666.22 (3rd cent.)

συνάξητε *PApoll.* 26.12 (A.D. 713)

ἐνάξοιμι *PCairMasp.* 163.31 (A.D. 569)

σύναξαι (for -ε, 2 sg. impt.) *POxy.* 1866.5 (6th/7th cent.)

συνάξατε *PApoll.* 9.12 (before A.D. 704)

ἄξαι *POxy.* 1864.12 (7th cent.); cf. *Archiv* v, p. 393, #312.4, mag. (A.D. 131)

ἀνάξαι *POxy.* 707.23 (ca. A.D. 136); *PRyl.* 427 frag. 14.7 (A.D. 198-209?); *PCairMasp.* 97 R.37 (6th cent.); etc.

ϛυνάξας *POxy.* 1414.21 (A.D. 270-75)

διάξας *PCairMasp.* 89 V.2, so duplic. 294.3, with συνδιήγαγεν 4 (6th cent.)

ἄξασθαι *PGiss.* 57.6 (6th/7th cent.)

but προσήγαγον *POxy.* 125.6 (A.D. 560)

[μ]ετήγαγον *BGU* 614.18 (A.D. 217)

π[ρο]σήγαγες *PCairMasp.* 156.20-21 (A.D. 570)

ἐ[π]ήγαγεν *POxy.* 2111.7 (ca. A.D. 135)

συνδιήγαγεν *PCairMasp.* 294 (duplic. of 89 V).4 (6th cent.)

ἄγαγε *PCairMasp.* 282.7 (6th cent.?)

μεταγαγεῖν *POxy.* 244.3 (A.D. 23)

ἀπαγαγεῖν *POxy.* 1468.25 (ca. A.D. 258)

καταγαγεῖν *BGU* 92 = *WChr.* 427.14 (A.D. 187); *POxy.* 144 = *MChr.* 343.12 (A.D. 580)

ἀναγαγεῖν *PAmh.* 154.7 (late 6th/7th cent.)

ἀγαγών *PRossGeorg.* ii, 43.24 = *PLBat.* xvii, 14.31 (2nd cent.?)

ἐπαγαγών *BGU* 45.11 (A.D. 203); *PBon.* 22 a1.11 (6th/7th cent.); etc.

ἐπαγαγόντες *POxy.* 2234.12-13 (A.D. 31)

ἀγαγόντων *PCairMasp.* 2 iii.10 (A.D. 567: *BL* i, 100)

προσαγαγόντων *PThead.* 13 i.4-5 (A.D. 322/3)

ἠγαγόμην *PCairMasp.* 155.10 (6th cent.?)

b. λείπω (compounds):[1]

κατέλειψα *BGU* 1141.17 (prob. 13 B.C.); *PGiss.* 69.6 (A.D. 118/19);

---

[1] Cf. also from the mag. papp. καταλείψης *PGM* 4.710 (4th cent.); καταλείψη *PGM* 3.632, w. ἐκλιπεῖν 349 (after Λ.D. 300); καταλείψας *PGM* 2.182 (4th cent.); but καταλιπών *PGM* 3.260 (after A.D. 300); *PGM* 4.1391 part. rest., w. -οῦσαν 2480 (4th cent.). The sigm.

sim. *PRossGeorg.* iii, 1.18 (A.D. 270: *BL* iii, 156); *PGiss.* 35.9 (ca. A.D. 285/6)

κατέλειψεν *PLond.* 177 = *MChr.* 57.6 (A.D. 40/41); *CPR* 102.11 (1st/2nd cent.); *POxy.* 2563.36-37 (ca. A.D. 170); *PCairIsidor.* 64.5,6 (ca. A.D. 298); *POxy.* 131.23 (6th/7th cent.)

καταλίψω (subj.) *SB* 7260 = *PMich.* 121 R II ii.6 abbrev. (A.D. 42); *PMich.* 321.13,15 (A.D. 42)

   καταλίψης *POxy.* 2153.22 (3rd cent.); *POxy.* 120 V.6-7 (4th cent.); etc.

   καταλίψη *PMich.* 322a.20 (A.D. 46); sim. *SB* 9373.8 (2nd cent.)

ἀπολιψάτω *SB* 1068 (n.d.)

καταλεῖψαι *PMilVogl.* 61.10-11 (2nd cent.); *BGU* 164.13 (2nd/3rd cent.); *PMon.* 11.50 (A.D. 586); etc.

καταλείψας *BGU* 467.6 (A.D. 177)

   παραλείψας *SB* 7520.22 (A.D. 710); *PWürzb.* 20.10 (Arab.)

but κατέλιπον *PStrassb.* 226.11 (A.D. 90-91); (δι-) *BGU* 747 = *WChr.* 35 i.7 (A.D. 139); (κατ-) *PMich.* 501.16 part. rest. (2nd cent.)

ἐνκατέλιπε *POxy.* 281 = *MChr.* 66.21-22 (A.D. 20-50); sim. *SB* 10476.4 (5th/6th cent.)

παραλίπης *PBaden* 37 = *PSarap.* 90.19 (prob. A.D. 108)

προλιπῖν *PMich.* 586.11 (ca. A.D. 30)

   προλιπεῖν *BGU* 586.16 (A.D. 302: *BL* i, 54); (ἀπο-) *POxy.* 472.47 (ca. A.D. 130); (κατα-) *POxy.* 705 = *WChr.* 407.74 (A.D. 199/200?: *BL* ii, 96)

ἀπολιπών *SB* 7568 = *PMich.* 232.5 (A.D. 36); (κατα-) *PMich.* 525.10 (A.D. 119-24); *PTebt.* 326 = *MChr.* 325.6 (A.D. 226); *PMich.* 602.14 (late 3rd cent.); etc.

c. Other verbs.

1) αἱρέω:[1]

   [ἀ]φῄρησαν *PCairIsidor.* 77.17-18 (A.D. 320)
     ἀναιρῆσαι *PAmh.* 142 = *MChr.* 65.8 (after A.D. 341)
     αἱρήσασθαι *BGU* 315.12 (Byz.)
   but ἑλών *POslo* 155.17 (2nd cent.)

---

aor. of λείπω is found in Ar. (frag. 965 = Antiph. 32), but elsewh. only late: (compds.) Plb. Str. etc.; (simple) Ptol. Luc. etc. (Veitch & *LSJ*, s.vv.; Rutherford, *Phryn.*, 343 [p. 468, but discussed on p. 217]). This sigm. aor. is not found in the Att. or Asia Minor inscrr. (*MS*, 183; Schweizer, 183; Nachmanson, 165), but is found in the Ptol. papp. in the 1st cent. B.C. and in the NT (in both only in the compd. κατα-) and early Xtn. lit. (Mayser i², 2, 138; *BDF*, § 75). It is the M.Gr. form (Jannaris, § 996.152; Mirambel, *Gram.*, 152; cf. Psaltes, 220).

[1] ἥρησα Q.S. Byz.Chron. (Veitch & *LSJ*, s.v.; Psaltes, 220). Cf. also from the mag. papp. ἀφαιρήσας *PGM* 13.66,576 (ca. A.D. 346), but ἀνεῖλεν *PGM* 4.2450-1 (4th cent.).

ἕλοιτο *SB* 7033 = *PPrinc.* 82.14 (A.D. 481)
ἀφελέσθαι *POxy.* 237 vii.41 (A.D. 186); etc.; for additional exx.,
see below, pp. 344-5.

2) ἁμαρτάνω:[1]

ἡμάρτησα *PGissBibl.* 30.20 (3rd/4th cent.); *PLond.* 1914.27 (A.D. 335?)
ἁμαρτῆσαι *PCairMasp.* 24 R.37 (ca. A.D. 551)
but διήμαρ[τ]ε *POxy.* 473 = *WChr.* 33.6 (A.D. 138-60)
ἁμαρτεῖν *PPhil.* 32.18 (late 1st cent.?)
διαμαρτεῖν *PRyl.* 624.9 (A.D. 317-23)

3) βιόω:[2]

συνεβίωσα *POxy.* 281 = *MChr.* 66.6 (A.D. 20-50); *POxy.* 282 = *MChr.*
117.4-5 part. rest. (A.D. 30-35); *PRyl.* 659.5 (A.D. 320: *BL* iii, 163)
cf. ἐβίωσεν and sim. frequently on mummy labels and tombstones,
e.g., *SB* 1190.1; 1191.3 (3rd cent.); 6123 (Rom.); etc.
βιώσας *PFay.* 19.12, with βιῶναι 13, letter of Hadrian (2nd cent.)
βιώσασα *PThead.* 19.13 (A.D. 316-20: *JJP* ii, 60)
βιωσάντων *PCairMasp.* 295 i.18 (6th cent.)
ἀπεβιώσατο *PLond.* 1708.84 (A.D. 567?)
but ἐβίω *SB* 6135.3, mummy label (n.d.)
βιῶναι *PFay.* 19.13: see βιώσας above; *PCairMasp.* 283 i.14 (before
A.D. 548); *PCairMasp.* 2 iii.23 (A.D. 567: *BL* i, 100); *PCairMasp.*
352 V.6 (6th cent.)
and also ἐπέζησεν *PFlor.* 61 = *MChr.* 80.48 (A.D. 85)
ἐπέζωσε (for ἐπέζησε) *PFouad* 75.10 (A.D. 64)
cf. ἔζησεν *SB* 34.2; sim. 175.9, inscr. (late 2nd cent.: *Hermes*
43, 560)
ἔζησα[ν] *PHamb.* 89.5 (2nd/3rd cent.)
ζήσω (subj.) *POxy.* 937.5 (3rd cent.)
ζῆσαι *PCairMasp.* 2 iii.14, with βιῶναι iii.23 (A.D. 567: *BL* i, 100);
PCairMasp. 151-2.66 (A.D. 570)
ζήσας *SB* 173.6, inscr. (ca. A.D. 200); *SB* 3982.2, inscr. (n.d.)
ἐπιζήσας *PGissBibl.* 46 x.1 (early 3rd cent.)
ἐπιζήσαντι *POxy.* 493 = *MChr.* 307.3,6,8,11 part. rest. (early
2nd cent.)

_____

[1] ἡμάρτησα Emp. (dbtfl.) *AP* (Pall./Luc.) D.S.; ἥμαρτον Thgn. Pi. Att. etc. (Veitch
& *LSJ*, s.v.).
[2] ἐβίωσα is found in Hdt. Pl. X. Arist. etc., but ἐβίων is preferred by earlier writers
(Veitch & *LSJ*, s.v.). ἔζησα is also class. (Hp. etc.), ἔζωσα Hdt. Both ἐβίωσα and ἔζησα
are found elsewh. in the Koine (Hauser, 114-15; Crönert, 247, 257; Psaltes, 224).

4) γαμέω:[1]

  ἐγάμησες *PHamb.* 88.4: *BL* v, 40 (mid 2nd cent.)
  ἐγάμησ[εν] *PRossGeorg.* iii, 10.12 (4th/5th cent.)
  γαμήσῃ *PMich.* 243.5 (A.D. 14-37); (clearly) *SB* 6266 = 6704.18
    (A.D. 538)
  γαμῆσε (for -σαι) *PSI* 967.17 (1st/2nd cent.)
  γαμῆσαι *SB* 7253 = *PMich.* 221.16 (ca. A.D. 296)
  ἡ γαμήσασα *PAmh.* 152.12 (5th/early 6th cent.)
but ἔγημα *PCairPreis.* 2.6 (A.D. 362)
  ἔγημον (for ἔγημαν), ἔγημεν *PLond.* 1708.43,163 (A.D. 567?)
  γῆμαι, τ[ῆς γ]ημαμ[έ]νης *PLips.* 41 R = *MChr.* 300.5; 9, sim. 11
    part. rest. (2nd half 4th cent.)
  γήμαντα *PHeid.* 237.18 (mid 3rd cent.: *BL* v, 43)

Both aorist formations are found in *BGU* 1210 (mid 2nd cent.), with γῆμαι
(23).70 & (49).133; γήμαντες (48).132, etc.; ἔγημ[εν] (51).136; γαμ[ῆ] (45).123;
and γαμήσῃ (29).86.

5) γινώσκω:[2]

  γνώσας, ἀνέγνοσα *POxy.* 1874.6,8 (6th cent.)
  γνώσωμεν *POxy.* 1937.7 (6th/7th cent.)
but ἀνέγνων *POxy.* 1188.28 (A.D. 13); *BGU* 1079 = *WChr.* 60.8-9 (A.D.
    41); *BGU* 136 = *MChr.* 86.27 (A.D. 135); *PPar.* 69 = *WChr.* 41
    i.8,10, etc. (A.D. 232)
  παρανέγνων *PCairMasp.* 324.12 (6th cent.)
  ἔγνωμεν *BGU* 1073 = *MChr.* 198.14 (A.D. 275)
  γνῶ (subj.) *PFlor.* 156.6 (3rd cent.)
    ἀναγνῶσι *POxy.* 1837.2 (early 6th cent.)
  γνῶθι *PFay.* 110.16 (A.D. 94)
    ἀναγνώτω *PFlor.* 61 = *MChr.* 80.24 (A.D. 85)
  γνῶναι *POxy.* 1865.12 (6th/7th cent.)

6) διδράσκω:[3]

  ἀπέδρασεν *PLond.* 1465 descr. (8th cent.)

---

[1] Cf. also from the mag. papp. γαμήσῃ *PGM* 5.330 (4th cent.); γαμῆσαι *PGM* **73.4**
(2nd cent.). ἐγάμησα 'gave in marriage' is found in Men., 'married' in Luc. D.S. LXX, NT,
Byz.Chron. (Veitch & *LSJ*, s.v.; *BDF*, § 75; Psaltes, 220).

[2] The simple ἔγνωσα is first found in the Koine, but the compd. ἀν- 'induce,' 'persuade,'
is Ion.: Hdt. (Veitch & *LSJ*, s.vv.; Schwyzer i, 756). ἀνέγνωσα is found once in the Ptol.
papp. and 5 times in the Byz.Chron. (Mayser i², 2, 140; Crönert, 248, n. 2; Psaltes, 220).

[3] Cf. also from the mag. papp. ἀποδράσας *PGM* 4.2152 (4th cent.), w. δραμεῖν 2320,
δραμόν (for δραμών) 2904, and ἔδραμες *PGM* 62.5 (late 3rd cent.). This sigm. aor. is found
as a v.l. in some class. authors (X. etc.) and in late Gr. (Ael. etc.) (Veitch & *LSJ*, s.vv.;
Psaltes, 220).

ἀποδρᾶσαι *PLond.* 1393 = *SB* 7241.5 (Arab.)
ἀποδράσαντος *PMich.* 515.3 (late 3rd cent.)
  δράσαντα *POxy.* 1423.6-7 (4th cent.)
but ἀπέδρα *POxy.* 298.5 part. rest. (1st cent.); *POxy.* 472.21 (ca. A.D. 130); *PFay.* 203 descr. = *PCairPreis.* 1.6 (2nd cent.); cf. also on late tombstone inscrr. *SB* 7906.7 (5th cent.); 7428.11 (A.D. 857: *BL* v, 100); *SB* 6035 = 8765.10-11 (A.D. 1181); etc.
ἀνέδραμεν *PLond.* 1730.9 (A.D. 585)
[δ]ιαδρᾶναι *BGU* 1147 = *MChr.* 103.30 (13 B.C.)
ἀποδράντος, ἀποδράντων *POxy.* 1415.5,6 (late 3rd cent.)

7) εὑρίσκω:[1]

εὑρήσῃς (or = εὑρήσεις?) *PMich.* 511.20 (1st half 3rd cent.)
  εὑρήσῃ *PSI* 177.10 (2nd/3rd cent.)
but ηὗρον/εὗρον, etc. passim (for examples, see above, pp. 240-1, and below, p. 343)

8) ἔχω (converse of σχῶ as future: see above, p. 288):[2]

παρέξας *BGU* 48.8 (2nd/3rd cent.?: *BL* i, 11)
  cf. ἔξωσιν (subj.) *PMur.* 116.8 (1st half 2nd cent.?)
  ἀνέξασθαι *PJand.* 96.12 (3rd cent.)
but ἔσχον, etc. passim (for examples, see below, p. 342)

9) κράζω:[3]

προέκραξεν *BGU* 1141.48 (prob. 13 B.C.)
  ἔκραξεν *PLond.* 113 (11b) (i, 224).2 (6th/7th cent.)
ἀνακράξαντες (for -άντων) *BGU* 1201.11 (A.D. 2)

10) λαμβάνω:[4]

ἐλάβ⟦ασ⟧εν *PRossGeorg.* iv, Anh. (p. 100).6 (A.D. 619-29)
  λαβῆ[σ]αι (or λαβῆ[ν]αι with Kapsomenakis, 91, n. 2: *BL* iii, 133) *POxy.* 937.18 (3rd cent.)
but ἔλαβον, etc. passim (see examples below, pp. 341-2).

11) πυνθάνομαι:[5]

πεύσασα *PCairMasp.* 5.7 (ca. A.D. 567)
but ἐπυθόμην *BGU* 424.6 (2nd/3rd cent.)

---

[1] This sigm. aor. is found in Man. and Sch.A. (Veitch & *LSJ*, s.v.).
[2] This sigm. aor. is not attested elsewh.; ἔσχησα is a f.l. in Nonn. (*LSJ*, s.v.).
[3] This sigm. aor. is late and rare: Thphr. etc. (Veitch & *LSJ*, s.v.).
[4] Forms of ἔλη(μ)ψα are found sporadically in Koine authors (Veitch, s.v.; Crönert, 266, n. 3; Psaltes, 222-3).
[5] Cf. opt. πεύσαιντο Byz.Chron. (Psaltes, 221).

ἐπύθετο *BGU* 82.9 (A.D. 185); *BGU* 893.26 part. rest. (2nd/3rd cent.)
πυθοῦ *PFlor*. 61 = *MChr*. 80.47 part. rest. (A.D. 85); *PFlor*. 194.10
   (A.D. 259)
πυθέσθαι *POxy*. 930 = *WChr*. 138.12-13 (2nd/3rd cent.); etc.

12) φέρω:[1]

   ἄ[π]οισον *PLBat*. xvi, 31.4 (A.D. 149)
   but ἤνεγκον etc. passim (see below, pp. 338-40)

13) χαίρω:[2]

   ἐχάρησα *PMich*. 464.19 (A.D. 99)
      cf. ἐχάρισα (for -ησα) *SB* 1524.2-3, sim. 5-6, inscr. (4th/6th cent.)
      χαιρησάμενοι *BGU* 747 = *WChr*. 35 ii.3 (A.D. 139)
   but ἐχάρην *SB* 6823.3 (A.D. 41-54); *SB* 7660.7 (ca. A.D. 100); *PMich*.
   474.2 (early 2nd cent.); *BGU* 332.6 (2nd/3rd cent.); *PAmh*. 145 =
   WChr. 53.17 (ca. A.D. 400); etc.

The substitution of sigmatic aorists in many verbs for the classical thematic aorists reflects a tendency to extend the more common aorist formation at the expense of the less common and so to regularize the aorist with the future and other tenses of most verbs. This is the converse of the tendency of verbs with contract futures in classical Greek to form a sigmatic future on the model of the aorist. This mutual influence of future and aorist led to the frequent interchange of endings between these tenses[3] and to the occasional substitution of one tense for the other (if not simply misspellings in the endings), e.g., ἵνα μὴ ... παρέξονται *BGU* 1655.41-42 (A.D. 169); ἵνα ἀποδώσι (for -σει), ἵνα ... γενέσοντε (for γενήσονται) *PLond*. 1917.16,21-22 (ca. A.D. 330-40).[4]

2. The aorists of ὄμνυμι/ὀμνύω[5] and φέρω show stem variation.

a. The normal ὤμοσα (for examples without the temporal augment, see above, p. 232) is spelled with a stem vowel -α- in these instances:[6]

   ὤμασα *SB* 10293.26 (A.D. 198); *POxy*. 1265.26 (A.D. 336); *SB* 8951 =
   PSI 1341.20 (2nd hand), 21 (3rd hand) (5th cent.)
   ὄμασα *PStrassb*. 42 = *WChr*. 210.18 (A.D. 310)
   ὠμάσαμεν *POxy*. 2767.25-26 (A.D. 323)

---

[1] ἀνοῖσαι is prob. in Hdt.; οἶσαι is found in codd. of Ph. (*LSJ*, s.v.).
[2] ἐχαίρησα occurs in Plu. (Veitch & *LSJ*, s.v.), but I have not found ἐχάρησα elsewh.
[3] See below, pp. 332-4.
[4] For further exx., see Horn, 124.
[5] For the transfer of -μι verbs to the thematic -ω conjugation, see below, pp. 375-85.
[6] For stem variation in the pf. of this verb, see below, p. 305.

b. The reduplicated aorist ἤνεγκον/ἤνεγκα[1] is spelled in various ways. The variations reflect phonological changes rather than inherited dialectal forms.[2] They all represent the one spoken form /enik-/. These variations, with references to examples and interpretation in Volume I: *Phonology*, are as follows:

1) ενενκ- (Vol. i, 170)

2) ενεκ-/ενικ- (Vol. i, 116)

3) ενειγκ- (Vol. i, 256)

4) ενιγκ-/ενινκ-/ενιγ- (Vol. i, 250)

5) ενηγκ-/ενηκ-/ενηχ- (Vol. i, 246)

6) ενεκκ- (Vol. i, 171-2)

E. FORMATION OF THE PERFECT STEM[3]

Considerable variation is found in the formation of the perfect stem of individual verbs, especially in competing -κ- and root perfects, aspirated perfects, and perfects formed by Attic reduplication. There is also an increasing tendency for the simple perfect to be replaced by periphrastic constructions.

1. -κ- perfects.

A late Greek -κ- perfect is used more frequently than the older aspirated perfect in γράφω, and several older, partially dialectal, -κ- perfects are found along with the root perfect in τυγχάνω, δείδω, πείθω, ἀκούω, and ἀπόλλυμι.

a. γράφω:

> διαγεγράφηκεν *OTait* 450.1 (A.D. 19); *OWilb-Brk.* 5.1 (A.D. 20); *WO* 7.1 (A.D. 26); *OStrassb.* 119.1 (A.D. 43); *Archiv* v, p. 170, #1.1 (A.D. 63); etc.
> γεγράφηκα *PFuadCrawford* 6.22 (3rd cent?); *BGU* 1035 = *WChr.* 23.14 (5th cent.); *SB* 9138.4 (6th cent.); *PApoll.* 26.2 (A.D. 713); etc.
> γεγράφηκας *PAlexGiss.* 48.3 part. rest. (ca. A.D. 120); *PJand.* 103. 7 part. rest. (6th cent.); sim. *PWürzb.* 21 A.16 (2nd cent.)

---

[1] For the variation in 1st and 2nd aor. endings, see below, pp. 338-40.

[2] For dialectal ἐν(ε)ικ-, see Schwyzer i, 744-5; Chantraine[2], § 184; Buck, *GD*, § 144a.

[3] Schwyzer i, 764-79; Chantraine[2], § 209-32; Buck, *GD*, § 146-8; *MS*, 184-6; Schweizer, 184-8; Nachmanson, 159-62; Hauser, 115-18; Mayser i[2], 2, 145-55; Psaltes, 229-33.

γεγράφηκεν *PRossGeorg.* iii, 15.2,3 part. rest. (6th cent.); *PGot.*
29.2 (6th/7th cent.); *BGU* 605.1 (7th/8th cent.); *PApoll.* 69.
12 (A.D. 703-15); etc.

γεγραφήκαμεν *PLond.* 1332.18; 1333.21 part. rest. (both A.D.
708); 1354.15 (A.D. 710)

γεγραφήκασι *PFay.* 117.27 (A.D. 108)

γεγραφήκειν[1] *BGU* 1141.28 (prob. 13 B.C.)

[ἐ]γεγραφήκεις *PMich.* 489.5-6 (2nd cent.)

καταγεγραφηκέναι *PCairGoodsp.* 13.3 (A.D. 341); *SB* 5174.3 (A.D.
512); 5175.2-3 (A.D. 513); *PMon.* 4-5 V.8 (A.D. 581); *PPar.* 21.19
(A.D. 616); etc.

γεγραφηκώς *POxy.* 1666.4 (3rd cent.)

but γέγραφα *PMich.* 340.78 (A.D. 45/46); *SB* 4224.35 (A.D. 138-61);
PCairMasp. 60 = *WChr.* 297.6 (6th cent.); etc.

γεγραφέναι, ἀντιγεγραφέναι *POxy.* 2199.14,17-18 (A.D. 123?)

γεγραφέναι *PAberd.* 30.12 (ca. A.D. 139); *SB* 9387.9 (2nd/3rd
cent.); etc.

καταγεγραφέναι *PBerlZill.* 6.19 (A.D. 527-65); *PMon.* 9.29 (A.D.
585); etc.

διαγεγραφώς *SB* 5673.13 (A.D. 147)

This late perfect of γράφω, found frequently already in the Ptolemaic papyri
and elsewhere in the Koine,[2] probably arose, as Mayser suggests, on the analogy
of decomposita in -γραφέω, although these decomposita are only infrequently
used in the perfect, e.g., κεχειρογραφηκέναι *BGU* 5 ii.13 (ca. A.D. 138); *PFlor.*
6.18 (A.D. 210). It represents a further extension of the -κ- perfect formation,
with the -η- as a formative element, to a consonantal stem.[3]

b. τυγχάνω:[4]

τετεύχηκα *POxy.* 2343.9 (ca. A.D. 288); *PLond.* 412 = *PAbinn.* 55.15
part. rest. (A.D. 351)

but παρατε[τε]υχέναι *Archiv* ii, p. 125 b.11, sim. 24 (A.D. 124/5)

τετευχυῖαν *POxy.* 91.19 (A.D. 187)

παρατετευχότα *POxy.* 113.14 (2nd cent.)

ἐπιτετευχότας *BGU* 332.6 (2nd/3rd cent.)

---

[1] For the omission of temp. augm. in the ppf., see above, p. 224.

[2] Veitch & *LSJ*, s.v.; Mayser i², 2, 150; Crönert, 248(-9), n. 3; Psaltes, 231.

[3] For the origin of the -κ- perfect within Gr. and its extension from the sg. of verb
stems in long vowels and diphthongs (cf. the three -κ- aorists) to the pl. and subsequent
transfer to consonantal stems, see Schwyzer i, 765, 774-6; Chantraine², § 224, 230-1.

[4] τετεύχηκα is intrans. in Hom. and both intrans. and trans. in Att.; it occurs earlier
than the aspirated pf. τέτευχα (D. etc.) which became freq. in later Gr. (Veitch & *LSJ*, s.v.).

c. The -κ- perfect participle of δείδω, rare in classical prose,[1] is found along with δεδιώς:

δεδοικώ[ς] *BGU* 361 iii.6 (A.D. 184)
but δείδω *PMerton* 81.32 (2nd cent.)
δεδειώς *PCairMasp.* 312.9 (A.D. 567)
[δεδ]ι̣ότες (?) *PCairMasp.* 9 R.8 (6th cent.)

d. The -κ- perfect of πείθω, in accordance with classical usage,[2] is used in the sense of "persuade," "satisfy," etc., while πέποιθα is used in the intransitive present sense of "trust," "be confident of":

πέπε[ι]κάς με ἀργυρίωι *SB* 5231.2 (A.D. 11); sim. *SB* 5247.3 part. rest. (A.D. 47)
but πέποιθα *PHermRees* 8.14 (4th cent.)
[ὡς βοηθη]θήσεται παρ' αὐτοῦ πέποιθεν *POxy.* 1101.19 (A.D. 367-70)
τῇ ἑαυτοῦ δυνάμι πε[πυ]θώς *PGen.* 3 = *MChr.* 122.20-21 (A.D. 175-80)

e. ἀκούω occurs in a variant of the Doric and Laconian ἄκουκα[3] along with the regular ἀκήκοα formed by Attic reduplication:

ἤκ[ου]κα *PGissBibl.* 31.21-22 (4th cent.)
but ἀκήκοα *POxy.* 2273.7 part. rest.: *BL* iv, 64 (late 3rd cent.); *PCairMasp.* 89 V.28 (Byz.)
ἀκηκ[ο]έναι *PRossGeorg.* ii, 43.19-20 = *PLBat.* xvii, 14.26-27 (2nd cent.)
ἀκηκοότος *PBrem.* 48.11 (A.D. 118)
τοῖς ... ἀκηκωάσι *sic SB* 7404.69-70 = *PLBat.* vi, 24.105 (up to A.D. 124)

f. (ἀπ-)όλλυμι:[4]

[ἀπο]λελωκέναι *sic* (transitive) *POxy.* 1716.12-13 (A.D. 333)
ἀπολωλεκέναι *PLips.* 35, above line 15 (ca. A.D. 375)

---

[1] Veitch & *LSJ*, s.vv. This verb was gradually replaced by φοβοῦμαι, which alone survives in MGr. (Jannaris, § 968).

[2] Veitch & *LSJ*, s.v.

[3] ἄκουκα also occurs in Plu., and a pass. ἤκουσμαι in D.H. Anon.ap.Demetr. and perh. Luc., and as a compd. in J.; a late Ion. ἀκήκουκα is found in Hdt. (Veitch & *LSJ*, s.v.). ἠκουκέναι, orig. read in *POxy.* 237 vii.23 (A.D. 186), is better taken as ἠνυκέναι: *BL* i, 318.

[4] This -κ- perfect is attested in Antiph. Hdt. Lys. Th. Ar., ppf. D. v.l. (Veitch, s.v. ὄλλυμι).

but ἀπολωλένα[ι] (intransitive) *POxy*. 486 = *MChr*. 59.32 (A.D. 131); sim. *PCairMasp*. 166.18 (A.D. 568)

ὀλωλότα *POxy*. 1873.7, highflown style (late 5th cent.)

ἀπολωλότων *StudPal*. v, 6.21 (3rd cent.)

Note. In the perfect of γίνομαι, both γέγονα and γεγένημαι are used, as in Attic,[1] without distinction in meaning. γέγονα is alone used in some formulae, e.g., γέγονε εἴς με in subscriptions to contracts, but both forms are used in parallel constructions, e.g., ἐδήλωσεν γεγονέναι σε ἐπιτ(ηρητὴν) μισθ(ώσεως) *PMeyer* 3.12 (A.D. 148); ὅπως κουράτωρ γεγένηται *PBouriant* 20 = *MChr*. 96 ii.13-14 (A.D. 350).[2]

2. Aspirated perfects.

a. The perfect εἴρηκα appears frequently in an aspirated form εἴρηχα, but the regular -κ- forms are equally common:

εἴρηχας *PFay*. 111.9 (A.D. 95/96); *SB* 4293.6 (Rom.)

εἴρηχες *PMich*. 510.7-8,23 (2nd/3rd cent.); *PMich*. 514.12 (3rd cent.)

ἤρηχες, ἤρηχεν *BGU* 261.17,22 (ca. A.D. 105: cf. *PMich*. 202)

εἴρηχε, εἴρηχεν *PFay*. 123.19-20,22 (after A.D. 110: *BL* iv, 29)

    εἴριχε *SB* 9249.12, with εἴρικε 7 (2nd/3rd cent.)

    ἴρηχε *BGU* 597.23 (A.D. 75)

εἴρηχαν *BGU* 595.13 (ca. A.D. 70-80)

but ἴρηκα *BGU* 843.11 (1st/2nd cent.); *PSI* 829.13 (4th cent.?)

εἴρηκα *PMich*. 492.19 (2nd cent.)

εἴρηκας *PSI* 974.8, with εἴρηκα 16 (late 1st/early 2nd cent.)

    εἴρηκες *SB* 9276.6 (1st/2nd cent.); *POxy*. 2149.8, with εἴρηκα 24 (2nd/3rd cent.); *POxy*. 2599.9,17,23,31,33 (3rd/4th cent.)

εἴρηκε *PFay*. 109.3 (early 1st cent.)

εἰρήκασιν *PHermRees* 25.13 (5th cent.)

These aspirated forms, too frequent to be merely orthographic variants,[3] are not attested elsewhere in Greek. They may have arisen on the analogy of εἴληφα and εἴληχα, and represent a further extension of the aspirated perfects proper to Attic-Ionic.[4]

Note. In the middle, forms of εἴρημαι usually serve as the perfect of λέγω,

---

[1] Veitch & *LSJ*, s.v.

[2] See further exx. in Preisigke, *WB*, s.v.

[3] There is only an occasional interchange of aspirated and voiceless stops intervocalically (see Vol. i, 90-95).

[4] These were formed in class. times from the 3rd pl. pf. mid.-pass. in -φαται/-το, -χα-ται/-το, often to express a resultative sense (Schweizer i, 771-2; Chantraine[2], § 228-9).

as in the best Attic, in the meaning "say," e.g., ὡς εἴρηται *POxy.* 2479.9 (6th cent.); 1843.9 (6th/7th cent.); 1864.8 (7th cent.); etc.; ὡς ἀνείρηται *SB* 7619 = *PRein.* 103.6 (A.D. 26); *PFlor.* 81.5 (A.D. 103); ὁ προειρημένος *POxy.* 1257.15 (3rd cent.); τὰ ἀπειρημένα *PAmh.* 77 = *WChr.* 277.8 (A.D. 139); *BGU* 786 ii.4 (2nd cent.); etc. But forms of λέλεγμαι are also used in the same sense, as well as in the meaning "collect."[1]

b. λαμβάνω forms the perfect regularly in εἴληφα, e.g., παρείληφα *PStrassb.* 247.18 (A.D. 551); παρείληφαν (for -ασι) *BGU* 153 = *MChr.* 261.17 (A.D. 152); εἰληφέναι *PMich.* 194.11 (A.D. 61); παρειληφότα *POxy.* 1102.8 (ca. A.D. 146). But sporadic alternative formations are found, as ἔλαμφα in π[αρ]ελάμφαμεν παρά σοι *SB* 4661.14 (Byz.).

c. λαγχάνω rarely appears in the Attic perfect εἴληχα,[2] e.g., τῶν ... εἰληχότων *POxy.* 1186.5 (4th cent.). It is normally found in divisions of property contracts in the poetic-Ionic and Hellenistic perfect λέλογχα (with orthographic variants):[3]

λέλογχα *PMich.* 318-20.1, sim. 3,5 (A.D. 14-37); sim. *PMich.* 323-5.29, 32,34 (A.D. 47)

λέλογχεν *PMich.* 317.5 (A.D. 14-37)

λελόνχασι *PSI* 903.19 (A.D. 47)

λέλονχαν *PMich.* 323-5 (duplic. of *PSI* 903).19 (A.D. 47)

λελογχέναι *PTebt.* 382.5,10 (prob. 30-27 B.C.: *BL* iii, 242); *PTebt.* 383.14,19 (A.D. 46); *BGU* 1037.24 (A.D. 48: *BL* i, 90); *PMich.* 557.10 (A.D. 116); *POxy.* 1637.11,13,24 (A.D. 257-9); *PLips.* 26.7 part. rest. (early 4th cent.); etc.

λελονχέναι *PSI* 697.7 (2nd cent.); *PFlor.* 50.25,63 (A.D. 268); *PStrassb.* 29.8,36 (A.D. 289); etc.

λελοχέναι *PCairMasp.* 313.30 part. rest., 33, with λελογχέναι 53,64 (6th cent.)

λελογχυῖης *PFlor.* 50.3 (A.D. 268)

d. A new aspirated perfect is dubiously attested for πιπράσκω in [πέπ]ραχα *PThead.* 3.4 (A.D. 299); πέπραχες *SB* 9194.7 (late 3rd cent.); and πέπραχεν *SB* 5357.5 (n.d.). The regular -κ- perfect is found elsewhere, e.g., πέπρακα *BGU* 1079 = *WChr.* 60.16 (A.D. 41); πέπρακες *SB* 9017 (8).8 (1st/2nd cent.); πεπρακότα *BGU* 1078 = *WChr.* 59.2-3 (A.D. 39).

---

[1] For exx., see reduplication above, p. 247. Cf. also from the mag. papp. προείρηται *PGM* 13.441 (ca. A.D. 346); προήρηται *sic PGM* 37.18 (4th cent.); προειρημένα *PGM* 1.296 (4th/5th cent.); τὰ ... εἰρημένα *PGM* 4.737 (4th cent.); etc.

[2] εἴληχα is used reg. in Trag. and Att. prose, and is the only form in the Att. inscrr. (Veitch & *LSJ*, s.v.; *MS*, 185).

[3] λέλογχα is found in Ep. Lesb. Dor. & late Att. prose (Veitch & *LSJ*, s.v.).

e. Other aspirated perfects are regular, e.g., μετηλλαχότος *BGU* 577.12 (A.D. 201/2); πεπομφέναι *PRein.* 116.3 (3rd cent.); συντεταχέναι *POxy.* 106 = *MChr.* 308.6 (A.D. 135).

3. Perfects formed by Attic reduplication.¹

In addition to ἀκήκοα and (ἀπ-)όλωλα, which also appear in -κ- forms,² a non-Attic perfect ἀγείοχα (with orthographic variants) is used in place of ἦχα, ἐλήλυθα is preserved in its regular form, and ἀλήλιφα, ἐνήνοχα, and ὀμώμοκα are found with frequent variations.

a. ἀγείοχα, variously spelled ἀγίοχα, ἀγείωχα, ἀγίωχα, ἠγείωχα, ἀγέωκα, etc., all phonetically equivalent orthographic variants of the earlier ἀγήγοχα, reduplicated like ἀγαγεῖν,³ replaces ἦχα as the normal perfect of ἄγω as elsewhere in the Koine:⁴

ἀγείοχα *POxy.* 283.14 (A.D. 45)
    παραγείωχα *StudPal.* xxii, 3.5 (2nd cent.)
        [παραγεί]ωχα, παραγέωκα *StudPal.* xxii, 4 ii.6; iii.5-6 (A.D. 127/8)
    εἰσηγείωχας *SB* 7579.5 (A.D. 99/100?)
ἀγείοχεν *SB* 9050 i.5 (1st/2nd cent.)
    ἐπαγείωχ(εν) *PLBat.* vi, 25.4 (A.D. 129)
ἀγίωχαν *SB* 6611 = *PLBat.* vi, 20.27 (A.D. 120/1)
ἀγιωχέναι *PPhil.* 1.39 (ca. A.D. 103-24)
    καταγειοχέναι *PLips.* 105 = *WChr.* 237.17 (1st/2nd cent.); *PLips.* 106.17 (1st/2nd cent.); *SB* 7515.265,322,649 abbrev. (A.D. 155)
    καταγιωχέναι *PTebt.* 470.6 (A.D. 111-13); sim. *PCol.* 1 R 4 i.6-7; vii.8-9; ix.10-11 (A.D. 155)
ἀναγιοχότας *BGU* 2060.13 (A.D. 180)

b. ἐλήλυθα is found in its regular forms, e.g., ἐλήλυθα *BGU* 27 = *WChr.* 445.6 (2nd/3rd cent.); *PCairMasp.* 89 V.22 (Byz.); ἐληλύθαμεν *POxy.* 1881.13 (A.D. 427); ἐπεληλύθασι *PMich.* 422.23 (A.D. 197); προσεληλυθέναι *POxy.* 1667.9-10, sim. 14 (3rd cent.); διεληλυθότει *PMich.* 341.6 (A.D. 47).

---

¹ Cf. reduplication above, p. 248.
² See above, p. 299-300.
³ The spelling ἀγήγοχα (= Dor. ἀγάγοχα) is still found in the Ptol. papp. (along w. various spellings wo. the 2nd intervocalic γ), as well as in Asia Minor inscrr. and some Koine authors (Veitch & *LSJ*, s.v.; Mayser i², 2, 104-5; Schweizer, 171, 186; Crönert, 243, n. 1). For the origin of this and sim. perfects formed by Att. redupl., see Schwyzer i, 650, Zus. 3; 766; Chantraine², § 212.
⁴ ἦχα is retained in Plb. and Stob., but the pf. w. Att. redupl. is much more freq. in other authors and in the non-literary Koine (*ibidd.* and Schmid iv, 602, for D.C. and Aristid.).

c. (ἐν)αλήλιφα occurs in the variant form ἐνήλεπα *POxy*. 294.15 (A.D. 22), with omission of the Attic reduplication and change of the stem vowel and consonant. The Attic reduplication is also omitted in the middle ἤλιμε (= ἤλειμ- μαι) *POxy*. 528.11 (2nd cent.). It is added above the line (presumably by the same hand) in ἀπ᾽αλ᾽ήλειπται *POxy*. 34 V = *MChr*. 188 i.14 (A.D. 127).

d. ἐνήνοχα appears occasionally with the stem vowel changed to ε (some-times replaced by η or υ[1]) but spellings with o are more common:

ἀνενήνεχα *PMich*. 554.43 (A.D. 81-96)
  προενήνεχα *POxy*. 1288.12 (4th cent.)
ἐπενήνυχα *PSI* 871.26 (A.D. 66)
  προσενήνεχαιν (= -χεν) *PMich*. 322a.17 (A.D. 46)
    ἐνήνυχε *POxy*. 2353.6 (A.D. 32)
      προσενήνυχεν *PMich*. 121 R IV vii.4 (A.D. 42)
        παρεισενήνυχεν *SB* 9824.7-8 (A.D. 114/33)
      ἐνήνεχε *SB* 9249.6 (2nd/3rd cent.)
  ἐνήνεχαν *PMich*. 482.6 (A.D. 133)
  συνανενυχέναι *SB* 7031 — *PMich*. 186.38 (3rd hand), with ἀνενηνο-
    χέναι 31 (2nd hand) (A.D. 72)
      ἀνενηνηχέναι, συνανενεχέναι *SB* 7032 = *PMich*. 187.33 (2nd
      hand), 41 (3rd hand) (A.D. 75)
  ἐνηνυχώς *POxy*. 2725.8 (A.D. 71)
  ἀνανηνυγμένη[2] *PLond*. 1168 (iii, 135-8).28 (2nd hand), with ἀνενηνεγ-
    μένηι 24 (4th hand) (A.D. 44: *BL* i, 282)
    cf. προσενενυχ(θέντων) *SB* 7260 iii g = *PMich*. 121 R III vii.3
    (A.D. 42)
but μετονήνοχα sic *PTebt*. 397 = *PMich*. 321.28 (A.D. 198)
  προσ[ε]νήνοχα *PFlor*. 323.6 (A.D. 525)
  ἀνενήνοχεν *BGU* 1058 = *MChr*. 170.48 (13 B.C.)
    ἐνήνοχεν *PMich*. 480.7 (early 2nd cent.)
    προενήνοχεν *SB* 4425 iv.2 (2nd cent.)
    διενήνοχεν *StudPal*. v, 53 = *WChr*. 39.15-16 (A.D. 267); *PBeatty-
      Panop*. 2.225 (A.D. 300)
  ἀνενηνόχαμεν *PFlor*. 33.9 (early 4th cent.)
    προσηνενόχαμεν *PMichael*. 41.6 (A.D. 539/54); *PCairMasp*. 32.28
    part. rest. (A.D. 551)
  ἀνενηνόχασιν *BGU* 1124.5, sim. 25 (18 B.C.)
    ἐνηνόχασιν *PGrenf*. ii, 73 = *WChr*. 127.8 (prob. early 4th cent.)
    δ[ι]ενηνόχασιν *PCairMasp*. 312.50 (A.D. 567)
  ἐνενηνοχ(έναι) *PAmh*. 68 = *WChr*. 374.63 (A.D. 81-96)

---

[1] For the interchange of ε and η, see Vol. i, 242-9; for the interchange of ε and υ, see Vol. i, 273-5.

[2] For the false de-augmentation, see above, pp. 234-5.

ἀπενηνοχ(έναι) *SB* 5233.10 (ca. A.D. 14)

ἀνενηνοχέναι *PMich.* 584.34 (2nd hand), 40 (3rd hand), 46 (4th hand) (A.D. 84)

προσενηνοχέναι *PSI* 1027.16-17 (A.D. 151); *PSI* 1117.18 (2nd cent.)

διενηνοχέναι *PStrassb.* 138 = *SB* 8020.6 (A.D. 325)

διενηνοχότα *PCairMasp.* 28 = *MChr.* 382.10 (ca. A.D. 551)

cf. also ἀνενή<νο>χαν *PStrassb.* 217.6 (early 2nd cent.)

προσενηναχέναι *PLBat.* ii, 5.16 (A.D. 305)

The [e]/[i] vowel in this perfect active may have arisen on the analogy of the perfect middle-passive ἐνήνεγμαι.

e. Similarly, ὀμώμοκα appears occasionally with the stem vowel ε, perhaps through dissimilation. The formative -κ- is sometimes aspirated to -χ-:

ὀμώμοκα *POxy.* 77.26-27 (A.D. 223); etc.

ὀμόμεκα *BGU* 543.21 (27 B.C.); *PErl.* 23.5 (2nd cent.)

συνομόμεκα *SB* 7174 = *PMich.* 233.25 (A.D. 24: *BL* v, 69)

ὀμομέκα[μεν], ὀμώμεκα, [ὀμώ]μοκα, ὀμωμόκαμεν *PSI* 53.26-27 (1st hand); 68,143,159,169, etc. (2nd hand) (A.D. 132/3)

ὀμώμεκα *POxy.* 251.29-30 (A.D. 44); *POxy.* 2958.22 (A.D. 99); *POxy.* 478 = *WChr.* 218.44 (A.D. 132); *POxy.* 1198.33 (A.D. 150); *POxy.* 1030 = *WChr.* 36.22-23 (A.D. 212); etc.

ὠμόμεκα *PSI* 1358.16 (A.D. 212)

ὠμομέκαμεν *PSI* 282.26 (A.D. 183)

ὠμώμεκα *PBaden* 24.9 (A.D. 224)

συνομώνεκα[1] *PTebt.* 298 = *WChr.* 90.80 (A.D. 107/8)

ὀμώμεχα, ὠμόμεχα *PTebt.* 316 = *WChr.* 148.26 (2nd hand), 104 (4th hand) (A.D. 99)

ὀμώμεχα *PFouad* 22 ii.24 part. rest. (A.D. 125); *BGU* 891 R.27 (A.D. 144)

συνομόμεχα *PTebt.* 293 = *WChr.* 75.25 (2nd hand), 26-27 (3rd hand) (ca. A.D. 187)

ὀμώμοχα *PRyl.* 82.17 (1st hand), with ὀμόμακα[2] 19 (2nd hand), ὀμώμοκα 20 (3rd hand), 21 (4th hand), 22-23 (5th hand) (A.D. 113)

ὠμωμόχαμεν *BGU* 2085.19 (2nd hand) (A.D. 119)

ὀμομοχότος *PBerlLeihg.* 10.11 (A.D. 120)

The fluctuation in spelling in these perfects formed by Attic reduplication suggests that the stem vowel was a central vowel /ə/.[3]

---

[1] For the substitution of ν for μ, see Vol. i, 119.

[2] Cf. the change of ο to α also in the aor. ὤμασα, etc., above, p. 296.

[3] Cf. Vol. i, 289-92.

4. Stem variation in the formation of other perfects.

a. σ seems to be inserted in the perfect middle-passive of συναίρω in συν-ῆρσθαι *BGU* 975.15 (A.D. 45); *PLBat.* vi, 13.10 part. rest., 35,53 (A.D. 113/1); *PLips.* 27 = *MChr.* 293.15 (1st hand), 33 (3rd hand), with [σ]υνῆρσμαι 38 (4th hand) (A.D. 123); and συνῆρστθαι *sic SB* 9740.17 (A.D. 177); the correct form συνῆρμαι occurs in *CPR* 23 = *MChr.* 294.15 (2nd hand), 22 part. rest. (3rd hand) (prob. A.D. 138-61) and συνῆρθαι *PSI* 921 R.28 (A.D. 143/4); cf. also ἦρται *PLond.* 235 = *PAbinn.* 29.12 (ca. A.D. 346).[1]

b. Confusion of perfect active and perfect middle-passive forms may underlie the form κεκομίκασ[θ]αι *PMich.* 476.6 (early 2nd cent.).

c. Confusion of perfect middle and aorist passive is found in μεμετρήσθημεν *PMich.* 395 i.5 (A.D. 183) and μεμετρηθ( ) with personal subject *PMich.* 396.6 (A.D. 186?).

5. Periphrastic construction.[2]

a. The perfect subjunctive and optative, both active and middle-passive, are formed periphrastically by means of the subjunctive or optative of εἰμί and the perfect participle:

> ἐὰν ἦς πεπρακώς *SB* 9017 (8).10-11 (1st/2nd cent.)
> αἰὰν ἦς εἰληφώς *POxy.* 1583.8 (2nd cent.)
> ἐὰν ... ἦ μεμηνυκώς *PTebt.* 297.11-12 (ca. A.D. 123)
> ἐὰν δὲ ἦν [πρ]οτετεκνώς (for ἦ προτετεκνωκώς) *BGU* 1210 (45).125; sim. (19).61 (mid 2nd cent.)
> ἵν᾽ ὦ εὐεργετημένος *POxy.* 2234.24-25 (A.D. 31); sim. *PLond.* 177 = *MChr.* 57.26 (A.D. 40/41); *PLond.* 363 (ii, 170-1).9 (1st/2nd cent.); *POxy.* 486 = *MChr.* 59.16 (A.D. 131); *POxy.* 2411.37-38 (prob. ca. A.D. 173); *POxy.* 1117.18 (ca. A.D. 178); etc.
> ἵν᾽ ὦ βεβοηθημένος *POxy.* 2342.32 (A.D. 102); sim. *PMich.* 174.19-22 part. rest. (A.D. 145-7); *POxy.* 488.33 (late 2nd/3rd cent.); etc.

---

[1] These forms, all governing τὴν ... συνβίωσιν, were taken by Mitteis in *MChr.* as forms not of συναίρω but of συναιρέω; Preisigke, *WB*, followed Mitteis in listing these forms s.v. συναιρέω. But Hunt, aided by the appearance of the contr. fut. συχαρεῖται in *PTebt.* 809.4-5 (156 B.C.), derived these forms from συναίρω; in this he was followed by *LSJ*. On phonological and morphological grounds, the insertion of σ in the pf. mid. is far more likely than syncope involving an accentual shift to derive these forms from συνηρῆσθαι (< συναιρέω).

[2] The question whether this use of εἰμί + the aor. ptc. appeared in connection w. the decline and loss of the perfect as a tense system is answered in the negative by G. Björck in ΗΝ ΔΙΔΑΣΚΩΝ: *Die Periphrastischen Konstructionen im Griechischen*, p. 80. Its use is stylistic, and will be treated further in Vol. iii, *Syntax*.

ἵνα ... ὦ πεφιλανθρωπημένος *PMich.* 489.10 (2nd cent.)
ἐὰν ἦς περιεσπασμένος *SB* 7987.11 (A.D. 81-96)
μ[εμ]νησμένος ἦς *SB* 9387.16 (2nd/3rd cent.)
εἴησαν ἀκηκοότες *PMon.* 6.38 (A.D. 583)
γεγραμμένα εἴη *BGU* 326 = *MChr.* 316 i.15 (A.D. 189)
εἴ[η κεχ]ειροτονημένος *PStrassb.* 276.19 (early 3rd cent.)

b. The aorist participle is occasionally substituted for the perfect participle:

ἵν' ἦς μοι τελείαν χάριτα παρέξας *BGU* 48.7-8 (2nd/3rd cent.?)
ἐὰν οὖν μὴ ἦς λαβών *PTebt.* 423.18 (early 3rd cent.)
ἐὰ‹ν› μὴ ἦς ποτίσας *PFay.* 131.16-17 (3rd/early 4th cent.)
ἐὰν ἦν παυσάμενος τοῦ ἀχύρου *PLond.* 948 V (iii, 209-10).3-4 (A.D. 257)
ἐὰν ... ἦν κοπείς *PFlor.* 175.14 (A.D. 255)
ἐὰν ἦσάν τι παθόντες ἀνθρώπ[ι]νον *PTebt.* 333 = *MChr.* 115.13 (A.D. 216)

c. The perfect and pluperfect indicative are also sometimes formed periphrastically by means of the present or imperfect indicative of εἰμί and the perfect participle:

εἰ δὲ ἦν ... [τ]ετελ[ε]υτηκ[ώ]ς (if not subj.) *POxy.* 496 = *MChr.* 287.11
    (A.D. 127)
ἐσ[μ]ὲν δι[α]δεδωκότες *PMich.* 524.6, with ἵν' ὦμεν εὐεργετημένοι
    15-16 (A.D. 98)
ἦν γεγραμμένα *PMich.* 480.10 (early 2nd cent.)
    ἤμην ἐνδεδυμένο‹ς› *POxy.* 285.10-11 (ca. A.D. 50)
        ἤμην ἐρρωμένος *PRossGeorg.* ii, 26.2 (A.D. 160)
    πάλαι ἂν ἀπηλλαγμένοι ἦσμεν (for ἦμεν) *PMich.* 512.5 (early 3rd
        cent.)

d. The aorist participle is sometimes substituted for the perfect participle:

εἰμὶ ἠναγκασθ[είς] *sic* *PMich.* 530.4 (3rd/4th cent.)
ἦς ... ἀναβάς, ἤμην διδαχθείς *SB* 6262.16,17 (3rd cent.)
    εἰ ἦς ἐπιδημήσασα *POxy.* 1682.9 (4th cent.)
    ἦν ἀποσιωπήσας *StudPal.* v, 25 ii.4 (3rd cent.)
    ἤμεθα γράψαντες *PFouad* 86.12 (6th cent.)
    ἦμεν διαστείλαντες *PLond.* 1346.4-5 (A.D. 710)
    δινὰ ἦσαν γράψαντες *PLond.* 1914.35-36 (A.D. 335?)

e. The perfect infinitive active is also formed periphrastically by means of the infinitive of εἰμί and the perfect active participle in ὥστε εἶναι ἡ ['Αμμωνάριο]ν [καὶ] ἡ 'Ωφελοῦς εὐπιθεῖς γεγονυῖαι καὶ ἀπεσχηκυῖαι *POxy.* 268 = *MChr.* 299.6 (A.D. 58).

f. The future perfect formation is virtually extinct. The form γεγονησ[ό]-μενον *SB* 7814.32-33 (A.D. 256) may be a relic of this formation.[1] Elsewhere, the future perfect is formed periphrastically by means of the future of εἰμί and the perfect participle, e.g., ἔσομαι τετευχώς *SB* 6663.37 (prob. 6/5 B.C.); ἔσῃ μοι κεχαρισμένος *POxy.* 1061.20 (22 B.C.); *PMerton* 62.9-10 part. rest. (A.D. 6); ἐσόμεθα εἰδότες *PSI* 898.3 (4th cent.); etc., or with the aorist participle: ἔσῃ χάριν μεγάλην πο[ι]ήσας *PBaden* 33.9-10 (2nd cent.). ἔχω is also used periphrastically with the future participle passive in ἔχει δοθησόμενα "he would have them given me..." *POxy.* 1875.13 (6th/7th cent.).[2]

These examples of periphrastic construction with a form of εἰμί and the perfect participle (especially passive) represent a middle stage in the gradual replacement of the perfect system by periphrasis. Periphrasis in the perfect tense, found early in Greek (e.g., Homeric τετελεσμένον ἐστί), was originally expressive, but became merely an equivalent substitute for the corresponding simple forms. It predominated in classical Attic in the formation of the perfect subjunctive and optative active, the perfect subjunctive and optative middle and passive of consonant stem verbs (γεγραμμένος ᾖ/εἴη but κεκτῶμαι, etc.), and in the future perfect. It spread to the third person plural indicative (and not infrequently to the third person singular) of the pluperfect, and led eventually, aided by the gradual diminution of difference in nuance between aorist and perfect in the Koine,[3] to the elimination of the perfect inflectional system in Modern Greek except for the perfect participle passive used periphrastically with forms of εἰμί (ἔχω).[4]

F. FORMATION OF THE AORIST (AND FUTURE) PASSIVE STEM[5]

The language of the papyri follows the preference of the Koine in general for second aorist passive forms. There is little increase in this tendency, however, and in Byzantine documents, some first aorist passive forms reappear. Variants of some aorist passive forms are also found.

---

[1] Cf. also from the mag. papp. κεκράξομαι *PGM* 5.270 (4th cent.).

[2] The fut. pf. was lost early in the Koine. It survived only in poet. Att. inscrr. of the 6th cent. B.C. (*MS*, 187) and is not attested in Asia Minor inscrr. (Schweizer, 188). Two exx. are found in the Ptol. papp. and inscrr. (Mayser i², 2, 155). No certain exx. are found in the Herc. papp. or in most Koine authors, but some relics are attested in Ascl. Str. Onos. (Crönert, 211 & n. 1). In the LXX, one certain ex. is found; in the NT, only in an inferior reading (*BDF*, § 65.1b). In MGr., the fut. pf. is expressed periphrastically by means of θὰ ἔχω and the pass. ptc. or an invariable root form (Thumb, *Handbook*, § 228; Mirambel, *Gram.*, 133, 136; Maspero 105, 107). See further Schwyzer i, 783; Chantraine², § 300.

[3] Cf. Schwyzer i, 779; Chantraine², § 231; Dieterich, 235; Psaltes, 229-30; Hatzidakis, *Einl.*, 204-5; Chantraine, *Histoire du parfait grec*, 246-52; Mandilaras, 217-21.

[4] Cf. Schwyzer i, 811-13; Chantraine², § 227, 231; *MS*, 166; Mayser i², 2, 87; Psaltes, 230-1; Thumb, *Handbook*, § 227; Mirambel, *Gram.*, 133-7; Maspero, 99-111.

[5] Schwyzer i, 756-64; Chantraine², § 185-92; *MS*, 186-7; Schweizer, 188-91; Nachmanson, 161-71; Hauser, 118-20; Mayser i², 2, 155-65; Crönert, 231-6; *BDF*, § 76; Psaltes, 225-9.

1. The use of the first and second aorist passive.

a. The second aorist (and future) passive formation is used predominantly or exclusively 1) in most verbs in which the second aorist passive was preferred or used exclusively in Attic; 2) in many verbs in which both the first and second aorist passive formations were used in Attic; 3) in many verbs in which the first aorist passive was preferred or used exclusively in Attic; 4) in other verbs in which an aorist passive is not attested in Attic.

1) Verbs in which the second aorist passive was preferred or used exclusively in Attic:

διεγράφην *BGU* 102.2 (A.D. 161: *BL* i, 20)
    ἐγράφη *BGU* 580.1 part. rest. (A.D. 2); *BGU* 891 R.25 (A.D. 135/6);
        PFlor. 52.24 (A.D. 376); *PBaden* 91.13,34 part. rest. (A.D. 471);
        SB 5609.4 (A.D. 735: *BL* v, 97); etc.
    ὑπεγράφη *PLond*. 1157 V (1) = *WChr*. 375.24 (A.D. 246)
γραφήτωι *sic POxy*. 1188.27 (A.D. 13)
γραφῆναι *PBerlLeihg*. 10.13 (A.D. 120); *BGU* 448 == *MChr*. 310.20 (2nd
    half 2nd cent.); *POxy*. 237 vii.10 (A.D. 186); *PAntin*. 188.7 (6th/7th
    cent.); etc.
    καταγραφῆναι *BGU* 50 = *MChr*. 205.8 (A.D. 115)
γραφῖσαν *BGU* 82.8 (A.D. 185)
    τὰ γραφέντα *PMich*. 479.13-14 (early 2nd cent.); *BGU* 484.10
        (A.D. 201/2); *POxy*. 1852.1 (6th/7th cent.); *POxy*. 1937.1
        (6th/7th cent.); etc.
but τὰ γραφθέντα *StudPal*. xx, 223.1 (6th/7th cent.)[1]
δαρῇς *POxy*. 2339.7 (1st cent.)
    δαρήσ[ει] *POxy*. 653 = *MChr*. 90.26 (A.D. 160-2)[2]
ἐκλέπην, ἐκλάπην, and once κλεφ(θέν), see above, p. 262.[3]
κοπῆναι *PRyl*. 236.24 (A.D. 256)
    ἀποκοπῆναι *PCairMasp*. 151-2.299 (A.D. 570)
κοπείς *PFlor*. 175.14 (A.D. 255)
    ἐκκοπείσης *SB* 7517.6 (prob. A.D. 211/12)

---

[1] The 2 aor. pass. is normal in class. lit. and is used excl. in the Att. and Perg. inscrr. and in the Ptol. papp.; but a 1 aor. appears in a 5th cent. B.C. inscr. from Miletus and (in compds.) in Archim. Gal. etc. (Veitch & *LSJ*, s.vv.; *MS*, 187; Schweizer, 190; Mayser i², 2, 160; Crönert, 232, n. 7). Cf. also from the mag. papp. ἐνεγράφη *PGM* 13.691 (ca. A.D. 346) and τὰ καταγραφέντα *PGM* 12.382 (A.D. 300-50). The 2 aor. pass. has survived in the MGr. γράφηκα, θὰ γραφῶ (Mirambel, *Gram.*, 138) along w. γράφτηκα < γράφθηκα (see Thumb, *Handbook*, § 207-8).

[2] A 1 aor. pass. is attested only in Nicoch.; the fut. pass. is late: NT, Luc. (Veitch & *LSJ*, s.v.).

[3] The 1 aor. pass. is found in E. and Hdt., but the 2 aor. pass. ἐκλάπην is reg. in Att. prose (Veitch & *LSJ*, s.v.).

κοπέντα *PFlor.* 153.3 (A.D. 268); sim. *PMerton* 92.17 (A.D. 324)
κοπεῖσαν *BGU* 14 iii.12 (A.D. 255)[1]
cf. κοφέντα *SB* 7368.34, sim. 25, with ἐϰκοφέναι 20,21 part. rest., and
ἐϰϰόφ[θαι] 28, sim. 29-30 (late 2nd/early 3rd cent.)
συνμανῆναι *SB* 9136.8 (4th cent.)[2]
πληγ[ῆ]ναι *PFlor.* 59.4 (A.D. 225/41)
πληγέντες *BGU* 163.7 (A.D. 108)
cf. πλ[α]γεῖσα *SB* 1267.6, inscr. (A.D. 8)[3]
but ἐπιπλ[η]χθῆναι *POslo* 17.13-14 (A.D. 138+)
ἐπιπληχθέντος *PAberd.* 177.3 (2nd cent.)
πληθέντων (for πληχθέντων?) *SB* 9415 (18).6-7 (3rd cent.)
ἐπιπληχθήσηι *POxy.* 2339.9 (1st cent.)
σαπῆ *SB* 7992 = *PSI* 1332.18 (2nd/3rd cent.); *POxy.* 2273.15 (late 3rd cent.)
κατασαπ[έ]γτ[ων] *StudPal.* v, 6.16 (3rd cent.)[4]
σπαρῆναι *PRyl.* 243.9 (2nd cent.); *PRyl.* 388 V.2 (3rd cent.?)
σπαρησομένων *PHamb.* 62 = *PLBat.* vi, 23.9 (A.D. 123); *PStrassb.*
267.28 (A.D. 126-8); *PAmh.* 91.22 (A.D. 159)[5]
ἐπεστάλην *PGiss.* 11 = *WChr.* 444.4-5 (A.D. 118)
ἐπεστάλης *BGU* 200.4 (A.D. 183)
συναπεστάλημεν *PSI* 1248.33 (A.D. 235)
ἐστάλη[σα]ν *BGU* 821.6 (2nd cent.)
σταλῆναι *PAntin.* 188.5 (6th/7th cent.)
ἐπισταλῆναι *PMerton* 80.11 (2nd cent.); *POxy.* 54 = *WChr.* 34.15
(A.D. 201); *PHamb.* 19.5 (A.D. 225); *POxy.* 1031.8-9 (A.D.
228); etc.
ἀποσταλῆναι *PCairIsidor.* 65.9 (A.D. 298/9)
ἀποσταλείς *PCairMasp.* 282.10 (6th cent.?)
ἀποσταλέντα *PPrinc.* 183.14 (A.D. 345)
ἐπισταλέντα *PTebt.* 397 = *MChr.* 321.4 (A.D. 198)
σταλεῖσαν *POxy.* 1843.18 (6th/7th cent.)
ἀποσταλέντων, -τος *PCairMasp.* 291.3,6 (6th cent.?)
ἐπισταλεῖσι *BGU* 8 = *WChr.* 170 ii.29 (ca. A.D. 248)

---

[1] This reg. 2 aor. pass. has survived in the MGr. κόπηκα, θὰ κοπῶ Mirambel, *Gram.*,
139). ἐκόφθησαν, orig. read in *PLond.* 242.4-5 (A.D. 346), was corrected to ἐκέρθησαν in
BL i, 267, and so appears in the re-edition in *PAbinn.* 48.
[2] ἐμάνην E. Hdt. S. Ar. Isoc. Pl. X. D. Is. etc. (Veitch & *LSJ*, s.v.).
[3] ἐπλήγην is common in Att. and Ion., and also πλᾶγην in compds. in the sense 'strike
w. terror or amazement'; πλᾱγείς is Dor. (Veitch & *LSJ*, s.v.). Cf. also from the mag. papp.
πληγῆς *PGM* 36.76 (4th cent.); ἐκπλαγῆναι *PGM* 4.572-3 (4th cent.); ἐκπλαγήσει *PGM*
7.921 (3rd cent.).
[4] ἐσάπην Hes. Hdt. Pl. (Veitch & *LSJ*, s.v.).
[5] ἐσπάρην S. Th. (Veitch & *LSJ*, s.v.). Cf. also from the mag. papp. ἐσπάρης *PGM*
4.2978 (4th cent.); ἐσπάρη *PGM* 13.492 (ca. A.D. 346).

310   Conjugation

σταλήσεται (confusion of construction for σταλῆναι) PLond. 1727.42
    (A.D. 583/4)¹
ἐπετράπην POxy. 51.5 (A.D. 173)
    ἐτράπη POxy. 935 = WChr. 119.5 (3rd cent.)
    ἐπετράπηι PLBat. vi, 15.32 (ca. A.D. 114)
    προτραπήτω, προτραπῶσιν POxy. 1413.5,9;17 (A.D. 270-5)
    προτραπῆναι POxy. 1416.5 part. rest., 6 (ca. A.D. 298: BL v, 78)
        τραπῆναι CPR 233 = WChr. 42.7 (A.D. 314)
        ἐκτραπῆναι PRyl. 133.22 part. rest. (A.D. 33); PStrassb. 259.12
            part. rest. (2nd cent.); SB 9136.8 (4th cent.); etc.
    ἐπιτραπησόμενα BGU 1021.16,17 part. rest. (3rd cent.)²
ἐφάνη BGU 1138 = MChr. 100.11 (19/18 B.C.); SB 6.13 (A.D. 216);
    POxy. 58 = WChr. 378.4 (A.D. 288); etc.
    ἀνεφάνη POxy. 939 = WChr. 128.4 (4th cent.)
    φανῶσι PMich. 322a.33 (A.D. 46); BGU 136 = MChr. 86.25 (A.D. 135)
    φανείη PChic. 2 = MChr. 217.10 (early 2nd cent.); POxy. 136 =
        WChr. 383.36 (A.D. 583)
    φανῆναι POxy. 1854.7 (6th/7th cent.); SB 8988.101, with φανέντος 65
        (A.D. 647)
    φανεί'ς′ PLeit. 5.16 (ca. A.D. 180); PCairMasp. 295 iii.3 (6th cent.)
        φανέν BGU 562 = WChr. 220.19 (after A.D. 138); SB 7558.24
            (A.D. 172/3?)
        φανέντος POxy. 708 = WChr. 432.5 (A.D. 188)
        διαφανέντος PMich. 426.21 (A.D. 199/200?)
        ἀναφανέντος PMich. 530.9 (3rd/4th cent.)
        φανέντες SB 9050 v.6 (1st/2nd cent.)
        φανέντας PFay. 107.10-11 (A.D. 133)
but ἀποφανθέντα CPR 233.10 = WChr. 42.3 (A.D. 314); PLond. 971
    = MChr. 95.8 (4th cent.)³
διεφθάρη POxy. 74.14 (A.D. 116); PAmh. 73 = PSarap. 4.6 (A.D.
    129/30); POxy. 1458.17 (A.D. 216/17)
    ἐφθάρησ(αν) PStrassb. 24 = PSarap. 52.15,39,48 part. rest. (A.D. 118)
    διαφθαρῆναι POxy. 95 = MChr. 267.35 part. rest. (A.D. 129); BGU
        98.19-20 (A.D. 211); POxy. 161 = POxy. 938.4 (late 3rd/4th cent.)

¹ The 1 aor. pass. is very rare, found in the compd. ἀπο- in Cret. inscrr. and Sch.Od.
(Veitch & LSJ, s.v.). The mag. papp. have only the 2 aor., e.g., διασταλήτω PGM 4.2471
(4th cent.). The 2 aor. pass. is preserved in MGr. στάληκα, θὰ σταλῶ (Mirambel, Gram.,
139), along w. στάλθηκα (Maspero, 139).
² ἐτράπην A. Ar. etc.; ἐτρέφην Hom., once E.; Ion. τραφθῆναι Od. Hdt. (Veitch &
LSJ, s.v.).
³ The 1 aor. pass. is rare in class. prose, in Att. appar. strictly pass. 'was shown, made
known' (Veitch & LSJ, s.v.). Cf. also from the mag. papp. ἐφάνθης PGM 11a.14 (4th/5th
cent.), but ἐφάνης PGM 2.115 (4th cent.); ἐφάνη PGM 13.175,197,476,491 (ca. A.D. 346);
φανείς PGM 4.653 (4th cent.); συνεφάνη, συνφανέντι PGM 13.395,552; [ἐ]μφανῆναι PGM
7.407 (3rd cent.); etc. The 2 aor. pass. is preserved in the MGr. φάνηκα, θὰ φανῶ (Thumb,
Handbook, § 207; Mirambel, Gram., 139; Maspero, 139).

φθαρέντων *POxy.* 1912.144 abbrev., 148,150 (late 6th cent.)[1]
ἐχάρην (intrans.) *PMich.* 473.4 part. rest., 26 (early 2nd cent.); *PMich.* 495.11 (2nd cent.); *PHamb.* 88.3 (mid 2nd cent.); *BGU* 615.5 (2nd cent.); *POxy.* 1676.4 (3rd cent.); etc.[2]

2) Verbs in which both the first and second aorist passive formations were used in Attic:

συνηλλάγην *BGU* 1062 = *WChr.* 276.29,32,33 (A.D. 236/7)
   ἠλλάγη *BGU* 361 iii.24 (A.D. 184)
      ἀπηλλάγη *PRyl.* 128.12 (ca. A.D. 30); *POxy.* 2187.23 (A.D. 304)
   ἀπηλλάγησαν *BGU* 969 i.11-12 (A.D. 142?)
      [συ]νηλλάγησαν *POxy.* 1839.3 (6th cent.)
   ἀπαλλαγῶμεν *POxy.* 267 = *MChr.* 281.17,20 part. rest. (A.D. 36)
      ἀπαλλαγῇ *SB* 7529.7 (2nd/3rd cent.)
   διαλλάγηθι *PGiss.* 17 = *WChr.* 481.13 (A.D. 117-38); *PMich.* 502.8 (2nd cent.)
   ἀπαλλαγῆναι *SB* 9353.16 (A.D. 140); *SB* 7558.11 (A.D. 172/3?); *PGissBibl.* 29.23 (3rd cent.); *POxy.* 1865.3 (6th/7th cent.); *PAntin.* 193.4 (7th cent.); etc.
      ἀλλαγῆνε (= -ναι) *PMich.* 493.11 (2nd cent.)
   ἀλλαγεῖσα *POxy.* 1631 V (A.D. 280)
      συναλλαγέντων *PTebt.* 329.10 (A.D. 139)
         ἀπαλλαγέντων *PMon.* 14.57 (A.D. 594)
   ἀπαλλαγήσομαι *PMich.* 493.15 (2nd cent.)
but ἀπελλάχθην (for ἀπηλλάχθη) *POxy.* 893 — *MChr.* 99.9 (late 6th/7th cent.)
   ἀπηλλάχθη *POxy.* 1119 = *WChr.* 397.16 (A.D. 253: *BL* i, 332)
   ἀπαλλαχθῆναι *PSI* 47.7 (6th cent.?)
   ἀλλαχθήσονται *SB* 10199.9 (ca. A.D. 219-24)[3]
ἐβλάβην *PMich.* 473.31,33 (early 2nd cent.); *PFlor.* 382.63 (A.D. 222/3); *PFlor.* 57 = *Archiv* iv, 437-8.63 (A.D. 223/5)
   [ἐ]β[λ]άβης *PHamb.* 29.24 (after A.D. 94)
   βλαβῶσιν *PFlor.* 151.11 (A.D. 267)
   βλαβῆναι *POxy.* 2344.7 (ca. A.D. 336); *PCairMasp.* 167.50 (6th cent.); *PCairMasp.* 295 ii.20 (6th cent.); *PCairMasp.* 151-2.129 (A.D. 570)

---

[1] ἐφθάρην S. Th. Pl. etc. (Veitch & *LSJ*, s.v.).

[2] For the new sigm. aor. act. ἐχάρησα, see above, p. 296. The 2 aor. pass. appears in Hom. Simon. Ar. Pl. etc. and is preserved in the MGr. χάρηκα, θὰ χαρῶ (Veitch & *LSJ*, s.v.; Thumb, *Handbook*, § 207; Mirambel, *Gram.*, 139; Maspero, 139).

[3] Att. prose writers preferred the 2 aor. pass., Hdt. and Trag. the 1 aor. pass., although the converse is not rare (Veitch & *LSJ*, s.v.). The 2 aor. pass. is alone used in the Att. and Magn. inscrr. and in the Ptol. papp. (*MS*, 187; Nachmanson, 170; Mayser i², 2, 160, 168). The mag. papp. have ἀλλαχθήσῃ *PGM* 4.2173 (4th cent.), but ἀλλαγέντος *PGM* 22a.5 (4th/5th cent.); ἀπαλλαγήσεται *PGM* 15.245-6 (ca. A.D. 346).

βλαβήσεται *POxy.* 1405.11 (A.D. 236/7: *BL* iv, 61)[1]
ἐμίγη *POxy.* 1734.15 (late 2nd/3rd cent.)
παραμιγήτω *POxy.* 2985.4 (2nd/3rd cent.)[2]
ἐξεπλέκη (for -πλάκη, with the vocalism of the pres. extended to the
    aor. pass. as in κλεπ-[3] if not actually ἐξεκλέπη) *PSI* 93.16 (3rd cent.)
[μετ?ε]στράφη *PFlor.* 376.25 (3rd cent.)
    στρ[α]φείς *POxy.* 33 = *WChr.* 20 i.6 (late 2nd cent.)
        ἀναστραφέντες *POxy.* 71 ii.12 (A.D. 303)
        ἀναστραφέντων *PLond.* 358 = *MChr.* 52.12 (ca. A.D. 150); etc.[4]
ἐτρίβη *PFlor.* 378.19 (5th cent.?)
    προστριβῆναι *PMon.* 6.66 (A.D. 583)
    [κα]τατριβέντω(ν) *StudPal.* viii, 1027.2-3 (6th cent.)[5]

Note. λέγω, of which the second aorist passive was preferred in the best
Attic prose except in the meaning "say," follows the Attic distribution:[6]

a) In the meanings "collect, enroll, select":

προσανελέγη *SB* 4425 A v.1 (2nd cent.)
    κατελέγημεν *PHermRees* 14.2 (late 4th cent.)
    κατελέγησαν *POxy.* 2407.15, sim. 17,24,46 (late 3rd cent.)
    cf. ἀπολεγῇ *BGU* 1564.11-12 (A.D. 138)

b) In the meanings "say, mention":

διελέχθην *PFlor.* 132.3 (A.D. 257); *PLBat.* xi, 26.6-7 (3rd cent.); *PHerm-
    Rees* 48.2 (5th cent.)
    διελέχθη *POxy.* 2155.17 (4th cent.)

---

[1] Both the 1 & 2 aor. pass. are in common use in class. Gr., w. both forms in Th. Pl.;
both forms are also found in the Ptol. papp., but only the 2 aor. at Herc. (Veitch & *LSJ*,
s.v.; Mayser i², 2, 161; Crönert, 232).

[2] Cf. also from the mag. papp. μίγητι *PGM* 62.17 (late 3rd cent.); μιγῆναι *PGM* 4.2934-5
(4th cent.); συνμιγῆναι *PGM* 7.911 (3rd cent.). Both the 1 & 2 aor. pass. are found in Att.,
incl. Trag., but the 2 aor. pass. is more common, as in Hom. (Veitch & *LSJ*, s.v.).

[3] See above, p. 262. Both the 1 & 2 aor. pass. are found in Att., incl. Trag. Forms with
-ε- are freq. v.ll. in class. authors, accepted in Tim., and are normal in the Ptol. papp.
(Veitch & *LSJ*, s.v.; Mayser i², 2, 160).

[4] Cf. also from the mag. papp. ἀποστραφῇς *PGM* 13.620-1 (ca. A.D. 346); στραφείς
PGM 70.16 (late 3rd/early 4th cent.), and the 2 fut. pass. στραφήσονται *PGM* 4.633 (4th
cent.). The 1 aor. pass. is found once each in Att. Com. and prose (Ar. & Pl.). Only the 2
aor. pass. is normally used in later inscrr., the Ptol. papp., and MGr. (Veitch & *LSJ*, s.v.;
Mayser i², 2, 161; Mirambel, *Gram.*, 139; Maspero, 139).

[5] The 1 aor. pass. is also used in good Att. poet. and prose, but the 2 aor. pass. is more
freq. (Veitch & *LSJ*, s.v.). It is alone found in the Ptol. papp. (Mayser i², 2, 161). Both forms
are found in Koine authors (Crönert, 235 & n. 7).

[6] Both the 1 & 2 aor. pass. formations occur, however, in Ion. and Dor. inscrr. and in
the Ptol. papp. (Schweizer, 190; Nachmanson, 171; Mayser i², 2, 162; Crönert, 233 & nn.
2-3). For the Att. usage, see Veitch & *LSJ*, s.vv. simple & compd.; *MS*, 187.

διαλεχθῆναι *PSI* 93.21 (3rd cent.); *PFouad* 87.9 (6th cent.)
διαλεχθείς *POxy.* 1349 descr. (4th cent.); sim. *WO* 1220.10 (2nd/3rd cent.?)
προλεχθείς *PCairMasp.* 32.63 (A.D. 551); *PLond.* 1676.43 (A.D. 566-73); *PMon.* 1.17 (A.D. 574)
λεχθέντος *PMon.* 1.35 twice (A.D. 574)
προλεχθείσης *SB* 5941.12 (A.D. 509); *SB* 4669.9 (A.D. 614)
λεχθείσης *PLond.* 1345.26 (A.D. 710)
προλεχθέντι *PCairMasp.* 151-2.126, sim. 276, with προειρημέ(νῳ) 133-4 (A.D. 570); *PMon.* 14.90 (A.D. 594)
λεχθέντα *PStrassb.* 20 = *PStrassb.* 280.7 (A.D. 273); *PFouad* 87.15, with διαλεχθῆναι 9 (6th cent.)
λεκθέντα (for λεχθέν) *POxy.* 1348 descr. (late 3rd cent.)
προλεχθέντα *PLBat.* xiii, 13.10 (A.D. 421)
διαλεχθέντα *PVars.* 29.1 (6th cent.)
προλεχθεῖσαν *BGU* 405.11 (A.D. 348)
λεχθέντων καὶ ἀντιλεχθέντων *PMon.* 14.31 (A.D. 594)
προλεχθέντων *PLond.* 1660.21 (ca. A.D. 553)

3) Verbs in which the first aorist passive was preferred or used exclusively in Attic:[1]

παρηγγέλη *BGU* 647.5 (A.D. 130); sim. *PFlor.* 184.5 (3rd cent.)
ἀπηγγέλη *POxy.* 486 = *MChr.* 59.31 (A.D. 131); sim. *PAntin.* 87.7 (late 3rd cent.)
παραγγελῆναι *POxy.* 1411.8-9 part. rest. (A.D. 260); *POxy.* 2235.23 (ca. A.D. 346)
ἀγγελείς, εἰσαγγελέντες *PFlor.* 2 part. = *WChr.* 401.8-9,171 (A.D. 265)
εἰσαγγελέντος *BGU* 16 = *WChr.* 114.10-11 (A.D. 159/60)
καταγγελείσης *POxy.* 1274.6 (3rd cent.)
παρανγελέντας *POxy.* 1032.18-19 (A.D. 162)
but παρεγγέλθην sic *PCairMasp.* 76.8 (Byz.); corr. *PApoll.* 35.3 (ca. A.D. 713)
παραγγελθείς *PCairMasp.* 87.17 (A.D. 543)[2]
ἡρπάγησαν *BGU* 341.13: *BL* i, 40, with ἁρπασ[θέντας] 12 (2nd cent.)
ἁρπαγέντα *PLips.* 40 iii.7 (late 4th/early 5th cent.)

---

[1] λημφείη *POslo* 18.4 (A.D. 162), πεμφῆναι *PRossGeorg.* iii, 18 R.10 (6th/7th cent.), and πεμφέντος *BGU* 646 = *WChr.* 490.2 (A.D. 193); *POxy.* 2018.10 (6th cent.) are more likely instances of the omission of one of two contiguous aspirates than exx. of a new aor. pass. formation, esp. since in the last document cited πεμθέντος occurs 8 times and the correct πεμφθέντος 5 times, but ἐλήμφη and κατελήμφη are found in codd. (Crönert, 68, n. 1).

[2] The 1 aor. pass. was normal in Ion. & Att. class. authors and in the Att. inscrr.; it is found along w. the 2 aor. pass. in Ion. inscrr. and some Koine authors (excl. in Str. and Ascl.). The 2 aor. pass. begins to appear in Att. inscrr. from the 5th cent. B.C. on and is used excl. in the Ptol. and Herc. papp., LXX, and NT (Veitch & *LSJ*, s.v.; *MS*, 187; Schweizer, 191; Mayser i², 2, 160, 166; Crönert, 231 & n. 8; *BDF*, § 76.1).

but καθηρπασθέν[τα] *PThead.* 23 = *PAbinn.* 44.14 (A.D. 342)[1]
ἐβ[ρέχ]η *PRossGeorg.* ii, 22.1 (ca. A.D. 154-9)
   ἐβρέχησαν *PGiss.* 60 v.12 (A.D. 118)
   βρεχέντων *WChr.* 341 = *PFlor.* 331.6 (A.D. 177)[2]
κατακρυβῇ *PMich.* 520.9 (4th cent.)
   cf. ἀποκρυπέντα *PLond.* 1343.37 (A.D. 709)[3]
ἐπιλαχέντος *PLond.* 1345.39 (A.D. 710)
   λαχέντα *SB* 4755.2 (Byz.)[4]
ἠνύγη (for ἠνοίγη) *BGU* 1655.60 (A.D. 169); *BGU* 326 = *MChr.* 316
   ii.10 (A.D. 194); *POxy.* 2348.51 (A.D. 224)
   ἀνυγείσης *PSI* 1258.15 (3rd cent.)
but ἠνοίχθη *PHamb.* 73.19 (2nd cent.)
   ἀνοιχθε[ίσ]ης *PRyl.* 109.8-9 (A.D. 235)[5]
περειορυγήτωσαν, ὀρυγῆνε (for -αι) *POxy.* 121.6-7,8 (3rd cent.)
but ἀνωρυχθ(είσης) *POxy.* 1917.111 (6th cent.)[6]
πτυγεῖσαν *PGen.* 10.17: *BL* i, 158 (A.D. 323)
but ἐπτύχθη *SB* 5174.23 part. rest.; 5175.25 (A.D. 512 & 513)[7]
στεφῆναι *PRyl.* 77.46 (A.D. 192)[8]
ἀποφραγῆναι *POxy.* 1409.16 (A.D. 278); *SB* 6000 V.29 (6th cent.)[9]

τάσσω, normally also first aorist passive in Attic, is found in the second aorist passive predominantly in the simple verb and in most compounds, but in the first aorist passive in the compounds προσ- and συν-, while both formations are used in the compound ὑπο- without apparent distinction.

---

[1] The 1 aor. pass. is normal in class. Gr.; the 2 aor. is late: Lyc. Str. Apollod. etc. and the NT, along w. the 1 aor. (Veitch & *LSJ*, s.v.; *BDF*, § 76.1).

[2] This 2 aor. pass. w. the vocalism ε seems to appear first in the Ptol. papp., along w. one ex. of the 1 aor. (Mayser i², 2, 161-2). An earlier 2 aor. pass. ἐβράχην is found in Hp. and Arist. (and Anacr.?), w. βρεχήσεται in the LXX and the mag. papp., e.g., *PGM* 4.291 (4th cent.). The class. Att. form was ἐβρέχθην, wh. also occurs in Arist. (Veitch & *LSJ*, s.v.; cf. Schwyzer i, 760; Chantraine², § 192). The 2 aor. pass. with the vocalism α is preserved in MGr. in βράχηκα, θὰ βραχῶ (Mirambel, *Gram.*, 138; Maspero, 138).

[3] The 1 aor. pass. is found in Ep. and E., but the 2 aor. pass. is used by Aesop. and S. (ptc.); the 2 fut. pass. is also found in E. and the LXX (Veitch & *LSJ*, s.v.).

[4] I have not found this aor. pass. formation elsewhere.

[5] Cf. also from the mag. papp. ἠνοίγη *PGM* 12.325 (A.D. 300-50); ἠνύγη 13.531 (ca. A.D. 346); ἠνοίγησαν *PGM* 12.324; 36.298 part. rest. (4th cent.); ἀνοιγήσεται *PGM* 4.358 (4th cent.); etc.; the 1 aor. occurs only in ἀνοιχθήτω *PGM* 13.295 (ca. A.D. 346). The 2 aor. pass. is late, occurring in Luc. Ps.-Callisth. and the NT, along w. the 1 aor. pass. (Veitch & *LSJ*, s.v.; *BDF*, § 76.1; Dieterich, 211). Only the 1 aor. pass. is attested in the Ptol. papp. (Mayser i², 2, 188).

[6] Cf. also from the mag. papp. ὀρυγέντ[ο]ς *PGM* 2.37 (4th cent.), etc., The 2 aor. pass. is late, occurring in the Ptol. papp., NT, Orig. etc. (Veitch & *LSJ*, s.v.; Mayser i², 2, 160; *BDF*, § 76.1).

[7] The 2 aor. pass. is known from Hp. (ἀν-), who also uses the 1 aor. pass., alone attested in Att. (Veitch & *LSJ*, s.v.).

[8] The 1 aor. pass. is used by E.; no 2 aor. pass. is attested elsewhere.

[9] The 2 aor. pass. is also found in the NT and Koine authors (Veitch & *LSJ*, s.v.; *BDF*, § 76.1; Crönert, 236 & n. 1).

a) Second aorist forms:

ἐτάγη *BGU* 457 = *WChr.* 252.6 (A.D. 132/3); *WChr.* 217.8 (A.D. 172/3); *POxy.* 2186.2 (A.D. 260); etc.

ἐτάγη(σαν) *BGU* 1028.24 (2nd cent.)

ταγῇ *PMich.* 538.11 (A.D. 126)

ταγῆναι *PTebt.* 299.23 (ca. A.D. 50); *BGU* 254.18 (A.D. 160); *PSI* 105.15 (late 2nd cent.); *BGU* 2021.8 (A.D. 215); etc.

ταγείς *POxy.* 2902 ii.5 (A.D. 272); *POxy.* 2912.9 (late 3rd cent.)

  ταγέντος *PMon.* 1.37 twice (A.D. 574)

  ταγεῖσαι *PTebt.* 337.2 (late 2nd/early 3rd cent.)

ἀποταγῆναι *PLond.* 214 = *WChr.* 177.23 (A.D. 270-75)

διετάγην *SB* 7352 = *PMich.* 490.11,22 (2nd cent.)

  διαταγέντα *POxy.* 2111.23 (ca. A.D. 135)

    διαταγεῖσαν *POxy.* 75.30 (A.D. 129)

    δ[ι]αταγῖσαι *PFay.* 97 part. = *MChr.* 315.13, sim. 32 (A.D. 78)

ἐκταγέντος *PCairMasp.* 169.16 (6th cent.)

ἐνετάγη *POxy.* 2936.9 (A.D. 271/2)

  ἐνταγ[ῆναι] *POxy.* 2896.7 (A.D. 268-70)

  ἐνταγείς *POxy.* 2898 ii.9-10 (A.D. 270-1); (clearly) *POxy.* 2911.11-12 (late 3rd cent.)

ἐ[π]ιτα[γ]ῆναι *BGU* 616.5 (n.d.)

κατατάγῆναι *POxy.* 1642.43 (A.D. 289); *WChr.* 470 = *PMon.* 2.7 (A.D. 578)

  καταταγέντι *BGU* 1074.19,21,24 (A.D. 275); *POxy.* 1415.8 (late 3rd cent)

ὑποταγῆναι *PHarris* 67 ii.14 (ca. A.D. 150?); *BGU* 646 = *WChr.* 490.4-5 (A.D. 193); *POxy.* 2228.28,36 (A.D. 285: *BL* v, 81)

b) First aorist forms:

ταχθείς *POxy.* 2895 i.5; ii.10 (A.D. 269/70)

προσετάχθημεν *PLips.* 58.5 (A.D. 371)

  προσταχθῇ *POxy.* 2347.8 (A.D. 362)

  προ[σ]ταχθείς *SB* 9840 = *PLBat.* xiii, 10.7 (4th cent.)

    προσταχθέντος *PStrassb.* 262.3, sim. 4 (4th cent.)

    προσταχθέντα *SB* 6824 = *PMich.* 157.11 (A.D. 250); *PRyl.* 112c.8 part. emended (A.D. 250); etc.

    [προ]σταχθέντων *BGU* 432 i.8 (A.D. 190)

    προσταχθεῖσι *SB* 4295 A.7 (A.D. 303); sim. *PLips.* 61 = *WChr.* 187.8 (A.D. 375); *PLips.* 62 ii = *WChr.* 188.4 (A.D. 385)

συνταχθείσης *PBouriant* 20 = *PAbinn.* 63.23 (A.D. 350)

  συντακτείσῃ (for -ταχθ-¹) *POxy.* 1470.13 (A.D. 336)

  συνταχθέν *PCairMasp.* 168.63 (6th cent.)

ὑποταχθῆναι *POxy.* 237 vi.34 (A.D. 186)

---

¹ Cf. Vol. i, 89.

A similar pattern is observed in this verb in Asia Minor inscriptions,[1] but in the Ptolemaic papyri, the simple verb and the compounds προσ-, συν-, and ὑπο- (and προσκατα-) appear in the second aorist passive, while δια- and κατα- appear in the first aorist passive, the usages of δια- and κατα- therefore being reversed. The second aorist passive is moreover used along with the first aorist passive in the compounds προσ- and συν-, and exclusively in ὑπο-.[2]

4) Verbs in which an aorist passive is not attested in Attic:

ἐγνάφη *POxy.* 1346 descr. (2nd cent.?)
    γναφῶσιν *PMich.* 501.11 (2nd cent.)
    κναφήτω *POxy.* 2156.18 (late 4th/5th cent.)
ἐσκύλην *POslo* 162.6-7 (4th cent.)
    σκυλῶ *PFlor.* 332.15 (2nd cent.)
    σκυλῆς *PSI* 1404.16 (A.D. 41/42); *POslo* 60.3 (2nd cent.); *PTebt.* 421.11 (3rd cent.); *POxy.* 941.3 part. rest. (6th cent.)
    συγσκυλῇ *POxy.* 2275.19 (1st half 4th cent.)
    σκυλῆτε *PStrassb.* 346.22 (2nd cent.)
    [σ]κύληθι *POxy.* 1669.13 (3rd cent.)
    συνσκύληθι *POxy.* 63.12 (2nd/3rd cent.)
    σκύλλητι *PSI* 900.17 (3rd/4th cent.)
    σκυλῆναι *SB* 4317.22 (ca. A.D. 200); *PLBat.* xiii, 19.3-4 (3rd cent.); *SB* 7993 = *PSI* 1333.10 (3rd cent.); *POxy.* 123.10 (3rd/4th cent.); *PFuadCrawford* 9.12 (3rd/4th cent.?); *PApoll.* 72.6 (A.D. 703-15); etc.[3]
ἐπιφυῆναι *PLond.* 1724.57 (A.D. 578-82); *PMon.* 1.46 (A.D. 574); 9.80 (A.D. 585); 14.90 (A.D. 594)
    φυήσεται *POxy.* 2554, frag. 1 ii.3 (3rd cent.)
    φυησομένωι *PFlor.* 20 = *WChr.* 359.20 (A.D. 127)[4]

b. Conversely, the first aorist passive formation is retained in καίω, in which a second aorist passive is found elsewhere in classical Greek and in the Koine, and is preferred in ζεύγνυμι, in which the second aorist passive was preferred in Attic:

[1] Schweizer, 190-1.
[2] Mayser i², 2, 162. The 2 aor. pass. is used almost excl. in the NT (*BDF*, § 76.1) and is the form in the mag. papp.: ὑπετάγη *PGM* 2.101 (4th cent.); ὑπετάγησαν *PGM* 13.744 (ca. A.D. 346); ὑποταγήσεται *PGM* 4.3080 (4th cent.). Elsewh. in Gr., the 2 aor. pass. is comparatively rare in this verb and is never found in the Att. inscrr. (Veitch & *LSJ*, s.vv. simple & compd.; *MS*, 187; Crönert, 235 & n. 6).
[3] An aor. pass. (2 aor.) is also found in inscrr. from various places; a 1 aor. pass. is found in Eust. (*LSJ*, s.v.).
[4] For the replacement of the intrans. root aor. ἔφυν by this 2 aor. pass. formation in the Koine, see *BDF*, § 76.2. The exx. cited in the subj. from E. Hp. Pl. in Veitch, s.v., are better attributed to ἔφυν (cf. *LSJ*, s.v.). There is one ex. of the new aor. pass. in the Ptol. papp. (Mayser i², 2, 161).

ὑποκαυθῆναι *PFlor.* 127.4-5 (A.D. 256)[1]

ἐζεύχθην *SB* 6222.18 (late 3rd cent.)

    συνζεύχθημεν sic *PLond.* 1727.9 (A.D. 583/4)

       ἀπεσευχθησεμεν (for ἀπεζεύχθημεν) *PCairMasp.* 121.10 (A.D. 573)

     παρεζεύχθησαν *PRyl.* 237.4 (mid 3rd cent.)

     ἀποζευχθῆναι *POxy.* 237 vii.25 (A.D. 186)

but ἀπεζύγημε‵ν′ *PLond.* 1712.10 (A.D. 569)

     ἀπεζύγη[σαν] *PCairMasp.* 154 R.10 (A.D. 527-65)[2]

It is significant that here the second aorist passive formations recur in Byzantine times, in direct opposition to the distribution in verbs whose second aorist passive predominates in Roman documents. This reflects a tendency to revert to the more Attic forms in Byzantine documents.

This evidence for the use of the first and second aorist passive forms in the papyri of the Roman and Byzantine periods reflects the tendency of the non-literary Koine to employ the second aorist passive in many more verbs than in classical Greek.[3] This tendency is a reversal of the general extension of the first aorist passive forms in Greek, few in Homer but regular in subsequent secondary formations. The late classical and Koine second aorist passives are mainly back-formations from first aorist passives, often with retention of the vowel grade of the first aorist passive.[4] These new formations may be archaistic, as Schwyzer suggests;[5] it seems unlikely that they represent Ionic influence, as implied by Chantraine,[6] because very few are first attested in Ionic.[7] Most are first found in inscriptions (including Attic) or papyri, or in Koine authors, including the Atticists.[8] The Modern Greek aorist passive generally corresponds to the classical first and second aorist passives, but a few changes and a few new formations occur.[9]

2. Some variation occurs in the formation of the aorist passive stem of δύναμαι, which has both the Attic and Ionic forms of the first aorist passive

---

[1] The non-Attic 2 aor. pass. is found in Ep. and Ion. and late prose: Plu. Ps.-Callisth. etc., and in the NT and Apostolic Fathers (Veitch, *LSJ*, *BAG*, s.v.; Crönert, 234 & n. 3; *BDF*, § 76.1). Only the 1 aor. pass. is attested in the Ptol. papp. (Mayser i², 2, 182). Both forms are found in the mag. papp.: κα[τα]καήσεται *PGM* 12.56 (A.D. 300-50); κατεκαύθ[η] *PGM* 20.7 (1st cent. B.C.).

[2] The 1 aor. pass. is found in Hdt. and Trag., but is rare in Att. prose; the 2 aor. pass. is more commonly used both in Trag. and prose (Veitch & *LSJ*, s.v.).

[3] Cf. the footnotes to the indiv. verbs above.

[4] E.g., ἠγγέλην, ἐβρέχην.

[5] i, 760.

[6] § 192.

[7] E.g., ἐβράχην (not ἐβρέχην) and ἐπτύγην, both found in Hp.

[8] E.g., ἠγγέλην is first attested in an Att. inscr. of the 5th cent. B.C.; ἐβρέχην, ὠρύγην, ἐλάχην, ἐστέφην appar. first in the Ptol. or later papp.; ἡρπάγην, ἠνοίγην, ἐφράγην in the papp. and Koine lit. (Luc. etc.). E. also seems to have had a predilection for 2 aor. pass. forms, as ἐτάγην and ἠγγέλην.

[9] See esp. Thumb, *Handbook*, § 207-8; Mirambel, *Gram.*, 139.

in the papyri of the Roman and Byzantine periods, with occasional hybrid forms arising from a confusion of the two. Both forms are also found in the New Testament and in the Ptolemaic papyri; in the latter, the Ionic form is confined to the indicative, with the Attic form mainly in the subjunctive and participle.[1] No such distribution is found in the papyri of the Roman and Byzantine periods.

a. The Attic aorist passive ἐδυνήθην (ἠδυνήθην[2]) is the most common form:

ἠδυνήθην *PRein.* 44 = *MChr.* 82.33 (A.D. 117-38); *PMich.* 478.8 part. rest. (early 2nd cent.); *PMich.* 486.5 (2nd cent.); etc.

ἐδυνήθην *PRyl.* 113.29 (A.D. 133); *PStrassb.* 233.5 (2nd half 3rd cent.); *SB* 7872.13 (A.D. 324-37); etc.

ἐδυνήθη *POxy.* 2784.10 (3rd cent.); *POxy.* 1495.12 (4th cent.); *PAntin.* 94.6,22 (6th cent.); etc.

ἐδυνήθημεν *POxy.* 128.5 (6th/7th cent.); sim. *PGen.* 54 = *PAbinn.* 35.20 (ca. A.D. 346)

ἐδυνήθητε *PVars.* 28.3 (6th cent.)

ἐδυνήθη[σ]αν *PCairMasp.* 333.26, sim. 14-15 (6th cent.)

δυνηθῶ *POxy.* 1272.22 (A.D. 144); *PMich.* 175.21 (A.D. 193); *PHarris* 68 AB.12 (A.D. 225); *PMerton* 91.18 (A.D. 316); *PMichael.* 38.12 (6th cent.)

δυνηθῆς *PMilVogl.* 24.6 (A.D. 117); *PWürzb.* 22 = *PSarap.* 97.15 (A.D. 117-38); *POxy.* 1294.10 (late 2nd/early 3rd cent.); *PMerton* 93.25 (4th cent.); etc.

δυνηθῇ *PFlor.* 149.6-7 (A.D. 267); *POxy.* 2130.28 (A.D. 267); *PCair-Isidor.* 75.20 (A.D. 316); etc.

δυνηθῶμεν *PGiss.* 46.13 (A.D. 117-38); *POxy.* 1117.22 (ca. A.D. 178); *POxy.* 62 V = *WChr.* 278.15-16 (mid 3rd cent.: *BL* iv, 58); *PLBat.* xvi, 32.18 (A.D. 305); etc.

δυνηθῶσι *PLBat.* xiii, 14.5 (2nd cent.)

δυνηθείην *POxy.* 237 iv.12 (A.D. 186)

δυνηθείημεν *POxy.* 1469.3 (A.D. 298)

δυνηθῆναι *PMich.* 529.15 (A.D. 232-6); *PHeid.* 237.20 (mid 3rd cent.: *BL* v, 43); *POxy.* 71 i = *MChr.* 62.21 (A.D. 303); etc.

δυνηθέντες *SB* 5681.25 (A.D. 623?: *BL* ii, 2, 120)

b. The Epic, Ionic, Lyric ἐδυνάσθην (only in late Greek augmented ἠ-[3]) is also found occasionally:[4]

---

[1] Mayser i², 2, 94, 156, 158; *BDF*, § 101, s.v.

[2] For the variation in the augment and for further exx., see above, pp. 230-1.

[3] Veitch, s.v. ἐδυνάσθη may orig. have been *metri grat.* for *-άθη (Schwyzer i, 762).

[4] Both forms are also found wo. appar. distinction in the mag. papp., e.g., μὴ δυνασθῇ *PGM* 7.911, w. μὴ δυνηθῇ 909, δυνηθῶσιν 938 (3rd cent.); ἵνα μὴ δυνηθῇ *PGM* 61.17 (late 3rd cent.); *PGM* 4.354 (4th cent.).

ἠδυνάσθην *POxy.* 743.36 (2 B.C.)

ἠδυνάσθη *Archiv* v, p. 381, #56.4 (prob. late 1st cent.)

δυνασθῶ *PSI* 967.11-12 (1st/2nd cent.); *SB* 9017 (31).17 (1st/2nd cent.)

δυνασθῇς *PMich.* 476.29 (early 2nd cent.); *PMich.* 507.4 (2nd/3rd cent.); *PMeyer* 22.3 (3rd/4th cent.); *PMichael.* 39.11 (Byz.); etc.

[δ]υνασθῇ *SB* 10200.14 (ca. A.D. 250)

δυνασθῶμεν *PMich.* 421.22 (A.D. 41-54); *PHamb.* 86.9 (2nd cent.); (for fut.) *POxy.* 1069.16, with δυνασθῇ 29-30 (3rd cent.)

δυνασθῶσιν *PGen.* 62 = *PAbinn.* 16.8 (ca. A.D. 346)

δυνασθῆναι *PMich.* 226.32-33 (A.D. 37)

c. Confusion between the two formations is reflected in the hybrid forms δυνησθῇ *PMich.* 464.21-22 (A.D. 99) and δυναθῇ *PMich.* 518.5 (1st half 4th cent.).

VII. VOICE[1]

Analogical levelling in mixed verbal systems brought about the occasional use of active futures in verbs which formed only a future middle in classical Greek. New aorist and future passive formations were created in some verbs which had only an aorist or future middle in classical Greek. Some classical deponent verbs occasionally have active forms.

A. FUTURE ACTIVE FOR FUTURE MIDDLE

Some future active forms are found in active verbs which in classical Greek had only a future middle (*futura medii*). This phenomenon is not so frequent in the papyri as in the New Testament and Koine literature, but is more frequent than in the Ptolemaic papyri, in which only one such new formation is attested.[2] The following forms occur:

> ἕως ἀκούσω *POxy.* 294.15-16 (A.D. 22)
>> ἀκούσεις *PMich.* 477.39 (early 2nd cent.)
>> ὑπακούσειν *BGU* 747 = *WChr.* 35 ii.2 (A.D. 139); *POxy.* 1667.11 (3rd cent.)[3]
>> perhaps also κατηχευσεν (for κατακούσειν?) *PLond.* 239 = *PAbinn.* 31.9 (ca. A.D. 346)[4]
> but ἀκουσόμεθα *PJand.* 101.4 (5th/6th cent.)
> ἀπαντήσο *sic PGen.* 56 = *PAbinn.* 37.24 (ca. A.D. 346)
>> ἀπαντήσειν *PLips.* 53.8 (A.D. 372)[5]

---

[1] Schwyzer i, 756-63, 779-83; Chantraine[2], § 185-92, 293-301; Mayser i[2], 2, 130, 157-8; Crönert, 230-1, 236-8; *BDF*, § 77-79.

[2] (ἐκφεύξειν) Mayser i[2], 2, 130. Cf. *BDF*, § 77; Crönert, 230-1.

[3] Cf. also from the mag. papp. ἀκούσεις *PGM* 3.453,456 (A.D. 300+); ἀκούσει (3 sg.) *PGM* 1.187 (4th/5th cent.). The fut. act. of this verb is first attested as a v.l. in Hyp. and then in Lyc. and other authors. It is a freq. variant in the NT (Veitch & *LSJ*, s.v.; *BDF*, § 77).

[4] But Kapsomenakis, 29, Anm. 1, takes it as a 2 sg. aor. impt.

[5] The fut. mid. is alone attested in the compd. ἀπ- in class. Att. The fut. act. is found in the Herc. papp. and other Koine authors, along w. the mid., and excl. in the NT in ἀπ- and συν- (Veitch & *LSJ*, s.v.; Crönert, 230; *BDF*, § 77).

ἐπικλαύσω *PAmh.* 154.9 (late 6th/7th cent.)[1]
ἀναπλεύσω *BGU* 601.17 (2nd cent.); *SB* 4317.8 (ca. A.D. 200)
    ἀναπλεύσειν *PAmh.* 131 = *PSarap.* 80.7-8 (early 2nd cent.)
    ἀναπλεύσοντα *PTebt.* 317 = *MChr.* 348.14 (A.D. 174/5)[2]
σπουδάσεις (fut. as impt.) *POxy.* 7456.8 (A.D. 16)[3]

Other examples are found in inscriptions and magical papyri.[4]

This slight increase in the number of late active future formations in verbs which had only a future middle in classical Greek represents the levelling of an irregular element in these mixed verbal systems. Verbs whose primary reference was to a physical action, functional or organic, formed a future middle in Attic.[5] But this usually lone middle form in an otherwise active conjugational system was an anomaly which tended to be regularized in late Greek.[6] It was eliminated in Modern Greek.[7]

B. NEW AORIST PASSIVE FORMATIONS

1. The following post-classical aorist and future passive formations of deponent and other intransitive verbs are found in the papyri of the Roman and Byzantine periods:

ᾐσθάνθην *PMich.* 486.7 (2nd cent.)[8]
ἐβουλήθην, etc., see above, p. 229.
    βουληθησομέν[ην] *PCairMasp.* 151-2.176 (A.D. 570)[9]
ἐγαμήθηι *POxy.* 361 descr. (A.D. 76/77)
    [ἐγ]αμήθη, γαμηθῇ *PStrassb.* 41 = *MChr.* 93.16,25 (ca. A.D. 250)
    γαμηθῇ *POxy.* 907 = *MChr.* 317.20 (A.D. 276)
    γαμηθῆναι *PGrenf.* ii, 76 = *MChr.* 295.11 (A.D. 305/6)

---

[1] The fut. act. is found in D.H. etc.; both voices are used in the NT (Veitch & *LSJ*, s.v.; *BDF*, § 77).

[2] The fut. act. is late but widespread (Veitch & *LSJ*, s.v.).

[3] The fut. act. is found in Plb. D.S. and later authors, and in the NT (Veitch & *LSJ*, s.v.; *BDF*, § 77).

[4] E.g., in very late inscrr., as in the NT, ἁμαρτήσει *SB* 7429.11; 7430.13; 7432 (all 11th/12th cent.). Cf. also ἁμαρτίσει *SB* 4949.19 (A.D. 753); sim. 5716.17 (A.D. 1172?); etc. In the mag. papp., θαυμάσεις is found in *PGM* 4.161,233,2298,3170-71 (4th cent.); *PGM* 13.252 (A.D. 346); sim. *PGM* 36.75 (4th cent.).

[5] Rutherford, *Phryn.*, 381, 383; cf. *KB* i, 2, 243-5. This was a particularly old type of fut. in Gr., very freq. and stable in Att., and also found in other dialects (Schwyzer i, 779, 781-2).

[6] Cf. Crönert, 230-1; *BDF*, § 77; Dieterich, 204-5; Psaltes, 218-19.

[7] Cf. Hatzidakis, *Einl.*, 197.

[8] The aor. pass. form is found in scholiasts, w. the fut. and aor. pass. in the LXX, etc. (Veitch & *LSJ*, s.v.).

[9] The aor. pass. form is found in Att. in S. inscrr. etc., but the fut. pass. is late: v.l. Aristid. Gal. (Veitch & *LSJ*, s.v.).

γαμηθεῖσα *PBrem.* 39.10 (2nd cent.)[1]
ἐλυπήθην *PMich.* 487.5 (2nd cent.); *POxy.* 115 = *WChr.* 479.3 (2nd
cent.); *SB* 8090.5 (2nd/3rd cent.); *POxy.* 1676.10 (3rd cent.); etc.
ἐλυπήθη *PMich.* 497.15 (2nd cent.)
ἐλυπήθημεν *PFouad* 80.4 (4th cent.)
μαχεσθῆναι *PFouad* 79.12-13 (3rd/4th cent.)[2]
μελ ηθῆς *PMich.* 466.35 (A.D. 107); see further below, pp. 366-7[3]

This is a continuation of the tendency throughout the history of Greek to
extend the -θη- formation to more and more verbs. Even classical Attic has
an aorist passive in many verbs which in Epic are found only in the aorist
middle, as ἐβουλήθην and ἐδυνήθην.[4]

2. The aorist passive of διαλέγομαι is preferred, as in classical Greek and
in the Ptolemaic papyri, not the aorist middle as common elsewhere in the
Koine.[5] For examples of this aorist passive formation, see above, pp. 313-14.

3. Conversely, the aorist middle of ἀρνέομαι is preferred to the classical
aorist passive formation in the papyri as elsewhere in the Koine:[6]

ἀπαρνηθέντες 'illegitimate' *PGrenf.* i, 53 = *WChr.* 131.35-36 (4th cent.)
but ἠρνήσατο *PFlor.* 61 = *MChr.* 80.49 (A.D. 85); *PMich.* 466.14 (A.D.
107); *PPhil.* 2 i.6 part. rest. (2nd cent.)
ἀρνήσωνται *SB* 8945.26 (late 3rd cent.)
ἀρνήσασθαι *PLond.* 1912.41 (A.D. 41); *BGU* 195.22-23 (A.D. 161)
ἀρνησάμενος *POxy.* 237 viii.14 (A.D. 186)

4. The aorist passive of ἀποκρίνομαι in the meaning "answer" is found only
sporadically; the classical aorist middle is preferred:[7]

---

[1] The aor. pass. formation is normal in the NT and elsewh. in the Koine: Plu. etc.
(Veitch & *LSJ*, s.v.; *BDF*, § 78, 101 s.v.).

[2] The aor. pass. formation is found in Plu. Paus., the fut. pass. only Sch.rec.A. (Veitch
& *LSJ*, s.v.).

[3] This aor. pass. formation is attested in S. *AP*, Flb. Ps.-Callisth., the fut. pass. as a
v.l. in Aeschin. X. D.H. and in the LXX, D.S. (Veitch & *LSJ*, s.v.).

[4] Cf. Schwyzer i, 757, 760; Chantraine[2], § 189, 192; Hatzidakis, *Einl.*, 193-4. Such aor.
pass. formations as appear in Att. are also used in the papyri, e.g., ἐγενήθην, ἐδεήθην,
ἤσθην, ἐπορεύθην, ἐφοβήθην.

[5] Cf. Veitch & *LSJ*, s.v.; *MS*, 193; Crönert, 237; *BDF*, § 78. The aor. mid. of this verb
was used in Ep. in the sense of 'pondered,' in late prose in the sense of 'discussed.' As in
the simple λέγω in the meaning 'say,' the 1 aor. pass. formation is always used in this compd.
(see above, pp. 313-14).

[6] The aor. pass. formation is preferred in Att. The aor. mid. is Ep.-Ion., and is found
in many inscrr. Only the aor. mid. is found in the Ptol. papp. and in the NT (Veitch & *LSJ*,
s.v.; Crönert, 236 & n. 7; *BDF*, § 78; Mayser i[2], 2, 170).

[7] The aor. pass. formation was used in this verb in the sense 'to be separated' in Hom.
Archil. Hdt. etc., but in the sense 'answered' (condemned by Phryn. 86), it is unknown in

ἀπεκρείθη *SB* 8247.4 (1st cent.)
but ἀπεκριν[ά]μην *PGiss.* 40 ii = *MChr.* 378.8 (A.D. 215)

    ἀπεκρίνατο *PSI* 1100.17,20,22 (A.D. 161); *SB* 7558.22 (A.D. 172/3?);
    PMich. 365.15 (A.D. 194); *POxy.* 2341.13,14-15 part. rest. (A.D.
    208); sim. *BGU* 969 i.16 part. rest. (A.D. 142?); *BGU* 592 i.3 part.
    rest. (2nd cent.); *BGU* 361 iii.6,29 (A.D. 184); *BGU* 388 = *MChr.*
    91 ii.17,30-31 (2nd half 2nd cent.); *PAntin.* 87.12 part. rest., 15
    (late 3rd cent.); etc.

    ἀποκρίνασθαι *PFlor.* 294.39 (6th cent.)
    ἀποκρειναμένων *PAmh.* 66.37 (A.D. 124); *POxy.* 237 vii.33, with
    ἀπεκρείνατο vii.25 (A.D. 186)

C. THE FUTURE MIDDLE AND PASSIVE

1. The future middle, originally serving for the passive as well, was replaced
by special future passive formations built on the first and second aorist passive
and ceased to be used in a passive sense by the fourth century B.C.[1] Analogous
futures, passive in form, were likewise substituted for the future middle in many
deponent and intransitive verbs, e.g., φανήσεται *POxy.* 237 v.16 (A.D. 186),[2]
φυησομένωι *PFlor.* 20 = *WChr.* 359.20 (A.D. 127).

2. The future middle formation is generally retained in the papyri, however,
as in the New Testament and elsewhere in the Koine, in γενήσομαι, δυνήσομαι,
and πορεύσομαι:[3]

    γενήσεται *PSI* 737.12 (2nd/3rd cent.?); *PLond.* 1032 (iii, 283).4 (6th/7th
    cent.)
    γενήσονται *POxy.* 1672.8 (A.D. 37-41)
    γενήσεσθαι *PMilVogl.* 76.9 (2nd cent.)
    γενησόμενον, -ους *PCairMasp.* 312.31 (A.D. 567)
        γενησομένου *PGiss.* 56.16 abbrev. (6th cent.); *StudPal.* xx, 218.24
        (7th cent.)
        γενησομένην *PHermRees* 12.3 (2nd/early 3rd cent.: *BL* v, 44);
        PAmh. 154.9 (late 6th/7th cent.)

---

earlier Att., exc. Pherecr. Pl.; after Macho ap. Ath. it became very freq. throughout the
Koine, esp. in inscrr., the Ptol. papp., LXX, and NT (Veitch & *LSJ*, s.v.; Nachmanson,
168; Hauser, 119; Mayser i², 2, 158; *BDF*, § 78; Crönert, 236). It is found excl. in the mag.
papp.: ἀποκριθῆς *PGM* 7.330 (3rd cent.); ἀποκρίθητι *PGM* 4.1032 (4th cent.); ἀποκρι-
θήσεται *PGM* 12.159 (A.D. 300-50); 4.231,249-50 (4th cent.); 1.160 part. rest. (4th/5th cent.).

[1] Schwyzer i, 756, 763; Chantraine², § 299. The formation in -(θ)ήσομαι was itself orig.
intransitive.

[2] Cf. also from the mag. papp. φανήσεται *PGM* 4.249,549,3253 (4th cent.); 7.349 (3rd
cent.). Both forms are found in the *NT* (*BDF*, § 79; cf. Crönert, 238).

[3] Cf. *BDF*, § 79; Crönert, 237-8; Mayser i², 2, 158-9 (the fut. of γίνομαι is not attested).

ἐπιγενησομέ[ν]ων *BGU* 8 ii.4 (ca. A.D. 248)

δυνήσομαι *SB* 8252 = *PFouad* 26.14 (A.D. 157-9); *SB* 9558.11 (A.D. 325)

δυνήσεται *PCairIsidor.* 62.20 (A.D. 296); *POxy.* 2187.29 (A.D. 304); *PBouriant* 20 = *PAbinn.* 63.41 (A.D. 350); etc.

δυνησόμεθα *PCairMasp.* 313.13 (6th cent.)

δυνησομένο(υ) *PCairMasp.* 97 R.49 (6th cent.)

δυνησομένη *SB* 5763.49 (A.D. 647)

δυνησομένους *PCairMasp.* 314 i.21; sim. ii.13 (ca. A.D. 527); *PCairMasp.* 151-2.244 (A.D. 570)

δυνηθήσομαι *PLond.* 897 (iii, 206-7).13 (A.D. 84)[1]

πορεύσομαι *PCairMasp.* 151-2.259 (A.D. 570)[2]

D. ACTIVE FORMS OF DEPONENT VERBS

1. ἀσπάζομαι is occasionally found with active forms (often along with middle forms) in private letters:[3]

ἀσπάζω, ἀσπάδι (for -ζει) *POxy.* 1670.20,24 (3rd cent.)

ἀσπάζω *SB* 6262.20,22 (3rd cent.); *PJand.* 117.10 (3rd cent.); *POxy.* 2682.18,21, with ἀσπάζαιται (for -εται) 15,16 (3rd/4th cent.); *PSI* 900.18-19, with ἀσπασώμεθα 18 (3rd/4th cent.)

ἀσπάσζο sic *SB* 7662.24, with ἀσπάσζετε (for -ζεται) 21 (late 2nd cent.)

ἀσπάζομεν, ἄσπασον *POxy.* 1158.18,20 (3rd cent.)

αἰσπάζομεν sic *PHarris* 158 V.1 (5th/6th cent.)

ἄσπαζε *PMich.* 493.19, with ἀσπάζετε (for -ται) 21 (2nd cent.); *POxy.* 1218.9-10, with [ἀσ]πάζονται 13 (3rd cent.); *PIFAO* ii, 40.10 (3rd cent.); *PGissBibl.* 32.19, with ἀσ[π]άζονται 28 (3rd/4th cent.); etc.

ἀσπάζετε *SB* 7356 = *PMich.* 203.36, with ἀσπάζου 29, [ἀ]σπάζεται (3 sg.) 35 (A.D. 98-117)

ἄσπασον *SB* 7244.29 part. rest., 32 (mid 3rd cent.); *SB* 7243 = *SB* 9746.7 part. rest. (early 4th cent.)

ἀσπάσατε *PMich.* 211.10, with ἀσπάζεται 11-12 (2nd/3rd cent.)

---

[1] This fut. pass. formation is also found in some Koine authors (Veitch & *LSJ*, s.v.; Crönert, 237, n. 5).

[2] A fut. pass. formation πορευθήσομαι is found in an Att. inscr. of 376-61 B.C. and in the LXX (*MS*, 193; *LSJ*, s.v.).

[3] Some other exx. of act. forms of ἀσπάζομαι are only apparent, e.g., ἄσπασε = ἄσπασαι, w. interchange of αι and ε (see Vol. i, 192-3) *POxy.* 1583.12 (2nd cent.). One act. form of this verb is also found in the Byz.Chron. and is noted in Hsch. (Psaltes, 247; *LSJ*, s.v. *ad fin.*).

2. Active forms of other deponent verbs are found occasionally:[1]

βούλεις *PLond.* 1927.57 (mid 4th cent.)
    βούλῃς *POxy.* 1593.14 (4th cent.)
    βούλητε *MChr.* 361.10 (A.D. 360)
    β[ο]υλήσῃς *PBaden* 43.23 (3rd cent.)
ἕως παραγένω *PSI* 1557.8 (A.D. 214)
δέο *POxy.* 1295.10 (2nd/early 3rd cent.)
    δεήσει *POxy.* 1417.15 (early 4th cent.)
    ἐδέησεν "ask" *POxy.* 1257.17 (3rd cent.); (clearly) *PLond.* 1915.10
    (ca. A.D. 330-40)
δύνῃς *PSI* 972.20 (4th cent.?)
    δυνήσατε *PLond.* 1916.24 (ca. A.D. 330-40)[2]
ἐργάζουσιν *PSI* 825.11 (4th/5th cent.)
ἔρχω *PJand.* 22.2 (A.D. 619-29)
[ε]ὐλαβεῖν *BGU* 665 ii.4 (1st cent.)
εὔξω *PLond.* 418 = *PAbinn.* 7.12 (ca. A.D. 346)
ἡγήσα[ς] (ptc.) *PFay.* 111.19 (A.D. 95/96)
[ἐ]κόμιζον *PMich.* 474.12 (early 2nd cent.)
ἔκτησα *PLond.* 77 = *MChr.* 319.72,74, with κτᾶσθαι 35 (late 6th cent.)
    ἀνεκτῆσαι *PCornell* 20a.7 (ed. -σ<θ>αι) (A.D. 303)[3]
λήμψῃς *PGiss.* 105.20 (5th cent.)
λοιποῦ[με]ν *PBrem.* 58.7 (ca. A.D. 117)
ἐὰν μάχουσιν *PPar.* 18.10 (3rd cent.: *BL* iv, 67)
μέμφη (= μέμφει for μέμφεται) *BGU* 822.13 (ca. A.D. 105: cf. *PMich.*
    202)
    μέμφε *PMich.* 473.7 (early 2nd cent.)
    ἔμεμφαι (for -ε?) *PMerton* 81.16 (2nd cent.)
μεμίσθωμεν *PLBat.* xi, 11.24 (A.D. 453)
    μ[ι]σ[θ]ῶσαι *PMich.* 185.5 (A.D. 122)
ῥύσει *PLond.* 413 = *PAbinn.* 6.4 (ca. A.D. 346)
χρήσω *PCairMasp.* 77.17 (6th cent.)
    ἔχρησεν *PMich.* 492.17 (2nd cent.)

The above evidence for voice reflects a process of simplification in the use of active, middle, and passive forms.[4] The gradual substitution of aorist and future passive for aorist and future middle formations, found from Homer to classical times, led to the extension of these aorist and future passive formations to deponent and other intransitive verbs which did not have a true passive

---

[1] Parallel exx. are found occ. in the Ptol. papp. (Mayser i², 2, 164-5).
[2] Cf. Ljungvik, *Syntax*, 102 & n. 1. Perh. also ἐκδύνηκα (= ἐδύνηκα?) *PSI* 967.18 (1st/2nd cent.).
[3] Act. forms of this verb are also found in Koine lit. (Crönert, 265, n. 3).
[4] See esp. Hatzidakis, *Einl.*, 193-200; Rutherford, *Phryn.*, 186-93.

meaning. But the aorist middle was preferred in other verbs, e.g., ἀρνέομαι, because it was considered "more Attic" in post-classical Greek.[1] The force of the middle was gradually lost, leading to the occasional appearance of active forms of deponent verbs and eventually to the elimination of the middle voice as a morphemic system in Modern Greek, where it is identified formally with the passive voice.[2]

---

[1] Cf. Schmid iv, **603**.

[2] Chantraine², § **339**; Thumb, *Handbook*, § **175**; Jannaris, § **673**, **675**. The mid. is retained in many deponents and reflexives wh. however are conjugated throughout in exactly the same way as the pass. voice of transitive verbs (Thumb, *Handbook*, § **176**-7).

VIII. THE ENDINGS OF THEMATIC VERBS[1]

There is much analogical levelling in the interchange of endings of the various tense systems of thematic verbs. The endings of the first aorist are used for those of the second aorist, perfect, and imperfect; those of the present, imperfect, and second aorist for those of the first aorist and perfect. The present, future, and aorist are sometimes confused, especially in the infinitive and imperative. In addition, the subjunctive is often confused with the indicative, the imperative with the infinitive, and less regular endings tend to be replaced by more regular ones. This levelling and confusion of moods and tenses reflects a transitional period, when alternate formations of a particular tense were being eliminated, and tenses similar in meaning and form were beginning to be identified. In Modern Greek, the different aorist actives have been combined, the perfect and future systems replaced by periphrastic constructions, the subjunctive partially identified with the indicative in pronunciation, the optative and infinitive lost, the imperative limited to the second person, and the participle greatly reduced in function and form.

A. THE ENDINGS OF THE PRESENT

1. Endings of the first aorist sometimes appear in the present system (outside of the imperfect, for which see below, p. 332), e.g., θεσπίζαι *PCair-Masp.* 352 V.1 (6th cent.); ἁρμόζαι *PMon.* 1.43: *BL* i, 310 (A.D. 574); ἀσπάζα[σ]θαι *SB* 7247 = *PMich.* 214.16 (A.D. 296); προσχαρίζασθαι *PLond.* 1708.222 (A.D. 567?); λογιζάμενος *POxy.* 2283.6 (A.D. 586). These isolated occurrences are not morphologically significant. They are probably due either to an inadvertent confusion of tenses (the aorist occurs in the same verb three lines earlier in the Michigan document), or to a phonological interchange of ο and α.[2] The form ἤκαμεν *PCairMasp.* 9 R.6 (ca. A.D. 552) and *PLond.* 1674.5

---

[1] Schwyzer i, 657-72; Chantraine², § 338-55; Buck, *GD*, § 138-9, 144, 145; *MS*, 165-9; Schweizer, 165-9; Nachmanson, 148-50; Hauser, 104; Mayser i², 2, 80-92; Crönert, 210-20; *BDF*, § 80-87; Psaltes, 209-15.

[2] See Vol. i, 286-9.

(ca. A.D. 570) represents the use of perfect endings according to the sense of this verb.[1]

2. The present infinitive of both barytone and contract verbs sometimes ends in -ει or -ι, sometimes in -εν.

a. Forms in -ει:

μετάγει *POxy.* 259 = *MChr.* 101.19 (A.D. 23)
ἐγχειρεῖ *SB* 7617 = *PRein.* 103.23 = *PRyl.* 178.5 (A.D. 26)
εὑρίσκει *PMich.* 202.14-15, corr. 17 (A.D. 105)
ἐνοχλεῖ *PTebt.* 286 = *MChr.* 83.8 (A.D. 121-38)
ἔχει *PStrassb.* 54.5 (A.D. 153/4): *BGU* 1049.20 (A.D. 342)
   προσέχει *PGiss.* 54 = *WChr.* 420.17 (4th/5th cent.)
χαίρει *POxy.* 1646.8 (A.D. 268/9); *PBerlZill.* 12.2 (3rd/4th cent.)
ὀφείλει *PFlor.* 53.6: *BL* i, 140 (A.D. 327)

b. Forms in -ι:

χαίρι *WO* 1010.3 (22/21 B.C.); *WO* 1058.2 (A.D. 90?); *PMich.* 204.2,
   with ἡμέρα‹ν› 9 (A.D. 127); *PHamb.* 39 A iii.21 (A.D. 179); etc.
φυλάσσι *POxy.* 729.11 (A.D. 137)
ἔχι *PThead.* 3.16 (A.D. 299)

c. Forms in -εν:

τροφεύεν *BGU* 1058 = *MChr.* 170.26 (13 B.C.)
χαίρεν *BGU* 1208 i.1 (27/26 B.C.); *SB* 7331.2 (late 1st/early 2nd cent.);
   PIFAO ii, 45.2 (1st/2nd cent.); *PLond.* 920 (iii, 172-3).10 (A.D. 176);
   POxy. 1761.2 (late 2nd/3rd cent.); *SB* 9415 (10).2 (3rd cent.); *SB*
   10279.2 (4th cent.); etc.
εὐδοκῶεν *PMich.* 322a.44 (A.D. 46)
οἰκονομῶεν *PLBat.* vi, 13.55, with οἰκονομῖν 14 part. rest., 42 (A.D. 113/14);
   BGU 1049.20 (A.D. 342)
ὑένεν (for ὑγιαίνειν) *PBerlZill.* 12.4 (3rd/4th cent.)
cf. ἀνοίγεν *SB* 5888.2-3, inscr. (n.d.)

These present infinitives in -εν are paralleled to some extent in the future and second aorist active infinitives.[2] It seems unlikely that they reflect ancient

---

[1] This late pf. conjugation of ἥκω is also found in the LXX, NT, J. Philostr. Scymn. and in the Ptol. papp. (Veitch & *LSJ*, s.v.; *BDF*, § 101, s.v.; Mayser i², 2, 148).

[2] See below, pp. 334-5, 346.

dialectal infinitives in -εν,[1] especially since there are no traces of these forms in the Ptolemaic papyri.[2] Nor do they seem to be merely instances of the phonological interchange of ει and ε before a nasal[3] because Greek verbs appear as loanwords in Coptic in the form -ε.[4] This spelling is found in χαίρε (for χαίρειν) *OTait* 2016.4 (A.D. 177). Perhaps bilingual interference is operative here, but it is unclear whether the Coptic form was derived from the Greek infinitive or imperative or was just a short form. In any case, there could have been little distinction in pronunciation between -(ε)ιν and -εν in stressed or unstressed syllables.

3. The form κέλευεν *PLond.* 405 = *PAbinn.* 11.13-14 (ca. A.D. 346) seems less likely an infinitive in -εν (with *BL* i, 268 and ed. *PAbinn.* n. ad loc.) than a present imperative with addition of -ν. This addition of a superfluous -ν is paralleled in first aorist imperatives with present endings.[5]

B. THE ENDINGS OF THE IMPERFECT

1. The ending -σαν, originating in the third person plural imperfect ἦσαν and in the sigmatic aorists, as ἔλυσαν, and extended early to the imperfect of -μι verbs, as ἐτίθεσαν,[6] is found occasionally in the papyri as widely elsewhere in the Koine[7] also in the imperfect of thematic verbs, including contract verbs:

> ἐκ<ρ>άζοσαν *POxy.* 717.11 (late 1st cent. B.C.)
> ὠφείλοσαν (for ὤφειλον or ὤφειλαν) *BGU* 2047.5 (A.D. 8)
> κατε[ί]χοσαν *PMich.* 421.18-19 (A.D. 41-54)[8]
> προεγάμουσαν *BGU* 251.4 part. rest. (A.D. 81); *BGU* 183 = *MChr.* 313.6 (same hand) (A.D. 85)
> ἤτουσαν *PPrinc.* 71.4: *BL* iii, 150 (3rd cent.)
> ἠξίουσαν *BGU* 1024 vi.12: *BL* i, 89, corr. elsewhere (late 4th cent.: *BL* i, 88)

---

[1] This infin. ending occurred in Arc. and in the language of some Dor. speakers (Chantraine[2], § 328).

[2] Mayser i[2], 2, 193.

[3] See Vol. i, 256-62.

[4] Schwyzer i, 807; Steindorff, 130-1; Böhlig, 46-47, 129; Böhlig, *Akten d. XI. intern. Byz.-Kongresses*, 65-66; cf. Introd. to Morphology above, p. XXI.

[5] See below, pp. 349-53.

[6] Schwyzer i, 665-6; Chantraine[2], § 353.

[7] Sim. forms are found in late inscrr. of various dialects, in the Ptol. papp., and in the LXX, NT, and some Koine authors (*ibidd.*; Buck, *GD*, § 138; Schweizer, 166; Nachmanson, 148-9; Mayser i[2], 2, 83-84; *BDF*, § 84.2; Jannaris, § 791; Crönert, 210; Kretschmer, *Entst.*, 9; Thumb, *Hell.*, 198-9).

[8] The forms εἴχοσαν in *AP* and ἔσχοσαν in Scymn. are called Alexandrian Greek forms of the 3 pl. impf. and aor. (Veitch & *LSJ*, s.v.).

2. In other imperfect forms, there is a transfer of endings from the first aorist, as elsewhere in the Koine:[1]

εἶχα *PCairIsidor.* 65.5 (A.D. 298/9); *PBouriant* 25.9 (5th cent.)
    εἴχαμεν *POxy.* 2873.9 (A.D. 62); *POxy.* 162 = *POxy.* 942.3 (6th/7th cent.); etc.
    εἴχατε *POxy.* 1585.2 (late 2nd/early 3rd cent.)
    εἶχαν *PRyl.* 238.11 (A.D. 262); *SB* 9622.19 (A.D. 343); *PSI* 71.10 (6th cent.)
    προεῖχαν *PGrenf.* ii, 41 = *MChr.* 183.5 (A.D. 46)
ἔλεγας *BGU* 595.9 (ca. A.D. 70-80)
    ἐλέγαμεν *BGU* 1673.16,19, with aor. ἐξαίβαλαν 9, etc. (2nd cent.)
    ἔλεγαν *PBrem.* 64.5 (ca. A.D. 117); *PBaden* 85a.15 (2nd cent.); *PErl.* 119.7 (3rd cent.)
ὠφείλαμεν *BGU* 515 = *WChr.* 268.5 (A.D. 193)
    ὤφειλαν *CPR* 14 = *StudPal.* xxii, 172.14 (A.D. 166)
    ὤφιλαν *PTebt.* 397 = *MChr.* 321.24 (A.D. 198)
    ὄφειλαν *PAmh.* 110.18 (A.D. 75)
ἐποτίζαμ(εν), συνεκομίζαμεν, συνελέγαμεν *BGU* 698.16,21,25 (2nd cent.)
ἐβάσταζαν *BGU* 454.12 (A.D. 193)
ἤμελλα *PBouriant* 23.13 (late 2nd cent.); *POxy.* 1160.15 (late 3rd/early 4th cent.)
παρατέμνας *PVars.* 26.15-16 (4th/5th cent.)
ἐχαρίζατο *PCairMasp.* 9 R above line 3 (6th cent.); *PLond.* 1674.3 (ca. A.D. 570)
ἐξειργάζατο *PCairMasp.* 97 V d.43, exercise in style (6th cent.)

3. Conversely, imperfect or second aorist endings are found sporadically in first aorist forms, e.g., ὄμοσον (for ὄμοσα) *PCairMasp.* 328 v.26; vi.25 (A.D. 521); κλαύσετε (for κλαύσατε) *SB* 9673 c.8, inscr. (30 B.C. - A.D. 14).

4. Present endings in the imperfect are read in ἐλέγει *BGU* 261.20 (ca. A.D. 205: cf. *PMich.* 202) and perhaps ἐβάλλειν *BGU* 1676.9 (2nd cent.).

C. THE ENDINGS OF THE FUTURE

Endings of the first aorist are likewise occasionally substituted for those of the future, mainly in the infinitive middle and in the participle. Future endings

---

[1] εἴχαμεν (2nd cent.) and two uncertain exx. are found in the Ptol. papp. (Mayser i², 2, 84-85, 144). No exx. are found, however, at Magn. or at Perg. exc. in a pres. ptc. if so interpreted (Schweizer, 182). Few instances are found in mss. of the LXX and nowhere attested unanimously; the NT has several exx., but likewise never unanimously (*BDF*, § 82). Two exx. are found in Att. inscrr. of Rom. times (*MS*, 184). See further Dieterich, 240-44; Jannaris, § 789, 794-5.

are conversely substituted for those of the first aorist occasionally in the infinitive active and middle.[1] This limited exchange of endings between future and aorist is paralleled to a lesser extent in the Ptolemaic papyri and elsewhere in the Koine.[2]

1. First aorist endings are found in the future infinitive middle, not only in instances in which syntactical confusion could be a cause, as in ἀξιῶ ἀναγράψασθαι *PMich.* 171.16-17 (A.D. 58), next to ἀξιῶ ἀναγράψεσθ[α]ι *PMich.* 170.12-13 (A.D. 49), but also very frequently in instances in which the aorist ending is added to a specifically future stem:

> ἐπελεύσασθαι *SB* 5275.18 (A.D. 11); *PMich.* 250.6 (A.D. 18); *PSI* 905.11 (A.D. 26/27); *POxy.* 1282.29 (A.D. 83): *PLBat.* vi, 9.16-17 (A.D. 107); *PLips.* 27 = *MChr.* 293.27-28,35 (A.D. 123); *PMilVogl.* 85.24-25 (A.D. 138); *CPR* 139.10 (2nd cent.); *POxy.* 1200.28 (A.D. 270: *BL* ii, 2, 99); *POxy.* 2770.13 (A.D. 304); *PCairGoodsp.* 13.11 (A.D. 341); *PMon.* 8.27 (late 6th cent.); etc.
>
> παρέξασθαι *PSI* 1118.17 abbrev. (A.D. 25/37); *PMich.* 583.15, corr. 21 (A.D. 78); *PSI* 897.29 (A.D. 93); *POxy.* 270 = *MChr.* 236.8,39 (A.D. 94); *PStrassb.* 151 = *SB* 8941.16 (ca. A.D. 100: cf. *BL* v, 134); *CPR* 191.7 (2nd cent.); *PMich.* 428.7 (A.D. 154): *BGU* 709.14 (A.D. 138-61); *PBouriant* 15.164 (A.D. 138-61: *BL* iv, 10); *PHamb.* 15.11 (A.D. 209); *CPR* 175.18 (1st half 3rd cent.); *PThead.* 2.10,11 (A.D. 305); 1.12 (A.D. 306); etc.
>
> ἔσασθαι *POxy.* 260 = *MChr.* 74.11 part. rest. (A.D. 59); *PFlor.* 370.2 (A.D. 132)
>
> παρέσασθαι *PTebt.* 411.10 (2nd cent.)
>
> παραλήμψασθαι *PLBat.* vi, 15.150 (ca. A.D. 114)
>
> ἀντιλήμψασθαι *PLond.* 301 = *MChr.* 340.6-7 (A.D. 138-61); *PJand.* 33.12 (A.D. 180-92)
>
> ἀναλήμψασθαι *PFay.* 20.14 (late 3rd/early 4th cent.)
>
> ἀξιωθήσασθαι *PLBat.* xvi, 35.25 (A.D. 144)

2. First aorist endings are also found occasionally in the participle, active and middle.

a. Active:

> τὰ ἐξ αὐτῶν περιεσόμενα πάν[τα] ἔτι δὲ καὶ οἰκονομήσαντα περ[ὶ] αὐτῶν *PFlor.* 86 = *MChr.* 247.24 (late 1st cent.)

---

[1] See below, pp. 352-3.

[2] Mayser i², 2, 163-4; Schmid i, 96; ii, 51-52; iv, 619; Dieterich, 244-5; Hatzidakis, *Einl.*, 190-93.

συνέστησά σοι (for σε) ... φροντιοῦντά μου τῶν ... ὑπαρχόντων καὶ
ἀπαιτήσαντα τοὺς μισθωτάς ... μισθώσαντα ἢ αὐτουργήσαντα ... καὶ
πάντα ἐπιτελέσαντα ... καὶ ... ποιησάμεν[ο]ν *BGU* 300 = *MChr.*
345.3-9 (A.D. 148)

δηλώσαντα (fut. ptc. of purpose) *PWürzb.* 9.70 (A.D. 161-9)

ἐποίσαντες *PCairGoodsp.* 14.9 (A.D. 343)

[δ]ίδομαι καὶ εἰσαγγέλλω τὸν ἑξῆς ἐγγεγραμμένον λιτουργὸν λιτουργήσαντ[α] *PLips.* 65 = *WChr.* 404.9-10 (A.D. 390)

τὸν δὲ τολμήσαντα ἐγκαλεῖν σοι ... *PMon.* 11.56 (A.D. 586)

b. Middle:

ἀπέστειλα πρός σε τὸν ἀγροφύλακα διηγησάμενός (for -όν) σοι *PRein.*
48.3-5 (2nd cent.)

δικασάμενον (fut. ptc. of purpose "to stand trial") *PMich.* 365.13 (A.D.
194)

ὑποδεξάμενα (for -όμενα) *PBeattyPanop.* 2.104-5 (A.D. 300)

There was probably no distinction in pronunciation between the forms -εσθαι
and -ασθαι and between the forms -σοντα and -σαντα, -όμενος and -άμενος in
view of the frequent interchange of α with ε and ο.[1]

3. The future infinitive active, like the present infinitive active, sometimes
ends in -ει or -ι, in -εν or -ε, and in Byzantine documents in the anomalous
spellings -ειεν or -ιεν.

a. Forms in -ει:

ἀποδώσει *PBouriant* 20 = *PAbinn.* 63.7 (A.D. 350)
ἐμμενεῖ *PMerton* 125.5 (6th cent.)
παρέξει *PMon.* 11.57 (A.D. 586)

b. Forms in -ι:

βεβαιώσι *PMich.* 251.35 (A.D. 19)
παραστήσι *PRyl.* 94.11 (A.D. 14-37)
τελέσι *PGrenf.* ii, 41 = *MChr.* 183.9 (A.D. 46)

c. Forms in -εν:

κατηχεύσεν (for κατακούσειν?) *PLond.* 239 = *PAbinn.* 31.9 (ca. A.D. 346)
ἐλευθερώσεν *SB* 8994.14 (6th cent.)

---

[1] See Vol. i, 278-90.

d. Forms in -ε:

ἐκτινάξε *SB* 9024.19 (late 3rd/early 4th cent.)

e. Forms in -ιεν:

ἐκστήσιεν *BGU* 917.20 (A.D. 348)

f. Forms in -ειεν:

ἐγκαλέσειεν *PMon.* 9.79 (A.D. 585); *PMon.* 12.41 (A.D. 590/1?)
ὠφελήσειεν *PMon.* 11.57 (A.D. 586)
ὀφελέσειεν *PMon.* 12.44 (A.D. 590/1?)

There was probably little if any distinction in pronunciation among all these spellings in view of the frequent loss of final -ν, the occasional interchange of (ε)ι and ε, and widespread contraction in speech.[1]

D. THE ENDINGS OF THE AORIST ACTIVE AND MIDDLE

1. The thematic (second) aorist.

a. Replacement of the second aorist endings by those of the first aorist.

The endings of the first aorist are very frequently substituted for those of the second aorist. This phenomenon, paralleled throughout the Koine,[2] led to the fusion of these two aorist inflections in the Modern Greek universal aorist paradigm -α, -ες, -ε, -αμε, -ατε (-ετε), -αν(ε).[3]

This fusion of the first and second aorist endings originated in the use of both sets of endings in classical Greek, varying according to dialect, in the two verbs εἶπον/εἶπα and ἤνεγκον/ἤνεικα.[4] The presence of some first aorist endings in these verbs in classical Attic, and the gradual increase in the frequency of their occurrence in post-classical inscriptions, can be attributed to the influence of other dialects, especially Ionic.[5] The next stage in the extension of the endings of the first aorist to other thematic aorists is less clear. Schwyzer and Blass-Debrunner-Funk, on the evidence of the manuscripts of the Septuagint and

---

[1] See Vol. i, 111-14, 249-62, 295-302.
[2] *MS*, 184; Schweizer, 181-3; Nachmanson, 166-7; Hauser, 144; Mayser i², 2, 84, Anm. 2; *BDF*, § 80-81; Dieterich, 237-9; Psaltes, 209-11.
[3] Thumb, *Handbook*, § 214; Mirambel, *Gram.*, 122; Jannaris, § 797; Maspero, 92-93.
[4] See the indiv. footnotes to these verbs below.
[5] Schwyzer i, 744-5.

New Testament, see the transition in ἔπεσαν/ἔπεσα, formed on the analogy
ἐτέλεσε : ἐτέλεσα(ν) :: ἔπεσε : ἔπεσα(ν),[1] followed by εἷλε : εἷλα(ν) on the
analogy of ἤγγειλε : ἤγγειλα(ν).[2]

The evidence of the papyri of the Roman and Byzantine periods indicates
that ἔπεσον and εἷλον are rarely used with first aorist endings;[3] ἦλθον and
ἔλαβον are the second aorist formations found most frequently with first aorist
endings, except for ἤνεγκον. These verbs are, of course, among the most frequently used aorists of this type. Other second aorists have first aorist endings
in approximately the same frequency as their occurrence. In aorist middle formations, first aorist endings are most frequent in ἐγενόμην. This evidence indicates a general movement of all second aorist formations towards the use of
first aorist endings rather than individual analogical formations.

The first aorist endings most frequently used are those of the first person
singular, first person plural and third person plural, the last especially in
ἦλθον. First aorist endings are rarely found (except in εἶπον and ἤνεγκον)
in the imperative, infinitive, and participle active, but they are very frequent
in the participle (middle) of ἐγενόμην.

1) εἶπον/εἶπα.

The usage of classical Attic serves as the basis for the usage of the papyri,
with first aorist forms found in approximately the relative frequency of their
use in other classical dialects.[4] εἶπα is less common than εἶπον, while εἶπας

---

[1] Schwyzer i, 753; Debrunner, *Geschichte*, 113. *BDF*, § 80, less plausibly make the ana-
logue ἔλυσεν : ἔλυσαν.

[2] Or εἷλε : εἷλα(ν) :: ἔστειλε : ἔστειλα(ν) Debrunner, *ibid.*

[3] ἔπεσαν is found, however, more freq. in late lit. in Orph., codd. of Plu., Ach.Tat.
(dub.l.), and in Byz. authors, as Malalas, as well as in the LXX & NT (Veitch & *LSJ*, s.v.).
But in these same sources, such other forms as ἔφυγαν, εὗραν, εἵλατο, ἦλθαν, ἐφάγαμεν,
etc., also occur (Veitch, *ibid.*). In fact, ἔπεσα seems only weakly attested in the NT compared with the freq. occurrence of ἔβαλαν, εἶδα, etc. (*BDF*, § 81).

[4] In class. Att., the 1 sg. εἶπον was preferred, but 2 sg. εἶπας, and appar. 2 aor. forms
in the pl. In Hom., the 2 aor. endings are used throughout, but εἶπας is restored by Aristarch.
In Ion. (Hdt.), 1 aor. forms are used, but 3 pl. εἶπον is a standard variant of εἶπαν. The
opt. is usu. 2 aor., w. -αιμι, etc., dbtfl. in Hdt., rare elsewh. Impt. εἰπέ is preferred in
Poet.-Ion., Trag., and X., while the dual εἴπατον, and εἰπάτω and εἴπατε are Att. and
common to most dialects, but with the corresp. 2 aor. forms also used in Poet.-Ion. and Pl.
The infin. was εἰπεῖν, exc. in Hdt. and Pi. The ptc. was εἰπών in class. Att., but εἴπας in
Hdt. Hp. and later Att. The 1 aor. mid. occurs in the indic., ptc., and infin. occ. in
Poet.-Ion., Arist., and later authors; a 2 aor. infin. mid. occurs in J. (Schwyzer i, 745;
Veitch, s.v. εἴπω; *LSJ*, s.v. εἶπον). In the Att. inscrr., the impt. -άτω is found in compds.
along with -έτω 350-250 B.C., with the ptc. εἴπας ca. 300 B.C., but the infin. is always εἰπεῖν
(*MS*, 184). 1 aor. forms are freq. elsewh. in the Koine (Schweizer, 182; Nachmanson, 164-5),
incl. in the Ptol. papp., where the 1 aor. forms predominate over the 2 aor. forms by 13 : 3,
although the infin. is generally εἰπεῖν (Mayser i², 2, 135). The NT has 2 aor. forms in the
infin. and ptc. wo. exception, but elsewh. 1 aor. forms in sim. frequency to those in the
Rom. & Byz. papp. (*BDF*, § 81.1). The 2 aor. prevails w. few exceptions in Koine authors

and εἶπαν are comparatively more common. Both forms of the second person singular imperative are found, but first aorist forms prevail in the third person and in the plural. Both forms of the participle are used, but the infinitive is regularly εἰπεῖν:

εἶπα *SB* 8247.17 (1st cent.); *PMich.* 473.16 (early 2nd cent.); *POxy.* 121.3 (3rd cent.); *PLond.* 239 = *PAbinn.* 31.10 (ca. A.D. 346); sim. *PAlex.* 28.22 (3rd cent.)

but εἶπον *POxy.* 294.26 (A.D. 22); *BGU* 665 ii.8 (1st cent.); *PSI* 742.2,8 (5th/6th cent.); *PSI* 1430.6 (7th cent.); etc.

προεῖπον *SB* 7252 = *PMich.* 220.17-18 (A.D. 296); *POxy.* 2187.22 (A.D. 304); *POxy.* 2268.13 (late 5th cent.)

εἶπας *SB* 7616 = *PBon.* 44.5 (2nd cent.); *POxy.* 1063.7, with εἶπον (impt.) 4, εἰπόντα 9 (2nd/3rd cent.): *PSI* 1260.25 (3rd cent.); *POslo* 63.7 (3rd cent.); *POxy.* 1777.3 (late 4th cent.)

but εἶπες *PMich.* 488.17 (2nd cent.); *PSI* 1430.5 (7th cent.)

προείπαμεν *POxy.* 1033 = *WChr.* 476.15 (A.D. 392); *PCairMasp.* 1.32 (A.D. 514); *BGU* 836 = *WChr.* 471.11 (A.D. 527-65); etc.

εἶπαν *PLond.* 414 = *PAbinn.* 5.13 (ca. A.D. 346); *POxy.* 903.8,10 (4th cent.); *SB* 9868.4, with 1 sg. εἶπο[ν] 3 (early 8th cent.)

εἶπον (impt.) *POxy.* 1063.4, as above (2nd/3rd cent.); *PLond.* 410 = *PAbinn.* 34.18 (ca. A.D. 346)

εἰπάτω *POxy.* 2341.21 (A.D. 208)

εἴπατε *POxy.* 533.14,15,22 (late 2nd/early 3rd cent.); *POxy.* 1590.4,11 part. rest. (4th cent.)

but εἰπέ *BGU* 388 = *MChr.* 91 ii.20 (2nd half 2nd cent.); *PSI* 973.4,8 (6th cent.); sim. *POxy.* 1837.15 (early 6th cent.); *PSI* 836.15 (6th cent.); etc.

πρόσειπε *PLond.* 409 = *PAbinn.* 10.27 (ca. A.D. 346); *POxy.* 2731. 6,8 (4th/5th cent.)

εἰπεῖν *POxy.* 2187.16 (A.D. 304); *POxy.* 941.6 (6th cent.), *PAntin.* 1881.16 (6th/7th cent.); etc.

ἀντειπεῖν *POxy.* 237 v.13 (A.D. 186); sim. *PMich.* 511.15 (1st half 3rd cent.)

προσειπεῖν *PLond.* 409 = *PAbinn.* 10.3 (ca. A.D. 346); *POxy.* 2731.5 (4th/5th cent.); *POxy.* 2156.5 (late 4th/5th cent.)

εἶπας, ἴπας (ptc. more likely than 2 sg. indic.) *BGU* 1673.8,10, with ἐξαίβαλαν 9, ἐλέγαμεν (impf.) 16,19, etc. (2nd cent.)

εἴπας *PSI Omaggio* 11.17,20 (3rd cent.)

εἴπαντος *PGiss.* 11 = *WChr.* 444.8 (A.D. 118)

(Crönert, 233). The mag. papp. have 2 sg. εἶπες *PGMXtn.* 15b.9 (n.d.); 2 aor. impt. εἰπέ 9 times, and both 1 & 2 aor. ptc. εἴπας, εἴπαντος and εἰπών, εἰπόντος, etc., frequently. The MGr. form is εἶπα, conjugated according to the above-mentioned unified paradigm, but the impt. retains the old 2 aor. in πές, πέτε (Schwyzer i, 745; Thumb, *Handbook*, § 215, 218; Mirambel, *Gram.*, 139; Maspero, 127).

εἴπαντα *POxy.* 1481.6 (early 2nd cent.)
but εἰπώ(ν) *PRyl.* 231.3 (A.D. 40)
    εἰπόντος *PMich.* 466.27 (A.D. 107); *BGU* 136 = *MChr.* 86.5 (A.D.
    135); *BGU* 114 = *MChr.* 372 i.18-19, with εἰπούσης i.6 (2nd cent.)
    εἰπόντων *BGU* 82.10 (A.D. 185)

2) ἤνεγκον/ἤνεγκα.[1]

The usage of the papyri follows that of most of the classical dialects in preferring the first aorist forms. But second aorist forms are used occasionally, as in Attic, in the imperative, more frequently in the infinitive, where the first aorist endings are post-classical, and in the participle, where the endings of the second aorist were preferred in Attic.[2] The middle is predominantly first aorist.

    ἤνεγκα *PTebt.* 314.4 (2nd cent.); *PLips.* 40 iii.17 (late 4th/early 5th cent.)
    προσήνεγκα *PLond.* 178 (ii, 207-8).6-7 part. rest. (A.D. 145); *POxy.*
        237 vi.14 (A.D. 186); *PTebt.* 334.6 (A.D. 200/1)
    ἐπήνεγκα *POxy.* 516.14 (A.D. 160); *POxy.* 237 v.9 part. rest. (A.D.
        186); *POxy.* 899 = *WChr.* 361.50 part. rest. (A.D. 200); *POxy.*
        1119 = *WChr.* 397.30 (A.D. 253: *BL* i, 332); *POxy.* 2343.1 (ca.
        A.D. 288); sim. *PVars.* 10 iii.21 (A.D. 156); etc.
    ἐπήγε[γ]κας *MChr.* 372 vi.16-17 (2nd cent.)
    παρήνεγκας *PBeattyPanop.* 1.46 (A.D. 298)
    ἐνεν[έ]γκαμεν *SB* 5672.17 (A.D. 156/7)
    ἀνηνέγκαμεν, ἐπηνέγκατε *POxy.* 1115.6,12 (A.D. 284)

---

[1] For variations in the spelling of the aor. stem of this verb, see above, p. 297.

[2] ἤνεγκον is more common than ἤνεγκα in Trag. and Com. in the simple, but the 2 aor. is attested beyond doubt only in the 1 sg. In prose, it is found as a certain reading only once in a compd. (Isoc.), where it is possibly used to avoid hiatus. Elsewh. the 1 aor. indic. forms were used. Both opt. forms were used in Att. The impt. ἔνεγκε is found in E. Ar. X. and later, as Luc., while ἔνεγκον is rarely used. 1 aor. forms alone occur in the 3 sg. and in the pl. The infin. is generally 2 aor., w. the 1 aor. form in Arist. and later authors. The ptc. is more commonly 2 aor. (Pi. E. S. Th. D. etc.), with the 1 aor. in compds. in Att. and as simple in Arist. The aor. mid. occurs uniformly in 1 aor. forms exc. for the 2 sg. impt., and the infin. in Hell. authors (Veitch & *LSJ*, s.v.). The Att. inscrr. have the 3 pl. indic. ἀπήνεγκον shortly after 403 B.C., but other indic. forms are excl. 1 aor. The impt. is always the previously unattested -έτω, the ptc. only 1 aor., the infin. always 2 aor. (*MS*, 183). For Perg., see Schweizer, 182. The Magn. inscrr. invariably have the 1 aor. exc. in the infin. (Nachmanson, 165). The Lyc. inscrr. have the 1 aor. more freq. in all moods (Hauser, 114). In the Ptol. papp., the 1 aor. prevails over the 2 aor. by 10 : 1; only 1 aor. forms occur exc. in the 2 sg. impt. and in many exx. of the infin. act. (Mayser, i², 2, 136-7). Koine authors use the 1 aor. exc. in the infin. and sts. in the ptc. (Crönert, 235). The mag. papp. have προσήνεγκα *PGM* 4.187-8 (4th cent.); 1 aor. impt. ἔνεγκον *PGM* 7.636 part. rest. (3rd cent.); *PGM* 4.372; μετένεγκον *PGM* 1.837 (4th/5th cent.), but 2 aor. impt. ἔνεγκε *PGM* 31b.9 (1st cent.); 1 aor. infin. κατενέγκαι *PGM* 74.8 (2nd/3rd cent.), but 2 aor. infin. ἐνεγκεῖν *PGM* 4.2097; 1.105-6, w. κατενεγκεῖν 123-4; 1 aor. ptc. ἀπενέγκας *PGM* 5.332 (4th cent.), but 2 aor. ptc. ἐνεγκών *PGM* 1.83. The NT always has the 1 aor. exc. in the infin. (*BDF*, § 81.2).

κατηνέγκατε *POxy.* 65.3 (3rd/early 4th cent.)

ἤνεγκαν *POxy.* 1164.6 (6th/7th cent.); *POxy.* 1861.9 (6th/7th cent.); *POxy.* 1863.7 (7th cent.)

    ἀνήνεγκαν *PMich.* 194.15 (A.D. 61); *POxy.* 2228.37 (A.D. 285: *BL* v, 81)

    ἐπήνεγκαν *BGU* 36 = *MChr.* 125.11 part. rest. (A.D. 98-117); *PTebt.* 331.10 part. rest. (ca. A.D. 131); etc.

ἔνεγκον (impt.) *POxy.* 298.30 (1st cent.); *PGissBibl.* 20.36 (1st half 2nd cent.); *SB* 7247 = *PMich.* 214.20,30,31 (A.D. 296); *SB* 7248 = *PMich.* 216.10,22 part. rest. (A.D. 296); *SB* 7472 = *PLBat.* i, 3.12 (± A.D. 530); etc.

    ἐξένικον (for ἐξένεγκον) *BGU* 229.4; 230.4 (2nd/3rd cent.)

    ἀνένεγκον *PMich.* 511.19 (1st half 3rd cent.); *PPrinc.* 103.5 (5th cent.); etc.

but ἔνεγκεν (prob. for ἔνεγκε) *POxy.* 1297.16 (4th cent.)

    ἀν[ά]νεγκε *PHamb.* 87.12 (early 2nd cent.)

εἰσενεγκάτω *PRyl.* 77.37 (A.D. 192)

ἐνέγκατε *POxy.* 1887.12 (A.D. 538)

but ἰσενενκέτωσαν *BGU* 1655.20 (A.D. 169)

ἐνέγκαι *POxy.* 1760.19 (2nd cent.); *BGU* 396.10 (Arab.: *BL* i, 44); *PLond.* 1339.14; 1343.12 (A.D. 709); etc.

    ἀνενέγκαι *POxy.* 1672.10 (A.D. 37-41); *PSAAthen.* 61.7 (1st cent.); *PMich.* 511.19 (1st half 3rd cent.)

    μετενέγκαι *POxy.* 728.11 (A.D. 142); *POxy.* 1482.8 (2nd cent.); *PMichael.* 17.3,5 (2nd/3rd cent.); sim. *PLond.* 236 = *PAbinn.* 4.12 (ca. A.D. 346); etc.

but ἐνεγκεῖν *PLond.* 1705.12 (1st half 6th cent.); *PPrinc.* 89.4 (6th cent.); *PLond.* 1660.13 part. rest. (ca. A.D. 553); *POxy.* 134.24 (A.D. 569); *POxy.* 144 = *MChr.* 343.15 (A.D. 580)

    εἰσενεγκεῖν *PSI* 285.12 (A.D. 294?); *PLond.* 1663.17 (6th cent.); *POxy.* 136 = *WChr.* 383.27 (A.D. 583)

    ἀπενεγκεῖν *SB* 7249 = *PMich.* 217.24 (A.D. 296); *PLond.* 1714.46 (A.D. 570)

    προσανενεγκεῖν *PGrenf.* i, 64.3 (6th/7th cent.); *POxy.* 128.7 (6th/7th cent.); etc.

ἐνέγκας (ptc.) *Archiv* v, pp. 381-2, #56.8 (prob. late 1st cent.); *POxy.* 2276.20 (late 3rd/4th cent.); *POxy.* 1854.2 (6th/7th cent.)

ἐνένκας *POxy.* 1293.19 (A.D. 117-38)

ἐνέγκαντες *POxy.* 1068.9 (3rd cent.); *POxy.* 1863.5, with ἤνεγκαν 7 (7th cent.)

but ἀνενεγκών *POxy.* 237 vi.30 (A.D. 186)

    ἐπενεγκών *POxy.* 1885.8 (A.D. 509)

    ἐνεγκόντος, ἐνενκε[ῖν] *PMich.* 617.7,7-8 (A.D. 145/6)

        προσενεγκόντος *PHermRees* 18.2 (A.D. 323?)

ἀνενεγκούσης, παρ[εν]εγκόντος *POxy.* 237 iv.35,36 (A.D. 186)

διενεγκόντα *PCairMasp.* 28 = *MChr.* 382.3 (and 12 for διενέγκουσι) (ca. A.D. 551)

ἐνεγκόντων *POxy.* 1164.7 (6th/7th cent.)

προσηνενκάμην *BGU* 970 = *MChr.* 242.14 (A.D. 177)

ἀπηνέγκατο *SB* 7376.28-29 (A.D. 3); *PRyl.* 125.22 (A.D. 28/29); *PRyl.* 119.11,27 (A.D. 54-67); *PMich.* 423-4.21 (A.D. 197); *PAntin.* 35 ii.12 (late 3rd cent.); etc.

προσηνέγκατο *PMilVogl.* 184.13 (A.D. 41-54?); *POxy.* 266 = *MChr.* 292.9 (A.D. 96); *BGU* 5 ii.12 (ca. A.D. 138); etc.

ἀπενεγκάμεθα *POxy.* 653 = *MChr.* 90.13 (A.D. 160-62)

προηνεγκάμεθα *POxy.* 1252 R.33,36 (A.D. 288-95)

προηνέγκαντο *POxy.* 97 = *MChr.* 347.12 (A.D. 115/16)

but προηνέγκεσθαι (for -σθε) *POxy.* 2110.38 (A.D. 370)

προσενέγκασθαι *SB* 9264 = *PMilVogl.* 71.21 (A.D. 161-80)

ἀπενέγκασθαι *PSAAthen.* 17.14 (A.D. 225)

προϲενεγκάμεν[ο]ϲ *POxy.* 2407.33, with [εἰσ]ένεγκον and [εἰ]σένεγκον (impt.) 50,51 (late 3rd cent.)

προσενεγκαμένου *POxy.* 237 vii.26, with ἐνέγκαντος (for ἐνέγκαντα: *BL* i, 318) 26-27 (A.D. 186)

προϲενεγκαμένων *PPrinc.* 124.12 (A.D. 130/1)

3) Other second aorist formations with first aorist endings:

ἦλθα *BGU* 814.13 (3rd cent.); *PLond.* 418 = *PAbinn.* 7.11 (ca. A.D. 346); *PRossGeorg.* iv, Anh. (p. 100).5,7 (A.D. 619-29); etc.

ἀπῆλθα *PBaden* 100.6-7 (late 1st cent.); *BGU* 814.27,30,31 (3rd cent.); *PGen.* 56 = *PAbinn.* 37.13 (ca. A.D. 346); etc.

ἐξῆλθα *POslo* 155.1 (2nd cent.); *PLond.* 404 = *PAbinn.* 25.4 (ca. A.D. 346); *POxy.* 1349 descr. (4th cent.); etc.

ἀνῆλθα *POxy.* 1773.12 part. rest. (3rd cent.); *PPrinc.* 98.4 (4th cent.); etc.

ἦλθας *BGU* 530.11 (1st cent.); *SB* 4630.10 (2nd cent.); *POxy.* 1483.3 (late 2nd/early 3rd cent.); *SB* 7248 = *PMich.* 216.9, with ἐλθῖν also 9 (A.D. 296); *POxy.* 903.13,14, with ἀπῆλθας 20-21 (4th cent.); etc.

ἤλθαμεν *POxy.* 743.24-25 (2 B.C.); *POxy.* 2342.17, with ἐλθεῖν 13 (A.D. 102); *SB* 9451 = *PSI* 1412.7-8 (2nd/3rd cent.); etc.

ἀπήλθαμεν *BGU* 1676.3-4 (2nd cent.); *PLond.* 988 (iii, 243-4).11 (3rd cent.: *BL* i, 293)

εἰσήλθαμεν *POxy.* 1670.17 (3rd cent.)

κατεισήλθαμεν *SB* 4284.8 (A.D. 207)

ὑπεισήλθαμεν *PCairMasp.* 313.26 (6th cent.)

ἀνήλθατε *PGrenf.* ii, 77 = *WChr.* 498.13 (late 3rd cent.)

ἦλθαν *PFlor.* 322.153,158,163 (A.D. 258?); *SB* 7252 = *PMich.* 220.
26 (A.D. 296); *PLond.* 236 = *PAbinn.* 4.17 (ca. A.D. 346);
PAntin. 44.11 (late 4th/5th cent.); *PCairMasp.* 62.1 (twice) (6th
cent.); *POxy.* 1164.1, with ἐλθεῖν 8 (6th/7th cent.); etc.

ἐπῆλθαν *PFay.* 108.10 (ca. A.D. 171); *PTebt.* 332.4-5 (A.D. 176);
   BGU 454.8-9 (A.D. 193); *PGen.* 16 = *WChr.* 354.23, with
   -ελθεῖν 20 (A.D. 207); *PGen.* 49 = *PAbinn.* 57.17 (ca. A.D.
   346); *PCairGoodsp.* 15.13 (A.D. 362); *PSI* 876.9 (5th/6th
   cent.); etc.

εἰσῆλθαν *PGen.* 3 = *MChr.* 122.17, with ἐπελθών 11-12 (A.D.
   175-80); *POxy.* 123.14 (3rd/4th cent.)

ἐξῆλθαν *PMich.* 492.7 (2nd cent.); *POxy.* 1490.8 (late 3rd cent.);
   PHermRees 48.9 (5th cent.)

ἐλθάτω *POxy.* 123.20 (3rd/4th cent.)

ἀπέλθατε *PLond.* 1032 (iii, 283).10, with ἀπελθεῖν 9 (6th/7th cent.)

ἀνελθάτωσαν *POslo* 88.15-16 (late 4th cent.)[1]

ἔλαβα *PSAAthen.* 61.11 (1st cent.); *BGU* 261.18 (ca. A.D. 105: cf. *PMich.*
202); *SB* 7572.2-3 (prob. 1st half 2nd cent.); *BGU* 423 = *WChr.*
480.9 (2nd cent.); *PFouad* 45.15 (A.D. 153); *PMich.* 224.6366 (A.D.
172-3); *BGU* 814.6 (3rd cent.); *BGU* 1082.4 (4th cent.); *PBerlZill.*
13.3 (6th cent.); *POxy.* 922.26 (late 6th/early 7th cent.); etc.

παρέλαβα *OTaitPetr.* 271.3 (A.D. 43/44); *POxy.* 2567.10 (A.D. 253);
   PCairIsidor. 50.31 (3rd hand), with παρέλαβον 6,22,38 (1st hand),
   46 (4th hand) (A.D. 310); *PFlor.* 60.8 (A.D. 319); *PRein.* 108.14
   part. rest. (6th cent.); etc.

παρέλαβα, συνπαρέλαβα *PRyl.* 189.7;8,9 (A.D. 128)

ἐξέλαβα *BGU* 562 = *WChr.* 220.21 (A.D. 117+)

κατέλαβα *PMich.* 492.18-19 (2nd cent.); *SB* 9251.9 (2nd/3rd cent.);
   PRein. 117.11 (late 3rd cent.)

ἔλαβα, κατέλαβα *PMich.* 514.9,15 (3rd cent.)

ἔλαβας *SB* 5218.7 (A.D. 156); *PMeyer* 22.10 (3rd/4th cent.)

ἐλάβαμεν *PHamb.* 39 E ii.4 (A.D. 179); *PHarris* 110.5-6 (4th cent.);
   StudPal. iii, 344.3 (6th/7th cent.); *PJand.* 23.4 (6th/7th cent.);
   etc.

παρελάβαμεν *BGU* 697 = *WChr.* 321.21 (A.D. 145); *PBas.* 2.15
   part. rest., sim. 20 (A.D. 190); *OMich.* 234.4 (A.D. 274/9);
   235.3; 236.3 (both A.D. 288); *PMerton* 31.2,9 (A.D. 307);
   PCairIsidor. 41.90-91 part. rest. (A.D. 312); 48.4; 49.5 (both
   A.D. 309); *PNYU* 4a.6,22 part. rest. (A.D. 312 & 319); *POxy.*
   1963.12 (ca. A.D. 500); etc.

---

[1] Forms of ἦλθον w. 1 aor. endings in the indic. and impt. are also found in the LXX,
NT, the Ptol. papp., and the Herc. papp. (Veitch & *LSJ*, s.v.; *BDF*, § 81.3; Mayser i², 2, 84,
136; Crönert, 233). Cf. also ἦλθαν *PDura* 55 B.7 (A.D. 218-22), and from the mag. papp.
ἀνήλθαμεν *PGMXtn.* 7.28, w. ἀνήρθατε (for ἀνήλθατε) 26-27 and 3 pl. ἀνῆρθαν 23 (5th cent).

ἐπελάβαμεν *PStrassb.* 183.3 (4th cent.)

κατελάβαμεν *POxy.* 162 = *POxy.* 942.1 (6th/7th cent.)

ἔλαβαν *POxy.* 1068.9 (3rd cent.); *PMeyer* 21.11 (3rd/4th cent.); *PSI* 1081.14 (3rd/4th cent.); 1082.19 (4th cent.?); *PMerton* 38.9 (mid 4th cent.); *POxy.* 1854.1 (6th/7th cent.); *POxy.* 1867.4 (7th cent.); etc.

κατέλαβαν *SB* 7374 = *POslo* 21.8 (A.D. 71)

παρέλαβαν *PLond.* 333 = *MChr.* 176.24-25 part. rest. (A.D. 166); *PSI* 961.16 (A.D. 176); *POxy.* 2136.11 (A.D. 291); etc.

συνπαρέλαβαν *PSI* 1100.9 (A.D. 161)

λάβα(τε) *StudPal.* viii, 1195.4 (A.D. 725: *BL* i, 417)

λαβάμενοι *PLBat.* vi, 37.9 (A.D. 167)[1]

ἀπέσχα *PStrassb.* 132 = *SB* 8014.22-23,25-26,28-29,46 (all 2nd hand), with ἀπέσχον 5 (1st hand) and 12 (2nd hand!) (A.D. 262-7)

ἐπέσχα *SB* 9025.4 (2nd cent.)

ἔσχας *PSI* 1073.3 (A.D. 389)

ἔσχαμεν *WO* 504.2 abbrev. (A.D. 112); *PTebt.* 640 V (late 2nd/early 3rd cent.); *BGU* 381.6 (2nd/3rd cent.); *POxy.* 2798.4 part. rest. (A.D. 304/5); *PCairIsidor.* 41.60 (A.D. 302-5); *PNYU* 5.4,23,53 (1st half 4th cent.); *StudPal.* iii, 201.2 (4th cent.); *StudPal.* iii, 68.1 (7th cent.); etc.

ἀπέσχαμεν *POxy.* 1696.22 (A.D. 197); *PStrassb.* 175.3 (A.D. 209); *SB* 7624 = *PCairIsidor.* 111.5 part. rest. (A.D. 298); *POxy.* 2798.14 (A.D. 304/5); *POxy.* 2270.16-17 (early 5th cent.); etc.

κατέσχαμεν *PGen.* 54 = *PAbinn.* 35.22 (ca. A.D. 346)

συναπέσχαμεν *PAlex.ined.* 536 (p. 26).7 (Rom.)

ἔσχαν *POxy.* 2240.26 (A.D. 211); *POxy.* 1831.3 (late 5th cent.)

ἀπέσχαν *CPR* 5 = *StudPal.* xx, 10.3 (A.D. 168)

παρέσχαν *POxy.* 2668.11 (A.D. 311); sim. *StudPal.* viii, 830, 835, 847, etc, (6th-8th cent.)[2]

ἔβαλα *POxy.* 2729.18 (4th cent.); *POxy.* 1862.45 (7th cent.); *PRossGeorg.* v, 64.5 (7th cent.)

συνέβαλα *PRossGeorg.* iii, 4.14 (3rd cent.)

ἀπέβαλα *PLond.* 240 = *PAbinn.* 51.12 (A.D. 346); *SB* 4650.14 (n.d.)

ὑπέβαλα *PMich.* 624.9 (early 6th cent.)

ἐπέβαλα *PHermRees* 67.11 (6th cent.)

ἔβαλας *POxy.* 2783.7-8 (3rd cent.)

ἐπέβαλαν *PRein.* 47.10 (2nd cent.)

ἐξαίβαλαν *BGU* 1673.9 (2nd cent.)

ἔβαλαν *PApoll.* 63.12 (A.D. 703-15)

---

[1] Forms of ἔλαβον w. 1 aor. endings are also found in the NT (*BDF*, § 81) and in the mag. papp., e.g., ἔλαβας *PGM* 36.327 (4th cent.).

[2] Forms of ἔσχον w. 1 aor. endings are also found in Att. poetic and other Koine inscrr. (*MS*, 184; *LSJ*, s.v.).

ἀμφιβάλαι *PSAAthen.* 9.13 (before A.D. 704); *PSI* 1266.12 (=
PApoll. 9.13) (before A.D. 704)

ἐνεβαλάμην *PSAAthen.* 63.4 (2nd cent.)

ἐπεβάλατο *PGissBibl.* 27.9 (3rd cent.)

ἐμβαλαμένου *POxy.* 157.3 (6th cent.)

καταβαλάμενον *PLond.* 1359.6 (A.D. 710)[1]

εἴδαμεν *SB* 6824 = *PMich.* 157.18 (A.D. 250); *SB* 4435.14; 4436.15-16;
4439.16; 4440.17; 4441.2; etc. (A.D. 250); *POxy.* 52.14-15 part. rest.
(A.D. 325)

συνείδαμεν *SB* 4712.14 (Byz.); 4672.21 (Arab.)[2]

εὕραμεν *PPrinc.* 67.3 (1st/2nd cent.); *PAlex.* 26.16-17 (2nd/3rd cent.);
PMich. 512.2 (early 3rd cent.); *POxy.* 2274.10 (3rd cent.); *PSI* 1080.4
(3rd cent.?); *SB* 6222.12;14,34 part. rest. (late 3rd cent.); *PLond.*
1359.6 (A.D. 710); etc.

ηὕραμεν *PCairMasp.* 4.5 (ca. A.D. 552: *BL* i, 100); *PLond.* 1380
= *WChr.* 285.7 (A.D. 710/11)

εὕραν *SB* 9203.11 (A.D. 222-35); *PCairIsidor.* 75.14 (A.D. 316);
PLond. 403 = *PAbinn.* 49.13 (A.D. 346)

ηὕραν *SB* 7520.17 (A.D. 710)

εὕρασθαι *POxy.* 1204.13 (A.D. 299)[3]

ἀπέθανα *PRossGeorg.* iv, Anh. (p. 100).3 (A.D. 619-29)

ἀπαίθαναν *POxy.* 922.20, with ἀποθανόντος 10, ἀποθανών 21 (late
6th/early 7th cent.)[4]

ἔμαθα *PLond.* 243 = *PAbinn.* 8.20 (ca. A.D. 346)

ἐμάθαμεν *POxy.* 1032.25, with μαθών 49 (A.D. 162)

ἔμαθαν *POslo* 179.6 (early 3rd cent.)

ἔπαθα *PLond.* 240 = *PAbinn.* 51.13 (A.D. 346); *PRossGeorg.* iv, Anh.
(p. 100).1 (A.D. 619-29)

ἐπάθαμεν *BGU* 798.9 (Byz.)

ἔπαθαν *PTebt.* 333 = *MChr.* 115.11 (A.D. 216); *POxy.* 2783.20 (3rd
cent.); *POxy.* 1874.13 (6th cent.)

ἐνεπέσαμεν *PSI* 829.7 (4th cent.?)[5]

[ἀ]πήγαγα *PGen.* 56 = *PAbinn.* 37.9 (ca. A.D. 346)

ὠφείλαμεν *BGU* 813.7 (2nd cent.)

ὀφίλατε *BGU* 44.8 (A.D. 102)

ἐτύχαμεν *PStrassb.* 196.10 (2nd cent.)

ἐν[έ]τυχαν *PCairIsidor.* 126.9 (prob. A.D. 308/9)

---

[1] Forms of ἔβαλον w. 1 aor. endings are also found in the Magn. inscrr., the LXX, and
NT (Nachmanson, 166-7; *BDF*, § 81.3).

[2] Forms of εἶδον w. 1 aor. endings are found in the codd. of various Koine authors and
of the NT (Crönert, 233 & n. 4; *BDF*, § 81.3).

[3] Forms of ηὗρον w. 1 aor. endings are found in Att. poetic inscrr., the Ptol. papp.,
and the *NT* (*MS*, 184; Mayser i², 2, 137; *BDF*, § 81.3).

[4] Forms of ἀπέθανον w. 1 aor. endings are also found in the NT (*BDF*, § 81.3).

[5] For forms of ἔπεσον w. 1 aor. endings elsewh. in the Koine, see above, p. 336, n. 3.

ἐφάγαμεν *PGissBibl.* 25.21 (3rd cent.)

   ἔφαγαν *PHamb.* 86.14 (2nd cent.)

      κατέφαγαν *PRyl.* 152.13-14 (A.D. 42); *PStrassb.* 181.13 (A.D. 166)

   φάγαι *POxy.* 1297.10 (4th cent.)

κατέφυγα *POxy.* 2479.26 (6th cent.)

   [προσ]εφύγαμεν *PLBat.* vi, 15.72 (ca. A.D. 114)

      κατεφύγαμεν *BGU* 1572.10 (A.D. 139)

   ἔφυγαν *PSI* 1266.6 = *PApoll.* 9.7 part. rest. (before A.D. 704); *PApoll.* 18.4 (ca. A.D. 705-6)

ἐγενάμην *POxy.* 933.14-15 (2nd cent.); *POxy.* 1062.11 (2nd cent.); *SB* 7562 = *PSI* 1241.8 (A.D. 159); *PAlex.* 28.15 (3rd cent.); *PLBat.* xiii, 18.7-8 (4th cent.); *PLond.* 77 = *MChr.* 319.72 (late 6th cent.); sim. *PMich.* 209.7 (late 2nd/early 3rd cent.); etc.

   παρεγενάμην *SB* 7352 = *PMich.* 490.21 (2nd cent.); *POxy.* 131.13 (6th/7th cent.); *POxy.* 1855.8 (6th/7th cent.)

   [συνε]γενάμην *POxy.* 2419.6 (6th cent.)

   γενάμενος *PMich.* 121 R II iv.1 (A.D. 42); *PHamb.* 88.8 (mid 2nd cent.); *PMich.* 487.3 (2nd cent.); *OMich.* 153.3 (2nd cent.); *PMich.* 209.13-14,16 (late 2nd/early 3rd cent.); *PCairMasp.* 279.16 (ca. A.D. 570); etc.[1]

      παραγενάμενος *PMich.* 474.13 part. rest. (early 2nd cent.); *POxy.* 2981.3-4 (2nd cent.); *PMich.* 482.24 (A.D. 133); *BGU* 531 ii.17 part. rest. (2nd cent.)

      γεναμένου *PPar.* 17.23 (A.D. 154); *BGU* 21 ii.2 (A.D. 340); *POxy.* 1941.5 (5th cent.); 1962.5 (A.D. 500); 1960.4 (A.D. 511); *StudPal.* iii, 410.1 (6th cent.); etc.

      γεναμένης *PMich.* 340.41 (A.D. 45/46); *POxy.* 2583.13 (2nd cent.); *BGU* 835.19 (A.D. 217); *POxy.* 1985.9 (A.D. 543); *PLond.* 1676.68 (A.D. 566-73); *POxy.* 137.13 (A.D. 584); *PAntin.* 188.19 (6th/7th cent.); *PLBat.* xiii, 20.6 (6th/7th cent.)

      γεναμένων *SB* 9314 = *PMilVogl.* 129.4 abbrev. (A.D. 135); *PMich.* 423.15 (A.D. 197); etc.[2]

εἵλατο *PBeattyPanop.* 1.276 (A.D. 298); *PCairMasp.* 294.15 and above 17 = duplic. of 89 V.16 ἐξείλατο (6th cent.)

ὑφείλατο *MChr.* 372 ii.10 (2nd cent.)

ἀφείλατο *PLips.* 40 iii.23, with ἀφελόμενοι iii.12 (late 4th/early 5th cent.); *PCairMasp.* 2 ii.9 (A.D. 567: *BL* i, 100).

εἱλάμεθα *BGU* 362 = *WChr.* 96 v.6 (A.D. 215)

   ἀνειλάμεθα *PRossGeorg.* v, 15-16 i.4 (A.D. 209?)

εἵλασθε *POxy.* 1415.31 (late 3rd cent.)

---

[1] Cf. also from the mag. papp. γενάμενος *PGM* 4.875 (4th cent.); *PGM* **36**.106 (4th cent.).

[2] Ptc. forms of ἐγενόμην w. 1 aor. endings are also found in the Ptol. papp., the LXX, and the NT, as well as in Asia Minor inscrr. and in the codd. of J. (Mayser i², 2, 135; *BDF*, § 81.3; Schweizer, 181; Crönert, 232, n. 6).

εἵλαντο *PVars.* 29.3 (6th cent.); *PLond.* 1707.5 (A.D. 566)
    ἀνείλαντο *BGU* 1135.6 part. rest. (10 B.C.); *BGU* 140 = *MChr.*
        373.11-12 part. rest. (A.D. 119)
    ὑφείλαντο *PFay.* 107.2 (A.D. 133); (ὑφίλαντο) *PGen.* 3 = *MChr.*
        122.18 (A.D. 175-80); *BGU* 388 = *MChr.* 91 i.42-43 part. rest.,
        with ὑφελόμενοι i.35 & ὑφελομένη ii.38 (2nd half 2nd cent.)
    διλάμενος (for διελόμενος) *POxy.* 2283.10 (A.D. 586)[1]
ἰκάμ[ην] *BGU* 843.6 (1st/2nd cent.)

These examples of first aorist endings in thematic aorists, still comparatively rare in the first century but frequent from the early second century on, are found in various types of documents, most often in private letters, but also frequently in receipts and orders, in petitions, contracts, and occasionally in official records and correspondence. The variety of verbs and verb forms in which these endings occur illustrates the general tendency to replace endings of the second aorist by those of the first aorist, leading to the amalgamation of these two inflectional types in Modern Greek.

b. When the endings of the second aorist are used, the ending -σαν is sometimes found in the third person plural, as in the imperfect:[2]

εὕροσαν *BGU* 1201.15,16-17 (A.D. 2)
εἴποσαν *SB* 8247.11 (1st cent.)
ἔσχροσαν *SB* 10218.25 (A.D. 98-117)
ἤλθοσαν *PSI* 798.8 (2nd/3rd cent.); *PSI* 842.4 (4th cent.?)
    ἐπήλθοσαν *BGU* 36 = *MChr.* 125.9 (A.D. 98-117); *BGU* 436.8-9
        part. rest. (duplic. of preceding: for the date, see *BL* i, 45)[3]

The -σαν ending with the thematic vowel is transferred to the first aorist of αἴρω in ἤροσαν *PRyl.* 127.14 (A.D. 29); 129.11-12 (A.D. 30); 136.8 (A.D. 34); 142.19 (A.D. 37); and, with a change of o to ω, in ἤρωσαν *PMich.* 230.8 (A.D. 48).[4]

c. The normal second person singular second aorist imperative of ἔχω, namely σχές, arising from the addition of -ς perhaps originally on the analogy of θές,[5] and used regularly in classical Greek except sometimes in compounds,[6]

---

[1] Forms of εἱλόμην w. 1 aor. endings are also found in the NT and in inscrr. and codd. of Koine authors (*BDF*, § 81.3; *LSJ*, s.v.).

[2] See above, p. 331.

[3] But ἐπεξήλθοσαν orig. read in *POxy.* 2182.9 has been corr. to ἐπεξῆλθος (= -θες) ἄν; see Youtie, 'Textual Criticism,' 42.

[4] Cf. *LSJ*, s.v., who cite the same form from the LXX as 3 pl. aor. The ending -οσει in ἐὰν εἴποσει *BGU* 597.6 (A.D. 75) is simply an orthographic variant of the regular subj. -ωσι (*BL* i, 55).

[5] Schwyzer i, 800, n. 1.

[6] E.g., by E. (Veitch & *LSJ*, s.v.).

preserves the -ς in documentary papyri, as in πρόσχες (for πρόσσχες) *BGU* 830.12-13 (1st cent.) and παράσχες *PRyl*. 240.4 (3rd cent.); *PFlor*. 120.5,7 (A.D. 254); *PFlor*. 247.5 (A.D. 256); *PFlor*. 137.4-5 (A.D. 263); *PFlor*. 140.7 (A.D. 264); *PStrassb*. 32 = *PFlor*. 134**.19 (A.D. 261); *PMerton* 34.3 (A.D. 346/7); etc. Compare also παράσχεις (impt.) *BGU* 1682.12 (ca. A.D. 300).[1]

d. The second aorist infinitive active in -ειν sometimes appears in -εν, parallel to the same phenomenon observed in the ending of the present infinitive:[2]

> ἀντιλαβῖν *PLond*. 239 = *PAbinn*. 31.23, with κατηχεύσεν (for κατα-
> κούσειν?) 9 (ca. A.D. 346)
> εἰπῖν *POxy*. 1033 = *WChr*. 476.11 (A.D. 392)
> cf. ἀνενεγκῖν *SB* 3558.5, mummy label (n.d.)

e. Endings of the perfect are also sometimes substituted for those of the second aorist active in the third person plural of the indicative and in the participle.

1) The perfect ending -ασι is sometimes found in the third person plural of second aorist stems:

> ἐπήλθασι *BGU* 275.5 (A.D. 215)
> ἤλθασιν, ἀπήλθασιν *PLond*. 1914.9,10;15 (A.D. 335?)
> ἀπίλθασιν *PRossGeorg*. iv, Anh. (p. 100).4 (A.D. 619-29)
> παρελάβασιν *PGissBibl*. 27.6 (3rd cent.)
> εἴπασιν *StudPal*. xx, 262.7: *BL* ii, 2, 166 (7th cent.)

The occurrence of -ασι in the second aorist but apparently never in the first aorist[3] seems significant in view of the frequent replacement of -ασι in the perfect[4] by -αν of the first aorist but apparently never by -ον of the second aorist. In this particular, the first aorist prevails over both the second aorist and the perfect, while the perfect itself prevails over the second aorist.

---

[1] Cf. also κατάσχες *SB* 7452.20, lead tablet love charm (not later than 3rd cent.). But some fluctuation is found in the mag. papp., e.g., κατάσχες *PGM* 13.804 (A.D. 346); *PGM* 4.332,372-3 (4th cent.); *PGM* 5.363,369 (4th cent.); πρόσχες *PGMXtn*. 5c.1 (5th/6th cent.); etc.; but κατάσχε *PGM* 7.404 (3rd cent.). Only παράσχες is attested in the Byz.Chron. (Psaltes, 215).

[2] See above, pp. 330-1.

[3] However, Jannaris, § 793, finds the ending -ασι in the -κ- aor. of -μι verbs in early Xtn. lit. and much later (after A.D. 1000) in sigm. aorists.

[4] See below, pp. 354-5.

2) The second aorist participle active is occasionally formed like a perfect participle in Byzantine documents:

ἀπελθώς *PThead.* 51.2-3,7 part. rest. (4th cent.)
   ἐλθότος *PCairMasp.* 322.4 (6th cent.); *PApoll.* 39.5 (ca. A.D. 708/9)
      cf. ἰσελθότος *PColt* 146.1 (6th/7th cent.)
   ἐλθότι *PAntin.* 33.7, etc. five times (A.D. 346?)
   εἰσελθότα *PLond.* 1384.36 (A.D. 710?)
   ἀπελθότες *OMich.* 356.1 (A.D. 299/300: *BL* iv, 113)
   ἀπελθότων *BGU* 836 = *WChr.* 471.5 (A.D. 527-65)
   ἐπελθότας *PCairMasp.* 356.1 (6th cent.)
[λ]αβώς *PThead.* 51.4 (4th cent.)
   ἀντιλαβότος *PErl.* 120.9 (6th/7th cent.)
   παραλαβότα *BGU* 151.4 (Xtn.)
   καταλαβότων *PLond.* 1350.8 (A.D. 710)
     προλαβότων *SB* 10459.4 (early 8th cent.)
   ἐλαβότας[1] *PPrinc.* 100.4 (4th cent.)
βαλότος *POxy.* 1890.22 (A.D. 508)
εἰπότος *PCairMasp.* 322.4 (6th cent.)
ἀποθανότος, ἀποθανότα *PApoll.* 24.3,4 (A.D. 710)
φυγότα *PLond.* 1384.38 (A.D. 710?)
μαθότες *PApoll.* 63.26 (A.D. 703-15)

The comparative frequency of these forms, together with the mutual inter-ference of second aorist and perfect observed in other forms, suggests that these participles represent analogical formations.[2] But this analogy is probably limited to the orthographic level outside of the nominative; there could hardly have been a distinction in pronunciation between -οντα and -οτα, etc., in view of the frequent omission of ν before a dental stop and its apparently widespread loss in pronunciation in this position.[3] This is supported by frequent examples of the loss of ν in other participial forms, e.g., λύσατι (for λύσαντι), ὁμολογούτων (for ὁμολογούντων), etc.,[4] where there can be little question of confusion with the perfect tense.[5] The nominatives in -ώς may represent actual analogical formations, but there may have been no distinction in pronunciation between -ως and -ων if both final -ς and -ν were silent letters.[6]

3) Influence of the perfect, if not semantic confusion, is also found in the hybrid second aorist infinitive active ἰδαίνε, phonologically equivalent to εἰ-

---

[1] For the transferred augment, see above, p. 225.
[2] So Kapsomenakis, 91. This interpretation is supported by the exemplary quality of the orthography of most of the documents in which these forms occur.
[3] See Vol. i, 116-19. Most of the exx. cited appear in the editions as -ο ‹ν› τ-.
[4] See Vol. i, p. 116.
[5] So Palmer, p. 2.
[6] See Vol. i, pp. 131-2.

δέναι, for ἰδεῖν in *PLond*. 1917.7: *BL* iii, 100 (ca. A.D. 330-40). On the other hand, the infinitive παρασχῖναι (for παρασχεῖν) *PGen*. 62 = *PAbinn*. 16.10 (ca. A.D. 346), although almost the converse of the loss of -αι in some perfect infinitives,[1] seems to reflect a confusion with the infinitive ending of the second aorist passive -ῆναι.[2]

2. The athematic (first) aorist.

a. Endings of the second aorist (and imperfect) are also found for those of the first aorist. This phenomenon, however, takes a different form from the converse above. Here the substitution of second aorist endings for those of the first aorist is not a general development but is virtually restricted to particular endings, namely, the second person singular indicative both active and middle, and the second and third person imperative active. Some interference is also found in the infinitive active.

1) The second person singular indicative active ending -ες of the second aorist and imperfect is quite often substituted for the ending -ας of the first aorist throughout the Roman and Byzantine periods:

> ἔγραψες *BGU* 261.24-25 (ca. A.D. 105: cf. *PMich*. 202); *BGU* 38.13-14 (2nd/3rd cent.: *BL* i, 10); *PGissBibl*. 25.7 (3rd cent.); *POxy*. 1160.18,24 (late 3rd/early 4th cent.); *StudPal*. xx, 82.8 (4th cent.); *PBerlZill*. 13.7 (6th cent.); *PJand*. 23.1,10 (6th/7th cent.); *POxy*. 1867.14 (7th cent.); *PApoll*. 61.1 (A.D. 703-15); etc.
> ἀντέγραψες *PMich*. 466.8-9 (A.D. 107); *SB* 9194.7-8 (late 3rd cent.)
> ἔπεμψες *SB* 7356 = *PMich*. 203.4 (A.D. 98-117); *PMich*. 482.25 (A.D. 133); *PMich*. 484.5 (2nd cent.); *PAberd*. 70.4-5 part. rest. (2nd cent.); *POxy*. 1489.4 (late 3rd cent.); *PMich*. 519.7-8 part. rest. (4th cent.); *PJand*. 126.1 (ca. A.D. 400); *POxy*. 1863.16 (7th cent.); etc.
> ἀπόστιλες *PBerlZill*. 10.1 (1st/2nd cent.); sim. *PLBat*. xiii, 18.33 (4th cent.)
> εὐπόρησε[ς] *PMich*. 464.18 (A.D. 99)
> ἐμέτρησες *SB* 9486 = *PMilVogl*. 217.4 (A.D. 125)
> ἔβλαψες *PMich*. 473.17, with ἔπεμψας 4 (early 2nd cent.)
> ἐποίησες, ἀπένηχες, ἔπεμψε[ς], ἔπλευσες *POxy*. 119.2,11,13 (2nd/3rd cent.)
> ἠγόρασες *POxy*. 2729.21 (4th cent.)
> ὄμωσες *POxy*. 1868.3 (6th/7th cent.)

Similarly also in the -κ aorist:

> παρέδωκες *PFlor*. 254.16-17 (A.D. 259)

---

[1] See below, p. 356.
[2] Parallel 2 aor. act. infinitives in -ῆναι are cited from Byz. authors by Psaltes, 215(-16), n. 2.

ἔδωκες *PSI* 237.13 (5th/6th cent.)
ἀφῆκες *POxy.* 1067.5 (3rd cent.); *BGU* 814.18 (3rd cent.); *POxy.* 2729.30 (4th cent.)

This phenomenon, widely paralleled in inscriptions but not very common in the Ptolemaic papyri or in Koine literature,[1] may have come about through the influence of the common third person ending -ε(ν). It led to the retention of this ending -ες in the predominantly -α- inflection of the Modern Greek aorist.[2]

2) The second person singular indicative middle ending -ω is sometimes replaced by the ending -ου of the second aorist and imperfect:[3]

ἐκομίσου *POxy.* 300.6 (late 1st cent.)
[ἐ]στρατεύσου *SB* 7354.6 (early 2nd cent.)
ἐμισθώσου *PSI* 822.9 (2nd cent.); *POxy.* 1280.7 (4th cent.)
διεπέμψου *PTebt.* 413.5 (2nd/3rd cent.)
ἀπεγράψου *POxy.* 1157.24-25 (late 3rd cent.)
ἐτάξου *PRein.* 55.9 (3rd/4th cent.)
ἠσπάσου *PGrenf.* i, 53 — *WChr.* 131.12 (4th cent.)
ἐδέξου *BGU* 984.9 (4th cent.); *PStrassb.* 35.7,17 (4th/5th cent.); cf. *PColt* 47.5 (before A.D. 605?); 161.4 (7th cent.)
ἐποιήσου *PLond.* 113 (1) (i, 199-204).90 (6th cent.)
cf. διεμαρτυρήσου *PColt* 19.3-4 (A.D. 548)

Other persons of the first aorist indicative middle are found with second aorist endings only sporadically, as ἀπεγραψόμην *BGU* 421.3 (A.D. 160/1); ἐσημιοσόμην *SB* 6956.7 (n.d.); διαπέμψετο *sic POxy.* 1068.7 (3rd cent.).

3) The second person singular imperative active[4] ending -ον is occasionally replaced by the ending -ε of the second aorist and present. This ending is further sometimes written -αι, which may possibly represent an analogical formation on the model of the aorist infinitive, or the infinitive itself used as an imperative, but is in fact indistinguishable in speech from the ending -ε. A further ending -εν is also found, as in present imperatives,[5] which here might

---

[1] It is found only once in the Ptol. papp., is extremely weakly attested in the NT, and is not found at all in the Byz.Chron., but is attested occ. in other Koine and Byz. authors (Mayser i², 2, 81-82; *BDF*, § 83.2; Psaltes, 212; Jannaris, § 798; Dieterich, 239).

[2] Thumb, *Handbook*, § 214; Mirambel, *Gram.*, 122; Jannaris, § 797; Maspero, 92-93.

[3] This phenomenon is found repeatedly in the Ptol. papp. (Mayser i², 2, 91-92), and also in the mag. papp., as ἐχαρίσου *PGM* 35.23 (5th cent.). It may be phonologically motivated: see Vol. i, 210.

[4] Dbtfl. exx. of the substitution of the ending -ου of the 2 aor. impt. mid. for that of the 1 aor. are also found in the papp., as πέμψου (if mid.) *PFlor.* 240.13 (A.D. 263).

[5] p. 331.

represent a contamination of the ending -ε with the historically correct ending -ον, but is probably only an orthographic variant of the ending -ον in view of the occasional change of o to ε in final syllables, including before -ν.[1] This suggests, in further light of the apparently widespread loss of final -ν in pronunciation,[2] that while analogical causes were operating for the substitution of the second aorist and present ending for the first aorist ending in the second person singular imperative,[3] the various endings -ον, -ε, -αι, and -εν (-αιν) were possibly all identified in pronunciation in the speech of the writers of the documents in which the variant spellings occur, and therefore strictly orthographic variants of the same aorist imperatival morpheme {-ε}.

Many of the following examples occur in asyndetic and paratactic constructions, in which it is not altogether clear whether the form in question, spelled -αι, -ε, or -εν, is really an imperative or an infinitive. In other instances, the form in question may be an imperative middle -αι.

a) The ending -ε:

ὑπόμεινε *PGiss.* 19.16 (A.D. 115: *BL* v, 34)

περίμεινε (corrected from περίμεινον!) *PSI* 1100.28 (A.D. 161)

ἦ (= εἰ) δοκῖ σοι, κύριέ μου, πέμψε μοι κέρμα *POxy.* 1220.5-7 (3rd cent.); sim. *PStrassb.* 73.20 (3rd cent.); *PFlor.* 210.13 (3rd cent.)

καὶ πέμψε τὸ ἀλύσιον *PMeyer* 22.7 (3rd/4th cent.)[4]

κἂν διὰ λόγου μοι πέμψε εἰ ... *PLips.* 110.12-13 (prob. 3rd/4th cent.) cf. the ambiguous but possibly impt.[5] καλῶς οὖν ποιήσις πέμψε μοι αὐτὰ ... ἀπάλλαξε ... *BGU* 335.3-6 (Byz.?)

εἰ δὲ θέλεις, ἀπόστειλε ἐφ᾽ ἡμᾶς τὰ κτήνη (no apodosis) *POxy.* 2153.19-20: *BL* iii, 141 (3rd cent.)

---

[1] See Vol. i, 289-91, and cf. *PRyl.* 242 cited under c) below, in which 5 other changes of o to ε, 3 before -ν and 2 before -ς, are found in addition to this change in the impt. A converse phonological substitution of a -(σ)ον ending for -(σ)εν is found, e.g., in ἐπετέλεσον (for ἐπετέλεσεν) *PMich.* 228.16 (A.D. 47) and *PMich.* 230.18, with ἐξέπεσον (for -σεν) 19-20 (A.D. 48).

[2] See Vol. i, 111-14. Simple loss of -ν in the 1 aor. impt. act. is also found in such exx. as γράψο μοι *SB* 5218.13 (A.D. 156).

[3] The primary ending -ε (pl. -ετε) has replaced the ending -ον of the 1 aor. impt. act. in the impt. in MGr., exc. dialectally. This primary ending -ε is found once already in the Ptol. papp., and is also attested occ. elsewh. in the Koine (Schwyzer i, 803-4; Mayser i[2], 2, 89; Jannaris, § 813; Psaltes, 212).

[4] This very incorrectly spelled letter also has the impt. γράψα μοι in line 9. This might poss. represent an aor. impt. in -α as -στα, διάβα, etc., on the analogy γράψα : γράψατε :: λέγε : λέγετε, but in view of the extremely unreliable orthography of this letter and the presence of the impt. πέμψε in 7, γράψα is perh. better taken as an intended form in -αι, with loss of the final -ι.

[5] Cf. Harsing, 53-54, where καλῶς οὖν ποιήσεις is shown to govern various constructions, most freq. a complementary infin., but also a paratactic impt. See further the use of this and sim. expressions in Ljungvik, *Beiträge*, 95-99.

μὴ πισθεὶς οὖν τοῖς καρπώναις τὴν τρύγην ποίησε καὶ οὕτως μοι ἐπίστειλον ... *PFay.* 133 = *PFlor.* 134*.13 (A.D. 260)

συνχώρησε αὐτοῦ τούτω τὸ ἄβαξ (for τοῦτο τὸ ἄπαξ) *PLond.* 417 = *PAbinn.* 32.7-8 (ca. A.D. 346)

cf. also ὤψε *PGMXtn.* 6c.2-7 (8 times) (5th cent.)

b) The ending -αι:

αἰάν συ δώξῃ, πέμσαι αὐτῷ *PFay.* 117.6-7, with πέμ[σ]ον 13 (A.D. 108)

ἐὰν δοκῇ σοι, πέμψαι τὸ ἀπόχρον Ἰσᾶτος καὶ παραλάβωμεν τὸ ἐλάδιον λυπὸν ἐὰν δόξῃ σοι *PFay.* 123.11-14 (after A.D. 110: *BL* iv, 29)

ἐὰν δέ σέ τι κατέχῃ, διάπεμψαί μοι αὐτά *PTebt.* 315 = *WChr.* 71.20 (2nd cent.)

καὶ ἐὰ<ν> λάβητε φαγόν, πέμψαι ἐμοί *PFay.* 127.14-15 (2nd/3rd cent.)

πέμψαι πάντας τοὺς κένους ... *PRossGeorg.* v, 5.10 (3rd cent.)

but προνοῆσαι in εὐθέ[ω]ς προνοῆσαι πέμψαι *PSI* 821.2 (2nd/3rd cent.) is probably middle,[1] and καταξίωσαι in καταξίωσαι οὖν ἡ σὴ ἀδελφότης ἀγώρασών μοι ... καὶ ἀπόστειλον *PSI* 1430.7-8 (7th cent.), which the editor takes as an aorist imperative, is probably a misspelling of the subjunctive καταξιώσῃ.[2]

c) The ending -εν:

κατάγραψεν ὠνὴν Ζωίλῳ ... *POxy.* 327.2: *BL* i, 321 (late 1st cent.)

λοιπὸν οὖν παράνγιλεν τοῖς πρεσβυτέροις μὴ ἔχιν πρᾶγμα [π]ρὸς τὸν ἄνθρωπον τοῦτον *SB* 7331.7-10: cf. *BL* iii, 183 (late 1st/early 2nd cent.)

ἆρεν *PRyl.* 435 V.2,3 (2nd cent.)

δήλοσεν *SB* 7662.8 (late 2nd cent.)

λαλοῦντος περὶ σοῦ ὅτι πέμψεν ἐπὶ τὴν πενθερά<ν> σου ... (text <ἔ> πεμψεν[3]) *PFay.* 126.4-8: cf. *BL* iii, 54 (2nd/3rd cent.)

πέμψεν *SB* 7572.5, with Διενυσίαν (for Διονυσίαν) 12 (prob. 1st half 2nd cent.); *PMich.* 511.12-13 (1st half 3rd cent.); *OTait* 2002.9, with τὸ περισσέν (for -όν) also 9 (Rom.)

πέμψεν μοι λάβανον *PRyl.* 242.6, with five other changes of ο to ε (3rd cent.)

κόψεν *OTait* 2471.7 (2nd/3rd cent.)

ἐντεῦθεν δὲ διέγραψεν Σ[ι]λβανῷ *PFlor.* 254.12-13: *BL* ι, 154 (A.D. 259)

---

[1] For the preference of Att. writers (also inscrr. and papp.) for the mid. of this verb, see *LSJ*, s.v.

[2] For sim. subjunctives in -αι and the interchange of αι and η(ι) in general, see Vol. i, 247-9.

[3] For the interpretation of this form as an impt., cf. Kapsomenakis, 27-29; Kapsomenos, "Ἔρευναι," 363-4.

κέλευεν *PLond.* 405 = *PAbinn.* 11.14 (ca. A.D. 346)

φρώντισεν τοὺς [ ], χάρισεν ἡμῖν τὰ φο[ ] ταῦτα *SB* 6270.19,28 (6th/7th cent.)

4) The third person imperative singular and plural ending -άτω(σαν) is sometimes replaced by the ending -έτω(σαν) of the second aorist and present:

ἀλλαξέτω *BGU* 597.10-11 (A.D. 75)

ἀνανκασέτω *POxy.* 121.7-8 (3rd cent.)

ποιησ{σ}έτω *PMeyer* 22.5 (3rd/4th cent.)

cf. also ἐκκλεινέτω *POxy.* 2193.11-12 (5th/6th cent.) in a loose quotation from Job 36.19, where ἐκκλινάτω stands in the text of the LXX

σπουδασέτωσαν *PFay.* 112.18 (A.D. 99)

ὑποστραφέτωσαν *PGiss.* 40 ii = *MChr.* 378.8 (A.D. 215)

5) The first aorist infinitive active ending -αι is sometimes curiously replaced by -εν. This spelling could represent the frequent change of αι to ε, with the erroneous addition of final -ν.[1] But in view of the occasional change of the present and second aorist infinitive ending -ειν to -εν,[2] and the apparent identification of ε and ι in /i/ before ν,[3] this spelling may represent the substitution of the present and second aorist infinitive ending -ειν for that of the first aorist. This phenomenon of -ειν in the first aorist infinitive is found elsewhere in the Koine,[4] and resulted in the sole Modern Greek remnant of the classical infinitive being formed in -ει on the aorist stem, as γράψει.[5]

πέμψεν *PMich.* 520.5 (4th cent.)

γράψεν *PStrassb.* 35.8,17 (4th/5th cent.)

γράψεν, πέμψεν, ποιῆσεν *BGU* 948.7;10,11;14 (prob. 4th/5th cent.)[6]

ἀντιγράψεν, ποιῆσεν, δοῦνεν *PHarris* 158 R.2; V.3; R.1,3,4 & V.4 (5th/6th cent.)

ἀποστῖλεν *SB* 7168.7 (5th/6th cent.)[7]

The ending -ειν is actually found in such examples as φθάνομεν ἀποδείξειν *PGrenf.* i, 53 = *WChr.* 131.32-33 (4th cent.), the ending -ιν (= -ειν) in καὶ οὐκ αἰθέλη (= ἐθέλει: *BL* iii, 238) ἡ κύρα μου πέμψιν μοι ... *StudPal.* xx, 223.4-5

---

[1] See Vol. i, 111-14, 191-3.

[2] See above, pp. 330-1, 346.

[3] See Vol. i, 249-62 and cf. above, pp. 330-1.

[4] Cf. Dieterich, 245; Hatzidakis, *Einl.*, 190-93.

[5] Thumb, *Handbook*, § 227; Mirambel, *Gram.*, 119, 122, 126; Hatzidakis, *Einl.*, 190.

[6] The ed., n. ad loc., refers to these as fut. infinitives. In form they might be fut., but an aor. infin. is generally required by the context. Syntactical confusion may underlie these forms, but the fact remains that infinitives in -(σ)εν are sts. found where an aor. infin. is expected.

[7] Cf. also from the mag. papp. μὴ ἐάσῃς αὐτὸν λαλῆσεν *PGMOstr.* 1.4-5,10 (late Rom.).

(6th/7th cent.),[1] the ending -ει in παρακαλ[ῶ γρά]ψει *POxy.* 294.28-29 (A.D. 22), and the ending -ι in μὴ ἐᾶσαι ... καὶ μὴ πέμψι *PSI* 1266.6-7 = *PApoll.* 9.7-8 (before A.D. 704). Parallels in the infinitive middle, as ἔθος δ' ἐστὶν τὸν ἔχοντα ἰδίους ὄνους τούτοις ἀπεργάσεσθαι *BGU* 969 i.23-24 (A.D. 142?) and σπούδασον διαπέμψεσθα[ι] *PSI* 92.8-9 (3rd cent.) are the converse of the frequent substitution of the ending of the first aorist infinitive middle for that of the future.[2]

This manifold evidence for the interchange of endings between the first aorist on the one hand and the second aorist and imperfect (or present and future) on the other reflects the mutual interference of these tense systems in post-classical Greek. This led to the loss of the future as a morphemic system and to the identification of the endings of both aorists and the imperfect in Modern Greek.[3]

E. THE ENDINGS OF THE PERFECT

The endings of the perfect active are also frequently replaced by those of other tenses, principally the second person singular -ας by the ending -ες of the second aorist and imperfect, and the third person plural -ασι by the ending -αν of the first aorist. Some variation in the formation of the perfect infinitive is also found.

1. The second person singular -ας, like the corresponding ending -ας of the first aorist,[4] is frequently replaced by the ending -ες of the second aorist and imperfect, a phenomenon also found occasionally elsewhere in the Koine:[5]

> μεμέτρηκες *OTait* 1168.2 (15 B.C.)
> ἀπέσταλκες *BGU* 1141.29-30, with ἀπέσταλκας 12 (prob. 13 B.C.)
> παρείληφες *POxy.* 742.4 (2 B.C.)
> ἡγώρακες *OTait* 1095.3 (A.D. 69); 1096.3-4 (1st cent.); sim. *WO* 1056.5 (A.D. 113)
> οἶδες[6] *BGU* 923.11 (1st/2nd cent.); *SB* 7356 = *PMich.* 203.28 part. rest. (A.D. 98-117); *PMich.* 476.17 (early 2nd cent.); *PTebt.* 568 descr. (2nd/early 3rd cent.); *POxy.* 1067.20 (3rd cent.); *BGU* 380.15-16 (3rd cent.); *SB* 9867.6 (3rd cent.); *PMich.* 514.8 (3rd cent.); *POxy.* 2926.3 (late 3rd cent.); *POxy.* 2682.13 (3rd/4th cent.); *POxy.* 2275.7

---

[1] Cf. also in the same line κελεύει οὖν ἡ κύρα μου πέμψον μο[ι] ... where πέμψον is an aor. impt. used paratactically, as also in line 3.

[2] See above, p. 333.

[3] Thumb, *Handbook*, § 225; Mirambel, *Gram.*, 122; Maspero, 86.

[4] See above, pp. 348-9.

[5] This substitution of -ες for -ας in the pf. is not common before Xtn. times. There is one ex. in a lit. pap. of the Ptol. period, and several exx. in the NT (Mayser i², 2, 81-82; Crönert, 210; *BDF*, § 83.2; cf. Schwyzer i, 767).

[6] For the form οἶδας instead of οἶσθα in the papp., see below, p. 409. Cf. also οἶδες in the mag. papp.: *PGM* 4.1442 (4th cent.).

(1st half 4th cent.); *PSI* 831.28 (4th cent.: *BL* vi, 180); *PSI* 1161.5, with οἶδας 11 (4th cent.); *POxy.* 1683.13 (late 4th cent.); *PSI* 742.7 (5th/6th cent.); *POxy.* 1837.10 (early 6th cent.); *PJand.* 23.2,11 (6th/7th cent.); etc.

ἠρώτηκες *POxy.* 1155.6-7 (A.D. 104)

δέδωκες, ἤρηχες, οἶδες *BGU* 261.14,17,23, with ἔγραψες 24-25 (ca. A.D. 105: cf. *PMich.* 202)

 δέδωκες *POxy.* 1295.17 (2nd/early 3rd cent.); *PLond.* 414 = *PAbinn.* 5.9-10 (ca. A.D. 346); *POxy.* 903.30 (4th cent.); *PLips.* 87.3; 88.4; 89.3 (late 4th cent.); *StudPal.* iii, 293.2 (5th/6th cent.); *StudPal.* viii, 1280.1 (6th cent.); *POxy.* 2995.2 (6th cent.); *PLond.* 1789.3 (6th cent.); 1753.1 (6th/7th cent.); *SB* 7520.7 (A.D. 710); etc.

εἴρηχες *PMich.* 510.7-8,23 (2nd/3rd cent.)

 εἴρηκες *POxy.* 2149.8 (2nd/3rd cent.)

πεποί<η>κες, γεγράφηκες *PWürzb.* 21 A.14,16 (2nd cent.)

 οἶδες, εἴρηχες, πεποίηκες *PMich.* 514.8,12,17-18 (3rd cent.)

ἦρκες *SB* 7248 = *PMich.* 216.28 (A.D. 296)

ἠξίωκες *PLips.* 110.11 (prob. 3rd/4th cent.)

Cf. also the ending -ης (probably = -ες):[1]

 οἶδης *PLond.* 410 = *PAbinn.* 34.13; *PGen.* 54 = *PAbinn.* 35.3, with οἶδας 4 (both ca. A.D. 346); *PRossGeorg.* v, 8.5 (4th/5th cent.)

διαγέγραφης (not ppf.) *PMerton* 61.1 (8 B.C.)

2. The third person plural indicative active ending -ασι is occasionally replaced by the ending -αν of the first aorist:

 ἀνενήνεχαν *BGU* 1053 = *MChr.* 105 ii.14-15 (13 B.C.)

 ἀγείοχαν *PRyl.* 603.4 (7 B.C.)

 ἀποδέδωκαν *BGU* 1200.20 (2/1 B.C.)

  ἀναδέδωκαν *PLBat.* vi, 9.15, with ἀπέσχηκαν 17 (A.D. 107); *SB* 9369 = *PSI* 1324.19 (A.D. 173); *PMich.* 529.11 (A.D. 232-6); *PLond.* 251 = *PAbinn.* 64.6 (ca. A.D. 346); *PLond.* 251 = *MChr.* 270.6 (A.D. 337-50); etc.

  δέδωκαν *PErl.* 116.6 part. rest. (3rd cent.); *POxy.* 1933.13 (6th cent.)

  ἐπιδέδωκαν *PLond.* 408 = *PAbinn.* 18.16-17 (ca. A.D. 346)

  παραδέδωκαν *PAmh.* 142 = *MChr.* 65.12 (after A.D. 341); *SB* 8246.33 twice, with καταπεφεύγασιν 34 (A.D. 335: *BL* v, 102)

 καταγέγραφαν *BGU* 1001.4 (30 B.C. - 14 A.D.: *BL* i, 86)

  μετεπιγέγραφαν *BGU* 328 i.6 (A.D. 138/9)

 ἐπαφεῖκαν *PRyl.* 147.17 (A.D. 39)

  ἀφεῖκαν *POxy.* 722 = *MChr.* 358.6 (A.D. 91/107)

 λέλονχαν *PMich.* 323-5.19, with -ασι 27 (A.D. 47)

---

[1] For the interchange of η and ε, see Vol. i, 242-9.

εἴληφαν *BGU* 1118.22 (22 B.C.); *PMich.* 333-4.11 (A.D. 52); *PAlex.* 7.11
 part. rest. (A.D. 113: *BL* v, 3)
 παρείληφαν *BGU* 1121.25 (5 B.C.); *BGU* 538.22 (A.D. 100); *StudPal.*
  xxii, 48.22 (A.D. 152); *BGU* 153 = *MChr.* 261.17 (A.D. 152); etc.
εἴρηχαν *BGU* 595.13 (ca. A.D. 70-80)
 εἴρηκαν *PHamb.* 89.6 part. rest. (2nd/3rd cent.); *PSI* 1562.2 (4th cent.)
γέγοναν *BGU* 597.19 (A.D. 75)
ἀφήλπακαν (for ἀφήρπακαν) *PAmh.* 125 introd. (late 1st cent.)
ἔφθακαν *POxy.* 1293.25 (A.D. 117-38)
μεθέστακαν *PSI* 822.6-7 (2nd cent.)
 ἕστακαν, πέπρακαν *PMichMichael.* 28 = *SB* 11130.8,32 (3rd/4th cent.)
 παρέστηκαν *PSI* 95.14 (3rd cent.)
εὕρηκαν *BGU* 821.4-5 (2nd cent.)
ἐλήλυθαν *SB* 9025.8 (2nd cent.)
 ἐπελήλυθαν *POxy.* 901 = *MChr.* 72.13 (A.D. 336)
καικίνηκαν *POxy.* 528.13-14 (2nd cent.)
ἀπήτηκαν *POxy.* 530.4 (2nd cent.)
πεπλάνηκαν *POxy.* 119.12: *BL* i, 316 (2nd/3rd cent.)
πεποίηκαν *POxy.* 2784.14 (3rd cent.)
καταβέβληκαν *PVars.* 29.6: *BL* iv, 103 (6th cent.)
οἴδαν *PJand.* 23.13 (6th/7th cent.)
ἀγώρακαν *BGU* 605.2 (7th/8th cent.)
cf. also πέπωκαν *POxy.* 465.37, astrol. (late 2nd cent.); ἐνπέπρηκαν *SB*
 8319.8-9, inscr. (Rom.)
but conversely ἐδώκασι *CPJ* 159a ii.6 (A.D. 180-93?)

This replacement of the ending -ασι by -αν is paralleled in late inscriptions
of classical dialects and widely elsewhere in the Koine.[1] The presence of -αν
in the third person plural completes the identification of the inflection of the
perfect indicative with that of the first aorist. The ending -αν seems to have
been so common in Egypt that the second-century A.D. philosopher Sextus
Empiricus was able to call these formations a specific trait of the Alexandrian
dialect.[2]

3. Endings of the present/future or imperfect/second aorist are substituted
sporadically for those of the perfect, as the third person present/future ending
-ουσι for -ασι in τεθελήκουσι *PAmh.* 130.16-17 (A.D. 70), and the first person
singular imperfect/second aorist ending -ον for -α in πέπρακον *BGU* 22.21

---

[1] Schwyzer i, 666; Buck, *GD*, § 104; Schweizer, 167; Nachmanson, 149; Mayser i², 2,
84-85 (from the 2nd cent. B.C.); Crönert, 210; *BDF*, § 83.1; Dieterich, 235-6; Jannaris, § 786;
Psaltes, 212-13; Hatzidakis, *Einl.*, 111-12, 185; Kapsomenakis, 75, n. 1.

[2] Thumb, *Hell.*, 170, who rightly calls attention to the widespread use of -αν for -ασι
elsewh. in the Koine, and suggests that both forms must have been in common use, since
both have survived in MGr. (p. 198). Cf. also Mayser i², 2, 84 & n. 2. Dieterich, 235-6, cites
parallels from Lac. Delph. Cret. and Asia Minor inscrr.

(A.D. 114) and εἴληφον *PLBat.* xiii, 18.26, corr. 29-30 (4th cent.); εἰδόντες *PAntin.* 198.2 (6th/7th cent.). Such isolated forms may be accidental, but they are paralleled elsewhere in Greek.[1]

4. For the form γεγόνασμεν *BGU* 1198 ii.13 (5/4 B.C.) and *PRossGeorg.* iii, 4.18 (3rd cent.), see above, p. 268.

5. The perfect infinitive sometimes loses the final -αι and so becomes identified with the occasional ending -εν (probably phonetically equivalent to -ειν) of the thematic (present, future, and second aorist) infinitives:[2]

ἰδέν *PMich.* 250.1 (A.D. 18)
εἰδέν *PTebt.* 397.29 (A.D. 198)
πεπρακέν *CPR* 220.4 (1st cent.)
ἀντ[ιγ]εγρ[α]φέν *PJand.* 53 iii.6 (ca. A.D. 96/98)
παρακεχωρηκέν *PMilVogl.* 26.6 (A.D. 127/8)
ἐξῳκονομηκέν *MChr.* 88 ii.32-iii.1 (before A.D. 141)

These examples generally occur, however, in very poorly written documents.

F. THE ENDINGS OF THE PLUPERFECT

The first person singular regularly ends in -ειν, e.g., ἐσχήκειν *PMich.* 476.10 (early 2nd cent.); *BGU* 465 i.6; ii.7 (A.D. 137); *POxy.* 1474.13 (A.D. 216); εἰρήκειν *PAlexGiss.* 38.7 (ca. A.D. 120); ἀπεστάλκειν *POxy.* 530.18 (2nd cent.); *PLond.* 853a = *PSarap.* 98.12 (early 2nd cent.); *SB* 6298.12 (2nd cent.); etc. Occasional forms in -ην, as πεπόνφην[3] *PTebt.* 414.9-10 (2nd cent.) and ἀπεληλύτην (for -θειν[4]) *SB* 7353 = *PMich.* 491.7-8 (ca. A.D. 200) are orthographic variants of the normal ending -ειν[5] and cannot be considered reflections of the old Attic endings -η, -ης.[6]

G. THE ENDINGS OF THE AORIST PASSIVE

The endings of the aorist passive are formed regularly, with only sporadic abnormalities which are not morphologically significant.

---

[1] Forms of the pf. inflected like the pres. are often used by the Sicilian Dor. writers Theocr. Epich. and Archim. and occur in some inscrr. and sporadically in the Ptol. papp. (Buck, *GD*, § 147.1; Mayser i², 2, 163). παρείληφον is found in the Byz.Chron. (Psaltes, 212).

[2] See above, pp. 330-1, 346, 352.

[3] For sim. exx. of unassimilated ν before a labial stop, see Vol. i, 171.

[4] For the interchange of τ and θ, incl. intervocalically, see Vol. i, 86-96.

[5] For the interchange of ει and η, see Vol. i, 256-62.

[6] In the Ptol. papp., this ending fluctuates between -ειν and -ην throughout the three centuries; -η is never attested, but -ει seems to occur once (loss of final -ν). Mayser takes these forms to be phonetically identical even for the Ptol. period (i², 2, 80-81).

1. A hybrid form of the aorist passive stem with middle endings, paralleled in two examples from the Ptolemaic papyri,[1] is found in ἐκληρόθημαι *SB* 4755.1 (Byz.).

2. The second person singular imperative sometimes ends in simple -θι for -θητι as in ἐπιμελήθι *POxy.* 744.6-7 (1 B.C.); *PSI* 888.3 part. rest. (4th cent.?); cf. also μνήσθι *PLBat.* xi, 28.1 (4th/5th cent.: *BL* v, 63). This form may have arisen on the analogy of the imperative ending -θι in ἴσθι, βῆθι, γνῶθι, etc. But the forms in -θητι are normal, e.g., μνήσθητι *PJand.* 103.14 (6th cent.).[2]

3. Forms of the infinitive in -η instead of -ῆναι, as in ἀποδοθῆ *PMich.* 312.42 (A.D. 34) and ἐρημωθῆ *POxy.* 2268.5 (late 5th cent.) may be connected with the occasional shortened forms of infinitives of other tenses, but since they occur only sporadically they are more likely scribal errors.

H. PARTICULAR PERSONAL ENDINGS

1. The second person singular middle-passive.

a. The second person singular middle-passive primary ending fluctuates between the classical Attic ending -η(ι) and the post-classical Attic -ει, arising originally ca. 378 B.C. as a result of the general shortening of the long diphthong ηι to ει.[3] Forms in -ι are also found:

> βούλη (indic.) *PPrinc.* 162.3 (A.D. 89/90); *PMerton* 28.22 (late 3rd cent.); *PMerton* 32.4-5 (early 4th cent.); *PLond.* 405 = *PAbinn.* 11.13 (ca. A.D. 346); *PGen.* 62 = *PAbinn.* 16.16 (ca. A.D. 346); *PSI* 783.8 (A.D. 357); *POxy.* 925 = *WChr.* 132.5 (5th/6th cent.); *PBaden* 30.9 (A.D. 577?); etc.
> (subj.) *PMich.* 276.24,31,40 (A.D. 47); *POxy.* 2134.24 (ca. A.D. 170); *POxy.* 1665.17-18 (3rd cent.); etc.
> βούλει (indic.) *SB* 7461.10 (A.D. 45); *PGiss.* 47 = *WChr.* 326.18,27 (A.D. 117-38); *POxy.* 2594.11 (2nd cent.); *POslo* 156.5 (2nd cent.); *POxy.* 2788.9 (3rd cent.); *BGU* 1080 = *WChr.* 478.16 (3rd cent.); *PGen.* 50 = *PAbinn.* 12.18 (ca. A.D. 346); *PPrinc.* 100.12 (4th cent.); *POxy.* 2156.14 (late 4th/5th cent.); *PCairMasp.* 97 R.27 (6th cent.); *SB* 4491.4 (6th/7th cent.); etc.[4]

---

[1] Mayser i², 2, 163.

[2] -θητι is still preserved as the aor. impt. pass. in Pontos, whereas elsewh. in MGr. the impt. is -σου on the analogy of -ου of the pres. impt. mid.-pass. (Jannaris, § 814).

[3] *MS*, 165; Schwyzer i, 668.

[4] In the mag. papp. (*PGM* i-ii), the indic. is βούλει 21 times, βούλη twice (*PGM* 7.918 [3rd cent.]; *PGMXtn.* 1.5 [5th/6th cent.]); the subj. is βούλη 15 times, βούλει twice (*PGM* 12.316 [A.D. 300-50]; *PGM* 4.222 [4th cent.]).

βούλει (subj.) *PAlexGiss.* 46.17 (ca. A.D. 120); *PLond.* 231 = *PAbinn.*
   9.14 (ca. A.D. 346); etc.
βούλι (indic.) *BGU* 530.7 (1st cent.); *PGen.* 55 = *PAbinn.* 30.23
   (ca. A.D. 346); *PAbinn.* 41.6 (ca. A.D. 346)
ἔση *PMerton* 62.10 (A.D. 6); *POxy.* 1672.15 (A.D. 37-41); *SB* 7615 =
   PBon. 43.10 (1st cent.); *BGU* 596.12 (A.D. 84); etc.
αἱρῇ (subj.) *BGU* 13 = *MChr.* 265.11 (A.D. 289)
οἴει *CPR* 20 = *StudPal.* xx, 54 i.18 (A.D. 250)
ἐλεύσει *POxy.* 937.25 (3rd cent.)

The fluctuation in this ending, paralleled in the Ptolemaic papyri and
occasionally in manuscripts of the New Testament,[1] is now purely orthographic.[2]

b. The ending -σαι, sometimes restored in thematic verbs elsewhere in the
Koine,[3] is found only rarely in these verbs in the papyri, as in the future
χαρίεσαι (for χαρίσει) *POxy.* 292.9 (ca. A.D. 25). For δύνησαι *BGU* 424.8 (2nd/
3rd cent.), see below, p. 385.

2. The personal ending of the first person plural middle appears as -μεσθα
instead of -μεθα in δυνάμεσθα *PRossGeorg.* iii, 4.11 (with ἀνακρινόμεθα 24)
(3rd cent.) and ἐπεξερχόμεσθα *PMon.* 13.37 (A.D. 594). This ending, paralleled
by one example in the Ptolemaic papyri,[4] is not a survival of the Epic and
Tragic ending -μεσθα but an independent analogical formation from -μεθα
after -σθε.[5] The -σ- is preserved in the Modern Greek -μαστε (dialectally
-μεστα).[6]

I. ENDINGS OF THE SUBJUNCTIVE

1. Forms of the indicative are frequently substituted for those of the subjunctive, e.g., ἐὰν οὖν θέλεις *POxy.* 1668.20-21 (3rd cent.); ἠὰν καλῶς πράξει
SB 7251 = *PMich.* 219.10 (A.D. 296); ἵνα ... ἀνελθοῦσι *PFlor.* 175.27-29 (A.D.
255); ἐὰν οἶδες *PJand.* 20 V.1 (6th/7th cent.); ἵνα πάθομεν *POxy.* 1855.8 (6th/7th
cent.); ἵνα σε ἀσπάζομαι *BGU* 1081.3 (2nd/3rd cent.); εὕνα ... διαπέμψεται
POxy. 1068.5 (3rd cent.); etc. The converse also occurs occasionally, e.g., εἰ

---

[1] Mayser i², 2, 90-91; *BDF*, § 27. Cf. Crönert, 37; Chantraine,² § 344.
[2] Cf. the parallel phenomenon in the augment of verbs beg. with αι- above, pp. 238(-9)
& n. 2.
[3] Schwyzer i, 668-9; *BDF*, § 87, w. lit.; Jannaris, § 773; Psaltes, 209.
[4] Mayser i², 2, 92, Anm. 9.
[5] So Schwyzer i, 670.
[6] Thumb, *Handbook*, § 219-20; Mirambel, *Gram.*, 122; Maspero, 93, 95. Cf. also Kapsomenakis, 47, n. 1; Chantraine², § 349.

καὶ συνβῇ *POxy.* 904.4 (5th cent.); εἰ δὲ δόξῃ αὐτοῖς ἐπελ[θεῖν] *PPar.* 20.29 (A.D. 600); εἰ δὲ ἴδῃς αὐτόν *PLond.* 1032 (iii, 283).6 (6th/7th cent.). Although the phonological identification of several endings, as -εις/-ῃς, -ει/-ῃ, and -ομεν/-ωμεν may have been a contributing factor, this phenomenon is syntactic in nature and will be treated in detail in Volume III.[1] This confusion of indicative and subjunctive, paralleled throughout the Koine,[2] resulted in the elimination of the subjunctive as a morphemic system and its replacement in Modern Greek by the endings of the indicative used with the subjunctive particle νά (ancient ἵνα), so that the endings of the present subjunctive coincide with those of the indicative and the aorist subjunctive with those of the future.[3]

2. The replacement of the ending of the third person plural -σι by -ν (corresponding to the replacement of the perfect ending -ασι by -αν[4]) is found in ἃς ἐὰν μεταξὺ ἀγάγων (for ἀγάγωσι) *BGU* 265 = *WChr.* 459.9 (A.D. 148). This phenomenon, paralleled once each in the present and aorist subjunctive in the Ptolemaic papyri as well as in the Septuagint,[5] spread eventually to the indicative as well, so that all third person plural active endings in Modern Greek, primary as well as secondary, end in -ν(ε).[6]

J. THE ENDINGS OF THE OPTATIVE

The optative, despite its gradual loss in post-classical Greek,[7] is by no means rare in the papyri of the Roman period, and becomes quite common in the Byzantine period.[8]

---

[1] Further exx. of the confusion of indic. and subj. may be found in Horn, 64-67; Kapsomenakis, 102, n. 1; Mandilaras, 245-8.

[2] Forms of the indic. begin to be used for the subj. in the act. and mid. from 343 B.C. on in the Att. inscrr. with the identification in pronunciation of ῃ and ει (*MS*, 166). See further Mayser i², 2, 86; Jannaris, § 779; Dieterich, 205; Hatzidakis, *Einl.*, 216-19; Schwyzer i, 789, Zus.; Chantraine,² § 309.

[3] Thumb, *Handbook*, § 179, 213; Mirambel, *Gram.*, 122, 124.

[4] pp. 354-5.

[5] Mayser i², 2, 87; Crönert, 210, n. 5.

[6] Mirambel, *Gram.*, 122. The use of -ουν for -ουσι in the pres. indic. is found occ. elsewh. in the Koine (Crönert, 210, n. 5; Dieterich, 247; Psaltes, 209; Jannaris § 777; Schwyzer i, 666; Hatzidakis, *Einl.*, 111-12).

[7] The opt. is retained in MGr. only in stereotyped forms, as in the lit. ὃ μὴ γένοιτο or ὁ θεὸς φυλάξοι (Mirambel, *Gram.*, 164). Its loss in the later Koine was the result of simplification in the use of the moods in syntax (cf. Schwyzer i, 797, Zus. 2).

[8] See esp. Harsing, *De Optativi in Chartis Aegyptiis Usu* (1910). His general remarks on p. 19 remain valid; his statistics brought up to date follow the same proportions. Thus one finds that 1) verbs with optative forms are those wh. are used most frequently in colloquial speech; 2) there are many exx. of the pres. opt. of contr. verbs in -έω; 3) there are optatives of six -μι verbs (δείκνυμι, δίδωμι, δύναμαι, εἰμί, ἵστημι, τίθημι), in which the pres. opt. is most common; 4) there are absolutely more forms of the pres. than of the aor. opt., but of the pres. the vast majority are of εἰμί, with the result that the aor. opt.

1. The endings of the present and second aorist optative of non-contract verbs are regular in -μι, e.g., μάθοιμι *PGen.* 1.15 (A.D. 213: *BL* i, 156); κατα-λάβοιμι *PLond.* 213 = *WChr.* 267 V.9 (3rd cent.); χαίροις *POxy.* 526.1 (2nd cent.); *POxy.* 1063.1 (2nd/3rd cent.); *BGU* 931.1 (prob. 3rd/4th cent.); εὕροις *PCairMasp.* 28 = *MChr.* 382.20 (ca. A.D. 551); εἴποι *POxy.* 472.20 (ca. A.D. 130); [ἀπ]ολαμβάνοι *BGU* 2070 R i.28 (mid 2nd cent.); ἀπολάβοιμεν *PHermRees* 5.27-28 (4th cent.); ἔχοιτε *POxy.* 60 = *WChr.* 43.9-10 (A.D. 323); θέλοιεν *POxy.* 237 vii.23 (A.D. 186); σώζοιεν *PBaden* 39 iii = *PSarap.* 89.14 (early 2nd cent.); *POxy.* 2561.20 (A.D. 293-305); γένοιτο *POxy.* 118.38 (late 3rd cent.); *POxy.* 925 = *WChr.* 132.7, Xtn. prayer (5th/6th cent.); ἡγοῖτο *PCairIsidor.* 74.23-24 part. rest. (A.D. 315); *PMerton* 91.21 (A.D. 316); ὑποδέχοιντο *POxy.* 1409.19 (A.D. 278); etc. Orthographic variations occur occasionally, e.g., χαίρυς (for χαίροις) *POxy.* 2274.1 (3rd cent.). But the athematic optative of contract verbs -οιην,[1] as in δοκοίην *SB* 7347.33 (2nd cent.); διατελοίης *PStrassb.* 286.14 (mid 4th cent.); ἐπιχειροίη *POxy.* 1119 = *WChr.* 397.24 (A.D. 253: *BL* i, 332), used already in classical Greek in the simple of the second aorist of ἔχω and so retained in the papyri, as σχοίης *POxy.* 939 = *WChr.* 128.10 (4th cent.),[2] is sometimes substituted for the thematic optative in -οιμι, as in τυχοίην *POxy.* 2237.17 (A.D. 498).

2. The language of the papyri of the Roman and Byzantine periods, in sharp contrast to that of the Ptolemaic papyri,[3] regularly employs the so-called Aeolic forms of the first aorist optative,[4] often with the orthographic variant ι for ει, e.g., κελεύσειας *PLips.* 38 = *MChr.* 97 i.3 (A.D. 390); ποιήσιας *PFlor.* 384.32 (5th cent.?); δόξειε *PTebt.* 326 = *MChr.* 325.13 (A.D. 266); ἀποδεί-ξειεν *PBerlZill.* 4.17 (4th cent.); δόξιεν *SB* 9187.14-15 (A.D. 317/18); ποιήσιεν *CPR* 19 = *StudPal.* xx, 86.24 (A.D. 330); [ἐγ]καλέσειαν *POxy.* 2111.44-45 (ca. A.D. 135); πειθαρχήσιαν *POxy.* 1411.16 (A.D. 260); etc. The reappearance of these early (pre-fourth century B.C.) Attic forms in the papyri of Roman and Byzantine times must be attributed to Atticistic influence.[5]

---

is the more living, esp. in Byz. times; 5) the pf. opt. is replaced by a periphrastic construction of the pf. ptc. and opt. of εἰμί (see above, p. 306), and the fut. opt. is very rare. For statistics for the Ptol. papp., see Mayser ii, 1, 289, n. 1; 295-6. In the NT, the opt. appears with any frequency, exc. for the opt. of wish in Paul, only in the Lucan corpus, owing to the influence of the lit. language (*BDF*, § 65.2).

[1] Cf. Chantraine[2], § 312. The contr. opt. is generally preserved throughout the Koine (*MS*, 166; Schweizer, 191; Nachmanson, 148). Both thematic and athematic forms are found, however, in -έω verbs in the Ptol. papp. (Mayser i[2], 2, 88). For the fluctuating usage of some Koine authors, see Crönert, 217, n. 1.

[2] σχοίην is the reg. Att. form, w. -σχοιμι found occ. in compds. in E. S. (lyr.) Th. Pl. (Veitch & *LSJ*, s.v.).

[3] In the Ptol. papp., the Aeol. forms are found only sporadically in official documents, and then only in the 3 sg. (Mayser i[2], 2, 87-88).

[4] On the 'Aeolic' forms (found mainly in Att.-Ion., but also sts. in Hom. Lesb. El.), see Schwyzer i, 766-7; Chantraine[2], § 313; Buck, *GD*, § 152.4; *MS*, 166.

[5] In Koine lit., non-Aeol. forms occur in the 2 sg. in Phld. Aristid. Philostr.Jun. etc., Aeol. forms in Str. J. The Aeol. forms of the 3 sg. were more common. However, many

3. Future optative forms are found in θέλω in ἐθελήσοις *PMichael.* 41.42 (A.D. 539/54) and ἐθελήσοιμεν *PCairMasp.* 158.21 (A.D. 568) and in ἀσθενέω in ἀσθενήσοιμι *SB* 5114.40 and ἀσθενήσοιμεν *SB* 5113.19 (both 7th cent.).

4. The aorist optative passive is regular in -είην, etc., e.g., ὀφθείην *PAntin.* 91.9 (6th cent.); δυνηθείης *POxy.* 939 = *WChr.* 128.15 (4th cent.); φανείη *BGU* 2031.24 (A.D. 180/92). The form βουληθείοις *StudPal.* iii, 255.4 (6th cent.) is probably simply a misspelling for -ειης.[1]

K. THE ENDINGS OF THE IMPERATIVE

The ending -σαν has replaced the classical Attic-Ionic ending in all third person imperatives in the papyri as almost universally elsewhere in the Koine from ca. 300 B.C. on,[2] e.g., καταφερέτωσαν *POxy.* 1415.1 (late 3rd cent.); συμβιούτωσαν *POxy.* 496 = *MChr.* 287.8 (A.D. 127); ἐλθέτωσαν *PAmh.* 66.43 (A.D. 124); εἰπάτωσαν *SB* 7696.55 (A.D. 250); κρατείσθωσαν *PLond.* 359 (ii.150).6 (1st/2nd cent.); κομισάσθωσαν *PLBat.* xiii, 18.20-21 (4th cent.); πεμφθήτωσαν, κατασχεθήτωσαν *PMarmarica* iv.21 & v.36; vi.24 (A.D. 190/1?); περειορυγήτωσαν *POxy.* 121.6-7 (3rd cent.); ἔστωσαν *CPR* 1 = *StudPal.* xx, 1.22 (A.D. 83/84); ἀφέτωσαν *BGU* 597.25 (A.D. 75); etc.

This adoption of the secondary ending -σαν is the final stage of evolution of the third person imperative in Greek. Originally formed by the addition of a particle *-tod*, becoming -τω, this third person imperative was pluralized either by the addition of a final -ν from the third person plural indicative (Homeric, Attic-Ionic ἔστων) or by being changed to the third person plural middle ending -ντω (West Greek), or to a combination of the two (the regular Attic-Ionic -ντων). Finally, this -ντων complex was replaced by the ending -σαν added to the original -τω along with its thematic vowel (preserved in the third person singular imperative).[3] This popular third plural ending -σαν spread likewise to the imperfect and to the second aorist.[4]

---

authors who adopt this usage also use the non Aeol. forms more or less freq. Only NT writers seem to use the non Aeol. forms excl. (*BDF*, § 85, for the NT reff.; these non-Aeolic forms are erroneously termed 'normal in Hellenistic'). Later authors also use the Aeol. forms excl., as Synes. Just. The 3 pl. is also generally the Aeol. form, but the non-Aeol. form is occ. used. On the other hand, some authors use virtually only the non-Aeol. form, as Str. Phld. Aristid. Ael. Just. See Crönert's comprehensive treatment, pp. 211-14, sts. unclear bec. of his distinction betw. Aeol. and 'Attic' forms, while in fact Att. authors generally used the Aeol. forms.

[1] For the occ. interchange of η and οι, see Vol. i, 265-7.

[2] The ending -σαν first appears in the Att. inscrr. from 300 B.C. on when it soon predominates (*MS*, 167). It is the sole form of the impt. throughout the Asia Minor inscrr. (Schweizer, 167-9; Nachmanson, 149-50; Hauser, 104). It is found excl. in the Ptol. papp. w. the exception of sporadic and dbtfl. hybrid forms (Mayser i², 2 89-90). It is reg. in the NT and in most Koine authors (*BDF*, § 84.1; Crönert, 219; Psaltes, 213-14). But the ancient forms are retained by some Koine authors, as Onos. Aristid. Luc. (Crönert, 219, n. 2).

[3] So already E. Th. X. (Schwyzer i 801-2; Chantraine², § 318-20; Buck, *GD*, § 140).

[4] See above, pp. 331, 345.

L. THE ENDINGS OF THE INFINITIVE

The endings of the infinitive are treated above under the individual tenses, including the interchange of endings between the infinitives of the first aorist and of the second aorist, present, and future, and the tendency to form the infinitive active of all three tenses, and perhaps of the perfect as well, in -εν. This ending, which is possibly a short form of the infinitive, is probably phonetically equivalent not only to the infinitives in -ειν, but also to the first aorist infinitive in -αι.[1] The infinitive is generally lost in Modern Greek, except for the remnant of the first aorist infinitive active (now ending in -ει) used in periphrastic constructions, and some relics of ancient present infinitives used substantively, as τὸ φαγί, τὸ φιλί.[2]

---

[1] See above, pp. 330-1, 334-5, 346, 352-3.
[2] Thumb, *Handbook*, § 181; Mirambel, *Gram.*, 119, 122, 126, 164.

IX. CONTRACT VERBS[1]

The confusion of the different classes of contract verbs, which led to the partial merger of those in -άω and -έω and to the general loss of those in -όω in Modern Greek, is reflected in the substitution of forms of -έω verbs for corresponding -άω forms and in other sporadic transfers of inflectional type. Some fluctuation in the use of contract and non-contract forms is also found in monosyllabic -έω stems. In addition, analogical levelling is found to a limited extent within each contract type.

A. CONFUSION OF THE DIFFERENT CLASSES OF CONTRACT VERBS

1. Verbs in -άω are occasionally found with forms of -έω verbs:

ἐνγυοῦμε (for ἐγγυῶμαι) *PLond.* 246 = *PAbinn.* 61.5-6,15-16 (Λ.D. 346)
   ἐγγυούμεθα *SB* 4658.10 (Byz.)
   cf. ἐγγυῆσθαι (= ἐγγυεῖσθαι in pronunciation) *PFlor.* 34.9,16 (A.D. 342)
ὑφωροῦμε (for ὑφορῶμαι) *PGen.* 17.14 (ca. A.D. 207)
προσδοκοῦμεν *POxy.* 1299.7, with εὐχαριστῶ[μεν] 5-6 (4th cent.); cf. also *PColt* 162.6 (6th cent.)
   προσδοκοῦσιν *POxy.* 1855.16 (6th/7th cent.)
   προσδοκεῖν *PCairMasp.* 324.8 (6th cent.)[2]
ἀγαποῦμεν *PLond.* 418 = *PAbinn.* 7.9 (ca. A.D. 346)
   ἀγαποὐντων *PFouad* 87.31 abbrev. (6th cent.); 89.10 (6th cent.)
   ἀγαποῦντας *BGU* 984.25 (4th cent.)
ἀγωνιοῦμεν *BGU* 449.4-5 (2nd/3rd cent.)

---

[1] Schwyzer i, 683-6, 717-30; Chantraine[2], § 284-92; Buck, *GD*, § 158-9, 161; Mayser i[2], 2, 113-18; Crönert, 220-24; *BDF*, § 88-91; Psaltes, 233-6.

[2] Preisigke unnecessarily classifies these and some other forms under independent headings. Although parallels are found elsewh. in the Koine (cf. Crönert, 222, nn. 3-6; *BDF*, § 90), these forms are for the most part only occasional and reflect transfer of inflectional contract type rather than alternative denominative or deverbative formations.

ἀπαντοῦντι *PLond.* 233 = *PAbinn.* 58.6 (A.D. 345)

   ἀπαντούντων *PGen.* 55 = *PAbinn.* 30.9 (ca. A.D. 346)

ἐρωτουμένης *PCairMasp.* 89 V.29 (6th cent.)

μελετο(υ)μένην *PCairMasp.* 97 V d.83 (6th cent.)

τολμοῦντες (for τολμῶντας) *PLond.* 245 = *PAbinn.* 45.19 (A.D. 343)

   and sim. *PAbinn.* 47.16-17; 49.21; 51.17; 52.19-20; 53.15-16; 54.31

   (all ca. A.D. 346)

διαιτ[ο]υμένων *POxy.* 496 = *MChr.* 287.12 (A.D. 127)

2. Verbs in -έω appear only sporadically with forms of -άω verbs, as ὁμο-λογῶμεν (for -οῦμεν indic.) *PRyl.* 160c, ii.34 (A.D. 32); sim. *POxy.* 1835.7,9 (late 5th/early 6th cent.); εὐχαριστῶ[μεν] *POxy.* 1299.5-6, with προσδοκοῦμεν 7 (4th cent.); εὐθυμῶντος *PRossGeorg.* iii, 10.5 (4th/5th cent.); ποιωμένη *POxy.* 1473.24 (A.D. 201).[1]

3. Verbs in -όω appear sporadically with forms of -άω verbs, not only in the present (contract) system, as ζημιᾶσθαι *BGU* 1044.13-14 (4th cent.), but also in other tense forms, e.g., ἠλλοτρίασεν *POxy.* 2267.8 (A.D. 360).

On the other hand, the -έω denominative τιθηνέω appears in the form of an aorist passive on the model of -όω verbs in τοῦ τιτθηνωθῆναι *PLond.* 1708.184a (A.D. 567?).[2]

This limited transfer of inflectional types in contract verbs appears to represent the beginning of the confusion of conjugation which resulted in the merger of most of the ancient -άω and -έω contract verbs into one Modern Greek inflectional type -ῶ, -ᾶς, -ᾶ, -οῦμε, -ᾶτε, -οῦν(ε); impf. -οῦσα, etc. (a second type -ῶ, -εῖς, -εῖ, -οῦμε, -εῖτε, -οῦν(ε), impf. -οῦσα, etc., is retained in relatively few verbs).[3] The confusion of contract classes is by no means general in the papyri but is confined mainly to the transfer of -άω verbs to the -έω inflection and virtually only when the resultant is -ου-. This pattern is similar to that observed in ancient Ionic and to some extent in Doric and other dialects, where the phenomenon was caused by the phonetic shift of αο and αω to εο and εω before contraction.[4] These forms in the papyri appear to be the result of ana-logical levelling between the two classes of contract verbs, with the replacement

---

[1] For the formation of ἐποφθαλμιάω from -μέω, see Palmer, 124.

[2] The forms διαπλανῶναι (for -ῆσαι) *PMich.* 228.15 (A.D. 47) and αἱρῶται (for αἱρῆται) *POxy.* 496 = *MChr.* 287.15 (A.D. 127) are anomalous.

[3] Thumb, *Handbook,* § 199, 237-50; Mirambel, *Gram.,* 122-3, 140-5; Maspero, 111-18. For this confusion of inflectional contr. types in the Koine and its connection with the MGr. system, see Schwyzer i, 728-9; Chantraine², § 286 Remarque; Mayser i², 2, 117-18; *BDF,* § 90; Crönert, 221-3; Psaltes, 233-4; Thumb, *Hell.,* 15, 68, 244; Hatzidakis, *Einl.,* 128-9; Jannaris, § 849-63.

[4] Schwyzer i, 728; Chantraine², § 286; Buck, *GD,* § 161.2.

of ω by ου perhaps, as Jannaris suggested,[1] because ου was the more frequent ending in contract verbs, occurring as it did in the -όω verbs as well as in the numerous -έω verbs. The substitution of ου for ω in these verb forms, however, may have been nothing more than the result of analogical influence on the orthographic level. In the speech of many writers of the papyri, ω and ου appear to have been identified in pronunciation, particularly before a nasal or σ, in which positions these changes occur.[2]

B. CONTRACT AND NON–CONTRACT FORMS OF THE SAME STEM

1. -κύρω/-κυρέω.[3]

a. προσκυρέω is not clearly attested from papyri of any period.[4] The non-contracted προσκύρω is alone used in the Ptolemaic papyri,[5] and in absence of direct evidence for the use of contract forms of this verb in papyri of the Roman and Byzantine periods, the ambiguous third person plural present προσκυροῦσιν *PPrinc.* 119.36 (ca. A.D. 325: *ZPE* 8 [1971], 15) and the participle προσκυρούσῃ *BGU* 275.6-7 (A.D. 215) can be assumed to derive from the non-contracted προσκύρω (as can the equally ambiguous example in -ει from the Ptolemaic papyri) rather than from -κυρέω with Preisigke.[6]

b. συγκύρω/συγκυρέω 'be attached to,' 'belong to.'

1) Forms of the non-contract συγκύρω, regular in the Ptolemaic papyri,[7] are frequent throughout the Roman period:

συνκύροντα *PMich.* 307.3, so duplic. *PSI* 914.3 (1st cent.); *PMich.* 584.7 (A.D. 84); *CPR* 102.13, with συνκυρούντων 14 (1st/2nd cent.); *PLBat.* xiii, 11.16 (A.D. 138); *BGU* 1583.12 (A.D. 203); *PRyl.* 99.5 (3rd cent.); *CPR* 9 i.4; ii.5; iii.5 (A.D. 271); etc.

cf. also συνκοίραντα *CPR* 28 = *MChr.* 312.10 (A.D. 110)

συνκύραντα *PMich.* 272.3 (A.D. 45/46)

---

[1] § 850-850ᵇ.

[2] See Vol. i, 208-11, 213-14.

[3] See esp. P. M. Fraser, "-ΚΥΡΩ and -ΚΥΡΕΩ: A Lexicographical Note," *Eranos* 49 (1951), 102-8.

[4] So Fraser, 103.

[5] Mayser i², 2, 115.

[6] *WB*, s.v. προσκυρ(έ)ω is to be distinguished from προσκυρόω, where the -κυρόω is a denominative from the o-stem noun κῦρος (Schwyzer i, 727, n. 2).

[7] Mayser i², 2, 115.

συνκύρωντα *PLond.* 154 (ii, 178-80).21 (A.D. 68)

συνκυρόντων *SB* 5108 = *PRyl.* 160.2 (A.D. 28/29); *POxy.* 2720.17 (A.D.
41-54); *PMich.* 335.3 (A.D. 56); *PFay.* 100.11 (A.D. 99); *PRyl.* 155.9,10
(A.D. 138-61); *BGU* 901.10 (2nd/3rd cent.); *PFlor.* 56 = *MChr.*
241.14 (A.D. 234); etc.

cf. also συνκυρώντων *PMich.* 122 II.4; sim. II.7 (A.D. 49); *PMich.*
295.6 (1st cent.); *PMich.* 297.2 (1st cent.)

συνκυρόντον (for -ων) *PSI* 917.5 = *PMich.* 282.3-4 (1st cent.)

συνκοιρώντων *PMich.* 585.12 (A.D. 87)

συνκυριώντων *PRyl.* 160b.7 (A.D. 37)

συνκυριόντων *PStrassb.* 208.14 (A.D. 75)

2) Forms of the contract συγκυρέω, without distinction in meaning from
the non-contract forms, are attested occasionally during the Roman period[1]
and are normal during the Byzantine:[2]

συνκυροῦντα *POxy.* 907 = *MChr.* 317.9,13 (A.D. 276)

συνκυρούντων *SB* 7260 iii a.1 = *PMich.* 121 R III i.1 (A.D. 42); *CPR*
11.8 (A.D. 108); *PSI* 705.8 (3rd cent.); *PSI* 698.6 (A.D. 392); sim.
PLond. 1724.32 (A.D. 578-82); *PMon.* 11.63 (A.D. 586); etc.

3) Ambiguous, and so to be judged according to the prevailing form of the
period, are [σ]υνκυρουσῶν *PLond.* 604 (iii, 70-76).2 (A.D. 47); τοῖς συνκύρουσι
POxy. 104.14 (A.D. 96); συνκύρουσι πᾶσει *POxy.* 1699.7 (A.D. 240-80).

2. (ἐπι)μέλομαι/(ἐπι)μελέομαι.

a. The non-contract ἐπιμέλομαι, alone attested, with one possible exception,
in the Ptolemaic papyri,[3] is found in ἐπιμέλεσθαι *PHeid.* 48b = *PSarap.* 84.2
(early 2nd cent.); *PTebt.* 616 descr. (2nd cent.); and ἐπιμελόμενον *PBrem.* 5.5
(A.D. 117-19).[4] But contract forms are found in ἐπιμελεῖσθαι *POxy.* 2190.38
(late 1st cent.) and ἐπιμελουμένης *PMon.* 8.3 (late 6th cent.); ἐπιμελούμενοι

---

[1] *Pace* Fraser, 105.

[2] But not all of Preisigke's reff. to συγκυρέω are necessarily derived from -κυρέω as
opposed to -κύρω. Exx. involving the fem. ptc. or dat. pl. of the neut. ptc. are of course
ambiguous.

[3] Mayser i[2], 2, 115. The late Att. ἐπιμελέομαι, wh. is required by meter in E. and
prevails in codd. of Ar. Pl. X. and is used almost excl. in Att. inscrr. from 380 B.C. on, is a
deverbative back-formation from the tenses in -η- (Schwyzer i, 721; Veitch & *LSJ*, s.v.;
MS, 175). This contr. formation is also found in Asia Minor inscrr. (Schweizer, 174-5). Both
forms are found in Koine lit. (Crönert, 223 & n. 4).

[4] Cf. also ἐπιμέλωσθε (read ἐπιμέλεσθε w. Kapsomenos, "'Ερευναι," 339) *BGU* 1078
= *WChr.* 59.11 (A.D. 39) and ἐπιμέλ[ε]τε *PMich.* 219.11 (A.D. 296).

PHermRees 5.18 (4th cent.). Ambiguous are the occurrences of the imperative ἐπιμέλου, e.g., *POslo* 47.14 (A.D. 1); *PMerton* 62.13 (A.D. 6); *PMich.* 464.16 (A.D. 99); *PFay.* 119.24 (ca. A.D. 100); *PMich.* 207.11 (2nd cent.); *PTebt.* 397 = *MChr.* 321.20 (A.D. 198); etc. The other tense systems are formed in -η-, as ἐπιμελήσεσθαι *POxy.* 2190.21 (late 1st cent.); ἐπιμελήσαντο[ς] *PSI* 893.7-8 (A.D. 315).

b. The compounds καταμελέω and παραμελέω are contract formations as normally elsewhere in Greek, as κα[τ]αμελεῖν *BGU* 195.19 (A.D. 161); παρα-μελούντω[ν] *PSI* 47.3 (6th cent.?). The other tenses are formed regularly in -η-, as [πα]ραμελήσουσειν *PMerton* 38.15-16 (mid 4th cent.); παραμελήσειεν *PBouriant* 20 = *PAbinn.* 63.41 (A.D. 350); παραμεληθέντα *PBeattyPanop.* 2.224 (A.D. 300).

c. The compound μεταμέλομαι is also used in a contract formation in contrast to its usage elsewhere in Greek in μεταμελεῖσθαι *PMichael.* 41.49 (A.D. 539/54); *PCairMasp.* 340 V.94 (6th cent.). Its other tenses are formed regularly in -η-, as μεταμεληθῆναι *PMon.* 8.28-29,31 (late 6th cent.) and (with -σ-[1]) μεταμελησθῆναι *PThead.* 51.15-16 (4th cent.).

3. Like the Ptolemaic papyri, the papyri of the Roman and Byzantine periods have only the contract form ἀποστερέω in the active and middle-passive, but the non-contract simple deponent στέρομαι:[2]

> ἀποστερεῖν *BGU* 1139.15 (5 B.C.); *PRyl.* 114.26 (ca. A.D. 280); *PAntin.* 99b.17 (early 4th cent.)
> ἀπο[στε]ρεῖτ[αι] *POxy.* 471.1-2 (2nd cent.)
> ἀποστερεῖσθαι *PCairMasp.* 24 R.22 (ca. A.D. 551)
> στέρεσθαι *BGU* 1050 = *MChr.* 286.24; *BGU* 1051.33 part. emended; *BGU* 1052.31; 1098.40; 1101.18 (all ca. 13 B.C.)
> στέρωνται (for στέρονται), στέρεσθαι *BGU* 1210 (60).155, (102).231 (mid 2nd cent.)

The other tenses are formed in -ε- or -η-; see above, p. 256.

Perhaps on the analogy of στέρομαι, συνιστορέω is found in the middle participle in the form συνιστερόμενος (for -ιστορ-) *POxy.* 2349.23 (A.D. 70) besides the normal contract forms, e.g., ἐξιστοροῦσα *POxy.* 486 = *MChr.* 59.12 (A.D. 131).

---

[1] For the insertion of -σ-, see above, pp. 268-9.

[2] Mayser i[2], 2, 115. This usage of the papp. accords w. the normal use of class. and Koine Gr. lit., although contr. forms are occ. found in late Gr. in the simple deponent as well as in act. and mid. forms of the compds. (Veitch & *LSJ*, s.v.).

4. Some normally non-contract verbs appear sporadically in forms which resemble contract formations, e.g., ὑπεραίρω in τῶν ὑπεραιρούντων τὸν ἀριθμὸ(ν) τῶν ἱερέων *PLond.* 347 (ii, 70-71).6-7 (A.D. 201), perhaps under the influence of αἱρέω; στέλλω in στ[ελ]ούμε[ν]ῳ[ν] *SB* 7634.21-22 (A.D. 249); and βλάπτω in βλαπτουμένο(υ) *PCairMasp.* 329 ii.6 (A.D. 524/5: *BL* iv, 15).

In the analysis of contract and non-contract formations of individual verbs in the papyri, the apparent identification of ω and ο with ου in the speech of many writers is a factor.[1] It is possible that there was no distinction in pronunciation between forms fluctuating between these spellings. It is significant that most fluctuations between contract and non-contract forms in the papyri involve these sounds.

C. PECULIARITIES WITHIN THE DIFFERENT CLASSES OF CONTRACT VERBS

1. -άω verbs.

a. χράομαι, which in classical Attic contracted αε to η instead of to α,[2] frequently contracts to α in the papyri of the Roman and Byzantine periods, as in Ionic and late Attic beginning with Aristotle and in the Koine in general.[3] This contraction serves to bring the paradigm of χράομαι into line with that of the denominative -άω verbs and is therefore more likely an independent analogical development within the Koine than an Ionic legacy.[4]

1) Contraction to α:

> χράσθω *POxy.* 502.29 (A.D. 164); *POxy.* 1207.15 (A.D. 175/6?); *POxy.* 912.16 (A.D. 235); *POxy.* 1036.25 (A.D. 273)
> χράσθωσαν *PGiss.* 49.26 (3rd cent.)
> χρᾶσθαι *SB* 7031 = *PMich.* 186.24 (A.D. 72); *SB* 7032 = *PMich.* 187.22 (A.D. 75); *POxy.* 104.8 (A.D. 96); *PBrem.* 68.8 (A.D. 99); *POxy.* 2410.6 (A.D. 120); *PFlor.* 1 = *MChr.* 243.7 (A.D. 153); *POxy.* 2722.28 (A.D. 154); *BGU* 2127.14 (A.D. 156); *POxy.* 2134.22 part. rest. (ca. A.D. 170); *PLond.* 932 (iii, 148-50).7 abbrev. (A.D. 211); *PFouad* 39.7 (A.D. 244-9); *POxy.* 1208.19 (A.D. 291); *PLips.* 26.10 part. rest. (early 4th cent.); *PMon.* 4-5 V.30 (A.D. 581); 9.75 (A.D. 585); 13.47

---

[1] See Vol. 1, 208-14.

[2] Veitch & *LSJ*, s.v.

[3] Schwyzer i, 675; Buck, *GD*, § 161a; *MS*, 175; Mayser i², 2, 114; Crönert, 223 & n. 2; Psaltes, 235.

[4] So also Thumb, *Hell.*, 64.

(A.D. 594); *SB* 5112.50 (A.D. 618?); *SB* 8987.29 (A.D. 644-5); cf. *PDura* 26.15 (A.D. 227)[1]

2) Classical Attic forms:

ἀπόχρηται *PRossGeorg.* v, 51.13 (2nd cent.)

χρῆσθαι *BGU* 1210 (34).97 (mid 2nd cent.); *POxy.* 237 v.38 (A.D. 186); *PLBat.* xvi, 2.24 (early 3rd cent.); *BGU* 614.19 part. rest. (A.D. 217); *POxy.* 2104.9 (A.D. 241?); *POxy.* 2280.16,18 (2nd half 3rd cent.); *PBeattyPanop.* 2.240 (A.D. 300); *PMichael.* 41.53 (A.D. 539/54); *PLond.* 991 (iii, 257-8).15 (6th cent.); *PLond.* 483 (ii, 323-9).45 (A.D. 616)

3) The -αο- forms of χράομαι are regularly contracted to -ω-:

χρώμεθα *BGU* 925 = *WChr.* 27.22-23 (2nd cent.)

χρῶνται (indic.) *PHamb.* 6 = *WChr.* 320.13 (A.D. 129)

χρῶνται (subj.) *PGiss.* 87.8 (ca. A.D. 117); *BGU* 140 = *MChr.* 373.32 (A.D. 119)

χρώμενος *POxy.* 285.9-10 (ca. A.D. 50); *POxy.* 237 v.37 (A.D. 186); *PMich.* 423-4.5 (A.D. 197); sim. *BGU* 98.21: cf. *BL* i, 19 (A.D. 211); *PSI* 222.6 (4th cent.?: *BL* iii, 221).

χρώμενον *PAmh.* 99b.16 part. rest. (A.D. 179); *PGrenf.* ii, 74.13 part. rest. (A.D. 302)

χρώμενοι *PRein.* 52.5 (3rd/4th cent.); *PLips.* 33 ii = *MChr.* 55.13 (A.D. 368)

χρωμένους *BGU* 987 — *MChr.* 269.13 part. rest. (1st half 1st cent.); *PMich.* 326.52 (A.D. 48); *CPR* 9 i.12; ii.13; iii.14 (A.D. 271); *PLips.* 3 = *MChr.* 172.12 (A.D. 256); *PLips.* 4 = *MChr.* 171 i.14 part. rest. (A.D. 293); *CPR* 10 = *MChr.* 145.5 (A.D. 322/3); *PCairGoodsp.* 13.10 (A.D. 341)

But the anomalous form χρωωμένους occurs in *POxy.* 1029.25 (only mistake) (A.D. 107),[2] and the Ionic form χρεώμενοι is read in *PMerton* 91.13 (A.D. 316).[3] This latter isolated form can hardly be an Ionicism; it may be influenced by the verb χρεωστῶ occurring frequently in the papyri, e.g., *POxy.* 71 i = *MChr.* 62.15 (A.D. 303).

---

[1] The mag. papp. have only χρᾶσθαι *PGM* 4.794,796 (4th cent.); *PGM* 5.385,392 (4th cent.).

[2] See Vol. i, 300.

[3] The copies of this petition, Cairo 57063 & 57385, have χρησάμενοι (ed., n. ad loc.).

b. ζάω[1] is conjugated regularly as in Attic for the most part, including the infinitive ζῆν:[2]

ζῆς (indic.) *PLBat.* i, 13.15 (2nd cent.)

ζῇ *PSI* 1263.1,5 (2nd cent.); *BGU* 1655.32 (A.D. 169); *POxy.* 1648.53 (late 2nd cent.); *POxy.* 1839.2 (6th cent.); *POxy.* 1840.5 (6th cent.); *POxy.* 943.7 (6th cent.); etc.; cf. *PGM* 26.9 (3rd/4th cent.)
ζῦ (= ζῇ) *SB* 7695.4 (6th/7th cent.)
ζῶμεν *POxy.* 1117.19 (ca. A.D. 178); *SB* 4650.12 (n.d.)
ἔζη *POxy.* 131.4 (6th/7th cent.); *PGrenf.* i, 65.2 (6th/7th cent.)
ζῇ (subj.) *POxy.* 490.5 (A.D. 124); *POxy.* 491 = *MChr.* 304.5 (A.D. 126); *POxy.* 492.6 (A.D. 130); *PSI* 1263.14 (2nd cent.)
ζῶμεν *PSI* 210.2 (4th/5th cent.)
ζῆν *PMich.* 228.23 (A.D. 47); *PMich.* 229.30 (A.D. 48); *PBaden* 51.2 (early 2nd cent.); *POxy.* 472.7 (ca. A.D. 130); *BGU* 242 = *MChr.* 116.16 (A.D. 186-8: *BL* i, 434); *PStrassb.* 128 = *SB* 7684.8 (A.D. 186); *PSI* 1360.3 (2nd/3rd cent.); *POxy.* 1557.12 (A.D. 255); *SB* 9622.18 (A.D. 343); *POxy.* 1885.10,11 (A.D. 509); etc.
διαζῆν *PMich.* 174.21 (A.D. 145-7)
ἐπιζῆν *POxy.* 472.13 (ca. A.D. 130)
ζῶν *POxy.* 2131.10 (A.D. 207); *PLond.* 77 = *MChr.* 319.10, with ζῆν 14 (late 6th cent.)
cf. ζῶντος *PGMXtn.* 5a.11 (4th cent.)
ζόντος *PGMXtn.* 5b.25 (5th cent.)
τοῖς ζῶσι *SB* 5198.7, tombstone (Rom.)

An anomalous imperative ζώτω is found in *PMeyer* 20.21 (1st half 3rd cent.). This verb is still inflected {zo}, {zis}, {zi} (ζῶ, ζεῖς/ζῆς, ζεῖ/ζῇ) in Modern Greek.[3]

2. -έω verbs.

a. Monosyllabic Ϝ stems, which contract only to ει in Attic,[4] sometimes fail to contract even to ει in the papyri, as limitedly elsewhere in the Koine.[5]

---

[1] From *ζηϳω < *gw-io as the aor. ἐβίων (Chantraine[2], § 277).

[2] Some verbs in -άω, notably πεινάω and διψάω, have the infin. in -ᾶν instead of -ῆν in the Koine (Chantraine[2], § 277; *BDF*, § 88; Crönert, 222; Phryn. 42 (Rutherford, 132-7).

[3] Thumb, *Handbook*, § 250; Jannaris, § 830.

[4] Schwyzer i, 685; Chantraine[2], § 275; Veitch & *LSJ*, s.vv.; *MS*, 176; Rutherford, *Phryn.*, 296-303.

[5] *BDF*, § 89; Crönert, 221; cf. Phryn. 195-7 (Rutherford, *ibid.*); Jannaris, § 835. Conversely, in the Ptol. papp., not only forms wh. contract to ει are found contracted, but sts. also the 2nd & 3rd sg. pres. subj. πλῆις, πλῆι, in place of the reg. πλέηις, πλέηι (Mayser i[2], 2, 113-14). Omission of all contraction is normal in these verbs in MGr. (Jannaris, § 835).

This omission of contraction serves to make the paradigm parisyllabic. This phenomenon is found only occasionally and has not yet become the regular inflection:

πλέετ[ε] (impt.) *PGissBibl.* 46 ii.1 (early 3rd cent.)
    πλέειν *PMon.* 4-5 V.29 (A.D. 581)
    ἐνπλέε[ι]ν *PSI* 298.11 (early 4th cent.)[1]
but ἀγαπλεῖ *PSarap.* 83.20 (early 2nd cent.)
    πλεῖν *PSI* 1242.12 (1st cent. B.C./1st cent. A.D.); *PLond.* 854 = *WChr.* 117.3 (2nd cent.); *PBeattyPanop.* 2.105 (A.D. 300)
    ἀναπλεῖν *PAmh.* 135 = *PSarap.* 96.11 (A.D. 129); *PMerton* 23.12-13 (2nd cent.)
    ἐκπλεῖν *BGU* 1210 (66).165, (67).168 part. rest. (mid 2nd cent.)
    ἐνπ[λ]εῖν *POxy.* 2347.6 (A.D. 362)
      ἐμπλεῖν *PLond.* 1713.37 (A.D. 569); 1714.37 (A.D. 570)
    καταπλεῖν *PBrem.* 48.11 (A.D. 118); (clearly) *PBrem.* 50.7-8 (A.D. 117-38); *PMich.* 516.6 part. emended (late 3rd cent.)
πλεῖσθαι *POxy.* 2182.31 (A.D. 166)
δέεται *BGU* 926.2 (A.D. 188); *PApoll.* 11.4 (A.D. 705)
    δέετε (for -ται) *PSI* 1103.3 (2nd/3rd cent.: *BL* iii, 228); *POxy.* 1415.23 (late 3rd cent.)[2]
    δέεσθαι *PSI* 299.17 part. rest. (late 3rd cent.); *PCairMasp.* 28 = *MChr.* 382.7 (ca. A.D. 551)
    προσδέεσθα[ι] *PFouad* 39.10 (A.D. 244-9)
    ἐνδέαισθαι *PCairMasp.* 154 V.2 (A.D. 527-65)
but δεῖν *POxy.* 2104.18 (A.D. 241?); *PLips.* 35.8,21 (ca. A.D. 375); etc.
    ἔδει *POxy.* 237 viii.29 (A.D. 186); *POxy.* 2407.21 part. rest., 30 (late 3rd cent.)
    δεῖται *PStrassb.* 5.16: *BL* i, 404 (A.D. 262); *SB* 7438.8 (A.D. 527-65)
    ἐ[ν]δεῖ[σθ]αι *PAmh.* 81 = *MChr.* 54.14 (A.D. 247)
συμπγέειν *PCairMasp.* 158.16 (A.D. 568); *PCairMasp.* 159-60.23 (A.D. 568)[3]
συνχέειν *PBeattyPanop.* 1.232,265 (A.D. 298)
    ἀποχέεται *CPR* 22 = *StudPal.* xx, 7.19 (after A.D. 150)[4]
    cf. also the parisyllabic ἐκχιεῖται *PSI* 1143.15 (A.D. 164)
    ἀποχεί[ε]ται *PRyl.* 154.14, with εἰσχεῖτα[ι] 18 (A.D. 66)
    ἐκχείετε *CPR* 189.6 (2nd cent.)
but ἐκχεῖται *CPR* 1 = *MChr.* 220.8,10 part. rest. (A.D. 83/84)

---

[1] Cf. also from the mag. papp. πλέειν *PGMXtn.* 29a.3 Gr.-Eg. lit. pap. (3rd cent.).

[2] Cf. also from the mag. papp. δέεται *PGM* 4.650 (4th cent.).

[3] Cf. also from the mag. papp. πνεέτω *PGM* 4.2117 (4th cent.).

[4] Cf. also from the mag. papp. προσχέεται *PGM* 7.235 (3rd cent.); ἐπίχεε *PGM* 2.56 (4th cent.). See also χέω and variants in the formation of the pres. stem above, p. 276.

b. Conversely, the subjunctive δέη is contracted to δῇ in *PFay.* 109.5 (early 1st cent.); *POxy.* 62 V = *WChr.* 278.16 (mid 3rd cent.: *BL* iv, 58); *PSI* 95.9 (3rd cent.); *PGiss.* 103.18 (after A.D. 309). But the regular δέη is found elsewhere, e.g., *SB* 3924.16 (A.D. 19); *POxy.* 525.5 (early 2nd cent.); *POxy.* 2192.15 (2nd cent.); *PFay.* 125.8-9 (2nd cent.); *BGU* 245 ii.5 (2nd cent.?); *BGU* 614.26 (A.D. 217); etc., as well as δέητε (for δέηται) *POxy.* 2600.10 (3rd/4th cent.); προσδέηται *POxy.* 743.33 (2 B.C.); etc.

c. Participles appear in contract forms sporadically, e.g., πλοῦντα *PHamb.* 104.3 (2nd/3rd cent.); ἀποδοῦγτι (for ἀποδέοντι) *PFay.* 20.2 (late 3rd/early 4th cent.). Elsewhere the regular non-contract forms are found, e.g., ἀναπλέοντα *BGU* 451.7-8 (1st/2nd cent.); *PGiss.* 14.7 (ca. A.D. 117); καταπλέοντα *SB* 4653.8 (A.D. 240/1); καταπλεούσας *PSI* 97.2 (6th cent.); δέουσαν *PTebt.* 332.18 (A.D. 176); τὰ δέοντ[α] *BGU* 251.5 (A.D. 81); τὸ ἀποδέον *BGU* 1564.13 (A.D. 138).

d. Conversely, δέω 'bind' remains uncontracted in the participle of the compound [σ]υνδέοντα *CPR* 232.17 (2nd/3rd cent.).

3. -όω verbs.

a. The infinitive of -όω verbs frequently ends in -οῖν:

> μεταμισθοῖν *PRyl.* 600.26 (3rd hand), with μεταμισθῦν 15 (1st hand) (8 B.C.); *PLond.* 1168 (iii, 135-8).9,12 (A.D. 44: *BL* i, 282); *POxy.* 2351.61 (A.D. 112); *PRossGeorg.* ii, 19.51 (A.D. 141); *POxy.* 101.48 (A.D. 142); *PStrassb.* 387.11 part. rest. (2nd cent.); *PMerton* 76.39 (A.D. 181); *PFlor.* 383.30 (A.D. 232-4); *PFlor.* 24.27 (mid 3rd cent.: *BL* iii, 55); etc.
>
> μεμισθοῖν sic *PLond.* 1164 (iii, 154-67) h.19 (A.D. 212)
> ἐκμισθοῖν *PYale* 68.10 (A.D. 204); *POxy.* 1705.14 (A.D. 298)
> μισθοῖν *PSI* 1040.33 (3rd cent.)
> ἐξαλλοτριοῖν, μισθοῖν *PMich.* 322a.30,31 (1st hand), 39 (2nd hand), 41,42 (3rd hand) (A.D. 46)
> ἐκσαλλοτριοῖν *PMich.* 321.22 (A.D. 42)
> βεβαιοῖν *SB* 9831.13 part. rest. (late 1st cent.); *PHamb.* 62 = *PLBat.* vi, 23.17 (A.D. 123)
> συμβιοῖν *PMilVogl.* 85.13 (A.D. 138); (συν-) *SB* 9381 = *PMilVogl.* 185.19-20 (A.D. 139)
> βιοῖν *PMich.* 174.12 (A.D. 145-7)
> μαστιγοῖν *POxy.* 1643.11 (A.D. 298)
> ἀναπληροῖν *POxy.* 900 = *WChr.* 437.10,18 (A.D. 322)
> πληροῖν *POxy.* 904.5 (5th cent.)
>> πληροῖ (for πληροῖν) *PPrinc.* 119.52: *ZPE* 8 (1971).22 (ca. A.D. 325)
> δηλοῖν *PLond.* 231 = *PAbinn.* 9.13 (ca. A.D. 346)

This infinitive in -οῖν, which is weakly attested in the Septuagint and the New Testament and occasionally elsewhere in the Koine,[1] is a result of the increasingly widespread pronunciation of οι as [i].[2] This pronunciation rendered -οῖν phonetically identical with the usual infinitive ending -ειν, with the -ο- perhaps retained on orthographic grounds corresponding to the -οι of the indicative singular, etc., on the analogy ποιεῖ : ποιεῖν :: μισθοῖ : μισθοῖν.[3]

b. The -οι ending of the indicative is extended to the present imperative in δήλοι, πα[ρά]δηλοι (for -δηλου if not for δήλωσον as in 26,33) *PFlor.* 175.10,14 (A.D. 255).

---

[1] *BDF*, § 91; Crönert, 220, n. 2; Psaltes, 234-5; Hatzidakis, *Einl.*, 193. It is not found in the Ptol. papp. (Mayser i², 2, 116).

[2] See Vol. i, 262-73.

[3] So *BDF*, § 91.

X. -MI VERBS[1]

The -μι verbs tend towards the thematic inflection in the papyri of the Roman and Byzantine periods, not only in the use of thematic endings or thematic formations built on different stems in the present system, but also in various forms of the aorist and perfect systems of the greater -μι verbs. In addition, analogical levelling is found within the various systems and even among the different types of athematic verbs. These phenomena reflect an early stage in the process through which all -μι verbs except εἰμί lost their athematic inflection in the transition from ancient to Modern Greek.

A. THE PRESENT SYSTEM

Active and deponent -μι verbs tend towards a thematic inflection in the present system. Foremost among these are the verbs in -(ν)υμι, most of which even in classical Greek had competing formations either in -ύω, as ὀμνύω, or formations constructed on different stems, as (ἀν)οίγω. Next most frequently affected are the greater -μι verbs ἵστημι, ἵημι, τίθημι, δίδωμι. The deponent δύναμαι is also frequently conjugated thematically.

1. Verbs in -(ν)υμι.

a. ὄμνυμι.

1) Thematic forms, already used as by-forms in classical Attic prose writers,[2]

---

[1] Schwyzer i, 673-83, 686-99; Chantraine[2], § 181, 217, 232, 234-43; Buck, *GD* § 138-40, 151, 154, 160, 163; *MS* 188-91; Schweizer, 176-8; Nachmanson, 155-8; Mayser i[2], 2, 121-7; Crönert, 238-41; *BDF*, § 92-100; Psaltes, 236-41.

[2] Athematic forms of ὄμνυμι are used excl. in the pres. indic. in Trag. and Ar., but Hdt. and Att. prose writers, incl. X. D. Lycurg., also have thematic forms of ὀμνύω, as do the lesser comic poets Antiph. Pherecr. etc.,; thematic forms are also found in the infin. and ptc. in the Att. and Perg. inscrr. (Veitch & *LSJ*, s.v.; *MS*, 191; Schweizer, 178; cf. Schwyzer i, 698-9; Chantraine[2], § 252).

are found most frequently in the first person singular and plural (which occur much more frequently than the other persons) and also in the participle:

> ὀμνύω *PRein.* 99.2 (30 B.C. - A.D. 14); *POxy.* 259 = *MChr.* 101.4 (A.D. 23); *PMich.* 176.20 (A.D. 91); *BGU* 581 = *MChr.* 354.5 (A.D. 133); *StudPal.* xx, 11.36 (A.D. 175); *PLeit.* 12.11 (A.D. 210/11); *POxy.* 1264.18-19 (A.D. 272); *SB* 9219.7 (A.D. 319); etc.
>
> ὀμνύομεν *SB* 7174 = *PMich.* 233.13 (A.D. 24: *BL* v, 69); *PAmh.* 68 = *WChr.* 374.33 (A.D. 81-96); *BGU* 2037.6 (1st half 2nd cent.); *PAntin.* 37.3 (A.D. 209/10); *PHibeh* 216.5 (A.D. 212); *PFlor.* 4 = *WChr.* 206.28 (A.D. 245); *POxy.* 85 ii.12-13; iv.13-14 (A.D. 338); etc.
>
> ὀμνύων *OStrassb.* 776.9-10 (early Rom.); *BGU* 92 = *WChr.* 427.9 part. emended (A.D. 187); *PWürzb.* 16.5 (A.D. 349); *PLond.* 1728.14 (A.D. 584/5); 1729.24 (A.D. 584); *PCairMasp.* 97 V d.54 (6th cent.); etc.
>
> ὀμνύουσα *PFlor.* 32b = *WChr.* 228.19 (A.D. 298); *PMon.* 9.21 (A.D. 585)
>
> ὀμνυούσῃ *PBrem.* 61.8 (ca. A.D. 117)
>
> ὀμνύοντες *BGU* 16 = *WChr.* 114.13-14 part. rest. (A.D. 159/60); *PCairMasp.* 1.33 (A.D. 514); *PCairMasp.* 296.5 (A.D. 535)
>
> διομνύοντα *BGU* 647.22, with ὀμνύτες *sic* 8 (A.D. 130)

ἐπωμνύετο *PFlor.* 214.7: *BL* i, 153 (A.D. 255)

2) Athematic forms also occur. These are not so common in the indicative, but are normal in the infinitive and participle:[1]

> ὄμνυμι *BGU* 248.12-13 (1st cent.: *BL* i, 32); *PLBat.* xvi, 17.24 part. rest. (A.D. 106); *PCornell* 20.16,36, etc. (A.D. 302); *SB* 7673 = *PCairIsidor.* 8.12 (A.D. 309); sim. -μει *PMich.* 613.7 (A.D. 415); *PSI* 1265.13 (A.D. 426/41)
>
> [ἐ]ξόμνυμι, ὀμνύς *PLond.* 1647.9,15 (A.D. 298)
>
> ἐπόμνυμι *PErl.* 79.8 (6th cent.)
>
> ὄμνυνμεν *sic* *PCairIsidor.* 9.9-10 (ca. A.D. 310)

ὀμνύαι *CPR* 232.26 (2nd/3rd cent.)

> ὀμνύς *PGrenf.* ii, 79 i.4; ii.5 (late 3rd cent.); *SB* 2267.5 (ca. A.D. 300); *PAmh.* 138 = *MChr.* 342.6 (A.D. 326); *POxy.* 83 = *WChr.* 430.5 (A.D. 327); *PLBat.* xi, 1 i.6; ii.5 (A.D. 338); *POslo* 113.7 (A.D. 346); *POxy.* 2347.2 (A.D. 362); etc.
>
> ὀμνύντες *POxy.* 1255.11-12 (A.D. 292); *PFlor.* 54.6 (A.D. 314); *POxy.* 2767.7 (A.D. 323); *BGU* 21 i.7 (A.D. 340); *PLips.* 54 = *WChr.* 467.5 (ca. A.D. 376); *PCairMasp.* 314 iii.10 (ca. A.D. 527); etc.
>
> ἐπομνύμενος *POxy.* 1880.13 (A.D. 427); *SB* 5273 = *StudPal.* xx, 128.7 (A.D. 487); *SB* 9152.5 (A.D. 492); *PCairMasp.* 328 iv.6; v.6, etc.

---

[1] Cf. also from the mag. papp. ὄμνυμι *PGM* 4.851 (4th cent.).

(A.D. 521); *PLond.* 1660.34 (ca. A.D. 553); *POxy.* 199 = *PLond.* 778
(iii, 279-80).11 (A.D. 568); *PSI* 59.8 (A.D. 596: *BL* i, 390); etc.
ὑπομνύμενος *POxy.* 2420.10 (A.D. 610)
ἐπομνύμενοι *POxy.* 1881.15 (A.D. 427); *PCairMasp.* 328 iii.6 (A.D. 521);
PCairMasp. 94.8 (A.D. 553); 169bis.33 part. rest. (A.D. 569); *PSI*
52.11 (6th cent.?); etc.

b. δείκνυμι.

1) Thematic forms of δείκνυμι, used already by Hesiod and in Attic prose,[1]
are sometimes found in the present indicative and participle:[2]

παραδεικνύω *SB* 7817 = *PSI* 1328.63 part. rest. (A.D. 201); *PJand.*
145.3 (A.D. 224)
ἐπιδεικνύω *PAmh.* 142 = *MChr.* 65.13 (after A.D. 341)
ὑποδεικνύεις *PSI* 742.10 (5th/6th cent.)
δεικνύει *PGiss.* 40 ii = *WChr.* 22.28 (A.D. 215)
παραδεικνύουσι *BGU* 915.10 (1st/2nd cent.: *BL* i, 83)
ἀποδεικνύων *PCairMasp.* 281.6 (6th cent.?)
ἐπιδεικνύουσα *POxy.* 2111.16 (ca. A.D. 135)
ἀποδικνυούσης *PSI* 698.17 (A.D. 392)
ἀποδικνύοντες *PLond.* 1349 = *WChr.* 284.28 (A.D. 710)
κατ[αδει]κνυόντων *BGU* 12 = *WChr.* 389.25-26 (A.D. 181/2)
δικνέοντε (for δεικνύονται) *PLond.* 1926.11 (mid 4th cent.)

2) Athematic forms are retained in the present indicative and imperative
active, in the infinitive passive, and in the participle active and middle-passive:

ὑποδείκνυμ[ι], ἀποδεικνύς *PMich.* 616.16 (ca. A.D. 182)
ἐ[ν]δείκνυμι *POxy.* 136 = *WChr.* 383.24 (A.D. 583)
διαδίκνυσι *POxy.* 472.11 (ca. A.D. 130)
ὑποδίκνυῳ *POxy.* 1066.21 (3rd cent.)
ὑποδεικνύς *BGU* 361 ii.29 (A.D. 184)
δεικνύς *POxy.* 2892 i.14 (A.D. 269); *POxy.* 2913 ii.13; iii.8 (A.D. 269)
ἐπιδικνύς *POxy.* 2902 ii.10 (A.D. 272)
ὑποδικνύντος *PThead.* 13 ii.2 (A.D. 321)
δεικνύντι *CPR* 232.33 (2nd/3rd cent.)
δεικνύντα *POxy.* 471.75 (2nd cent.)
ἐπιδείκνυσθε *SB* 3924.34 (A.D. 19)
δείκνυνται *PStrassb.* 169.4 (2nd cent.)

---

[1] Incl. X. Pl. and the Att. orators (Veitch & *LSJ*, s.v.).
[2] Cf. also the thematic infin. and ptc. in the mag. papp., e.g., δεικνύειν *PGM* 4.772
(4th cent.); δεικνύων *PGM* 4.785; 7.524 (3rd cent.); 22.32 (4th cent.); but ὑποδείκνυται
PGM 8.65-66 (4th/5th cent.), and ἐπιδεικνύμενος *PGM* 4.2448 (4th cent.).

παραδίκνυσθαι *SB* 7599.29 (A.D. 95)
ἐπιδείκνυσθαι *POxy.* 42 = *WChr.* 154.5 (A.D. 323)
ἐνδείκνυσθα[ι] *PLond.* 1711.38 (A.D. 566-73)
διγνυμέν[ων] *SB* 5761.28 (A.D. 91-96)
ἐπιδεικνυμένων *POxy.* 2190.35 (late 1st cent.)

c. ὄλλυμι retains the athematic inflection in ὤλλυτο *POxy.* 472.7-8 (ca. A.D. 130) and ἀπόλλυται *BGU* 1024 iv.26 (late 4th cent.: *BL* i, 88).[1]

This transition of the -νυμι verbs ὄμνυμι and δείκνυμι to the thematic inflection began early in Greek, apparently from the forms of the third person plural present and imperfect indicative and the participle in consonantal stems having the aspect of thematic forms -νυ[ϝ]οντι, -νυ[ϝ]ον, -νυ[ϝ]οντ- < IE *nuwe/onti, *nuwe/ont, *nuwont-.[2] While these apparently thematic forms were themselves partially replaced in Attic-Ionic by athematic forms (e.g., δεικνύασι, ἐδείκνυσαν, δεικνύντ-), the original forms remained in competition[3] and occasioned new analogical thematic formations, so that even in the period of the best Attic, ὄμνυμι/ὀμνύω, δείκνυμι/δεικνύω, etc., offered competing athematic and thematic forms throughout the active of the present system. The thematic forms gradually came to predominate in the inscriptions, papyri, and literary works of the Koine,[4] and eventually resulted in the complete disappearance of the athematic inflection in Modern Greek.[5]

2. The greater -μι verbs.

a. Thematic forms of ἵστημι, based on several collateral stems, are found occasionally in the present system.

1) A contract stem ἱστα-, found in particular forms throughout classical literature and in the Koine,[6] is reflected in the following forms:

---

[1] ὀλλύω is found only in the pres., rarely in the simple verb (Archil. Com. Frag.), more freq. in compds. (Hp. Th. Isoc. Pl. X.) (Veitch & *LSJ*, s.v.).

[2] Schwyzer i, 698; Chantraine², § 252, 334. This explanation was first developed by Meillet (Schwyzer i, 699).

[3] E.g., δεικνύουσι Hdt. Isoc. Is. (in composition); ἐδείκνυον Hdt. Antiph. Aeschin. D.; δεικνύων X. D. (Veitch, s.v.).

[4] *MS*, 191; Schweizer, 178; Nachmanson, 155-6; Mayser i², 2, 121; *BDF*, § 92; Crönert, 239-40 & n. 1 on each page. In general, the act. tends to have the thematic formation, esp. in the pres., most commonly in the 1 sg.; the mid.-pass. tends to retain the athematic formation. Cf. further ⲁⲓⲕⲛⲉⲧⲉ as a Gr. loanword in Copt. (Böhlig, *Akten*, 66).

[5] Cf. Chantraine², § 177; Jannaris, § 936-7; Thumb, *Handbook*, § 198. For (ἀν)οἴγνυμι/ (ἀν)οἴγω and μ(ε)ίγνυμι/μίσγω, see formation of the pres. stem above, pp. 280-1.

[6] This stem, prob. an analogical back-formation from the subj. ἱστῶ, is found (rarely) in the *Il.* (impt. only), Hdt. Ar. Ctes. Pl. Them. etc. (Veitch & *LSJ*, s.v.; Crönert, 259(-60), n. 5). It occurs several times in the Ptol. papp., as well as in the LXX and Koine lit. and in the NT, where it is a less freq. variant than ἱστάνω (Mayser i², 2, 123; Crönert, *ibid.*, *BDF*, § 93; Psaltes, 236).

καθιστῶμεν (pres. indic.) PVindobWorp 3.21 (A.D. 321)
συνείστα (impf.) POxy. 2349.21 (A.D. 70)
   cf. ἀποκαθείστα PAntin. 42.22 (A.D. 542)
ἀποκαθιστᾶν POxy. 904.5 (5th cent.)
ϛυνιστῶϋ PRyl. 604.17 (3rd cent.)
   προσιστῶν PLond. 1383.7 (ca. A.D. 709)
   καθιστῶντο(ς) PLond. 131 R = SB 9699.546 (A.D. 78/79)
   ἐφιστῶν᾽τι᾽ PMerton 76.23 (A.D. 181)
   ἱστῶσι (ptc.) POxy. 2580.9 (early 3rd cent.)
   καθιστώντας PCairMasp. 323.13 (6th cent.)

2) A contract stem ἱστε- is reflected in the late forms ἀφιστοῦμεν POxy. 2270.18 (early 5th cent.) and παριστούντω[ν] SB 7241.43 (A.D. 697-712), unless they are instances of the transfer of some -άω verbs to the -έω inflectional type noted in Contract Verbs above.[1]

3) A late present stem ἱσταν-, frequent in Koine literature and the New Testament,[2] is inflected thematically in the infinitive active and in the middle-passive indicative and participle:[3]

   ἀφιστάνιν BGU 1127.19 (18 B.C.); sim. BGU 1130.20 part. rest. (4 B.C.);
      PMilVogl. 26.15-16 (A.D. 127/8); CPR 189.20 (2nd cent.)
   ἀφιστάνειν BGU 542.15 (A.D. 165); CPR 5 = StudPal. xx, 10.14
      part. rest. (A.D. 168); SB 10571.21 part. rest. (A.D. 194); PGiss.
      51.20 (A.D. 202); etc.
   καθισ[τ]άνειν BGU 1074 = SB 5225.4 (A.D. 275)
   ἀνιστάνειν, [καθι]στάνειν POxy. 2476.2,6 (A.D. 288: BL v, 82)
   συννιστανόμεθα sic PAlex. 25.8 (2nd cent.)
   συνιστανόμενος POxy. 727.25 (A.D. 154)
   ἐξιστανόμενος POxy. 1405.24 part. rest. (A.D. 230/7. BL iv, 61);
      CPR 202 = StudPal. xx, 54 i.6, with ἀφισταμένῳ (for -εστ-) 15
      (A.D. 250)
   ἀφιστανομένη καὶ ἐξιστανομένη PRyl. 117.22 (A.D. 269)
   ἀφιστανομένου PSI 292.15, with ἐξιστανομέγ[ους] 4, ἐξιστάμενος 18,
      συνεστάναι 20 (3rd cent.)

---

  [1] pp. 363-5.
  [2] This stem, an analogical back-formation from the infin. ἱστάναι, occurs for the first time in the Ptol. papp. (3rd cent. B.C.) (Mayser i², 2, 123). It is also found in Att. and Asia Minor inscrr. and occ. in Koine authors, the LXX, NT, and Byz.Chron. (MS, 177; Nachmanson, 157; Veitch, s.v.; Dieterich, 218; Crönert, 259(-60), n. 5; BDF, § 93; Psaltes, 242). It is also found as a v.l. in compds. in Is. Lys., but it was prob. introduced by copyists (LSJ, s.v.).
  [3] Cf. also from the mag. papp. the pres. impt. mid. συνιστάνου PGM 13.29 (A.D. 346) and the mid.-pass. ptc. ἱστανόμενος PGM 4.257 (4th cent.); ἀνιστανόμενος PGM 13.117, with ἀνιστάμενος 673 (A.D. 346).

καθισταν όμενον (for -μενος) *PLBat.* iii, 16.12-13 (6th/7th cent.)
καθιστ[α]νάμενοι sic *PAmh.* 70 = *WChr.* 149.4 (A.D. 114-17)
κατιστανομένων sic *BGU* 747 = *WChr.* 35 V.1 (A.D. 139)
προισταν ομέγ[ο]ις *POxy.* 2569.22 (A.D. 265)

4) A simple stem σταν-,[1] without the initial reduplication of the present,
is reflected in ἀποστάνομαι *PGen.* 53 = *PAbinn.* 36.21 (ca. A.D. 346).

5) στήκω,[2] an analogical back-formation from the perfect ἕστηκα, and an
anticipation of the Modern Greek στέκω, is found in the participle in ἐπιστή-
κων *PMich.* 515.2 (late 3rd cent.) and στήγων sic *PLips.* 40 ii.4 (late 4th/
early 5th cent.).

6) στατίζω, the poetic form of ἵστημι,[3] is found in the following forms:

στατίζοντος *POxy.* 2130.21 (A.D. 267); *POxy.* 65.1 (3rd/early 4th cent.)
στατίζοντι *POxy.* 2130.23 (A.D. 267); *PCairIsidor.* 139 descr. abbrev.;
    62.1 part. rest.; sim. 63.1 (all A.D. 296)
στατίζοντο (for -οντα) *POxy.* 2187.8 (A.D. 304)
στατιζόντων *PBerlZill.* 4.22 (4th cent.)

7) Other thematic present formations competing with ἵστημι are found in
decomposita in -στατέω (and -όω in ἀναστατόω); see Palmer 125, 133.

b. τίθημι.

1) New thematic forms (contract and non-contract) are found in the present
indicative and participle active and middle-passive:

περιτιθεῖς *BGU* 1141.19 (prob. 13 B.C.)
    ὑποτιθοῦσα *BGU* 350.13 (A.D. 98-117); *PRyl.* 162.28 (A.D. 159)
    συντιθοῦν[τες] *PFlor.* 322.42 (A.D. 258?)
        κατατιθο(ῦντες) *POxy.* 1732.7 (late 2nd cent.)
        ἐπιτίθο(ντες) *POxy.* 985 descr.: *BL* iii, 133 (2nd half 1st cent.)

---

[1] Some occurrences of this stem in compds. are found in the Att. inscrr. of Rom. times
and in the NT (*MS*, 177; *BDF*, § 93).

[2] Pres. forms of this stem are also found in the LXX, NT, and Koine lit., incl. the
Byz.Chron. (Veitch & *LSJ*, s.v.; *BDF*, § 93; Psaltes, 245). Cf. also from the mag. papp.
στήκεις *PGM* 4.728 (4th cent.); impt. στῆκε *PGM* 4.923; ptc. στήκων *PGM* 36.273 (4th
cent.).

[3] στατίζω is found in Trag. Arist. Str. etc.; it is not freq. (*LSJ*, s.v.). Cf. Palmer, 141.

ὑποτίθοντας PMich. 428.9 (A.D. 154)
παρακατατίθομαι BGU 326 = MChr. 316 i.16 (A.D. 189)
παρατίθομαι PCairIsidor. 29.3 (1st quarter 4th cent.)
[ἀ]ποτιθόμεθ[α], ἀποτιθομένου PMich. 175.8,12-13, with ἀποτί-
    θεσθαι 16-17 (A.D. 193)
ὑπερτίθοντε (for -ται) BGU 984.12 (4th cent.)
παρατιθόμενος PLond. 239 = PAbinn. 31.7 (ca. A.D. 346)[1]

2) Athematic forms are more common, however, e.g., παρατίθημι POxy. 2110.6 (A.D. 370); τίθεντο[2] PPar. 20.4 (A.D. 600); παρατίθεμαι POxy. 1663.8 (2nd/3rd cent.); ὑποτίθεσθαι PMich. 322a.30,31,39 (1st hand), sim. 41,42 (2nd hand) (A.D. 46); ὑπερτιθέμεν[ο]ς POxy. 86 = WChr. 46.15 (A.D. 338); etc.

Thematic forms of τίθημι in the second person singular present imperative τίθει and in the second and third person singular imperfect ἐτίθεις, ἐτίθει (as if from a contract formation τιθέω) are regular in classical Attic, and corresponding forms of the second and third person singular present are found in Poetic-Ionic.[3] Other thematic forms are generally later.[4]

c. Thematic forms of ἵημι are found only rarely:[5]

εἰ ... ἀφίω (if not subj. ἀφιῶ) PPrinc. 73.10 (3rd cent.)
ἐὰν ... συνίεις PLond. 1346.15 (A.D. 710)
    εἰ ... συνίεις PLond. 1348.14 (A.D. 710)
    εἰ συνήεις PLond. 1359.14 (A.D. 710)
μὴ ἄφιε POxy. 1758.12 (2nd cent.)
ἀφίονται PMich. 174.6 (A.D. 145-7)
cf. also ἀφῶ (= ἀφίημι) SB 8536.13,20 (late 6th cent.)
    ἀφεῖ (for ἀφίει) SB 9121.4 (1st cent.)

Of these, the imperative is poetic (Tim. Thg.),[6] the first person singular is paralleled in the Septuagint and in the Apostolic Fathers,[7] and the third person plural in the Ptolemaic papyri.[8] Many thematic forms of this verb were in use in classical Greek, especially in Epic and Ionic, formed either

---

[1] Cf. also from the mag. papp. παρατιθῶν PGM 4.334-5 (4th cent.); PGM 1.169 (4th/5th cent.).
[2] For the omission of the syll. augm., see above, p. 225.
[3] Veitch, s.v. τιθέω; LSJ, s.v. τίθημι; Schwyzer i, 687.
[4] Veitch & LSJ, Mayser, ibidd.; BDF, § 94.1; Crönert, 277-8; Psaltes, 236.
[5] Cf. also from the mag. papp. ἀφίομεν PGMOstr. 4.10 (4th cent.); παραφίων PGM 13.347 (A.D. 346); ἀφίων PGM 2.112 (4th cent.).
[6] Veitch, s.v. ἵω; LSJ, s.v. ἵημι. The pl. ἵετε is reg. in Att. (Ar. etc.), while the Att. sg. is also thematic in ἵει, as if from a contr. formation (Ar. Pl. etc.).
[7] BDF, § 94.2.
[8] Mayser i[2], 2, 124.

from the pure stem ἱ-, as the Homeric first person singular imperfect ξύν-ιον, or from a contract stem ἱε-, as the Attic second and third person singular imperfect.[1] Other thematic forms occur later.[2]

d. δίδωμι.

1) Thematic forms of δίδωμι appear frequently in the present indicative and participle active and are also found occasionally in the imperfect and imperative, and in the passive.[3]

> δίδω (or διδῶ) *SB* 9121.7 (1st cent.); *BGU* 261.21, with δίδι (impt.) 23
> (ca. A.D. 105: cf. *PMich.* 202); *POxy.* 121.23 (3rd cent.); *POxy.*
> 936.17 (3rd cent.); *PMich.* 515.4 (late 3rd cent.); *PCairIsidor.* 133.10
> (last quarter 3rd cent.); *PPrinc.* 168.3 (3rd/4th cent.); *SB* 6264.8
> (Rom.); *PAbinn.* 24.11 (ca. A.D. 346); *PLond.* 453 (ii, 319-20).10
> (4th cent.); *POxy.* 1683.19 part. rest. (late 4th cent.); etc.
> δίδωι *SB* 9646 = *PMilVogl.* 218.8 (2nd cent.)
> μεταδείδω *PMerton* 112.14 (2nd cent.)
> δίδι (or διδῖ) (3 sg.) *BGU* 38.19 (2nd/3rd cent.: *BL* i, 10)
>> δίδει *PBerlZill.* 11.16 (3rd cent.)
>> ἀποδίδει *PGrenf.* ii, 91.7 (6th/7th cent.)
> διδοῦμεν (or δίδουμεν) *PLond.* 414 = *PAbinn.* 5.16 (ca. A.D. 346)
>> ἀναδιδοῦμεν *PLond.* 1075 (iii, 281-2).15, with ἀναδίδομ[εν] 24
>> (7th cent.)
>> ἀποδιδοῦμεν *PLond.* 1343.18, with ἀποδιδοῦντες 23 (A.D. 709);
>> *PLond.* 1349 = *WChr.* 284.26 part. rest. (A.D. 710); *PRoss-
>> Georg.* iv, 8.10, with διδῶν 13 (A.D. 711); *SB* 7241.28 abbrev.
>> (A.D. 697/712)
> δίδουσιν (or διδοῦσιν) *PMichael.* 41.40 (A.D. 539/54)
> ἐδείδι (for ἐδίδου) *BGU* 602.6 (prob. 2nd cent.)
>> ἐδίδι *PLond.* 418 = *PAbinn.* 7.18 (ca. A.D. 346)
> διδῇ (or δίδη) *PCairIsidor.* 132.5 (3rd cent.)
>> ἐκδίδη *PSI* 1266.8 = *PApoll.* 9.9 (before A.D. 704)
> δίδι (for δίδου impt.) *SB* 7660.32 (ca. A.D. 100); *BGU* 261.23, with δίδω
> 21 (ca. A.D. 105: cf. *PMich.* 202); *POxy.* 2982.18 (2nd/3rd cent.)
> δείδι *POxy.* 1185.12, with δείδου 9 (ca. A.D. 200)
> δίδων (or διδῶν) *PLond.* 1338 = *WChr.* 255.26 (A.D. 709); *PLond.* 1393.54
> (8th cent.); *PLond.* 1382.25 = *PRossGeorg.* iv, 1.30, with παραδιδ[ο]ῦ-
> μεν 26 (A.D. 710); 8.13 (A.D. 711); 11.6 (A.D. 711)
>> ἐκδίδων, μὴ δίδων *PLond.* 1393 = *SB* 7241.11,54, with ἀποδιδοῦ-
>> με(ν) 28 (A.D. 697/712)
>> ἐκδίδων *PLond.* 1391 = *PRossGeorg.* iv, 6.11 (A.D. 710)

---

[1] Veitch, s.v. ἱέω, ἵημι, ἵω; *LSJ*, s.v. ἵημι.
[2] Veitch & *LSJ*, ibidd.; *MS*, 188; Mayser i², 2, 124; *BDF*, § 94.2; Crönert, 258, n. 3.
[3] Thematic forms of the pres. of δίδωμι are also found in the mag. papp., as δίδεις *PGM* 12.255 (A.D. 300-350).

διδοῦντος *SB* 7341.20,36 (A.D. 3); *BGU* 86 = *MChr.* 306.22 (A.D.155);
    BGU 2041.11 (A.D. 201); *PGrenf.* i, 54.11: *BL* i, 183 (A.D. 378)[1]
ἀναδιδοῦντος *PStrassb.* 187.4-5 part. rest. (2nd cent.); *PSI* 900.15
    (3rd/4th cent.); *POxy.* 2156.8 (late 4th/5th cent.); sim. *PRyl.*
    242.7-8 (3rd cent.)
παραδιδοῦντος *PFlor.* 31.10 (A.D. 312)
ἀποδιδοῦντος *PRossGeorg.* iv, 2.16 (A.D. 711)
διδοῦντι *SB* 10279.5 (4th cent.)
    ἀναδιδοῦντι *POxy.* 532.11 (2nd cent.); *POxy.* 2726.12-13 (2nd
    cent.); *PRyl.* 240.3 (3rd cent.); *POxy.* 1773.17 (for -οῦσι)
    (3rd cent.); *PMich.* 515.2 (late 3rd cent.); *POxy.* 1770.15 (late
    3rd cent.); *POxy.* 2577.4-5 (3rd/4th cent.); *PSI* 236.35 (3rd/4th
    cent.); *POxy.* 2275.5 part. rest. (1st half 4th cent.); *PHermRees*
    13.5-6 part. rest. (4th cent.); *StudPal.* viii, 968.3 (4th cent.); etc.
διδοῦντα *POxy.* 136 = *WChr.* 383.35 (A.D. 583); *SB* 7240.12 (A.D.
    697/712)
    ἀνδιδοῦντα *sic BGU* 44.15, with διδόντα 14 (A.D. 102)
    ἀναδιδοῦντα *POxy.* 1848.2 (6th/7th cent.)
διδοῦντες *PMerton* 128.3 (3rd cent.)
ἀποδιδοῦντων *PLBat.* vi, 24.50-51 (up to A.D. 124)
διδοῦσι *OStrassb.* 788.7 (prob. 2nd cent.)
δίδεται *POxy.* 191 descr. = *POxy.* 1053.13 abbrev. (late 6th/early 7th
    cent.); *PLond.* 1349 = *WChr.* 284.17 (A.D. 710)

    2) The forms ἐπιδίδωμεν *BGU* 108 R = *WChr.* 227.3 (A.D. 203/4); δίδωμε
SB 7168.6 (5th/6th cent.); ἀποδίδωμαι *SB* 7360.11 (A.D. 214); δ[ί]δωται *PSarap.*
103a = *SB* 9733.7 (A.D. 90-133); and δίδυμε *PRyl.* 135.13 (A.D. 34), could
represent thematic formations, but may be merely orthographic variants of the
athematic δίδωμι.

    3) Regular athematic forms are still common, however, e.g., δίδομεν *POxy.*
2232.8 (A.D. 316); ἀναδιδο{α}μεν *PHeid.* 224 = *SB* 9544.5 (A.D. 322); διδόασιν
POxy. 1467.3 (A.D. 263); διδότω *POxy.* 34 V = *MChr.* 188 ii.6 (A.D. 127);
διδόναι *PMich.* 466.39 (A.D. 107); etc.

    Thematic forms of δίδωμι, like those of τίθημι and ἵημι, are found in Homer
and in Poetic-Ionic in the second and third person singular and third person
plural of the present, and even in Attic in the second person singular imperative
and in the singular of the imperfect.[2] Other thematic forms are generally later.[3]

---

    [1] Cf. also δειδοῦντος *PDura* 26.25 (A.D. 227).
    [2] Veitch, s.vv. διδόω, δίδωμι; *LSJ*, s.v. δίδωμι; Schwyzer i, 687; *MS*, 188; Chantraine[2],
§ 242.
    [3] The first occurrence of the thematic ptc. is in the Ptol. papp., where a contr. 3 pl.
pres. is also found (Mayser i[2], 2, 124). A dbtfl. ex. of διδῶ appears in the NT, along w. ἐδί-
δετο, and 3 pl. impf. act. ἐδίδουν (*BDF*, § 94). The 3 sg. pres. is paralleled in Koine authors
(Crönert, 250, n. 3). Cf. also Phryn. 220 (Rutherford, pp. 315-37).

4) A possible analogical athematic formation of the present indicative is ἐ[π]ιδίδημι (for ἐπιδίδωμι) *PFay.* 29.13-14 (A.D. 73).

5) The present imperative δίδος appears for δίδου in *PSarap.* 83.18 (early 2nd cent.).

6) The present subjunctive appears rarely in διδοῖς, διδοῖ (with orthographic variants), parallel to the aorist subjunctive δοῖς, δοῖ (for which, see below, pp. 388-9):

> ἀποδιδῦς (= -διδοῖς) *PFay.* 124.22 (2nd cent.)
> διδοῖ *BGU* 822.6 (ca. A.D. 105: cf. *PMich.* 202); *PAmh.* 132 = *PSarap.* 81.6-7 (early 2nd cent.)
>> διδῦ (= διδοῖ) *SB* 9450.2 (2nd/3rd cent.); *PSI* 1413.2 (2nd/3rd cent.) perhaps also διδῖ *SB* 9451 = *PSI* 1412.14 (2nd/3rd cent.) and ἀποδιδῖ (if not for -διδῇ) *PGen.* 51 = *PAbinn.* 19.25 (ca. A.D. 346)

3. The deponent δύναμαι.

a. δύναμαι likewise has thematic formations built on the normal stem. These occur in the present indicative (mainly in the first and second person singular) and in the participle:

> δύνομαι *SB* 7737.6 (1st cent.); *PPhil.* 33.13 (prob. 1st cent.: *BL* iv, 70); *BGU* 923.14 (1st/2nd cent.); *PMich.* 477.11 part. rest. (early 2nd cent.); *BGU* 388 = *MChr.* 91 ii.8, with δύνασαι i.9, etc. (2nd half 2nd cent.); *BGU* 246.10 (2nd/3rd cent.); *POxy.* 130.16 (6th cent.); *POxy.* 1844.4 (6th/7th cent.); *PLond.* 1081 (iii, 282-3).8 part. rest. (7th cent.); etc.
>> δύνη *BGU* 1079 = *WChr.* 60.27 (A.D. 41); *PMich.* 577.10 (A.D. 41-68); *POxy.* 2190.49 (late 1st cent.); *PMich.* 204.6 (A.D. 127); 523.16 (2nd/3rd cent.); *PHarris* 108.7 (3rd cent.); *PMerton* 28.9,20 (late 3rd cent.); *POxy.* 1157.7,11 (late 3rd cent.); *POxy.* 1865.4 (6th/7th cent.); etc.[1]
>> δύνης *POxy.* 2612.5 (A.D. 285-90); *PSI* 972.20 (4th cent.?)

---

[1] Cf. also from the mag. papp. δύνη *PGM* 14.21 (A.D. 200-50); *PGM* 7.691 (3rd cent.); but δύνασαι *PGM* 13.945 (ca. A.D. 346); 4.538 part. rest., 2097 (4th cent.). δύνη, found in Pythag. and late prose from Plb. on, and as a v.l. in E. S. (Veitch & *LSJ*, s.v.), in place of the reg. class. Att. δύνασαι, prob. represents the beg. of the transition of δύναμαι to the thematic inflection (Schwyzer i, 668; Chantraine², § 344). It is usual in the Ptol. papp. (Mayser i², 2, 91). δύνησαι (p. 385) seems to represent the restoration of the -σαι ending in the thematic formation.

δύγαιται (for δύνεται?) *PBas.* 16.8 (1st half 3rd cent.)

δυνόμεθα *PFlor.* 195.14 (3rd cent.); *POxy.* 1668.22 (3rd cent.); *PTebt.* 417.12 (3rd cent.)

cf. δυνώμεθα (indic. = δυνόμεθα) *PColt* 75.4 (7th cent.)

δύνονται *BGU* 1085 ii.5-6 (A.D. 161-80); *POxy.* 1773.32 (3rd cent.)

[ἐ]δύγετο *PMilVogl.* 25 ii.21 (A.D. 126/7)

δυνόμενος *BGU* 159 = *WChr.* 408.5 (A.D. 216); *BGU* 614.20 part. rest.: *BL* i, 56 (A.D. 217); *SB* 7468.11 (A.D. 221); *PMerton* 91.15 (A.D. 316)

δυνομένη *PCairIsidor.* 77.22 (A.D. 320)

δυνόμενοι, δυνόμενος *PMerton* 92.12,18 (A.D. 324)

δυνομένων *PLond.* 77 = *MChr.* 319.42 (late 6th cent.)

b. Athematic forms are normal in the present system, however:

δύναμαι *BGU* 648 = *WChr.* 360.16 (A.D. 164/96)

δύνασαι *PAlex.* 25.22 (2nd cent.); *SB* 7992 = *PSI* 1332.21 (2nd/3rd cent.); *POxy.* 2985.6 (2nd/3rd cent.); *POxy.* 1473.21 (A.D. 201); *PStrassb.* 224.8 (after A.D. 212); *PJand.* 97.12 (mid 3rd cent.); *POxy.* 2783.22-23 (3rd cent.); *PAmh.* 136.16 (3rd cent.); *PMichael.* 38.8 (6th cent.); etc.

δύνησαι *BGU* 424.8 (2nd/3rd cent.)

δύναται *PFlor.* 61 = *MChr.* 80.42 (A.D. 85); *PMich.* 477.18, with δύνομ[αι] 11 (early 2nd cent.); *POxy.* 2340.23 (A.D. 192); etc.

δυνάμεθα *POxy.* 162 = *POxy.* 942.4 (6th/7th cent.)

δύνανται *SB* 16.18 (A.D. 155/6)

δύνασθαι *PMich.* 174.18-19 (A.D. 145-7)

δυνάμενον *PMich.* 205.11-12 (2nd cent.)

c. An irregular subjunctive form is found in δύνημαι *PLond.* 897 (iii, 206-7). 6 (A.D. 84). Cf. also δ{ι}ννάσει (for δυνάσῃ) *PHamb.* 104.4-5: *BL* iii, 76 (2nd/3rd cent.).

The thematic inflection of δύναμαι seems to have arisen from the subjunctive δύνωμαι. The thematic inflection is frequent in the Koine[1] and normal in Modern Greek (although μπορῶ is more frequently used).[2]

---

[1] The earliest occurrence of the thematic δύνομαι (apart from δύνῃ, cf. preceding note) seems to be in the Ptol. papp. (3rd cent. B.C.) (Mayser i², 2, 125). δύνομαι is also found in the LXX, but in the NT it occurs only in one family of mss., w. the exception of the 2 sg. δύνῃ, wh. is found along with δύνασαι (*BDF*, § 93).

[2] Schwyzer i, 693-4; Thumb, *Handbook*, § 198; Jannaris, § 996.54.

B. OTHER ATHEMATIC TENSES

1. The second aorist active and middle.

a. The indicative active.

1) The -χ- aorist formations have become normal in the plural.[1] Relics of the classical second aorist may be orthographic variants of the new sigmatic aorist ἔδωσα (see the following):

>ἐδώκατε *SB* 7368.46, with ἔδοσαν 44 (late 2nd/early 3rd cent.)
>>ἔδωκαν *BGU* 415 = *MChr.* 178.26 (A.D. 102: *BL* i, 44); *POxy.* 237 vii.41 (A.D. 186)
>>παρέδωκαν *SB* 7376.23 (A.D. 3)
>>ἐπέδωκαν *BGU* 613 = *MChr.* 89.18 (A.D. 138-61); *POxy.* 1630.8 (A.D. 222?); *PFlor.* 119.2 (A.D. 254)
>but ἔδοσαν *PPhil.* 3.5 (A.D. 144?)
>>παρέδοσαν *SB* 8444.15, inscr. (edict of A.D. 68); *MChr.* 102.1, inscr. (A.D. 68)
>>ἀπέδοσαν *PGiss.* 46.4,9 (A.D. 117-38)
>>cf. also [ἀ]πεδοῦμεν *PMich.* 149 vi.10, with ἀπϙδοῦνται 11, astrol. (2nd cent.)
>ἐπέθηκαν *BGU* 759 = *PSarap.* 1.13 (A.D. 125)
>>προ[σ]έθηκαν *BGU* 903.16 (A.D. 169/70?)
>but ἔθεσαν *PAntin.* 153 i (a).7, semi-literary (6th cent.)
>ἐπαφεῖκαν *PStrassb.* 181.10 (A.D. 166)

2) Occasional examples of a new sigmatic aorist ἔδωσα are also found.[2] These occur mainly in the subjunctive, but are also found in other moods:

>ἔδωσεν *POxy.* 1066.12 (3rd cent.); *POxy.* 1874.14 (6th cent.)

---

[1] It is an oversimplification to call the -χ- stem pl. Hellenistic and the 2 aor. forms Attic. The class. usage is: ἔδομεν Ar. Isoc.; ἔδοτε Lys. And. Aeschin.; ἔδοσαν A. Lys. Th. Ar. Pl.; ἐδώκαμεν, ἐδώκατε, ἔδωκαν D. etc.; ἔδοσαν & ἔδωκαν only Lys.; ἐθήκαμεν, ἐθήκατε X. D. etc. (rare); ἔθετε And.; ἥκαμεν, ἥκατε Aeschin. D. Is. (rare) (Veitch, s.vv.). In the Att. inscrr., -χ- forms appear in the pl. only from 385 B.C. on, but are reg. from 300 B.C., although 2 aor. forms again occur in competition in Rom. times (*MS*, 188-9). At Perg. and Magn., only -χ- forms occur (3 pl.), although 2 aor. forms are found in the pl. elsewh. in Asia Minor (Schweizer, 183-4; Nachmanson, 166; Hauser, 114). In the Ptol. papp., only -χ- forms are found in both the sg. and pl. (Mayser i², 2, 142-3). In the NT, παρέδοσαν occurs in the very lit. prooemium of Luke, but elsewh. only the -χ- forms (*BDF*, § 95.1). Koine authors vary in their use of these forms, but in the Herc. papp., the 2 aor. act. is preserved only in the 3 pl.; the 1 & 2 pl. have the -χ- aor. (Crönert, 240, & n. 2).

[2] Cf. Schwyzer i, 742, 755, 814; Chantraine², § 181; Crönert, 251; *BDF*, § 95.1; Psaltes, 239; Dieterich, 220-1. Veitch, s.v., gives some exx. of the aor. subj. in later lit. and an opt. δύσαιμι in a Sch.A. Cf. also from the mag. papp. δώσῃς *PGM* 7.622 (3rd cent.); δώσητε *PGM* 35.16 (5th cent.).

ἵνα δώσω SB 9194.11 (late 3rd cent.); PJand. 18.6 (6th/7th cent.)
ἐὰν δὲ μὴ ἀποδόσω BGU 635.8 (A.D. 139)
δώσῃς POxy. 599 descr. (late 1st/2nd cent.); PGen. 46 = PAbinn.
59.15 (A.D. 345); (BGU 1035 =) WChr. 23.15 (5th cent.); PLond.
1334 = PRossGeorg. iv, 3.17 (A.D. 709); PLond. 1353.27 (A.D.
710); etc.
δόσῃς BGU 546.2 (Byz.); PLond. 113 (11b) (i, 224).5 (6th/7th cent.)
παραδόσῃς PCairMasp. 322.1 (6th cent.)
δώσῃ PRossGeorg. v, 4.12 (2nd cent.); PSI 1428.12 (6th cent.); PCair-
Masp. 200.3 (6th cent.?); PJand. 24.2 (6th/7th cent.); PApoll.
14.7 (ca. A.D. 705/6); 46.6 (A.D. 703-15); etc.
δόσῃ PMichael. 38.10 (6th cent.); BGU 546.1 (Byz.); POxy. 1862.21
(7th cent.)
ἀπ[ο]δώ[σ]ωμε(ν) POxy. 1855.14 (6th/7th cent.)
ἵνα δώσατε, ἵνα δώσῃ PSI 1266.2,7 = PApoll. 9.3,8 (8th cent.)
δώσωσιν POxy. 1854.2 (6th/7th cent.); PLond. 1335.10 (A.D. 709)
παραδώσατε (impt.) SB 5640.13; 5641.10 abbrev. (both ca. A.D. 710)
ἵνα παραδώσηται PLond. 1917.12 (ca. A.D. 330-40)
cf. also δωσῆσαι (for δῶσαι) SB 9868.3 (early 8th cent.)
ἀποδώσατε PRein. 43.14,16-17 (A.D. 102) seems to be future for -δώσετε.[1]

Modern Greek has preserved the -κ- aorist ἔδωκα, but the sigmatic aorist ἔδωσα is more common.[2]

3) A sigmatic aorist of ἀφίημι is attested in ἀφῆσαι POxy. 2353.14 (A.D. 32) and μὴ ἀφήσις BGU 814.27 (3rd cent.).

4) The transitive first aorist and the intransitive second aorist of ἵστημι are retained as in classical Greek, e.g., ἔστησεν PBaden 37 = PSarap. 90.14 part. rest. (A.D. 107-12); συνέστησα POxy. 724 = WChr. 140.2 (A.D. 155); POxy. 509 ? (late 2nd cent.); στῆσαι PRein. 44 = MChr. 82.33 (A.D. 117-38); με[τ]α[σ]τῆσαι BGU 36 = MChr. 125.13 (A.D. 117-38); παραστῆσαι PMich. 174.19 (A.D. 145-7); ἀπ[ο]-καταστῆσαι POxy. 1665.14,20 (3rd cent.); συνεστήσατο BGU 22.15 (A.D. 114); etc.; συνέστην POxy. 2231.44 (A.D. 241); περιέστην POxy. 902 = MChr. 72.12 (ca. A.D. 465); ἐξέστης POxy. 1672.3 (A.D. 37-41); ἀντ[ε]κατέστη POxy. 97 = MChr. 347.9 (A.D. 115/16); [π]αρέστη PMich. 527.16 (A.D. 186-8); στῆναι POxy. 1631.14 (A.D. 280); προστῆναι PLeit. 2.2-3 (late 2nd cent.); POxy. 891.12-13 (A.D. 294); περιστῆναι POxy. 899 = WChr. 361.14 (A.D. 200); ἀναστῆναι POxy. 1161.9-10 (4th cent.); ἐπιστάντος PAntin. 96.3 (6th cent.); ἐπιστάντες PLBat. xiii, 8.7 (A.D. 421); etc. But στῆσαι is used intransitively for στῆναι in POxy. 1102.17 (ca. A.D. 146).

---

[1] A hybrid form διδώσα[με]ν read in SB 7366.43 (A.D. 200) may also poss. reflect the sigm. aor. formation.

[2] Schwyzer i, 814; Thumb, Handbook, § 202; Mirambel, Gram., 139; Maspero, 138.

b. The subjunctive.

1) The subjunctive of the second aorist of δίδωμι sometimes retains its classical inflection:[1]

δῷς *POxy.* 653 = *MChr.* 90.28 (A.D. 160-2); *PSI* 1101.6 (A.D. 271); *PSI* 1413.1, with διδῦ 2 (2nd/3rd cent.)

μεταδῷς *PPhil.* 33.6, with ἀναγνοῖς 17 (prob. 1st cent.: *BL* iv, 70) ἀναδῷς *POxy.* 1063.14 (2nd/3rd cent.)

δῶι (3 sg.) *BGU* 531 ii.5 (A.D. 70-80: Olsson, #43, p. 128)

ἀποδῶι *POxy.* 278 = *MChr.* 165.22 (A.D. 17); *PMich.* 567.19 (A.D. 91); *BGU* 339 = *MChr.* 250.16,21-22 (A.D. 128)

δῶ *PHarris* 155.9 (5th/6th cent.)

ἀποδῶ *POxy.* 270 = *MChr.* 236.28 (A.D. 94); *BGU* 2042.15 (A.D. 105); *POxy.* 485 = *MChr.* 246.19-20, with ἀπ[ο]δοῖ 22 (A.D. 178)

μεταδῶ *BGU* 1047 iv.10 (A.D. 117-38); *PLond.* 908 = *MChr.* 229.32, with ἀποδοῖ 33 (A.D. 139)

ἀποδῶμεν, ἀποδῶσι *PMich.* 333-4.40 (2nd hand), 26 (1st hand) (A.D. 52) ἀναδῶτε *PFay.* 26.16 (A.D. 150)

2) More commonly, however, it is inflected δοῖς, δοῖ in the singular, on the analogy of contract verbs in -όω:[2]

δοῖς *PTebt.* 409.5 (A.D. 5); *SB* 7600.11, with δῦ[ς] 15 (A.D. 16); *PLips.* 106.18 (A.D. 98); *SB* 7268 descr. (A.D. 98-117); *SB* 4294.9 (Rom.)

παραδοῖς *POxy.* 2981.13-14 (2nd cent.); *PSI Omaggio* 12.3 (3rd cent.)

δοῖ *PRyl.* 229.4,5 (A.D. 38); *PPrinc.* 163.6 (2nd cent.); *BGU* 246 above line 16 (2nd/3rd cent.); *POxy.* 2680.14 (2nd/3rd cent.); cf. *SB* 3892.3 mummy label (3rd cent.); etc.

παραδοῖ *POxy.* 742.9 (2 B.C.); *PHamb.* 71.20 (A.D. 149); *PBas.* 5.9 (3rd cent.)

προσμεταδοῖ *POxy.* 68 = *MChr.* 228.34 (A.D. 131)

ἀποδοῖ *PMichael.* 9 A.12 (ca. A.D. 92); *PFlor.* 86 = *MChr.* 247.18,21 (late 1st cent.); *PStrassb.* 525.18 (A.D. 98-117); *PMich.* 572.23 (A.D. 131); *POxy.* 728.18 (A.D. 142); *PVindobWorp* 10.4,16 (A.D. 143/4); *BGU* 741 = *MChr.* 244.27 part. rest. (A.D. 143/4); *PSI* 941.8 (2nd cent.); *PFlor.* 1 = *MChr.* 243.6 (A.D. 153); *SB* 5125.12 (A.D. 238); etc.

---

[1] Cf. also from the mag. papp. [με]ταδῷς *PGM* 1.130 (4th/5th cent.).

[2] Cf. also from the mag. papp. δοῖς *PGM* 71.4 (late 2nd/early 3rd cent.); ἀποδοῖς *PGM* 12.76 (A.D. 300-50); δοῖ *PGM* 4.1809 (4th cent.).

3) This new subjunctive formation appears occasionally in the phonetically equivalent orthographic variant υ for οι:[1]

δῦς *POxy.* 269 ii.9,11, with δῦ 8 (A.D. 57); *BGU* 811.5 (A.D. 98-103); *SB* 7356 = *PMich.* 203.28 (A.D. 98-117); *POxy.* 936.12 (3rd cent.); *BGU* 816.17 (3rd cent.);

δῦ (for δῦς?) *SB* 9017 (28).6 (1st/2nd cent.)

δῦ *PMich.* 244.7 (A.D. 43); *SB* 9636.14 (A.D. 136); *PMich.* 510.24 (2nd/3rd cent.); *PTebt.* 420.23 (3rd cent.)

ἀποδῦ *PFay.* 112.7 (A.D. 99)

4) Later, these same forms {dis, di}[2] appear in the spelling δῆς, δῆ on the analogy of the more normal subjunctive endings:[3]

δῆς *OTait* 2475.5 (2nd/3rd cent.); *POxy.* 2599.34 (3rd/4th cent.); *PGen.* 46 = *PAbinn.* 59.12 (A.D. 345); *PLond.* 418 = *PAbinn.* 7.22 (ca. A.D. 346); *PGen.* 53 = *PAbinn.* 36.12 (ca. A.D. 346); *POxy.* 2729.23 (4th cent.)

δῆ *POxy.* 1069.35 (3rd cent.); *POxy.* 1158.14 (3rd cent.); *PFlor.* 259.7 (3rd cent.)

ἀποδῆ *PMich.* 566.19 (A.D. 86)

It is significant that three of these examples come from the Abinnaeus archive in which there are many examples of the transfer of contract verbs in -άω to the -έω type.[4]

5) The corresponding athematic aorist subjunctive of γινώσκω, found normally in its classical forms γνῶς *POxy.* 1682.6 (4th cent.); καταγνῶς *PMich.* 480.12 (early 2nd cent.); ἐπιγνῷς *PMilVogl.* 25 ii.23 (A.D. 126/7); *BGU* 2060.7 (A.D. 180), is likewise sometimes inflected γνοῖς, γνοῖ:

γνοῖς *PMich.* 479.17 (early 2nd cent.)

ἐπιγνοῖς *POxy.* 1155.12 part. emended (A.D. 104); *POxy.* 932.8 (late 2nd cent.)

ἀναγνοῖς ... καταγνοῖς *POxy.* 1062.13,14 (2nd cent.)

ἀναγνοῖς *PLond.* 1917.3 (ca. A.D. 330-40)

ἐπιγνοῖ *SB* 9484.9 (2nd cent.)

---

[1] See Vol. i, 197-9. Cf. also from the mag. papp. δῦς (if not for δός impt.) *PGM* 71.4 (twice) (late 2nd/early 3rd cent.).

[2] For the interchange of υ and οι with η, see Vol. i, 262-7.

[3] Cf. also from the mag. papp. [ἵ]να ἀνταποδῆς *PGM* 3.7, w. ἀνταποδοῖς 115 (after A.D. 300).

[4] See above, pp. 363-4.

This new aorist subjunctive, first attested in δοῖς, δοῖ in Ptolemaic papyri from the third century B.C.,[1] is an analogical formation reflecting the transfer of -μι verbs to a thematic conjugation rather than a purely orthographic phenomenon,[2] supported by the identity in pronunciation of the old third person singular δῶι (δῷ) with the first person singular δῶ.[3]

c. The optative.

The aorist optative is the regular classical -οίην, etc., not the usual Hellenistic -ῴην,[4] e.g., ἀποδοίην *PLond.* 1774.15 (A.D. 570); 1716.4 part. rest. (A.D. 570?); δοίης *POxy.* 1587.8 (late 3rd cent.); μεταδοίης *PHarris* 160.15 (early 4th cent.); ἀποδοίης *SB* 5656 = *PCairMasp.* 305.20 (A.D. 568); δοίη *PMichael.* 43.10 (A.D. 526); *PLond.* 113 (1) (i, 199-204).21 (6th cent.); δοῖεν *PHermRees* 3.21 (4th cent.).[5] The Hellenistic form δῴην, etc., seems to have arisen less on the analogy of ἔδωκα[6] than on the analogy of the optative of contract verbs in -άω, as τιμῴην. This ending was sometimes extended in late Greek to other verbs, including contract verbs in -έω, as in ποιῴη.[7] Its failure to displace δοίην, etc., in the papyri may be connected with the popularity of the thematic forms of the present and aorist subjunctive. Since those thematic forms resembled the corresponding forms of contract -όω verbs, the optative -οίην, likewise identical with the present optative of contract -όω verbs, would have appeared regular.

d. The imperative.

---

[1] Mayser i[2], 2, 86-87. Subj. δοῖς, γνοῖς, etc., are also found in the NT, along w. the reg. δῷς (*BDF*, § 95.2) and occ. in inscrr. (*MS*, 190 [from 3rd cent. A.D.]; Schweizer, 192, Anm.). This subj. may have been Ion., along w. the contr. forms of the pres. indic. διδοῖς, διδοῖ, spreading by analogy to γνοῖς, etc. (so Crönert, 215-17; cf. further Schweizer, 793). The forms διδοῖς, διδοῖ, classified by Mayser as optatives (i[2], 2, 88) may also be subj.

[2] Mayser i[2], 2, 86-87, explained these forms as purely orthographic variants of δῶις, δῶι (and therefore more corr. accented δοῖς, δοῖ). This explanation, based on the phonetic identity of ωι and οι, may have been valid for the Ptol. period; but by the beg. of the Rom. period, the long diphthongs in -ι were identified with their corresp. simple vowels (Vol. i, 183-6), while οι was monophthongized and identified with υ (Vol. i, 197-9).

[3] So *BDF*, § 95.2.

[4] The opt. δῴην, to be dist. from the Hom. subj. δώη(ς), is attested as a vl.. in Hes. Hdt. X. D. etc. The earliest occurrence of -ῴην in an athematic aor. is ἀναβιῴην in Ar. (*BDF*, § 95.2). There is no certain ex. of δῴην in the Ptol. papp. (Mayser i[2], 2, 88), but this form is common in the LXX and NT (*BDF*, *ibid.*) and is found, at least in compds., in various Koine authors and inscrr. (Crönert, 215, n. 2, to wh. add Aristeas 110). Sim., γνῴης, etc., is found in Koine authors and in codd. of Arist. etc. (Crönert, 215, n. 1). Cf. also from the mag. papp. δόη (for δῴη) *PGM* 40.4 (4th cent.).

[5] Cf. also from the mag. papp. γνοίης *PGM* 4.2108 (4th cent.).

[6] Schwyzer i, 795.

[7] Cf. Moeris, p. 208; Schweizer, 191.

1) The athematic aorist imperatives of ἵστημι and βαίνω sometimes appear in compounds as -στα and -βα:[1]

σύστα *PMich.* 210.4 (2nd/early 3rd cent.)
ἀνάβα *SB* 9120.12 (1st cent.); *PHamb.* 87.6-7 (early 2nd cent.); *SB* 6299.2 (2nd cent.)
διάβα *PFay.* 110.15 (A.D. 94)
κατάβα, ἀνάβα *POxy.* 2719.6,7 (3rd cent.)
cf. also ὕπα (for ὕπαγε) *PSAAthen.* 62.11 (1st/2nd cent.)

The prime analogate of these imperative forms is -βα, found already in classical Attic,[2] apparently contracted from βα-ε, which originally may have been the imperative of an alternative present formation *βάω,[3] but came to be understood as aorist. -βα is the only imperative retained in Greek loanwords in the Sahidic Coptic New Testament; in all other words, the infinitive (in -ε[4]) is adopted for the imperative.[5] The imperative -βα is likewise preserved in Modern Greek, and led to the use of the ending -α in some present imperatives, as στέκα, τρέχα, φεύγα.[6]

2) The second aorist imperative of δίδωμι appears occasionally as δές, plural -δετε:

δές *OTait* 1994.2 (2nd cent.?); 2002.1 (Rom.); 2471.6 (2nd/3rd cent.); *PMich.* 588.8 (mid 3rd cent.); *PMeyer* 22.3 (3rd/4th cent.); *PHerm-Rees* 15.5 (late 4th/early 5th cent.)
ἀπόδες *PSI* 967 V.21 (1st/2nd cent.)
ἐπίδες *SB* 9272.8 (1st/2nd cent.)
παράδες *SB* 9251.4, with δός also 4 (2nd/3rd cent.); *BGU* 775.9 (3rd cent.: *BL* i, 65); cf. *SB* 2052.3-4, mummy label (n.d.)

---

[1] Cf. also συνπαράστατε *SB* 7452.6, lead tablet love charm (not later than 3rd cent.), and from the mag. papp. συνίστα, παράστα *PGM* 2.73,79 (4th cent.); ἀνάστα *PGM* 7.238 part. rest., 621 (3rd cent.); *PGM* 8.99 (4th/5th cent.), along w. the simple στῆθι, e.g., *PGM* 2.86 (4th cent.); 13.250,262 (ca. A.D. 346); 4.68 (4th cent.); ἀνάβα *PGM* 7.441 (3rd cent.); 61.5 (late 3rd cent.), along w. ἔμβηθι *PGM* 7.561 (3rd cent.); κατάβηθι *PGM* 4.2493 (4th cent.).

[2] -βα is found in compds. in E. (3 times), Thgn. Ar., while pl. βᾶτε is found in the simple in A. S. (Veitch & *LSJ*, s.v.). -στᾱ is first attested in ἀπόστᾱ in fragg. of Men. (Veitch, s.v.). -στα, -στατε are also found in the LXX, in addition to στῆθι (but always -βηθι), and -βα, -στα along w. -βηθι, -στηθι in the NT (*BDF*, § 95.3). See further Schwyzer, 676, n. 1; Crönert, 260 & n. 2; Psaltes, 238-9; Thumb, *Hell.*, 207. These forms are not found in the Ptol. papp.

[3] Schwyzer i, 676.

[4] See above, p. 331.

[5] Böhlig, 134.

[6] Thumb, *Handbook*, § 196, 218; Jannaris, § 830[b]; Mirambel, *Gram.*, 139.

μετάδες *PTebt*. 416 = *WChr*. 98.16 (3rd cent.); (clearly) *PTebt·*
420.22, with δός 24 (3rd cent.)

παρ[ά]δετε *BGU* 360.7-8 (A.D. 108/9)

ἀνάδεται (for ἀνάδετε) *PJand*. 9.34 (2nd cent.)

Although these forms reflect the phonological interchange of ο and ε, especially common in final syllables before ς,[1] they are the result of the analogy at least on the orthographic level of the imperatives θές, θέτε of τίθημι.[2] This imperative does not seems to occur elsewhere in Greek. The classical imperative δός has been preserved in Modern Greek.[3]

3) The second aorist imperative of ἵημι (in compounds) generally retains its classical form ἕς, e.g., ἄφες *POxy*. 932.5 (late 2nd cent.). An orthographic variant ἄφος occurs in *POxy*. 1346 descr. (2nd cent.?). This isolated spelling could be the result of analogy on the orthographic level with δός, but can hardly be considered morphologically significant in view of the interchange of ο and ε in final syllables before -ς.[4] The Modern Greek contracted form ἄς (= ἄφες)[5] is first attested in *PAmh*. 153.7: *BL* i, 5 (late 6th/7th cent.) and *PRossGeorg*. iii, 22.9 (7th cent.).

e. The infinitive.

The second aorist infinitive of δίδωμι is very frequently written δῶναι in both simple and compound use:

> δῶναι *PFay*. 109.4 (early 1st cent.); *BGU* 824.13 (A.D. 55/56); *PGiss*. 11 = *WChr*. 444.16-17 (A.D. 118); *BGU* 326 = *MChr*. 316 i.14 (A.D. 189); *PJand*. 98.7 (3rd cent.); *PMerton* 28.9 (late 3rd cent.); *PGen*. 11 = *PAbinn*. 62.10 (A.D. 350); *SB* 4650.21, with δοῦναι 19 (n.d.); etc.
>
> ἀποδῶναι *PLond*. 361 R (ii, 169-70).9 (late 1st cent.); *BGU* 36 = *MChr*. 125.7 (A.D. 98-117); *PMich*. 605.15 (A.D. 117); *PMich*. 488.15-16 (2nd cent.); *BGU* 970 = *MChr*. 242.24 (A.D. 177); *PFlor*. 167 R.12 (3rd cent.); etc.

---

[1] See Vol. i, 289-92. The spelling παράδους *PSI* 460.6 (3rd/4th cent.) is prob. an instance of the freq. interchange of ο and ου (Vol. i, 211-14) rather than a 'contaminazione volgare di παραδίδου con παράδος' (ed., n. ad loc.).

[2] δός itself was prob. orig. *δές (as θές, ἕς), and became δός by levelling with the -ο- of the paradigm (Schwyzer i, 800).

[3] Now usu. δῶς or δῶσε (or δό) (Thumb, *Handbook*, § 217; Mirambel, *Gram.*, 139). The MGr. impt. δές is from (ἰ)δέ+ς 'look.'

[4] See Vol. i, 289-92.

[5] Thumb, *Handbook*, § 194.

ἀνταποδῶναι SB 5247.23 (A.D. 47)

ἐκδῶναι PFay. 34.5 (A.D. 161)

μεταδῶναι BGU 970 = MChr. 242.25 (A.D. 177); SB 7630 = PSI
    1325.11 (A.D. 176/80); PMich. 615.25 (ca. A.D. 259); POxy. 123.11
    (3rd/4th cent.); etc.

παραδῶναι POxy. 910.39 (A.D. 197); PMich. 604.19 (A.D. 223); cf. SB
    9126.5, mummy label (3rd cent.)

ἐπιδῶναι PLeit. 13.15-16 (mid 3rd cent.)

The phonetically equivalent spelling δõναι also occurs:

δõναι SB 9826.12 (2nd cent.)

ἀποδõναι BGU 595.4 (ca. A.D. 70-80); POxy. 68 = MChr. 228.24, with
    μεταδοῦναι 30 (A.D. 131)

ἐπιδõνα[ι] POxy. 2343.11 (ca. A.D. 288)

The regular δοῦναι is still normal, however, e.g., δοῦναι PMich. 346b.6 (A.D. 16); POxy. 2276.12 (late 3rd/4th cent.); PJand. 23.13 (6th/7th cent.); παραδοῦναι POxy. 2114.14 (A.D. 316); POxy. 2347.8,10 (A.D. 362); ἐκδοῦναι POxy. 1859.2 (6th/7th cent.).

The spelling δõναι is too common to be simply the result of an interchange of ου and ω. It represents at least an orthographic alternative, although there may not have been any distinction in pronunciation between δõναι and δοῦναι among many speakers because of Egyptian interference.[1] It seems less likely connected with the old Arcadian infinitive δῶναι[2] than a post-classical formation modelled on γνῶναι.[3] This analogy is supported by the identity of the subjunctives δῶ, δῷς and γνῶ, γνῷς (papyri also δῶ, δοῖς; γνῶ, γνοῖς), and by the occasional converse spelling of the second aorist infinitive of γινώσκω as γνοῦναι, e.g., BGU 846.16 (2nd cent.); ἀναγνοῦναι POxy. 743.18 (2 B.C.), instead of the normal γνῶναι, e.g., ἐπιγνῶναι PPhil. 33.9 (prob. 1st cent.: BL iv, 70); PPar. 21b.26 (A.D. 592); 21.48 (A.D. 616).[4]

f. The participle.

The second aorist participle of δίδωμι sometimes has a thematic form, as δοῦντες PTebt. 420.6 (3rd cent.); ἀναδοῦντα SB 4809.2 (Byz.). If these examples

---

[1] See Vol. i, 208-14.

[2] Cf. Schwyzer i, 808.

[3] So BDF, § 95.1.

[4] In the Koine, δῶναι is first attested in a 3rd cent. B.C. inscr. from Orchomenos (LSJ, s.v.). It occurs twice in cod. B of the LXX (w. -γνοῦναι once) (Crönert, 251, n. 2), and once in a cod. of the NT (BDF, § 95.1). It is also found in an ostr. from the end of the Ptol. period, while γνοῦναι appears twice in the Ptol. papp. (Mayser i², 2, 140). Cf. also from the mag. papp. μεταπαραδῶναι PGM 4.501 (4th cent.).

are not instances of the frequent interchange of o and oυ,[1] they reflect, like similar forms in the present participle,[2] the transfer of -μι verbs to the thematic conjugation.

ġ. The indicative middle.

1) The second aorist middle of δίδωμι sometimes forms the third person singular in -ετο instead of -οτο:

> ἐξέδετο *PMich.* 121 R II viii.1; V II.12; XI.13; XII.6 abbrev. (A.D. 42);
> *PMich.* 237.7,34 (A.D. 43); *PMich.* 123 R XII.11; XIV.42 (A.D.
> 45-47); *PTebt.* 442.5: *ZPE* 7 (1971), 2 (A.D. 113); *StudPal.* xxii, 40.4
> (A.D. 150); *PSI* 288.8 (2nd cent.); *CPR* 222.18 (2nd cent.); *BGU*
> 159 = *WChr.* 408.3, with δυνόμενος 5 (A.D. 216); *SB* 7634.11 (A.D.
> 249); *POxy.* 1273.1 (A.D. 260)
> ἀπέδετο *PStrassb.* 79.1 (16/15 B.C.); *CPR* 191.12 part. rest. (2nd cent.);
> *PLond.* 1164 (iii, 154-67) f.18 (A.D. 212)

These forms[3] may have arisen on the analogy of the -ε- in ἔθετο. They could equally reflect the general transition of δίδωμι and other -μι verbs to a thematic inflection.

2) Thematic forms of the second aorist of τίθημι are also found sporadically, as παρέθοντο *PSI* 447.16 (A.D. 167).

2. The perfect.

a. ἵστημι.

1) The intransitive second perfect of ἵστημι is retained in the papyri as generally elsewhere in the Koine[4] in the participle and rarely in the infinitive:

> παρεστώς *POslo* 18.1 (A.D. 162); *POxy.* 1204.13 (A.D. 299)

---

[1] See Vol. i, 211-14.

[2] See above, pp. 382-3.

[3] A sim. ex. of ἀπέδετο is found in the Ptol. papp., explained by Mayser as either vowel weakening in the unstressed syll. or better a spontaneous interchange w. ἀπέθετο (i², 2, 140). ἀπέδετο is also read in Ph. (Crönert, 251, n. 3), and is found in the Delph. inscrr., where it is interpreted by Rüsch, 156, as an ex. of vowel assimilation in unstressed syllables.

[4] *MS*, 189-90; Schweizer, 185; Nachmanson, 159; Mayser i², 2, 146-7; Crönert, 261(-2), n. 1; *BDF*, § 96. The use of the 2 pf. ptc. in the Ptol. papp. is common only in the 1st cent. B.C.; earlier, the 1 pf. ptc. predominates, exc. in ἐνεστώς (Mayser, *ibid.*). The neut. ptc. ἑστός from ἑσταός corresponds to the masc. ἑστώς as -κώς : -κός (*BDF*, *ibid.*).

προεστώς POxy. 2721.5 (A.D. 234); POxy. 1275.8-9 (3rd cent.)
καθεστώς POxy. 1407.10 (late 3rd cent.)
ἐνεστός POxy. 245.6 (A.D. 26); PLond. 151 (ii, 215-16).7 (2nd cent.);
    BGU 237.4 (A.D. 164/5); BGU 28.18 (A.D. 183); POxy. 102.7 (A.D.
    306); POxy. 103.6 (A.D. 316); POxy. 1630.4 (A.D. 222?); POxy. 1632.9
    (A.D. 353); etc.
    καθεστός POxy. 68 = MChr. 228.32 (A.D. 131)
ἐνοστῶτος sic POxy. 2579.2 (A.D. 313?)
συνεστῶτος PLips. 28 = MChr. 363.4 (A.D. 381)
    π[ρο]εστῶτος PCairMasp. 168.60 (6th cent.); 170.7 abbrev. (A.D.
    564?)
ἐνεστώσης PMich. 323-5.19, so copy PSI 903.19 (A.D. 47); SB 4434.22
    (A.D. 117-38); SB 4416.6 (ca. A.D. 157)
ἐνεστώση PFlor. 53.10 (A.D. 327)
ἑστῶτα PBouriant 20 = PAbinn. 63.44, with συνέστηκεν 7, ἔστηκεν 25
    (A.D. 350)
    ἐφεστῶτα PCairMasp. 169bis.17 (A.D. 569)
    προεστῶτα PCairMasp. 151-2.148 (A.D. 570)
ἑστῶτες PLond. 755 V (iii, 221-3).2,37 (4th cent.)
π[αρ]εστώτων PRyl. 77.33 (A.D. 192)
    [π]ροεστώτων POxy. 1450.24 (A.D. 249/50)
    ἀντικαθεστώτων PLips. 34.18,20; 35.19,21-22 part. rest. (both ca.
    A.D. 375)
    ἐφεστώτων PHamb. 23.10 (A.D. 569)
προεστῶσει PRyl. 122.6-7 (A.D. 127)
    συνεστῶσι PBon. 24a.9 (A.D. 135)
    ἐφεστῶσι PSI 460.6-7 (3rd/4th cent.)
ἐφαιστώσαις PLips. 16.18 (A.D. 138); (ἐν-) PAmh. 93 = WChr. 314.23
    (A.D. 181)
    ἐφεστιώσαις BGU 393.16 (A.D. 168); (clearly) PCairMasp. 302.16
    (A.D. 555)
καθεστῶτας POxy. 2603.14-15 (4th cent.)
ἐφεστώσας POxy. 912.27 (A.D. 235)
καθεστάναι PLond. 354 (ii, 163-5).22 (ca. 10 B.C.); POxy. 1418.11 part.
    rest. (A.D. 247)
    συνεστάναι PThead. 20 ii.3 (4th cent.)

2) The first perfect is used in the indicative, and sporadically in the participle:[1]

---

[1] Cf. also from the mag. papp. ἔστηκε PGM 4.1474 (4th cent.); συνέστηκεν PGM
4.1769; 13.76,588 (ca. A.D. 346); παρέστηκεν PGM 13.104,660-1 part. emended (A.D.
346); παρεστήκασι PGM 1.199, sim. 208 (late 4th/5th cent.); PGM 4.1204; ἑστηκυιῶν
PGM 4.30-31; but ἑστός freq., e.g., παρεστώς PGM 4.2384,3166; συνπαρεστῶτι PGM
13.550-1 (A.D. 346); ἑστῶτα PGM 13.52,422; παρεστῶτας PGM 13.124-5,682; ἑστάνα[ι]
PGM 3.697 (A.D. 300+); etc.

ἕστηκα *SB* 8246.9 (A.D. 335: *BL* v, 102)
 ἀποσυνέστηκα *BGU* 191.3 (A.D. 143)
 ἐξέστηκα *PSI* 822.14 (2nd cent.)
 καθέστηκα *PAmh.* 82.14 (late 3rd/early 4th cent.); *POxy.* 902 =
  MChr. 72.3 (ca. A.D. 465); *PCairMasp.* 295 iii.11 (6th cent.);
  PCairMasp. 89 V.30 (Byz.)
ἕστηκεν *PBouriant* 20 = *PAbinn.* 63.25, with συνέστηκεν 7, ἑστῶτα
  44 (A.D. 350); *PLips.* 38 = *MChr.* 97 i.3 (A.D. 390)
 ἐνέστηκεν *SB* 8005.13 (2nd cent.)
 συνέστηκεν *POxy.* 653 = *MChr.* 90.11 part. rest. (A.D. 160-2);
  PBouriant 20 = *PAbinn.* 63.7, with ἕστηκεν 25, ἑστῶτα 44
  (A.D. 350)
 καθέστηκεν *PSI* 285.6 (A.D. 294?); *PLond.* 971 = *MChr.* 95.15
  (4th cent.); *PCairMasp.* 294.1 (6th cent.); *SB* 6000 V.24 (6th
  cent.); *PSI* 76.6 (A.D. 574-8); *POxy.* 1869.9 (6th/7th cent.);
  etc.
καθεστήκατε *BGU* 1027 xxvi = *WChr.* 424 i.11 (late 4th cent.:
  BL i, 88)
ἐπεσστήκασι *sic PFay.* 20.20 (late 3rd/early 4th cent.)
 καθεστήκασι *SB* 9150.39 (5th cent.); sim. *POxy.* 1876.7 (ca. A.D.
  480); 1877.6 part. rest. (ca. A.D. 488); *PCairMasp.* 89 V.7
  part. rest., 9; so duplic. *PCairMasp.* 294.7,9 (6th cent.)
συγηστήκι, συνηστήκι (for συνειστήκει ppf.) *PLBat.* vi, 13.11,36 (A.D.
  113/14)
 συνηστήκει *PMilVogl.* 85.10 (A.D. 138)
ἐνεστηκός *POxy.* 1457.5-6 (4/3 B.C.)
 καθεστηκότι *PLond.* 971 = *MChr.* 95.7 (4th cent.)

3) The late transitive first perfect ἕστακα,[1] probably formed from the perfect passive ἕσταμαι (cf. τέθεικα from τέθειμαι below),[2] is found in the indicative, infinitive, and participle:

συνέστακας *PFay.* 109.9 (early 1st cent.)
 συνέστακε *PMich.* 498.15 (2nd cent.); *BGU* 816.4-5 (3rd cent.)
 κατέστακε *POxy.* 528.21-22 (2nd cent.)
 παρέστακε *PLond.* 197 V.8: *BL* i, 251 (3rd cent.)
συνεστάκαμεν *PLond.* 255 = *WChr.* 272.10 (A.D. 136)
 παραστάκαμεν *sic PStrassb.* 171.11 (early 3rd cent.)

---

[1] The trans. pf. ἕστακα, to be dist. from the intrans. Dor. ἕστᾱκα (= Att. ἕστηκα) of the choruses of A. and S., is found in compds. already in Hyp. and Pl. (Veitch & *LSJ*, s.v.). Forms of ἕστᾱκα are also found in the Ptol. papp., the LXX, NT, Asia Minor inscrr. of Rom. times, and in various Koine authors (Mayser i², 2, 146-8; *BDF*, § 97.1; Schweizer, 184-5; Crönert, 260 & n. 3; Dieterich, 218).

[2] Schwyzer i, 775: Chantraine², § 230.

ἐστάκαται (for -τε?) *POxy.* 2729.25 (4th cent.)

ἔστακαν *PMichMichael.* 28 (now = *SB* 11130).8 (3rd/4th cent.)

μεθέστακαν *PSI* 822.6-7, with ἐξέστηκα 14 (2nd cent.)

καθεστάκειν *PBrem.* 53.16-17 (A.D. 114)

μεθεστακέναι, συνεστακέναι *PLond.* 354 (ii, 163-5).10,13 part. rest. (ca. 10 B.C.)

συνεστακέναι *PFouad* 35.3-4 (A.D. 48); *POxy.* 94 = *MChr.* 344.6 (A.D. 83); *POxy.* 364 descr. (A.D. 94); *POxy.* 97 = *MChr.* 347.2 part. rest. (A.D. 115/16); *PLBat.* vi, 27.10 part. rest. (A.D. 132); *POxy.* 726.12-13 (A.D. 135); *PLond.* 306 = *WChr.* 263.8-9 (A.D. 145); *POxy.* 727.12 (A.D. 154); etc.

ἀποσυνεστακέναι *PMich.* 604.12 (A.D. 223); *POxy.* 1274.9 (3rd cent.)

συνεστακότι *POxy.* 2349.25 (A.D. 70); *POxy.* 505 = *MChr.* 350.5 (2nd cent.)

συνεστακυίᾳ *POxy.* 261 = *MChr.* 346.16, with συνεστακέναι 13 (A.D. 55)

4) The form ἔσταμαι (mostly passive), common in Hellenistic Greek,[1] is found in the papyri in the infinitive and participle passive:

ἐστάσθαι *POxy.* 2351.62-63 (A.D. 112); *POxy.* 725.46 (A.D. 183); *PLond.* 1164 (iii, 154-67) f.28 (A.D. 212)

μετεστάσθαι *PBaden* 37 = *PSarap.* 90.6-7 (prob. A.D. 108)

συνεσταμένος *POxy.* 243 = *MChr.* 182.1-2 (A.D. 79); *POxy.* 1105.1 (A.D. 81-96)

καθεσταμένος *PBaden* 18.18 (A.D. 61/62); sim. *POxy.* 2856.1 2 (A.D. 91/92)

ἐσταμένον *CPR* 206 i.10 (A.D. 138-61); *CPR* 111.12 part. rest.; 114.17 (both 2nd cent.)

ἐσταμένου *POxy.* 278 = *MChr.* 165.9 part. rest., with ἐσταμένην 20 (A.D. 17); *PMich.* 256.4 (A.D. 29/30); *PGen.* 10.13 (A.D. 323)

καθεσταμένου *POxy.* 1434.1 (A.D. 107/8)

συνεσταμένου, προσυγεσταμένον *POxy.* 2349.3,29 (A.D. 70)

ἐσταμένην *PMich.* 253.9-10; 257.7 (A.D. 30); *POxy.* 264 = *MChr.* 266.7 abbrev. (A.D. 54); etc.

ἐσταμέναι *POxy.* 104.19 (A.D. 96)

ἐσταμένων *SB* 7619 = *PRein.* 103.9 (A.D. 26); *PLond.* 131 R (= *SB* 9699).68 (A.D. 78/79)

μεθεστα[μ]ένων *SB* 7404.44 = *PLBat.* vi, 24.86 (up to A.D. 124)

---

[1] ἔσταμαι is likewise late, first attested as a v.l. in Pl. (Veitch & *LSJ*, s.v.; Schwyzer i, 770; Chantraine[2], § 222). It is found in the Ptol. papp. sporadically in the 3rd cent., freq. in the 2nd-1st cent. (Mayser i[2], 2, 152-3). It is also common in the NT and Koine lit. and inscrr. from Rom. times (*BDF*, § 97.1; Crönert, 262(-3), n .2; *MS*, 190; Schweizer, 188; Nachmanson, 162; Rüsch, 219).

καθεσταμένους *PLond.* 1166 (iii, 104-5).12 (A.D. 42)

καθεστ[α]μένας *PBaden* 38 = *PSarap.* 16.5 (A.D. 105/6)

ἐσταμένας *PLBat.* xvi, 15.10 (A.D. 236)

b. τίθημι.

1) The perfect middle-passive is regularly τέθειμαι (after εἶμαι[1]):

τέθειμαι *POxy.* 504.41 (early 2nd cent.); *PRyl.* 159.34 (A.D. 31/32)

προτέθειμαι *PHarris* 62.22 (A.D. 151)

κατατέθειμαι *POxy.* 507.24 (A.D. 169)

προστεθεῖσθαι *BGU* 8 ii.15,21 (ca. A.D. 248)

συντεθεῖσθαι *POxy.* 140 = *WChr.* 438.8 (A.D. 550); *POxy.* 1894.8
(A.D. 573); *POxy.* 136 = *WChr.* 383.12 (A.D. 583); *POxy.* 2239.8
(A.D. 598)

ἀποτεθειμένα *PRyl.* 125.14 (A.D. 28/29)

ὑποτε[θ]ειμένα *BGU* 446 = *MChr.* 257.15 (A.D. 169-77: *BL* iii, 13)

The form παρακατατέθεμαι *POxy.* 907 = *MChr.* 317.7 (A.D. 276) is rather
a simple error or phonological variant of the regular form[2] than a reflection of
the ancient dialectal τέθεμαι.[3]

2) The perfect active is accordingly τέθεικα, sometimes spelled τέθικα;
τέθηκα is rare and doubtful:[4]

[π]αρατέθεικα *POxy.* 326 = *SB* 10241 R.9 (A.D. 45)

ἀποτέθεικα *POxy.* 1482.21 (2nd cent.)

προστεθείκαμεν *PGrenf.* i, 53 = *WChr.* 131.30 (4th cent.)

προστεθεικέναι *BGU* 660 i.17 (2nd cent.)

διατεθεικέναι *PLBat.* i, 20.3 (3rd cent.)

ἀποτεθεικώς *PCairMasp.* 2 iii.20 (A.D. 567: *BL* i, 100)

τέθικα *SB* 10476.13 (5th/6th cent.)

but ἀνα[τ]έθηκα *BGU* 388 = *MChr.* 91 i.43 (2nd half 2nd cent.)

τέθικας *PFay.* 119.17 (ca. A.D. 100)

---

[1] Schwyzer i, 775; Chantraine[2], § 221.

[2] For the interchange of ει and ε, incl. before nasals, see Vol. i, 256-9, 261-2.

[3] As Phocian (Schwyzer i, 770, 775).

[4] For the identification of ει and ι, see Vol. i, 189-91. For τέθηκα vs. τέθεικα, see *LSJ*,
s.vv. The former is the reg. form in Att. inscrr., w. the latter not appearing before the 1st
cent. B.C. (*MS*, 189). Both forms are found at Perg., but only the latter at Magn., Lyc.,
and (w. one exception) in the Ptol. papp. (Schweizer, 184; Nachmanson, 159; Hauser, 115;
Mayser i[2], 2, 145). τέθεικα is also used in the NT and in Koine authors (also τέθηκα) (*BDF*,
§ 97.2; Crönert, 278 & n. 3).

ἐπανατέθικεν *PSI* 286.7-8 (3rd/4th cent.)

ὑποτέτικεν *sic PRyl.* 606.38 (late 3rd cent.)

τίτιχε *sic PLond.* 414 = *PAbinn.* 5.11 (ca. A.D. 346)

c. ἵημι.

A new perfect active formation in compounds is -ίωκα, attested in ἀφίωκα *PMich.* 473.24 (early 2nd cent.) and ἐπαφίωκεν *PRossGeorg.* iii, 1.20 (A.D. 270: *BL* iii, 156). This form seems to be phonetically identical with the Doric-Hellenistic perfect ἕωκα.[1] But the classical Attic form (sometimes with ι for ει) is normal, e.g., ἀφῖκες *PCairIsidor.* 133.6 (last quarter 3rd cent.); ἀφεῖκεν *PLBat.* xiii, 24.3 (A.D. 98-117); *POxy.* 723.2 (A.D. 138-61); παρεῖ[κε]ν *POxy.* 1202.15-16 (A.D. 217); ἀφεῖκαν *POxy.* 722 = *MChr.* 358.6 (A.D. 91/107).

d. θνήσκω.

The athematic perfect of θνήσκω[2] is found in θεθνάναι *sic POxy.* 130.12 (6th cent.).[3]

3. Other tenses.

Some anomalous future formations of δίδωμι are found along with the regular δώσω, e.g., δίσω *PFlor.* 209.7 (3rd cent.), probably a misspelling for δήσω formed on the analogy of θήσω,[4] and διδώσω *StudPal.* iii, 381 V (6th cent.), more likely a contamination of the normal present and future stems of δίδωμι than (with Kapsomenakis[5]) a survival of the Homeric form.

---

[1] For the appar. identification of (esp. prevocalic) ε and ι, see Vol. i, 249-56, 261-2. For the Dor. form (w. the proper vocalism of the pf. act. corresp. to εἶμαι), see Veitch & *LSJ*, s.v.; Schwyzer i, 345, 770, n. 1, 775 & n. 12, Chantraine², § 221; Buck, *GD*, § 146), ἀφέωκεν is found once in the Ptol. papp. along w. the reg. εἶκα (Mayser i², 2, 96, 148). Cf. *BDF*, § 97.3.

[2] This athematic pf. is also preserved in the NT (infin.) and occ. in Koine lit. (infin. & ptc.) (*BDF*, § 96; Crönert, 258, n. 1). Appar. only -κ- forms are used in the Ptol. papp. (no infin. attested) (Mayser i², 2, 180).

[3] For the redupl., see above, p. 244. Other exx. of this athematic pf. are found in the mag. papp., as τεθνεώτων *PGM* 5.300 (4th cent.). The thematic forms also occur, as τεθνηκότων *PGM* 12.219 (A.D. 300-50); 4.1914 (4th cent.).

[4] Cf. other formation of δίδωμι on the analogy of τίθημι, e.g., the 2 aor. impt. δές and the 3 sg. indic. mid.-pass. ἀπέδετο. See further Kapsomenakis, 16, n. 1, who sees in this form an anticipation of the MGr. dialectal ἔδικα or ἔδισα (for ἔδωκα, ἔδωσα). He also adduces δίσομαι *PMeyer* 23.11, cited above in connection w. δέομαι.

[5] *Ibid.*

C. IRREGULAR VERBS

1. εἰμί.[1]

The verb "to be" is conjugated for the most part as in Attic. The variations which occur are the result of phonological developments within the Egyptian Koine, analogical levelling within the paradigm of εἰμί, or reflect the initial stage of the transfer of εἰμί to the deponent inflection which is found in the Modern Greek paradigm εἶμαι, εἶσαι, εἶναι, εἴμεθα, εἶσθε, εἶναι.[2]

a. The present indicative.

1) The first person singular appears in the spelling ἦμε in *PRossGeorg.* iii, 10.22 (4th/5th cent.), and in the spelling -ιμαι in the compound συμπάριμαι *PLips.* 3 = *MChr.* 172 i.17 (A.D. 256).[3] These spellings, both representing the form {imε}, are phonetically equivalent anticipations of the Modern Greek εἶμαι.[4] Other variants of the regular εἰμί are merely orthographic, as ἰμεί *SB* 2266.19 (4th cent.).

2) The second person singular.

a) The second person singular is regularly the Attic εἶ, e.g., *BGU* 1079 = *WChr.* 60.32 (A.D. 41); *POxy.* 40.9 (late 2nd/early 3rd cent.); *SB* 5676.17 (ca. A.D. 232); *POxy.* 2407.50 (late 3rd cent.); *PHermRees* 18.5 (A.D. 323?); etc. The spelling ἶ, as in *SB* 4947.10, love charm (not later than 3rd cent.), is only an orthographic variant.

b) The Homeric ἐσσί[5] as *second* person (for third person ἐσσί, see below) does not appear in the documentary papyri.[6]

c) The Ionic εἶς[7] likewise does not seem to occur. The form εἶς in *PGot.* 21.2, theol. frag. (6th/7th cent.) is better read εἶ χ(αί).[8]

d) But the Modern Greek εἶσαι seems to occur already in *PJand.* 101.8 (not before 5th cent.).[9]

---

[1] Schwyzer i, 676-8; Chantraine[2], § 235-7; Buck, *GD*, § 160, 163; *MS*, 190-1; Schweizer, 177-8; Nachmanson, 157-8; Hauser, 109; Mayser i[2], 2, 86, 90, 127; Crönert, 253; *BDF*, § 98; Psaltes, 239-41.

[2] Thumb, *Handbook*, § 224; Mirambel, *Gram.*, 129-30; Maspero, 96.

[3] Cf. also ἴμαι *PLund.* iv, 12.16, mag. (4th cent.).

[4] Cf. also ἴμε on an inscr. of A.D. 314 (Dieterich, 227).

[5] Cf. Veitch & *LSJ*, s.v.; Schwyzer i, 321, 659, 677; Chantraine[2], § 235; Buck, *GD*, § 138.

[6] But ἐσσί is read in the mag. papp. in *PGM* 3.218 (A.D. 300+).

[7] Cf. Veitch & *LSJ*, s.v.

[8] See A. Debrunner, "εἶς 'du bist' in einem Papyrus?" *IF* 56 (1938), 177. εἶς is read, however, in the mag. papp. in *PGM* 1.95 (4th/5th cent.).

[9] εἶσαι is also used in place of εἶ in the Byz.Chron. (Psaltes, 239-40).

3) The third person singular.

a) The third person singular is normally ἐστί(ν), but the form ἐσσί is used unmistakably for the third person in *BGU* 602.8 (prob. 2nd cent.); *SB* 8027.10 (2nd/3rd cent.); *BGU* 385 = *WChr.* 100.6 (2nd/3rd cent.); (ἐσσίν) *POxy.* 2154.18 (4th cent.). This form ἐσσί as third person seems to appear elsewhere only in an Aeolic inscription[1] in construction with a nominative plural neuter, where it might be an analogous formation of the third person plural rather than an assibilated Lesbian form of ἐστί.[2] The occurrence of this form in the papyri is the result of the assibilation of τ after σ in the pronunciation of some of the writers of the papyri, a phenomenon also observed in other words in which the cluster στ occurs.[3]

b) The form ἔνι (and its phonetic equivalent ἔνει), for ἔνεστι with the preposition used without an accompanying verb, as in the Homeric and Tragic ἄνα 'up,' etc.,[4] occurs occasionally, most often after a negative,[5] generally in the meaning "there is (not.)"

i. Negative:

οὐδὲν ἁμάρτημα ἔνει *BGU* 1141.8 (13 B.C.)
ὧδε γὰρ ἔνι *PMich.* 465.28 (A.D. 107)
ο <ὐ> δὲ ἐν τῇ Θώλθει χορτοπάτημα ἔνει *POxy.* 2986.8-9 (2nd/3rd cent.)
καὶ οὐκέτι φόβος οὐδὲ εἷς ἔνει *POxy.* 1668.19-20 (3rd cent.)
οὐδὲν δύσκολον ἔνι ἐπὶ τῆς οἰκίας σου *POxy.* 1218.5-6 (3rd cent.)
[ὅτι ἀπρ]έπιά (for -ειά) ἐστιν καὶ οὐκ ἔνι "neque decet neque fieri potest" *PJand.* 11.8 (4th cent.?: *BL* i, 197)
καὶ οὐκ ἔνι *PSI* 837.9 (3rd/4th cent.)
οὐδαὶ (for οὐδὲ) οὐκ ἔνι (i.e., μάτια σιδήρου) *POxy.* 2729.18 (4th cent.)
ἱροφῖα οὐκ ἔνι τοῖς βόες *sic* *PAmh.* 143.5 6 (4th cent.)
τόκον (for τόπον or στίχον) οὐκ ἔν[ι] *BGU* 1024 v.20 (late 4th cent.: *BL* i, 88)
ἐπιδὴ ἐν Ἀλεξανδρίᾳ οὐκ ἔνει *PStrassb.* 35.20 (4th/5th cent.)
ἄνεμός ἐστιν καὶ οὐκ ἔνι ἐμποδισμός *SB* 9607.5 (6th cent.)
ὅτι πλοῖον οὐκ ἔνι εἰς τὸν ὅρμον *POxy.* 1867.15 (7th cent.)

---

[1] See Schwyzer i, 270, n. 1.

[2] Schwyzer i, 677, n. 3.

[3] See Vol. i, 66.

[4] Schwyzer i, 388. ἔνι for ἔνεστι is found freq. in the Att. inscrr. and elsewh. in the Koine (*MS*, 190; Dieterich, 225-6). It occurs in the mag. papp. in the spelling ἔνη *PGMXtn.* 7.17 (5th cent.).

[5] Six exx. of ἔνι are found in the NT, all negative (*BDF*, § 98), as are all the exx. in Hatzidakis, *Einl.*, 207, but in some Koine authors, ἔνι is used wo. a negative (Crönert, 253 & n. 2).

ii. Positive:

περὶ δὲ παπύρων ἔνι παρ᾽ ἡμεῖν *POslo* 159.16 (3rd cent.)
καὶ ἐν αὐτοῖς [τ]ὸ ἀδίκημα ἔνι *SB* 9415 (18).20-22 (3rd cent.)
ἢ (for εἰ) δέ τι ἔνει *PMichael.* 39.17 (Byz.)

This form, rather than the classical Greek infinitive, may be the origin of
the Modern Greek third person singular and plural εἶναι {inε},[1] but the phonetic
metathesis can only be explained if the final [e] sound arose by means of
progressive assimilation to the initial [ε-], with *subsequent* analogical levelling
of the initial ε- with the εἰ- [i] of the other forms, as Jannaris suggests.[2]

4) The first person plural is normally the regular ἐσμέν, e.g., *PTebt.* 316 =
WChr. 148.13,16 (A.D. 99); *POxy.* 33 = *WChr.* 20 v.5 (late 2nd cent.); etc.,
but orthographic variations occur, as the omission of final -ν in ἐσμέ *POxy.*
1299.6 (4th cent.); *PPrinc.* 120.6 (6th cent.).[3]

5) The third person plural is regularly εἰσίν, e.g., *PMich.* 323-5.26, so copy
PSI 903.25 (A.D. 47). The form ᾽σιν in the phrase ἀρούρων ὧν κεκληρωιμένοι
᾽σίν *PMich.* 326.14, sim. 46 (A.D. 48) is a result of aphaeresis or haplography.[4]
The form ἔνουσι is found in καὶ γὰρ πολλοὶ ᾽Οξυριγχῖται ἔνουσι ἔνθαδε *POxy.*
2595.6-7 (3rd cent.) and ἔνουσιν (rather than ἐνοῦσιν) οἱ στρουθοῦ *sic* *PLond.*
239 = *PAbinn.* 31.15 (ca. A.D. 346). This form is probably a thematic variant
of ἔνεισιν rather than a plural of ἔνι above.

b. The imperfect.

1) The first person singular is regularly ἤμην, as in the New Testament and
the Ptolemaic papyri,[5] instead of the Attic ἦ (contracted from the Epic-Ionic
ἦα) or ἦν, e.g., ἤμην *POxy.* 285.10 (ca. A.D. 50); *POxy.* 1582.5 (2nd cent.);
POxy. 526.3 (2nd cent.); *PAlex.* 28.22 (3rd cent.); *PLBat.* xi, 26.4 (3rd cent.);
PLips. 40 ii.5,6; iii.15 (late 4th/early 5th cent.); etc.; ἀπήμην *POxy.* 1204.23
(A.D. 299); παρήμην *PLBat.* vi, 49a ii.10 (prob. A.D. 205); *PNYU* 1.11 (A.D.
299+); *PCairMasp.* 126.59,67 part. rest., 74 (A.D. 541); *PGron.* 10.30, sim. 28
(prob. 6th cent.: *BL* v, 39); etc. The imperfect form ἤμην with middle-passive

---

[1] So Schwyzer i, 678; Chantraine[2], § 237; *BDF*, § 98.
[2] p. 250, n. 1. ἔνι, however, is retained dialectally in MGr. (Pontos, Cyprus) (Thumb,
Handbook, § 224).
[3] See Vol. i, 111-14.
[4] Cf. sim. exx. of other persons of the indic. in Vol. i, 319.
[5] *BDF*, § 98; Mayser i[2], 2, 127.

endings is found even in codices of Attic authors.¹ It served to distinguish the first and third persons of the singular.²

2) The second person singular is normally the late Greek ἦς;³ the classical Attic ἦσθα⁴ is found only rarely:

> ἦς *PFlor.* 61 = *MChr.* 80.59 (A.D. 85); *PGiss.* 79 iv.7 (ca. A.D. 117); *SB* 6262.16 (3rd cent.); *POxy.* 1489.7 (late 3rd cent.); *POxy.* 1682.9 (4th cent.); etc.
>
> παρῆς *POxy.* 2182.5 (A.D. 166)
>
> ἦσθα *POxy.* 471.131 (2nd cent.)
>
> > perhaps also ἦσα (subj. for ἦσθα?: see below, p. 404) *PLond.* 897 (iii, 206-7).9: *BL* i, 288 (A.D. 84)⁵
> >
> > cf. also the hybrid ἦσθας *PFlor.* 382.13 (A.D. 222/3)

This last form, with the addition of -ς on the model of other second person singular endings, is also attested in late Attic.⁶

3) The third person singular is normally the regular Attic ἦν, e.g., *POxy.* 2190.43 (late 1st cent.); *POxy.* 2419.4,7 (6th cent.); etc. But a form ἦ occurs several times:

> τότε γὰρ οὔπω κατάπλους ἦ αὐτῶν *BGU* 1674.6-7 (2nd cent.)
>
> ἐφ᾽ ὃν χρόνο[ν] περιῆ *PLBat.* vi, 15.61 (ca. A.D. 114)
>
> ἡνίκα περιῆ *POxy.* 68 = *MChr.* 228.21 (A.D. 131); *PRyl.* 656.7 (A.D. 300)
>
> ταῦτα δὲ πάντα ϲυγενῆι *POxy.* 929.12-13 (late 2nd/3rd cent.)

This form is not connected with the old Aeolic third person singular ἦ,⁷ but probably came to be used as a result of the confusion arising from the frequent use of ἦν for the third person singular subjunctive ἦ(ι).⁸ There may have been no distinction in pronunciation between the two written forms ἦν and ἦ(ι) in view of the frequent omission of final -ν and the complete loss of the long diphthongs in -ι.⁹

---

¹ E.g., E. Lys. X. Hyp. (Veitch & *LSJ*, s.v.; Schwyzer i, 127, 678; Chantraine², § 237; Rutherford, *Phryn.*, 240-44). For the Koine, see further Schweizer, 178; Schmid iv, 599; Dieterich, 223-4.

² Schwyzer i, 678. According to Kretschmer, *Entst.*, 12-13, it is a NWGr. element of the Koine.

³ This form has no connection with the old Greek ἦς, attested, e.g., in Anacr., but is a new formation from ἦν (Schwyzer i, 662, n. 4). ἦς is a v.l. in Pi., and occurs along with ἦσθα in the LXX, NT, and Byz.Chron. (*LSJ*, s.v.; *BDF*, § 98; Psaltes, 239). The 2 sg. is not attested in the Ptol. papp. (Mayser i², 2, 127).

⁴ ἦσθα is retained among Koine authors in J. Luc. (Crönert, 253, n. 5).

⁵ Cf. also from the mag. papp. ἦσα (impf.) *PGM* 4.2721 (4th cent.).

⁶ E.g., in Men. (*LSJ*, s.v.; Schwyzer i, 127, 662).

⁷ Schwyzer i, 677.

⁸ So Mayser i², 2, 86. See below, p. 405.

⁹ See Vol. i, 111-14, 183-6.

4) The first person plural is normally the classical ἦμεν *PSI* 1242.12 (1st cent. B.C./1st cent. A.D.); *POxy.* 2732.13 (6th cent.?); παρῆμεν *PCornell* 20.25, 43-44, etc. (A.D. 302). But a middle form ἤμεθα (after ἤμην) is found in *SB* 9238.15 (A.D. 198-211); *POxy.* 162 = *POxy.* 942.3 (6th/7th cent.).[1] Another analogical form ἦσμεν, with the -σ- introduced presumably from ἦσθα, ἦστε (= ἦτε), ἦσαν,[2] is found in *PMich.* 512.5 (early 3rd cent.).

5) The second person plural is regularly ἦτε, but ἦστε[3] (which may be indic. in place of subj.) is read in ἐὰν ... ἦστε ἐμβαλόμενοι *PSI* 1557.21 (A.D. 214).

6) The third person plural is regularly the Attic ἦσαν, e.g., παρῆσαν *POxy.* 122.6-7 (late 3rd/4th cent.). An anomalous form presumably modeled on the third person plural primary ending -σι[4] occurs in ἦσιν *PLond.* 1914.16 (A.D. 335?) and ἦσει *PLond.* 1170 V (iii, 193-205).388,471,492,498,506,507 (A.D. 258/ 9). The substitution of ει- for η- is found in εἶσαν *SB* 7168.4 (5th/6th cent.).

c. The subjunctive.

The subjunctive in general follows the regular Attic inflection (usually without the -ι adscript in the second and third person singular[5]). But the following peculiarities appear.

1) The first person singular appears as ὦμε in *PLips.* 110.14 (prob. 3rd/4th cent.). This form, in connection with the indicative forms εἶμαι and εἶσαι above, reflects the transition of εἰμί to the deponent inflection. It is phonetically identical with ὦμαι.[6]

2) The second person singular, normally ἦς, e.g., *BGU* 48.7 (2nd/3rd cent.?: *BL* i, 11), apparently occurs as ἦσα in *PLond.* 897 (iii, 206-7).9: *BL* i, 288 (A.D. 84). This form is probably a misspelling of the imperfect indicative ἦσθα.[7] The present indicative apparently used for the subjunctive in the second person singular in ἵν' εἶ *PRyl.* 658.13 (early 4th cent.) might be better restored as ἵν' εἶ[δῆς].

---

[1] ἤμεθα is also found in the Ptol. papp. and in the LXX and NT (Mayser i², 2, 127; *LSJ*, s.v.; *BDF*, § 98).

[2] So ed., n. ad loc.

[3] ἦστε Ar., ἦτε Pl. (*LSJ*, s.v.).

[4] Cf. Olsson, *Aegyptus* 7 (1926), 109-10.

[5] For the identification of the long diphthongs in -ι with their corresp. simple vowels, see Vol. i, 183-6.

[6] For the identification of αι and ε, see Vol. i, 191-3. The form ὦμαι as 1 sg. subj. is found once in the Ptol. papp. (126 B.C.) (Mayser i², 2, 127).

[7] So *BL* i, 288. For ἦσθα in the impf., see above, p. 403.

3) The third person singular frequently appears as ἦν, with the erroneous addition of final -ν, making the form identical in spelling with that of the third person singular of the imperfect. This form ἦν is found very frequently:[1]

ἦν (subj.) *POxy.* 1061.13 (22 B.C.); *POxy.* 744.9,10 (1 B.C.); *PMich.* 585.16,35 (A.D. 87); *PMich.* 477.13 (early 2nd cent.); *PSarap.* 103 bis (pp. 316-17).12 (early 2nd cent.); *POxy.* 1757.14,18 (after A.D. 138); *PFouad* 54.30 (A.D. 142?); *BGU* 300 = *MChr.* 345.5 (A.D. 148); *PHamb.* 88.11 (mid 2nd cent.); *PStrassb.* 187.7,9 (2nd cent.); *PFouad* 77.34 (2nd cent.); *POxy.* 1760.16,17 (2nd cent.); *POslo* 155.14 (2nd cent.); *BGU* 821.6 (2nd cent.); *BGU* 1210 (19).61; (45).125 (mid 2nd cent.); *BGU* 2052.6 (2nd cent.); *BGU* 821.6 (2nd cent.); *PMich.* 487.14 (2nd cent.); *POxy.* 2411.51 (ca. A.D. 173); *POxy.* 237 vii.28 (A.D. 186); *SB* 7349.5 (late 2nd/early 3rd cent.); *POxy.* 1294.16 (late 2nd/early 3rd cent.); *POxy.* 63.18 (2nd/3rd cent.); *PMich.* 602.10 (early 3rd cent.); *PMich.* 511.12 (1st half 3rd cent.); *PFlor.* 89.14 (3rd cent.); *POxy.* 1273.33 (A.D. 260); *PGrenf.* i, 53 = *WChr.* 131.30 (4th cent.); etc.

περιῆν *POxy.* 496 = *MChr.* 287.9 (A.D. 127)

προσῆν *POxy.* 34 V — *MChr.* 188 i.7 (A.D. 127)

ἐνῆν *PBaden* 36 i = *PSarap.* 85.7 (early 2nd cent.); *BGU* 48.13 (2nd/3rd cent.?: *BL* i, 11); *SB* 7242 = *PRossGeorg.* iii, 3.15 (3rd cent.); etc.

This form, which is not attested in classical dialectal or Koine inscriptions but is found in the Ptolemaic papyri,[2] may be phonetically equivalent to the regular ἦ, in light of the frequent loss and erroneous addition of final -ν.[3] The widespread and frequent addition of -ν to this form, however, and its complete absence from other third person singular subjunctive forms, indicates the analogical influence on the orthographic level of the form ἦν of the third person singular imperfect, which itself sometimes conversely appears as ἦ (see above, p. 403).

4) The first person plural appears as ὤμεθα, with middle-passive ending, in ἵν' ὤμεθα εὐεργετημένοι *PLBat.* vi, 37.22 (A.D. 167). This form again reflects the tendency towards the inflection of εἰμί as a deponent.

5) The third person plural is regular in ὦσιν, e.g., *POxy.* 36 = *WChr.* 273 iii.5 (2nd/early 3rd cent.). Only orthographic variants occur, e.g., ὦσειν *PMich.* 254-5.2 (A.D. 30/31).

---

[1] Cf. also from the mag. papp. ἵνα...ἦν *PGM* 5.165 (4th cent.); *PGM* 4.731 (4th cent.); etc.

[2] Mayser i², 2, 86, Anm. 4. See further Horn, 27-30.

[3] See Vol. i, 111-14.

d. The optative.

The optative normally follows the regular Attic inflection εἴην, εἴης, εἴη in the singular, e.g., εἴην *BGU* 92 = *WChr.* 427.18 (A.D. 187); ἀπείη *POxy.* 125.16 (A.D. 560). Most variations which occur are only orthographic, e.g., εἴηι *POxy.* 251.26 (A.D. 44). But the following forms are significant.

1) A thematic primary middle-passive ending occurs in the first person singular in εἴημαι *SB* 7988 = *PSI* 1329.22 (A.D. 212).

2) A thematic secondary middle-passive ending appears in the third person singular in ὃ μὴ εἴοιτο in the sense of γένοιτο *SB* 5294 = *StudPal.* xx, 35.7 (A.D. 235).

3) The thematic active ending -οι is found in the third person singular in ὃ μὴ εἴοι σοι γένοιτο *POxy.* 1680.8 (late 3rd/early 4th cent.) and perhaps also *PLond.* 991 (iii, 257-8).19 (6th cent.). This spelling εἴοι is phonetically equivalent to the regular form εἴη.[1] If not the result of homoioteleuton and correctly read, it may reflect an influence on the orthographic level of the optative of thematic verbs.

4) In the plural, the optative fluctuates, as in Attic, between the forms εἴημεν, εἴησαν and εἶμεν, εἶεν:

> εἴημεν *POxy.* 1252 R.29 (A.D. 288-95); *PCairIsidor.* 9.13 (ca. A.D. 310); etc.
>
> εἶμεν *PLond.* 1247 (iii, 225-6).16 (A.D. 345)
>
> εἴησαν *PLond.* 1249 (iii, 227-8).4-5 (A.D. 346: *BL* i, 290); *PMon.* 6.38 (A.D. 583)
>
> > εἶεν *BGU* 113 = *WChr.* 458.4 (A.D. 140); *PSI* 1039.15 (3rd cent.); *PCairIsidor.* 66.16 (A.D. 299)

The expanded forms εἴημεν, etc.,[2] represent analogical formations after the singular εἴην, etc.,[3] with an early extension in the third person plural of the -σαν ending of the imperfect ἦσαν and sigmatic aorists.[4]

---

[1] For the occ. interchange of η and οι, see Vol. i, 265-7.

[2] εἴημεν is the more common Att. form; εἴητε occurs in Andoc. Lys., εἴησαν in Antiph. Th. X. and Hdt., while εἶεν is Ep.-Ion., and also Th. Pl. X. (Veitch & *LSJ*, s.v.). εἴησαν is also found in the Herc. papp. (Crönert, 253) and excl. in the Ptol. papp. (Mayser i², 2, 87).

[3] Schwyzer i, 419.

[4] Schwyzer i, 665. Cf. above, pp. 331, 361.

e. The imperative.

1) The third person singular imperative is regularly ἔστω, e.g., *POxy.* 36 = *WChr.* 273 ii.12 (2nd/early 3rd cent.); *PFlor.* 167 V.19 (mid 3rd cent.); *PLond.* 233 = *PAbinn.* 58.13 (A.D. 345). Orthographic variants occur, especially the erroneous addition of an -ι adscript, as in ἐξέστωι τῶι προστάτηι *PMich.* 243.3 (A.D. 14-37).

2) But a new form ἤτω also occurs:[1]

ἤτω *POxy.* 533.11, poss. also 9 part. rest. *pace BL* i, 325 (late 2nd/early 3rd cent.); *POxy.* 2983.26 (2nd/3rd cent.); *BGU* 276.24 (2nd/3rd cent.?); *PFlor.* 166.5 (mid 3rd cent.); 175.8 (A.D. 255); 181.38 (3rd cent.); *BGU* 419 = *WChr.* 373.13 (A.D. 276/7); etc.

This form came into use in Hellenistic times.[2] It represents an extension of the η- of the imperfect to the imperative.

3) ἐσθέτω is also read in *SB* 9490 = *PMilVogl.* 202.3 (2nd cent.).

4) For the third person plural imperative ἔστωσαν, see above, p. 361.

f. The infinitive.

The present infinitive is regular in εἶναι. An abbreviated form εἶν is found in *PTebt.* 316 = *WChr.* 148.80, but correctly written εἶναι 46, etc. (A.D. 99). This is a blunder in an atrociously written signature, not a survival of the West Ionic and Chian dialectal form.[3]

g. The future.

The future is in general inflected according to the Attic pattern. For the second person singular ἔσῃ, e.g., *SB* 7354.9 (early 2nd cent.), see above, p. 358;

---

[1] This new impt. is found 11 times in the mag. papp.: *PGM* 7.425.428,542 (w. ἔστω 544), 600,844 (3rd cent.); *PGM* 4.2188,2881,3117,3133 (twice) (4th cent.); *PGM* 5.325 (4th cent.). ἔστω occurs 16 times (*PGM* i-ii) and παρέστω *PGM* 4.2743,2761,2783 (4th cent.). ἤτωσαν is also found in *PGM* 13.126 (ca. A.D. 346). Note also the occ. appearance in the mag. papp. of the form ἔσο for the 2 sg. impt. in place of the reg. ἴσθι, e.g., *PGM* 2.165 (4th cent.); *PGM* 3.213 (after A.D. 300). This latter form is also found in Hell. lit., as Plu. M.Ant. Hld. Porph. and Byz.Chron. (Schwyzer i, 678; *LSJ*, s.v.; Psaltes, 239).

[2] ἤτω appears once in Pl. as an inferior reading for ἴτω (*LSJ*, s.v.) and as a v.l. in Hp. (Veitch, s.v.). Later, it is established for Aret., the LXX, NT, and Byz.Chron. (Veitch, s.v.; *BDF*, § 98; Psaltes, 239). It is also found in late Att. and Asia Minor inscrr. (*MS*, 191; Schweizer, 177-8; Nachmanson, 158; Dieterich, 227).

[3] Schwyzer i, 87, 678; Buck, *GD*, § 160. It also occurs in some Koine inscrr. (Crönert, 253, n. 4).

note also the orthographic variant ἔσει *PMichael.* 20.6 (A.D. 277); παρέσει *BGU* 624.21 (A.D. 284-95). For the occasional appearance of ἔσασθαι (with first aorist endings) for ἔσεσθαι in the infinitive, see above, p. 333.

An active form seems to occur in ἔσο (for ἔσομαι?) *PMerton* 45.6 (late 5th/6th cent.).

2. εἶμι.[1]

The classical Attic inflection of εἶμι is retained, with only sporadic variants, mainly orthographic.

a. The present indicative appears as εἶμι *POxy.* 529.17 (2nd cent.) and ἶμι *SB* 7352 = *PMich.* 490.12 (2nd cent.).

b. The imperfect is the late Attic-Ionic -ῄειν in the singular, not the older ᾖα,[2] e.g., μετῄειν *POxy.* 71 i = *MChr.* 62.9 (A.D. 303). The plural ἀπῄειμεν, rare and doubted in classical Greek,[3] is found in *PCairMasp.* 9 V.27 (6th cent.) and *PLond.* 1674.67 (ca. A.D. 570).

c. The second person singular imperative is regular in -ιθι, e.g., πρόσιθι *PMich.* 530.28 (3rd/4th cent.).[4] The third person singular imperative is regular in -ίτω: ἀπίτω *POxy.* 2857.27 (A.D. 134); *StudPal.* i, p. 7, i.29 (A.D. 480); δόλος, φθόνος, πονηρὸς ἀπίτω ἀπέστω = *dolus malus abesto POxy.* 1901.54-55 (6th cent.); sim. (ἀπείτω) *PLond.* 77 = *MChr.* 319.65 (late 6th cent.). The third person plural imperative is -ίτωσαν, e.g., προσίτωσαν *PBeattyPanop.* 2.158 (A.D. 300).

d. The infinitive is normally -ιέναι, e.g., ἐπιέναι *POxy.* 2349.13 (A.D. 70); ἀπιέναι *PCairMasp.* 2 ii.2 (A.D. 567: *BL* i, 100), with orthographic variants, e.g., ἐξειέναι *PLips.* 110.5 (prob. 3rd/4th cent.). But other variants occur in προῖναι *BGU* 1210 (71).182 (mid 2nd cent.) and π[ρ]οσεῖναι *SB* 7517.7 (prob. A.D. 211/12).

e. The participle is regular, e.g., ἐξιών *POxy.* 472.2 (ca. A.D. 130); *POxy.* 1662.8 (A.D. 246); εἰσιόν *PMich.* 311.14,35 part. rest. (A.D. 34); (with crasis)

---

[1] Schwyzer i, 674; Chantraine², § 234; Schweizer, 177; Nachmanson, 157; Hauser, 108-9; Mayser i², 2, 126-7; Crönert, 253-4; *BDF*, § 99.1. For εἶμι and ἐλεύσομαι in the fut., see above, pp. 288-9.

[2] Schwyzer i, 674; *LSJ*, s.v. ᾖειν occurs as a simple only in Luc., but in compds. in Pl. X. D. etc.; ᾖα is found in Pl. X. D. (Veitch, s.v.).

[3] Veitch, s.v.

[4] Cf. also from the mag. papp. ἴθι *PGM* 3.249 (A.D. 300+); 13.100,655 (ca. A.D. 346); 4.2543,2548 (4th cent.); ἄπιθι *PGM* 4.45,252,2041; [πρόσ]ιθι *PGM* 1.77 (4th/5th cent.).

τοὐπιόν *POxy.* 83 = *WChr.* 430.14 (A.D. 327); ἐξιόντα *PWürzb.* 8.6 (A.D. 158); etc. Only orthographic variations occur, e.g., ἐπειόντα *POxy.* 237 vii.11 (A.D. 186).

3. οἶδα.[1]

οἶδα appears in an advanced stage of analogical levelling, with the second person singular οἶδας instead of οἶσθα and the -α- of the singular extended to the plural to replace the ancient zero-grade forms. The verb is extinct in Modern Greek except in stereotyped phrases, as Κύριος οἶδε 'God knows !'[2]

a. The perfect (present) indicative.

1) The first person singular.

The form οἶδον, a back-formation from οἶδες, οἶδε as if imperfect or second aorist, occurs in *PLBat.* xi, 28.4 (4th/5th cent.: *BL* v, 63).

2) The second person singular.

a) The second person singular is standardized by the ending -ας of the regular perfect tenses and appears normally as οἶδας:

> οἶδας *BGU* 37.6 (A.D. 51); *PFlor.* 61 = *MChr.* 80.36 (A.D. 85); *POxy.* 2190.54 (late 1st cent.); *SB* 7354.9 (early 2nd cent.); *BGU* 388 = *MChr.* 91 ii.20 (2nd half 2nd cent.); *POxy.* 33 = *WChr.* 20 ii.4; v.9, 10-11 part. rest. (late 2nd cent.); *PMich.* 209.11 (late 2nd/early 3rd cent.); *SB* 7993 = *PSI* 1333.3 (3rd cent.); *PRyl.* 692.28; 695.14; 696.9 (late 3rd cent.); *PLBat.* xi, 27.7 (3rd/4th cent.); *PLond.* 243 = *PAbinn.* 8.14; *PLond.* 408 = *PAbinn.* 18.7,18; *PAbinn.* 20.8 (all ca. A.D. 346); *PPrinc.* 98.19 (4th cent.); etc.

This form is already found once in Homer and occasionally in classical Poetic-Ionic authors,[3] and represents the analogical levelling of the old perfect ending -σθα to -ας, as happened much earlier in the regular perfects.[4]

---

[1] Schwyzer i, 662, 767-9, etc.; Chantraine[2], § 213-17, etc.; Schweizer, 166; Nachmanson, 160; Mayser i[2], 2, 81, 89, 102, 130, 145, 149; Crönert, 270; *BDF*, § 99.2.

[2] Jannaris, § 970[b].

[3] *LSJ*, s.v. εἴδω B; Veitch, s.v. This is the usu. form in the Ptol. papp. and NT (Mayser i[2], 2, 81; *BDF*, § 99.2), but only οἶσθα(ς) is found in the Herc. papp., while other Koine authors used either form (Crönert, 270 & n. 2). The Byz.Chron. have only οἶδας (Psaltes, 241).

[4] Schwyzer i, 662.

b) Occasional variations of οἶδας are also found.

i. Further analogical levelling takes place to produce the form οἶδες, with the second person singular ending of the second aorist and imperfect. For examples of this form, see above, pp. 353-4.

ii. The form οἶδης also occurs in *PLond.* 410 = *PAbinn.* 34.13; *PGen.* 54 = *PAbinn.* 35.3, with οἶδας 4 (both ca. A.D. 346) and *PRossGeorg.* v, 8.5 (4th/5th cent.).[1] This form is not connected with the old Aeolic form οἶδης[2] but probably represents a change of η to ε.[3]

c) The old second person singular οἶσθα is preserved in *POxy.* 1119 = *WChr.* 397.15 part. rest. and unclear (A.D. 253: *BL* i, 332) and *PHermRees* 2.3 (4th cent.). Further, the form οἶσθας is read in *PSI* 685.3 (A.D. 324-7: *BL* v, 123). This form, parallel to ἦσθας above,[4] is found in classical poets,[5] and represents an addition of -ς to the second person singular on the analogy of other second person singular endings.

3) The inflection of the singular spreads to the plural, so that the normal forms of the first and second persons are οἴδαμεν, οἴδατε, although the zero-grade forms are still found occasionally in the Byzantine period as exclusively in the third person plural:

> οἴδαμεν *POxy.* 2353.11-12 (A.D. 32); *PCairIsidor.* 73.6 (A.D. 314); *PLond.* 413 = *PAbinn.* 6.5 (ca. A.D. 346); *POxy.* 1777.5 (late 4th cent.); *POxy.* 1868.2 (6th/7th cent.); etc.[6]
> but ἴσμεν *SB* 9218.5 (A.D. 319/20); *PLips.* 41 R = *MChr.* 300.9 (2nd half 4th cent.); *PCairMasp.* 3.22 (A.D. 567: *BL* i, 100); *PLond.* 1713.19, so copy *PFlor.* 93.13 (A.D. 569); *PCairMasp.* 311.15 (A.D. 569/70?) εἴσμεν *SB* 8246.11,27 (A.D. 335: *BL* v, 102); *PBouriant* 20 = *PAbinn.* 63.42 (A.D. 350); *PLips.* 40 ii.4 (late 4th/early 5th cent.); *PHermRees* 29.11 (A.D. 586)
> 'σμεν *PBouriant* 20 = *PAbinn.* 63 iii.5 (A.D. 350)
> οἴδατε *POxy.* 2788.19 (3rd cent.); *PTebt.* 420.4 (3rd cent.); *POxy.* 156.6 (6th cent.); *PApoll.* 46.8 (A.D. 703-15); etc.
> but ἴστε *PGen.* 14.17 (Byz.); *PBeattyPanop.* 2.106,219 (A.D. 300); *PApoll.* 70.5 (A.D. 714); (as subj.) *POxy.* 2416.7 (6th/7th cent.)
> ἴσασι *BGU* 163.14 (A.D. 108)

---

[1] See above, p. 354.
[2] Cf. Schwyzer i, 680.
[3] For the interchange of η and ε, see Vol. i, 242-9.
[4] p. 403.
[5] Schwyzer i, 662. An ex. is also noted from the 3rd cent. B.C. in the Ptol. papp. (never οἶσθα) (Mayser i², 2, 81).
[6] Cf. also from the mag. papp. οἴδαμεν *PGM* 3.591 (after A.D. 300), etc.

These forms reflect the tendency in Greek to level the inherited IE vowel gradation in the perfect system. This levelling took place in the perfect between Homer and the classical Attic authors in most other verbs, so that ἴσμεν, ἴστε, etc., were the only common remnants of the zero-grade plural of the perfect in Attic.[1] The subsequent loss of vowel gradation in this verb is a further example of analogical levelling in the Koine.

b. The pluperfect (imperfect).

1) The first person singular is the best Attic prose ᾔδειν,[2] e.g., *PHermRees* 12.4 (2nd/early 3rd cent.: *BL* v, 44). It occurs with several orthographic variations, including ᾔδιν *PLBat.* vi, 24.84 (up to A.D. 124), εἴδην *POxy.* 2339. 17 (1st cent.), and οἴδειν *SB* 9106.4 (5th cent.); *PCairMasp.* 155.14 part. rest. (6th cent.?). This last form might reflect a confusion of οἶδα and ᾔδειν on the orthographic level, but in view of the frequent interchange of οι and (ε)ι,[3] there was probably just the one spoken form [idin].

2) The second person singular appears as ᾔδεις in *BGU* 388 = *MChr.* 91 ii.30 (2nd half 2nd cent.). This form, used in preference to ᾔδεισθα in the best Attic,[4] is comparable to οἶδας from οἶσθα in the perfect (present).

c. The subjunctive is regular in εἰδῶ, etc., e.g., *PMich.* 465.6 (A.D. 107). Orthographic variations also occur, e.g., εἰδῶι *BGU* 248.25 (1st cent.: *BL* i, 32), and ἰδῇ (for εἰδῇ) *POxy.* 68 = *MChr.* 228.31 (A.D. 131).

d. The optative is regular in εἰδείην, etc., e.g., εἰδείης *POxy.* 2666 i.19 (ca. A.D. 308/9); εἰδεῖεν *PStrassb.* 511.13 (A.D. 169).

e. The imperative is also inflected regularly, with orthographic variants:

> ἴσθι *POxy.* 2190.44 (late 1st cent.); *PBrem.* 53.29 (A.D. 114); *PBrem.* 63.25 (ca. A.D. 117); *POslo* 55.3 (2nd/3rd cent.); *PMerton* 24.9 (ca. A.D. 200); *POxy.* 2681.5 (3rd cent.); *POxy.* 892 = *WChr.* 49.4 (A.D. 338); *POxy.* 2156.13 (late 4th/5th cent.); etc.
>
> εἴσθι *PBrem.* 55.8 (ca. A.D. 117); *BGU* 151.2 (Xtn.)

---

[1] Cf. Schwyzer i, 767; Chantraine[2], § 217, 219. The forms οἴδαμεν, etc., are found, however, in Hdt. Ph. and as v.ll. in some Att. authors (Veitch & *LSJ*, s.v.). They are the only forms found in the Ptol. papp. (incl. one ex. of the 3 pl. οἴδασιν) and, w. one exception each of ἴστε and ἴσασι, in the NT (Mayser i[2], 2, 149; *BDF*, § 99.2). They are not freq., however, in Koine authors, who in general prefer the zero-grade forms (Crönert, 270, n. 3).

[2] E.g., Antiph. Lys. Aeschin. D.; ᾔδη is found, however, in S. Ar. Pl. X. etc. (Veitch & *LSJ*, s.v.).

[3] Vol. i, 272-3.

[4] E.g., Ar. Is. D. etc. (Veitch & *LSJ*, s.v.). εἰδησσθα has been suggested (ed., n. ad loc.) for [εἴ]δης σύ *PMerton* 80.12 (2nd cent.).

but οἶδε *PLBat.* xiii, 19.6 (3rd cent.)
ἴστω *POxy.* 1409.21 (A.D. 278)
ἴστε *PBeattyPanop.* 2.106,219 (A.D. 300)
ἴστωσαν *PHamb.* 29.8 (after A.D. 94); *PFay.* 20.10 (late 3rd/early 4th cent.)

f. The infinitive is likewise regular in εἰδέναι, apart from orthographic variations and the variation (ε)ἰδέν above, p. 356.

g. The participle is regular in εἰδώς, etc., but the form οἰδότος (cf. the pluperfect οἴδειν above, p. 411) occurs in *SB* 9455.11 (early 6th cent.).

h. The regular future is attested in εἴση *POxy.* 2192.40 (2nd cent.).

4. φημί.[1]

φημί shows similar analogical levelling. It is also extinct in Modern Greek.[2]

a. The present indicative.

1) The second person singular is φής, e.g., *PMich.* 486.6 (2nd cent.); *PCol.* 123 = *SB* 9526.56 (A.D. 200); *POxy.* 1502.6 (ca. A.D. 260/1); *SB* 8246.22 (A.D. 335: *BL* v, 102); *PBouriant* 20 = *PAbinn.* 63.17 (after A.D. 350). Any distinction between the forms φήις and φής is lost in both the orthography and the pronunciation of the papyri of the Roman and Byzantine periods.[3]

2) The third person singular is φησί(ν), e.g., *POxy.* 2192.30,38 (2nd cent.); *POxy.* 2340.16 (A.D. 192); *POxy.* 2194.6 (5th/6th cent.); etc.

3) In the plural, the stem vowel -α- is retained, e.g., φαμέν *POxy.* 472.31 (ca. A.D. 130); *POxy.* 471.48 (2nd cent.); *PCairMasp.* 169.17 (6th cent.).

b. The imperfect indicative.

1) The first person singular is regular in ἔφην, e.g., *POxy.* 2981.13 (2nd cent.); *SB* 7997 = *PSI* 1259.10 (2nd/3rd cent.); *PSI* 696.5 (3rd cent.);

---

[1] Schwyzer i, 674-5, etc.; Chantraine², § 238-9, 343, etc.; *MS*, 177; Schweizer, 177; Nachmanson, 157; Mayser i², 2, 81, 83, 125-6; Crönert, 281-2; *BDF*, § 99.3.

[2] Jannaris, § 976ᵇ.

[3] φήις is in fact read in *PSI* 846 i.7 (2nd/3rd cent.), wh. seems to be a text of Ar. φής is attested in A.D. (Schwyzer i, 659, n. 7). Both forms seem to have arisen from *φᾱσι w. loss of the intervocalic -σ- to φᾱι, Ion. φηι, w. subsequent addition of -ς on the analogy of other 2 sg. endings (Chantraine², § 343).

POxy. 1469.14 (A.D. 298); *POxy.* 1101.11 (A.D. 367-70); *PCairMasp.* 87.298 part. rest. (A.D. 543); προέφην *PCairMasp.* 151-2.44 (A.D. 570).

2) The second person singular is normally ἔφης, e.g., *POxy.* 2996.30 (2nd cent.?); *MChr.* 372 v.11 (2nd cent.), as in the Ptolemaic papyri.[1] But the form ἔφησθα appears in *POxy.* 2343.9,11 (ca. A.D. 288). The -σθα ending, normal in Attic,[2] is not original here, but is a survival of the productive poetic ending -θα added simply to the usual form of the second person singular.[3]

3) The third person singular is the regular ἔφη, e.g., *POxy.* 2582.5 (A.D. 49); *SB* 6995.15 (A.D. 124); *SB* 6996.11,29 (ca. A.D. 127); *POxy.* 472.2 (ca. A.D. 130); *POxy.* 1418.20 (A.D. 247); *PGen.* 76.11 (3rd/4th cent.); *PLond.* 1708.227 (A.D. 567?); *POxy.* 1869.1 (6th/7th cent.); etc. But orthographic variations occur, including the addition of false -ι adscript in ἔφηι *POxy.* 2339. 26 (1st cent.); *SB* 7368.12,41,46 (late 2nd/early 3rd cent.), and the addition of -ν in ἔφην *PMich.* 236.3 (early 1st cent.).

4) In the plural, the stem vowel -α- is normally retained, as in ἔφαμεν *PPrinc.* 119.29 (ca. A.D. 325: *ZPE* 8 [1971], 15); ἔφασαν *POxy.* 2111.34 (ca. A.D. 135); *POslo* 17.7 (A.D. 136); *SB* 7516.14 (ca. A.D. 140-50); *BGU* 2070 R I.23 (mid 2nd cent.); *SB* 8004.5 (early 3rd cent.); *POxy.* 2276.8 (late 3rd/4th cent.); *PLond.* 1708.141,144,154, etc. (A.D. 567?); etc. But the stem vowel -η- appears in προέφημεν *PCairMasp.* 2 ii.11 (A.D. 567: *BL* i, 100).

c. The infinitive is regular in φάναι *POxy.* 2788.9 (3rd cent.); *PFlor.* 127.2 (A.D. 256).

d. The active participle is regular in φάς, e.g., *SB* 5232.32 part. rest. (A.D. 14/15), and the middle participle in φάμενος, e.g., *PRyl.* 88.27 (A.D. 156); φαμένου *BGU* 427.23 (A.D. 159); φαμένης *POxy.* 2133.29 (late 3rd cent.).

5. ἧμαι.[4]

ἧμαι occurs only in πάρημαι and in κάθημαι and double compounds.[5]

---

[1] Mayser i[2], 2, 81.

[2] E.g., Ar. Pl. X. Aeschin. D. (Veitch & *LSJ*, s.v.).

[3] Chantraine[2], § 343. Both forms are used elsewh. in the Koine. Cf. Phryn., 125 (Rutherford, 225-8); Schmid ii, 33.

[4] Schwyzer i, 127, 668, 679-89; Chantraine[2], § 240, 307, 311; Schweizer, 177; Mayser i[2], 2, 108, 125; Crönert, 263; *BDF*, § 100.

[5] In the Ptol. papp., the simple ἧμαι is still used, but only in poetry (Mayser i[2], 2, 125).

a. The second person singular indicative appears as κάθη *POxy.* 33 = *WChr.* 20 iii.13 (late 2nd cent.); *POxy.* 1160.24-25 (late 3rd/early 4th cent.), instead of the Attic κάθησαι, where the -σ- is retained because it was part of the stem (*ἠσ-σαι).[1] This form κάθη, found already in late Attic,[2] represents the beginning of the transfer of this compound to the thematic inflection, resulting in the Modern Greek κάθο(υ)μαι,[3] with consequent loss of the simple ἧμαι from the living language.

b. The other forms of this verb in the papyri are the regular Attic forms, constructed on the analogy of the apparent ἡ- stem of ἧμαι < *ἧσμαι,[4] as κάθηται *PMich.* 466.48 (A.D. 107); καθήμεθα *POxy.* 1854.10 (6th/7th cent.); καθῆσθαι *PSI* 822.12 (2nd cent.); καθήμενος *SB* 7356 = *PMich.* 203.15 (A.D. 98-117).

6. κεῖμαι.[5]

κεῖμαι occurs very frequently in composition and is conjugated regularly according to the Attic inflection in the indicative, with only orthographic variants:

ἐπίκεισαι *PRyl.* 243.7 (2nd cent.)
  κεῖται *POxy.* 1479.4 (late 1st cent. B.C.); *POxy.* 293.7 (A.D. 27);
    POxy. 114.3,11 part. rest. (2nd/3rd cent.); *POxy.* 1297.4,7,13-14
    (4th cent.); etc.
  πρόκειται, πρόκιται, passim
  κεῖνται *SB* 9213 i.6 (A.D. 215)
  διάκινται *PMich.* 464.9 (A.D. 99)

But a new contracted form of the subjunctive seems to occur in παρα-κῶντ(αι) *PFlor.* 92 = *MChr.* 223.3 (A.D. 84).[6]

An imperative κατάκου in *PGM* 13.136,695 (ca. A.D. 346) is a new form in place of κατάκεισο.[7]

Other forms are also regular with only orthographic variants, e.g., κείσθω *PCairMasp.* 97 V d.76 (6th cent.); ὑποκεῖσθαι *POxy.* 59.12 (A.D. 292); προ-κίμεναι *PMich.* 303.4 (1st cent.); ἀποκείμενα *POxy.* 1413.14 (A.D. 270-5).

This verb has been transferred to the thematic conjugation in Modern Greek in the form κείτομαι.[8]

---

[1] Schwyzer i, 668, 680.

[2] κάθη seems to be first attested in Hyp. It is used in the NT (Schwyzer i, 680; Veitch & *LSJ*, s.v.; *BDF*, § 100).

[3] Schwyzer i, 680; Mirambel, *Gram.*, 162.

[4] Schwyzer, *ibid.*

[5] Schwyzer i, 679; Chantraine[2], § 240, 304-5; Schweizer, 177; Nachmanson, 157; Mayser i[2], 2, 125; Crönert, 264; *BDF*, § 100.

[6] See Kapsomenakis, 67. For the subj., cf. προσκέωνται Hp., κατα- Luc. (Veitch, s.v.).

[7] Kapsomenakis, 66-67.

[8] Schwyzer i, 679; Jannaris, § 963; Kapsomenakis, *ibid.*

SUMMARY OF CONJUGATION

The above evidence for conjugation indicates a morphemic structure in the language of the papyri of the Roman and Byzantine periods different from that of classical Attic in the loss of certain forms, in the adoption of some elements from other dialects, and in the regularization of many inflectional paradigms.

A. AUGMENT AND REDUPLICATION

1. The occasional loss of both syllabic and temporal augment and reduplication in compounds and simple verbs, combined with the occasional transfer of augmented and reduplicated forms to other moods and tenses, indicates a degree of uncertainty about the use of these morphemes (pp. 223-48).

2. Some uncertainty is also indicated by irregularities in the place of augment and reduplication in some compound verbs (pp. 248-54).

Classical Attic Greek	Roman-Byzantine Papyri	Modern Greek
ἔγραψα {egrapsa}	(ἔ)γραψα {(e)γrapsa}	ἔγραψα {′eγrapsa}
ἐγράψαμεν {egrapsamen}	(ἔ)γράψαμεν {(e)γrapsamɛ(n)}	γράψαμε {γrapsame}
ἤθελον {ēthelon}	ἤθελον {ithɛlon}	ἤθελα {iθela}
ἔπιον {epion}	ἔπιον {epion}	ἤπια {ipia}
ἤγγειλα {ēŋgeila}	-ἤγγειλα/-ἄγγειλα/-ἔγγειλα {-i(ŋ)gila/-a(ŋ)gila/-ɛ(ŋ)gila}	ἄγγειλα {agila}
ἦλθον {ēlthon}	ἦλθον/ἔλθον {ilthon/ɛlthon}	ἦρθα {irθα}
ηὖρον {hēuron}	ηὖρον/εὖρον {(h)euron/(h)ɛuron}	ηὖρα {ivra}
ἀνήνεγκον {anēneŋkon}	ἀνήνεγκον/ἀνένεγκον/ἀνανέγκης {anini(ŋ)kon/anɛni(ŋ)kon/anani(ŋ)kis}	ἔφερα {efera}

Classical Attic Greek	Roman-Byzantine Papyri	Modern Greek
γεγραμμένος {gegr-}	(γε)γραμμένος {(jε)γτ-}	γραμμένο {γτ-}
(κ)έκτημαι {(k)ekt-}	κέκτημαι {kεkt-}	κτημένο {kt-}
ἀκήκοα {akēkoa}	ἀκήκοα/ἤκουκα	(ἔχω) ἀκούσει
ἀνέωιξα {aneōiksa}	ἤνοιξα {inyksa}	ἄνοιξα {aniksa}
ἠνάγκασα {ēnaŋkasa}	ἠνάγκασα/ἀνήγκασα	ἀνάγκασα {anagasa}
	{ina(ŋ)kasa/ani(ŋ)kasa}	

B. TENSE FORMATION

1. There is a tendency to extend a single stem vowel or consonant throughout the paradigm in many verbs whose stem was modified in the formation of tenses in classical Greek (pp. 255-71).

2. Several late present formations arising through phonetic alterations, the addition or loss of suffixes, or as a result of back-formation from other tense stems, have survived in Modern Greek or developed into other forms (pp. 271-84).

3. The tendency towards regularization led to the replacement of many contract futures by sigmatic futures, and to the elimination of some other futures formed on different stems by the formation of new futures on stems of other tenses within the paradigm (pp. 284-90).

4. The tendency towards regularization likewise led to the replacement of some ancient root aorists by new sigmatic aorists, some of which have survived in Modern Greek (pp. 290-7).

5. Considerable variation is found in the formation of the perfect stem of individual verbs, especially in competing -κ- and root perfects, aspirated perfects, and perfects formed by Attic reduplication. In addition, there is a tendency to replace the perfect by means of periphrastic constructions which led to the complete loss of the perfect system in Modern Greek except for the perfect passive participle used in similar periphrastic constructions (pp. 297-308).

6. The language of the papyri follows the preference of the Koine in general for second aorist passive formations, but some classical Attic first aorist passive formations recur in Byzantine times. The classical distribution is followed in general in Modern Greek. In addition, new aorist passive formations are found, and Ionic forms occur along with Attic forms of the aorist of δύναμαι (pp. 308-20).

Classical Attic Greek	*Roman-Byzantine Papyri*	*Modern Greek*
ἐφόρησα {ephorēsa}	ἐφόρεσα {ephorεsa}	φόρεσα {foresa}
ἐβάρυνα {ebaryna}	ἐβάρεσα {εβarεsa}	(βάρυνα {varina}
		(βάρεσα {varesa}
ἐπόνησα {eponēsa}	ἐπόνησα {eponisa}	πόνεσα {ponesa}
ἐπήινεσα {epēinesa}	(ἐπ)ήνησα {(εp)inisa}	παίνεσα {penesa}
ἐκλάπην {eklapēn}	ἐκλέπην/ἐκλάπην	κλέφτηκα {kleftika}
	{εklεpin/εklapin}	
ἐσήμηνα {esēmēna}	ἐσήμανα/ἐσήμηνα	σήμανα {simana}
	{εsimana/εsimina}	
(ἐξ)ῆραι {ērai}	(ἐξ)ᾶραι {εksarε}	ἦρα {ira}
ἐβάστασα {ebastasa}	ἐβάστασα/-ξα {εβasta(k)sa}	βάσταξα {vastaksa}
ἥρπασα {hērpasa}	ἥρπασα/-ξα {(h)irpa(k)sa}	ἄρπαξα {arpaksa}
ἐσπούδασα {espoudasa}	ἐσπούδασα {espudasa}	σπούδαξα {spuðaksa}
σεσημασμένος {-sēmasm-}	σεσημημμένος {-simim-}	σημασμένο {simasm-}
κάω {kaō}	κάω/καίω {kao/kεo}	καίω {keo}
κλάω {klaō}	κλαίω {klεo}	κλαίω {kleo}
χέω {kheō}	χέω/χύω/χοίζω	χύνω {çino}
	{khεo/khyo/khoizo}	
ἐθέλω {ethelō}	(ἐ)θέλω {(ε)thεlo}	θέλω {θelo}
αὐξ(άν)ω {auks(an)ō}	αὐξ(άν)ω {auks(an)o}	αὐξαίνω {afkseno}
δύομαι {dyomai}	δύομαι/δύνω	ντύνω {dino}
	{dyomε/dyno}	
ἀλέω {aleō}	ἀλήθω {alitho}	ἀλέθω {aleθo}
οἴγνυμι/οἴγω	ἀνοίγω {anyγo}	ἀνοίγω {aniγo}
{oiŋnymi/oigō}		
καλῶ {kalō}	καλέσω {kalεso}	θὰ καλέσω {θa kaleso}
τελῶ {telō}	τελέσω {telεso}	θὰ τελέσω {θa teleso}
ἐλπιῶ {elpiō}	ἐλπίσω {εlpiso}	θὰ ἐλπίσω {θa elpiso}
μενῶ {menō}	μενῶ {mεno}	θὰ μείνω {θa mino}
οἴσω {oisō}	οἴσω/ἐνεγκῶ {εni(ŋ)ko}	θὰ φέρω {θa fero}
σχήσω/ἕξω	ἕξω/σχῶ {(h)εkso/sk(h)o}	θὰ ἔχω {θa eχo}
{skhēsō/heksō}		
εἶμι, ἐλεύσομαι	εἶμι, ἐλεύσομαι, ἔλθω	θὰ ἔρθω {θa erθo}
ἔλιπον {elipon}	-ἔλιπον, -ἔλειψα	ἔλειψα {elipsa}
	{-εlipon, -εlipsa}	

Classical Attic Greek	*Roman-Byzantine Papyri*	*Modern Greek*
ἐκόπην {ekopēn}	ἐκόπην {εkopin}	κόπηκα {kopika}
ἐγράφην {egraphēn}	γραφθέντα, ἐγράφην	γράφ(τ)ηκα {γraf(t)ika}
ἀνεῴχθην {aneōikthēn}	ἠνοίγην {inyjin}	ἀνοίχτηκα {anixtika}
ἐβρέχθην/ἐβράχην	ἐβρέχην {εβrεkhin}	βράχηκα {vraçika}
ἐκαύθην {ekauthēn}	ἐκαύθην {εkauthin}	κάηκα {kaika}

C. VOICE

1. Analogical levelling brought about the occasional use of future actives in verbs which formed only a future middle in classical Greek (pp. 321-2).

2. Some new aorist and future passive formations appear in verbs which had only an aorist or future middle in classical Greek (pp. 322-5).

3. In addition, some classical deponent verbs occasionally have active forms (pp. 325-7).

Classical Attic Greek	*Roman-Byzantine Papyri*	*Modern Greek*
ἀκούσομαι	ἀκούσομαι/ἀκούσω	θὰ ἀκούσω
ἀπαντήσομαι	ἀπαντήσω	θὰ ἀπαντήσω
ἠσθανόμην	ἠσθάνθην	αἰσθάνθηκα
ἐγενόμην	ἐγενόμην/ἐγενήθην	γίνηκα
γενήσομαι	γενήσομαι	θὰ γινῶ
φανοῦμαι	φανήσομαι	θὰ φανῶ

D. ENDINGS

1. Analogical levelling led to a frequent interchange of endings among the various tenses and moods of thematic verbs. The endings of the first aorist are used for those of the imperfect, future, perfect, and especially second aorist; those of the present, future, and second aorist for those of the first aorist and perfect; those of the perfect for those of the second aorist. This levelling led to the simplified conjugational system of Modern Greek with its two basic sets of endings (pp. 329-57).

2. Additional analogical formations are found in individual personal endings and in the imperative and infinitive (pp. 357-63).

Classical Attic Greek	*Roman-Byzantine Papyri*	*Modern Greek*
εἶχον {eikhon}	εἶχον/εἶχα {ikhon/ikha}	εἶχα {ixa}
ἦλθον {ēlthon}	ἦλθον/ἦλθα {ilthon/iltha}	ἦρθα {irϑa}
ἔλαβον {elabon}	ἔλαβον/ἔλαβα {elabon/elaba}	ἔλαβα {elava}
ἔπαθον {epathon}	ἔπαθον/ἔπαθα {epathon/epatha}	ἔπαθα {epaϑa}
ἐγενόμην {egenomēn}	ἐγενόμην/ἐγενάμην {egenomin/egenamin}	ἔγινα {eɣina}
ἔπεμψας {epempsas}	ἔπεμψας/-ες {epempsas/-es}	ἔπεμψες {epempses}
ἔγραψας {egrapsas}	ἔγραψας/-ες {eɣrapsas/-es}	ἔγραψες {eɣrapses}
ἔδωκας {edōkas}	-έδωκας/-ες {-edokas/-es}	ἔδωκες {edokes}
πέμψον {pempson}	πέμψον/-ε(ν)/-αι {pempson/-e}	πέμψε {pempse}
μεῖνον {mcinon}	μεῖνον/-ε {minon/-e}	μεῖνε {mine}
γράψαι {grapsai}	γράψαι/-εν {ɣrapse/-i(n)}	γράψει {ɣrapsi}
δεῖξαι {deiksai}	-δείξαι/-ειν {-ðikse/-i(n)}	δείξει {ðiksi}
εἰλήφασι {eilēphāsi}	εἰλήφασι/-αν {iliphasi/-an}	—
δέδωκας {dedōkas}	δέδωκας/-ες {dedokas/-es}	—
βούληι {boulēi}	βούλη/-ει {βouli}	-εσαι {-ese}
ἐρχόμεθα {erkhometha}	ἐρχόμε(σ)θα {erkhome(s)t(h)a}	ἐρχούμαστε {erxumaste}
(ἐὰν) θέληις {thelēis}	(ἐὰν) θέλης/-εις {thelis}	(νὰ) θέλεις {ϑelis}
ἀγάγωσι {agagōsi}	ἀγάγωσι/-ων {aɣaɣosi/-on}	-ουν(ε) {-un(e)}
ἐλθόντων {elthontōn}	ἐλθέτωσαν {elthetosan}	
χαίρειν {khairein}	χαίρε(ι)ν {kherin}	—

E. CONTRACT VERBS

1. Reciprocal interference among the different classes of contract verbs is indicated to a limited degree by the identification of certain forms of -άω verbs with the corresponding -έω forms and by other occasional transfers of inflectional type (pp. 363-5).

2. Fluctuation between contract and non-contract forms of some verbs is found (pp. 365-8).

3. Some irregular verbs within the individual contract classes have been regularized either by the adoption of the predominant vowel of the contract class or by the extension of non-contract formations throughout the paradigm (pp. 368-73). -

Classical Attic Greek	*Roman-Byzantine Papyri*	*Modern Greek*
ἀγαπῶντας {agapōntas}	ἀγαπῶντας/-οῦντας {aγapo(n)tas/aγapu(n)tas}	ἀγαπῶντας/-οῦντας {aγapondas/-undas}
ἀπαντῶμεν {apantōmen}	ἀπαντῶμεν/-οῦμεν {apa(n)tomɛn/-umɛn}	ἀπαντοῦμε {apandume}
εὐχαριστοῦμεν {eukharistoumen}	εὐχαριστοῦμεν/-ῶμεν {ɛukharistumɛ(n)/-omen}	εὐχαριστοῦμε {efxaristume}
ζῆις {zēis}	ζῆ(ς) {zi(s)}	ζεῖς/ζῆς {zis}
πλεῖς {pleis}	πλέεις {pleis}	πλέεις {pleis}
δηλοῦν {dēloun}	δηλοῦν/δηλοῖν {dilun/dilyn}	δηλών(ω) {ðilono}

F. –MI VERBS

1. -μι verbs show a definite tendency towards thematic inflection, especially in the present system by use of thematic endings or thematic formations built on collateral stems, as also by similar phenomena in other tense systems (pp. 375-85, 388-90, 393-4, 413-14).

2. In addition, analogical levelling is found within the individual tense systems, especially in the extension of the first aorist and perfect formations at the expense of the second formations, and also between the different types of athematic verbs, especially between the greater -μι verbs and the athematic root aorists of thematic verbs (pp. 386-7, 390-3, 394-414).

Classical Attic Greek	*Roman-Byzantine Papyri*	*Modern Greek*
ὄμνυμι {omnȳmi}	ὄμνυμι/ὀμνύω {omnymi/omnyo}	ὀμώνω {omono}
ἵστημι {histēmi}	ἵστημι {(h)istimi} (ἰ)στά(ν)ω {(hi)sta(n)o} στήκω {stiko}	——— στήνω {stino} στέκω {steko}

Classical Attic Greek	*Roman-Byzantine Papyri*	*Modern Greek*
τίθημι {tithēmi}	τίθημι/τιθῶ {tithimi/titho}	θέτω {θeto}
ἀφίημι {aphiēmi}	ἀφίημι/ἀφίω {aphi(i)mi/aphio}	ἀφήνω {afino}
δίδωμι {didōmi}	δίδωμι/διδῶ {didomi/dido}	δίνω {ðino}
ἔδοσαν {edosan}	{ἔδωκαν {εdokan} {ἔδωσε {εdosε}	{ἔδωκαν {eðokan} {ἔδωσε {eðose}
ἔθεσαν {ethesan}	ἔθηκαν {εthịkan}	{ἔθεκαν {eθekan} {ἔθεσαν {eθesan}
ἄφεισαν {apheisan}	ἄφηκαν {aphikan}	{ἄφηκαν {afikan} {ἄφησαν {afisan}
δός {dos}	δός/δές {dǝs}	δῶσ(ε) {ðos(e)}
στῆθι {stēthi}	-στα {-sta}	—
βῆθι {bēthi}	-βα {-βa}	-έβα {-eva}
εἰμί {eimi}	εἰμί/ἦμε {imi/imε}	εἶμαι {ime}
εἶ {ei}	εἶ/εἶσαι {i/isε}	εἶσαι {ise}
ἐστί {esti}	ἐσ(τ)ί/ἔνι {εs(t)i/εni}	εἶναι {ine}
ἐσμέν {esmen}	ἐσμέ(ν) {εsmε(n)}	εἴμαστε {imaste}
ἦ(ν) {ē(n)}	-ήμην {imin}	εἴμουν(α) {imun(a)}

INDEX OF GREEK WORDS AND FORMS

Words are listed in their dictionary form, followed by the forms in which they appear in the grammar. Compound verbs are listed only under the simple verb if it is in use, unless the preverb itself is affected.

'Ααρών indecl. 104

ἀβαρής: ἀβαρός (for -ές) 138

ἀββᾶς: ἀββᾶς, gen. ἀββᾶ, ἀβᾶ, dat. ἀββᾷ, acc. ἀββᾶ, ἀβᾶν, ἀββᾶν (for dat.) 20

'Αβδέλλ(α) indecl. 104

'Αβίκλας: gen. 'Αβίκλα 13

ἀβλαβής: ἀβλαβῆν 135, ἀβλαβές (for fem.) 137

ἀβόλλης *abolla*: ἀβόλλης, -ην 15-16

'Αβραάμ: 'Αβραάμ indecl. 104, 'Αβραάμις 25 n. 2, 'Αβρααμίου, -ίῳ 104

ἀβροχέω: ἠβροχηκυίης 132

ἄβυσσος: ἡ ἄβυσσος, τῆς ἀβύσσου, τὴν ἄβυσσον 38 n. 2

ἀγαθός: ἀγαθωτάτῳ, ἀγαθότατον, ἀγαθώτατον, ἀγαθοτάτην 146-7

ἀγαπάω: ἀγαποῦμεν, ἀγαπούντων, ἀγαποῦντας 363, ἠγαπημενότ[ερον] 146

ἀγγέλλω: παράγγειλα[ς], παρέγγιλα, παρεγγέλθην 233, ιmpt.? παράνγιλεν 351, παρεγγέλθην *sic*, παραγγελθείς; -ηγγέλη, -αγγελῆναι, ἀγγελεῖς, etc. 313

ἀγήρως: ἀγέρον (for -ων acc:), ἀγή[ρ]ως 126 & n. 2

ἀγοράζω: ἀγοράννο 280, προσαγο[ρ]άσωι 287, ἠγόρασες 348, ἐγόρακα 233, ἠγόρακες 353, ἀγώρακαν 233, 355

ἀγορεύω: ὑπαγόρευσα, ὑπεγόρευσα, -έσαμεν 233, ἀπηγορευομένου 234

ἀγράμματος: ἀγρά|μου (for -μάτου) 90

'Αγρίππας: gen. 'Αγρίππα 13

ἄγω: impt. ὗπα 391, infin. μετάγει 330, ἦξα, ἄξω, -άξοιμι, -άξατε, ἄξαι, -άξας, ἄξασθαι, -ήγαγον, ἀγάγης, ἀγάγε, -αγαγεῖν, ἀγαγών, etc. 290 & n. 6, 291, [ἀ]-πήγαγα 343, ἀγάγων (for -ωσι) 359, ἀγείοχα, -αγείωχα, -αγέωκα, -ηγείωχας, -αγιωχέναι, -αγιοχότας etc. 302, ἀγείοχαν 354

ἀγωνιάω: ἀγωνιοῦμεν 363

'Αδάμ indecl. 104

ἀδελφιδοῦς: ἀδελφιδοῦς, -οῦ, -ῷ, -οῦ(ν), -οῖ, -ῶν, -οῖς, -οῦς, ἀδελφιδέος 36, τοῦ ... ἀδελφιδοῦς, τῷ ... ἀδελφιδῇ (= -εῖ?), ὁ ... ἀδελφιδός 37

ἀδιαίρετος: διῃρέτων 237

ἀδιαφορέω: ἀδιαφορηθῆναι 257

ἀδιούτωρ *adiutor*: ἀδιούτορος, -ορι 48

'Λειάν indecl. 104

ἄθλιος: ἀθλίας gen., ἀθλίαν 105

ἀθρός: ἀθρόον, ἀθρῶων, ἀθρῶως, ἀθρός 121

Αἰγόκερως: Αἰγόκερως, gen. -κερωι (-κερως), dat. -κερω(ι) etc., acc. -κερω(ι) 32

Αἴγυπτος: τῇ Αἰγύπτῳ, τὴν Αἴγυπτον 38

αἰδώς: αἰδοῦς, αἰδοῖ, αἰδῶ 69

αἰκίζω: ἠκίσατο, -αντο 237

Αἴλουρᾶς: gen. Αἰλουρᾶ, dat. -ᾷ 16

Αἰνείας: Αἰνείου 12

αἰνέω: συνήνεσεν, [συ]ναινέσαντ[ο]ς, παραινέσαι, ἐπαινεθήσει 259

αἴξ: αἴγαν 45, acc. αἴγες 47

αἶρα: αἴρης 5

αἱρέω: αἱρῇ 358, αἱρῶται (for -ῆται) 364 n. 2, ἀναιλούμεθα (for ἀνήρ-) 237, ἀφελοῦμαι 287 n. 3, [ἀ]φήρησαν, ἀφαιρήσας, ἀναιρῆσαι, αἱρήσασθαι 292 & n. 1, διῖλον 235, ἑλών 292, ἕλοιτο, ἀφελέσθαι 293, εἴλατο, -άμεθα, -ασθε, -αντο, -άμενος etc. 344-5, εἰλάσθαι 234, διαιρήκαμεν 237, διείρημαι, -ίρημαι, -ήρημαι etc. 238-9, ἀνταναίρησαι 237

αἴρω: ὑπεραιρούντων *sic* 367, συναρεῖται 305 n. 4, ἄρης, ἄρη, ἄρον (ἄρρον), ἄραι, ἄρας etc. 264 n. 2, 265, ἄρεν impt.? 351, ἤροσαν 345, ἤρκες 354, [σ]υνῆρσμαι, συνῆρσθαι etc. 305

αἰσθ(άν)ομαι: αἰσθέσθωσαν, ἔσθη (for αἴσ-

ῥήσι[ς], ἐβάρησα, βεβαρημένη, βαρηθῶσιν etc. 258, βαρεθῆναι also 261 n. 2

βαρύς: βαρυτάτης. -η, -ην 147

βάσανος: τὰς βασάνους, βάσανα 40

βασιλεύς: βασιλός (nom.), -έων 86

βασκαύλης *vasculum*: πασκαύλιν, pl. βάσκυλα 24

βαστάζω: ἐβάσταζαν 332, βαστάξεις, ἐβάσταξα, βάσταξον, βαστάξαι, βαστάξαντες, ἐβάστασε, βαστάσης, βαστασάντων, ἐβαστάχθη, διαβασταγῆναι etc. 265 & n. 3, 266

βάτελλα *patella*: βατέλλης 9; see also πάτελλον

βαφεύς: βαφῖ 85

βέβαιος: βεβαία, -αν, acc. pl. -ας 109

βεβαιόω: βεβαιοῖν 372, βαιώσω 242 n. 3, infin. βεβαιώσι 334

βεβαίωσις: gen. βεβεωσης 75, dat. βαιώση 242 n. 3

βέλτιστος: βελτίστου, -η, -ον, -α etc. 155

βελτίων: βελτίου (for dat.), -ίονα, -(ε)ιον 152

βενεφικιάριος *beneficiarius*: βενεφικιᾶρις 27

βεστίον/βέστη *vestis* 23 n. 3

Βησᾶς: gen. Βησᾶ & -ᾶτος, dat. -ᾷ 17

βιάρχης: gen. βιάρχη 14

βιβάζω: ἐκβιβάσω 287, ἐμβάσαι 242 n. 3

βίβλος: fem. βίβλου, -ῳ 38

βικεννάλιον *vicennale* 50

Βικτωρίνη: Βικτωρίνη, -ης, Βικτορίνης 10; see also Οὐικτωρείνα

βίος: τὸ βίον 42

βιόω: βιοῖν 372, βιοῦντες (for dat.) 131, συμβιούτωσαν 361, βίω(σεν) 225, ἐβίωσεν, βιώσας, βιωσάντων, ἀπεβιώσατο, ἐβίω, βιῶναι 293

Βίων 65

βλάβος: τοῦ ... βλάβος 66, βλάβεσσι 47

βλάπτω: βλαπτουμένο(υ) 368, ἔβλαψες 348, καταβεβλαμένα *sic* 246, ἐβλάβην, βλαβήσεται etc. 311-12

βοηθέω: ἔχει βοηθῆσαι 290, ὦ βεβοηθημένος 305

βοΐδιον: βούδια & βο(ε)ίδια, βουδίῳ[ν] 82 n. 4

βορρᾶς: βορρᾶ nom. & gen., dat. -ᾷ, acc. -ᾶ & -ᾶν, cf. mag. βορέας, -έᾳ, -έαν 20 & n. 3, 21

βότρυς: βότρυας 80

βουκελλάριος *bucellarius* 24

βουκελλάτης *bucella*: βουκελλατῶν 24

βούλομαι: βούλει/βούλη (indic. & subj.) 357 & n. 4, 358, βούλεις, -ης, -ητε, β[ο]υλήσης 326, ἠβούλετο, ἐβουλόμην, ἐβουλήθην etc. 229, ἐβουλήθημεν, -ητε, -ησαν 230, ἐβουλήθην, βουληθησομέν[ην] 322, βουληθείοις 361

βοῦς: βοός, βοῦν, βόες, βοῶν, βοῦσι & βόεσι, βόας & βόες etc. 47, 82-83

βοωτρόφος: βοωτρόφος 82 n. 4

βραδύς: βραδύτερον, -α 147

βραχύς: βραχύτατον, -ων, -ας 147

βρέουιον *breve* 50

βρέχω: ἐβ[ρέχ]η, ἐβρέχησαν, βρεχέντων, βρεχήσεται 314 & n. 2

βύσσος: masc. βύσσου 39

βῶλος: masc. βῶλ(ου) 39

Γάλβα/Γάλβας *Galba*: gen. Γάλβα 13

γαμέω: προεγάμουσαν 331, ἐγάμησες, γαμῆσαι, γαμήσασα, ἔγημα, γῆμαι, γήμαντα etc. 294 & n. 1, ἐγαμήθην, γαμηθῇ, -θῆναι, -θεῖσα etc. 322-3

γάμος: γάμον γάμον 211

γάριον: γάριον, γαρίου, γάρια 99

γάρος/γάρον/τὸ γάρος: ὁ γάρος, γάρου, γάρον; γάρους, acc. γάρος 99

γέλως: γέλωτα, γέλωσι 69

Γέμελλα: gen. Γεμέλλης & -ας 11

γεμίζω: ἐγέμησεν 262

γένημα: γενημάτου 44

γένυς: γένι (for γένυν) 80

γεοῦχος: τῆς γεούχου, τῇ & τῷ γεούχῳ 41

γεραιός: γερα(ίτερος) 149

γέρανος: masc. γεράνους 40

γέρας: γερῶν, γέρα 69

γέρδιος: γέρδιος & γέρδις, γερδίωι, γέρδιν 27

Γέτας *Geta*: gen. Γέτα 13

γεύω: γεγευσαμένους 243

γέφυρα: γεφύρης, -η 5

γεωργέω: γεωργηκ[ότ]ων 243

Γεώργιος: Γεώργις 25 n. 2

γί(γ)νομαι: γενέσοντε (for -ήσονται) 296, γενήσεται, -εσθαι, -όμενον etc. 324, ἐπιγενησομέ[ν]ων 325, παραγένω 326, παραγεν[ό]μην 224, ἐγενάμην, γενάμενος etc. 344 & n. 1, γένοιτο 360, γέγονε, γεγονέναι, γεγένηται 300, γέγοναν 355, γεγόνει 224, γεγόνασμεν 268, γεγονυ(ε)ίης, -η, -ην 132,

133, εἶναι ... γεγονυῖαι 306, γεγονησ[ό]-
μενον 307

γι(γ)νώσκω: ἀνάγνω 224, γνώσκς, ἀνέγνωσα, γνώσωμεν, ἀνέγνων, γνῶ, γνῶθι, γνῶναι etc. 294, γνῶς, γνοῖς, ἐπιγνοῖ etc. 389,
γνοίης 390 n. 5, γνοῦναι etc. 393, διαιγνωσκέναι (= διε-) 268

γῆρας: gen. γήρους & γήρως, dat. γήρᾳ,
γήρι, γήρῳ 68

γλεῦκος: gen. γλεύκου 43

γλυκύς: κλυκύου (for γλυκέος) 127, [γλ]ύ-
κιον 152, γλυκυτάτηι nom. 116, γλυκυτάτη, -ης, -οις 147-8

γλύφω: γεγλ[υμ]μένους 246

γναφεύς: γναφέος, γναφέα 85, γναφέων 86

γνάφισσα: γναφίσᾳ 6

γνάφω: ἐγνάφη, γναφῶσιν, κναφήτω 316

γνωρίζω: γνωριεῖς, γνωριεῖται (for -τε) 286

γνώριμος: γνωρίμην 109

γόμος: γόμ(ον) μίαν, τὸν γόμον 42

γονεύς: γονέων, γονέοιν, γονεῦσι, acc. γονεῖς
& γονέας etc. 86

γόνυ: γόνατι, [γ]ούνατι etc. 91

γραῖα: γρεᾶ 81

γράμμα: γράμμα (for pl.), γράμματα (for
sg.) 89

γραμματεύς: gen. γραμματέου 44, γραμματέος, -έους, -έα 85, acc. γραμματεῖς 86

γραῦς: γραῦς, γραός, γραῦν, γραῶν 81

γράφω: εἰμὶ γράφων 284, ἤμελλα ... γράφειν
(= ἔγραφον) 284, ἤγραψ[α] 231, ὑπώγραψα, γράψεν 224, indic. γράψας 225, διάγραψεν, κατάγραψεν 223, ἔγραψες 348,
354, subj. γράψω 289, impt. γράψο,
γράψα 350, impt. (?) κατάγραψεν, διέγραψεν 351, infin. γράψεν 352, infin.
[γρά]ψει 353, ἀπεγραψόμην 349, ἀπεγράψου 349, ἀναγράψασθαι, ἀναγράψεσθ[α]ι
333, ἤμεθα, ἦσαν γράψαντες 306, γεγρά-
φηκα, -ας etc. 297, γεγράφεκα 261 n. 2,
γεγράφηκες 354, γεγραφήκειν, γεγράφειν
etc. 224, γεγράφηκεν, -ήκειν, -ηκέναι,
-ηκώς, γέγραφα, -φέναι, -φώς etc. 298,
γέγραφα, γέγραμμαι, ἐπεγραμμένῳ, ἐγραμμένον 246 & n. 1, pf. διαγέγραφης, -γέγρα-
φαν 354, infin. ἀντ[ιγ]εγρ[α]φέν 356, ὑπογεγραφυίης 132, γραμένος 242, ἦν γεγραμμένα, γεγραμμένα εἴη 306, διεγράφην,
γραφήτω, -ῆναι, γραφέντα & γραφθέντα

etc. 308 & n. 1, παρεσυνγραφῇ 252,
διαγεγραφεῖσαι 243

γύης/γύος: nom. γύης, gen. γύου & γύοου,
dat. γύωι & γύει, acc. γύν, γῆν; cf. γύης,
γύας 94 & n. 4, 95

γυνή: γυνή (for gen.), γυνή/γυνῇ (for dat.)
52, γυναῖκαν 45, acc. γυναῖκες 46

γυψίον: γυψίον, γύψιος (= γυψίου?) 102

γύψος: τῆι γύψοι, τὸν & τὴν γύψον, τὸ γύπσος
40, γύψου, τὸν γύψον, τὸ γύπσος 101

δάκρυ: δάκρυσιν 80

δαλματική *dalmatica*: δαλματική, -κῆς etc.,
δελματικόν, -κά 8-9, δερματίκιν 28

δάμαλις: δ[ά]μαλις, δάμαλιν etc., δαμάλην,
δαμάλ(αι) 77

δανίζω: δεδανικυίη 133

Δανιήλ/Δανιήλιος: gen. Δανιήλ, Δανιηλίου,
-ίῳ 104

δαπανάω: δαπανάσης, -ήσης 256

δαπάνημα: δαπάνημα (for pl.) 89

Δαυίδ: Δαυείδ indecl. 104

δείδω: δείδω, δεδειώς etc., δεδοικώ[ς] 299

δείκνυμι: -δείκνυμι, -υς, -υ, -ύς, -υσθε,
-υνται etc., δεικνύω, -ύεις, -ύει, -ύειν,
-ύων, -ύμενος etc. 377 & n. 2, 378,
ἀποδειγμένου 242, ἀποδείξειν 352, ἀπο-
δείξειεν 360, ἐπειδιχθέντων 131

δεῖνα: nom. δ(ε)ῖνα, gen. δῖνος/δ(ε)ίνατος,
dat. τῖνι (for δεῖνι), acc. δ(ε)ῖνα, indecl.
δεῖνα, δῆνα etc. 182 & n. 2

δεῖπνον (τό): δῖπνον 96

δεκαδύο, see δώδεκα

δεκαείς, see ἕνδεκα

δεκαεννέα: δεκαεννέα 196

δεκαέξ: δεκαέξ 196

δεκαεπτά: [δ]εκαεπτά 196

δεκαοκτώ: δεκαοκτώ, δεχοκτώ 196

δεκαπέντε: δεκαπέντε 196; see also πεντεκαίδεκα

δεκατέσσαρες: δεκατέσσαρες, -τέσσαρα, -τεσ-
σάρων, -τέσσαρας 195

δεκατρεῖς: δεκατρεῖς, -τριῶν 195

δέκατος: δέκα (for δεκάτη), τρί[τ]ο[υ καὶ]
δεκάτο[υ], τετάρτη καὶ δεκάτη, πέμπτον
καὶ δέκατον 202 & n. 4

δέλτα: τοῦ, τῶι Δέλτα 103

δέλτος: ἡ & ὁ δέλτος 40 & n. 7

δέν negative 186

δένδρον (τό): δέδρον *sic*, δένδρα 102

νόμην, ἠδυνήθην/ἠδυνάσθην, οἰδηνήθημεν etc. 230, ἐδυνάμην, ἐδυνήθην, αἰδυνήθημεν etc. 231, ἠδυνήθην/ἠδυνάσθην etc. 318 & n. 4, 319, δυνηθείης 361

δύ(ν)ω: δύνει, δύνων etc., ἔνδυνε, ἀναδύομα[ι], ἀνεδύετο, ἐνδεδύσ[ε]τε, ἐνδιδύσκειν 279 & n. 2, ἤμην ἐνδεδυμένο<ς> 306

δύο: ἅπαξ δύο (= δίς) 210, δύο δύο 211, δύο/δύω 186, δύωι, δύοι, δύας, δύα, gen. δύο, δύω, δούω 187, δυοῖν, δυεῖν, δυῶν, δυσ(ε)ί(ν) 188, δυσ(ε)ί, δύο (dat.) 189, δυοῖν 3

δυ(ο)τριακοστόν: δυοτριακοστόν, δυοδριακοστόν, -τοῦ, δυοτρ(ε)ίαντον, δυτριακοστόν, -τοῦ, δυδριακοστόν, -τοῦ 207

δυσχεραίνω: ἐδυσχέρανεν 264

δυσωπέω: ἐδυσωπήσαμεν 248 n. 2

δώδεκα: δώδεκα, δυόδεκα, δωούδεκα, δεκαδύο, -δύω, -δίου, -δυσί 195

δωδέκατος: δωδέκατον 206, δωτέκ(α)τ(ον) 207, δωδεκάτου, δυωδέκατον, δυο-, δωδεκάδου 202

Δῶμνα: Δῶμνα, Δόμνη 9

ἑαυτοῦ: ἑα(υ)τούς, ἑαυτῆς etc. 1 pers. reflex. pron. 167-8, ἁτῶν, ἑαυτούς, ἑατήν etc. 2 pers. reflex. pron. 169, ἑαυτῶν, ἑαυτός, ἑαυτό etc. for pers. pron. 170 & n. 6, 171, ἑαυτούς etc. for reciprocal pron. 171

ἐάω: ἔασα, ἔασε(ν), εἰάσης, εἴασες 235 & n. 3, ἐάσαι, εἴασα 255

ἑβδομήκοντα: εὑδόκοντα 198, ὁδ(δ)ομήκοντα, ἑχδεμήκοντα, ἑπτύκοντα 197 & n. 7

ἑβδομηκοστόδυος: ἑβδομηκοστοδύο 209

ἕβδομος: ἑβδόμη 205

ἐγγενής: ἐνγενούς 138

ἐγγίζω: ἔγγισαν 234

ἔγγιστος: ἔγγιστος, -η <ς>, ἔγγιστα etc. 155

ἔγγραφος: ἐγγέγραφον 243 n. 1

ἐγγυάω: ἐνγυοῦμε (for -ῶμαι), -ούμεθα, -ῆσθαι (for -εῖσθαι) 363, ἐνεγύησας, -άμην, ἐνγεγύημαι etc. 252, ἐνεγυήκα[μεν] 244

ἔγγυος: fem. ἐνγύου 41

ἐγδοχεύς: ἐγδοχέων, acc. -εῖς 86

ἔγκυος: fem. ἐνκύου 111 n. 3

ἐγώ: ἐμοῦ, ἐμέ, με, μοι, ἐμέν(α)(ν) 161-2, ἐγώ (for acc.) 163

ἐθελοκακέω: ἐθελοκακεῖν 277

ἐθέλω, see θέλω

εἶδος: εἴδεσσι 47

εἰκάς: εἰκάς, πέντε καὶ εἰκάδι, [ἑβδό]μην καὶ εἰκάδα 205

εἰκοσαπεντάρουρος: εἰκοσαπενταρούρων 193

εἴκοσι: εἴκοσι μιᾶς, τέσσαρες 196

εἰκοσιπέντε: πέντε καὶ εἴκοσι 196

εἰκοσιτέσσαρες: dat. -ες 193

εἰκοσιτέταρτος: εἰκοσιτοτα|σαρακοσογδ(οον) 209

εἰκοστόγδοος: εἰκοσθόγδ[οον] 208

εἰκοστός: ἑνὸς καὶ εἰκοστοῦ, πρώτου καὶ εἰκοστοῦ etc., δευτέρας κίκοστῆς, εἰκοσεβδόμωι, εἴκοσι ἑβδόμου 204

εἰκοστοτέταρτος: εἰκ(οσ)τ(οτέταρτον) 207

εἴκω: εἶξα 237

εἰκών: ἰκόνος, εἰκόνα, εἰκόνες, ἰκόνων, εἰκόνας 65

εἴλη: εἴλαν 4

εἰμί: ἤμε, -ιμαι, ἰμεί, εἶ, ἴ, εἶς, εἶσαι etc. 400, ἐσσί 401, ἔν(ε)ι 401-2, ἐσμέ(ν), (εἰ)σίν, ἔνουσι(ν), ἤμην 402, ἧς, ἧσ(θ)α(ς), ἦν, ἦ 403, ἦ(σ)μεν, ἤμεθα, ἦ(σ)τε, -ῆσαν, ἦσιν, ἦσει, εἶσαν, ὦμε, ἧς, ἦσα 404, ἦν sub'., ὤμεθα, ὦσ(ε)ιν 405, εἴην, εἴημαι, εἴοι(το) etc. 406, ἔστω, ἤτω, ἐσθέτω, εἶν<αι>, ἔση etc. 407, ἔσει 408, παρούσᾳ 132, ὄντες (for fem.) 130, ἔση 358, ἔσασθαι 333

εἶμι: εἶμι fut. 289, (ε)ἴμι, μετήειν, ἀπήειμεν, πρόσιθι, ἀπ(ε)ίτω, προσίτωσαν, ἐπιέναι, προῖναι, ἐξιών etc. 408, ἐπιέναι 289, εἰσιόντος, -ούσης 288, τοὐπιόν, ἐξιόντα, ἐπειόντα 409, ἀνιοῦσιν 289

εἴργω: καθεῖρξαν 237

εἷς: for τις, for def. art. 181, ἕνα neut. 183-4, ἔναν 184, ἔνον, ἔνες, μίας acc.?, μία neut.? 185, ἀνὰ ἓν ἕν 210, μίαν 211, μίαν ἥμισυ 205

εἰσάκτης: εἰσάκτον 15

ἐκεῖνος: ἐκεῖνο 177

ἐκκαιδέκατος: ἐκκαίδεκα (for -άτου) 204, ἐκκαιδεκάτου, -τον, ἐξκαιδεκάτου etc. 203

ἑκούσιος: ἑκουσίου, -ίῳ, -ιον, -ίᾳ 111

ἔκπλους: ἔκπλουν 34

ἑκών: ἑκών (for fem.) 113

ἐλάδιον: *eladi* (ἐλάδι) 28

ἐλασσόω: ἐλαττουμένου 130

ἐλάσσων: ἐλάσσονος, -ονι, ἔλασσον, ἐλάσσω, ἐλάττω etc. 152

λίμης *limes*: λιμήτ[ο]υ, λιμίτου, λιμέτου, Λιμίτου 49

λίμνος: τῆς λίμνου 39

λιμός: τῇ λιμῷ, λειμοῦ γεν[ομ]ένου, τῷ ... λιμῷ 41

λιμπάνω: παραλειμπά[ν]ω, καταλιμπάνειν, καταλιμπάνων, ἀπολειμπάνεσθαι, ἀπολειμπανόμενον etc. 278 & n. 2

λινοῦς: λινᾶ (for -ῆ) 115, λινῆ, -οῦ, -οῦν, -ῆν, -οῦς etc. 117

λιτουργέω: λιτουργήσαντ[α] 334

λίτρα: λί(τρα) χωρικά, τὸ λί(τρον) etc. 4, gen. λείτρης & λείτρας 5

λίψ: τὸ λίβυς 48

λογάριον: λογάριν 28

λογίζομαι: λογιζάμενος 329, ἀπελογησά[μην] 262

Λουκίλλα *Lucilla*: Λουκίλλη[ς], -ᾳ 11

Λύκαινα: Λυκαίνης, -ῃ, -αν 9

Λυκαρίαινα: Λυκαρίαινα, -ης 9

λυπέω: λοιποῦ[με]ν 326, ἐλυπήθην etc. 323

λυχναψία: λυχναψί<α>ν 4

λωδίκιον (*lodix*): λωδῖκιν 27

λωρῖκα *lorica*: λωρεῖκος nom., λωρίκαν, -ων 8

Μααμήτ indecl. 104

μαγίς: acc. μαγίδες 46

μαγίστερ/μαγίστρος/μαγίστωρ *magister*: μαγίστερ, μαγίστρου, μαγίσστορος, μαγίστερος, μαγίστρω, μαγίστωρι, μαγίστερι, μαγίστερα, μάγιστρε voc., μαγίστρων, μαγίστερσι 23-24

μαγιστρότης *magistratus*: μαγιστρότητος 50

μάγκιψ *manceps*: μάγκιψ 49

Μαικήνας: gen. Μαικήνα 13

μαίνομαι: ἐμηνά[μ]ην 264, συνμανῆναι 309

μάκαρ: voc. μάκαρ 142 n. 3

μακάριος: μακαρίας gen. 106, [μ]ακαριωτάτης 155 n. 3

Μακάριος: nom. Μακάρις, Μακάρι, gen. Μακάρι 26

μακάριστος: μακάριστος 155 n. 3

Μακρῖνα: Μακρῖνα, Μακρίνας 10

μακροφυής: μακροφυοῦ[ν] 138

Μαλλίτης: gen. Μαλλίτη & Μαλλίτου 14

μανδήλη *mantele*: μανδήλην 8

μανθάνω: ἔμαθα, -αμεν, -αν 343, μάθοιμι 360, μαθότες 347

μᾶνιξ *manica*: μάνικες 9

Μαξίμα: Μαξίμα, gen. -ας & -ης, dat. -ᾳ & -ῃ 11

Μαρεψῆμις: nom. Μαρεψῆμις, gen. -ήμιος & -ήμεως 79

Μαριάμ/Μαρία: Μαριάμ indecl., Μαρία, -ίας, -ίᾳ 104

Μαρκέλλα: Μαρκέλλης, -αν 9

Μαροέμμα: Μαροέμμα 10

Μαρρῆς: gen. Μαρρήους, -είους, -έους, -ήου, dat. Μαρῆτι, acc. Μαρρῆν 74

μαρτυρέω: διεμαρτυρήσου 349

μαρτυροποιέω: ἐμαρτυροποιεῖτο 248 n. 2

μάρτυς: μάρτυς, -υν, -υρα, -υρες, -ύρων, -υσι, -υρας 63 & n. 4, nom. μάρτυρος, acc. -ων (for -ον), dat. -οις 64

μασγιδᾶς: gen. μασγιδᾶ 19

μαστιγόω: μαστιγοῖν 372

Ματρέας: gen. Ματρέου & Ματρέα 13

ματρῶνα *matrona*: ματρώνας, -ᾳ 7

μαφόρ(τ)ιον *maforte*: μαφόρτιν 27, μαφόρ(τ)ιον 50

μαχαιρᾶς: μαχερᾶς, μαχαιρᾶ 19

μάχομαι: μάχουσιν (for subj.) 326, μαχεσάμην 224, μαχησάμην 260, μαχεσθῆναι 260, 323

μεγαλόπολις: gen. μεγαλωπόλεος 75

μεγαλοπρεπής: μεγαλοπρεπεστάτου 148

μεγαλοφυής: μεγαλοφυῆ 137

μέγας: μεγάλου, μέγαν, indecl. μέγα 143 & n. 3, μείζονος, μίσονος, μίζονα, μείζω etc. 153, μειζότερος, -ᾳ, -ου, -(ῳ), -ῃ, -ον, -αις 158, μεγάλου μεγάλου 159, μεγίστη, -ον, -ε, -ων, [-ας] 156, μεγιστότατος 158

μ(ε)ίγνυμι/μίσγω: καταμίσ[γ]ουσι, μίσγε, σμίγων, συμμίσγεται, μί[σ]γεσθα[ι], περιμίγνυνται, μιγνύναι, μείγνυσθ[αι], ἐπιμιγνύων 281 & nn. 1, 3, ἐμίγη, μίγητι, παραμιγήτω, μιγῆναι etc. 312 & n. 2

μείζων, see μέγας

μείνω: ὑπόμεινε, περίμεινε 350

μείς/μήν: μείς 65, μῆναν 46, μῆνον 44, μῆναις (= -ες for -ας) 47

μελαγχρής: μελανχρής 123

μελάγχρους: μελάγχρους 123

μελανόχροος/-χρους/-χρως: μελανόχροον, -χρου, -χρουν, -χρωτα 123

μέλας: [μέ]λας, μέλανος, μέλανα, -ας, μελαίνης, -αν etc., μέλαν, μελάν[ων] 129, μελανόν, -οῦ, -ῆς, -ήν, -ῶν 130 & n. 1

πλακουντᾶς: πλακουντᾶ, -ᾷ, -ᾶν & -ᾶ,
-ᾶσ(ι) 19
πλανάω: διαπλανῶναι (for -ῆσαι) 364 n. 2,
πεπλάνηκαν 355
πλατύς: πλατύτερον 147
πλείων: πλείονος, -ονα, πλεῖον, πλέον, πλῆον,
πλείονες, οἱ/αἱ πλείους, πλ(ε)ίονα, -όνων,
-οσι, -ονας, τὰς πλείους/πλείως, τὰ πλείω/
πλύω(ι), πλείω ἔλατ[το]ν, πλεοέλαττον,
πλέω ἔλαττον 153-4, πλεωτέραν, πλειοτέραν 158
πλεῖστος: πλείστου, -ον, -α, -οις 157
πλέκω: ἐξεπλέκη 312
πλέω: πλέετ[ε] impt., πλέειν, ἀναπλεῖ,
πλεῖν, πλεῖσθαι etc. 371 & n. 1, πλοῦντα,
ἀναπλέοντα etc. 372, ἀναπλεύσω, -σειν,
-σοντα 322, ἔπλευσες 348
πλήρης: indecl. πλήρης 138 n. 6, 139,
πλήρ(ε)ις, πλήρη, -εσι, -ες etc. 139, gen.
πλήρου & -ος, -ους, acc. pl. fem. πλήρους, neut. pl. πλῆρα; πληράτου, πλήρατα
140, πληρεστάτῳ 148
πληροφορέω: πληροφορήσω subj., [π]ληρο-
φορέσαι 257
πληρόω: πληροῖ(ν), ἀναπληροῖν 372, πλήρωσεν 225, πεπλήρωσα 244, ἐπλήρωκα,
ἐπληρῶσθ[αι] 243, πεπλήρωμαι, πεπλη-
ρῶσθαι 246
πλήσσω: πληγῆς, πληγ[ῆ]ναι & ἐκπλαγῆναι,
πληγέντες, ἐκπλαγήσει, ἐπιπλ[η]χθῆναι,
-πληχθέντος, -θήσηι etc. 309 & n. 3
πλίνθος: fem. πλίνθου, -ον, -οις, -ους, masc.
πλίνθους 41 & n. 3
πλοῖον: πλοίῳ, πλοῖν, πλῦν 28
πλοῦς: πλοῦ 33, πλοῦν 34
πλοῦτος: masc. πλούτου, -ῳ, -ον, neut.
πλοῦτος, -ει 100
πνέω: συμπνέειν, πνεέτω 371 & n. 3
πόθεν for ὅθεν 182
ποιέω: ποιωμένη 364, fut. ποιησάμεν[ο]ν
334, ἐποίησες 348, ἐποίησου 349, ποιήσιας, -ιεν 360, ποίησε 351, ποιησσέτω,
infin. ποιῆσεν 352, ptc. ἐποιήσας 225,
ἔσῃ ... πο[ι]ήσας 307, πεποί<η>κες 354,
πεποίηκαν 355, πεποίηκειν 224, ποιηκώς
243
ποιμήν: ποιμένον 44
ποῖος: ποίου, ποῖον & ποῖν 182
πόλις: gen. πόλις & πόλιος 75
Πολυκράτης: Πολυκράτους, -ην 70

πολύς: neut. πολύν 143, πολλύς, -ύν, -ύ 144
πολλὰ πολλὰ πολλά 21
πονέω: ἐπόνη[σα], [πο]νήσαντι, ἐκπονέσασιν
καταπεπονῆσθαι, -πονηθῆναι 259
πορεύομαι: πορεύσομαι 325
πόρτα *porta*: πόρτα, πώρτας 7
πορτᾶς: πορτᾶ(τος) 19
πόρτος *portus*: Πόρτου, -ον 25
πορφυροῦς: πορφυροῦς, -ᾶ, -οῦν, -ῆν, -ῶν,
φόρφυρεν etc. 118, πορφυρῆν 115
πόσος: πόσον, πόσου, ποσ[άσδε] (for τοσάσδε) 182
ποταμίτης: ποτ[α]μίτοις 15
ποταμοφυλακίς: ποταμοφυλακίδου 44
ποταμός: neut. ποταμόν 43
ποτίζω: ἐποτίζαμ(εν) 332, ἧς ποτίσας 306
πού as rel. pron. (dbtfl.) 179 n. 6
πούς: ποδός fem. 48, πόδον 44
πρᾶγμα: indecl. 89, gen. pl. πράγμων 90,
κατὰ πρᾶγμα πρᾶγμα 211
πράκτωρ: acc. πράκτορες 47
πρᾶξις: gen. πράξεος 75, 85
πρᾶος: παρᾶος, πρᾶον, πρᾶως, πραΰς, πραΰν,
πρηΰν 144 & n. 2
πρᾶσις: gen. πρᾶσις & πράσιο(ς) 75
πράσσω: πράξει for subj. 358, εἰσπράξαντο
224, acc. διαπράξαντες 131, ἧς πεπρα-
κώς 305
Πρεῖσκα: Πρείσκας 10
πρεσβευτής: πρεσβευτής, -τοῦ, -τῇ, -τήν 93
πρέσβυς: πραίβυς, πρέσβεα, nom. & acc.
πρέσβεις, πρέσβεων & πρέβεων 93, πρέσβεα, πρέσβεων 81, πρεσβύτερος, -ου, -αν
147, πρεσβυτερωτέρα 157
πρεσβύτης: πρεσβύτης, -τῃ, -την 93
πριγκιπᾶλις *principalis*: nom. πριγκ[ι]πᾶλις
& πριγκιπᾶρις, dat. πρινκιπαλίῳ & πριν-
κιπαρίῳ, pl. πρινκιπαλίων, -ίοις 49
πρίγκιψ *princeps*: πρινκίπῳ 49
Πρισκίλλα: Πρισκίλλης 10
προκήρυξις: προκηρύξεος 75
Προκόνδα: Προκόνδῃ 10
προνοητής: προνοητοί 15
προσδοκάω: προσδοκοῦμεν, -οῦσιν, -εῖν 363,
ἐπροσδόκων 252
προσεχής: προσεχέστερον 148
προστασία: προστασί<α>ν 4
προστάτης: voc. πρόστατα 14
προσφιλής: προσφιλεστάτην 148
πρόσωπον: masc. πρόσουπον *sic* 43

πρῷρα: gen. πρῴρας 5
πρῶτος: πρώτιστα 157
Πτολεμαῖος: Πτολεμαῖς, -αῖν 26
πτύσσω: ἐπτύχθη, πτυγεῖσαν 314
πυνθάνομαι: πεύσασα, ἐπυθόμην, ἐπύθετο, πυθοῦ, πυθέσθαι 295-6
πυρέσσω: πεπυρέχειν 224
πυροσιτόχροος: πυροσειτόχροο[ς] 125
πυρρόχρους/-χρωμος: πυρρόχρους, -χρωμον, φυρόχρωμον 125
πωλέω: πωλέσῃ, πώλησον 258
πῶς for ὅπως 182

ῥαβδίζω: ἐράβδισαν 246
ῥάβδος: τὴν ῥάβδον 39
ῥάδιος: ῥᾷον 154
Ῥαχήλ indecl. 104
Ῥεβέκκα: Ῥεβέκκας 104
ῥέω: συνερευκώς 246
ῥήγνυμι: διέρηξεν 246, 268, καταρήξ[α]ντες 268, κατέρρηχεν 246
ῥίπτω: ἔριψεν, ἐρριμμένας, ἀπέριψεν, ῥέριμμαι, ἀπορέριπται 246 & n. 2
ῥίς/ῥίν 65
ῥόγα (erogatio): ῥόγας, -αν 7
ῥύομαι: ῥύσει 326
ῥυπαρός: fem. ῥυπαροῦ 112
ῥώννυμι: ἔρρωται, -νται, -σο, -σθαι, -μένην, ἔρωσο, -σθαι, -μένος 246 & n. 3, ἤμην ἐρρωμένος 306

Σαβεῖνα: Σαβείνης & -ας, Σαβίνη 11
σάγμα: pl. σάγμα 89
σαγματᾶς: σαγματᾶν 19
σάκελλα sacellum: σακέλλης, -η 7
σαλπιγκτής: σαλπικτής, -τοῦ, -τῇ, σαλπιγκ[τοῦ], σαλπιστής 267 n. 7
Σαραπίαινα: Σαραπιαίνης 10
Σάραπις: Σαράπιδος, -ιδι & -ι, -ιν 57
Σαραπίων 65
Σαταβοῦς: Σαταβοῦς, -οῦτος, -οῦ[τι], -οῦν 60
Σατυρίαινα: Σατυριαίνης 10
σαφής: σαφέστερον 148
σβέννυμι: ἐσβέσθαι 245
σεαυτοῦ: σεαυτοῦ, -ῷ, σαυτοῦ, -ῆς, -ῷ, -όν, -ήν, σατοῦ, -ῷ 168, σατόν, -έν, -ήν, σεαστῆς, ἐσεαυτοῦ 169, σεαυτῇ (for 3rd pers.) 170 n. 6
σείω: διασείσθην 223

Σεκοῦνδα: Σεκούνδης & -ας 11
Σεκουντίλλα: Σεκουντίλλας 10
σεμίδαλις: σεμιδάρεως, -άλεως, σιμιδάλ(εως), σιμιδαλίῳ, σεμίδ[αλ]ιν 78
σεμνοπρεπής: σεμνοπρεπεστάτης, -τάτη<ν> 148
Σεναμουνία: Σ[ε]ναμουνίης 3
Σεναπολλῶς: Σεναπολλῶς, -ῶτο(ς) 61
Σενοκῶμις: gen. Σενοκώμεος 75
Σεουηρίνα: Σεουηρίνας 10
Σέργιος: Σέργις 25 & n. 2
Σερηνίλλα: Σερηνίλλης & -ας, Σερηνίλα 11
σημαίνω: ἐσήμανα, σημανῶ, σήμανον, σημᾶναι, σημάνας, ἐσήμηνα, σημῆναι etc. 263, ὑπεσημηνάμην, ἐπεσημήνατο, κατασημηνάμενος etc. 264, σεσημαμμένης, -οις, κατασεσημημμένα 268 n. 5
σημειόω: ἐσημιοσόμην 349
σήπω: σαπῇ, κατασαπ[έ]ντ[ων] 309
σθένος: τὴν ... στῆνος 48
σιαγών: σιαγόναν 46
σιγγουλάριος singularis 50
σίγνιφερ/σιγνίφερος signifer: σιγνιφέρου, σιγνιφέρι 24
σιδηροῦς: [σι]δηρᾶ, -ᾶς, -ᾶν, -αῖς, -ᾶς, -οῦ, -οῦν, -όν, σιδηραίου 118 & n. 2
σιλίγν(ι)ον (siligo): 23 n. 3, σιλίγ[ν]ων 48
σίναπι: σίναπι, gen. σινάπεως, σινήπεως, σινάπευς, οἰνάπις, dat. σίναπι 77-78
σιτομέτρης: σιτομέτρο[ς], σιτομέτροις 15
σῖτος 95, fem. σῖτον 42
σιτόχροος/-χρους/-χρωμος: σιτοχρόου, -όους, σιτόχρων, σειτόχρωμο[ς] 125
σιωπάω: ἦν ἀποσιωπήσας 306
σκάλη scala: σκάλη 8
σκέπη: σκέπης, -η & -ι, -ην 93
σκέπτομαι: σκέπτομαι, σκεπτόμεν<ος> 282 n. 7, ἐπισκεπτύμενος 283, σκέψομαι, σκέψη, ἐσκεψάμην, σκέψηται, σκέψασθαι, σκεψάμενος, ἐπεσκεμμένο[ν] etc. 270 & n. 2, ἐπισκεμμένας 243
σκευάζω: παρασκευάσατε 224, ἠσκεουασμένης 231
σκοπέω: σκοπῶ, σκόπει, σκοπεῖν, σκοποῦσαν, ἐπισκοποῦμαι, ἐπισκωποῦ etc. 283, ἐσκόπησα, σκόπησον, σκοπῆσαι, σκοπήσας, σκοπηθῆναι 270
σκορπίζω: ἐσκορπισμέναι 245
σκρείβας scriba: σκρ(ε)ίβας, gen. -ου & -α, dat. -ᾳ, acc. -αν & -α, ἰσκ[ρ]ίβαις 12

Φιλοῦς: Φιλοῦς, -οῦτος, -οῦν 60
Φιλώτας: gen. Φιλώτου & -α 13-14
φλοῦς: φλοῦν, φλοῦυν, φλοός, φλωός, φλόα 36
φοβέω: φοβεθείς/φοβηθείς 258
φόβος: masc. φόβος, -ον, neut. φόβος 100
Φοιβάμμων 65
φορέω: φορέσεις, ἐφόρεσα, φορέσῃς, ἐκφορήσῃ, ἐξεφόρησεν, διαφορηθῇ 257
φόρησις: φορήσε(ως) 257
φόριμος: fem. φορίμης & φορίμου 110
φόρος: gen. φώρους 23
φράσσω: ἀποφραγῆναι 314
φρέαρ: φρέαρ & φρέαν nom., φρέατος, φρέαθος, φρέατρος, φρέατι, φρέατρα 90 & n. 6
φρικώδης: φρικωδέστατον 148
φρίξ: masc./neut. φρικός 48
φρόνιμος: fem. φρονίμη & φρόνιμος 110
φροντίζω: φροντίσει, φροντιεῖ, -ιοῦμεν 286, impt. φρώντισεν 352
φροντιστής: gen. φρο<ν>τιστῇ 14
φυγάς: φυγάς, -άδων, -άδας 143
φυλάσσω: infin. φυλάσσι 330
φυτεύω: καταφύτευσεν 224
φύω: ἐπιφυῆναι, φυήσεται 317, φυησομένωι 316, 324
φωνέω: ἐπροσφώνησεν 252, προσφων[ή]σατε 224, σωμφο[νημένην] sic 242, συμπεφωνηθεῖσα[ν] 243

Χαιρᾶς: Χαιρᾶ & -ᾶτος, -ᾷ & -ᾶτι 18
Χαιρήμων: Χαι[ρή]μωνος, Χαι[ρ]ήμωνι 65
χαίρω. χαίροις, χαίρους (— -οις) 360; infin. χαίρεν & χαίρ(ε)ι 330, χαίρε 331; ἐχάρην 296, 311, ἐχάρησα, -ισα, χαιρησάμενοι 296
Χαλέδ indecl. 104
χάλκεος/χαλκοῦς: χάλκεος, -εον; χαλκοῦς, -οῦν, -ῆ, -ῆν, -οῖ, -αῖ, -ᾶ 119 & n. 1, χαλκοῦν 117
χάλκωμα: pl. χάλκωμα 89
Χάρης: Χάρητος & -ήτου, -ῆτι 60
χαρίζω: ἐχαρίζατο 332, προσχαρίζασθαι 329, χαρίσομαι, -εται, χαριῇ(ι)/χαριεῖ/χαρειεῖς/ χαρίεσαι, χαριε<ι>ται, χαριεῖσθε 286, χαρίεσαι also 358, χάρισεν 352, ἐχαρίσου 349 n. 3, ἔσει χαριζόμενος 290, ἔσῃ … κεχαρισμένος 307
χάρις: acc. χάριν/χάριτα(ν) 52 & n. 4

χαρτάριον: χαρτάριν 28
χάρτης: χάρτην, χάρτον, χάρτοις, χάρτεσι 15 & n. 3
χεῖλος: pl. χείλεα & χείλη 67 n. 1
χειμών: χειμῶναν 46
χείρ: χεῖραν 46, χερός, χερί, χέρα(ν), χέρας 64, acc. χέρες 47
χειρίζω: infin. ἐγχειρεῖ 330
χειρικός: χερικήν 64
χειρογραφία: χερογραφ[ίαν] 64
χειρόγραφον: masc. χειρόγραφον 43
χειροτονέω: εἴ[η κεχ]ειροτονημένος 306
χειρόω: ἐπιχειροίη 360
χείρων: χεῖρον 154, χέρι[ο]ν, χείρονα, χείρω, χείρονας 155 & n. 2
χειρωνάξιον: χερωναξίου 64
χέρσος: fem. χ[έ]ρσος, χέρσου, χέρσον, χέρσας 110
Χεῦς: Χεῦς, Χεῦτος, Χεῦτι, Χεῦν 59
χέω: συνχέειν, ἀποχέεται, ἐκχιεῖται, ἐπίχεε etc. 371 & n. 4, ἐκχύοντες, [ἐ]κχοίζουσι, ἐκχοεῖσαι, ἐχοισμένης, ἐπίχυν(ν)ε 276 & nn. 4-5, ὑποχυμένος 242
χίλιοι: χιλείας 199
χιτών: χιθώνους 45
χλοῦς: acc. pl. χλοῦς 36
χλωροῦς: acc. pl. fem. χλωρᾶς 119
χοίζω: see χέω
χοῖνιξ: acc. χοίνικες, χοινίκεσι 47
χοῦς (measure): nom. χοῦς, χόος, gen. χοός, χοῦν, χό(ες), χόε(ς), χόε[ς], χῶες; χοέως, χοεῖς, χω[ῶ]ν, χοέων, χοέσι, acc. χο(ε)ῖς/χωεῖς/χοέας 83-84
χοῦς (excavated earth): χοῦ & χοός, χοῦν 35
χράω: χρήσω, ἔχρησεν 326, χράσθω, χράσθωσαν, χρᾶσθαι 368 & n. 5, ἀπόχρηται, χρώμεθα, χρῶνται, χρῆσθαι, χρώμενος, χρησάμενοι etc. 369 & n. 2
χρέος: nom./acc. χρέος/χρέως, gen. χρέους, pl. χρέα 67
χρεωστῶ: χρεωστῶ 369
χρή: ἐχρῆν, ἐ[χ]ρῆι, ἐχρῆ, χρῆν etc. 226
χρῆ(ι)ζω 273
χρῆμα: χρῆμα (for dat.) 89
χρήσιμος: χρησίμην 108
χρηστήριον: χρηστηρίοισι 23
χρόνος: neut. χρόνον 42